THE ALCHEMY OF POETRY

A READER'S GUIDE TO UNDERSTANDING POETRY

ELIZABETH GUY, PH.D.

First Rider Publishing

Contents

Dedication   v

Introduction   1

  1 Poetry Confronting Art: Ekphrastic Poetry   3

  2 Making Life Easier to Bear: The Sonnet   51

  3 Go Seek the Kingdom: Pilgrimage and Poetry   82

  4 Poetry with a Divine Will: Numinous Poetry   135

  5 Troubled Pleasure: The Romantics   179

  6 A Singularness of Heart: Pre-Raphaelite Poetry   262

  7 As We See Ourselves: Australian Poetry   320

  8 A Terrible Beauty is Born: Irish Poetry   360

  9 A Life Worth Living: The Russian Silver Age   402

  10 Poetry that Saves a Nation: Nobel Laureates   449

  11 List of Poems   515

Acknowledgements   520

The Alchemy of Poetry

Copyright © 2020 by Elizabeth Guy

First published in USA by Dreaming Big Publications in 2020.
First published in Australia by First Rider Publishing in 2021.

All rights reserved. This book or any portion thereof may not be reproduced or used in any manner whatsoever without the express written permission of the publisher except for the use of brief quotations in a book review.

Cover designed by The Social Designer Australasia Pty Ltd.

Printed in Australia.

ISBN- 978-0-6451113-09

firstriderpublishing.com.au

*To
Peter and Elaine Guy,
my parents,
who believed I could ... even before I did*

Introduction

A thing of beauty is a joy for ever:
Its loveliness increases; it will never
Pass into nothingness; but still will keep
A bower quiet for us, and a sleep
Full of sweet dreams, and health, and quiet breathing.

from *Endymion* by John Keats

Poetry makes sense of life; it offers us truths; it brings us unimagined worlds; and it liberates our pain. This distilled and concentrated Art form creates a "bower quiet", which in turn offers us "sweet dreams, and health, and quiet breathing". I want to share with you some of the most beautiful poems I have read. I have shaped this assortment of poems, that you cannot live your life without reading, into ten categories. Within each, there are approximately a dozen or so poems to which I offer a close analytical reading. I have taught poetry for over 30 years to adults and tertiary and secondary students in Australia, Fiji, Scotland, and Chile. When I was in my mid-30s, I wrote a PhD on poetry at Sydney University. Throughout this time, I have loved the intensity and power of great poetry. I have found in moments of great joy or sadness that it is poetry which says the impossible, ensuring that the poignancy and loveliness of our humanity never passes into nothingness. Moreover, I think great Art is a "joy forever" and belongs to everyone; thus, it is crucial that we continue the dialogue between ourselves and the poems. It is in this dialogue that we witness the alchemy of poetry: the way it transmutes from a language form and feature to a universal elixir, an undiscovered gold and, most significantly, "A thing of beauty".

I can't remember a time when there wasn't poetry: from the Irish lullabies my mother sang when we were put to bed, to my first hard cover 1968 edition of *Poems to Read to Young Australians* (with Mary Quant designs on the inside cover) and from the ritual of prayers at Catholic mass, to the radio jingles of the 60s and 70s. I went to school in a time where an elocution teacher would come once a week and teach us extracts from long poems. Teachers throughout my schooling asked us to write our own verse – ghastly evidence remains in my parents' home to this day. Later, in boarding school, a librarian asked me if I had ever read Pablo Neruda and handed me his *Selected Poems*. I never gave it back. How could I? He put his hand into my heaped up heart and pledged his life-long love affair to me:

...I leave you here
what I had and did not have,
what I am and what I'm not.
My love is a child crying
afraid to leave your arms,
I leave him to you forever:
you, most beautiful of women.

from *Autumn Testament* by Pablo Neruda

The book falls open to this poem every time. The spine split. There's still the Dewey code waiting hopefully on the inside cover: Ch 861.44 NER. What was the name of that librarian? She said she loved Neruda and hadn't even put this new book on the shelves yet, and I was to bring it straight back. What can you do? And then there were the heavily mascaraed years of writing poetry and going to poetry readings. I remember once my father took me all the way into town, to Hyde Park, where Les Murray and budding poets like myself were to read their poetry aloud.

I can't remember what poem I chose, having taken several with me, but I do remember Les Murray looked nothing like his poetry. I read a poem of mine, and he watched on. Later, after reading many, many poems of his, he got up to leave and passed me with this sole comment: "Don't stop." I did stop, I can just about hear your sigh of relief. Later, I wrote my PhD on Nobel Prize winning poets. I mean really...why bother writing poetry when you are up against those giants.

I concentrated on Seamus Heaney, Derek Walcott, and, of course, Pablo Neruda. By that stage, I had lived and worked in Chile, and I had a best friend who remembered him when her father, another poet, had visited him in his home at Isla Negra. My friend told me Neruda would put her and her sister in a big wooden barrel and roll them about on the beach, just down from his house. She said he was so much fun and larger than life. Of course, I was never supposed to write a PhD on poetry, but I went into a bookshop up in Paddington and found Heaney's *New Selected Poems 1966-1987*. That was the beginning of the end for me. Heaney led me to Derek Walcott who led me back to Neruda. So, it was the Nobel Laureate triumvir of Neruda and Heaney and Walcott with their poetics of the nation state that gave rise to five years of writing a dissertation. Oh and of course a place of belonging that has always remained my true country.

So, I taught poetry. Some students came to it with hesitant, tentative steps while others were already believers. Wherever I seemed to go, the world was in need of poetry. I taught it in the University of Santiago in Chile, in the University of the South Pacific in Fiji, in the University of Sterling in Scotland, and in Sydney University and the University of Technology Sydney. I taught poetry in Adult Education Courses both in NSW and WA and then in Sydney high schools. I remember being asked to give a paper on my dissertation in Fiji. It was advertised as *No Man is an Island*, and I sat around with a group of people, talked poetry, and drank cava. Later, I heard what one of the students had said to someone as he left: they're talking about poetry like it is religion:

The word goes round Repins,
the murmur goes round Lorenzinis,
at Tattersalls, men look up from sheets of numbers,
the Stock Exchange scribblers forget the chalk in their hands,
and men with bread in their pockets leave the Greek Club:
There's a fellow crying in Martin Place. They can't stop him.

from *An Absolutely Ordinary Rainbow* by Les Murray

Well of course poetry is a religion, and it cannot be stopped. Poetry offers ritual and cadence: sacrifice and secrets. Poetry offers a nation state: a place within a place when it no longer confers sovereignty upon you. Poetry is sacred and profane and thus it is at once sublime and mighty. It is audacious and disturbing but always – and this applies to all great poetry – yours. Mine. Ours. Of course, as a teacher of literature and language I have had to listen to a colleague or two say, "Why teach poetry?" A question that, if it wasn't so sad, would be laughable. It puts me on the battlefield because what is the point of living if there is no Art? And poetry is the most concentrated of all Art. It is the oldest of all literary forms. Without poetry we are an idiotic, uncivilised people telling tales "full of sound and fury, signifying nothing". Poetry is, in one crowded hour, the only one in the room. So, we read poetry to face the truth. To stand there and dig in, to stumble over words we don't get, to find a phrase that flicks a light on in our memory, to cat-paw over and over an image that was laid down long ago. Most of all, we read poetry to remind ourselves of what really matters: to witness the soaring light that tears up our small lives.

I

Poetry Confronting Art: Ekphrastic Poetry

Without a conversation, there can be no art. Both artists and audiences must keep company with or live amongst art in order for it to become familiar and be known. I am compelled by the conversation that is generated by visual arts. It only seems natural that I would be drawn to a genre of poetry that engages with seen or imagined masterpieces. "Ekphrasis" comes from Greek and refers to the speaking out or offering a vivid description of art. Throughout time, poets have engaged in the conversation provoked by visual arts, just as visual artists have been inspired by poetry to create paintings and sculpture. These 12 poems that I want to share with you in this chapter could be, for the most part, classified as ekphrastic poems.

The first poem looks back at the Dutch Golden Age where Auden dialogues with Brueghel's *Landscape with the Fall of Icarus* and wonders about our place in the landscape of suffering. Two decades later Williams considers the same painting but sees only our longing to be free while remaining forever trapped. We then move to Corn, who tells his own complicated life story through the observation of 22 Vermeer paintings. The fin de siecle's rising genre of Realism and Impressionism take us to Markham's discursive engagement with Millais' *The Man with the Hoe* and the way he makes us see ourselves within the painting. We then move to Olzmann's ekphrastic poem on Rodin's *The Thinker* which is a meditation on the seduction of original art. Next, Ronk's sonnet on Matisse's *Woman with a Hat* is a revelation about the plasticity of time as art is being created and viewed. The next two ekphrastic poems are from Modernism: Leader has a talk with Hopper's *Girl at Sewing Machine*, and Williams writes a poem that seven years later will inspire the artist, Demeuth, to paint a portrait of Williams: *I Saw the Figure 5 in Gold*. The last poems speak to the art from Classical Antiquity. While working for Rodin in Paris, Rilke took the opportunity to see *Apollo's Torso* in the Louvre. His poem tells us that life changes utterly when it collides with masterpieces of art. Homer's notional ekphrastic poem *The Shield of Achilles* shows us how we, the listener, become part of the art being created. And Keats, who never saw Sosibios' *Grecian Urn*, writes his poem about the completely fulfilling purpose of living your whole life in the pursuit of beauty in order to know truth. Finally, Shelley did visit the Uffizi in Florence to view Da Vinci's *Medusa*, and his ekphrastic ode confronts us with the radical politics behind the narrative.

All of these visual art masterpieces are springboards from which the poet proves great art offers contemporary enlightenment and metaphysical transformation. Ekphrastic poetry is a rich and fulfilling way to listen to the conversation between the arts. Moreover, I hope you see much more than just what I am saying in this dialogue that I have commenced with you.

Musee des Beaux Arts by W. H. Auden (1938)

About suffering they were never wrong,
The old Masters: how well they understood
Its human position: how it takes place
While someone else is eating or opening a window or just walking dully along;
How, when the aged are reverently, passionately waiting
For the miraculous birth, there always must be
Children who did not specially want it to happen, skating
On a pond at the edge of the wood:
They never forgot
That even the dreadful martyrdom must run its course
Anyhow in a corner, some untidy spot
Where the dogs go on with their doggy life and the torturer's horse
Scratches its innocent behind on a tree.

In Brueghel's Icarus, for instance: how everything turns away
Quite leisurely from the disaster; the ploughman may
Have heard the splash, the forsaken cry,
But for him it was not an important failure; the sun shone
As it had to on the white legs disappearing into the green
Water, and the expensive delicate ship that must have seen
Something amazing, a boy falling out of the sky,
Had somewhere to get to and sailed calmly on.

Landscape with the Fall of Icarus: Oil on canvas (73.5 by 112 centimeters) in the Royal Museum of Fine Arts of Belgium, Brussels. Attributed to Pieter Brueghel although recent research suggests that it is perhaps a copy of Brueghel's lost original from 1560.

Landscape with the Fall of Icarus is not in the Louvre, but it once was. In 1794, following the battle of Fleurus, works of art were seized from what is now known as Belgium and removed to the Louvre. It wasn't until 1815 that they were returned in an act of restitution. The Museum of Beaux Arts had been open since 1803, and this is where we find the Brueghel painting today. Brueghel was known as the peasant painter and focused on the ordinary people, a result of the Protestant Reformation. His genre paintings depict scenes of everyday life. Brueghel's figures are solid and warm; his landscapes drew on Virgil's notion that landscape is given meaning by the labors of its people. Paintings from the 16th century Flanders are narratives with a wide range of visual cues from which we see more and more. Brueghel was influenced by the multitude of proverbs that circulated within his society. He lived and worked in Antwerp, which was a place of politics and trade. Brueghel rendered an accurate representation of the simple life and in some ways generated a sympathy toward the narratives he painted.

Musee des Beaux Arts is a muscular poem by the English modernist W. H. Auden and is composed of 21 lines and two stanzas, each containing one sentence. I am employing all my powers of resistance in not calling it a sonnet: despite its symmetrical shape, the way it invites meditation, focuses on one subject and contains a volta. Perhaps we could call this a free verse poem or the center panel of a triptych: on the right-hand side, the tale from Ovid and on its left the painting by Brueghel. The tale from Ovid's *Metamorphoses* Book VIII tells of Daedalus and his son Icarus who made their escape from Crete on wings that were held together with bee's wax. The tale is deeply moving. The father sheds tears before he flies ahead after carefully instructing his son to travel between the extremes of the sun and the earth. Icarus is young and exuberant with this newfound freedom and so ignores his father's pleas. The son flies too close to the sun, the bee's wax melts, wings disintegrate, and Icarus falls to Earth. The father wretchedly sees all: now no longer entrapped on Crete, he is entrapped in grief. This is a story to remind us that we cannot aspire to God; the star at the center of the solar system was always regarded thusly by poets. The young should not ignore the instructions of the old; this allegory requires us to be cautious and take the middle ground.

Auden, like many of us, is fascinated by the idea of suffering at the heart of this tale. Yet Auden is not focused on the suffering of a father and son entrapped on an island with no escape; or the misery of Daedalus who yearns to set foot on his native soil; or the heightened anxiety of a parent who suspects his son is vulnerable to the pending perils; or the unimaginable travail of watching a child die; or the grief of burying one's child; or the anguish of a life without one's child. Auden cannot be focused on this suffering of Daedalus or Icarus because Brueghel is not. Brueghel is captivated by Ovid's tale where "some angler catching fish with a quivering rod, or a shepherd leaning on his crook, or a ploughman resting on the handles of his plough, saw them, perhaps, and stool there amazed, believing them to be gods able to travel the sky". Brueghel's intent is to convey the fact that humanity has always and will always suffer from indifference. Auden's poem confronts this truth head on.

The first stanza deals with a singular premise that the great artists have always understood humanity's indifference to suffering. Auden rearranges the order of the sentence: "About suffering they were never wrong, / The old Masters." Instead of the usual pattern of subject followed by the predicate we have the predicate, object, and verb followed by the subject. The subject names the central concern of the sentence, the verb states what the subject does, and the object receives the action of the verb. Here, Auden leads with the object. Why? Suffering is at the forefront of Auden's mind; moreover, it may be surmised to be at the forefront of the old Masters' minds. The old Masters, painters who worked in Europe between the years of 1450 to 1800, were fully trained and Masters of their artists' guild. Those artists of the early Netherlandish paintings, such as Pieter

Brueghel the Elder and then on into the Dutch Golden Age, were all old Masters. Auden moves on to add "how well they understood / Its human position". I'm intrigued by the use of the word "position", suggesting that suffering has a locus in our imagination and in our world. So, in less than three lines, it is suggested that suffering has its own specific location (especially in humanity's imagination). The entire 13 lines of this first stanza comprise one sentence that explores the proximal relationship humanity has with suffering. This long-demanding sentence (with its various clauses) takes us through four painterly moments that depict humanity's intimacy, but indifference, toward suffering.

Firstly, Auden takes us to a genre painting with the meticulous coverage of the mundane. So, we lean in and see "someone ... eating or opening a window / or just walking dully along" while suffering "takes place". Brueghel's own oeuvre is preoccupied with the ordinary labors and actions of ordinary people. Thus, the act of eating or opening a window or walking is worthy of art. It holds a mirror up to us, and we see the landscape of our own familiar and commonplace lives. It is in this mirror that we see our indifference to the place of suffering that is occurring at the exact same moment we are performing the rites of everyday living. Secondly, we are nudged before "the aged reverently, passionately waiting / For the miraculous birth". It is every parent's place to suffer as they await the birth of their child, and Auden's addition to this image is darkly ironic: "Children who did not specially want it to happen." The miraculous nature of birth is arbitrary. This takes us to our third painterly moment and that is of "Children...skating / On the pond at the edge of the wood". Here is a latent threat associated with the "edge of the wood", the site of unknown dangers. The 4th painterly image in this stanza is that of the martyrdom that plays out with the nonchalance of the dog and horse as failed witnesses. This "dreadful martyrdom must run its course / Anyhow in a corner", the unspeakable is relegated to the sidelines of our concern. Auden comments on human suffering occurring within the landscape of the ordinary, of the everyday, and the response to this is nothing more than insouciance and a getting on with life: "dogs go on with their doggy life."

The second stanza telescopes into the Brueghel painting *Landscape with the Fall of Icarus*. Like the first stanza, this is made up of one sentence. It has one unit of thought, which indicates that we fail to give witness to the amazing, the extraordinary, and the indefensible. I love the slow pace of the phrase "how everything turns away / Quite leisurely from the disaster". Here, form imitates content. The meandering of vowel sounds slows us down, and in an unhurried way, we deliberate upon Brueghel's interpretation of Ovid's tale. Brueghel is faithful to Ovid in that he depicts the "angler catching fish with a quivering rod, or a shepherd leaning on his crook, or a ploughman resting on the handles of his plough" but not as figures caught in amazement and certainly not left wondering whether Daedalus and Icarus were "gods able to travel the sky". Brueghel's characters are completely uninterested and unperturbed by what has happened. Indeed, all three of them face away from the fall of Icarus. Auden only mentions the ploughman who "may / Have heard the splash, the forsaken cry, / But for him it was not an important failure". The verb "may" suggests a possibility that Icarus' suffering was witnessed: the fact that both the sound of a splash and a cry are mentioned indicates it is most likely that the ploughman did hear this catastrophe, a boy falling from a sky, but it is not considered significant. Which begs the questions: what is? Are we immune to suffering? Brueghel's lower Netherlands knew of disease and brutal religious warfare just as Auden's England knew of the wasteland of World War I. Does excessive suffering have the same effect on us (in that we leisurely turn away)? What I find so touching about Brueghel's people is that he portrays them without judgement; there is a warmth and generosity about these flawed human beings who are, in many ways, us.

The redshirted ploughman initially hooks our attention in the center foreground, but our eyes soar up through the painting, taking in the land and sea and sun-drenched sky. The land and seascape are activated by the industry of human figures. The visual rhythm of the middle ground takes us from corrugated freshly ploughed soil, to the ploughman, to the shepherd leaning on his crook looking skywards, to islets, and then to the ship. Auden, at last and imitative of the way Brueghel positions the disaster in the corner of the canvas, moves his focus to Icarus in the final four lines of this poem. The sun, the eye of God, sheds singular light on Icarus and the ship sailing past. Does Auden suggest that God watches on equally indifferent? That this catastrophe can be reduced to "white legs disappearing into the green / Water" speaks to that moment of collision between death and life. It is also so utterly reductionist. There is sympathy but not sentimentality. These "white legs" are synonymous with the unknown, the unnamed, and the unrecorded carnage of war. It's curious that the barque sailing by in a world of busy trade and discovery is described as "the expensive delicate ship", as if a trophy of the wealthy sophisticated world. The irony is, of course, that it sailed "calmly on". Auden states that this ship "must", not "may", have seen the boy fall. In these final lines of the poem, we are unequivocally confronted by humanity's deliberate and calculated disinterest: to have seen "Something amazing" but not to care. Four years later, Eliot would write "we had the experience but missed the meaning": a true echo of Brueghel and Auden's take on Ovid's tale. Finally, it is worth reflecting on the title of both poem and painting: both situate place as the primary subject. Brueghel puts the word "Landscape" at the beginning of his title because it is the most significant consideration (more so than the Ovidian drama), and Auden's title is of course the painting in situ. Perhaps this suggests that it is our place of belonging that needs examination if we are to respond differently to that of the ploughman, the shepherd, and the angler.

Landscape with the Fall of Icarus by William Carlos Williams (1960)

According to Brueghel
when Icarus fell
it was spring

a farmer was ploughing
his field
the whole pageantry

of the year was
awake tingling
near

    the edge of the sea
    concerned
    with itself

    sweating in the sun
    that melted
    the wings' wax

    unsignificantly
    off the coast
    there was

    a splash quite unnoticed
    this was
    Icarus drowning

Some 22 years after Auden, the American Imagist poet William Carlos Williams publishes his ekphrastic poem in response to the same painting by Brueghel. The Imagist poets emerged out of the Modernist movement and were committed to clarity of expression through the use of precise visual images: choosing the exact word and not the decorative and attempting to write in the voice of the common people. Rather than making this easier to write, it in fact demanded exacting precision to get poetry right: to ensure an intellectual and emotional complexity in an instant in time. Williams writes a poem in seven three-line stanzas. The entire poem is a sentence but doesn't end, as it lacks a full stop. His poem is primarily about the landscape and the significance of the power of spring: ploughing in order to sow the earth, bright awakening light, the crystallised sea, the sweltering sun, and the splash off the coast. In all of this fecundity and life there is death: the central metaphor of great storytelling since time immemorial. Indeed, Icarus falls in line two, but he doesn't drown until 21 lines later. Our eyes and his lithe body fall down the page together; we give witness to a life descending to death.

    In the first stanza, we are taken to the central idea of the poem, which isn't Brueghel nor is it Icarus, but spring. In stanza two, we are clearly given the Brueghelian image of the ploughman, but in Williams' case, he is "a farmer", and it is "his field". The narrative is no longer about anonymous bystanders or observers but rather a person at the center of his own story, concerns, and responsibilities. This is someone doing what must be done in spring if there is to be sustenance and not famine. So, we move from Ovid's observers who stood there amazed and claiming Daedalus and Icarus to be gods when they took to the skies; to Auden's ploughman who "may have heard" and the ship that "must have seen"; to Williams' farmer who, in all actuality, didn't even notice. It was the "pageantry", the spectacle of spring, which held the farmer captivated. In other words, it was life, not death, which mesmerized and drove the farmer on.

    The third stanza anthropomorphizes this time of year as "awake" and "tingling". The canvas of the landscape truly does seem like it is roused and conscious when spring is at its zenith, where everything is budding and bursting into life. The palette of Brueghel's 1560 masterpiece is awash in teal greens, chiffon yellows, chestnut browns, and scarlet reds. These are colors of life and the bruised tragedy of a botched escape resulting in the death of someone's son. Williams rolls into stanza four by connecting the act of ploughing in spring to "the edge of the sea". This could perhaps be a nod to Auden's image of latent threat in "the edge of the wood", but the landscape in Williams' poem is far more benevolent than that of Auden's. Both Williams' poetic and Brueghel's painterly representation of this drama is powerfully aware of where the land ends and the sea begin, as well as what is and what is not naturally located in the skies. The tragedy of Icarus and Daedalus is that they disrupt this vital, natural order of things.

In stanza five, the verb "melted" is sandwiched between the sibilance of "sweating...sun" and the alliterative "w" in "wings' wax". So, the spectacle of spring becomes disquieting. This is a world that has a healthy respect for the elements of nature. It also makes us pause and realise that Icarus has been flying above this poem since line two, and it is now line 15 where the horror occurs. Our eye has been on the earth and the sea and now the power of the sun but at no point has it been guided to glimpse the catastrophe overhead. Why? Is it because the tragedy of Icarus falling is peripheral to the more central issue of productivity in the face of temperamental nature? Stanza six begins with "unsignificantly", an obsolete version of the word "insignificantly" and works as a type of volta, moving us from our focal point of spring back to the title's promise: the fall of Icarus. This archaic lexical choice reinforces the outdated and superseded significance of the tragedy of Icarus which occurs "off the coast" or nearly off canvas or vicariously in another temporality but certainly not ours.

Stanza seven reduces the significance of the metamorphoses of boy to bird to a watery death, in nothing but "a splash". This disturbingly reductionist end makes us realize how immaterial our own death will be in comparison to the birth and death of the seasons that have gone on and will go on throughout time. Despite being told that the splash was "quite unnoticed", both in the poetic and painterly representations, it is these very works of art that turn our attention once again to this tragedy. What is it about "Icarus drowning" that seems to continue on in our imaginations, imitated by Williams' choice to not use a full stop? This is a cautionary tale. Ovid begins his tales with "In nova fert animus mutates dicere formas / corpora" which can be translated as "I intend to speak of forms changed into new entities". Icarus changes from a landlocked, entrapped body to a body flying free and then to a body drowned. Typical of Ovid's epic poems, here we see the violence inflicted on a boy for his exuberance and thus he morphs into the natural landscape. Evident in all three representations is the meta-textuality of transformation; in Brueghel's painting, and Auden and Williams' poems, Icarus' transformation is subverted. What do we have here as we move from canvas to canvas across time? From Ovid we know Daedalus and Icarus are entrapped men; in Brueghel we see the way the ordinary worker is imprisoned in his own world of minutia; in Auden we read about our own sense of entrapment in a consciousness that doesn't care about suffering; and meanwhile Williams shows us that we remain trapped within a never ending canvas of seasons, which is more significant than us. The fall of Icarus as depicted in ekphrastic poetry reminds us that we long to be free while knowing we are trapped.

Seeing all the Vermeers by Alfred Corn (2002)

Met Museum, 1965, the first
I'll see, his Young Woman Sleeping.
Stage right, bright-threaded carpet flung over the table
where a plate of apples, crumpled napkin
and drained wineglass abut the recapped pitcher.
Propped by one hand, her leaning drowse,
behind which, a door opens on the dream, dim, bare
but for a console and framed mirror—or a painting
too shadowed to make out. Next to it,
(certitude) one window, shuttered for the duration...

That dream also timed me out, a lull in the boomeranging
hubbub of the staggering city I'd just moved to.

In the Frick's Officer and Laughing Girl, spring sunshine
entered left, partly blocked by the non-com suitor's hat-brim,
wide, dark as seduction, conquest. A map dotted with schooners
backed her fresh elations, the glass winking at them both.... He'd see
why, in a later day, crewcut recruits were shipping out to Nam;
and she, why the student left was up in arms against the war.

In '67, Ann and I spent a graduate year in Paris;
and lived in the Louvre, too, along with The Lace-maker—
self-effacing, monumental, an artisan
whose patience matched the painter's, inscribed
in tangling skeins of scarlet oil against an indigo
silk cushion. Silent excruciation
among toy spools framed the bald paradox
termed 'women's work', disgracing anything less
than entire devotion to labor entered into. (That May,
a million demonstrators marched up the Champs Elysées.)

From there to Amsterdam and The Little Street,
where innate civility distilled a local cordial, free
from upheaval, from dearth and opulence, each brick
distinct, their collectivity made credible
by a chalky varicosis that riddled foreground façades.
A century's successive mortars filled those cracks,

nor will the figures down on hands and knees in the foreground
stand up again till they've replaced that broken tile.

The Woman in Blue Reading a Letter calmed misgivings
with the global trust that swelled her body, a soft counterweight
to expeditions tracked across the weathered map behind.
A new-found Eden, festooned with portents, history
piloting ship and cargo across the wrinkling sea.

The Maidservant Pouring Milk's power to see
in threadbare clothes and plain features a meek radiance
made of caritas, doesn't need words... But since I do,
call her a velvet motet developed in blue, in scaled-down
yellow-green that I could hear, the resonant stillness
centered on movement's figment, cream paint paying out
a corded rivulet at the cruse's lip. Crusty loaves, nail-holes
in plaster, and knuckles roughened by scalds and scrubs
witnessed to the daily immolation, performed as first light
tolled matins from a Dutch-gold vessel hooked to the wall.

By train to Den Haag, to see the View of Delft's ink-black
medieval walls and bridge, barges anchored on a satin
water more pensive than the clouded blue above,
where one tall steeple took its accolade of sun.
(Proust's "patch of yellow wall" I couldn't find, though.)

The Girl in a Turban looked like Anne Wiazemsky,
Godard's new partner, whom we'd seen in his latest film.
Liquid eyes, half-parted lips, a brushstroke ancillary
to fable highlighting the weighty pearl at her earlobe,
her "Turkish" costume stage-worthy, if she ever chose to act.

By then it was set: No matter how many years or flights
it took, I'd see all of Vermeer—which helps explain
the Vienna stop we made that spring, and our instant beeline
to An Artist in His Studio (called, today, The Allegory of Fame).
What to make of the Artist's bloomers, outmoded even then—

and why would his model hold book and clarion, standing
before the mapped Low Countries? If that anesthetized mask

on the table near her denied the chandelier its candles,
then who hung a tapestried curtain in the left foreground?

Vermeer; but his meaning subverts comment, always
less hypnotic than the surface itself, a luminous
glaze adhering to receding frames in series,
chromatic theatres for featured roles that also kindle
fervour in their supporting actor, the secret soul.

Strike me dumb on first seeing The Astronomer
in Guy de Rothschild's study—well, a photograph of it
in an '80s coffee-table book, The Great Houses
of Paris. Not long after, thanks to philanthropy
and the tax structure, it devolved upon the state.
Semester break that winter, McC. and I jetted to France,
entered the Louvre's new glass pyramid and fought
dense crowds to where he hung, The Lace-maker's late consort.
In a brown studio, his fingers reading the globe,
he sat, immovably dutiful to calculations
devised ad hoc to safe-crack the star-studded zodiac.

I was one of the visitors tiptoeing
through Isabella Gardner's house in Boston
decades before the heist, which to this day
remains unsolved. But balance one instance
of good luck against a trip made to Ireland
in '86, missing by only a few months
the Beit Collection's Lady Writing a Letter.
Paid so often now, the compliment of theft
puts a keen edge on our art pilgrimages:
The icon may be gone when you arrive.

That fall, I lived in London's Camden Town,
writing on... call them stateside topics; and soon
tubed up to Kenwood House, relieved to find
their prime collectible unstolen—its potential
as ekphrastic plunder not apparent at the time.
(A sonnet, no less, completed earlier in New Haven,
qualified me for that satire on the Connecticut bard
besotted with Vermeer. Still, subjects could be barred
in advance only if they and poems were the same gadget.

Disbelief, you're suspended, even for the standard
gloat over shots knocked back at the Cedar Tavern,
ca. 1950, with Pollock and de Kooning.)

Here then was Kenwood's Lady with Guitar, in corkscrew
curls, lemon jacket trimmed with ermine, lounging
like some hippie denizen of Washington Square,
strumming for the nth time his second-hand Dylan...
Maybe they heard her, too, the National Gallery's
paired women portraits, each playing a virginal,
both in silk dresses, one seated, one standing—
Profane and Sacred Love, if the old allegory fits.

A trip from London to Edinburgh produced, beyond
the classic-Gothic limestone city grimed with soot,
an early Christ in the House of Mary and Martha,
conceived before the painter's parables began unfolding
at home in Delft. Still, Martha's proffered pannier is as real
as the bread it holds, and Jesus' open hand, rendered
against clean table linen, as strong and solid as Vermeer's.

A chill, damp March in Dresden with Chris.
We'd begun with the Berlin State Museum's holdings
and then trained down on our way to Prague.
The Gemäldegalerie, quiet as a church, listened
while beads of tarnished rain pelted the skylights.
Works known from reproductions offered themselves
to the grey ambient, visibly conscious
of having survived Allied firebombs fifty years
earlier and a post-war Ice Age that slammed home,
then froze every bolt in the Eastern sector.
Young Vermeer's The Procuress makes love for sale
push beyond the sour analogue
of art-as-commerce into distinct portraits,
comedic types you have and haven't seen before
caught up in cheerful barter while wine flows
at a balustrade draped with carpet and a fur cape.
The client's left hand could have been mine,
weighing down a pretty shoulder (and the bodice),
but not the right, poised to let fall a coin
into her open palm. Men's hunger for sex

and poverty's for comforts—an old story,
mean or tragic, and never finally resolved.

Having missed Her Majesty's The Music Lesson, lent
over the years to several exhibitions, guess who danced
when told that it would grace the show to end all shows
scheduled in Washington, the fall of '95.
And other hard-to-sees from Brunswick and Frankfurt—
jubilation—were included also, plus
apprentice works on pagan or religious themes.
Long caterpillar of a line, composed of hundreds
come to worship art and its obsessive love of life.
An hour's wait on aching legs, and in we go:
The Geographer, taking his place by The Astronomer;
Ireland's letter-writer, look, recaptured, and now restored
to the public; a View of Delft, cleaned so thoroughly
you couldn't miss that patch of yellow—not a wall,
Proust got it wrong, instead, a roof... Sheltering involuntary
memories of countless choked-up viewers,
whose gazes added one more laminate of homage
to a surface charged with how many hundred thousands now.

From the permanent collection—why?—I saw as though
I never had the Woman Weighing Gold, some twenty years
(gone, and still here) since that first visit (Walter with me)
to the National Gallery. By word-origin Galilees,
international through their holdings, these cathedrals
of art draw in the faithful that faith in art has summoned
for mutual appraisal, what we are seen in what we see.

Hence the scales at center canvas Vermeer suspended
from her fine-boned hand, the face all understanding
and, so, forgiving all. Nevertheless, the great maternal
judge weighs one gold (a ring? a coin?) against a smaller gold,
in gloom as dark as the Day of Wrath, whose millennial
trumpet tears away a final veil.
So human error
will yield, her calm demeanour says, to Pax caelestis
and dawn break forth in perpetual light transforming
breath, strife, treasure, theft, love, and the end of love,
into its own substance—strong, bright beam of Libra rising

step by step up the scale to Eden and a countenance
the soul, made visible, is now accorded grace to see.

Around us, heads bent toward a morning vintaged
more than three hundred years ago. Manifold delight
wearing Nikes, Levi's, parkas; students, grizzled veterans,
young mothers, teachers, painters—awestruck, whispering
Heavens! Just look at that! —his New World public.

Christ in the House of Martha and Mary (1654) Oil on canvas 160 x 142 cm National Gallery of Scotland, Edinburgh; The Procuress (1656) Oil on canvas 143 x 130 cm Gemaldegalerie Alte, Dresden; A Maid Asleep (1657) Oil on canvas 87.6 x 76.5 cm Metropolitan Museum of Art, New York; The Little Street (1657) Oil on canvas 53.4 x 44 cm Rijksmuseum, Amsterdam; Officer and Laughing Girl (1655) Oil on canvas 50.5 x 46 cm Frisk Collection, New York; The Milkmaid (1658) Oil on canvas 45.5 x 41 cm Rijksmuseum, Amsterdam; The Girl with a Glass of Wine (1959) Oil on canvas 78 x 67 cm Ulrich Museum, Brunswick; View of Delft (1660) Oil on canvas 98.5 x 117.5 cm Koninklijk Kabinet, The Hague; Woman in Blue Reading a Letter (1662) Oil on canvas 46.5 x 39 cm Rijksmuseum, Amsterdam; Woman Holding a Balance (1662) Oil on canvas 46.5 x 39 cm National Gallery, Washington; The Music Lesson (1662) Oil on canvas 73.3 x 64.5 cm The Royal Collection, Windsor Castle; Woman with a Pearl Necklace (1662) Oil on canvas 55 x 45 cm Gemaldegalerie Alte, Berlin; The Art of Painting (1662) Oil on canvas 120 x 100 cm Kunsthistorisches Museum, Vienna; Girl with a Pearl Earring (1665) Oil on canvas 46.5 x 40 cm Koninklijk Kabinet, The Hague; The Concert (1663) Oil on canvas 72.5 x 64.7 cm Isabella Stewart Gardner Museum, Boston; Astronomer (1668) Oil on canvas 50 x 45 cm Musee du Louvre, Paris; The Geographer (1668) Oil on canvas 53 x 46.6 cm Stadelsches Kunstinstitut, Frankfurt; The Lace-maker (1669) Oil on canvas 24.5 x 21 cm Musee du Louvre, Paris; The Guitar Player (1670) Oil on canvas 53 x 46.3 cm Kenwood House, London; Lady Writing a Letter with her Maid (1670) Oil on canvas 71.1 x 58.4 cm National Gallery of Ireland, Dublin; A Lady Standing at a Virginal (1670) Oil on canvas 51.7 x 45.2 cm National Gallery, London.

This is a visually sumptuous narrative poem that becomes a gallery through which we walk and view Vermeer's work. This free verse of ten stanzas stretches from 1965 to 1995. Corn takes us on a very intimate tour (sometimes alone, sometimes accompanied by Ann, his wife or later Walter or McM (his partners)), but at all times we are aware of the history of the world beyond the gallery corridors. This meandering narrative is an homage to 30 years and 11 different cities where Corn viewed half of the existing 34 Vermeers. His loquacious style and ambulant meter make his ekphrastic poem intimate and compelling.

In stanza one, we go upstairs into the "Met Museum 1965" to see "his *Young Sleeping Woman*". This first Vermeer sets up a "boomeranging / hubbub of the staggering city I'd just moved to" and thus a type of center or anchorage. From "bright-threaded carpet" in the foreground, to the young woman "Propped by one hand" in the mid ground, to the door opening behind her, to "a console and framed mirror – or a painting / too shadowed" in the background, we follow the composition.

She is young, dreaming, and sleeping momentarily with all the promise of possibility conveyed in the opened door. The uncertainty of what is beyond that moment and the suggestion of "one window, shuttered for the duration" indicate an almost apprehensive contemplation of the future. The poet refers to himself at the start and the end of the poem, which makes it clear that the frame of reference is personal.

Stanza two takes us a few blocks up 5th Avenue from the Met to the Frisk Collection to view *"Officer with Laughing Girl"*. It is the "spring sunshine / … partly blocked by the non-com suitor's hat-brim, / wide, dark as seduction, conquest" that sets up a hint of wariness, despite the joyful title. This non-commissioned officer obscures the light. His presence is disturbingly captured in the simile, "dark as seduction", suggesting flirtation and danger. This really is a painting of romance and intimacy with war. The officer in Vermeer's painting is wearing the attire of an officer in the First Anglo-Dutch War. The officer and the laughing girl are not looking at the "map dotted with schooners" behind them, nor do they notice the light through the "glass winking at them both". The tableau is about the ways in which we cannot see the signs of our times but rather only our own personal obsessions and interests. Some 300 years later, its 1965 when the United States rapidly increased its military forces in Vietnam: "crewcut recruits…shipping out to Nam." The lovers in the painting, like Corn and his wife in 1965 viewing the Vermeer, see themselves but not the oncoming threat of war.

By stanza three, we are two years along, the poet is accompanied by his wife, and we are at the Louvre in Paris observing *"The Lace-maker /* self-effacing, monumental, an artisan / whose patience matched the painter's". It is not only the painter's patience that is imitative of the lace-maker but the poet's patience. The lace-maker's "tangling skein" is "inscribed" in "scarlet oil". I can't help but see the poet making a poem about a painter making a painting about a lace maker making lace: a meta-art and palimpsest text. The focus now shifts to the "Silent excruciation" of work that is offered such dignity. The backdrop, of course, for the poet is the May 1968 Social Revolution in France where millions of workers, students, and other supporters protested against the de Gaulle regime. The stanza is concluded with parentheses as a way of offsetting the Vermeer to the political upheaval of 1968: "(That May, / a million demonstrators marched up the Champs Elysees.)" This is an effective ending to this idea of the significance of detail.

In stanza four, we head off into Amsterdam's Rijksmuseum to see three Vermeers. Firstly, "the innate civility distilled" in *"The Little Street"*; secondly, the "calmed misgivings" of *"The Woman in Blue Reading a Letter"*; and thirdly, the "threadbare clothes and plain features" of the *"Maidservant Pouring Milk"*. The first is a celebration of humble and hard work: "free / from upheaval, from dearth and opulence, each brick / distinct, their collectivity made credible / by a chalky varicosis." The façade of the little street is emblematic of the diligent attention to detail and indefatigable work ethic of those who people the streetscape: "nor will the figures down on their hands and knees in the foreground / stand up till they've replaced that broken tile."

The second Vermeer in the Rijksmuseum picks up on the dialogue between a pregnant woman, a letter, and the global world represented in the map behind her. Perhaps her regrets are salved by the contents of the letter. Hers may well be the "new-found Eden, festooned with portents…across the wrinkled sea"; a future burgeoning with both hope and augury. How can the metaphorical ocean before her be crossed smoothly? The third painting sets up the way in which the milkmaid requires no words but the poet does. Thus, we are flooded with a soundscape of praise for her, something close to sacred choral music: "a velvet motet." The music of the poem opens in the indigo "blue" of her overskirt and then is "scaled-down" to the "yellow-green" of her bodice until we arrive at the "resonant stillness" of "cream paint paying out / a corded rivulet at the cruse's lip". I love the collision of color in music and in painting.

Stanza five keeps us in the Netherlands as we train up into The Hague. We stand at "*View of Delft*'s ink-black / medieval walls and bridge" and recall Proust's "patch of yellow wall". This vignette is framed by a veritable contrast of color as we watch Corn, watch Proust, and watch Vermeer. The personification of the "water more pensive than the clouded blue above" and "one steeple took its accolade of sun" makes us consider the living soul of Delft, Vermeer's hometown.

We turn then to our next Vermeer in this same gallery. Again, Corn collides the experiential moment of viewing an artwork in the actual town of its conception, made some 300 years before, to the latest French New Wave film *La Chinoise* released by Jean-Luc Godard in 1967: "*Girl in the Turban* looked like Anne Wiazemsky / Godard's new partner...Liquid eyes, half-parted lips, a brushstroke ancillary / to fable highlighting the weighty pearl in her earlobe." Her eyes, bottom lip and earring all bear a fecund roundness and luster. The cultural interpretation of this painting may be that of an exotic other or odalisque, portraits typical of the Golden Age Dutch artistry: and as such are objects of desire that can be fetishized and possessed. The punctum or wound that establishes a relationship between the individual and the art, is for Corn, the art making, the "brushstroke" which is secondary, "ancillary", to her legend. It is as if he realises that the artist, just like the poet, will construct the self however he chooses. To see the maid servant modelled as exotic desire simply to fulfil Vermeer's requirements is perhaps an epiphany for Corn as he is coming to his own personal realizations that he too has been acting a part rather than being his true self. The girl in the turban's direct gaze is intimate, unguarded, and challenging. Despite the "'Turkish' costume stageworthy, if she ever chose to act", there is something deeply familiar and transferable about her desirous gaze sent out of the canvas to the viewer. It is a cinematic moment where everything falls away and instead of seeing a performer conveying the illusion of intimacy, Corn identifies something recognizable and defiant: a self-love refusing to perform as the other.

Stanza six confirms Corn's shift from performing as straight to being his true self, gay: "By then it was set." This stanza explores the seduction of surfaces which can distract us from the interior self. Corn tells of the stop in Vienna to see Vermeer's "*Artist in His Studio*". He then asks a series of *Cluedo* style questions: "What to make of the Artist's bloomers...Why would his model hold book and clarion...If that anesthetized mask...denied the chandelier its candles / then who hung a tapestried curtain." We ponder these seductive superficial questions as if the surface will render the deeper meanings this painting holds. The answer to all of this is given to us, "Vermeer ... his meaning subverts comment". The meaning is "less hypnotic than the surface itself"; so, we are asked to go beyond the surface, which may well seem mesmerizing, and consider what lies beneath if we want to understand our self. The surface, the "luminous / glaze" a Golden Age trope of "receding frames in series", is the beginning of the mise-abyme, where in a moment of meta-painting the "supporting actor", the artist, can come out from behind the canvas and be part of the performance of the art.

In other words, within his work, below the luminous glaze of the surface, is the artist, the poet, and the true self. Corn has come out from behind decades of performing as someone he is not.

By stanza seven we have moved from the late 60s to the early 80s and from Ann his wife to his third partner, the poet J. D. McClatchy. No longer is his soul secret but rather on display and treading upon the boards of his own stage. Indeed, somewhere between the "Guy de Rothschild's study" and "the Louvre's new glass pyramid" he and "McC…jetted to France" in search of *The Astronomer*. His playful quip at *The Lace-maker*, which he visited at the Louvre in 1967 with his wife Ann being *The Astronomer*'s former spouse is a nod to his own personal life. The image of "fingers reading the globe" as the astronomer sits "immovably dutiful to calculations" speaks to the finite detail of art making as much as it does about the subject of the composition. The palindromic rhyme of the last line, "ad hoc to safe-crack the star-studded zodiac" is heard in the plosive c of "hoc", "crack" and" zodiac", and the sibilant "star" and "studded". The palindrome suggests a circularity or completion. So, when *The Lace-maker* stands across from *The Astronomer* just as Anne and Corn in late 60s stand across from McM and Corn in the early 80s, we understand the way in which Corn sees his life framed by patterns of circularity which have led to his completion.

Stanza eight rambles across art heists in Boston and Ireland and then on to drunken arguments between de Kooning and Pollock at the Cedar Tavern in New York until we eventually view Vermeer's work in London and Edinburgh. It's an exploration of the edginess of the here and now because tomorrow it may all be gone. A lesson keenly learned at the "Isabella Gardner's house in Boston" as well as "the Beith Collection" in Ireland; in fact, the self-destructive competitive nature of de Kooning and Pollock's relationship knew all too well that the gift of art was transient because it was contingent on human beings. This is a quick survey of four Vermeers because the 5th, *The Concert*, remains stolen from Isabella Gardner's house. Indeed, "*Lady Writing a Letter*" in Ireland is paid "the compliment of theft" just months after he visits. We are then asked to consider the way in which art theft "puts a keen edge on our art pilgrimages: / The icon may be gone when you arrive". We move along on this journey to Kenwood House in London: its art collection playfully and self-referentially referred to as "ekphrastic plunder". It is here that Corn plunders "*Lady with Guitar*" using an unexpected simile: "lounging / like some hippie denizen of Washington Square / strumming for the nth time his second-hand Dylan." This is our realization that everything is theft; indeed, ekphrastic poetry is a great case in point. We pause here to wonder whether the *Lady seated at a Virginal* and *Lady standing at a Virginal*, a portrait pair made by Vermeer in 1670, over at "the National Gallery" can hear the strumming from *Lady with Guitar* hanging in Kenwood House up on Hampstead Heath. Finally, we move across to Edinburgh, "the classic-Gothic limestone city grimed with soot", in order to see one of Vermeer's early paintings, "*Christ in the House of Martha and Mary*". The artist's ability to render realistic skin tone and the life-like woven basket in paint are indicators of the messianic qualities that the poet believes the artist to possess. This conceit continues in this painting, Vermeer's second earliest, which is large and unlike his later genre pieces. That it is "conceived before the painter's parables began unfolding / at home in Delft", suggests Vermeer offered a type of salvation to this world with his art. The parallel concludes when the artist's hands are likened "as strong and solid" as those of Jesus.

Stanza nine moves us between Berlin and Prague, into the damp and rain-filled Dresden: "having survived Allied firebombs fifty years / earlier and a post-war Ice Age that slammed home / then froze every bolt in the Eastern Sector." This site is positioned as a place of suffering. *The Girl with a Pearl Necklace* from the "Berlin Sate Museum's holdings" gets no mention because it is the woman obtaining a prostitute for three men in "*The Procuress*" that holds all of Corn's attention. I wonder why they don't see *The Glass of Wine* in Berlin or *The Girl Reading a Letter by an Open Window* in Dresden? Initially, he pushes past the "sour analogue" of selling love or making art for commerce and focuses on the distinct portraits of the characters about the procuress and the drapery of rich carpet and fur. Yet before we know it, we are back at the moment of soliciting, where the poet himself identifies with the lascivious male on her right: "The client's hand could have been mine / weighing down a pretty shoulder (and the bodice)." In this cold forsaken German city, still scared by the past, Corn completes the meditation on this painting: "Man's hunger for sex / and poverty's for comforts – an old story / mean or tragic, and never finally resolved." Buying and selling is politics written on the body, on the city, on the history, and on art.

So, we finally arrive in the gallery of stanza ten: Washington 1995. Here is a gathering of Vermeers from all over: London, Brunswick, and Frankfurt, not to mention the permanent collection in the Washington National Gallery. To see all the Vermeers is expressed in the poet's exuberance: "guess who danced…jubilation." We view the well-restored and well-loved Vermeers as we "come to worship art and its obsessive love of life…whose gazes added one more laminate of homage / to a surface charged with how many hundred thousands now." The love of art is a religion. The poet goes on to prove this by referring to the etymology of the word gallery: "By word-origin Galiliees…these cathedrals / of art draw in the faithful that faith in art has summoned / for mutual appraisal, what we are seen in what we see." Here we consider how the galilee, which was originally a chapel and then a cathedral, houses our love, our obsession, and our faith. I pause here at the quintessential relationship between art, that is painting and poetry, and the experience of the numinous; painting and poetry has always been the medium by which we have traveled to know the scared. Moreover, art examines us as much as we examine it. In the final painting we look upon, *Woman Weighing Gold*, we note the scales are "suspended / from her fine-boned hand, the face all understanding… Nevertheless, the great maternal / judge weighs one gold…against a smaller gold". The image recalls a day of judgement where all our words and deeds will be assessed despite unconditional love and forgiveness. Her "calm demeanour" is read to say: "human error / will yield…to Pax caelestis." It is the choral rendition of heavenly peace that assures us of "transforming / breath, strife, treasure, theft, love and the end of love / into its own substance". This is the end point of Corn's 30 year narrative: where he has told a story of the celestial power of art and the tale of himself. We are left with the final moment in the cathedral of art with a Vermeer-esque tableau of "students, grizzled veterans, / young mothers, teachers, painters- awestruck, whispering / Heavens! Just look at that!" Indeed, this veritable motley collection of the faithful is Vermeer's "New World public".

The Man with the Hoe by Edwin Markham (1898)

Bowed by the weight of centuries he leans
Upon his hoe and gazes on the ground,

The emptiness of ages in his face,
And on his back, the burden of the world.
Who made him dead to rapture and despair,
A thing that grieves not and that never hopes,
Stolid and stunned, a brother to the ox?
Who loosened and let down this brutal jaw?
Whose was the hand that slanted back this brow?
Whose breath blew out the light within this brain?

Is this the Thing the Lord God made and gave
To have dominion over sea and land;
To trace the stars and search the heavens for power;
To feel the passion of Eternity?
Is this the dream He dreamed who shaped the suns
And marked their ways upon the ancient deep?
Down all the stretch of Hell to its last gulf
There is no shape more terrible than this--
More tongued with censure of the world's blind greed--
More filled with signs and portents for the soul--
More fraught with menace to the universe.

What gulfs between him and the seraphim!
Slave of the wheel of labor, what to him
Are Plato and the swing of the Pleiades?
What the long reaches of the peaks of song,
The rift of dawn, the reddening of the rose?
Through this dread shape the suffering ages look;
Time's tragedy is in that aching stoop;
Through this dread shape humanity betrayed,
Plundered, profaned and disinherited,
Cries protest to the Powers that made the world,
A protest that is also prophecy.

O masters, lords and rulers in all lands,
Is this the handiwork you give to God,
This monstrous thing distorted and soul-quenched?
How will you ever straighten up this shape;
Touch it again with immortality;
Give back the upward looking and the light;
Rebuild in it the music and the dream;

Make right the immemorial infamies,
Perfidious wrongs, immedicable woes?

O masters, lords and rulers in all lands,
How will the future reckon with this Man?
How answer his brute question in that hour
When whirlwinds of rebellion shake all shores?
How will it be with kingdoms and with kings--
With those who shaped him to the thing he is--
When this dumb Terror shall rise to judge the world,
After the silence of the centuries?

L'homme à la houe by Jean-François Millet. Oil on canvas 80 x 99.1 cm. 1860-62. Currently held at the Getty Center Los Angeles.

    Why do we stop at this painting by Millet and this poem by Markham? It is a reminder of the past and how reassuring it is that we are not back there: locked in the pattern of peasant hardship and boredom. The realism of both artist and poet renders easy access and reassures us that art is for us after all. Perhaps we stop at the poem because we need to be reminded of a historical period where revolution was on the brink of the 20th century and with it a dire need to end serfdom. I wonder at the political impact of painting and poetry and the way it forces us to confront suffering. Thus, human anguish reaches across time. This is a fin de siecle poem. The end of a century has an impact on the imagination of most. It is a Janus-faced time of reflection and aspiration. The arts in particular respond to that call to look back and consider what was, as well as look forward and articulate what could be. When Markham wrote this in 1898, the Western world was on the cusp of Modernity.
    Stanza one offers four lines of description of the man as he is before us in the Millet painting, and the next six lines ask four questions about who is responsible for this travesty. The man is without name or identity or any characteristic other than that of a peasant laborer. Those responsible, on the other hand, are named by the 4th and 5th stanzas, so on one level this poem really is a citation of what the ruling class has gotten horribly wrong. In many ways, the man with the hoe could be any one of us "bowed by the weight" of all that must be achieved as we lean upon the routines and expectations that make our life a replica of everyone else's life. Maybe the "emptiness of ages" is in our face because we have blown out the light. So, in answer to the question "Who made us 'dead to rapture and despair, / A thing'" the answer may be us. The clipped sibilance of "Stolid and stunned" imitates the plodding mindless paces of a beast of burden who is none other than a sibling to the man with the hoe: "a brother to the ox." The reference to the "loosened ... jaw" suggests guttural communication that inadequately responds to the world. The phrase "the hand that slanted back this brow" is emblematic of the hardship that the vast majority experienced in the times Millet and Markham lived. The most powerful question of this stanza is "Whose breath blew out the light

within this brain?" The plosive use of "breath blew" and "brain" makes us realize the violence of this act and the violation of the subject.

From stanza one to two, we move from a "man with hoe" as a powerless victim to a man with hoe as empowered and downtrodden. The second stanza is made up of two questions and then a five line answer. The two questions pose the comparison between the vast scope of the universe and the man with the hoe. He is referred to as "the Thing" loaded with potential action: "To have dominion…to trace…and search… To feel." These higher order verbs are not in the vocabulary of a man with a hoe whose repertoire is to weed, dig, and scrape. In contrast, these verbs evoke God and man's part in the omnipotent drama of the divine. Thus, we are left wondering whether this was indeed "the dream He dreamed". The anaphora in stanza two intensifies the emotion and drives the rhythm: "More tongued with censure…More filled with signs…More fraught with menace." We feel ourselves being hauled down a Dante-esque "stretch of Hell" to prove that "no shape is more terrible than this," which the "man with hoe" endures. What is interesting about the last three lines in stanza two is the quiet way in which the politics have crept up on us. This living hell is a result of "the world's blind greed", which will generate "signs and portents": so much so that this man with the hoe is "fraught with menace to the universe". There is something potentially threatening about the man with the hoe; indeed, his oppression makes the universe vulnerable. Therefore, subjugation of the spirit puts the world in peril.

Stanza three insists that the protest of the man with the hoe must now be heard as a prophecy. Markham commences with the verbing of "gulfs" to emphasise the abyss growing between the peasant and the angels: between his earth-bound existence and the celestial choirs above. Markham poses time honored questions about the value of philosophy and astrology to a mind shackled by the basic needs of survival: "what to him…Plato and…the Pleiades?" These are Socratic and Platonic questions, and from this, he moves to an Aristotelian conundrum which considers the value of aesthetics for those caught beneath "the wheel of labor". Thus, the alliterative r binding the sensory aesthetics of hearing, sight, and smell, "reaches…of song…rift of dawn, the reddening of the rose", is not for the man with the hoe. Indeed, his "dread shape", repeated twice in this stanza, is the lens through which all suffering can be contracted and known. Here is the image of eternal travail on earth. Markham asserts that the man with the hoe is the icon shaping the call for justice: "Humanity betrayed / Plundered, profaned and disinherited." This is an American *Internationale*, a working class *Masque of Anarchy*: "Cries protest to the Powers that made the world, / A protest that is also prophecy." In the last three lines of this climatic stanza, the plosives link together the message that the workers have been plundered and profaned by those in power.

In stanza four, Markham asserts that the ruling class is responsible for the welfare of those less fortunate, and, as such, they must answer to God for the violation of their duties. At the start of this stanza and the next, Markham names the addressees of this poem: "O masters, lords and rulers in all lands." There is no getting away from this direct address. The ruling elite's "handiwork" is "this monstrous Thing distorted and soul-quenched". The 16th century word, "handiwork", connects the actual hands of the ruling elites to what they have made. It is a very different philosophical framework to a liberal Western mindset of today because at the end of the 19th century the masters were responsible for the laborer's physical and metaphysical well-being. Furthermore, this responsibility comes off the back of Victorian thinking that considered it a Christian duty to improve the souls of the less fortunate. The proximity of the ruling elite's hands to the worker continues: "How will you ever straighten up this shape; / Touch it again with immortality." It is as if the worker's only hope for salvation is at the hands of the master. The ruling elite is faced with imperatives: "Give back…Rebuild…Make right." Therefore, those with power must give to the workers: enlightenment and hope, "Upward looking and the light"; aesthetics and aspiration, "the music and the dream"; and pride, justice, and happiness, "Make right the immemorial infamies, / Perfidious wrongs, immedicable woes".

Despite the end to the Age of Revolutions, the rising disquiet in China and Russia, not to mention the Spanish American War of 1889, Western society remained cautious about the emergence of an oppressed people who would not remain downtrodden. The 5th stanza looks directly at this conundrum. This final stanza poses three questions to the masters. In the first question, Markham asks the ruling elite what sort of future can be estimated or calculated with "this Man". The peasant with a hoe must be considered seriously because the whole of society's future is contingent upon the ways in which his humanity can be restored. The second question becomes more specific and reflects upon the winds of change that blow about the fin de siecle in Markham's America. By this stage, the nation's economic boom has plunged, unemployment is at an all-time high of 18.4 percent, the Reading Railroad has financially collapsed, money in circulation declines, and agricultural depression spreads. Here he asks about the influence of the "whirlwinds of rebellion" that "shake all shores?" The final question of the poem asks "How will it be" for the masters and for the nations when this *Frankenstein*'s monster rises up, a "dumb Terror". It is of our own making that this beast has grown and been hitherto without agency, without voice. In many ways, I hear Yeats' *Second Coming* some two decades later confirming the prophecy of this very stanza. Like "the rough beast that slouches towards Bethlehem", the second coming of Markham's "thing" is "to judge the world / After silence of the centuries": a terrifying prospect. What of the contemporary reader? We are left wondering how we have come from so little to so much and yet seem so spiritually bereft. Are we men with hoes forevermore?

Replica of The Thinker by Matthew Olzmann (2011)

By the doorstep of The Museum,
the Duplicate is frustrated.
Like the offspring of a rock star or senator,
no matter what he does, it's never enough.
He only wants to think dignified thoughts,
important thoughts, thoughts that will imprint
like an artist's signature on the memory of mankind.
But it's difficult, because when he thinks,
his head is filled with iron and bronze,
not neurons and God.

I too, feel like that.
You know how it works when you make a photocopy
of a photocopy? The original fights to be seen
but appears blurred in each new version.
Each morning, I sit at the kitchen table
the way my father must've years ago.
I've got my oatmeal and coffee,
my newspaper and blank stare.

The Replica

digs his right elbow into his left thigh,
his chin into his right fist, and then he thinks
as hard as his maker will allow. He tries to envision
patterns among celestial bodies, the mysteries
of Christ, X + Y, crossword puzzles, free will.
The expression on his face;
somewhere between agony and falling asleep.

Yet he holds this pose
as if no one will notice what frauds we are,
as if some world around him is about to make sense,
some answer has almost arrived. Almost.

Bronze sculpture by Auguste Rodin held variously (including Rodin Museum, Paris). 186 cm high and approximately 28 full size castings. First conceived as part of the Gates of Hell in 1880 but this casting did not appear until 1904.

I really like this perky little poem. In its simplicity, it is both elegant and complex. It's a poem deeply preoccupied with the dilemma of the unoriginal. Can a world without the original actually ever make sense? If there is no new, just a copy of a copy, as Baudrillard has taught us, then how does our uniqueness have authentic meaning? Rodin's *The Thinker* is a statue of daring largess, a magnificent epistemological wonder that has the effect of making us ponder the truth or the simulation of truth. All bets are off when it comes to this masterpiece of sculpture. There is so much uncertainty even about the origins of this masterpiece: the original title was *The Poet*...or maybe not; the original design was made for the *Gates of Hell* in a more miniature form...or maybe not; and the original idea was that this represented Dante before he enters Hell...or maybe not. There are multiple copies of *The Thinker* outside the entrances of museums across the globe. So, what are we seeing? A body, which is a copy of every other body hence we identify it as a body; copied by Rodin in a drawing; copied then as a clay model; copied in a sand cast; and copied in molten bronze. This was a collaborative process where Rodin's team of accomplished plaster casters, studio assistants, carvers, founders, and young sculptors seeking mentoring contributed to the emerging production of public works in sculpture, in particular in bronze. So, could we actually say that this masterpiece is made by Rodin? Furthermore, there is the potential to make even more copies with the casts still available. More importantly, why does the notion of original matter so much to us when it comes to valuing art? Let us consider these questions as we read Olzmann's poem.

In this airy free verse poem, we move from the public domain to the private: from "the doorstep of the Museum" to "the kitchen table". These binary settings give us a concrete context to cogitate the public and private fascination with replicas, copies, duplicates, reproductions, photocopies, facsimiles, prints, imitations, and fakes. When we first meet *The Thinker* within the poem, our expectations of an uber-man in a state of contemplation, albeit a naked one, are usurped by the personification of the statue as "frustrated". This is unexpected, and we are taken into the realm of the unanticipated when this mighty icon is likened to "the offspring of a rock star or senator". This transports an iconic fin de siecle masterpiece into something that belongs to the world of popular culture or contemporary politics. This simile conveys the idea that the Duplicate is "never enough". This is the heart of the poem: the idea that a replica is a lesser version of the original and can never fulfil the promise of the original. Olzmann explores the statue's desire to think; indeed, the word "thought" appears in triplet in quick succession. The statue's wish is folded neatly into a perfect self-referential simile: "thoughts that will imprint / like an artist's signature on the memory of mankind." Like Rodin's signature at the base of the statue or the founder's signature at the base of the plinth, Olzmann's signature beneath this poem is an attempt to nudge his art into mankind's memory. I love the quirky little disclaimer at the end of this stanza, that despite the desire and drive to think, "his head is filled with iron and bronze, / not neurons and God". What does this tell us about the seduction of art? That no matter how realistic or idealistic or illusory or seductive, art remains art.

In the next stanza we move between the contemplation of the sculpture and that of the poet. Olzmann asserts that we are all familiar with replica making: "You know how it works when you make a photocopy / of a photocopy?" Perhaps he is asking something more intrinsic about the way we constantly replicate the thoughts and actions of others. This very poem we read is a "photocopy / of a photocopy" in that it is a replica of Olzmann's original draft. There is another clue here in terms of what Olzmann is suggesting about duplicates and that is that "The original...appears blurred in each new version". Metaphorically this suggests the instability and transient nature of replicas: that in the capacity to endlessly reproduce there is a distancing from the actual original and therefore the suggestion that something is lost or made lesser. Olzmann offers a snapshot of himself at breakfast mirroring his father. The poet positions inaction directly across from inaction to replicate his father's morning: "I've got my oatmeal and coffee, / my newspaper and blank stare." These ordinary and familiar nouns belong to the domestic space of the poet and to the father and to us, but the "blank stare" is reminiscent of the inanimate Thinker and reminds us we too struggle to comprehend the meaning of connections no matter how hard we try.

At the start of the third stanza, we are invited to consider how *The Thinker* is positioned. Indeed, the arrangement of the statue's posture reads like a game of *Twister*: "digs his right elbow into his left thigh, / his chin into his right fist." The verb choice, "digs", is adroit because it is a reminder of the art making process of creating a bronze statue, digging into the clay and sand cast, but also suggesting the way in which the statue is digging in for the long haul as a public monument for centuries to come. Meanwhile, in keeping with the durability of the material of the statue, we read "he thinks / as hard as his maker will allow", suggesting that he can only be the sum of his parts. In other words, he needs to be *The Thinker* but is restricted by a head "filled with iron and bronze". In this stanza, we come across our third reference to God and *The Thinker*'s relationship with his maker. There is an ongoing reminder here that this creation is dependent on his creator; moreover, art is a version of, a duplicate of, or a copy of a miniature of artist or poet as God. The existential considerations attributed to *The Thinker*'s cognisance are similar to our own at various times: "patterns among celestial bodies, the mysteries / of Christ, X + Y, crossword puzzles, free will." This is a momentary meander through astrology, theology, mathematics, etymology, and psychology. We are left with *The Thinker*'s face: caught between the pain and fatigue of only ever doing this difficult interminable thinking.

In the final and brief stanza, we see the heroism of *The Thinker*, even if he remains slightly ridiculous. Despite the doubt, despite the dependency on a greater being, despite the unoriginality of his being, and despite his inability to think, "he holds his pose". It's the stoicism and silence that is so appealing. In a world where social media must express just about every single thought ever considered, there is something generous, contemplative, and silent about this heroic figure. The anaphora of "as if" in the antepenultimate and penultimate lines lead to suppositions upon which our lives are contingent: that "no one will notice what frauds we are" and the world "is about to make sense". If this is the state of cognisance for a statue without originality, then it is also true for us. The ultimate line suggests that *The Thinker* holds his pose in the hope that all will be revealed, but, in the repetition of the adverb "almost", we are reminded that full knowledge is forever just out of reach. Is it only the original that can give us complete closure? This poem contemplates the value of the original: whether this is Rodin's sculpture or the poet himself or even ourselves. Furthermore, *Replica of The Thinker* is an ontological exploration of the way in which we all bear a copy of the self within ourselves which is infinitely recurring: a poem of mise en abyme.

Why knowing is (& Matisse's Woman with a Hat) by Martha Ronk (2002)

Why knowing is a quality out of fashion and no one can decide to
but slips into it or ends up with a painting one has never
seen that quality of light before even before having seen it
in between pages of another book and not remembering who knows
or recognizing the questionable quality of light on her face
as she sits for a portrait and isn't allowed to move an inch
you recognize the red silk flower on her hat
and can almost place where you have seen that grey descending
through the light reversing foreground and background
as the directions escape one as the way you have to
live with anyone as she gets up finally from her chair
having written the whole of it in her head as the question

ignored for the hundredth time as a quality of knowing is
oddly resuscitated from a decade prior to this.

La Femme au Chateau is an oil on canvas by Henri Matisse (80.63 centimeters by 59.69 centimeters). Amelie Matisse, Henri's wife, was the model for this controversial painting that was first exhibited in 1905 at the Salon d'Automne. This painting was at the center of Fauvism: loose brushstrokes, unfinished style, and unnatural colors. It hangs in the San Francisco Museum of Modern Art.

This sardine squished sonnet, where time changes and meaning silver tails about, is a complex delight. Here is a meditation on experimentation. We simultaneously contemplate the experimentation of Ronk's art and Matisse's art; wedged in between is the explosion of Amelie's portrait. Ronk's sonnet is a contemporary poetic discursive practice of epistemology that confronts the fin de siecle practice of Impressionist art. Like Matisse, Ronk chooses to test the boundaries, and she does so in a single sentence sonnet, which, by the time we reach the phrase "having written the whole of it in her head", we realize is written from Amelie's perspective. I think the art of getting close to this poem is to recognize its Fauvist style: a wild beast of sorts. The lines have an unfinished quality to them, considerations are offered in unnatural colors, and there is a definite looseness to the poem's brushstrokes in order to allow space for our entry.

An easier entrée to the sonnet could have been: Why is knowing a quality out of fashion? Instead, we are asked to enter into this small room of intensity with an epistemological statement: "Why knowing is a quality out of fashion." The statement anticipates an explanation to follow with explanations of why discernment and understanding are not currently trendy. This makes me think about Matisse's *La Femme au Chateau*, which of course was not at all fashionable, neither the hat nor the painting, when it was exhibited in the early 20th century. Great art then, like now, can go in and out of fashion. The end of the opening line, "no one can decide to", leaves us with a cliff hanger: reflective of the way this painting at the time of hanging generated suspense and anxiety. The second line makes me think of Leo and Gertrude Stein who ended up with this painting, a type of accidental pairing. The third line speaks to the wonder of this painting where "one has never / seen that quality of light before". Enlightened, the Steins ended their collection of 19th century art when they saw this Matisse painting and commenced their 20th century collection upon its purchase. It is as if this "quality of light" was the window that opened up their gaze to the Moderns. It's not as if there wasn't light in the masterpieces of the 19th century but rather this "quality", this particular feature of light, opened up a whole new world. When the Steins bought and displayed this Matisse masterpiece, it made Picasso's *Girl with a Basket of Flowers*, which was hung in the Stein's apartment immediately beneath Matisse's *La Femme au Chateau*, look tame. Matisse's daubs of red, yellow, pink, and green on the face coupled with her direct and steady gaze at the observer is not only scandalously experimental but demanding of our reaction.

A great masterpiece lives and breathes: thus, art viewing is experiential. Seeing art in books is not the same as seeing it in situ: "having seen it / in between pages of another book." This poem takes us to the artist's easel and the model posing, in a hat, seated on a chair with the light streaming down her face. We are asked to consider whether it was this light that had people variously enthralled or enraged. The contemplation of the light continues: "recognizing the questionable quality of light on her face / as she sits for a portrait and isn't allowed to move an inch." We are now squarely in his studio as Matisse paints the tough minded Amelie. I like the way in which a sense of ambiguity has crept in to our observation of this moment. The quality of light is now "questionable" as it hits her face: lighting up a cacophony of unusual color combinations. Meanwhile, she must be motionless, quite lifeless, in order for the artist to capture her life. So present are we in this studio as Amelie is being painted that we are spoken to directly: "you recognise the red silk flower on her hat / and can almost place where you have seen that grey." This collapsing of two time schemes, one in which Matisse paints Amelie and the other as we observe the renowned painting, suggests that no matter what the era, the reaction to this masterpiece is both visceral and cerebral; it hauls us into its immediacy.

In *La Femme au Chateau* the art making is visible, and the brush strokes do not conform to the rigor and discipline of the early Impressionists. The idea of this "grey descending / through the light reversing foreground and background" indicates how the pallet behind the portrait is so lurid that it pushes out past the image of the woman. The background, the backstory, is more important than the subject. Yet the erratically executed art making eludes understanding of both the observer and the model, who in this case is the wife of a poor artist: "directions escape one as the way you have to / live with anyone." Thus, the portrait becomes enigmatic and its meaning defies capture. It is at this point that Madam Matisse "gets up finally from her chair / having written the whole of it in her head as the question / ignored for the hundredth time". The idea of the portrait walking away from itself is compelling. She has had time to ponder on what knowing is and has arranged these thoughts in her head. She is ignored because Matisse has his own obsessions; she is ignored because she is wife and step mother and artist's model; she is ignored because the painting isn't really about her at all; thus, she is ignored because she is not the subject.

Amelie does not pose the question: what is knowing? (an epistemological question that is at the heart of this masterpiece). Rather, she composes a statement in the penultimate line of the sonnet: "a quality of knowing is." It is a reverse mirror image of the opening line of the sonnet: "knowing is a quality." Why does she do this? I think after the hanging of *La Femme au Chateau* in the salon d'Automne the Matisses must have known that ignorance was in fashion. Additionally, hindsight shows that resistance and hostility can be revived into a state of enlightenment: "oddly resuscitated from a decade prior to this." This is also a reference to Matisse's daughter Marguerite who was born ten years before he painted *La Femme au Chateau* and contracted diphtheria where Matisse had to perform an emergency tracheotomy on the kitchen table. She was resuscitated and would later become the model for Picasso's *Girl with a Basket of Flowers*. Amelie knew that it was this incident and the subsequent closeness between father and child that gave Matisse absolute certainty in "a quality of knowing". Despite the uncertainty of the entire world around him he was sure about the direction of his art; furthermore, he trusted in the quality of light that had been granted him.

Girl at Sewing Machine by Mary Leader (1996)

It must be warm in the room, walls the color of over-steeped tea,

the sun high,
coating the yellow brick exterior of the apartment building,
angling in on
the girl, stripped down to camisole and petticoat, sewing.
She's a busty girl,
soft, no doubt perspiring, slippery under her breasts, moisture
trapped on the back
of her neck under all that chestnut hair. She doesn't notice,
though; you can see
she's intent on her seam. She doesn't slump over the machine
but bends from the hip,
her body as attuned as her hands. Her feet, though not shown
in the painting,
are bound to be pudgy, are probably bare, pumping the treadle
ka-chunk ka-chunk ka-chunk

but that's unconscious. Her point of concentration is the needle,
silver, quick,
its chick chick chick chick chick, necessity to keep the material
in perfect position,
position. What is she making? The fabric looks heavy and yet
billowy, like
whipped cream, or cumulus clouds; certain girls, while large, move
with grace (when nobody's
there) but in public, conceal, or try to conceal, their bodies
beneath long clothes.
They favor long hair, feeling it wimples and veils embarrassment.
Yes, I know this girl.
Only in her room, only when unseen, can she relax at all, peel off
a hot blouse,
a brown skirt, like the one heaped on her bed in the background,
take pleasure in

a good hairbrush, the bottle of scent on the dresser, the picture
of her own choosing
on the wall. Whatever she's making--let's go ahead and say it's
a dress for herself--
she is not, as you might think, dreaming of a party, a dance,
or a wedding. No, she's
deciding to flat-fell that seam--time-consuming, but worth it--
stronger, better-looking.

I'm sure she knows by now not to expect much attention from boys.
She's what? twenty?
eighteen? She will, in time, use many words to describe herself,
not all of them bad;
but not once will one of them be "pretty," or "lovely." Those
aren't for a fat girl
though she can take a mass of cloth, and a cast-iron machine,
and make a beautiful shape.

Girl at Sewing Machine by Edward Hopper, 1921. Oil on Canvas. 48 x 46 cm. Currently held in Thyssen-Bornemisza Museum Madrid.

    This is one of my favorite Hopper paintings, but I am rather partial to window series. Just imagine a whole exhibition dedicated to compositions of the window, where windows are portals to elsewhere, a kind of escape hatch for the subject and for the audience. Of course, windows were used as a technique by artists to let in light: highlighting certain elements of the painting's narrative. I think about the intensity of what the girl at the sewing machine is doing and how I am looking into an intimate feminine moment as she sits, stripped down to her underclothes, running up a seam on an old fashioned sewing machine. That which is behind her disappears off canvas; what's ahead of her is a drama for another artist. Here she is placed at the center of her private space: concentrating on attention to detail. She is a woman at her toilette, a woman at her private mending, a woman at her mirror, and a woman at her art. Hopper's art making, here in this painting, gives off an unfinished quality or lightness. Her curvaceous roundness casts soft relief to the angularity and fixity of the window frame, chair back, sewing table, and dark wooden dressing table. I love the color at the wall in the girl's bedroom where she sits and sews; it is an extravagant color at the end of the color spectrum. The interior is variations of the warm burned reds and bright oranges, which includes her hair, while the whites and yellows of the exterior light and brick work are similar in the fabric being sewn, her underclothes, and flesh. This painting is a whorl of sunshine.
    Mary Leader's poem is as warm as Hopper's painting. It is an intimate conversation between her and you. She draws you in and asks your view and opinion as if we are seeing this together. The entire poem is made up of three octets, and between each octet, like the run-on stitching of a sewing machine, enjambment sews us to the octet below. This poem pulls back the curtains of a small little interior drama. It's in the early 1920s, and the girl at the sewing machine seems independently self-contained in what appears to be an apartment, possibly New York City. Leader begins with a honeyed spotlight on a semi-naked woman intent on her feminine labors. The poet's voice from the onset is conversational and speculative; it is the quiet voice of an observer, of one who is familiar with this setting, character, and plotline. Our eye tracks the warmth of the room awash in "the color of over-steeped tea"; an apt metaphor as one could imagine the girl being distracted and letting the tea brew too long. The sun is "coating the yellow brick exterior…and angling in on / the girl" thus nature is painterly in its ambitions as it lights up the "busty girl, / soft, no doubt perspir-

ing, slippery under her breasts, moisture / trapped on the back / of her neck under all that chestnut hair".

Like a voyeur peeping through a door ajar, our gaze moves far beyond and below the visual to the imagined. The atmosphere is luscious. As in all nudes, or women at their toilette, the object of our gaze is unaware of our presence and gets on with her task at hand: "She doesn't notice." Her attention is completely focused on the machine, so the poet, who gazes with us, directly acknowledges our presence: "you can see... She...bends from the hip, / her body as attuned as her hands." We watch together the poise and concentration of this little seamstress. It is as if she has no interest in our observation or intent: only hers matters. What I love the best is the treadle pumping: "ka-chunk ka-chunk ka-chunk." This darling little onomatopoeia stitches us to her intensive labor and to Hopper's painting. We are there with her in this tight, intimate space.

Like the girl who lovingly bends over her work, this machine is warm and alive in its newly hatched efforts: "the needle, / silver, quick, / its chick chick chick chick chick." It is a little genre of sensuality: we feel the warmth of the room, see the girl at the sewing machine who also feels the interior heat and the fabric beneath her hands. Together we hear the soothing repetitious "ka-chunk" and "chick", assuring us of this reality. There are quiet momentary adjustments to keeping "the material / in perfect position/ position". The repetition imitates the double handling of the fabric as it slips beneath the needle foot. Curiously, it takes the poet this long to ask us "What is she making?", as if this is not as important as witnessing this bedroom intimacy. We billow about in the poet's meanderings concerning what "certain girls, while large" tend to do to "conceal, their bodies". This is an unexpected turn. The painting seems to voice the opposite. Hopper offers revelation not concealment: she is lit up and semi-naked with hair cascading unselfconsciously; she is a picture of health, youth, and feminine beauty, unaware of our ongoing voyeurism. Meanwhile, Leader's voice is sympathetic as she fleshes out the familiar girl she sees: "Yes, I know this girl." She speaks to a girl who prefers to cover her body and face in order to cover that which may be considered as unsightly. The fabric she sews is a metaphor for her body; thus, in effect, *she* is "billowy...whipped cream...cumulus clouds". Her hair "wimples and veils embarrassment". Hair as a symbol of sexual allure in women is used here, ironically, as a nun's headdress protecting the girl from unwanted objectification. Indeed, away from this gaze, including ours, she can "peel off / a hot blouse / a brown skirt", a strip tease of sorts.

By the third octet, we know we are inside the popular painterly subject of woman at her toilette but here in this room, where light and warmth have licked about the interior to reveal a woman uninterrupted and indifferent to our watchfulness, she reclaims the toilette with all its pleasures for herself alone and not for the male viewer. In other words, she moves from object to subject. Thus, in a meta-art moment, Leader states that the little seamstress will take pleasure in "the picture / of her own choosing". On the one hand, this is a nod to Hopper's painting of an interior and on the other hand is an assertion that this girl makes herself subject not object of the male gaze. Here, the girl at the sewing machine takes back her picture. The poet then invites us to be complicit in the hypothetical of what the girl sews: "let's go ahead and say it's / a dress for herself." We are told bluntly "she is not, as you might think, dreaming of a party, a dance, / or a wedding"; I love the way we are caught like a peeping Tom and chided for our romantic fantasies. Indeed, these are dashed immediately by the "flat-fell seam". This durable and sturdy join is her preoccupation. The rest of the octet deals with the way in which the girl is not an object for admiration and attention from the opposite sex. As a result of this, she will generate a particular coded language for herself: "She will, in time, use many words to describe herself... not once will one of them be "pretty," or "lovely." Those / aren't for a fat girl." So, we have vicariously agreed that this girl, who is somewhere between 18 and 20, will have a constrained notion of her beauty and allure. This is a sobering consideration and a reminder that we are complicit in making her the object of our gaze, despite thinking she was unaware and unconcerned about the power of objectification. In the end, the girl at the sewing machine, the girl intent on the making of her own art, regains agency and is subject. We read that she can make from "cloth, and a cast-iron machine...a beautiful shape"; therefore, while she can sail away from the strictures of our gaze, we are left behind.

The Great Figure by William Carlos Williams (1921)

Among the rain
and lights
I saw the figure 5
in gold
on a red
fire truck
moving
tense
unheeded
to gong clangs
siren howls
and wheels rumbling
through the dark city

I Saw the Figure 5 in Gold by Charles Demuth, 1928. Oil, graphite, ink and gold leaf on paperboard. 90.2 x 76.2 cm. Currently held in Metropolitan Museum of Art New York.

What a gem! Both the painting and the poem. I have had a life-long love affair with this poet. He shocks me with his boldness and his refusal to stick to the rules. His poems are Cornell's before they are Demuth's. They are deep insets of personal and intimate American art. In their brittle compact spaces, they seem monumental. Despite its miniature appearance, this poem towers over some of the wordier poetic snapshots of modern love or city life written by other poets. There is a surgical precision in Williams' word choice and grammatical arrangement. As for syntax, it is more than sparse; it is barely present. Aside from a veritable stack of 31 words in 13 lines, prime numbers in a mirror reflection, there is no obvious structural arrangement. Williams is a painterly poet and uses the words to create a clean and precise visual image. This poem is not strictly an ekphrastic poem as it isn't in response to Demuth: rather, this poem triggered this painting. It is Demuth's homage to Williams some seven years after *The Great Figure* was published. So, within Demuth's painting is a poem; within this poem is a city; within this city is a rainy night; within this rainy night is a red fire truck; within this red fire truck is movement; and within this movement is the figure "5". This poem is about this great figure: William Carlos Williams.

Let's start at the beginning where it is cold and wet and luminous. Already there is a shimmer that surrounds our expectations as we commence this poem: "Among the rain / and lights." The priming of this moment is still damp and yet we are promised clarity of vision, perhaps even enlightenment. Then the poet enters: "I saw." This is something that has already happened but was so impressive, so brilliant it must be committed to art and to time immemorial. What does it mean to see? To realize, to comprehend, to grasp, to recognize? It is an epiphany where we emerge out of blindness and into sight. It is a declaration that the universe can still surprise us and teach us the unexpected. I love how what he sees is "the figure 5". It's not "the number 5" or "the digit 5" or "the numeral 5". It is the voluptuous and curvaceous shape of both the word "figure" and the number "5". What other number could be comelier and sonsier? This fetching figure sure did stop Williams in his tracks. Both the painting and the poem catch me up on the gold. The phrase "in gold", and the gold leafing in Demuth's painting of the repeated and receding round form of the number "5", work explosively. Both these artworks, the poem and the painting, are glamorous and very New York City in the Roaring 20s. Gold leafing was of course used to iconize a subject that was considered sacred in order to invoke reverence. Furthermore, a fire truck, in a vibrant never sleeping city, would similarly be regarded as that promise of salvation. Up until this point, we have been telescoped into "5" from the context of rain and lights; now, we pull back slightly to see the location. The great figure is, somewhat curiously and unexpectedly, "on a red / fire truck".

Let's look at this color red, which is at the end of the color spectrum. It has long been associated with passion: Eros and Thanatos. Thus, it is the color of excitement and desire as well as danger and warning: it is Janus-faced. It draws our eye to it and demands response: hence the close proximity of the words "red" and "fire". This is code for sacrifice, courage, heat, anger, and hopefully joy. So, the lines that follow this red fire truck are surprising: "moving / tense / unheeded." The personification of the fire truck as "tense" reminds us of the cityscape awash in rain, people and traffic thus requiring a certain edgy awareness from the fire truck in its charge toward its destiny. It is a living, breathing, and emotive being. It is all verb and verve: a fiat of rescue. Yet, this movement is "unheeded": noticed but disregarded. Rather it is the sound of alarm that draws the gaze: "to gong clangs / siren howls / and wheels rumbling." The onomatopoeia and anthropomorphism generate a cacophony of apprehension. This is poem of strong visual contrasts. The drama happens "through the dark city": a place flooded with light at night. The rain is at one end of the poem, and the fire is somewhere at the other end. I think about the cold and black wet evening in contrast to the red and gold of the fire truck; I think about the racy vibrant city energy symbolized in sirens blaring; and I think about the vertical sheets of rain intersecting the horizontal charge of the speeding fire truck. Yet all the time I am wondering about the fire…where is it? It is somewhere off canvas, beyond the unwritten full stop: perhaps somewhere in Williams, in Demuth, in us.

There is one final observation that cannot be overlooked. As a result of considering the title of both Williams' poem and Demuth's painting, we are positioned to see the great figure "5". This number is a prime number, as are the 13 lines of the poem and the 31 words therein. Prime numbers are my favorite. If the shimmer and delight of this Demuth painting is an homage to, indeed a portrait of William Carlos Williams, then I need to think through this prime number as central to captivating his likeness. The painting is a mirror reflecting the poet and the number "5" dominates the canvas' center. If William Carlos Williams is the number "5", then he is a prime-numbered person: someone who cannot be divisible by anyone or anything. He cannot be broken down (nor is he made up of, as in a composite-numbered person, anything but himself as one). I definitely recognize this intractable monumental poet as the one I fell in love with years ago.

Archaic Torso of Apollo by Rainer Maria Rilke (1918)
Translated by Stephen Mitchell

We cannot know his legendary head
with eyes like ripening fruit. And yet his torso
is still suffused with brilliance from inside,
like a lamp, in which his gaze, now turned to low,

gleams in all its power. Otherwise
the curved breast could not dazzle you so, nor could
a smile run through the placid hips and thighs
to that dark center where procreation flared.

Otherwise this stone would seem defaced
beneath the translucent cascade of the shoulders
and would not glisten like a wild beast's fur:

would not, from all the borders of itself,
burst like a star: for here there is no place
that does not see you. You must change your life.

Torso of Apollo by Kanachos of Sicyon or Pythagoras, 480-470 BC. Unearthed in 1872 by O. Rayet and A. Thomas in the theatre at Miletus, a prosperous Hellenistic city in Asia Minor. In the following year, Edmond and Gustave de Rothschild, who had subsidized the expedition, presented it to the Louvre.

So much is already in the title of Rilke's poem: art from classic antiquity, a carved male torso and the god Apollo. The multiple appellations of the legendary Apollo, speak to believers' desire for a god to be all things for all people. Apollo was known as the god of beauty, poetry, music, truth, prophecy, healing, sun, light, and plague. It was his power that enabled Paris to kill the mighty, hitherto unconquerable, Achilles. Apollo was an oracular god, and the songs sung in his praise were known as "paeans." Let's get closer to his likeness in this marble statue in the Louvre: an exemplary piece of sculpture from the Early Classical Period. Although damaged and without head, legs and arms, this male torso demonstrates a radical break from male nudes of the Archaic period. Here we see a nude male poised frontally that is anatomically correct, with a stylized back and star shaped pubic area. The torso alone indicates the contrapposto position of the original work, standing with weight on the foot and leg that is placed slightly forward and the arms and shoulders twisting off axis from hips and legs. So, considering Apollo was an oracular god and paeans or songs of praise were made in his honor, it is only fitting that Rilke sings a song of praise to the godly creation of this masterpiece. Rilke's poem is not just describing what he is seeing or experiencing but rather asking us to contemplate the transcendent power of art.

Archaic Torso of Apollo is a sonnet. This small complex sonnet is inviting meditation on both Apollo the god as well as the marble male torso in the Louvre. Let's look structurally at the sonnet and consider a short overview before we conduct a close reading. The first sentence is a short assertion of what is in absence and, because it is the head of Apollo which is missing, we are asked to consider a castrated icon. Rather than explore the effigy's iconoclasm, the second sentence asserts that it is the masterpiece of art, suffused with enlightenment, that is worthy of our contemplation. The 3rd and 4th sentences are meandering meditations that prove that, without the enlightenment that art offers, we would not recognise pleasure, inspiration, and ourselves. With this thesis established, we are turned about in the short 5th sentence, which contains the sonnet's volta or turning point: "You must change your life." The reflection we see in art speaks directly to us. The imperative is that our lives must mirror this enlightenment witnessed in such wonders as the torso of Apollo. I think this is true: that life changes utterly when it collides with masterpieces (be it poetry or statuary). Great art is experiential, and it offers profound metaphysical transformation because great art is the source of enlightenment.

The first sentence speaks to that which is absent, a curiosity considering the legend of the god and the presence of the marble statue are both so intensely present. What is absent is the "legendary head / with eyes like ripening fruit". So, in the first moment, we are confronted with the idea of absence or castration: Apollo's fabled head is missing, and beheading is the deprivation of power, vitality, and vigor. Although that which is in absence might heighten our interest in the present, it also inevitably drags our eye to what we believe should be there, could be there, and would be there. In a visual schizophrenia, we are rapidly construing in the mind's eye the fabulous and famous head of this remarkable god while looking at the magnificent torso. So diligent is our mind's eye chiselling away at the imaginary marble to create the head, that we see the comparison Rilke makes between Apollo's eyes and ripening fruit. The use of the present participle "ripening" suggests the extant living quality of this masterpiece. Indeed, the "ripening fruit" is not only a visual imagery but proposes a smorgasbord of sensory responses: taste and smell and touch. Ripening is always moving towards the ripened, over ripe, and fermenting fruit. Apollo's eyes are burgeoning with life, but Rilke is also pointing toward mortality or an end point.

So, from what "We cannot know", we move to the next sentence that runs on from quatrain one to quatrain two. Despite Apollo being castrated, we are told "his torso / is still suffused with brilliance from inside". I love this paradox. The torso is charged with light and genius; it is the sun, imbued with burning power because this is the son of the god of gods. The torso is "still" bathed in light. So, this is not just an art work to be appreciated in a gallery; rather, this is a living breathing being that defies its cold stone inanimate form. From metaphor we move to simile in the exploration of this ancient indeed, archaic, marble torso: "like a lamp / in which his gaze, now turned to low, / gleams in all its power." The torso itself is the object that will offer us enlightenment; it will cast away the shadows that have hitherto hindered our illumination. Apollo's gaze is turned low because his eyes radiate intense agency. Is art imbued with power, or is it the subject depicted that conveys iconic power?

The third sentence of the sonnet completes the second quatrain. Rilke is suggesting that, without this luminosity emanating from the torso, "the curved breast could not dazzle you so". The torso then becomes a kind of epicenter for the inspiration of art: as if the epithets of his godhead such as aesthetics, poetry, music, and light are located within this part of the body. Yet it is the playful and cheeky comment in the next run on line, or enjambment, which arrests our contemporary predilection: "nor could / a smile run through the placid hips and thighs." The personification of the pelvic region heightens the observer's voyeuristic pleasure as it is both the object of desire and the beloved himself. Indeed, this runs "to that dark center where procreation flared." Again, and again we are reminded that this is not just a poem to an extraordinary work of art but a paean that sings praise to the godly capacity of the creator. Here we witness metamorphic limestone transformed into life. It is as if the marble statue itself has disseminated into an ekphrastic art form.

The first unrhymed tercet repeats the adverb "otherwise" to continue the contemplation of the marble effigy, Apollo. Without the enlightenment offered to us via Apollo's torso, "this stone would seem defaced". This is an interesting verb choice: "defaced". It suggests that without this light, the torso would seem a disfigured, ruined, and vandalised deformity. Rather than recognise this as a disfigurement, we ponder the translucency of the marble in the "cascade of shoulders / .... [that] glisten like a wild beast's fur". This wonderful paradox of marble being pellucid, nearly diaphanous, speaks to the alchemy of the sculptor. The simile of Apollo's shoulders compared to the fur of a "wild beast" is connotative of the muscular intensity and ferocity latent within the god.

The final unrhymed tercet completes this consideration of what we gaze on before us. From the containment of a marbled sculptured body, the object bursts forth as a luminous, incandescent and heavenly body: "from all the borders of itself / burst like a star." *Archaic Torso of Apollo* is one of Rilke's *New Poems* which considers objects so that the poem itself becomes a poetic object. Thus, in the penultimate sentence he writes, "there is no place / that does not see you"; in other words, the object and the poem are art, and art reflects us. Like a mirror, art sees us: hence our epiphany when we realise, we can see ourselves somewhere within the masterpiece.

The Iliad Book XVIII (The Shield of Achilles) by Homer 12th – 8th century BC
Translated by Ian Johnston

The first thing he created was a huge and sturdy shield,
all wonderfully crafted. Around its outer edge,
he fixed a triple rim, glittering in the light, [480]
attaching to it a silver carrying strap.
The shield had five layers. On the outer one,

with his great skill he fashioned many rich designs.
There he hammered out the earth, the heavens, the sea,

the untiring sun, the moon at the full, along with
every constellation which crowns the heavens—
the Pleiades, the Hyades, mighty Orion,
and the Bear, which some people call the Wain,
always circling in the same position, watching Orion,
the only stars that never bathe in Ocean stream.

Then he created two splendid cities of mortal men. [490] In one, there were feasts and weddings. By the light of blazing torches, people were leading the brides out from their homes and through the town to loud music of the bridal song. There were young lads dancing, whirling to the constant tunes of flutes and lyres, while all the women stood beside their doors, staring in admiration.

Then the people gathered
in the assembly, for a dispute had taken place.
Two men were arguing about blood-money owed
for a murdered man. One claimed he'd paid in full,
setting out his case before the people, but the other [500] was refusing any compensation. Both were keen to receive the judgment from an arbitration.

The crowd there cheered them on, some supporting one,
some the other, while heralds kept the throng controlled.
Meanwhile, elders were sitting there on polished stones
in the sacred circle, holding in their hands
the staffs they'd taken from the clear-voiced heralds.
With those they'd stand up there and render judgment,
each in his turn. In the center lay two golden talents,
to be awarded to the one among them all
who would deliver the most righteous verdict.

The second city was surrounded by two armies,
soldiers with glittering weapons. They were discussing [510] two alternatives, each
one pleasing some of them—whether to attack that city and plunder it,
or to accept as payment half of all the goods
contained in that fair town. But those under siege
who disagreed were arming for a secret ambush.
Their dear wives and children stood up on the walls
as a defence, along with those too old to fight.
The rest were leaving, led on by Pallas Athena

and Ares, both made of gold, dressed in golden clothes, large, beautiful, and armed—as is suitable for gods. They stood out above the smaller people with them. When the soldiers reached a spot which seemed all right for ambush, a place beside a river where the cattle [520]

came to drink, they stopped there, covered in shining bronze. Two scouts were stationed some distance from that army, waiting to catch sight of sheep and short-horned cattle. These soon appeared, followed by two herdsmen playing their flutes and not anticipating any danger. But those lying in ambush saw them and rushed out, quickly cutting off the herds of cattle and fine flocks of white-fleeced sheep, killing the herdsmen with them. When the besiegers sitting in their meeting place [530]

heard the great commotion coming from the cattle, they quickly climbed up behind their prancing horses and set out. They soon caught up with those attackers. Then they organized themselves for battle and fought along the river banks, men hitting one another with bronze-tipped spears. Strife and Confusion joined the fight, along with cruel Death, who seized one wounded man while still alive and then another man without a wound, while pulling the feet of one more corpse from the fight. The clothes Death wore around her shoulders were dyed red
with human blood. They even joined the slaughter
as living mortals, fighting there and hauling off
the bodies of dead men which each of them had killed. [540]

On that shield Hephaestus next set a soft and fallow field, fertile spacious farmland, which had been ploughed three times. Many laborers were wheeling ploughs across it, moving back and forth. As they reached the field's edge, they turned, and a man came up to offer them a cup of wine as sweet as honey. Then they'd turn back, down the furrow, eager to move through that deep soil and reach the field's edge once again. The land behind them was black, looking as though it had just been ploughed, though it was made of gold—an amazing piece of work!

Then he pictured on the shield a king's landed estate, [550] where harvesters were reaping corn, using sharp sickles.
Armfuls of corn were falling on the ground in rows,
one after the other. Binders were tying them up in sheaves with twisted straw. Three binders stood there.
Behind the reapers, boys were gathering the crop,
bringing it to sheaf-binders, keeping them busy.
Among them stood the king, a sceptre in his hand,
there by the stubble, saying nothing, but with pleasure
in his heart. Some distance off, under an oak tree,

heralds were setting up a feast, dressing a huge ox
which they'd just killed. Women were sprinkling white barley on the meat in large amounts for the workers' meal. [560]

Next, Hephaestus placed on that shield a vineyard, full of grapes made of splendid gold. The grapes were black, the poles supporting vines throughout were silver. Around it, he made a ditch of blue enamel, around that, a fence of tin. A single path led in, where the grape pickers came and went at harvest time. Young girls and carefree lads with wicker baskets were carrying off a crop as sweet as honey.
In the middle of them all, a boy with a clear-toned lyre
played pleasant music, singing the Song of Linos, [570] in his delicate fine voice. His comrades kept time, beating the ground behind him, singing and dancing.

Then he set on the shield a herd of straight-horned cattle, with cows crafted out of gold and tin. They were lowing as they hurried out from farm to pasture land, beside a rippling river lined with waving reeds.
The herdsmen walking by the cattle, four of them,
were also made of gold. Nine swift-footed dogs
ran on behind. But there, at the front of the herd,
two fearful lions had seized a bellowing bull. [580]

They were dragging him off, as he roared aloud.
The dogs and young men were chasing after them.
The lions, after ripping open the great ox's hide,
were gorging on its entrails, on its black blood,
as herdsmen kept trying in vain to chase them off,
setting their swift dogs on them. But, fearing the lions,
the dogs kept turning back before they nipped them,
and stood there barking, close by but out of reach.

Then the famous crippled god created there a pasture
in a lovely valley bottom, an open ground
for white-fleeced sheep, sheep folds, roofed huts, and pens.

Next on that shield, the celebrated lame god made [590] an elaborately crafted dancing floor, like the one Daedalus created long ago in spacious Cnossus,
for Ariadne with the lovely hair. On that floor,
young men and women whose bride price would require
many cattle were dancing, holding onto one another
by the wrists. The girls wore fine linen dresses,
the men lightly rubbed with oil wore woven tunics.
On their heads the girls had lovely flower garlands.

The men were carrying gold daggers on silver straps.
They turned with such a graceful ease on skilful feet,
just as a potter sits with a wheel between his hands, [600]
testing it, to make sure that it runs smoothly.
Then they would line up and run towards each other.
A large crowd stood around, enjoying the dancing magic,
as in the middle two acrobats led on the dance,
springing, and whirling, and tumbling.

On that shield, Hephaestus then depicted Ocean,
the mighty river, flowing all around the outer edge.

This powerhouse is one of the earliest examples of ekphrastic poetry. It provides insight into a mythological artwork and its creation. Here we have Hephaestus, the Greek god of blacksmiths and artisans, forging a shield for Achilles, whose armor has been taken by Hector. I love this moment in the battle outside the besieged city of Troy, which is all part and parcel of the passionate and confident storytelling in both *The Iliad* and *The Odyssey*. Of course, it is the uber-story from which all stories come to us in the Western imagination: Homer and the Bible are the two cornerstones to our narration of self. Homer is the source name given to oral epic poetry from the end of the 9th early 8th century BC; this was passed down and preserved eventually in writing.

In this particular extract, we see Homer's genius in the way he can bring to life a mythological artwork that had been hitherto unseen but only heard and imagined. This is ekphrastic poetry at its best. In some ways, the shield is an emblem of poetry and the act of its creation. It is a show piece of meta-art: art about the making of art. Here is a microcosm of the macrocosm of the universe, and as such, it is symbol of completion; its circular form imitates that very symbol. It is an exercise in complete and utter imagination of a masterpiece by the god of all artisans, Hephaestus. He made all weaponry for the gods, and some stories indicate that he was lame as a result of being thrown out of Olympus. Accordingly, he was brought up by Thetis, the mother of Achilles. Most interestingly is the idea that Hephaestus had special powers to create motion from that which he created. Let's start in the shield's center and move outwards.

i. *The earth, sea, sky, sun, moon and constellations (484-489)*. In the opening section, we are taken into the physical world of crafting art, and we are aware of the lame god's physical strength and tenacity as art takes shape before our eyes. Despite some intermittent references to Hephaestus, like any great artist, he is invisible to the art he creates. Moreover, the art itself, the shield, takes on a life of its own. It is a type of self-generating creativity. The "untiring sun" and the "moon at full" appear alongside each other as reminders of the completion and wholeness of this phenomenal shield. The sun is the symbol of day, enlightenment, power, and the masculine whereas and moon is the symbol of night, changeability, inconstancy, and the feminine. Here, contained on this shield for Achilles, exists the impossibility of opposites coexisting. Homeric Greeks were fascinated with astrology for time keeping purposes and later for astro-meteorology uses. So, we recognise the legendary "Pleiades, the Hyades, mighty Orion, / and the Bear, which some people call the Wain" as the "only stars that never bathe in Ocean stream". This reference is an example of the richly threaded oral history reflected that intensified audience reception. The shield is a palimpsest text, as is the poem, with layers of history, theology, psychology, astrology, and meteorology: all of which are ways to articulate an ontology and eschatology.

ii. *A city with a wedding and another with a battle (490-540)*. We are moving away from the center of the shield to observe the festivity of a wedding scene: "blazing torches", "loud music", "young lads dancing", and "women...staring in admiration." All is as it should be with the stage set for love and celebration, but this is turned on its head. To our surprise, we hear of men arguing over "blood-money owed / for a murdered man." The crowd swiftly turns their attention from the nuptial celebrations to the feud. This is an aberrant drama within a drama as the "elders...on polished stones / in the scared circle" arbitrate and ultimately reward the "righteous verdict". This moment in miniature is intriguing: it is every wedding where at some point the heightened emotion goes off the rails.

iii. Meanwhile, a city close by has troubles brewing: "surrounded by armies" with "glittering weapons." At this moment, the poem reflects military manoeuvre and theological legend. There is something deeply moving about "their dear wives and children" who face the oncoming invading army on the walls of their city "as a defence, along with those too old to fight". The depiction of these vulnerable but courageous motley crews left behind and the city's army setting out to ambush led by their gods "Pallas Athena/ and Ares ... dressed in golden clothes, / large, beautiful, and armed" generates great pathos. Most disturbingly, when the battle ensues along the riverbed outside the city, we hear of "Strife and Confusion join[ing] the fight, / along with cruel Death". The goddess of strife and confusion, Eris, and goddess of death, Atropos, must have been personal, intimate, and familiar to Homeric Greeks. The personification of death continues: "The clothes Death wore around her shoulders were dyed red with human blood." This is a staged drama with its setting and costuming clearly selected to maximise the majestic horror of warfare. Indeed, Eris and Atropos are so enamoured by the carnage about them that they too "joined the slaughter".

iv. *The ploughing of a field (541-549)*. Moving further from the center of the shield is this small reminder of Hephaestus toiling away on this masterpiece. Indeed, this meta-art moment is coupled with meta-commentary as the narrator, Homer, cries out to us, "an amazing piece of work"! This immediacy of real time creation, coupled with the narrator's commentary, makes me consider the value of an audience who would have not only made this epic tale valid by listening but ensured its longevity by handing it on from generation to generation. The metaphorical significance of the field being ploughed and re-ploughed in readiness for sowing and then for harvest are metaphors for preparing and creating the shield itself and thus the poem: "The land behind them / was black, looking as though it had just been ploughed, / though it was made of gold." Even in the description of the shield there is the magical moment of looking back on what has been created and despite its earthliness we note that it gleams as gold. Such efforts by laborers, listeners, gods, and poets require spiritual and physical replenishment which is offered in "wine as sweet as honey". This ambrosia is the drink of the gods and works as nourishment for those laboring to create.

v. *The harvest on a king's estate (550 – 560).* On this circumference of the shield, we see the extensive property of the king's estate with its images of a bounteous harvest. Note the "harvesters", "binders", "reapers", "heralds", and "women" gathering the corn and preparing the feast: a frenetic industry of activity. Meanwhile, "Among them stood the king, a sceptre in his hand, / there by the stubble, saying nothing, but with pleasure / in his heart". Look at that proximity of "sceptre" and "stubble" which in turn brings "pleasure". We have the symbol of rule and might alongside the harvesting of basic produce as indicators of a life well lived. The veneration of the mighty, powerful, and benevolent is at the heartland of the Homeric epic and is the reason why Achilles is worthy of such a shield.

vi. *Grape pickers in a vineyard (561-572).* We are invited to look closer now at the materials of this great artistic masterpiece: Apollo's shield. Here is a shield that is multi-layered in precious metals: gold, silver, blue enamel, and tin. This vineyard is a metaphor that weaves workers and readers in and about its tendrils. So, we are within the art and in some ways making it come alive. Now, we come to "a boy with a clear-toned lyre / played pleasant music, singing the Song/ of Linos,/ in his delicate fine voice". Singing works as a meta-poetic reference in poetry. It is a self-referential moment reminding us that we are also listening to lyric and meter. The "Song of Linos" is a dirge, and so, within this moment of bounty and celebration, the remembrance of loss is ever present. We, like the comrades on the shield and those gathered in Ancient Greece to hear this epic poem, join in keeping time "singing and dancing".

vii. *Herdsmen and their dogs protecting cattle from lions (573-586).* Pulling back further we notice that there's so much movement on this shimmering shield. Moreover, the poet works tirelessly to animate the drama: "cows...hurried", "rippling river", "waving reeds", "herdsmen walking" and "nine swift-footed dogs ran on". Into this ripe landscape appears "two fearful lions" that seize a "bellowing / bull"; it is a combat between strength, symbolised in the lion, and male virility, symbolised in the bull. The scene explodes into chaos, with the plosive noise of the bull bellowing, the "dogs and young men chasing" and "lions ripping open the great ox's hide /...gorging". I love the scene of the faithful dogs still attempting to frustrate the lions but keeping "out of reach". The very detail of the dogs shying away from their duty in fear of their own lives is rendered with exacting care.

viii. *A sheep farm (587-589).* This is a small interlude shaped into the shield where the audience may catch its breath and restore its heartbeat. At this moment, we are offered a calm bucolic scene with images of fertility and plenteousness: "a pasture/ in a lovely valley bottom, an open ground / for white-fleeced sheep, sheep folds, roofed huts, and pens." We are made aware of the presence of "the famous crippled god", Hephaestus, who is creating the shield.

ix. *A dance with young men and women (590-606).* Around this section of the shield we notice the proximity between "the celebrated lame god" and Daedalus. He was a descendent of Hephaestus and a great inventor, making the dance floor for Ariadne. The delicacy of detail is enchanting with the dancers "holding onto one another/ by the wrists"; the girls' "fine linen dresses" and "flower garlands"; and the men "lightly rubbed with oil wore woven tunics" and carrying "gold daggers on silver straps". Nothing is left to chance: indeed, the god is very much in the detail. Even in all this excess of creativity, Homer offers us another simile to understand the power of art making: "just as a potter sits with a wheel between his hands, / testing it, to make sure that it runs smoothly" these dancers danced. This reference to the creation of a masterpiece is tactile, familiar, and ever moving. Meanwhile "in the middle two acrobats led on the dance, / springing, and whirling, and tumbling"; the entertainer, like the master craftsman of Hephaestus and Homer, takes us leaping and twirling into the story of astounding acts of creation.

x. *The ocean (607-609)*. Around the final circumference of the shield is the ocean or "mighty river" which is a metaphor for the making of art. Looking back over these 123 lines of poetry, Hephaestus is referred to 13 times. Homer wants us to be deeply aware that we are witnessing the magic of art making. This shield before us is a mandala that can only exist because of the co-dependency of composer and responder. Overwhelmingly, this must be seen as the uber-ekphrastic poem because it confronts art located in legend, in myth, and in imagination.

Ode on a Grecian Urn by John Keats (1819)

Thou still unravished bride of quietness,
Thou foster-child of silence and slow time,
Sylvan historian, who canst thus express
A flowery tale more sweetly than our rhyme:
What leaf-fringed legend haunts about thy shape
Of deities or mortals, or of both,
In Tempe or the dales of Arcady?
What men or gods are these? What maidens loth?
What mad pursuit? What struggle to escape?
What pipes and timbrels? What wild ecstasy?

Heard melodies are sweet, but those unheard
Are sweeter; therefore, ye soft pipes, play on;
Not to the sensual ear, but, more endeared,
Pipe to the spirit ditties of no tone:
Fair youth, beneath the trees, thou canst not leave
Thy song, nor ever can those trees be bare;
Bold Lover, never, never canst thou kiss,
Though winning near the goal — yet, do not grieve;
She cannot fade, though thou hast not thy bliss,
Forever wilt thou love, and she be fair!

Ah, happy, happy boughs! that cannot shed
Your leaves, nor ever bid the Spring adieu;

And, happy melodist, unwearied,
Forever piping songs forever new;
More happy love! more happy, happy love!
Forever warm and still to be enjoyed,
Forever panting, and forever young;
All breathing human passion far above,
That leaves a heart high-sorrowful and cloyed,
A burning forehead, and a parching tongue.

Who are these coming to the sacrifice?
To what green altar, O mysterious priest,
Lead'st thou that heifer lowing at the skies,
And all her silken flanks with garlands dressed?
What little town by river or sea shore,
Or mountain-built with peaceful citadel,
Is emptied of this folk, this pious morn?
And, little town, thy streets for evermore
Will silent be; and not a soul to tell
Why thou art desolate, can e'er return.

O Attic shape! Fair attitude! with brede
Of marble men and maidens overwrought,
With forest branches and the trodden weed;
Thou, silent form, dost tease us out of thought
As doth eternity: Cold Pastoral!
When old age shall this generation waste,
Thou shalt remain, in midst of other woe
Than ours, a friend to man, to whom thou say'st,
"Beauty is truth, truth beauty, — that is all
Ye know on earth, and all ye need to know."

Sosibios, the Athenian sculptor, created this vase in the Roman Empire at the end of the Republic 50BC. This Neo Attic style displays a decorative repertoire with Apollo, Artemis, and Hermes standing near a burning brazier and presiding over a procession of Bacchic dancers.

    This is a voluptuous ode of five ten line stanzas, decimas, with an intricate rhyme scheme of a, b, a, b and variations of the combination of the final six lines c, d, e, d, c, e. An ode is a paean or song of praise. Keats probably only ever read about Sosibios' vase, but it must have ignited his imagination because this is a song of praise beyond compare! This Greek urn stands majestic and quiet in its marble whiteness now in the Louvre. Keats' 1819 ode brings to life an artwork that collides temporalities of the Ancient Greek Empire, the Roman Empire, the French Bourbons, Napoleonic pillaging, and English Romanticism.

We begin this ode as an apostrophe or direct address to the vase: "Thou still unravish'd bride of quietness." This would have to be one of the most exquisite openings of any love song that ever existed. The curvaceous sonsy vase is the object of love and promise. Yet the word "unravish'd" is the alarm at the center of this line, which addresses the bride who is guarded on either side by "still" and "quietness". Thus, the ode has commenced seconds before she is seized and carried off. Therefore, her beauty is both fleeting and immortalised. The sibilance runs through the first four lines, reiterating the quietude of this nubile bride: "foster… silence… slow / Sylvan historian… canst thus express / sweetly." She is described variously as an "unravish'd bride", a "foster-child of silence and slow time", and a "Sylvan historian". She moves between the state of unknowing to the state of knowing. She alone could tell a "tale more sweetly than our rhyme"; in other words, the story carved on her body is more valuable than anything Keats is capable of creating. No lover of such a beloved is going to turn his back on her without an attempt to seize this opportunity and carry her off. The following six lines of the decima contain seven questions that get shorter and shorter. The momentum nearly runs away from us in our breathless pursuit to gain knowledge. What we learn is that, written across her body, haunting "thy shape", is a "leaf-fring'd legend". At one level, this is the valley of Tempe and the hills of Arcadia: part of the imagined sites of belonging in Ancient Greek mythology. On another level, this is the mysterious beauteous body of a woman: to be wondered at and fetishized by young poets like the Romantic Keats. Playing out this bacchius fantasy are gods, men, and "maidens/ loth" in "mad pursuit". So, there is pursuit, a "struggle to escape" and "wild ecstasy" all to the rising tempo of music.

Decima two continues this conceit of music in the first four lines. Here, the poet argues that the evocation of music conveyed by our imagination far surpasses any literal tune or melody. The whimsy is that this very ode is mellifluous in its incantation and lyricism. The plosive imperative, "pipes play on", is taken up with gusto in the following six lines of the decima. Here we focus on the frieze about the belly of the vase and the way it holds the eternal motion and energy of desire: "Fair youth…you canst not / leave…nor ever can those trees be bare; / Bold Lover, never, never canst thou kiss." This is desire that will never ever be satiated. This is one part human one part deified passion. This is the chase with all its heart-racing hunger but without the catch, the ravishment. Note how the lover "though winning near the goal" will never actually attain his objective. Fingertips stretched, tantalizingly close, just a hair's breadth out of reach, nearly, just a little, just…not quite. The allure and tease remain forever while satisfaction and consummation will always be just out of reach. This is the nature of desire. Thus, we are assured that the catch will remain forever young: "She cannot fade…For ever wilt thou love, and she be fair!" Of course, in keeping with conventional poetic love, he the lover is active and will be subject of this pursuit in always loving, while she the Beloved is always object and passive. The alliterative connection of her as unable to "fade" but remain forever "fair" reminds us that the desire for the beautiful female object can only ever increase as a result of centuries of artistic paeans created by men. This is a song about male desire immortalised in works of art; such as Sosibios and Keats.

Decima three moves from the immortalisation of desire that can never fade, to an ecstasy of happiness. We move from the eternal explosive happiness of the limbs of the trees that will never know a winter, to the rapturous energised joy of the melodist who can play on uninterrupted, to the ecstatic febrile bliss of young lovers as they pursue the object of desire around and around unhindered. Six times we aspirate "happy" in the first five lines of this decima. This is an ode that brings to life the energy and passion of the many levels of exultant pleasure that can be achieved. This poem is precisely about the way in which we may need not "ever bid Spring adieu". Like the lesson great art teaches us, we can live a life in pursuit of beauty. This life will always offer happiness. The meta-poetic moment of the "happy melodist, unwearied, / For ever piping songs for ever new" is a reference to Keats' own desire to write on forevermore. Moreover, it is the lovers who reach the crescendo of happiness in "More happy love! More happy, happy love!" This line works as the center axis on which this entire ode turns. The physicality of the poem cannot be overlooked with the efforts of "panting", "breathing", and "a heart...cloy'd", not to mention "A burning forehead, and a parched tongue". The pursuit of beauty and thus happiness is exhausting!

Decima four takes a good look at the vase itself. We are caught by the opening question: "Who are these coming to the sacrifice?" It is an invitation to lean in and see the other narratives spinning about the rounded body of the vase. Initially, we see a "green altar", a "mysterious priest", and a "heifer lowing...her silken flanks with garlands". It is a reminder that passion is concerned with Thanatos as much as it is Eros. In other words, passion is constituted by death and love; hence, suffering must be at the interface of passion. A cost must be paid. We then note that the cost is citadels "emptied of this folk". I always feel this is a type of Hamlin in which all the beautiful youth are taken; lured away by the magic of the everlasting melody. There's something haunting our peripheral vision where "streets for evermore / ...silent...not a soul to tell / Why thou are desolate, can e'er return". Here is the conundrum. Until this point we have been seduced by the energy, desire, and excitement of the pursuit of passion and yet now we can sense the desolation and price of this hunger. We are reminded that these bold lovers and loth or reluctant beloveds can never return to an innocent state where they are sans desire.

In the final decima, we return to the apostrophe; the direct address to the vase. She is the epitome and quintessence of beauty; she is "O Attic shape". This is a nod to Sosibios' own Greek heritage at the endpoint of the Roman Empire, but it is also an emerging Western belief in the Hellenistic values of beauty. Despite the overly elaborate "marble men and maidens" and "forest branches and trodden weeds", she remains elusive. It is her "silent form", which is eternally provocative to artists, poets, collectors, and writers. Keats addresses her as he would a beloved who is tantalisingly out of reach: "Thou...dost tease us out of thought." Like many poets before him he compares her allure to eternity: tormentingly unfathomable. About her coveted voluptuous shape, we have read the idealised portrayal of country life: a "Cold Pastoral!" I can't help but think there is an exhaustion of the young lover at this point as he declares the object of his pursuit "Cold". She is forever taciturn and unsympathetic to his hunger. The line "when old age shall this generation waste" makes a clear division for the first time between that which is immortalised on the urn and those mortals who are viewing it. The urn's message is that the poetry of her beauty will sustain us: "Beauty is truth, truth beauty." In the spirit of this Attic love song, so steadily embracing the eternal pursuit of desire despite its cost, Keats leaves us with his axiom. The hunger for beauty is the hunger for truth and vice versa. The pursuit of beauty can only lead to the discovery of truth; the quest for truth can only ever lead to beauty. What else is there that we need to know?

On the Medusa of Leonardo Da Vinci by Percy Shelley (1819)

It lieth, gazing on the midnight sky,
Upon the cloudy mountain-peak supine;
Below, far lands are seen tremblingly;
Its horror and its beauty are divine.
Upon its lips and eyelids seems to lie
Loveliness like a shadow, from which shine,
Fiery and lurid, struggling underneath,
The agonies of anguish and of death.

Yet it is less the horror than the grace
Which turns the gazer's spirit into stone,
Whereon the lineaments of that dead face
Are graven, till the characters be grown
Into itself, and thought no more can trace;
'Tis the melodious hue of beauty thrown
Athwart the darkness and the glare of pain,
Which humanize and harmonize the strain.

And from its head as from one body grow,
As ... grass out of a watery rock,
Hairs which are vipers, and they curl and flow
And their long tangles in each other lock,
And with unending involutions show
Their mailed radiance, as it were to mock
The torture and the death within, and saw
The solid air with many a ragged jaw.

And, from a stone beside, a poisonous eft
Peeps idly into those Gorgonian eyes;
Whilst in the air a ghastly bat, bereft
Of sense, has flitted with a mad surprise
Out of the cave this hideous light had cleft,
And he comes hastening like a moth that hies
After a taper; and the midnight sky
Flares, a light more dread than obscurity.

'Tis the tempestuous loveliness of terror;
For from the serpents gleams a brazen glare
Kindled by that inextricable error,
Which makes a thrilling vapour of the air
Become a ... and ever-shifting mirror
Of all the beauty and the terror there—
A woman's countenance, with serpent-locks,
Gazing in death on Heaven from those wet rocks.

Head of Medusa, oil on wood 49cm x 74cm held in the Uffizi Gallery since 1753. Attributed to Leonardo Da Vinci.

This poem confronts the delicious relationship between beauty and horror. It is made up of five octaves with the rhyme scheme of a, b, a, b, a, b and the final couplet c, c locking in a truth. Shelley writes this darkling poem after a visit to Florence in 1819, it is a poem which explores the fascinating and familiar aftermath of a ghastly and violent act. Let's consider Medusa: Why has she morphed across the ages to represent different meanings for men and women? Here is a deeply familiar tale of a man violating a woman: decapitating her intellect and her voice. It should hardly surprise us that her physiognomy is so ghastly; it needs to be represented as a writhing head of snakes. Legend tells us that Medusa was raped by Poseidon in Athena's temple and as a result was punished by this goddess of wisdom and war. According to Ovid, Medusa's beauty was replaced with a countenance so hideous that Perseus needed a mirror in order to behead her. So, this is really a story about a woman, typically an object of beauty, becoming a female subject of horror: misogyny by any other name. Moreover, this is about a scapegoat for society's fear of miscegenation. This is about the ways in which women are to blame for getting in the way of the man's story: a tale of desire and terror. For some, Perseus momentarily restores Eden, for others his deed is motivated by vengeance.

The first octave of this ode is a multi-layering of masculine iterations made by Shelley, Da Vinci, and Ovid. Thus, we begin with "It": not "she" or "Medusa" but the object loaded with centuries of male fascination. The neutral pronoun makes her less powerful, less hideous, and less frightening. Such is the impact and drama of Medusa's death stare which sees all: "gazing in the moonlight sky, / Upon the cloudy mountain peak supine; / Below far lands are seen tremblingly." In the spirit of Romanticism, Shelley's landscape is awakened to the sublime powers: "Its horrors and its beauty are divine." Even in the first octave, Shelley cannot help himself but be enthralled, nearly in love, with this woman of all women: "lips and eyelids seem to lie / Loveliness like a shadow, from which shrine...agonies of anguish and of death." The alliterative connection between lips and lie and loveliness is a plaintive song to beauty lost. The mere shadow of her loveliness has resulted in art by men throughout the ages. This is the concupiscence of the eye "fiery and lurid" from as far back as Western imagination can go.

In octave two, we learn that Medusa's beauty is so pleasing that it seems divine, and it is this which cannot be looked upon. Shelley admits: "it is less the horror than the grace / which turns the gazer's spirit into stone." We hear in Exodus that God tells Moses he cannot look upon the face of God and live. So too was the fate of those who attempted to look on the face of Medusa. Shelley grapples with this enigma. He traces the "lineaments of that dead face", considering the way in which her beauty, liveliness, and potency are not extinguished by death but rather enhanced: "the melodious hue of beauty thrown / Athwart the darkness and the glare of pain." Beauty is light and is known in relation to its counterpoint: darkness. It is this moment of enlightenment that will "humanize and harmonize" the tension between Medusa's quick beauty and her legendary death. Curiously, it is not until she is dead that Medusa's potency can be fully tamed.

Octave three confirms my suspicions all along about Medusa's head of vipers. I always thought it suspicious that her beautiful tresses were replaced by innumerable phalluses. Was it this that made her truly terrifying? That her head was the site of male potency and power? Medusa was no longer the most beautiful woman known to man with the allure of her uncovered hair and ravishing face; she was now a gorgon with writhing snakes as hair. This image is not for the faint-hearted, yet it is fascinating: "they curl and flow / And their long tangles in each other lock." Indeed, this head of hair in the Da Vinic painting is depicted as a mass of orgasmic ecstasy. Shelley refers to their "unending involutions shew / Their mailed radiance". This is a spectacle of shining vipers with their metallic scaled vivacity; this is the aftermath of obsessive love and desire. It is the phallic over-inscription of Medusa's head that leaves us with such "ragged jaw", rough talk, on the subject. In other words, the vipers unequivocally signal her power.

In octave four, we see inside the gorgon sisters' lair and the final moments of the death scene. While Medusa is sleeping with her sisters, in this cave where they live like wild animals sheltering from predators, we note the presence of mice, bats, and newts. These are the witnesses to her beheading, but even these innocent bystanders are marked by the pejorative: "a poisonous eft / Peeps idly into those Gorgonian eyes / Whilst in the air a ghastly bat...flitted with mad surprise." Theirs is a state of innocence and yet just by association they are regarded as venomous and frightening. Shelley likens Perseus' stealth to "a moth that lies / After a taper": not exactly the courageous hero but rather a thief who comes in the night to steal back man's potency. The "midnight sky" is mentioned twice: first in octave one and now in octave four. We are reminded of the mighty canvas of darkness with all its connotations of the unknown upon which this drama unfolds. There is a momentary flare from the midnight sky that lights up "dread" not "obscurity"; thus, the Medusa drama is something to be feared but never forgotten.

In octave five, we are bombarded with paradox in order to heighten this moment of beauty and terror. In the first line, we see "this tempestuous loveliness of terror". Horror and dread generate an allure, a passion, which has sustained men throughout the ages. Here is the object of masculine desire and terror at its apotheosis. Perhaps men could not look upon her because it would be like looking into the mirror of themselves, with that phallic head of hers making them writhe with self-lust. Shelley reminds us that "from the serpents gleams a brazen glare". This audacious gaze of the serpent is disturbing because it suggests the uncharacteristic notion of female boldness. The serpent's gaze is also a mirror into which we are disinclined to look. This, coupled with "the inextricable error" of the "thrilling vapour of the air" from Medusa's mouth suggests life is still present. The paradox of death and life; terror and beauty; dread and reverence; and the phallus crowned feminine is mirrored in all of us. The final rhyming couplet leaves us with the unimaginable: "A woman's countenance, with serpent locks, / Gazing in death on heaven from those wet rocks." Medusa sees heaven and in so doing sees redemption, salvation, and respite after a life suffered at the hands of men.

2

Making Life Easier to Bear: The Sonnet

This chapter explores the sonnet across the visceral and cerebral landscapes of life: from Sicilian love songs to English varietals of Shakespearian or Spenserian sonnets and beyond. We will unpack sonnets from the 12th century through to modern day; from female and male sonneteers; from the rule abiding sonnet to its unruly bad boy doppelganger. The word sonnet comes from the Italian *sonetto*, meaning "a little sound, a little song"; indeed, its stateliness belies the modesty of the word's derivation. So, let's investigate these small square poems; these little mandalas inviting meditation; these art works of vivid symmetry. Each sonnet will fill you with surprise! Each is a pocket rocket. And to think ... all you really needed when life got a little unbearable was a sonnet!

Let's just remind ourselves of the structure of this delightful form. Traditionally, the sonnet is a poem of 14 lines in iambic pentameter linked by an intricate rhyme scheme. Every notable poet down throughout the ages has tried his or her hand at this clever and challenging enigmatic poem. Rhyme and meter are not offered to confine but rather to enable a virtuoso performance. The sonnet was originally introduced to the English from Sir Thomas Wyatt when he wrote *Whoso List to Hunt*. There are two traditional types of sonnets: the Italian or Petrarchan and the English or Shakespearean. The octet or octave in the Italian is designed with two quatrains and a rhyme scheme of a b b a, followed by the volta or turn, then the sestet which is made up of two tercets and a rhyme scheme of c d e c d e. The English sonnet is shaped into three quatrains with the rhyme scheme of a b a b c d c d e f e f and then the volta with the final couplet g g. The octet sets up the question or statement and the sestet either provides an answer or counterstatement.

Having said all of this, a sonnet need not be 14 lines nor written in iambic pentameter nor follow a distinct rhyme scheme, and the volta can occur in the most unexpected places. Yet the overarching feature is that the sonnet is a way of organizing one's thinking around one complex subject and offering both exploration and contemplation. Thus, the sonnet is an emblem of coherent meaning. I have decided to explore sonnets that loosely come under the categories of desire, devotion, doubt, and delight. You might find this corralling a little ineffectual as sonnets do have a life of their own, spirited entities that they are, and a tendency to become a little untethered and move over into other enclosures. In other words, the sonnets exploring the complexity of desire seem, at times, to also be interested in devotion and in so doing express doubt ... but at all times they remain an explosion of delight. Why do sonnets make life easier to bear? The craftsmanship of each of these little light boxes invites meditation and allows the reader space to breathe and dream and feel fully alive. A great sonnet is a cathedral or a symphony or a Guernica.

Sonnets of Desire

Leda and the Swan by W. B. Yeats (1923)

> A sudden blow: the great wings beating still
> Above the staggering girl, her thighs caressed
> By the dark webs, her nape caught in his bill,
> He holds her helpless breast upon his breast.
>
> How can those terrified vague fingers push
> The feathered glory from her loosening thighs?
> And how can body, laid in that white rush,
> But feel the strange heart beating where it lies?
>
> A shudder in the loins engendered there
> The broken wall, the burning roof and tower
> And Agamemnon dead.
>   Being so caught up,
> So mastered by the brute blood of the air,
> Did she put on his knowledge with his power
> Before the indifferent beak could let her drop?

How can a little poem house so much? This sonnet is about the Greek myth of Zeus impregnating Leda; it is about Yeats' passion for Maud Gonne; it is about the truth that violence begets violence; it is about nations created out of destruction; and it is about inheritance. I am sure *Leda and the Swan* houses so much more, but for our purposes, we are considering the way in which this sonnet, in all its chiselled bone and voluptuous flesh, contemplates the dark side of desire. Since the Hellenistic age, the mythology of Zeus, taking the form of a giant swan and impregnating Leda, has captured the people's imagination. Here is a way to consider the violation of a woman by the god of all gods, in order to beget the greatest beauty of antiquity, Helen. Zeus' capacity to take what he desired and make it his own was rendered with such force that Leda gave birth to the powerful double offspring not once but twice: Helen and Polydeuces as well as Castor and Clytemnestra. The violent drama this offspring would return to the world rivalled the violence from which they were begotten. Yeats publishes *Leda and the Swan* in 1923, some ten years after he imagined Maud Gonne as Helen of Troy in *No Second Troy*. Already the legend of Gonne's beauty and acumen permeate Yeats' poetics. Most interestingly is the fact that this poem is published the year Yeats is awarded the Nobel Laureate for giving expression to the spirit of his whole nation: a nation that was, that very year, separated into the Republic of Ireland and Ulster. This sonnet is the house of intimacy and bloodshed evoked by the dark desire of sex and violence. It is Greek drama, it is Ireland in Civil War, and it is our inheritance.

Let's look closely at this sonnet. Three words announce the attack which is then followed by three and a half lines outlining what happened. The swift and unexpected nature of "A sudden blow" belies the relentless and ongoing violent factionalism that continues to plague humanity since time immemorial. Leda's weak and infantile state makes her a non-threat, an easy target: "the staggering girl." She is the object of desire. The first stanza offers up momentary glimpses of her desirable flesh: "thighs…nape…breast." In contrast is the force and agency of her assailant: "great wings beating…caressed / By the dark webs…caught in his bill / He holds her." So, here is attack, rape and violence in the first half of the octet with a rhyme scheme of a b a b. In the Italian or Petrarchan sonnet, the octet sets up a problem, expresses desire, and reflects on experience. The second part of the octet evokes Leda's surrender to the attack. Her will has been overthrown and thus her surrender can only be regarded as a result of there being no other choice. Or is Yeats posing another way to regard this surrender? In this sonnet her surrender is conveyed in the adjective "vague" and in the verb "loosening". Without these words the first question posed, "How can those terrified … fingers push?", is rhetorical because it would be impossible for Leda to resist the "feathered glory" of Zeus. Yet with the added word "vague", the question stops being rhetorical and becomes a disturbing enquiry into the extent to which Leda also desired this violation. The second question posed in this second stanza, "how can body, laid in that white rush / But feel the strange heart beating where it lies?", indicates that it would be impossible for a "body" to not have full carnal knowledge. Innocence is long gone. Experience of attack and surrender has taken its place. Thus, the "white rush" gives life to knowledge of violent dark desire within both the attacker and the attacked, which will become the inheritance of humanity ever after. To sum up the darkness of the octet, Yeats is suggesting that we all long for self-violation.

It seems to me that the solution or outcome posed in the sestet is that we are all cursed. As if the dark desire, "A shudder in the loins", emanating from the act between Zeus and Leda, impregnates us all. So, while we are cursed to desire violation, it is ultimately because destruction leads to creation, symbolized in the birth of Leda's offspring and the writing of Yeats' poem. The sestet intensifies the exploration of the destructive elements of humanity's dark desires. The debris of war and the destruction of civilisation are captured in a synecdoche: "The broken wall, the burning roof and tower." The colossal impact of this culminates in Clytemnestra's dark desire: "And Agamemnon dead." Thus, we can see the way in which the destructive act of Zeus violating Leda creates ongoing waves of various impacts. The sestet has a rhyme scheme of c d e c d e and a brilliant volta mid-way through the 11th line. The turn of thought is not in the expected place between the octet and the sestet. Why? Yeats is troubled; indeed, we are all disturbed by this proximity between destruction and creation. He asks in the final question if Leda, in fact, desired the darkness that would fill her and become hers. You can hear Yeats unable to let it go: "Being so caught up, / So mastered by the brute blood of the air, / Did she put on his knowledge." He is leading the witness and building a case. This "brute blood", or violent aggression, is all pervasive and as such entraps and enslaves Leda to own this dark desire. Yeats is suggesting that to capture the unattainable can only happen with violent aggression and destruction. Paradoxically, the unattainable, be it Laura for Petrarch or Gonne for Yeats, keeps creativity alive. *Leda and the Swan* says much about the covetous desire for bodies and spaces hitherto not our own and only begotten through violence, but it says more about the intense relationship between destruction and creation. The longevity of this sizzling sonnet is that it asks us to contemplate this dark desire for destruction if we are to continue to create.

Who's Who by W. H. Auden (1934)

A shilling life will give you all the facts:
How Father beat him, how he ran away,
What were the struggles of his youth, what acts
Made him the greatest figure of his day;
Of how he fought, fished, hunted, worked all night,
Though giddy, climbed new mountains; named a sea;
Some of the last researchers even write
Love made him weep his pints like you and me.

With all his honours on, he sighed for one
Who, say astonished critics, lived at home;
Did little jobs about the house with skill
And nothing else; could whistle; would sit still
Or potter round the garden; answered some
Of his long marvellous letters but kept none.

A thumb nail sketch can tell you nothing and everything about a man. I love the sadness and quiet of this little sonnet. The way it begins in the heady heights of its title, an almanac containing the iterations of significant public lives, but ends with the poet's epistolary iterations long discarded. It is a contemplation of the insignificance of one's life to the one who cannot love you. Unrequited love is the talisman of grand desire. I have always liked Auden. His poetry is hard, exact, and unrelenting. Despite Auden's love for Christopher Isherwood or Chester Kallman, I like to consider this sonnet unanchored to biographical data and drifting across something more far reaching. This is a sonnet about how desire between two people is not always measured in equal parts. *Who's Who* is made up of the octet with the rhyme scheme of a b a b c d c d and the sestet, e f g g f e. This sonnet is a square box that is slid under the bed. You know it is there and, very occasionally, you reach in and pull it out. You know already what is inside this box: letters returned, thumbed snapshots, and a ticket stub from some concert long ago. You remember the ferocity of that love: the unsustainable world it created in which you both, or you thought both, needed nothing else. It's a cold memory of giving love that was not returned; an exhalation of love pining; and a sonnet of desire.

The octet is one sentence: one unit of thought. It is the poet sitting back talking to the reader about himself. Initially, this octet argues that "A shilling life will give you all the facts", and then, by the end of the sentence, he indicates that "the last researchers" offer more insights worth considering. Here is someone whose story is of constant and ongoing interest. On the one hand, a list of facts that sums up one's life at the grand cost of 12 pence seems paltry and renders nothing more than a caricature; but on the other hand, the academic pursuit to know more suggests a worthy topic full of inspiration and challenge. This person's identity is summed up in the three categories: struggles, actions, and emotional response. It's a reductionist history and yet one that is neutral enough to be just about anybody's curriculum vitae. The "struggles of his youth" are summed up in a pair: "How Father beat him, how he ran away." From adversity comes fortitude. Hence, these innocuous hardships forge a man and galvanize him into the actions of a significant, worthy public figure: "he fought, fished, hunted, worked all night…climbed new mountains; named a sea." He is the uber-action man: more legend than real. In fact, it is these actions that "Made him the greatest figure of his day". The high modality of this claim is seductive. Curiously, his humanity and vulnerability momentarily make him like us: "Love made him weep his pints like you and me." So, it is love or one's desire of a particular beloved that levels us all.

The following sentence makes up the sestet and explores the object of the poet's desire. Despite all the accolades given to the poet, he is thwarted by the singular struggle that cannot gain purchase: unrequited love. Most interestingly, the object of the poet's love has a very ordinary curriculum vitae. So ordinary in fact that it has "astonished critics". And it is that fact which ultimately enamours me to the object of his love. Here is someone who had no business inciting passion. Here is someone disturbingly commonplace, insignificant, and non-descript. Someone who "Lived at home; / Did little jobs about the house…could whistle; would sit still / Or potter round the garden". This list does not inspire confidence in the players of grand love. It is a record of the absolutely ordinary characteristics that make up our lives. After the curriculum vitae of the octet it is ironic that this is who the poet "sighed for". This long audible exhalation stretches on and on into a longing that will be never be requited.

The poet's very lament translates into the "marvellous letters" or indeed, this very sonnet created out of a love that is not returned. There is an insouciance in the way the object of his love "answered some" of these letters but more deliberately "kept none". I like the adjective of "marvellous" placed snuggly against his epistles: "his long marvellous letters." Did the beloved wonder at their content? Were they considered extraordinary and indeed astonishing (a more fitting response according to the critics)? Or did the beloved turn away to something more significant? At this point, I turn back to the palindromic nature of the title's statement: who is who. It suggests to me the interchangeable nature of identity. Put another way, the object is subject; the beloved is the lover; the ordinary is the legend. It's all just perspective. Therefore, to the critics, the significant self is perhaps the poet in the octet. Yet to the poet, the significant self is the beloved who remains disinterested in the poet. Structurally, there is a space between the octet (where the poet resides) and the sestet (where the object of desire remains visible but forever out of reach). This sonnet makes me contemplate the power of unrequited desire and the way in which yearning generates art.

Whoso List to Hunt, I know where is an Hind by Sir Thomas Wyatt (1530)

Whoso list to hunt, I know where is an hind
But as for me, hélas, I am no more.
The vain travail hath wearied me so sore,
I am of them that farthest cometh behind.
Yet may I by no means my wearied mind
Draw from the deer, but as she fleeth afore
Fainting I follow. I leave off therefore,
Since in a net I seek to hold the wind.
Who list her hunt, I put him out of doubt,
As well as I may spend his time in vain.
And graven with diamonds in letters plain
There is written, her fair neck round about:
Noli me tangere, for Caesar's I am,
And wild for to hold, though I seem tame.

This sonnet by Thomas Wyatt seems to be playful but beneath the surface lurks the dangers of dark desire. *Whoso List To Hunt* is a free imitation of Petrarch's *Una Candida Cerva Sopra L'erba*. In Petrarch's sonnet the deer uses her beauty to draw the poet to follow her under the "laurel's shade", a nod to Petrarch's muse and unrequited beloved, Laura. Wyatt, a diplomat who spent time in Italy, was instrumental in bringing the Italian sonnet to the English audience. His own obsession with Anne Boleyn, who eventually married King Henry VIII but later was executed for adultery, could well be the inspiration for the single conceit that controls this poem, which is that of the hunt. Indeed, while imprisoned for treason in 1536, Wyatt watched Boleyn's beheading, a sober reminder of the outcome of wrongful desire. In Petrarch's sonnet, the lover follows the hind until he falls into a stream, a good way to cool off. In Wyatt's sonnet he gives up this dangerous pursuit to others but then warns them off the trail entirely. Interestingly, in both Petrarch and Wyatt's sonnets, the kill is not theirs to make. The rhyme scheme is a b b a a b b a c d d c e e. The rhyming couplet at the end makes the sonnet distinctly English especially as it was written in the first half of the 16th century. There are a number of archaic words in this sonnet, making us aware that it is crafted in a completely different time and place. Yet desire for the beloved played out as a hunt, coupled with the tug and thrust of temptation and resistance, still fascinates us. Finally, it is interesting to consider that hunting is killing either for food or blood sport; either way it is a disturbing conceit to pursue when contemplating the woman of one's desire. Therefore, the beloved or the object of desire is prey, a target and game for the kill.

In the opening sentence, Wyatt laments that his hunting days are over but whoever else may wish to hunt he is prepared to offer advice because he knows "where is an hind". Is it longing or boasting, or a combination of both, which makes him give up this secret? On face value, it would seem that while he cannot go in for the kill, he is directing others to have their go. The deer, on the other hand, is placed on earth to be chased and stalked until it is finally captured and killed. Wyatt conveys his weary sorrow in having to relinquish what he has desired for so long in the exhalation of "helas" allowing us to see that he gives up the hunt reluctantly. The second sentence takes up this idea of fatigue with intensity because this is the aftermath of an unsuccessful pursuit of the beloved: "The vain travail has wearied me so sore / I am of them that farthest cometh behind." The archaic verb "sore" indicates how this laborious effort has impacted him, so much so that he can barely keep up with the other hunters. So, in the first two sentences, we learn a great deal about Wyatt: he is a failed hunter, he wants to offer up the whereabouts of the hind to his fellow hunters, and he is dismayed that he cannot keep up with the frenzied pack that is hunting her down.

Even in the third sentence, we hear of the poet's "wearied mind", not wanting to pull away from the hunt and so "Fainting I follow". This is some deer! Her allure and mesmeric quality have an all-consuming effect on him. His desire knows no bounds except that of physical collapse. Consequently, by the 4th sentence, he must "leave off" and give up the chase, the pursuit, the hunt. He reasons that she is uncatchable, and this is conveyed metaphorically: "in a net I seek to hold the wind." He confronts the impossibility of this capture. Like Petrarch, Wyatt constructs a hind that is alluring and fantastical, more imagined than real. For the poet, his muse is this object of desire, whether it be Laura for Petrarch or Boleyn for Wyatt. The object of desire must always be just beyond reach; otherwise, there will be no creation of poetry. We move into the sestet indicated by the slight shift in the rhyme scheme. Wyatt seems more concerned about his fellow hunters than he ever does about the targeted deer and as such decides it is only sporting that he lets his confreres know that her pursuit will be a waste of time: "Who list to hunt, I put him out of doubt, / As well as I may spend his time in vain." So, she is untouchable.

Both in the octet and the sestet we are cognizant of the hunter's apprehension that this pursuit has been futile, pointless, and useless. Why? Well the diamond studded collar about her "fair" neck is a fairly significant indicator that she is no ordinary deer but one that is already possessed by some wealthy indulgent master. The message engraved upon this collar, contained in the rhyming couplet, is the slam dunk of ownership; moreover, it sums up the division of State and Church, Henry VIII's unmitigated achievement. The Latin calque, "Noli me tangere" is translated as "do not touch me". This is an intertextual reference to Jesus' encounter with Mary Magdalene in John's Gospel 20:16—17: "Jesus saith unto her, Mary. She turned herself and saith unto him, Rabboni; which is to say Master. Jesus saith unto her, Touch me not; for I am not yet ascended to my Father." This curious phrase in Wyatt's poem is an iteration of ownership concerning the object of desire: the jewel encrusted manacle about her neck articulating "for Caesar's I am" and the instruction to not make profane what belongs to the sacred, renders those in pursuit impotent. The final line works as both a warning and a lure: "And wild for to hold though I seem tame." It is this imagined, unfettered passion, within the object of desire, which positions her as a target. Indeed, the juxtaposition of the hind as civilized, demure, and tame against that which she actually is, ravenous, uninhibited, and wild, increases her allure. Inaccessibility makes her, as an object of temptation, even greater. If ever there was a sonnet articulating a fantasy of desire, in all its blood lust, this would be it.

Clearances V by Seamus Heaney (1987)

> The cool that came off sheets just off the line
> Made me think the damp must still be in them
> But when I took corner of the linen
> And pulled against her, first straight down the hem
> And then diagonally, then flapped and shook
> A fabric like a sail in a cross-wind,
> They made a dried-out undulating thwack.
> So we'd stretch and fold and end up hand to hand
> For a split second as if nothing had happened
> For nothing had that had not always happened
> Beforehand, day by day, just touch and go,
> Coming close again by holding back
> In moves where I was x and she was o
> Inscribed in sheets she's sewn from ripped-out flour sacks.

I can't remember when I first read this sonnet. A long time ago, in a country far, far away, Heaney was an emeritus professor at the Scottish university in which I was working. He knew I was writing my PhD on three poets, and he was one. We talked about his poems and he was warm, personable, and humble. I was enthralled and delighted by his generosity. He was the Nobel Laureate of Northern Ireland for goodness sake! My time with Heaney was a graceful courtship. It was an ongoing and romantic pursuit of love: albeit decidedly one sided on my behalf. Or is it? Doesn't the poet love his readers and want them to know his inner self, his dreams and ambitions, his hopes and failed moments, his darkest secrets, and his exultant epiphanies? Heaney has the ability to create poetry that is so profoundly personal and intimate that when I read him, I know he has written the poem solely from him to me. Writing is a courtship between the writer and the reader. Getting that courtship right, stepping in and out of each other's lives, is something we practice every day. When I read this perfect sonnet, I see it as the courtship between mother and daughter; between sister and sister; between poet and student; between colleague and colleague; between teacher and student; and between the lover desirous of the beloved. Some days this courtship is graceful and filled with goodwill, so tuned to the needs of the other and so precise in its design that it is a joy.

This sonnet is part of an eight sonnet sequence and an elegiac tribute to his mother. A great poem never remains solely anchored to the poet's purpose or context or biography. A great poem, indeed, a great sonnet, becomes the domain of the reader and serves a purpose within the reader's context and biography. I love the way Heaney talks about how the cool that came off the sheets morphs into "a dried-out undulating thwack". Here touch wavers into sound. I love how what we think we are holding, not only changes shape as we interact with others, but makes us realize our first perceptions of what we were holding are often wrong. So, what seemed initially to be something personal and commonplace, like a "sheet", is in fact something suggestive of grandeur and adventure: "a sail in a cross-wind." This little 14 line dance is made up of two sentences. The first sentence is rich in verbs: where coolness comes off, sheets are taken off, dampness makes me think, I'm taking the corners, and there is pulling, flapping, and eventually shaking.

Heaney then offers us a second sentence that takes us somewhere else entirely. Desire for the other is like that. Initially you come to passion, believing it is all about the verbs: the doing and wanting and longing and pursuing and writing and speaking and listening and touching and devouring. Oh, and loving. You think this is desire but in a split second you know it is something more; you are utterly transformed by this relationship which is both delicate and robust: designed and spontaneous. It is this very tension that keeps desire ignited. Desire for the other is that graceful courtship that happens day by day; it's often touch and go, and it is all about coming close and holding back. It's so Heaney-esque for this sonnet to end with a volta. The lover is x, and the beloved is o. Is desire a game of tic-tac-toe? This sonnet explores how desire is playful and relational as well as a way of learning patience and strategy. This graceful courtship of desire is an experience where we get to contemplate how someone else thinks and feels.

Getting the courtship right is so important because without it there can be no folding of sheets in such eloquent precision. Without that graceful movement between each other, we might as well all pack up and leave those wondrous transformative sheets flapping in the breeze. Finally, at the end of the sonnet, I am told that these sheets are "sewn from ripped-out flour sacks". Why does he offer this detail up? Heaney wants to remind me that it was never ever about the sheets; it might be the reason we come together, but it's not really about the sheets. It is about context, emotional talismans, and the desire to know. Indeed, this sonnet is made up of two stanzas and two sentences, imitative of the two people in an intimate courtship. Heaney's sonnet demonstrates how desire is a thing of beauty.

Sonnets of Devotion

Maundy Thursday by Wilfred Owen (1915)

Between the brown hands of a server-lad
The silver cross was offered to be kissed.
The men came up, lugubrious, but not sad,
And knelt reluctantly, half-prejudiced.
(And kissing, kissed the emblem of a creed.)
Then mourning women knelt; meek mouths they had,
(And kissed the Body of the Christ indeed.)
Young children came, with eager lips and glad.
(These kissed a silver doll, immensely bright.)
Then I, too, knelt before that acolyte.
Above the crucifix I bent my head:
The Christ was thin, and cold, and very dead:

And yet I bowed, yea, kissed - my lips did cling.
(I kissed the warm live hand that held the thing.)

    This is a saturnine and pensive sonnet. It faithfully considers the tension between the secular and the sacred. Owen is loved because his poetry, and in particular his sonnets, are devoted to the truth. Dead at 25, one week before armistice was declared in May 1918, here was a young soldier and poet dedicated to the veracity of trench and gas warfare in World War I. When I think of Owen, I think of fidelity. Despite his youthfulness, or maybe because of it, his poetry has a constancy to it, and it offers an oeuvre that demonstrates textual integrity. There is something heartfelt in the idea of a young man as both soldier and poet. *Maundy Thursday* is a finely wrought contemplation of the way we hunger to connect to each other: whether it is through a shared belief system or the tangible touch of intimacy. Owen uses the Italian sonnet form and writes the sestet in rhyming couplets. Moreover, the four pairs of parentheses and the rhyming couplets stylistically imitate the act of kissing, which is referenced seven times throughout this poem. The volta occurs in the last line of the poem and as such declares the poet's true devotion to human life, warmth, and connection. This is a poem that in its title declares an awareness of the Christian rituals and calendar. Maundy Thursday is Holy Thursday of the Easter week and recollects the Last Supper. The word "Maundy" could be a derivative of the Latin *mendicare* meaning "to beg." I like to think about this sacred holy day begrimed by the desperate need of sustenance. Indeed, at the altar beneath the crucified Christ kneels the devotees, begging for nourishment and salvation.

    The rhyme scheme of the octet is a b a b c d c d. Men, women, and children crowd into these first eight lines, offering up devotion to the Christ in a state of crucifixion. Contextually, this poem is written pre-enlistment for Owen while he was teaching English and French in Bordeaux. Yet the intense focus on the suffering of Christ foreshadows Owen's singular fixation on the relentless and unredeemable suffering of humanity. The sonnet commences with a gorgeous juxtaposition of the altar boy's peasant like "brown hands" and the "silver cross", immediately signalling the chasm between humanity and salvation. Contrast drives this sonnet. To the veneration of the cross, the men come forth "lugubrious…reluctantly", women come "mourning…meek mouths", and the children come "eager…and glad". This is a community not bound by shared belief but rather obligation. Riddled throughout the octet is the inclination to kiss. The adults in particular make a dismal crew of devotees whereas the children are drawn to the spectacle of the event.

    The sestet primarily focuses on the poet. It is now no longer a shared experience with other men, women, and children, but an intimate moment of devotion. Here Christ is described as "thin, and cold, and very dead". It is an unexpected rendition of the messiah. Does infidelity lurk within the devotion of the sacred? Is it only human to doubt the meaning of the metaphysical? Despite this, or rather because of this, "I bowed…my lips did cling". In other words, in the face of such conflicting responses to the "emblem of a creed", the poet is also compelled to declare his commitment to what he believes. Contained in the last line is the volta, offering up the true cause of his devotion; we read that he cleaved to the "warm live hand that held the thing". The irony that he chose to kiss the living altar boy rather than the crucified Christ suggests devotion to the presence of something living and breathing rather than to religious ritual. Yet more interestingly for me is what unites the congregation of believers and doubters alike and that is the belief in salvation via intimate connection. The constant riposte in this sonnet is to "kiss". It links the octet to the sestet. Indeed, in each of the four parentheses is an aside concerning the act of kissing, as if such an intimate act needs to be done covertly, inside a syntactical cave. Perhaps the intimate act of a kiss is the ultimate emblem of love that drives all devotion.

Batter my heart, three-person'd God by John Donne (1609)

Batter my heart, three-person'd God
As yet but knock, breathe, shine, and seek to mend;
That I may rise and stand, o'erthrow me, and bend
Your force to break, blow, burn, and make me new.

I, like a usurp'd town to another due,
Labor to admit you, but oh, to no end;
Reason, your viceroy in me, me should defend,
But is captiv'd and proves weak or untrue.

Yet dearly I love you, and would be lov'd fain,
But am bethroth'd unto your enemy;
Divorce me, untie or break that knot again,
Take me to you, imprison me, for I,
Except you enthral me, never shall be free,
Nor ever chaste, except you ravish me.

When I was in boarding school, our English teacher, Sister Ellen, taught us this sonnet. I remember her passion as she wrestled with it and stripped back its enigmatic carapace. She was fearless: fast talking, quick gesturing, and spittle flying as she unpacked every word, metaphor, meter, and conceit. By the end, we were exhausted and strangely disturbed by a male poet wishing to be raped by God. I think we found Donne too odd to take seriously for the rest of our time there, and yet this sonnet, like all of Donne's poetry, remained with me throughout my life. I don't find this brief contemplation consoling in any way, but it certainly rearranges my idea of devotion. Here is a believer absolutely unwavering in his desire to be assaulted by God. It is supposed to be disturbing. We are meant to walk away bewildered and deeply uncomfortable by this craving, his yearning. The sonnet is so intimate and private that I wonder whether it is this which bothers me so much. The voice is that of a lover asking to be violated. For a class of young 17-year-old females, this was alarming to the extreme. Was this something we were expected to emulate? The power of this sonnet is that you can't get away from the personal intimate truth of the poet. You can't turn your back on the beautiful horror of this assault. You can't ever again think of devotion as something controlled, measured, and well ordered. This is one of the greatest battles to be fought, and there will be no prisoners.

It may be argued that Donne, influenced by the Jesuits, used Loyola's three part spiritual exercises to structure his sonnet. In the first quatrain, the penitent establishes a scene in which to meditate; in the second quatrain, he contemplates the truths that lie within this meditative scene; and in the final sestet, he directly addresses God in his petition and resignation to the Divine Will. The sonnet was probably written around 1609 during a time of financial, emotional, physical, and spiritual hardship. It was at this point that Donne moved from his practice of Catholicism to Anglicanism. The Jacobeans were staunchly religious and dominantly Anglican; to be Catholic was to be part of the minority and be faced with limited opportunities and poor regard. All in all, he wrote 19 Divine Sonnets or Divine Meditations, which were published posthumously in 1633. Donne uses the Petrarchan sonnet form in its two quatrain structure followed by a sestet, and yet, it is influenced by the Shakespearian sonnet with the rhyming couplets and other rhythm and structural patterns. Note the way the rhyme scheme follows in quatrain one: a b b c; then in quatrain two: c b b c; and finally, in the sestet as d e d e e e. What interests me is the way Donne chooses not to rhyme anything with the word "God" in the opening line, as if to indicate that God is singular, peerless, and incomparable. Throughout this sonnet, Donne plays out a few different metaphors: the battle, the town under siege, and the betrothed.

Whenever I have taught this sonnet, I always begin by asking the students to count up the number of verbs in the first quatrain. There are over a dozen verbs in these first four lines. From the onset, this sonnet packs a punch. Furthermore, Donne inverts the first iamb in the opening line so that we have four rather than five metrical feet, commencing with a strong rather than a weak stress. Donne makes up the iambic pentameter by packing six strong stresses into the second line: "Batter my heart, three-person'd God / As yet but knock, breathe, shine, and seek to mend." So, what's happening here? So far, "As yet", God has been a fairly lackluster opponent, seeking ways and means that are gentle and encouraging rather than one of assault and battery. In the early 17th century, the religious idea was that the contrite individual was in a holy battle with the full force of the holy trinity: "three-person'd God." The penitent man calls upon the full force of God to smash him down in order, paradoxically, for him to "rise and stand". The plosive "b" ratchets up the action so that at the end of the third line, God's battering is unrelenting: "bend...break, blow, burn." This is a power that cannot be borne, and yet, it is the only thing that will "make me new". So by the end of the first quatrain, the penitent has created a scene in which to meditate.

The second quatrain is linked to the first by the shared end rhyme. Here, the penitent contemplates the truths that lie within this embattled scene. From this first metaphor of the physical battle with God, we move to the simile of a town under siege. The penitent wrestles to let in the invading force despite his loyalty elsewhere: "I, like a usurp'd town to another due, / Labor to admit you, but oh, to no end." This is a dangerous idea considering that the Gunpowder Plot was narrowly thwarted only four years beforehand. It is radically subversive to contemplate egress to besiegers or invaders because it was an act of treason and disloyalty to the sovereign. As mentioned, the second phase of the Loyola Spiritual Exercise is to contemplate the truths in the mediated scene created. Surely the truth here is that to allow God entrance is first and foremost a declaration of allegiance to the holy Sovereign over and above the monarch. Meanwhile, the ineffective viceroy set there by God to defend against false gods is "captiv'd and proves weak or untrue". God's "Reason", living within the walls of the usurped town, who should have been exercising authority over the soul, was barricaded from offering any hope or salvation. This is surely a town under crisis. So, the other truth emerging from this contemplation is that God must battle and besiege the penitent because his viceroy is feeble and false.

In the spirit of the Loyola Spiritual Exercise, the sestet commences with a direct address to God in his petition and resignation to the Divine Will. The declaration of giving and wanting to receive love faithfully is heartfelt: "Yet dearly I love you, and would be lov'd fain." The adnominatio, repeating a word but in different forms, of *love* clearly places it at the center of the petition. The third and final metaphor is concerned with the betrothed. So, Donne has moved from the contrite self in holy battle with God to a town under siege laboring to let in God to the one who is "bethroth'd unto your enemy". So, the guilt-stricken penitent uses the powerful rule of three to list the ways he has abjectly failed God. The penitent confesses, with remorse and shame, the various ways in which he has perfidiously turned away from God. From these false bonds of love and loyalty he petitions God to "Divorce me, untie or break that knot" and most tellingly he adds the qualifier "again". What does this tell us? This is not a first offender but rather a vexatious and multiple-offender who has not given up hope. The penitent yearns to surrender to the Divine Will: "Take me to you." His desire to be in the grasp of God has driven this sonnet from beginning to end. He lays down his weapons, hoists the white flag and surrenders. The battle is over because he bows down to the mystery of God's love. Here is an enigmatic and paradoxical mystery whereby it is only in being captive that one can be free: "for I / Except you enthral me, never shall be free." Most unnervingly, it is only in being defiled that one can be made pure: "for I... Nor ever chaste, except you ravish me." We have penetrated this sonnet's armor with its clever structure, mesmeric rhyme, and strategic use of multiple metaphors, and yet, we are left somewhat overcome on the battlefield. Like Donne's penitent self, we are defeated and triumphant. Did I warn you that this sonnet takes no prisoners?

The world is too much with us by William Wordsworth (1802)

The world is too much with us; late and soon,
Getting and spending, we lay waste our powers;—
Little we see in Nature that is ours;
We have given our hearts away, a sordid boon!
This Sea that bares her bosom to the moon;
The winds that will be howling at all hours,
And are up-gathered now like sleeping flowers;
For this, for everything, we are out of tune;
It moves us not. Great God! I'd rather be
A Pagan suckled in a creed outworn;
So might I, standing on this pleasant lea,
Have glimpses that would make me less forlorn;
Have sight of Proteus rising from the sea;
Or hear old Triton blow his wreathed horn.

This little gem of perfection consecrates nature as our salvation. In a world teeming with the material demands of economic growth and profit, Wordsworth's observance of nature enables him to proselytize its sublime power. Written in 1802, when Wordsworth was 32, here is an Italian sonnet with a few variations. Firstly, in the heat of his rising frustration, we notice that the iambs have been inverted in lines 2 and 3 so that we commence with a stressed followed by unstressed meter; we also note the way the volta turns us about, not at the end of the octet and the start of the sestet, but mid-way into the first line of the sestet, as if to mimic the 11th hour prayer to consolidate his devotion. Wordsworth, as you probably know, is the grand poohbah of Romantic poetry. At this point in his life, he had just received an inheritance. Consequently, Wordsworth was able to return to France with his sister, Dorothy, and set up a fiscal arrangement that might benefit his daughter, Caroline, a child he had with his French mistress Annette Vallon in 1791. Moreover, on his return to Grasmere in the Lakes District, he was able to marry his childhood friend, Mary Hutchinson. When I think about the life of this seminal literary figure, I think about the way he was able to go on his multiple walking tours, travel abroad, be initially enamoured of the French Revolution, later despise its brutality, and all the while pursue a life of writing. Great talent was nurtured by money and leisure. Wordsworth defined poetry: "the spontaneous overflow of powerful feelings: it takes its origin from emotion recollected from tranquillity." I wonder what tranquillity would those under the grit and grime of the Industrial Revolution have experienced at this time? What tranquillity for those neck-deep in the blood bath of the first and second French revolutions? And what tranquillity for those impacted by the Napoleonic Wars? With this backdrop, let us consider nature's call to tranquil devotion as the one true salvation.

The sonnet is a symmetrical little contemplation that contains width, breadth, and depth. Indeed, every great sonnet is a mise en abyme: a box, within a box, within a box ad infinitum. In this Wordsworthian sonnet, we have the philosophy of Materialism at war with that of the metaphysical: the battle between the ontological world and its theological counterpart. So, let's see, in the theological context of Wordsworth's time, the world is regarded as the material or profane sphere as opposed to the spiritual transcendent sphere. The Romantic poets riled against this belief that everything is resultant of material interactions. Rather than be a devotee to the creed that the only things that exist are matter and energy, Wordsworth is committed to the metaphysical and the sublime. We exist, according to this sonnet, not for material gain and worldly pursuits but rather for the terror and beauty revealed to us in the sublime majesty of nature. All else is of little consequence. So ultimately, this sonnet is a box containing an ontological world.

The first two quatrains contained in the octet follow the Italian sonnet rhyme scheme of a b b a a b b a. The first line asserts its argument: "The world is too much with us." This squarely places before us an observance heightened in its criticism. From dawn to dusk, from birth to death, we are "Getting and spending". I like the use of the verb as present participle, suggesting we are driven by an immediacy and harried preoccupation to gain materially. For the consumer of today, this poem remains daringly relevant. Like a call to prayer, the sonnet is stating unequivocally that our priorities are wrong. The proof of this great travesty is that we "lay waste our powers". Put another way, our potential is a wasteland, and we have become the dystopic self. All that we could be has been utterly ruined. Paradoxically, it is our wretched blessing that is "a sordid boon", and thus, we are incapable of seeing our inheritance, which is in nature. Like the unfaithful who fail to remain observant and devotional, "We have given our hearts away". We are too materially connected to the world and thus we fail ourselves. This is a powerful and cogent argument that speaks to the contemporary concerns of readers today.

The second quatrain in this octet offers a window to nature because, up until this point, we have failed to see, smell, hear, taste, touch, and be spiritually transported. Hence, Wordsworth points beyond the window to exclaim "This"! This is his emotion recollected in tranquillity. The overflow of feeling is created by this experience of nature in its soundscape of sibilance, plosives, and aspirates: where the sea "bares her bosom" and the "winds…are up-gathered now like sleeping flowers". It is fantasia to which "we are out of tune" and thus cannot play our part. The energy of nature is palpable. The sea is laid bare and unpredictable in its lunar proclivities. The wind becomes wild wolves "howling at all hours", hungry and desperate, driving one to madness. Here is nature at its primordial supremacy. Yet all of this and more "moves us not". The sonnet challenges us to be in the world and experience the sublime power of nature.

We have now arrived at the sestet and volta of the sonnet. We move from the collective pronoun to the personal. Wordsworth is not positioned with his reader. Here, he cuts himself off and speaks with such vehemence and force because we remain unwilling to heed his message. The repetitious use of the guttural consonant in "Great God!" explodes up from the throat in sheer frustration. He remonstrates that he would "rather be / A Pagan". For it seems that beneath this argument is the notion that monotheism is an indoor pursuit and not one that experiences the sublime in nature nor in the real language of men. Thus, Wordsworth declares he would rather be the outsider, the marginalized, and the despised if it means he stands here on "this" grassy arable land in order to know the divine. He would rather have "glimpses" of all that is beyond the worldly, knowing it would heal his lost and hungry heart. Quite frankly, I would rather a bit of that as well! Indeed, such is Wordsworth's courage and devotion to the observance of the sublime majesty of nature, that he would rather see the son of the mighty Poseidon, "Proteus rising from the sea" and "hear" Poseidon's other son "Triton blow" his twisted conch shell, despite the cacophony it will create and the giants it will awaken. Regardless of the consequences, Wordsworth is devoted to the mystery of God as experienced in nature. This is the true meaning of awe: the horror and the terror of God's beauty.

In the Lost Province by Tom Paulin (1980)

As it comes back, brick by smoky brick,
I say to myself – strange I lived there
And I walked those streets. It is the Ormeau Road
On a summer's evening, a haze of absence
Over the caked city, that slumped smell
From the blackened gasworks. Ah, those brick canyons
Where Brookeborough unsheathes a sabre,
Shouting 'No Surrender' from the back of a lorry.

And the sky is a dry purple, and men
Are talking politics in a back room.
Is it too early or too late for change?
Certainly the province is most peaceful.
Who would dream of necessity, the angers
Of Leviathan, or the years of judgement.

I like the quiet stroll we take with Paulin down South Belfast via Ormeau Road, the site of his childhood. Published in 1980, this unrhymed Italian sonnet offers up a lull, a moment of meditative consideration, in the traumatic history of this place. Indeed, it is a devotional poem to place. The local residents of lower Ormeau Road, Market area, and the Donegal Pass down near the Belfast Gasworks have endured violent riots and mayhem over the past 100 years yet still remain steadfast and committed to their sense of place. Now there is no flag, no emblem, and no Orange Lodge Parade in an effort to reduce the violent interface of Catholics and Protestants. In 1972 in Ormeau Park, the oldest of all the city's parks, the politician William Craig from the Ulster Vanguard called on 100,000 followers to collect the names of Catholic men and women of this area who were against them so that they could liquidate the enemy. This is a snapshot of the sort of place it had been during the Troubles. In the late 1990s, the road was sealed off for two days after protest and rioting occurred. Members of the local Orange Lodge had been accused of triumphalism after five Catholic men were murdered in a local bookmaker's shop. This sonnet is wedged somewhere between these two moments in Paulin's local history: the 1972 Craig speech and the 1990 riots. I too have walked this street and others in Belfast and found it hard to come to terms with a country still in a state of civil war: a tribal complicity. It's curious to think about Paulin's parents choosing to go back to Belfast to raise their children, after many years living in England. Years later Paulin also makes his return to Belfast from Oxford University. There is a kind of nostalgia for Ormeau Road but a nostalgia at a distance, as if savagery is slumbering.

The octet is made up of three taut sentences. The opening meanders between memory of the experience and living the experience. There is a dreamlike quality to this image of Paulin heading down the Ormeau Road that starts at the Gasworks, now over a 130 years old: "As it comes back, brick by smoky brick, / I say to myself – strange I lived there." Memory floods back as he walks the streets, the plosive and guttural consonants in "back, brick by smoky brick" place us from the start in the colloquial tones of County Antrim. He has to assure himself he is there and that this is not some strange specter. This notion of displacement haunts his poetry. In the next sentence, he places us clearly and purposefully in the temporality of a well-known site of sectarian violence, but riots and protests are suspended momentarily with the "summer's evening". To be politically displaced intensifies one's devotion to place, whether this is lived through memory or actual visitations. Paulin captures that liminal site of existence in which many live in Northern Ireland.

There is a hiatus in this warzone. He walks us through a palimpsest text that is imprinted by centuries of struggle and work that sustained a life. As we continue with Paulin on his ambulatory musings of place and belonging, we come to see that devotion to place is not only underscored by commitment to peace but the ongoing intractable commitment to tribalism. Hence, this place of his is shrouded in "a haze of absence / Over the caked city, that slumped smell / From the blackened gasworks". In other words, the cease-fire is "caked", "slumped", and "blackened" by its unsustainability in such a place as Ormeau Road. The final sentence begins with a nostalgic exhalation that is heavy with irony: "Ah, those brick canyons / Where Brookeborough unsheathes a sabre, / Shouting 'No Surrender' from the back of a lorry." Time is plastic and the pleasant evening stroll bends into another temporality where Paulin imagines the brick kilns as canyons, dislocating us from the present into the past. Here, partisan politics and their violent charge into the future was de rigueur. Paulin recalls the Prime Minister of Northern Ireland from 1943-1963, Basil Stanlake Brooke, 1st Viscount Brookeborough, staunch Ulster Unionist and hard line anti Catholic, opposing any move to improve relations between Catholics and Protestants nor would he address the grievances of the Catholics in Northern Ireland. Brookeborough was in the 10th Hussars during World War I, hence the way in which his metaphorical World War I approach to politics is represented on the campaign trail. Paulin offers up two devotees to place: first William Craig and then Basil Stanlake Brooke, both leaders committed to sectarian violence and suffering in order to locate a place of belonging without Catholics in Northern Ireland.

The octet regards this street in Belfast as exhausted by the unrelenting charge into the battle. The shift in argument, promised to us in the Italian sonnet's volta at the sestet, takes us into a contemplation of surrender. The sunset places us in a liminal space in all its potentiality: "the sky is a dry purple, and men / Are talking politics in a back room." This is a moment of connection and dialogue between those not marked by the signatures of tribal difference. Their discussion is not articulated with weaponry or loudspeaker on the street but rather in the quiet stillness of domestic spaces. Indeed, the only question posed in the entire sonnet, is the only question worth asking: "Is it too early or too late for change?" This is the quintessential question for all of the island of Ireland. It is Paulin's three-line response to this question that leaves us both hopeful but deeply unsure. Initially his answer is assuring as he asserts the certainty of existing peace: "Certainly the province is most peaceful." Yet this is somewhat qualified by a quiet ironic statement suggesting that it is hard to imagine during this slumbering peace that anyone would awaken to the "dream of necessity", a reference to the protest against Home Rule articulated in the Ulster Covenant of 1912. Nor would anyone come away from this so called peace and wish for "the angers / Of Leviathan", otherwise understood as the reconfiguration of the Commonwealth as imagined by Hobbes in 1651. Furthermore, no one would want to end the sleep of peace and have back the *Troubles*, referred to here as the "years of judgement". Paulin's Ulster, although slumbering, still has within itself the compulsions, furies, and rulings of another time. Until this is resolved, it would be too early for complete peace and while blood continues to be shed, it is too late.

Sonnets of Doubt

Sonnet 68 by Lady Mary Wroth (1627)

My pain, still smothered in my grieved breast,

Seeks for some ease, yet cannot passage find
To be discharged of this unwelcome guest:
When most I strive, more fast his burdens bind,
Like to a Ship on Goodwin's cast by wind,
The more she strives, more deep in sand is pressed,
Till she be lost: so am I in this kind,
Sunk, and devoured, and swallowed by unrest,
Lost, shipwracked, spoiled, debarred of smallest hope,
Nothing of pleasure left; save thoughts have scope,
Which wander may. Go then, my thoughts, and cry
Hope's perished, Love tempest-beaten, Joy lost:
Killing Despair hath all these blessings crossed.
Yet Faith still cries, Love will not falsify.

I love the muscularity of this sonnet and the way Wroth pulls no punches. She omits the Petrarchan rhetoric for wooing and courtship in her sonnet. The Petrarchan sonnet has the male lover wooing the cold and unpitying beloved, but the Wrothian sonnet has the beloved unveiling what it is to be pursued and hounded by the male lover. I suggest she has grave doubts about the whole wooing courtship palaver. Wroth came from a distinguished literary family which included Sir Walter Raleigh and Sir Philip Sidney, sonneteers in their own right. Wroth penned a sonnet sequence and a prose romance; her work is an enduring legacy of the intellectual and creative accomplishments of a woman in Elizabethan England. Indeed, this sonnet is one of a sequence entitled *Pamphilia to Amphilanthus* and published in 1627. In this sonnet, the beloved explores her feelings about doubt, jealousy, and her unfaithful lover. Initially Wroth was trapped in an ill matched, unhappy marriage, arranged by James I, to a husband who did not share her passion for literature and the arts. When he and her son died, she lost the entail to the Wroth estate and moved on to a life contingent on the good will of others, including her cousin with whom she had two illegitimate children. She wrote and published, but her reputation for doing so was constantly under attack, despite Ben Jonson's lifelong public encouragement and support. Obscurity shrouds the latter part of her life. What matters to us here is this sonnet and its transgressive elements. Not only is the subject matter surprising, primarily because it is authored by the beloved and therefore offers an unexpected reading position on the lover's advancements, it also disrupts the Petrarchan and English sonnet structures. The first ten and a half lines of her sonnet explore her pain. The last three and a half lines are filled with the urgency and imperatives, suggesting that salvation can only be offered to her from her. Without a doubt this is one for the feminists!

Shipwrecks are central to the imagination of Wroth and offer both the metaphorical triggers of drowning and pillage. In the opening line, we commence with the image of Wroth being submerged beneath her suffering: "My pain, still smothered in my grieved breast." It is her lamenting heart that asphyxiates her sense of self. This sonnet is underscored by Pamphilia or Wroth or any beloved trying to determine who she really is in the light of suffering caused by the lover. She "cannot passage find"; put another way, she cannot surface from this lament, and she cannot find herself being anything other than this grief. In the third line, she continues this despair of not having the agency to rid herself of "this unwelcome guest". I want to pause here. This is a transgressive consideration that the lover is sorrow and penetrates her very being so that she becomes suffering. No longer is the beloved a passive adjunct to the lover, one who is a recipient of his advancements without power or discernment. On the one hand, she "Seeks for some ease"; on the other hand, the more she struggles, the more she becomes submerged: "When most I strive, more fast his burdens bind." The interplay between sibilance and plosive in this short line continues throughout the entire sonnet. The soft sibilant sound, suggestive of the beloved, wrestles against the harsh plosives, representative of the lover.

In the 5th line of *Sonnet 68*, Wroth digs into her contextual knowledge of shipwrecks off the Kentish coast, where she grew up at Penshurst. The Goodwin Sands were a dangerous entrance to the Strait of Dover in the south of England and one where hundreds of ships ran aground and lost cargo. Thus, the Goodwin Sands took the lives of castaways. Wroth's family and community would have devoured news and stories about such occurrences. Moreover, she joins a poetic conversation first established by Petrarch, then taken up by the English sonneteers, such as Wyatt and Sidney, where the dynamic of ships and galleys are used as metaphors to explore love and pain. Her simile stimulates the image of being cast adrift: "Like to a Ship on Goodwin's cast by wind, / The more she strives, more deep in sand is pressed." Wroth knows that her destiny is one of destruction if she is to remain submerged and drowning in this untenable state of suffering. This is reiterated by the surge of verbs which drown her: "Sunk, and devoured, and swallowed by unrest, / Lost, shipwracked, spoiled, debarred of smallest hope." Her sense of self is diminished and even the "smallest hope" is denied. Nothing is left. She is bereft, fixed, and destroyed. Only her "thoughts have scope". I see this ship smashed on the treachery of the rising sand bar. I see the wild howling waves and winds that begin to break up the galley and heave it to its watery grave. I see the desperation and despair of those on board who know they will drown and not survive.

It is at this impasse, where there is no hope and no one to hear her cries, where she desperately lifts up her voice. She, the beloved, rises up and takes command of her own wracked and sunken vessel. With fiery imperatives, like a boatswain commanding the crew to rally, she impels her thoughts to "Go then...and cry". Her cry is drama ridden and steeped in metaphor: "Hope's perished, Love tempest-beaten, Joy lost: / Killing Despair hath all these blessings crossed." The rhyming couplet locks in the truth that hope, love, and joy are no more; indeed, her anguish has overwhelmed these blessings that could have been hers. Yet in naming her condemned and dying self she somehow liberates it from its wracked state. It is in the last line of the sonnet that the volta appears and offers salvation: "Yet Faith still cries, Love will not falsify." The beloved realises *true* love cannot be disingenuous. Wroth navigates unchartered waters to find the means to save herself. It is in the suffering, which just about drowns her, that she comes to know true love will not be false; thus, the lover who wronged her never loved her. This is a sonnet about the discovery of selfhood when all seems lost and impossible. This is a love poem *by* the beloved where the object and subject of the poem is herself. Wroth defined herself through her writing and thus makes a powerful case today, for women to bring agency not passivity to their world: to be subject and not object in the dangerous waters of love. Indeed, Wroth's grave doubts about her lover have led her to a greater faith in herself.

Sonnet 73: That time of year thou mayst in me behold by William Shakespeare (1609)

That time of year thou mayst in me behold,
When yellow leaves, or none, or few do hang
Upon those boughs which shake against the cold,
Bare ruined choirs where late the sweet birds sang;
In me thou seest the twilight of such day
As after sunset fadeth in the west,
Which by and by black night doth take away
Death's second self that seals up all in rest;
In me thou seest the glowing of such fire
That on the ashes of his youth doth lie,
As the deathbed, whereon it must expire,
Consumed with that which it was nourished by;
This thou perceiv'st, which makes thy love more strong,
To love that well, which thou must leave ere long.

Doubt is a strange and quiet succubus. I think about Shakespeare growing old, dogged by the same anxieties all of us will suffer: who will care when I shake off this mortal coil? How will my passage across the straits be finally navigated? Is there love for me in the winter of my days? I think about all of Shakespeare's supremacy and yet here he is as vulnerable and doubt ridden as most of us; perhaps this is his true mark of genius. Maybe doubt keeps us human. Maybe doubt is not that which cripples us but enables us. I suggest that doubt is the source, ultimately, of the greatest art, the highest achievements, and the strongest passion. Doubt keeps us uncomfortable, hungry, and even desperate. It screws our courage to the sticking place. Doubt drives us to the darkest place and from this can emerge such creativity as *Sonnet 73*. Shakespeare wrote 154 sonnets, the first 126 are addressed to the Fair Youth and the rest to the Dark Lady. Much has been written about whether Shakespeare had a platonic or homoerotic relationship with the young man who is addressed as the Fair Youth. Indeed, published in 1609, these sonnets were dedicated to Mr. W. H. Whether this is Shakespeare's patron, William Herbert, Lady Mary Wroth's cousin, lover, and father of her two illegitimate children, or any other number of candidates considered by academics over the course of history, may never be known. What is known is that the object of Shakespeare's love generated great doubt and great poetry.

Sonnet 73 is made up of three quatrains and one couplet. The volta, which occurs between lines 12 and 13, offers up an epiphany or revelation. Shakespeare is inverting the conventional gender roles established in the Petrarchan sonnets to expose the lover as a poor, bare forked animal awash with doubt. Throughout the sonnet, we are constantly being made aware of the sands running through the hour glass; there is no attempt to conceal or obscure the ageing process. The lover who is old and approaching death beseeches his beloved to love him more, not despite aging but indeed because of it. The shortness of life makes the lover more precious, more desirable, and more essential. So we begin in quatrain one with the invitation to "behold", in quatrain two and three to "seest", and by the rhyming couplet to "perceiv'st". In other words, to gaze auspiciously, to then see with the eye, and finally to discern with the mind. We are asked to look deeply. We notice that the extended metaphor of time stretches across the sonnet. In quatrain one, we are cast into an autumnal, wintery time: "This time of year...When yellow leaves, or none, or few do hang / Upon the those boughs which shake against the cold." I see this lover in his dotage, bone thin and frail, his clothes draped loosely on his skeletal frame. This landscape is the pathetic fallacy of the lover. He is the place where once there was birdsong: an achingly poignant self-referential gesture to the poet in his prime. The word "choir" refers to the site between the altar and the nave of the cathedral or church and as such is the place made sacred and holy by song. Therefore "Bared ruined choirs" speaks to what once was: the sacred song of "sweet birds".

From the wintery landscape we move to quatrain two and the liminal time and space of dusk. Instead of the impressive observation of the aging bard in the first quatrain, we now reflect upon the lover as transient and passing: "In me thou seest the twilight of such day / As after sunset fadeth in the west." What is considered is the way the lover has been seen for some time as edging towards darkness and coming toward his end. This is not the virile lover of Petrarch's love sonnets but someone older and wiser and all too aware of his fading appeal. The lover is unequivocal in his admissions that not only will the twilight sky morph into the night sky but this "black night doth take away / Death's second self that seals up all in rest." In other words, the lover's death will eliminate any restful sanctuary and peace of sleep that could be a respite for those grieving. This is not exactly the wooing courtship we might have been expecting from lover to beloved. It is as if the urgency of time passing strips away the vanity of love and insists on its bare bones. This love sonnet is morphing into a box of *memento mori*.

Quatrain three takes us in from the cold landscape and darkened skies to the domestic and intimate bedroom. Rather than the erotic carnal space of sensuality, this is the time and place of the deathbed with its accompanying fireplace. When we move closer to this "glowing" fire we see "the ashes of his youth". Indeed, if you draw nearer, you will see how the ashes lie like the lover lies in his deathbed: both "must expire" and both "Consumed with that which it was nourished by". Thus, the heat of passion both creates and destroys. The last scenes evoked by these three quatrains shows us how the beloved must see the aged lover lying on his deathbed, a flickering ember of his former self. Hence it is with surprise that we turn the corner, thanks to the volta, and step into the rhyming couplet. The ingenious conceit is that the very truth of the lover "makes thy love more strong". Why? What is the truth? The truth in the lover that the beloved beholds is that to grow old and die is the beloved's truth as much as it is the lover's. Indeed, it is the veracity of this fact that ignites the fervor of the beloved to love the lover passionately in the time they have together here on earth. Thus, the beloved's love is aflame because he knows that the he too "must leave ere long". It is not pity or obligation or faithfulness that keeps the fire of their love alive but rather the knowledge that the beloved can see his own mortality reflected in the lover. It is the urgency of sands through the hour glass that spur the beloved to passionately pursue the lover, who is the love of his life, until he too can no longer "love that well". This is a sonnet that is riddled with doubt until the conjoining of the rhyming couplet in the final two lines.

Hope is the thing with feathers by Emily Dickinson (1891)

Hope is the thing with feathers –
That perches in the soul –
And sings the tune without the words-
And never stops – at all –

And sweetest – in the Gale – is heard –
And sore must be the storm –
That could abash the little Bird
That kept so many warm –

I've heard it in the chilliest land –
And on the strangest Sea –
Yet – never – in Extremity,
It asked a crumb – of me.

It's hard to resist Emily Dickinson. Her poems are puzzles, and this sonnet in particular is a complex box within a box within a box. I think there is something very fresh and modern about this American poet writing in the Victorian era. Her 1800 poems in total were unconventional, and thus, only a dozen were published in her lifetime. This sonnet is her 314th poem and was published posthumously. This is worthy of consideration. Here is a woman from a prominent family in Massachusetts who chooses herself and her writing over and above everything and everyone else. This self-belief is fascinating. Without significant publication or intense public accolade, Dickinson somehow manages to write on until she dies of Bright's disease at 56. To some, she is regarded as a recluse; to me, she is dedicated to her art: an unusual and atypical choice for a woman to make in her day. So, I am imagining that here is a sonneteer who has no doubt about herself in terms of being mortal and edging closer to death; she has no doubt that her writing is everything and utterly fulfilling; and she has no doubt that a quiet, withdrawn, and inconspicuous life is her bounty. What she does doubt is whether the belief and value systems affixed to her world are sufficiently fulfilling. This pensive sonnet considers the way in which certain virtues and values are not givens. Rather, a thinking individual must grapple with whether or not these virtues and values are indeed theirs and not simply an assumed inheritance. Nothing is begotten easy in the world of Dickinson; comfortable assumptions about goodness are replaced with spiky edged challenges that will make us reassess and indeed doubt whether we truly have virtue or values.

What does hope ask of us? Does it ask us to hang on, to trust, to be resilient, to fight, or to surrender? If hope asks nothing of the individual, then hope does not exist for that individual. Hope is an emotional way of thinking that assumes a past and a future. Without hope there is death and a finality to the individual who once had the imagination to believe. Every day our life is littered with the flotsam and jetsam of hope; it is the driftwood in our lives that we cling to in moments when we are floundering in doubt. I think it's interesting that some of us can see the driftwood more easily than others and know to hold on and to keep hoping. I also know that in some cases of extremity, there is nothing left in you as you cling on to hope. It is when one is most tested that hope asks the most from us. Belief in yourself or something beyond yourself generates hope; doubt in yourself or something beyond yourself generates despair. This sonnet suggests that despite our doubt, hope asks nothing of us but to exist. This sonnet is unconventional, typical of all Dickinson's poetry with its short lines, non-standardised capitalization and punctuation, and slant rhyme. This is where the stressed syllables of ending consonants match, but its preceding vowel sounds do not. This is a 12-lined sonnet made up of three quatrains and a volta that offers an abrupt epiphany in the final two lines.

In the opening line of quatrain one, we hit the Dickenson conundrum, which is that hope cannot be named. The dream or aspiration or desire for hope remains inarticulable. It can only be expressed with approximation. So, we are given an exquisite metaphor that hope "is the thing with feathers". The definite article indicates its recognizable value, one that is collectively understood and anticipated. In holding up the mirror to hope, Dickinson plays with the idea of the inadequacy of language and therefore fails to name it as anything other than an inanimate object that lacks a specific name. Hope certainly appears in its visual imagery as a bird, and yet, it is a thing: a material object without life or consciousness. So, are we then to understand that hope is a falsity? It is not something that has life but just the appearance of life with its "feathers" as it "perches" and "sings". Is the illusion of hope being a bird enough? If we believe it is this approximation, then will it fulfil our desire and be that which alights in our soul and whose song soars through our hearts? Indeed, this "tune...never stops – at all - ". In other words, if we believe in the illusion, it will sustain us eternally. This begs the question: but what if we cannot believe in the illusion of hope? Indeed, doubt offers little other than despair.

The use of the em dash, the most versatile of all punctuation marks, is telling. What we see from the start in Dickinson's sonnet is the overuse of the em dash, which replaces commas, parenthesis, and colons. Here, in quatrain one, each line ends with an em dash rather than a comma; the em dash is more emphatic and enhances readability. The em dash, which is more intrusive but less formal, replaces parentheses in the 4th line of quatrain one. The punctuation, along with the slant rhyme, never lets us forget the intrusive and emphatic poet who also remains enigmatic and inscrutable. The illusion of hope in quatrain two is so strong that it can withstand gale force winds and anything else a tempest of doubt can throw. In fact, the more testing the circumstances, the more tenaciously hope presents itself as the rescue to wracked lives. Moreover, the wordless tune of hope is "sweetest – in the Gale". This peculiarity of selecting certain nouns to be proper nouns, rather than common, heightens their value in our reading. What birdsong could be heard over the cacophony of wind and storms? Only that of our imagination, surely. Moreover, it is only the tumultuous rain, thunder, wind, and lightening that could defeat this song of hope, this internal birdsong: "And sore must be the storm - / That could abash the little Bird." It is here in the second quatrain that we sight another proper noun roosting in the third line: "Bird." Despite its vulnerability and insignificance in the stormy natural elements, the bird has the capacity to offer song and warmth in times of severe adversity. This is the sensual experience of hope to which we edge closer, more confidentially identifying what it is to which we cling. It is in naming that we attempt to take firm possession of the source of our rescue.

This sonnet is one sentence. The song, which runs from the first quatrain into the third, is an extended metaphor as well as a self-referential meta-poetic device. The song is the call of hope that is ever present as much as it is the voice of the poet. Here, on this page before us, perches a sonnet that exists as a result of attempting to articulate what is in the soul. Dickinson places herself in this final quatrain to emphasize her own pursuit of finding hope. She gives witness to its warmth "I've heard it in the chilliest land - / and on the strangest Sea -". She also gives witness, in the last two lines, that hope asked nothing of her: "Yet – never – in Extremity, / It asked a crumb – of me." The capitalization of "Extremity" towers over her and reduces everything else in her life to insignificance. When she is at the edge, the limit and the boundary of her capacity to endure, hope has been present. Hope flutters within and did not ask anything of her except perhaps to suspend doubt. I think this is really fascinating; if we have the power to imagine and believe in hope, then we have the capacity to rescue ourselves from doubt. Finally, this warm-blooded, fluttery sonnet gives flight to our instincts to soar above hesitations, misgivings and uncertainties which cage the spirit.

Long time a child by Hartley Coleridge (1851)

Long time a child, and still a child, when years
Had painted manhood on my cheek, was I;
For yet I lived like one not born to die:
A thriftless prodigal of smiles and tears,
No hope I needed, and I knew no fears.
But sleep, though sweet, is only sleep; and waking,
I walked to sleep no more; at once o'ertaking
The vanguard of my age, with all arrears
Of duty on my back. Nor child, nor man,
Nor youth, nor sage, I find my head is gray,
For I have lost the race I never ran;
A rathe December blights my lagging May;
And still I am child, though I be old:
Time is my debtor for the years untold.

Hartley Coleridge, Samuel Taylor Coleridge's eldest son, had an enchanted, unsettled then tragic life. Much has been written about his upbringing as a type of experimental uber Romantic Child followed by addiction, vagrancy, poverty, and loneliness. Hartley Coleridge inspired writing in the Romantic greats like William Wordsworth, Samuel Taylor Coleridge, Charles Lamb, Robert Southey, Thomas De Quincey, and William Hazlitt and yet never found the recognition he sought for his own writing. Once he was loved as an infant slumbering, the dear babe with gentle breath;

later he was abandoned as the extremely short and unattractive failure who never self-actualized. How poignant to begin with so much and end with so little. Did this prodigal son ever return home? I would argue that he did, and this sonnet is proof. Here we have a confessional sonnet with its private revelations about himself and the anguish he experiences. Its 14 lines have the rhyme scheme of a b b a a c c a d e d e f f and is made up of three sentences. It is a compact and intense meditation of the poet's truth.

The first sentence of this sonnet runs for five lines and reflects upon the consequence of having been the eternal youth. The poet considers the masque of manhood that has been merely "painted...on my cheek"; meanwhile, he remains "a child, and still a child". This idea of entrapment pervades the sonnet. Coleridge writes himself as a "thriftless prodigal of smiles and tears" connoting the indulgence and extravagance that plagued him all his life. What intrigues me most in this opening sentence is the middle line, which captures the mindset of each and every one of us: "I lived like one not born to die." Coleridge sums up the hubris of every person who has ever lived. In his honest appraisal of his own vice of living a life where he never grew up, he holds up a mirror to every individual. This *puer arternus*, the child-god forever young, exhibits the bi-polar characteristics of newness, potential, and hope as well as disorder, intoxication, and whimsy. The unconscious aspect of the *puer* is the *senex*, the older wiser man who exhibits discipline, control, responsibility, order, and the rational. Thus, while the *puer* had no "hope" nor "knew no fears" he had the discipline and order to create this candid sonnet: clearly suggesting that the prodigal did return.

Unlike the sweet babe forever slumbering beneath the ministry of frost, Hartley Coleridge is awakened to the angst that has been eternally strutted across the stage of life: "and waking, / I walked to sleep no more." Like the torment of Hamlet where procrastination thwarts action and lost opportunities continue to hound him, the poet knows that, for him, there can never be contented rest. It is as if all that was given allowed him to outdistance the "vanguard of my age". In other words, these advantages make Hartley Coleridge even more accountable, more answerable to the demands expected of him and more liable to pay back "all arrears". On some levels, this sonnet is heartbreaking. Having been given so much and yet so little, in terms of consistent parental love and care, having been so precocious and delightful in his youth and yet so despairing and hopeless in his adulthood, and having such weight of expectations placed upon him to only emerge as an exile and failure, all generate great sympathy. On a more significant level, this sonnet is the *senex* of the poet demonstrating a mature and measured understanding of self. This is not just peculiar to him but somehow, he has managed to show us ourselves, in all our puerile underdeveloped indulgent ways.

The third and last sentence of this sonnet takes us into the visage of what it is to be a man child: not "child, nor man, / Nor youth, nor sage." In this accumulation of what he is not, we see him in an in-between state, a type of limbo, where there is no hope for his success: only doubt about the value of his existence. This self that Hartley Coleridge confesses is caught somewhere between dormancy and actualization. Trapped in his beloved nature, the poet sees how eager winter "blights" his "lagging" spring. His adult self is hampered by his need to be the beloved Romantic Child; hence, Hartley Coleridge is the paradoxical self who remains the aged child. Most poignantly is the acknowledgement of failure: "For I have lost the race I never ran." Was it a choice to not participate, not to run? And whose race was it, really? I wonder about these questions. Hartley Coleridge failed to win the Newdigate Prize for English Verse or hold on to the Oriel fellowship he had initially won at Oxford. At the end of this sonnet, the rhyming couplet clicks tight on all the poet is not: "And still I am child, though I be old: / Time is my debtor for the years untold." Here in this final line Hartley Coleridge knows he must pay the highest price of all, the life he has squandered. In the dark night of his soul, I doubt whether there is much joy. Having said that, this gloriously honest and poignant sonnet is testimony to the struggles of a great poet. Without doubt, here is the returned prodigal son whose confessional strength make him more *senex* than *puer*.

Sonnets of Delight

The bright field by R. S. Thomas (1995)

I have seen the sun break through
to illuminate a small field
for a while, and gone my way
and forgotten it. But that was the
pearl of great price, the one field that had
treasure in it. I realise now
that I must give all that I have
to possess it. Life is not hurrying

on to a receding future, nor hankering after
an imagined past. It is the turning
aside like Moses to the miracle
of the lit bush, to a brightness
that seemed as transitory as your youth
once, but is the eternity that awaits you.

I remember driving into Wales on Christmas day. It had been raining, but when we crossed into Wales, everything was washed clean and the landscape rolled about us drying in the thin sunshine. I thought I had never seen green the way I saw those thick dark verdant hills; I had forgotten blue but then all about me was the lightest pellucid watercolor sky, and it filled me with so much joy. The lake stretching out to the right was dark and quiet and a castle keep rose up on my right. I drove on through the villages and thought I was in *Milk Wood* where Reverend Eli Jenkins would stumble out, avoiding my car, and send up a prayer for the beauty of his darling Wales. Later, as I listened to the lilt and wash of Welsh being spoken, I realized how I was a long, long way from England. Wales seemed a foreign and magical place: very different to the Scotland in which I had lived years beforehand. I say all this because I see the great R. S. Thomas, Welsh poet nominated for the Nobel Prize in 1996 and Anglican priest, as a luminous water color of so much exquisite Welsh sound and imagery.

Here we have an Italian free verse sonnet with a break in the text after the octet with an enjambment that links it neatly to the sestet below. The octet seems to offer us a physical moment of beauty contingent on its transience and our inability to hold it. The sestet flips the mirror and suggests that the very nature of impermanence makes beauty metaphysical. Let's have a closer look. We open with a glorious epiphany: "I have seen the sun break through." This is the way stories of great courage and struggle end; this is the promise of resurrection: the belief that we are worthy of illumination, love, and redemption. So, at this point in the opening line, we are done. It is the eschatological conclusion and one that leaves us reassured and even perhaps vindicated. What follows to complete that first sentence is wholly disruptive. This glorious moment, with no demands whatsoever, offers clarity to our small lives: "to illuminate a small field." Yet we forsake this gift and turn away and leave it ultimately "forgotten". The second sentence is key: "that was the / pearl of great price, the one field that had / treasure in it." Thomas interrupts his rather plain declarative language with the elegant simplicity of high modal metaphor: "pearl of great price." This field is a field, but it is also something beyond the literal. The aspirate in "pearl" and "price" is the exhalation of breath one makes in the moment of surprise: in that moment when we see the divine manifest. The third sentence of the octet connects the first and second sentences together: "I must give all that I have." In other words, this sunshine must be possessed no matter the cost. I love the imperative and hyperbole of this sentiment.

The octet and the sestet are conjoined by the enjambment of the 4th sentence. Do you notice that we can't hurry on but are momentarily suspended by the break in the text? The form imitates content; we can't rush forward because "life is not hurrying". What happens next is that we are disrupted when our expectations are not met. Thomas speaks about "a receding future" and an "imagined past", neither of which life moves quickly toward. The inversion of characteristics associated with the future and the past makes us sit up and wonder where it is that we are bent on arriving. The idea of the future as retreating further and further behind us and the notion of the past as merely an illusion means that the only moment that is real, is now. Meanwhile we are "hurrying" and "hankering", the alliterative "h" has a soothing sound, suggesting we are all seduced to choose movement over stillness, in an effort to know permanency over transience.

In the final sentence of the sonnet, Thomas proffers how to truly possess this treasure. Quietly, the poet suggests that in this lack of hurrying and hankering, in this stillness, we might turn "aside": not ahead, not behind, but to one side and face this "brightness". The ease in which possession can take place is mind boggling. It is right there beside us and within our reach. Thomas offers us two similes and one metaphor in this final section of the sonnet. Firstly, he asks us to turn aside "like Moses to the miracle / of the lit bush" in Exodus Chapter 3. We approach this bush which appears to be on fire, yet does not burn and God calls to Moses who answers: "Here I am." Put another way, to possess the sun breaking through a small field we need to say "Here I am". The second simile describes the fervor of this bright field "as transitory as your youth" and in so doing reminds us of the familiar yearning each one of us experiences for the pure, immortal and endlessly possible. In ending with a metaphor, Thomas leaves us with the final Ace: this sun breaking through, this bright field, this burning bush, this miraculous elucidation, this response to God, this sonnet that "awaits you". It is a treasure within your reach.

Rag and Bone by Norman MacCaig (1980)

That sun ray has raced to us
at those millions of miles an hour.
But when it reaches the floor of the room
it creeps slower than a philosopher,
it makes a bright puddle
that alters like an amoeba,
it climbs the door
as though it were afraid it would fall.

In a few moments it'll make this page
an assaulting dazzle. I'll pull a curtain
sideways. I'll snip
a few yards off those millions of miles
and, tailor of the universe, sit quietly
stitching my few ragged days together.

This Italian sonnet in free verse is just too delightful! So much comes to mind but not till after I watch the smash of day break; its slow easy dawdle up the interior of a room; its surprising jelly-like plop into the sestet below; its final blaze as a completed sonnet emerging onto this white page; and then finally a shining fairy tale. It is a compact, clever little light box that is absolutely delicious. And to think, as the Scottish MacCaig used to say, he could write a poem in the same time it took to smoke two fags. Let's start with the title, "Rag and Bone." In the mid-19th century, there were approximately one thousand rag and bone men in Edinburgh alone. They would collect unwanted household items and sell them to merchants: an industry of second-hand rags such as old material, shoes, fur, furniture, metal, and bone to be made into knife handles, toys, ornaments, and soap. This was a world of recycling, dictated by necessity. I like to think about MacCaig scavenging through his life and making something brilliant and shiny out of what would have ordinarily ended up as rubbish. At the end of the day, we are all rag and bone, but not all of us are making something as beautiful out of our lives as this sonnet.

Now, let's consider time. Here in this square box of contemplation, we note that the "sun ray has raced to us / at those millions of miles an hour"; moving at 300,000,000 meters a second. This offers us seconds, minutes, hours, and days. Then, as the earth rotates, time "creeps slower than a philosopher". Indeed, a little later still the sestet catches "a few moments" and "a few…days". What I like so much is how time is an illusion. On the one hand, it is measured by our obsessive and compulsive relationship with science, but on the other hand, time is measured by who and what we are: a bundle of rags and bones. Secondly, did you notice the light? We have "sun ray", "bright puddle", and "dazzle". The brightness is so nimble it can become anything we want it to be: enlightenment, life, clarity, and wonder. It can even become the sonnet itself. Thirdly, you must have seen the tailor? And not just any tailor but someone already in the legend of literature, *The Brave Little Tailor*, all the way from mid-19th century Germany Brothers Grimm. There, he sits in the sestet and with a "snip", "a few yards", and "quietly / stitching". He manages to sew his "ragged" life into something spectacular. So successful is he that we feel this spectacular garment about us as if it has always been our own. MacCaig shows us how sonnet writing is the rag and bone trade where everything old such as time, light, German fairy tales, and our bony and ragged selves, can be made new again.

In the first sentence of the octet, we have the straight talking, no nonsense fact of sunlight sprinting toward us. This is our life force, in all its urgency, reaching out to us. The second sentence rolls out gradually across six lines. It offers up dawn, with the slowness of the moving earth, coupled with the slowness of the sun's rays. This metaphorically shuffles across our interiority in all its sagacious deliberation. Light then morphs into another metaphor of "a bright puddle" and then alters into a simile "like an amoeba". At this point, light is illusory and personified: "it climbs the door... afraid it would fall." So, in our octet, we have form imitating content with the ray of light taking no time to reach us but the realization of its potency taking a long, long time to dawn on us! In contrast, the sonneteer promises us that before too long he will "make this page / an assaulting dazzle". I don't know whether I can remember a better definition of a poem. This moment of meta-poetry is the volta. Here we are reminded that we are inside the process of a poem being created. Moreover, this small square poem, filled with illumination, will be a physical punch of brilliance. A pugnacious jab but one that I believe will be his winning strike. I love the delightful preparation: "I'll pull a curtain / sideways." Put another way, he'll let extravagant light in and see what can be uncovered. In this last sentence, we swing right back to the first sentence of the octet. This brave little "tailor of the universe" dares to filch "a few yards off those millions of miles" so that the light will get to us quickly and in another form. In his quiet little shopfront, the poet outwits all his obstacles and exceeds his birthright to bring together the wonder of his day: sonnet making.

Sonnet by Elizabeth Bishop (1978)

Caught -- the bubble
in the spirit level,
a creature divided;
and the compass needle
wobbling and wavering,
undecided.
Freed -- the broken
thermometer's mercury
running away;
and the rainbow-bird
from the narrow bevel
of the empty mirror,
flying wherever
it feels like, gay!

By the time Bishop wrote this sonnet, she was living in the USA; moreover, it was written a year before her death at the age of 68. An immensely private person, Bishop completed her studies in English Literature at Vassar then traveled and lived overseas; indeed, for 15 of those years, she resided in Brazil. Her work is renowned for its precision and sharp edges. This poem is no exception. She well could have pinned this small sonnet to her wall and spent years going over it to ensure that no word was there that shouldn't have been. So, when I come to this 14-line sonnet, where the longest line is made up of only four words, I am deeply aware of the meticulous exactitude with which Bishop considers her world. I am charmed and captivated by this sonnet, and yet, I feel her control suggests something irrepressible that lurks at the periphery of her world. So, I am intrigued by that as well. What is the subject of this sonnet? Being captured or being freed are both states of duality. So often we are caught up in well-meaning pursuits that we fail to see how the instruments we use to measure our success are in fact hindering our progress. The four images before us explore the schizophrenic state of being caught or freed; however, at the peripheral edges lurk the irrepressible alternative to its more obvious outcome.

In many ways, this sonnet is a rabbit hole down which we run until we realize like Alice, we are in a Wonderland that seems quite upside down. In the first six lines of the sonnet, we consider two instruments: one for the determination of a perfectly level surface and the other for the purpose of finding true north. Rather than commencing with the octet at the start of the sonnet, we begin with the sestet; this in itself dislocates our bearings. If this sonnet has been turned on its head, then the sestet in which we find ourselves would be offering the answer or counterstatement to that which is found in the octet. Rather than start with the state of freedom, we begin with that of entrapment. The entire poem is a puzzle that will linger with you long after you have left it because, believe me, it will never leave you. To go down this sonnet, this rabbit hole, is to be both caught and freed from the way we may assess self-fulfilment.

"Caught" is the past participle of the verb "to catch" and as such indicates action that has taken place. Rather than begin traditionally with a definite or indefinite article that precedes the subject, verb, and object pattern of grammatically familiar sentences, we commence with a verb that is also the subject of the poem. The object is twofold and is imagined in the visual certainty of a spirit level and then a compass. These instruments convey a literal as well as a metaphorical outcome of capture. Literally, inside the spirit level's sealed glass tube, "the bubble" is caught; its function is to indicate whether the surface is perfectly level. This is shown when the bubble reaches the exact mid-way point in the tube and is represented as "a creature divided". When we consider this metaphorically, to be perfectly level, an individual must be split, fractured, and compromised. The sonnet suggests that those in pursuit of an evenly-balanced life are in fact caught in a bifurcation of themselves. The second image in the sestet is that of a magnetic "compass needle" with its alliterative "wobbling and wavering". Literally, while the compass shows direction relative to the geographic cardinal point, this needle is caught in its reaction to the magnetized north and is personified as being "undecided". Metaphorically, when navigating through life, we are caught in uncertainty and doubt despite the ways and means at our disposal that provide orientation. Thus, we are trapped in a bubble, in our pursuit of balance, and in a wavering needle in our efforts to find our bearings. We are creatures caught in the end rhyme of "divided" and "undecided".

"Freed", the past participle of the verb "free," not only commences the octet but also signals the volta to this sonnet. Here, the instruments used to assess ourselves are either broken or on a thin-sloping surface. Therefore, we are released from not only the exacting instruments of measurement but also the precise expectations we regard as essential for becoming fully human. The first image is "the broken / thermometer's mercury / running away"; its alliterative "m" is now unable to measure temperature, and it morphs into a deadly escapee. Literally, the element is liberated from the hermetically-sealed glass tube, but metaphorically, there is no assessment of the temperature, and as such, the individual is set free to respond in whatever way decided. The second image is the way in which we are freed from the "narrow bevel / of the empty mirror". Now this is interesting. The instrument by which we assess ourselves, the reflection summing up our appearance and identity, is actually empty. From the periphery of the mirror, flies our image as something wondrous, exotic, and free! The mirror is empty because the real self has taken flight in "the rainbow-bird ... flying wherever / it feels like, gay!" I am seeing rainbow macaws, parakeets, and parrots from Brazil's skyscape. Literally, the rainbow spectrum can be seen in the sloping surface of the glass, but metaphorically, this visual, glanced peripherally, is not empty but rather the individual absolutely fulfilled. The end rhyme of "away" and "gay" suggest the absolute joy and delight of what it is to experience freedom.

3

Go Seek the Kingdom: Pilgrimage and Poetry

"Pilgrim" has its origins in Latin in the word "peregrinus," denoting foreigner. A pilgrim is someone who travels to a sacred place. For the most part, it is a physical journey and one that is often difficult where the security of home is left behind and trust is placed in Divine Providence. Since Ancient Greece, pilgrimage has been a way to evoke and establish identity. Yet it also has come to provide a focus for worship with a political purpose of binding together participants. Throughout the Middle Ages, Christian pilgrims journeyed to Rome or the Holy Lands but then also to sites where saints or visions or miracles had transpired, such as Lourdes, Canterbury, Fatima, and Santiago de Compostela. Indeed, the term *palmer* emerged for pilgrims because of the palms the Christians would bring back after having undertaken a pilgrimage. Buddhists make pilgrimages to the historical places of Buddha's life in Nepal and India. Muslims travel to Mecca, Saudi Arabia to fulfill a once in a lifetime obligation. Hindus journey to certain sacred cities, mountains, rivers, caves, temples, and festivals throughout India. The journey to these sacred places for devotees often followed ancient trade routes, which disease, famine, and war frequently rerouted.

Pilgrimages continue to this day: whether undertaken as a way of retreating from the modern world or doing penance or taking time to reflect or seeking adventure. There are also secular pilgrimages to places of cultural or historical significance such as Auschwitz, Gettysburg Battlefield, the Mausoleum of Lenin, and Graceland to name a few. Literature has tracked the footsteps of pilgrims since ancient times. This difficult journey that is fraught with suffering, and an intense yearning for the goal, is an allegory for the renunciation of material pleasures in favor of the transcendent. A pilgrimage is a physical journey through time and space; it provides a metaphorical passage for the pilgrim. In undertaking this journey, the pilgrim experiences ritual transformation and may even be healed. The culmination of the pilgrimage is the arrival at the destination, which has been made sacred for many reasons but in particular because of the emotionally charged longing of the pilgrim. The end of the pilgrimage is the spiritual summit and can be perceived as the approach to God. Therefore, a pilgrimage is a physical undertaking in order to facilitate the inner spiritual journey to one's authentic home.

Early pilgrims...

The Odyssey by Homer (670 BC)
Translated by Robert Fagles

Sing to me of the man, Muse, the man of twists and turns
driven time and again off course, once he had plundered
the hallowed heights of Troy.
Many cities of men he saw and learned their minds,
many pains he suffered, heartsick on the open sea,
fighting to save his life and bring his comrades home.
but he could not save them from disaster, hard as he strove –
the recklessness of their own ways destroyed them all,
the blind fools, they devoured the cattle of the Sun
and the Sungod wiped from sight the day of their return.
Launch out on his story, Muse, daughter of Zeus,
start from where you will – sing for our time too.

By now,
all the survivors, all who avoided headlong death
were safe at home, escaped the wars and waves.
But one man alone...
His heart set on his wife and his return – Calypso,
the bewitching nymph, the lustrous goddess, held him back,
deep in her arching caverns, craving him for a husband.
But then, when the wheeling seasons brought the year around,
that year spun out by the gods when he should reach his home,
Ithaca – though not even there would he be free of trials,
even among his loved ones – then every god took pity,
all except Poseidon. He raged on, seething against
the great Odysseus till he reached his native land.

This poem extract is concerned with the pilgrimage home. Nowadays the term "odyssey" refers to a series of adventures marked by changes in fortune. This extract is the beginning of the great epic verse *The Odyssey*, attributed to the blind bard Homer from Chios in Greece, somewhere in the late 8th century BC. It is 12,109 lines of hexameter verse; the lines are made up of six metrical units broken down into dactyls, a long and two short units, and spondees, two long units. This tale of heroism and adventure resurfaced, after a thousand years of being lost to the West, in 14th century Italy from Byzantium via carefully preserved Greek manuscripts. Homeric language is an artificial poetic language and certainly not one that would have been used in daily practices of civics and commerce. Yet despite the archaisms and incongruities, the epic tale, as is its prequel *The Iliad*, is filled with speedy adventure, exciting action, and sympathetic sketches of humanity. Scenes of *The Odyssey* are also captured on vases dating back to 670 BC. The Greek hero of the Trojan War, Odysseus, leaves Troy to return to Ithaca, but this journey takes ten long years. Waiting at home is his long suffering wife, Penelope, and son Telemachus. Initially when he leaves the Greeks, he is an admiral of a small fleet, then he becomes a captain of a small ship, and then finally a shipwrecked sailor clinging to wreckage. He is driven off course repeatedly and is constantly under threat by Poseidon who pursues him. Odysseus is regularly entangled, allegedly against his will, in some love nest and is one of the most persuasive orators. His pilgrimage home is a test of endurance and strength.

The "Muse" is invoked to sing the song of Odysseus through the blind bard so that he is able to tell the epic poetic tale of this wandering hero. We are given a foreshadowing of what is to come in the first stanza: "driven time and again off course... many pains he suffered." This is a hero set upon by Poseidon and as a result must run the gauntlet of disasters. Does the suffering and this test of endurance intensify his desire to reach home? What does he learn along the journey that would constitute it as an uber-pilgrimage? I would suggest that he is tested physically, emotionally, intellectually, and spiritually. Despite this, he never loses sight of his destiny, and in order to reach his goal, he relinquishes the plunder that once seemed so important. This pilgrimage commences when Odysseus loses all his companions and embarks on his own individual journey: "he could not save them from disaster ... the recklessness of their own ways destroyed them all... they devoured the cattle of the Sun / and the Sun god wiped from sight the day of their return." On the island of Thrinacia, Odysseus' men committed sacrilege by eating the sacred cattle belonging to Helios; consequently, they perished, and their ships were destroyed. Homer asks the Muse to "Launch out on his story... start from where you will"; it is a reminder that the audience and the poet are subject to the whimsy of Calliope, one of the nine muses of art and science, all of whom were daughters of Zeus.

At the commencement of the second stanza, we are off and racing on the tail winds of the Greek archipelago. Unlike his fellow Greek warriors, this pilgrim has been blown off to the Achaeans and is vulnerable and "alone". Resultant of his ships being destroyed, Odysseus is washed ashore on to the island of Ogygia where he has remained enthralled for the past seven years by the "bewitching nymph, the lustrous goddess", Calypso. Eventually the gods allow Odysseus egress and yet we are told that "he should reach his home, / Ithaca – though not even there would he be free of trials" because of the fury of Poseidon's revenge. Odysseus fought against the Trojans who Poseidon supported (hence the god's animosity). Moreover, Odysseus blinded Polyphemus, Poseidon's son, and to add insult to injury, mocked him and accused him of being impious. So, the wrath of this god, the brother to the mighty Zeus, pursues Odysseus for ten years "till he reached his native land".

The Odyssey is the uber-pilgrimage text. From this, all other archetypal stories of pilgrims enduring the gauntlet of their journey emerge (in order to reach the higher truth at the end of their pilgrimage). Odysseus is a flawed pilgrim. He shows us his vulnerabilities as well as his resilience, and we see his cowardice as much as we see his courage. There are many times when he seems to have lost his way and is stripped of the help of those around him. He is every man and woman who has embarked on a pilgrimage to find that what was regarded initially as essential to survive at the start turned out not to matter. Paradoxically, in going forward, this pilgrim of all pilgrims is returning home. Odysseus' pilgrimage is that of Jesus of Nazareth and I suspect all prophets: the journey forward in the belief that this must be undertaken if enlightenment is to be achieved. Similarly, Jesus' pilgrimage had to ultimately be taken alone in his final hours where he also knew that he was en route home. I think Homer is an essential starting point from which we commence our journey to explore the poetics of the pilgrim. *The Odyssey* is asking us to consider the pilgrimage to a sacred place where we might be reconfigured, and this place is home.

Psalm 84 by Sons of Korah (535 BC)

How lovely is Your tabernacle, (1)
O Lord of hosts!
My soul longs, yes, even faints (2)
For the courts of the Lord:
My heart and my flesh cry out for the living God.
Even the sparrow has found a home, (3)
And the swallow a nest for herself,
Where she may lay her young –
Even Your altars, O Lord of hosts,
My King and my God.
Blessed is the man whose strength is in Your house: (4)
They will still be praising You. Selah
Blessed is the man whose strength is in You (5)
Whose heart is set on pilgrimage.
As they pass though the Valley of Weeping (6)
They make is a spring;
The rain also covers it with pools.
They go from strength to strength; (7)
Each one appears before God in Zion.
O Lord God of hosts, hear my prayer: (8)
Give ear, O Jacob! Selah
O God, behold our shield (9)
And look upon the face of Your anointed.
For a day in your court is better than a thousand. (10)
I would rather be a doorkeeper in the house of my God
Than dwell in the tents of wickedness.
For the Lord God is a sun and shield; (11)
The Lord will give grace and glory;
No good thing will He withhold

From those who walk uprightly.
O Lord of hosts(12)
Blessed is the man who trusts in You!

This poem explores the diaspora's pilgrimage home. Psalms are songs of praise, and biblical scholars now believe that King David did not write all 150 psalms in the Old Testament. *Psalm 84* is attributed to the Sons of Kora, who served the Lord in choral and orchestral music. The backstory to these psalmists is not pretty; according to the Book of Numbers, Kora led a rebellion against Moses and Aaron, but God killed the rebels except for the sons of Kora. It is little wonder that they became psalmists and were dedicated to singing God's praise. This particular psalm quietly indicates that we are all on a pilgrimage, to reach home. Composed in 535 BC, just after the Jews returned from Babylon to Canaan after 70 years of slavery, the Jews were then ordered to rebuild Jerusalem and the temple. In this year, they celebrated the Feast of the Tabernacle and began laying the stones of the temple to house the Ark of the Covenant, within which lay the tablets given to Moses by God.

Made up of 12 verses, the psalm exclaims the beauty of the earthly dwelling place of God, which is the Mishkin or tabernacle. To this residence, all believers long to journey. God is proclaimed as the "Lord of hosts!" from the Hebrew meaning "angelic armies;" so we are in no doubt that this is a metaphysical home of the angelic armies and to which we all yearn to reach. The psalmist sings of the personal desire to reach this destination: "My soul longs, yes, even faints... My heart and my flesh cry out." Expansive parallelism is used to amplify the first claim, which is that the pilgrim longs for the "living God". By verse three and four, we learn of the natural order of this longing for quintessential home. The symmetry invoked by the psalm is largely due to the use of parallelism, such as when the sparrow or swallow eventually finds its nest in order to "lay her young" is compared to the "Blessed... who dwell in Your house". The musical direction of exclamation, "Selah", ends verse four and later verse eight, reminding us that this is a song to be sung in praise of the Lord.

At the center of the song, we are assured that "Blessed *is* the man whose strength *is* in You, / Whose heart *is* set on pilgrimage". Joyous and holy is that person who believes in the Lord because they will be driven by love. This is about wanting something so badly that there is no way forward except one foot after the other to find the way home. The pilgrim must pass "through the Valley of Weeping", a symbolic place of suffering and one of mourning what has been forsaken. Yet the pilgrim will make "a spring" of this suffering because he is "set on" this path in the spirit of love. We hear in verse seven that the pilgrim goes "from strength to strength" and so calls out to the "God of hosts" to "hear my prayer". For the Lord to turn his face away or not to hear the call of his people is the fundamental fear expressed by the psalmist. Finally, we are reassured that the Lord will "give grace and glory", the guttural alliteration making concrete the promise of salvation: "No good *thing* will He withhold / From those who walk uprightly." The idea of movement permeates this psalm. It suggests the pilgrimage of the Jews from slavery in Egypt to the conquered land of Canaan but also the movement through the valley of weeping to the House of the Lord. The psalm also speaks to the ongoing journey of the pilgrim and the way this believer calls for the protection of the Lord of heavenly armies as he endures the travails of his journey homeward to the Promised Land.

Inferno Canto I by Dante Alighieri (1320)
Translated by Seamus Heaney

In the middle of the journey of our life
I found myself astray in a dark wood
where the straight road had been lost sight of.

How hard it is to say what it was like
in the thick of thickets, in a wood so dense and gnarled
the very thought of it renews my panic.

It is bitter almost as death itself is bitter.
But to rehearse the good it also brought me
I will speak about the other things I saw there.

How I got into it I cannot clearly say
for I was moving like a sleepwalker
the moment I stepped out of the right way,

But when I came to the bottom of a hill
standing off at the far end of that valley
where a great terror had disheartened me

I looked up, and saw how its shoulders glowed
already in the rays of the planet
which leads and keeps men straight on every road.

Then I sensed a quiet influence settling
into those depths in me that had been rocked
and pitifully troubled all night long

And as a survivor gasping on the sand
turns his head back to study in a daze
the dangerous combers, so my mind

Turned back, although it was reeling forward,
back to inspect a pass that had proved fatal
heretofore to everyone who entered.

This poem explores the lost and wandering pilgrim. Dante Alighieri wrote his most famous epic poem, *The Divine Comedy* between 1308 and 1320; it was completed a year before his death. Dante radically chose a serious subject, the redemption of humanity, and wrote it in the common language of his day rather than Latin. The term "Comedy" is used in the title because, in its day, poems were classified as either high tragedy or low comedy. Comedic poems had happy endings and were written in everyday language. Poems dealing with high tragedy, on the other hand, were concerned with serious matters and written in a poetic style. Therefore, Dante's title is a conceptual challenge in that he couples "Divine" with "comedy" suggesting both high tragedy and low comedy. *The Divine Comedy* is an epic narrative poem divided into the *Inferno*, *Purgatorio*, and *Paradiso*. It is one of the masterpieces of world literature and captures the Medieval Christian notion of the metaphysical world. At the start of the *Inferno*, we read of Dante who finds himself lost in a dark wood. Frightened after coming across a leopard then a lion then a she wolf, he puts his life in the hands of a shade, the great Roman poet Virgil. As Virgil existed prior to the birth of Christianity, he is unable to lead Dante to the safety of Heaven; this will become the purview of the muse and beloved Beatrice. For now, Virgil will take Dante safely through the nine concentric circles of torment located within the Earth. Thus, Dante is the veritable pilgrim who must descend into an inferno and face his own demons. He has a guide, but resilience and fortitude must also be his companions if he is ever to make his way home. Dante wrote in terza rima where each tercet's first and third line rhyme with the middle one of the preceding set and encloses the new rhyme-sound of the next. He composed 14,000 lines in an exacting form; indeed, each line is fanciful and patrician. Is the form itself the raison d'etre of the poem, or is the poet's vision of this metaphysical world the reason this poem is a masterpiece? Either way it makes for compelling reading and one that rearticulates the fate of the wandering pilgrim.

The opening tercet indicates that this is a narrative for the universal human experience, according to the Medieval Christian view. To find oneself in the collective center of life's journey, "In the middle of the journey of our life", would well have seemed apt in the early 14th century Italy. This was a time where Thomas Aquinas' *Summa Theologica*, published some 50 years beforehand, formed the cornerstone to the identity of the Catholic Church. This philosophical treatise dealt with the existence of God, Man's purpose, Christ, and the Sacraments. Indeed, Dante's epic verse is a song to Aquinas' theological teachings. Furthermore, at the time of writing, Dante was immersed in the political struggle between the Guelphs and the Ghibellines. He aligned himself with the Guelphs, who supported the Pope over the Roman Emperor. Dante was exiled from Florence in 1302 and remained so for the rest of his life. The exilic self, abandoned and lost, searching for the path homeward, haunts the epic narrative from start to finish. Thus, the protagonist Dante, who makes his perilous descent with Virgil, is the pilgrim traveling through the trajectory of the *Summa*. In the first tercet, the metaphorical layering of setting is ever present: "In the middle of the journey of our life / I found myself astray in a dark wood / where the straight road had been lost sight of." Despite the signposting available to the pilgrim, he finds himself adrift, astray, and run aground. Of course, the wood is "dark", and the "straight road" is "lost". We are all too aware of the dangers that lurk in the unknown places and the possibility to stray, should the path prove meandering and snaky. The great poem commences media res as if to remind all of us pilgrims, that we are already mid-journey, thus there is an urgency to find one's way home.

Dante begins in a place that, for all intents and purposes, seems like the end. It is a place from which he must escape. He intensifies the anxiety of this setting with excess: "the thick of thickets, in a wood so dense and gnarled". Its haunting quality is exacerbated because the very "thought of it renews my panic". The only way he can convey his terror is through a proximal description, hence the simile: "It is bitter almost as death itself is bitter." This is the liminal space of death and dying, but like all threshold spaces, it proffers the juxtaposition of death and life, of evil and good. He then recounts what occurred which led to his final epiphany at the end of the *The Divine Comedy*. He arrives at the bottom of the mountain dazed and confused: "cannot clearly say / for I was moving like a sleepwalker." He is in a philosophical crisis, "standing off" and gripped by "a great terror". This is man at the nexus of the Medieval Christian world. This somnambulist is not awake to his world and is without courage. Dante is overwhelmed by the mountain that he must climb if he is to escape; it stands before him like something living and monstrous with its "shoulders" glowing in dawn's backlight. These "rays" of light from God are what "keeps men straight on every road", but for Dante, they are obscured by the place in which he has found himself.

Here is a pilgrim filled with disquiet. His path ahead is obscurely lit. The route that has led him here cannot be distinguished. He is stuck between two worlds and is a pilgrim unsure how to move forward. Dante then speaks of "a quiet influence settling / into those depths in me that had been rocked / and pitifully troubled all night long". Is it at this point that he contemplates the pilgrimage to the place from which no one returns? Is this his journey into the dark night of his soul? Is he to contemplate the path which has "proved fatal / heretofore to everyone who entered"? This is the ultimate pilgrimage and one we all have to undertake. To avoid it is impossible. Later, in Canto I, Dante recounts his efforts to avoid it and how this led him to an encounter with wild beasts. Dante decides he must undertake the uber-pilgrimage into death and the afterlife if he is to survive: "And as a survivor gasping on the sand / turns his head back to study in a daze / the dangerous combers." The simile of a castaway grasping landfall represents the desperate gratitude he experiences but also the disbelief that he actually survived the ordeal. Like the pilgrim who looks back and reflects on the journey he made, Dante will consider the tempestuous tribulations that brought him to the ultimate Triune God. At the conclusion, this pilgrim understands what he sees, the face of God, but he is unable to express its mystery.

The Canterbury Tales: General Prologue by Geoffrey Chaucer (1392)

When April with his showers sweet with fruit
The drought of March has pierced unto the root
And bathed each vein with liquor that has power
To generate therein and sire the flower;
When Zephyr also has, with his sweet breath,
Quickened again, in every holt and health,
The tender shorts and buds, and the young sun

Into the Ram one halfhis course has run,
And many little birds make melody
That sleep through all the night with open eye
(So Nature pricks them on to ramp and rage) –
Then do folk long to go on pilgrimage,
And palmers to go seeking out strange strands,
To distant shrines well known in sundry lands.
And specially from every shire's end
Of England they to Canterbury wend,
The holy blessed martyr there to seek
Who helped them when they lay so ill and weak.

Befell that, in that season, on a day
In Southwark, at the Tabard, as I lay
Ready to start upon my pilgrimage
To Canterbury, full of devout homage,
There came at nightfall to that hostelry
Some nine and twenty in a company
Of sundry persons who had chanced to fall
In fellowship and pilgrims were they all
That toward Canterbury town would ride.
The rooms and stables spacious were and wide,
And well we there were eased, and of the best.
And briefly, when the sun had gone to rest,
So had I spoken with them, every one,
That I was of their fellowship anon,
And made agreement that we'd early rise
To take the road, as you I will apprise.

But none the less, whilst I have time and space,
Before yet farther in this tale I pace,
It seems to me accordant with reason
To inform you of the start of every one
Of all of these, as it appeared to me,
And who they were and what was their degree,
And even how arrayed there at the inn;
And with a knight thus will I first begin.
...
Now have I told you briefly, in a clause,
The state, the array, the number, and the cause

Of the assembling of this company
In Southwark, at this noble hostelry
Known as the Tabard Inn, hard by the Bell.
But now the time is come wherein to tell
How all we bore ourselves that very night
When at the hostelry we did alight.
And afterward the story I engage
To tell you of our common pilgrimage.
But first, I pray you, of your courtesy,
You'll not ascribe it to vulgarity
Though I speak plainly of this matter here,
Retailing you their words and means of cheer;
Nor though I use their very terms, nor lie.
For this thing do you know as well as I:
When one repeats a tale told by a man,
He must report, as nearly as he can,
Every least word, if he remember it,
However rude it be, or how unfit;
Or else he may be telling what's untrue,
Embellishing and fictionizing too.
He may not spare, although it were his brother;
He must as well say one word as another.
Christ spoke right broadly out, in holy writ,
And, you know well, there's nothing low in it.
And Plato says, to those able to read:
"The word should be the cousin to the deed."
Also, I pray that you'll forgive it me
If I have not set folk, in their degree
Here in this tale, by rank as they should stand.
My wits are not the best, you'll understand.

Great cheer our host gave to us, every one,
And to the supper set us all anon;
And served us then with victuals of the best.
Strong was the wine and pleasant to each guest.
A seemly man our good host was, withal,
Fit to have been a marshal in some hall;
He was a large man, with protruding eyes,
As fine a burgher as in Cheapside lies;
Bold in his speech, and wise, and right well taught,
And as to manhood, lacking there in naught.

Also, he was a very merry man,
And after meat, at playing he began,
Speaking of mirth among some other things,
When all of us had paid our reckonings;
And saying thus: "Now masters, verily
You are all welcome here, and heartily:
For by my truth, and telling you no lie,
I have not seen, this year, a company
Here in this inn, fitter for sport than now.
Fain would I make you happy, knew I how.
And of a game have I this moment thought
To give you joy, and it shall cost you naught.

"You go to Canterbury; may God speed
And the blest martyr soon requite your meed.
And well I know, as you go on your way,
You'll tell good tales and shape yourselves to play;
For truly there's no mirth nor comfort, none,
Riding the roads as dumb as is a stone;
And therefore will I furnish you a sport,
As I just said, to give you some comfort.
And if you like it, all, by one assent,
And will be ruled by me, of my judgment,
And will so do as I'll proceed to say,
Tomorrow, when you ride upon your way,
Then, by my father's spirit, who is dead,
If you're not gay, I'll give you up my head.
Hold up your hands, nor more about it speak."

Our full assenting was not far to seek;
We thought there was no reason to think twice,
And granted him his way without advice,
And bade him tell his verdict just and wise.
"Masters," quoth he, "here now is my advice;
But take it not, I pray you, in disdain;
This is the point, to put it short and plain,
That each of you, beguiling the long day,
Shall tell two stories as you wend your way
To Canterbury town; and each of you
On coming home, shall tell another two,
All of adventures he has known befall.

And he who plays his part the best of all,
That is to say, who tells upon the road
Tales of best sense, in most amusing mode,
Shall have a supper at the others' cost
Here in this room and sitting by this post,
When we come back again from Canterbury.
And now, the more to warrant you'll be merry,
I will myself, and gladly, with you ride
At my own cost, and I will be your guide.
But whosoever shall my rule gainsay
Shall pay for all that's bought along the way.
And if you are agreed that it be so,
Tell me at once, or if not, tell me no,
And I will act accordingly. No more."

Geoffrey Chaucer is considered the father of English Literature. He lived from 1343 to 1400 in England, and although much of what is written about his life is conjecture, it certainly makes curious reading. Chaucer was a civil servant, courtier, diplomat, author, philosopher, and astronomer, and more importantly, his writing legitimized Middle English vernacular at a time when French and Latin were the languages of court and writing. He traveled extensively and may well have made a pilgrimage to Santiago de Compostela. *The Canterbury Tales* is a collection of versified stories told by pilgrims en route to the shrine of St. Thomas Becket at Canterbury. These pilgrims meet Chaucer, the narrator, at the Tabard Inn in London who agrees to join them and take up the challenge of telling two tales a piece there and back as a way of entertaining each other on this somewhat tedious and even arduous pilgrimage. These tales told in narrative verse are distinctly English with their bawdy jokes and the way in which the respected are humorously undermined. Like Dante, Chaucer chooses to write in the vernacular, but Middle English is distinctly different to Modern English. The Great Vowel Shift, where the long vowels of Middle English changed and spelling was standardized, had yet to occur. This version we are considering is a Modern English version, which allows us to experience the same sort of easy accessibility the readers of Chaucer's day would have enjoyed. The pilgrims tell comedies, tragedies, romances, dirty stories, and biographies of the saints; they can be categorized into courtly romances, fabliaux, fables, sermons, and confessions. Although 83 manuscripts of *The Canterbury Tales* still exist, it reads as an incomplete (with only 24 tales told and no one winning the competition or reaching their destination). The *General Prologue* sets the scene of this remarkable ensemble of storytelling pilgrims.

At the very start of *The Canterbury Tales*, we are filled with the excessive energy and drive of spring. This forms the pathetic fallacy for the pilgrims who are spurned on, after the dormant winter, to be reborn as pilgrims: "When April with his showers sweet with fruit…When Zephyr also has, with his sweet breath…And many little birds make melody…Then do folk long to go on pilgrimage, / And palmers to go seeking out strange strands, / To distant shrines well known in sundry lands." In this cacophony of life, pilgrims are catalyzed into curiosity. The pilgrimage is both "strange" and "distant"; in other words, the journey is not to that which is familiar and intimately known but rather to a place where the individual is challenged. In this particular case, Chaucer mentions that these pilgrims wish to pay their respects to the saint "Who helped them when they lay so ill and weak". Are they en route because they are gratefully paying homage or because they wish to be on a Contiki Tour after convalescing through an English winter? In the second stanza, Chaucer observes these pilgrims as they gather at Southwark. Here we have the self, referentially the composer, establishing a narratorial role between himself and the reader. In contrast to some of the other pilgrims, we are in no doubt of Chaucer's authenticity as a pilgrim: "full of devout homage." Homage to what, one might ask. So, at this hostel, where they are all bustling about in anticipation of the start of the pilgrimage, they agree to include Chaucer in their party, because as he himself admits, "I was of their fellowship". The story line is seductively contemporary and easy; moreover, we have a narrator who we trust. This has all been conveyed in two short opening stanzas.

At the heart of the *General Prologue* is the introduction to the various pilgrims, all 29 of them. As readers, we believe ourselves to be in safe hands. The introduction of these characters has revealed their humanity rather than their religiosity: "Now have I told you briefly, in a clause, / The state, the array, the number, and the cause / Of the assembling of this company." Chaucer is speaking directly to us and even begs us for leniency in the art of storytelling; that is, he will be recounting what they said and did and as such cannot be judged as vulgar or ill-mannered. So in creating this illusion that he will carefully scribe the tales he hears and cannot be criticized, Chaucer is asking us to eavesdrop and be a voyeur with him: "I pray you, of your courtesy, / You'll not ascribe it to vulgarity…Retailing you their words." In other words, our scrutiny of the pilgrims is all done for the pleasure of entertainment. He justifies his ambition to "report…Every least word" with a Christ like honesty: "Christ spoke right broadly out, in holy writ, / And, you know well, there's nothing low in it." It is this type of ironic witticism that keeps us artfully aware of Chaucer's skills as a charismatic story teller.

In the last three stanzas of the *General Prologue*, we meet the Host of the Tabard Inn who throws the pilgrims a challenge. This larger than life merry host could be in many respects a narrative projection of Chaucer himself because it is the host who calls the pilgrims to the game of storytelling just as it is Chaucer who uses this small band of men and women to form the very fabric of *The Canterbury Tales*. We meet the host: "Fit to have been a marshal in some hall; / He was a large man, with protruding eyes, / As fine a burgher as in Cheapside lies; / Bold in his speech, and wise, and right well taught, / And as to manhood, lacking there in naught." Physically the host is formidable and worthy of the role of guide which he volunteers to be. This is not a religious seer or a spiritual confessor about to lead the pilgrims but an up and coming bourgeoisie, "burgher", from the financial district of London, "Cheapside". Furthermore, the pilgrimage they are about to undertake is an experience, as far as their new guide is concerned, where games should be played and enjoyed. He recognizes in this group of pilgrims that they are fit for the "sport" of the "game have I this moment thought". The spontaneity of this suggestion, if we are to believe it, is apparently at no cost to the pilgrims other than helping them wile away the time. One has to ask if the pilgrims could have been better off in quiet contemplation en route to their sacred destination but that would not have offered us such a unique, lively, and oftentimes irreligious collection of tales. The host knows that the pilgrims will be shaped by the game of this competition, which is to tell the best story in order to win free dinner and drinks on their return at his establishment: "You'll tell good tales and shape yourselves to play; / For truly there's no mirth nor comfort, none, / Riding the roads as dumb as is a stone." Hence the mental and physical hardship that must be endured on the pilgrimage is not to be the focus of their journey but rather free entertainment. Hard immutable silence, contained in the simile, is not the way forward for these pilgrims according to their new found guide. Indeed, his rule is absolute: "whosoever shall my rule gainsay / Shall pay for all that's bought along the way." Who's going to argue with that outcome?

So, the *General Prologue* introduces us to Chaucer, the narrator, the 29 pilgrims, and the host. Pilgrimage is a collective undertaking and one that requires a guide. The pilgrims are deeply flawed and human and represent us just as much as they do their medieval counterparts. Their desire for pilgrimage is to reach a sacred site and thus we have to presume the journey is undertaken for religious reasons. Yet, we very quickly see the lack of spirituality and religiosity in many if not most of the pilgrims. Not only does *The Canterbury Tales* contest the quixotic project of pilgrimage but it holds up a mirror to the contemporary pilgrim.

Renaissance pilgrims...

Romeo & Juliet Act 1 Scene 5 by William Shakespeare (1595)

Romeo: If I profane with my unworthiest hand
This holy shrine, the gentle fine is this:
My lips, two blushing pilgrims, ready stand
To smooth that rough touch with a tender kiss.
Juliet: Good pilgrim, you do wrong your hand too much,
Which mannerly devotion shows in this;
For saints have hands that pilgrims' hands do touch,
And palm to palm is holy palmers' kiss.
Romeo: Have not saints' lips, and holy palmers too?
Juliet: Ay, pilgrim, lips that they must use in prayer.
Romeo: O, then, dear saint, let lips do what hands do;
They pray, grant thou, lest faith turn to despair.
Juliet: Saints do not move, though grant for prayers' sake.
Romeo: Then move not, while my prayer's effect I take.

At the same time William Shakespeare was writing the tragedy *Romeo & Juliet* in 1595, he was writing the comedy *Midsummer Night's Dream*. The tragedy is a story of the "star cross'd lovers", Juliet Capulet and Romeo Montague set in Verona during a long established family and intergenerational feud, and it is an archetypal love story. When Shakespeare was writing this story, he had Ovid's *Pyramis and Thisbe* tale on his mind, specifically referenced in *Midsummer*. This is no surprise as we all know that Shakespeare plundered many a storyline for his plays including the long poem entitled *Romeus and Juliet* by the English poet Arthur Brooks. Shakespeare flourished during the reign of Elizabeth I as well as James I, and his contribution to the English Renaissance cannot be understated nor can we regard his genius as anything other than raw unadulterated talent. Born in 1564 to a glove maker in Stratford-upon-Avon, he went to a grammar school but pursued no other academic education. He left his wife and children to go to London to be an actor and a playwright and indeed became the most popular poet and playwright living. He returned to his family to die at 52 in 1616, after writing 154 sonnets and 37 plays. *Romeo and Juliet* is four frenetic days concerned with what we make sacred and what we seek to violate.

This sonnet we are looking at is found in the scene at the ball in the Capulet household: a scene of celebration and anticipation. The moment Romeo sees Juliet across a crowded room, he is smitten. He completely forgets Rosaline; indeed, he has never loved till now! Meanwhile Tybalt, a kinsman of Capulet, recognizes the voice of Romeo and calls for his rapier, but he of course is cut off at the pass by Juliet's father who wants no violence that night. This section from Act 1 scene 5 has happened so suddenly that we, along with the young lovers, are completely in a tail spin. Shakespeare uses 14 lines of iambic pentameter with the rhyme scheme of a b a b c b c b d e d e f f and a volta occurring at the commencement of the rhyming couplet. This sonnet plays with the tension between the profane and the sacred: and the body and the soul. I think this is why the first encounter is so charged. This sonnet seems to capture the very essence of the struggling pilgrim: being embodied but in pursuit of the metaphysical.

In the first two quatrains, Shakespeare establishes the problem. Romeo is concerned that his hands have "profane[d]" Juliet and so desires to pay the penalty, which is to kiss her. This is only logical because she is the saint before which Romeo, the pilgrim, has journeyed. In response Juliet, who will never be out witted or coerced, indicates that the touching together of his hand to hers is a type of kiss, thus they are already kissing by holding hands. The third quatrain responds to this dilemma when they agree that both saints and pilgrims have lips and the conjoining of these, in prayer, is a demonstration of faith. How could she, the sacred saint to whom he has pilgrimaged, deny him his faith, devotion, and prayers? In the rhyming couplet that concludes the sonnet we see the twist; she concedes in that she grants him his kiss, but she will not move, and he's okay with that…for now. Let's not forget that he has just met her for the first time 14 lines ago.

In the first quatrain, spoken solely by Romeo, the binary of the physical and metaphysical is established. Juliet is the sacred, "This holy shrine", before which he stands with "hand", "lips", and "kiss". Well he may be at the site of the sacred, but the physical is very much on his mind. In order to resolve the binary of the sacred and the profane, he regards his lips metaphorically as "two blushing pilgrims". He has risen above what motivates most young men, the satiation of sexual appetite, and offers himself as a pilgrim who is in awe of reaching his holy destiny. Yet there is something else. Just at the periphery is this reference to "that rough touch", the hungry groping and grappling by a young fiery lover desperate to satisfy his lust. Of course, we want to read this solemnity between young lovers as beauteous and poetic, but I can't help hear something a little racier.

In the second quatrain, spoken solely by Juliet, we see her pick up the gauntlet he has thrown down. He is arguing that as a devotee he should replace his coarse touch with his lips and offer a penitent kiss. In this quatrain, Juliet unexpectedly and unflinchingly accepts his "hand" because,

"Good pilgrim" that he is, his hand shows "devotion". I like to think about how young Juliet would have been, just past her first menstrual cycle. Until this point she is a child, now she is the significant pawn in the chess pieces of marriage for political alliance. Juliet not only accepts but indulges this young upstart, this intruder who is a stranger to her, by playing with his desires coquettishly: "For saints have hands that pilgrims' hands do touch, / And palm to palm is holy palmers' kiss." Not only does she affirm his choice to elevate her status to saint and his to pilgrim, she also assents to the kiss as a conjoining of palms. Her challenge to Romeo is unequivocal. In this very first point of contact with him she is outwitting his conceit. Indeed, the annunciation of the repeated plosive in "palm to palm is … palmers" flirtatiously imitates the kiss that poor Romeo so desperately seeks.

The final quatrain is a co-mingling of the voices of both Romeo and Juliet; hence the tension is rising. How will this juxtaposition between the sacred and the profane, between the metaphysical and the physical, be resolved? It is an impossibility. Yet here we have two very determined, well-matched young lovers who are palpably aware of desire. Romeo attempts to argue for the innocence of the kiss. He asks Juliet a question where the only answer can be yes; she gives him this answer and then some: "Ay, pilgrim, lips that they must use in prayer." So, while she heats up the passion with the answer yes, "Ay", she then qualifies her answer to assert lips are for praying. Again, she tantalizingly repeats "lips" in her answer but not as a synecdoche for desire but rather as a mouthpiece for prayer. In so doing, she is beating Romeo at his own game in extending the pilgrim metaphor. Yet Romeo is an indefatigable pilgrim and agrees that the prayer to his beloved saint, Juliet, must be granted "lest faith turn to despair". She has nowhere to go but offer the devoted and faithful pilgrim his request. Far be it for her to lead this pilgrim to a state of hopelessness.

The delightful rhyming couplet that concludes this sonnet is the complete kiss of two voices and presses the purpose of prayer and lust together: "for prayers' sake… my prayer's effect I take." In other words, the rhyming couplet puts belief into practice. The volta, the unexpected turn, has planted the kiss into place and has momentarily made these two stand still. The inverted repetition of Juliet's phrase, "not move" in Romeo's "move not" is a tactic agreement to halt their sparring lips so that the kiss can take place. There's something erotic and provocative in Juliet's concession to grant Romeo his prayer to kiss her but only to do so without moving the body. His response to this test is to embrace it so that he can take hold of her lips unassailed. The rest, as the they say, is history…he goes in for a second kiss because the first which "purged" him of "sin" is now on her lips, and so at her behest must take back the "Sin from thy lips". Her last comment, before they are interrupted by her Nurse, is that he kisses "by the book", a phrase used by Shakespeare to denote learnt by rote. She is telling him she is being left unsatisfied. Hello?! The profanity of these two emerging from a feud of such infamy is made sacred by a love that is intractable. This sonnet is about pilgrimages left unfulfilled. The journey to the site where the profane and physical are conjoined to the sacred and metaphysical is long and arduous. Yet, according to Shakespeare, it is electric and exciting!

The Passionate Man's Pilgrimage by Sir Walter Raleigh (1603)

Give me my scallop shell of quiet,

My staff of faith to walk upon,
My scrip of joy, immortal diet,
My bottle of salvation,
My gown of glory, hope's true gage,
And thus I'll take my pilgrimage.

Blood must be my body's balmer,
No other balm will there be given,
Whilst my soul, like a white palmer,
Travels to the land of heaven;
Over the silver mountains,
Where spring the nectar fountains;
And there I'll kiss
The bowl of bliss,
And drink my eternal fill
On every milken hill.
My soul will be a-dry before,
But after it will ne'er thirst more;
And by the happy blissful way
More peaceful pilgrims I shall see,
That have shook off their gowns of clay,
And go apparelled fresh like me.
I'll bring them first
To slake their thirst,
And then to taste those nectar suckets,
At the clear wells
Where sweetness dwells,
Drawn up by saints in crystal buckets.

And when our bottles and all we
Are fill'd with immortality,
Then the holy paths we'll travel,
Strew'd with rubies thick as gravel,
Ceilings of diamonds, sapphire floors,
High walls of coral, and pearl bowers.

From thence to heaven's bribeless hall
Where no corrupted voices brawl,
No conscience molten into gold,
Nor forg'd accusers bought and sold,
No cause deferr'd, nor vain-spent journey,

For there Christ is the king's attorney,
Who pleads for all without degrees,
And he hath angels, but no fees.
When the grand twelve million jury
Of our sins and sinful fury,
'Gainst our souls black verdicts give,
Christ pleads his death, and then we live.
Be thou my speaker, taintless pleader,
Unblotted lawyer, true proceeder,
Thou movest salvation even for alms,
Not with a bribed lawyer's palms.
And this is my eternal plea
To him that made heaven, earth, and sea,
Seeing my flesh must die so soon,
And want a head to dine next noon,
Just at the stroke when my veins start and spread,
Set on my soul an everlasting head.
Then am I ready, like a palmer fit,
To tread those blest paths which before I writ.

Sir Walter Raleigh had risen up the ranks due to favor shown him by Elizabeth I. He was a gentleman, writer, poet, scholar, politician, courtier, spy, and explorer of the Americas. Indeed, Raleigh was instrumental in the colonization of North America and pursued the legend of El Dorado when he traveled to South America. He had been imprisoned in the Tower in 1592 for three months at the displeasure of Elizabeth I because he had married one of her ladies-in-waiting without her permission. Raleigh resisted the Italian Renaissance influence on poetry with its ornamental poetic devices and complex intertextuality. Perhaps this was a political decision to privilege English Protestantism over and above the flamboyance of Continental Catholicism, but his poetry is written in Plain Style, which is simple, direct, and straightforward. *The Passionate Man's Pilgrimage* is attributed to Raleigh and was supposed to have been written in 1603 after a travesty trial where he defended himself against the accusations of high treason: a crime punishable by being hanged, drawn, and quartered. While he avoided this punishment, he did remain imprisoned in the Tower for 15 years. He managed to join another expedition to South America but violated the terms of his pardon by not avoiding conflict with the Spanish; thus, on his return, despite a number of opportunities to flee for his life, he surrender to James I, was imprisoned in the Tower and then beheaded. The title of the poem speaks to not just a man's pilgrimage toward his death but one who is "passionate". This adjective suggests that he is compelled or even ruled by strong emotion; moreover, he understands that love and death are intimately entwined and thus his journey toward the ultimate sacred site of rightful judgement, heaven, will be one of suffering for Eros and Thanatos.

The first short stanza of six lines does not employ the popular iambic pentameter of its day but rather an iambic tetrameter with varying metrical and rhythmic patterns. This allows a strong and direct voice to address Christ, "him that made heaven, earth, and sea", and vicariously, his listening readership. The first stanza lists the paraphernalia of the pilgrim: "Give me my scallop shell…My staff…My scrip…My bottle…My gown…And thus I'll take my pilgrimage." His request to God is stripped of any fanciful poetic device or allusion. His urgency is palpable. It is interesting to consider that in stark contrast to this humble pilgrim is Raleigh the vanquishing colonizer of the Americas with his hunger for gold. The trappings he demands are symbols and necessary items of a pilgrim, including the shell which is the traditional emblem of those returning from the sacred site of Saint James the Great in Compostela.

In the second stanza, made up of 22 lines, we see Christian mythology surrounding the pilgrim who "Travels to the land of heaven". This pilgrimage of the passionate man will mean that the body "must be" washed in blood so that the soul will be "like a white palmer" in order to find eternal life. To suffer en route is in keeping with the theological thinking of the day and is captured in the contrasting palette of the body being cleansed in red blood so that the soul remains pure white. The site of the sacred that this passionate pilgrim imagines is one that offers immortality: "Where spring the nectar fountains; / And there I'll kiss / The bowl of bliss, / And drink my eternal fill." The spring in Greek mythology quenched the poets and offered them inspiration and thus immortality, in that their works would be forever remembered. When writing this poem, Raleigh would be contemplating how he would be remembered. In his musings of the final leg of the pilgrimage, Raleigh muses the "happy, blissful" company of other "peaceful pilgrims" who "have shook off their gowns of clay, / And go apparelled fresh like me". Therefore, he sees himself as shucking off his human form, a reference to Genesis 2:7, where man is made human by God from clay. Again, we are reminded that he thirsted on this pilgrimage: "At the clear wells… Drawn up by saints in crystal buckets." This thirst would be quenched with the aid of heavenly bodies and offer everlasting life.

The third stanza, again made up of six lines, uses cumulative listing to convey the actual route this pilgrim takes to heaven. Curiously, in contrast to the first stanza where the humble pilgrim carries nothing more than his shell, walking staff, certificate of pilgrimage, a bottle, and a gown, we now see the riches of heaven that would rival the legend of El Dorado: "paths… Strew'd with rubies thick as gravel, / Ceilings of diamonds, sapphire floors, / High walls of coral, and pearl bowers." Rubies, diamonds, sapphires, coral, and pearls indicate Raleigh's aforementioned passion to find the legend as promised in the Americas. It is this personal and cultural contextual reference that adorns the path to Heaven.

The final stanza, made up of 24 lines, outlines the court of heaven where rightful judgement is bestowed upon the passionate pilgrim. This is in stark juxtaposition to the unjust treatment Raleigh received when tried for high treason in 1603. The anaphora of "no corrupted voices brawl, / No conscience molten into gold, / Nor forg'd accusers bought and sold, / No cause deferr'd, nor vain-spent journey" reiterates the corrupted British justice Raleigh experienced. The rhetoric is borne out of his own deep sense of jurisprudence; indeed, the outrage over his trial led to hearsay rules that we follow to this day. The parallelism Raleigh establishes between the earthly court of law and that of heaven is Christ as King's Counsel who prosecutes mercifully despite the "sins and sinful fury" of the pilgrim accused. Indeed, Christ has already died for the sins of all men and offered eternal life, thus mercy is a bygone conclusion: "our souls black verdicts give, / Christ pleads his death, and then we live." Raleigh calls upon "him that made heaven, earth, and sea" in the moment he is beheaded. Raleigh is a pilgrim, a believer, and as such knows that Christ will "Set on my soul an everlasting head". This prayer is poignant and heartfelt. It is written by a pilgrim who believes he is at death's door and to pass through he needs great courage. Raleigh knows that death will not only be violent and public but it will also violate his reputation. Thus, this poem is his immortal declaration as poet and loyal subject that he is a passionate pilgrim.

Hymn to God, My God, in My Sickness by John Donne (1631)

Since I am coming to that holy room,
    Where, with thy choir of saints for evermore,
I shall be made thy music; as I come
    I tune the instrument here at the door,
    And what I must do then, think here before.

Whilst my physicians by their love are grown
    Cosmographers, and I their map, who lie
Flat on this bed, that by them may be shown
    That this is my south-west discovery,
    Per fretum febris, by these straits to die,

I joy, that in these straits I see my west;
    For, though their currents yield return to none,
What shall my west hurt me? As west and east
    In all flat maps (and I am one) are one,
    So death doth touch the resurrection.

Is the Pacific Sea my home? Or are
    The eastern riches? Is Jerusalem?
Anyan, and Magellan, and Gibraltar,
    All straits, and none but straits, are ways to them,
    Whether where Japhet dwelt, or Cham, or Shem.

We think that Paradise and Calvary,
    Christ's cross, and Adam's tree, stood in one place;
Look, Lord, and find both Adams met in me;
    As the first Adam's sweat surrounds my face,
    May the last Adam's blood my soul embrace.

So, in his purple wrapp'd, receive me, Lord;
    By these his thorns, give me his other crown;

And as to others' souls I preach'd thy word,
    Be this my text, my sermon to mine own:
"Therefore that he may raise, the Lord throws down."

The pilgrim must ask time and time again: am I on the right path? The pilgrimage is a journey that invokes uncertainty not only about finding the right path to take but also accepting what the destination may entail. If all pilgrimages are a coming home of sorts then perhaps Donne's final poem asks: where is true home? There is no doubt that he is a weary and fevered pilgrim; moreover, his pilgrimage has navigated the dire straits of life. This hymn is not only offering praise to God, it is also offering a way for Donne to sing himself back to his true home. Donne was born in 1573 into a recusant Catholic family that had experienced persecution and martyrdom for the practice of their faith. Donne's mother was related to Thomas More, and Donne's brother was imprisoned and died of the Bubonic plague while serving a custodial sentence for harboring a Catholic priest. Donne studied at Oxford and Cambridge Universities but was unable to receive a degree because of his Catholicism. He then went and studied Law at Lincoln Inn, joined Waler Raleigh in raids on Cadiz, and then became the private secretary to Sir Thomas Egerton, the Lord Keeper of the Great Seal of England. It was during this time that Donne became an Anglican. However, his marriage to Egerton's 16-year-old niece led to his imprisonment followed by years of impoverishment. In 1610, he published *Pseudo-Martyr*, a treatise that argued for Roman Catholics to support James I while still remaining loyal to the Pope. Needless to say, this won him great favor with the King, but he was still refused reinstatement back at court; instead the King pressured Donne to be ordained as an Anglican priest. Donne then became the Dean of St Paul's Cathedral. Meanwhile his wife died aged 37, after giving birth to her 12th baby who also died.

    Donne is regarded as one of the great Metaphysical poets. This was a loosely grouped collection of poets who played with the complexities of the intellectual and personal. His friend and biographer, Izaac Walton believes *Hymn to God, My God, in My Sickness* was written eight days before Donne died in 1631. It is made up of six quintets with a rhyme scheme of a b c b b. This is a personal hymn because it is addressed to an intimate God, and it is conveyed by the poet in his most vulnerable state. The repetition in the title of "God" and "My" foregrounds the speaking position of the poet in close relationship with God. Quintet one begins media res; this abrupt opening is a typical device used by the Metaphysical poets as a way of startling the reader and coaxing a new perspective. Moreover, the gerund verb "coming" indicates the approach of a pilgrim to the holiest of all shrines: the afterlife. In this first quintet, Donne offers us the conceit of being made the music of God. Conceits are a violent yoking together of seemingly unconnected ideas. Here we observe his approach to eternity, captured in the metaphor "holy room", as one where he adjusts his soul in order to be allowed entry: "Where, with thy choir of saints for evermore, / I shall be made thy music; as I come? I tune the instrument." Donne anticipates conjoining with the communion of saints but the readiness of his soul, despite his desire, is in abeyance.

    The second quintet takes us to a second conceit and one that runs as an extended metaphor through the center of the poem. His physicians are "Cosmographers" and he "their map". As they read, the geography of his physical state (his suffering) is understood to be part and parcel of his journey toward death. His "south-west discovery" is the hot feverish journey toward death; this is made holy by the Latinate phrase, "per fretum febris" meaning "the fever across the strait." This tight, difficult passage is the final leg of the pilgrimage to his God. The enjambment from quintet two to quintet three continues this idea of sailing across this passage until he reaches his "joy" because he sees "my west". The notion of west and east are a reference to Christian mythology; the sun rises from the east and is the metaphorical site of Christ's birth and resurrection. Whereas the sun falls in the west, so this is associated with death. This paradox conveyed in Christianity and enjoyed by the Metaphysics, that in death there is life because we die to be born to eternal life. Donne poses a rhetorical question in the center of quintet three: "What shall my west hurt me?" The poet is reassuring himself that in death the material self can no longer be harmed. Indeed, to sharpen this very argument, Donne points out that flat maps can be wrapped around so that the furthest west edge touches the furthest east. This is also true in the minds of the faithful that death and eternal life touching each other: "As west and east / In all flat maps (and I am one) are one, / So death doth touch the resurrection."

We continue the conceit of the map in quintet four because the pilgrim is still not assured, despite the clever arguments that have preceded asserting that death is nothing to be feared. The three questions that crowd the start of quintet four speak to the anxiety surfacing for the pilgrim. The poem displays what it is to be vulnerable, human, and feverishly certain one moment and unsure the next; it offers an honesty that outstrips the cleverness of the poem. The poet is driven to ask: where is true home? The sites he names are representative of the Renaissance imagining of the East and as such are places of unknown riches. Yet each of these places, like eternity itself, must be reached via the difficult and narrow passage no matter where one begins the pilgrimage: "All straits, and none but straits, are ways to them, / Whether where Japhet dwelt, or Cham, or Shem." The reference to the sons of Noah, and their mythological connection to Asia, Africa, and Europe, suggests the universality of all people as they pilgrimage home.

The penultimate quintet takes us into the Christian symbols of Eden, the tree of knowledge, and Adam. This is paralleled to Calvary, the crucifixion, and Christ. Here Donne calls directly to his God with an imperative to recognize the physical and metaphysical self: "Look, Lord, and find both Adams met in me; / As the first Adam's sweat surrounds my face, / May the last Adam's blood my soul embrace." The suffering, feverish, and vulnerable pilgrim is resurrected into the second Adam, Christ his Lord.

In the final quintet, Donne knows his pilgrimage has led him to his true and right home. With the second address to the Lord, Donne requests he be received into eternal life wrapped in the power and royalty of Christ the King: "So, in his purple wrapp'd, receive me, Lord." The final three lines sum up this hymn as a sermon, which emerges out of Donne's experience as a pilgrim: "And as to others' souls I preach'd thy word, / Be this my text, my sermon to mine own." Donne leaves us with a paradox: "Therefore that he may raise, the Lord throws down." He is suggesting that in one's west is one's east, in one's suffering is one's ascendency, in one's death is one's eternal life. These are the axioms that have been wrestled out of the narrow and dangerous straits Donne has had to navigate as he takes his final pilgrimage.

The Pilgrim by John Bunyan (1684)

Who would true Valor see
Let him come hither;
One here will Constant be,
Come Wind, come Weather.
There's no Discouragement,
Shall make him once Relent,
His first avowed Intent,
To be a Pilgrim.

Who so beset him round,
With dismal Stories,
Do but themselves Confound;
His Strength the more is.
No Lion can him fright,
He'll with a Giant Fight,
But he will have a right,
To be a Pilgrim.

Hobgoblin, nor foul Fiend,
Can daunt his Spirit:
He knows, he at the end,
Shall Life Inherit.
Then Fancies fly away,
He'll fear not what men say,
He'll labor Night and Day,
To be a Pilgrim.

Usually we associate John Bunyan with the first novel ever written, *The Pilgrim's Progress*, which still remains popular and has never been out of print since its publication, Part 1 in 1678 and Part 2 in 1684. Yet he also wrote sermons, religious treatise, and approximately 74 poems. Bunyan was born in 1628 to a humble family and studied spasmodically at the local grammar school and then became a brazier like his father. At 15, he was drafted into the army during the English Civil War. During this time, he became deeply impressed with a Church that was both military and militant. He had a religious conversion after his stint in the army and pursued a faith that was Bible focused and without ceremony or tradition. He soon became a Puritan preacher and then a Baptist.

When the Stuart monarchy re-established itself, it was illegal to preach unless one was an ordained preacher, but Bunyan would not desist. He was arrested and spent more than 12 years in jail for being a dissenter. It was while he was incarcerated that Bunyan wrote. He was released along with 1000s of other non-conformists in 1672. Bunyan lived in a time where the Protestant Church did not support the literal idea of pilgrimage; however, as Bunyan was a Bible student, the idea of pilgrimage hit him with imaginative force. Bunyan was enthralled by the idea of pilgrimage in the Old and New Testament. In the Old Testament, a number of shrines had been established, and people were expected to go and worship during certain religious festivals and offer sacrifice. Indeed, Jerusalem was built on a hill and the *Songs of Ascent* in the Psalms 120 to 134 were songs for pilgrims to sing as they tramped off to the holy city. In the New Testament, believers were seen as pilgrims on their metaphoric ascent to the heavenly Jerusalem; as such, they were lifelong wanderers through this world in hope of the next. The word *sojourner* was used to denote the temporary residence a believer has in this world as they pilgrimage to heaven. Hence, the physical journey can often be symbolic of the spiritual journey of the struggle between doubt and faith.

Bunyan's poem, *The Pilgrim*, was originally published at the end of Part 2 of his novel, *A Pilgrim's Progress*. It is inspired by the Biblical reference in Hebrews 11:13: "These all died in faith, not having received the promises, but having seen them afar off, and were persuaded of *them*, and embraced *them*, and confessed that they were strangers and pilgrims on the earth." Bunyan's poem was later used frequently as a hymn. *The Pilgrim* is typical of Bunyan's unadorned style that speaks directly to the heart of the reader. It's written in three octaves in iambic trimeter, with three iambic feet, and the rhyming scheme of a b a b c c c d. The final line of each octet is repeated throughout. Like the novel, *The Pilgrim's Progress*, Bunyan takes virtues and converts them into allegories in order to convey his moral message. Here we are asked to consider *who* is the sufficiently committed to face the challenge of a pilgrimage: "There's no Discouragement, /Shall make him once Relent, / His first avowed Intent." We are assured in the rhyming triplet that this pilgrim is indefatigable.

In the second octet, we move from the elements of nature that hinder this pilgrim's progress to the obstacles of humans, animals, and the fantastical. Late English Renaissance writing explored the world of man's mortal enemies, such as fierce beasts and giants. Therefore, the pilgrim has the "right" to be on his pilgrimage despite the tales of caution told to him by others along his way: "Who so beset him round, / With dismal Stories ... His Strength the more is." It would seem that the stronger the threat, the greater is the pilgrim's resolve: "No Lion can him fright, / He'll with a Giant Fight." This does not seem like an ordinary mid-17th century pilgrim but someone super human, extraordinary and imbued with the grace of God.

In the final octet, Bunyan builds to a crescendo. Fearsome mythical creatures or evil demons cannot deter this pilgrim because, "He knows, he at the end, / Shall Life Inherit". This is a reference to the New Testament idea that the believer is in a constant state of pilgrimage throughout his life and no matter what suffering he endures, in the end, he will inherit eternal life. Bunyan himself endured persecution because he refused to conform to the ruling of the Protestant Church. His unpolished style of writing is central to the Puritan and Baptist notion of Plain Speaking and Bible wielding devotion, where suspicion of authority, tradition, and ceremony allows him a sure-footed high modal expression. The superficial transient feelings of this life are replaced by the deeply permanent knowledge of reaching the end point of the pilgrimage: "Then Fancies fly away, / He'll fear not what men say, / He'll labor Night and Day, / To be a Pilgrim." In these final lines of the poem, we are reminded again of the suffering and threat caused to the pilgrim by "what men say". The Renaissance humanism sought to create a society which was able to speak and write with eloquence and clarity; people were thus seen to be capable of engaging in civic life and persuading others to be virtuous. In many ways, Bunyan can be read as someone who idealized this aspect of his times and yet the political turmoil of his day undermined the very possibility of freedom of speech. Thus, the pilgrim knew that the road ahead was one of unflaggingly difficulty.

Romantic pilgrims...

Childe Harold's Pilgrimage from Canto IV by Lord Byron (1817)

CXXXVII
But I have lived, and have not lived in vain:
My mind may lose its force, my blood its fire,
And my frame perish even in conquering pain;
But there is that within me which shall tire
Torture and Time, and breathe when I expire;
Something unearthly, which they deem not of,
Like the remember'd tone of a mute lyre,
Shall on their soften'd spirits sink, and move
In hearts all rocky now the late remorse of love.

CXXXVIII
The seal is set. -- Now welcome, thou dread power!
Nameless, yet thus omnipotent, which here
Walk'st in the shadow of the midnight hour
With a deep awe, yet all distinct from fear;
Thy haunts are ever where dead walls rear
Their ivy mantles, and the solemn scene
Derives from thee a sense so deep and clear
That we become a part of what has been,
And grow unto the spot, all-seeing but unseen.

CXXXIX
And here the buzz of eager nations ran,
In murmur'd pity, or loud-roar'd applause,
As man was slaughter'd by his fellow man.
And wherefore slaughter'd? wherefore, but because
Such were the bloody Circus' genial laws,
And the imperial pleasure. -- Wherefore not?
What matters where we fall to fill the maws
Of worms -- on battle-plains or listed spot?
Both are but theatres where the chief actors rot.

CXL

I see before me the Gladiator lie:
He leans upon his hand -- his manly brow
Consents to death, but conquers agony,
And his droop'd head sinks gradually low --
And through his side the last drops, ebbing slow
From the red gash, fall heavy, one by one,
Like the first of a thunder-shower; and now
The arena swims around him -- he is gone,
Ere ceased the inhuman shout which hail'd the wretch who won.

CXLI

He heard it, but he heeded not -- his eyes
Were with his heart, and that was far away:
He reck'd not of the life he lost nor prize,
But where his rude hut by the Danube lay,
There were his young barbarians all at play,
There was their Dacian mother -- he, their sire,
Butcher'd to make a Roman holiday --
All this rush'd with his blood -- Shall he expire
And unavenged? -- Arise! ye Goths, and glut your ire!

CXLII

But here, where Murder breathed her bloody steam;
And here, where buzzing nations choked the ways,
And roar'd or murmur'd like a mountain stream
Dashing or winding as its torrent strays;
Here, where the Roman millions' blame or praise
Was death or life, the playthings of a crowd,
My voice sounds much -- and fall the stars' faint rays
On the arena void -- seats crush'd -- walls bow'd --
And galleries, where my steps seem echoes strangely loud.

CXLIII

A ruin -- yet what ruin! from its mass
Walls, palaces, half-cities, have been rear'd;
Yet oft the enormous skeleton ye pass,
And marvel where the spoil could have appear'd.
Hath it indeed been plunder'd, or but clear'd?
Alas! developed, opens the decay,

When the colossal fabric's form is near'd:
It will not bear the brightness of the day,
Which streams too much on all years, man, have reft away.

CXLIV

But when the rising moon begins to climb
Its topmost arch, and gently pauses there;
When the stars twinkle through the loops of time,
And the low night-breeze waves along the air,
The garland forest, which the gray walls wear,
Like laurels on the bald first Caesar's head;
When the light shines serene but doth not glare,
Then in this magic circle raise the dead:
Heroes have trod this spot -- 'tis on their dust ye tread.

Lord Byron published the 4th canto of *Childe Harold's Pilgrimage* in 1817. It contained 186 stanzas and captured the spirit of his overseas travels as he meditated upon the transience of the mighty empires and how our own immortality is erased. For Byron, art, architecture, and nature reflected transcendence. He was just 29 when he wrote the 4th section of this lengthy narrative poem, 7 years before his death. He was born George Gordon Noel Byron and lived in relatively basic conditions with a father who abandoned his children and wife and then died; meanwhile his mother belittled her son because he was born with a club foot. By the age of ten, his fortunes turned and he inherited a peerage and considerable wealth from a distant uncle; thus, he became Lord Byron of Nottinghamshire and eventually attended Cambridge and entered parliament.

A lover of the poetry of Alexander Pope, Byron was soon to develop a poetics that sympathized with neo-classicism, order, discipline, and clarity. His reputation grew with the publication of Canto I and II of *Childe Harold's Pilgrimage* in 1812. The poem emerged out of his travels from Portugal to Spain across the Mediterranean to Greece, Albania, and eventually on to Turkey. Here was a pilgrim who explored the familiar, in Spain and Portugal; the exotic, in Albania and Turley; and the violent, in the bullfights and the Albanian feuds. After the Napoleonic Wars and the French Revolution, Byron's poem expressed the *weltschmerz*, the world weariness, melancholia, and disillusionment, of his generation. *Childe Harold* received immediate critical acclaim, was translated into ten different languages, and was sold out in the first three days.

Byron returned to England with the first two Cantos published and delivered his famous maiden speech, *Frame Breakers*. In the three times he delivered speeches in parliament, the other two being the plea for Catholic Emancipation and the Right to Petition Parliament for Reform, he demonstrated that he had never lost touch with reality and that he was a free thinker who believed in equality for all. Despite his flamboyant notoriety for a luxurious and libertine lifestyle, not to mention his insatiable appetite for women, men, and even his step sister, Byron made extraordinary contributions to the poetic revolution of the Romantics and to the promotion of liberty for oppressed people everywhere.

The Byronic Hero emerges in *Childe Harold's Pilgrimage*; this is a construct of the intelligent, adaptable, mysterious, and cunning hero who struggles with integrity and authority. As a consequence, he is arrogant, cynical, and self-destructive. His sexual proclivities are legend. This results in society treating him as an outcast, and so he spends his days in exilic pilgrimage. *Childe Harold's Pilgrimage* from Canto I right through to Canto IV is written in the very challenging Spenserian stanzas, which are made up of 8 lines in iambic pentameter and the 9th line an Alexandrian, a 12-syllable iambic line with the rhyming scheme of a b a b b c b c c. The persona, Harold, travels in order to find himself after the wasted youth of his past; Harold reinvents himself as a result of the struggles and challenges he faces while on pilgrimage. Indeed, "childe" is a medieval term denoting a young man who goes on a quest in order to become a suitable candidate for knighthood.

Like much of the great Romantic poetry, the sentiments and concepts explored in *Childe Harold's Pilgrimage* speaks to our own contemporary context. This is a *romaunt*, a romantic story told in verse almost a quest for moral and intellectual certainty. These 8 stanzas, between stanzas 137and 144, explore the elegiac nature of our own transience. It is not great gestures that ensure our immorality, but rather, our transcendence is possible because of our brokenness and our connection to others and nature. Harold considers the Roman sites of ancient civilization, the Circus Maximus and the Colosseum, where various rulers assuaged the people's desire for public games, religious festivals, and sacrifice. The opening line in CXXXVII is deeply enigmatic and unresolved: "I have lived, and have not lived in vain." This encapsulates the pilgrim of every age who believes they have and have not achieved what they intended to achieve: that their life is and is not worthless and fruitless. The pilgrim must face their own immortality, their brokenness, and vulnerability if they are to know transcendence. In this particular stanza, Harold considers his decay and the surety of death: "My mind may lose its force, my blood its fire, / And my frame perish." The tricolon works here as an emblem of the trinity within Harold, not despite but because of his weakness. What remains in the shell of the man when he expires is "Something unearthly" which will "move / In hearts ... the late remorse of love". The pilgrim knows that love unexpressed will be a regret that will linger into eternity.

In stanza CXXXVIII, Harold faces the inevitability of death. Byron imagines awe, generated by Death, will far outstrip fear: "Now welcome, thou dread power! ... thus omnipotent... With a deep awe, yet all distinct from fear." Death is ever-present in the signatures of time passing, represented in the symbol of the Roman ruins to which he has made his pilgrimage. When Harold looks closer at the holy objects of this civilized past, time collapses, and he is both contemporary Romantic wanderer and Roman spectator: "we become a part of what has been...all-seeing but unseen." Then, in stanza CXXXIX, he is there standing shoulder to shoulder in the roar of the hungry Roman crowd baying for blood, "As man was slaughter'd by his fellow man". He answers his question, about why this is so, with chilling irony: "because / Such were the bloody Circus' genial laws, / And the imperial pleasure." The suffering of the powerless happens because of authority's desire to treat them as play things. Byron makes his contemporary political comment that the players all "rot" whether they die in the theatre of war or sport, so "What matters where we fall to fill the maws / Of worms". Concern for the lives of lesser beings that were cruelly extinguished by the more powerful would become his lightning rod for his parliamentary speeches.

Stanzas CXL and CXLI zoom in from the general to the specific, from the crowd to the individual, and from the victorious to the victim. In the acquiescence of death, the Gladiator "conquers agony" and with great precision and drama, "his droop'd head sinks ... through his side the last drops...The arena swims around him -- he is gone". This is an ancient Christ who has been given up to his enemy for sport. He is the English soldier caught up in so many battles they are too numerous to name. As he dies he hears "the inhuman shout which hail'd the wretch who won". It is this injustice that spurns Byron's idealism and surfaces in his parliamentary speeches. Moreover, it works as an enjambment into stanza CXLI where the great Gladiator takes no notice of the cruelty because his imagination transports him to his place of home: "He reck'd not of the life he lost nor prize, / But where his rude hut by the Danube lay, / There were his young barbarians all at play, / There was their Dacian mother -- he, their sire." This paradisiacal memory, one that shelters him in his dying, takes him back to his place of belonging prior to capture, enslavement, and brutal death. The Dracians bordered Germania in the south east and their capital is where modern Romania is today. Byron mobilizes scathing irony to showcase the vicissitudes of reality for those who come under the empire's desire: "Butcher'd to make a Roman holiday." Like all pilgrims, Harold now as a dying Gladiator, is moving toward the eternal place of longing.

In stanzas CXLII, CXLIII, and CXLIV we move back to the Roman crowd, then Harold walking amongst the ruins of Ancient Rome and on to the Romantic poet seeing the sublime in nature. This pilgrimage has given witness to the blood lust of the minions: "But here, where Murder breathed her bloody steam; / And here, where buzzing nations choked the ways, / And roar'd or murmur'd like a mountain stream / Dashing or winding as its torrent strays." The personification of this unlawful premeditated violent killing stains the very people caught up in its spectacle. Like the Roman Empire, contemporary war and everyday violence witnessed by Harold is realized as "playthings of a crowd". This very act of witness is central to the business of the pilgrim who journeys through such atrocities: "my steps seem echoes strangely loud."

In the next stanza, Byron notes the ways in which violence is our inheritance and is symbolically passed down from generation to generation in the same way the ancient ruins are cannibalized in order to rebuild "Walls, palaces, half-cities". Harold laments the ruination of such masterful architecture and engineering; he realizes that man has violently plundered this with no regard and thus no civility.

We leave these eight selected stanzas from Canto IV, all of which retain an elegiac tone, with an observation of "the rising moon" that casts a light over "this magic circle" of the dead. The Colosseum in its glory and perfection represents the sacred site to which this pilgrim has traveled and one that is holy: "Heroes have trod this spot -- 'tis on their dust ye tread." This site is the burial place for the overthrown and the oppressed, for the suffering and the despised, and for the brutalized and the enslaved. I think this is such an extraordinary example of how the journey to a historical site can result in profound and transcendent epiphanies that are life changing.

Landing of the Pilgrims by Felicia Dorothea Hemans (1820)

The breaking waves dashed high,

On a stern and rock-bound coast,
And the woods against a stormy sky
Their giant branches tossed;

And the heavy night hung dark
The hills and waters o'er,
When a band of exiles moored their bark
On the wild New England shore.

Not as the conqueror comes,
They, the true-hearted came;
Not with the roll of the stirring drums,
And the trumpet that sings of fame;

Not as the flying come,
In silence and in fear;--
They shook the depths of the desert gloom
With their hymns of lofty cheer.

Amidst the storm they sang,
And the stars heard, and the sea;
And the sounding aisles of the dim woods rang
To the anthem of the free!

The ocean eagle soared
From his nest by the white wave's foam;
And the rocking pines of the forest roared--
This was their welcome home!

There were men with hoary hair
Amidst that pilgrim band:
Why had they come to wither there,
Away from their childhood's land?

There was woman's fearless eye,
Lit by her deep love's truth;
There was manhood's brow serenely high,
And the fiery heart of youth.

What sought they thus afar?
Bright jewels of the mine?

The wealth of seas, the spoils of war?--
They sought a faith's pure shrine!

Ay, call it holy ground,
The soil where first they trod.
They have left unstained what there they found--
Freedom to worship God.

    Felicia Hemans wrote this rousing poem some 200 years after the Puritans established the Plymouth Colony in Massachusetts, New England in 1620. In the literary circles of her day, she was one of the most widely-published poets. Admired by William Wordsworth and Sir Walter Scott she managed to keep her household running, bringing up her five sons with no husband, solely on the earnings she made by publishing a poem each a year until she died of a weak heart coupled with rheumatic fever, at the age of 41, in 1835. Hemans was born in 1793 and was a child prodigy. She was married at 20, and some 6 years later her husband left her and went to live in Italy. Although Hemans never traveled, she imitated the sentiments of the Regency period and explored the themes of nature, childhood innocence, the heroic, the confines of domesticity, and freedom of thought. *Landing of the Pilgrims* was written around 1820 and considers the arrival of the Brownist separatist Puritans who originally fled England for the Netherlands between 1586 and 1605. Concerned they would lose their Englishness, these Puritans then set sail for North America in 1620 to establish a colony where they could practice their faith without the trappings, traditions, and organization of the central church. Yet, this poem is also about Hemans' England during Regency, impacted by the Napoleonic Wars and French Revolution; the enormous economic and social change brought about by the Industrial Revolution and British Parliamentary Reform; as well as the far reaching impact of the American War of Independence. Regency itself was a time of uncertainty. Thus, the achievements of pure-hearted individuals, albeit those hounded out of their own country, in establishing a place of belonging in the New World of the Americas, could now be read as an outcome of English tenacity and faith in God.

    In ten quatrains, with an a b a b rhyme scheme, Hemans captures the courage and fortitude of those in search of a place of freedom and belonging. Indeed, liberty is the central purpose for their pilgrimage, no matter their age or vulnerability. Her writing reflects the Romantic beliefs in the idealization and imagination of the individual as well as the sublime power of nature. Hemans takes an event that is sufficiently historical and one that occurred beyond English borders to turn a nation's gaze on what a small band of pilgrims are capable of finding: a new Jerusalem.

    In the first two quatrains, we have the establishment of setting. This place is imagined as liminal, existing between the known and the unknown, where the sea finishes and land emerges. This site tests the arrival of the pilgrims: "The breaking waves dashed high, / On a stern and rock-bound coast." It is not a hospitable Constable landscape but rather one filled with impediment and travail. It is a homecoming that is initially painted in "the heavy night hung dark" and not in the light shafts of Turner's seascapes. This is a place articulated as untamed and uninhabited with the arrival of the pilgrims by the end of quatrain two: "a band of exiles moored their bark / On the wild New

England shore." Hemans reflects her audience's perspective, which does not regard these men and women as invaders but rather virtuous people in pursuit of safety and freedom. Thus, they signal their arrival "Not with the roll of the stirring drums, / And the trumpet that sings of fame" but rather with "their hymns of lofty cheer". Her audience at the time may have read this with little concern for the impact it had on indigenous people of America because they, like Hemans, regarded this landscape as unpeopled and a "desert". Perhaps these are some of the clues as to why Hemans lost popularity after the 19th century.

The 5th and 6th quatrains become a song of praise to God sung by the pilgrims. They find inspiration in the tumultuous sky, sea, and landscape. Indeed, the new and unknown place of America's natural surrounds becomes the site in which their worship is conducted: "Amidst the storm they sang, / And the stars heard, and the sea; / And the sounding aisles of the dim woods rang / To the anthem of the free!" This is a radical departure from thinking that religious practice should take place under the auspicious of a centralized church with its traditions and rule. Moreover, the hymn has now transmogrified into an "anthem"; thus, it sings of their collective liberty experienced as a new and burgeoning nation. Here, nature shows the face of beauty in the sublime: in the soaring "ocean eagle" and "the rocking pines" offering salutation to the pilgrims on arrival. Hemans sets up questions in the 7th quatrain and answers them in the 8th, then again questions in the 9th, followed by answers in the 10th quatrain.

The question posed in quatrain seven is "why would these old men come to this strange place so far from their homeland to die?" In quatrain eight, the answer is because their faith is shared with a community of believers, demonstrated in women who are "Lit by her deep love's truth", the men whose noble resolve is conveyed in their "brow serenely high", as well as the passion of the younger generation evident in "the fiery heart of youth". Thus, their pilgrimage is more than a personal journey but one done for the greater good of others.

In quatrain nine, the questions are "why travel this far and for what ultimate gain?" The answer is immediate: "They sought a faith's pure shrine!" This is a reference to the Puritans themselves and their need to simplify and regulate the church. Quatrain ten elucidates this wondrous place as "holy ground" and remains forevermore a site upon which one has the "Freedom to worship God". I wonder whether Hemans felt she was making her own pilgrimage to a wild and woolly place as she continued to earn her own living and support her family. Her work does emerge in the era proceeding the publication of Mary Wollstonecraft's *The Vindication of the Rights of Women*. Hemans, like many of the first wave feminists, were probably doing battle every day with the liminal spaces in which they had to exist.

Song of Myself: Section 46 by Walt Whitman (1855)

I know I have the best of time and space - and that I was never measured,
and never will be measured.

I tramp a perpetual journey,
My signs are a rain-proof coat and good shoes and a staff cut from the woods;

No friend of mine takes his ease in my chair,
I have no chair, no church nor philosophy;
I lead no man to a dinner-table or library or exchange,
But each man and each woman of you I lead upon a knoll,
My left hand hooking you round the waist,
My right hand pointing to landscapes of continents, and a plain public road.

Not I, not anyone else can travel that road for you,
You must travel it for yourself.

It is not far ... it is within reach,
Perhaps you have been on it since you were born, and did not know,
Perhaps it is everywhere on water and on land.

Shoulder your duds, and I will mine, and let us hasten forth,
Wonderful cities and free nations we shall fetch as we go.

If you tire, give me both burdens, and rest the chuff of your hand on my hip,
And in due time you shall repay the same service to me;
For after we start we never lie by again.

This day before dawn I ascended a hill and looked at the crowded heaven,
And I said to my spirit,
When we become the enfolders of those orbs and the pleasure and knowledge of everything in them,
shall we be filled and satisfied then?
And my spirit said
No, we but level that lift to pass and continue beyond.

You are also asking me questions and I hear you;
I answer that I cannot answer ... you must find out for yourself.

Sit awhile wayfarer,
Here are biscuits to eat and here is milk to drink,
But as soon as you sleep and renew yourself in sweet clothes,
I will certainly kiss you with my goodbye kiss and open the gate for your egress hence.

Long enough have you dream'd contemptible dreams,
Now I wash the gum from your eyes,
You must habit yourself to the dazzle of the light and of every moment of your life.

Long have you timidly waded, holding a plank by the shore,

Now I will you to be a bold swimmer,
To jump off in the midst of the sea,
and rise again and nod to me and shout,
and laughingly dash with your hair.

Leaves of Grass, from which *Song of Myself* is taken, underwent six distinct editions in Walt Whitman's own lifetime. This collection of prose-like poems demonstrates his Biblical cadence, unusual symbols, proletarian hero persona, non-standardized grammar, and the intimate relationship with his nation, his soul, and the reader. Who was Walt Whitman? The persona he cultivated of himself is someone raw, rude, and representative of the common man; indeed, he identifies himself in his first edition as, "Walt Whitman, an American, one of the roughs, a kosmos, disorderly, fleshly, and sensual, no sentimentalist, no stander above men or women or apart from them, no more modest than immodest". Moreover, his vagabond life from job to job, his travels from his homeland of Long Island and Brooklyn to New Orleans, Washington, and other places, his faithful absorption of the popular culture of his day, and his firsthand experience of the American Civil War while working as a volunteer nurse, fueled his belief that the United States was a country made up of disparate parts. This first version of *Song of Myself Section 46* (the entire *Song of Myself* runs for some 1,350) is the poet calling to the masses in the newly urbanized America, to be alive to the new world. This new world is found in the reflective and intimate relationship one has with an immaterial connection with America. This free verse poem invites contemplation. This section of *Song of Myself* can be broken down into four different parts, but in keeping with the Whitmanesque style, one thought generates the next, one image flows to the next, and thus it is a mesmeric ongoing "yarp" singing of the pilgrimage to oneself.

The poem opens in high modal clarity and bold positive assertion. The voice of this dramatic monologue is "newly formed modern man," one who is self-made, like the autodidact and voracious reader of Whitman himself. He is someone who is self-reliant, generous, and a believer: "I know I have the best of time and space." He qualifies this statement immediately with an anti-stasis, "I was never measured, and never will be measured". In other words, he abhors the cautious sedentary life of the fixed and rigid self. His has been a life of traveling on foot from place to place. The simple and straight forward diction makes this poem accessible to the common man and attempts to poeticize the vernacular of the working person. The rule of three is then mobilized to indicate truth and completion in what he is saying: "a rain-proof coat and good shoes and a staff cut from the woods...I have no chair, no church nor philosophy; / I lead no man to a dinner-table or library or exchange." These are the signatures of freedom in contrast to that of entrapment. Indeed, it is his liberation from the excess of worldly commodities and conventional expectations that he is sufficiently elevated to lead me and you. Immediately, we are led by Whitman, "left hand hooking you round the waist" to the "knoll" from where America and other worlds can be seen and most importantly, the "plain public road" available to all.

What then follows is the call to me, the poet's friend. Ours is an intimate relationship, one where trust and belief in each other is quintessential. What is his destiny is mine: to travel "the perpetual journey" alone no matter those around me. This is captured when he asserts, "Not I, not anyone else can travel that road for you, / You must travel it for yourself". It is here in this section, that the pilgrimage is disclosed as "everywhere on water and on land" and one we have always been on since birth but "did not know". The conflation of the physical tramping of the pilgrim, and that of the metaphysical path taken solely by each one of us along the journey of life, is achieved seamlessly in Whitman's poem.

What I love is that, within these hallowed through lines of poetic philosophy, we have the imperative: "Shoulder your duds." We are called to carry our old and tattered garments as we move with the poet recognizing "Wonderful cities and free nations". Is this the new America hitherto born out of democracy and a desire for freedom? A nation already surging in the preliminary battles of what will ultimately become the American Civil War? Although this pilgrimage can only be one's sole personal experience, it is paradoxically undertaken by all, and as such, Whitman speaks to the sense of community, sisterhood, and brotherhood, which permeate this experience. This is a significant contribution Whitman makes to the poetic contemplation of pilgrimage: "If you tire, give me both burdens…And in due time you shall repay the same service to me." He reiterates that I am alone on my journey but there are many opportunities for each one of us to help each other along the pilgrimage.

In the next section of this poem, we see the way in which the poet ascends a hill before dawn to speak to his soul. The implications seem biblical. It is the poet prophet who trudges up the steep dark slope of his soul in order to understand the nature of his destiny. The symbolism of pre-dawn suggests the promise of enlightenment and it is in this anticipatory atmosphere that we overhear the immediate dialogue between the poet prophet and his soul. The poet's question seems self-evident and anticipates the response of *yes!* but this is not what prevails. If we summit the celestial body of heaven and earth, achieving the full and complete "pleasure and knowledge" of this experience, surely, we would be fulfilled and "satisfied". The answer is a resounding "No". This dialogue takes place beneath "the crowded heaven"; thus, the celestial constellation intensifies the sacred truth. The soul tells the poet that the summit reached levels out, and we must tramp on and "continue beyond". This is the point of enlightenment for both the poet and us.

In the final section of this selected extract from *Song of Myself*, we are preparing to embark on our own pilgrimage. We can hear the uncertainty within ourselves as we jostle about with our equipment, which we believe will help us on our way. Our doubt and hesitancy shapes into questions, from which the poet distances himself: "You are also asking me questions … I answer that I cannot answer … you must find out for yourself." The poet has already shown us that the questions must be asked to our *own* spirit or soul. Our insecurity and self-doubt as beginner pilgrim draw warmth and comradery from the poet to us and permeates the pages of this epic poem. We are invited to "Sit awhile" and we are called "wayfarer"; thus, we are all vagabonds that travel on foot from place to place. He offers us simple sustenance that will generate renewal: "Here are biscuits to eat and here is milk to drink… you sleep and renew yourself in sweet clothes." The poet shows us the way forward and does so with affectionate familiarity. Up until this point, our aspirations and hopes have been nothing more than "contemptible". A stirring adjective indicating that our lives' pursuits have lacked real value. What he offers is a quasi-religious conversion from darkness to the "dazzle of the light and of every moment of your life" made possible by him washing "the gum" from our eyes. This poet prophet can heal our blindness and offer us sight. Up until this point, we have been "timidly" wading close to the shore but we are to "jump off" now "in the midst of the sea, and rise again" shouting and laughing. This powerful metaphor disrupts our expectations. Pilgrimage is not contingent on the physical footfall on landscape but on the immersion into the unfathomable, from which redemption is promised.

The Pilgrim by Sophie Jewett (1896)

> *"Such a palmer ne'er was seene,*
> *Lesse Love himselfe had palmer beene."* Robert Greene

Pilgrim feet, pray whither bound?
Pilgrim eyes, pray whither bent?
Sandal-shod and travel-gowned,
Lo, I seek the way they went
Late who passed toward Holy Land.

Pilgrim, it was long ago;
None remains who saw that band;
Grass and forest overgrow
Every path their footing wore.
Men are wise; they seek no more
Roads that lead to Holy Land.
Proud his look, as who should say:
I shall find where lies the way.

Pilgrim, thou art fair of face,
Staff and scrip are not for thee;
Gentle pilgrim, of thy grace,
Leave thy quest, and bide with me.
Love shall serve thee, joy shall bless;
Thou wert made for tenderness:
God's green world is fair and sweet;
Not o'er sea and Eastern strand,
But where friend and lover meet
Lies the way to Holy Land.
Low his voice, his lashes wet:
One day if God will—not yet.

Pilgrim, pardon me and heed.
Men of old who took that way

Went for fame of goodly deed,
Or, if sooth the stories say,
Sandalled priest, or knight in selle,
Flying each in pain and hate,
Harassed by stout fiends of hell,
Sought his crime to expiate.
Prithee, Pilgrim, go not hence;
Clear thy brow, and white thy hand,
What shouldst thou with penitence?
Wherefore seek to Holy Land?
Stern the whisper on his lip:
Sin and shame are in my scrip.

Pilgrim, pass, since it must be;
Take thy staff, and have thy will;
Prayer and love shall follow thee;
I will watch thee o'er the hill.
What thy fortune God doth know;
By what paths thy feet must go.
Far and dim the distance lies,
Yet my spirit prophesies:
Not in vigil lone and late,
Bowed upon the tropic sand,
But within the city gate,
In the struggle of the street,
Suddenly thine eyes shall meet
His whose look is Holy Land.
Smiled the pilgrim, sad and sage:
Long must be my pilgrimage.

Sophia Jewett wrote this poem in 1896 when she was approximately 35 years of age. By this stage, she had been working for 15 years in the English Faculty at Wellesley College, Massachusetts, a Liberal Arts private college for women. Despite a 16-month tour of Italy and England at the age of 20 with the Calkins family, Jewett gained very little worldly experience. At seven, she had lost her mother and at nine, her father; her grandmother, who had taken in the Jewett children, died by the time Sophia was a young adolescent. She then found inspiration and counsel in the prominent Presbyterian minister, Dr. Wolcott Calkins, in Massachusetts and formed a strong attachment to his eldest daughter, Mary, who would go on to also teach at Wellesley College. Jewett's early poetry, written under the pseudonym of her mother's name, Ellen Burroughs, reflects her faith as well as her burgeoning young female affections for Mary Calkins. She never married, but it was believed by the students at Wellesley that she was in love with a colleague in the English Faculty, Miss Sherwood: a relationship that was later ended with the arrival of Miss Shackford. Jewett died after a brief illness at the age of 48.

The epigraph to *The Pilgrim* comes from the English poet, dramatist, and pamphleteer Robert Greene in his 1590 poem, *Never Too Late*. This Renaissance poem observes a pilgrim in his typical drab garb on his way to the Holy Land, and yet, when we look closer, we notice he is as powerful as a Titan and as a beautiful as Adonis. Indeed, the only thing spoiling this eye candy trudging along is the fact that he keeps crying and sighing. Why is such a godly creature, who is the very essence of virility and beauty, filled with lamentation while walking a pilgrimage? We discover it is because of his virility and beauty that he is indeed compelled to make a pilgrimage, as an act of penitence. Greene himself had undergone the Grand Tour and discovered therein a pilgrimage to debauchery.

Jewett's poem, *The Pilgrim*, is a conversation with Greene's poem, *Never Too Late*. I find it curious that she would take up this 300-year-old poem, exposing how pilgrimages to the Holy Land were the Grand Tour of the medieval period (with extracurricular activities of a secular and decadent nature). In her poem, Jewett is attempting to dissuade the pilgrim from going to the Holy Land, suggesting that it is no longer relevant for the modern person wishing to find God. She is arguing that the pilgrim should look to his own country, friends, and lovers, rather than Christ's grave in Calvary. Yet the pilgrim to whom she addresses her advice will not be turned back; his archaic terms and medieval apparel suggest his values are anachronistic to her Bostonian world of feminism and scholarship. Jewett continues to argue that the Holy Land is to be found in one's own life. This may well have been the case for Jewett, but I daresay it would hardly have been the case for the medieval pilgrim bent on achieving penitence or for the rakish libertine on the Grand Tour.

The Pilgrim is a conversation poem made up of five stanzas written for the most part in trochaic tetrameter. The poet asks the pilgrim four questions: "Pilgrim feet, pray whither bound? / Pilgrim eyes, pray whither bent? ... What shouldst thou with penitence? / Wherefore seek to Holy Land?" The responses to these questions are in keeping with the reader's assumptions surrounding the purpose of the medieval pilgrim: to reach a sacred destiny. In this case, the pilgrim moves "toward Holy Land" because he bears the weight of "sin and shame" and thus needs to do penitence. In stanza two onwards, Jewett's voice is clearly not one of mindless religious compliance but rather one of intellectually rigour, questioning conventions, and practices. Jewett argues that the practice of making a pilgrimage to the physical Holy Land is irrelevant and redundant: "it was long ago ... Grass and forest overgrow / Every path their footing wore". Despite the wise no longer seeking that path, this pilgrim will not be put off, and his determined nature is conveyed in his pride, "Proud his look", and self-belief, "*I shall find where lies the way*".

In stanzas three and four, the poet mounts two different arguments to persuade the pilgrim to desist. Fortuitously, the pilgrim is "fair of face" and as such should "bide with me", the poet, where "Love shall serve thee, joy shall bless". Greene's pilgrim is being addressed, one who "His face faire like Titans shine ... Adon was not thought more faire". This is one hot pilgrim. Jewett asserts that such a body was built to remain very much in the here and now of her world: "Not o'er sea and Eastern strand, / But where friend and lover meet / Lies the way to Holy Land." She has a seductive argument. Just as Greene's pilgrim shed "pearles of sorrow" so too in Jewett's poem "his lashes wet" are a constant sign of his distress. In the 4th stanza, Jewett asks the medieval pilgrim to consider the ambitions of pilgrims who have gone before him, all of whom have some "crime to expiate" and do battle with "stout fiends of hell". Unlike these "Sandalled priest, or knight in selle [sadle], / Flying each in pain and hate" who "Went for fame of goodly deed", she asks him to clear his conscience and relinquish the burden of purpose.

Greene's pilgrim is undeterred by Jewett's arguments, and so, by stanza five, she seemingly concedes that he may pass and continue on his medieval destiny to the Holy Land. We are in the heady fin de siecle of Boston and in the newly emerging progressive women's college of Wellesley with its motto, *Non Ministrari sed Ministrare*, Not to be ministered unto, but to minister. Thus, Jewett administers knowledge of her day and age to this tired maudlin pilgrim. She expresses this in spirited prophesy: "Not in vigil lone and late, / Bowed upon the tropic sand, / But within the city gate, / In the struggle of the street." This radicalized penitent would be someone living in the very throb and hub of modern life, connected to the struggles of the everyday worker and immersed in the concerns of a better society. Not someone whose religious observance removes him from others and from his country. Jewett's thesis is that it is in the struggle for social justice in one's own society that true pilgrimage is conducted. To all this wondrously liberating and truly inspiring vision, Greene's pilgrim can only smile "sad and sage" and concede that therefore for him "*Long must be my pilgrimage*". Progress and the future, certainly in the mind of Jewett, was a pilgrimage into the modern world, one where the pilgrim must fight for the commonweal.

Modern day pilgrims…

Poem in October by Dylan Thomas (1945)

It was my thirtieth year to heaven
Woke to my hearing from harbour and neighbour wood
And the mussel pooled and the heron
Priested shore
The morning beckon
With water praying and call of seagull and rook
And the knock of sailing boats on the webbed wall
Myself to set foot
That second
In the still sleeping town and set forth.

My birthday began with the water-
Birds and the birds of the winged trees flying my name
Above the farms and the white horses
And I rose
In a rainy autumn
And walked abroad in shower of all my days
High tide and the heron dived when I took the road

Over the border
And the gates
Of the town closed as the town awoke.

A springful of larks in a rolling
Cloud and the roadside bushes brimming with whistling
Blackbirds and the sun of October
Summery
On the hill's shoulder,
Here were fond climates and sweet singers suddenly
Come in the morning where I wandered and listened
To the rain wringing
Wind blow cold
In the wood faraway under me.

Pale rain over the dwindling harbour
And over the sea wet church the size of a snail
With its horns through mist and the castle
Brown as owls
But all the gardens
Of spring and summer were blooming in the tall tales
Beyond the border and under the lark full cloud.
There could I marvel
My birthday
Away but the weather turned around.

It turned away from the blithe country
And down the other air and the blue altered sky
Streamed again a wonder of summer
With apples
Pears and red currants
And I saw in the turning so clearly a child's
Forgotten mornings when he walked with his mother
Through the parables
Of sunlight
And the legends of the green chapels

And the twice told fields of infancy
That his tears burned my cheeks and his heart moved in mine.
These were the woods the river and the sea
Where a boy

In the listening
Summertime of the dead whispered the truth of his joy
To the trees and the stones and the fish in the tide.
And the mystery
Sang alive
Still in the water and singing birds.

And there could I marvel my birthday
Away but the weather turned around. And the true
Joy of the long dead child sang burning
In the sun.
It was my thirtieth
Year to heaven stood there then in the summer noon
Though the town below lay leaved with October blood.
O may my heart's truth
Still be sung
On this high hill in a year's turning

From 1941 to 1945, the Welsh poet Dylan Thomas lived with his wife, Caitlin Macnamara and young family, on the west coast of County Ceredigion where he completed *Poem in October*. I have always loved this poem; perhaps it is because I too am an October child. In this exquisite Hopkinesque lyric, Thomas sings his epiphany after the pilgrimage from the waking sea town to the hills beyond: a journey that mirrors his life's pilgrimage to uncover his "heart's truth". He writes seven decimas, and thus, in 70 lines, he ascends to heaven. The internal coupling of assonance and alliteration, as well as the compound adjectival or adverbial phrases, seduce the reader up into the vortex of Thomasonian world. This is a landscape filled with sound and imagery and symbol. It is paradoxical and impossible and exactly as it would only be. We move in exaltation and wonder with Thomas as he trudges forever upwards into his childhood in order to understand that the purity and innocence in the world seen then is the very epiphany the wayfarer has been moving toward all his life. What I love about Thomas is everything. I love his passion and care for language. I love his utter belief that the journey he is undertaking is precisely his destiny. I love how he is completely fearless.

The opening line of the very first decima begins at the high point of exaltation and exhilaration: "It was my thirtieth year to heaven." We are in no doubt of his belief that with every year, he is making his way closer and closer to paradise. This Promised Land is palpable and as real to him there in Wales on the west coast as it is to him in his childhood memories. Thomas is awoken to the sacred in nature: "the heron / Priested shore... With water praying." This site of belonging, which fills his very senses and ours, inspires him "to set foot... and set forth". Like a medieval pilgrim he commences his journey walking through the seasons of the present and past as well as the sights and sounds that orchestrate the ultimate epiphany. His purpose is to leave the "still sleeping town" of his existence and make the ascent.

In decima two, we realize that it is his birthday, so the celebration is not confined to the edenic landscape around him but to having been born. This pilgrim believes he is unambiguously called to make this pilgrimage: "the birds of the winged trees flying my name." The pilgrimage is such a personal undertaking and one that is for the most part done singularly and in the natural landscape. Thomas rises up out of the "rainy autumn / And walked abroad in shower of all my days". In many ways, this is his baptism and absolution. That he would never reach his 40th year to heaven makes the poetic notion of autumn, as the precursor of death, even more poignant. There is a sense of not turning back as he crosses "Over the border / And the gates / Of the town closed". The pilgrim can never return.

The world he witnesses is wondrous: roiling in sound and sight and symbol. By decima three, the sensory cornucopia is excessive: "A springful of larks in a rolling / Cloud... bushes brimming with whistling... the sun of October / Summery / On the hill's shoulder." This is the place of life, fertility, and youth; indeed, we are told that the rain and the wind is left "In the wood faraway under me".

In decima four, he looks back down on where he has come, as pilgrims do in their long musings. There is something deeply healing about ambulant meditation, and the pilgrims begin to see, sometimes for the first time, where they have come from and where they are headed. Thomas looks back on the signifiers of man's authority that in many ways indicate purpose and meaning: "the sea wet church the size of a snail / With its horns through mist and the castle / Brown as owls." The Church and State are reduced in stature. In its place, nature is brimming with the promise of life: "But all the gardens / Of spring and summer were blooming." It is no wonder that he believes it is here, amongst the signatures of natural life, that he can contemplate this phenomenal gift of life given him: "There could I marvel / My birthday." Yet it is the very power of Nature, with its capricious character, that makes this decision impossible: "but the weather turned around." Most pilgrims learn very early on that they are at the mercy of the weather; they have no control and must bend their will to the natural elements. It is at this point that we leave the purely physical and emotional realm and move into the metaphysical.

In decimas five and six, we walk with Thomas into a place that is numinous. This is a place of "other air" and an "altered sky". No longer are we in autumn ascending a hill above the town but rather in "a wonder of summer / With apples / Pears and red currants". A veritable feast of color and smell and taste! This vision gives way to another that is tantalisingly clear: "a child's / Forgotten mornings when he walked with his mother / Through the parables / Of sunlight / And the legends of the green chapels." It is more than a memory; it is the poet on his 13th birthday ascending the hill and actually seeing revelation unfurl. Spiritual lessons are taught while walking and in the intimate familial relationship such as that between mother and son. The symbols of morning and sunlight imbue this moment with hallowed beauty. Even the enchantment of Lud's Church, one of the green chapels, enters the frame of this magical place. Legend has it that the green chapels were protected at different times by Sir Gawaine, Robin Hood, and Bonnie Prince Charlie.

In the penultimate decima, the 30-year-old poet and his child self are conflated; hence, this poem and the parables witnessed as a child are the "twice told fields of infancy". The awakening of the child is and always was the awakening of the poet: "his tears burned my cheeks and his heart moved in mine." Moreover, the revelations of childhood remain the alpha and omega of all that is laid bare in the life of a poet. Thomas knows that it is in this very landscape of "listening / Summertime" that "the truth of his joy", the meaning of his epiphany, can be poeticized. He has traveled to the place in himself, landscaped by the familiar and familial, where the mystery of love is ever present: "the mystery / Sang alive."

The final decima brings us to the summit. Just when Thomas chooses to celebrate his birthday in this epiphanic mystical site that conflates the past with the present as well as the child with the adult, a place where the truth of joy is all encompassing, "the weather turned around". It is like a scene where we move from the metaphysical, "the long dead child sang burning / In the sun", to the physical as he reaches the pinnacle of his ascent. This nadir is enigmatic and strangely inscrutable: "stood there then in the summer noon / Though the town below lay leaved with October blood." Thus, time splices into the fertile promise of summer at its zenith and the autumnal sacrifice as prelude to death. Indeed, it is because of the transient and elusive nature of the epiphany that it is all the more desired. This pilgrim, the 30-year-old Welsh poet, with all his demons and suffering, ends this lyric with a prayer: "O may my heart's truth / Still be sung / On this high hill in a year's turning." This is the prayer of every pilgrim: to never forget the euphoric insight gained at the summit of one's pilgrimage. What a poem!

Funeral Rites by Seamus Heaney (1975)

I
I shouldered a kind of manhood,
stepping in to lift the coffins
of dead relations.
They had been laid out
in tainted rooms,
their eyelids glistening,
their dough-white hands
shackled in rosary beads.
Their puffed knuckles
had unwrinkled, the nails
were darkened, the wrists
obediently sloped.
The dulse-brown shroud,
the quilted satin cribs:
I knelt courteously,
admiring it all,
as wax melted down
and veined the candles,
the flames hovering
to the women hovering
behind me.

And always, in a corner,
the coffin lid,
its nail-heads dressed
with little gleaming crosses.
Dear soapstone masks,
kissing their igloo brows
had to suffice
before the nails were sunk
and the black glacier
of each funeral
pushed away.

II
Now as news comes in
of each neighbourly murder
we pine for ceremony,
customary rhythms:
the temperate footsteps
of a cortège, winding past
each blinded home.
I would restore
the great chambers of Boyne,
prepare a sepulchre
under the cup-marked stones.
Out of side-streets and bye-roads
purring family cars
nose into line,
the whole country tunes
to the muffled drumming
of ten thousand engines.
Somnambulant women,
left behind, move
through emptied kitchens
imagining our slow triumph
towards the mounds.
Quiet as a serpent
in its grassy boulevard,
the procession drags its tail
out of the Gap of the North
as its head already enters
the megalithic doorway.

III
When they have put the stone
back in its mouth
we will drive north again
past Strang and Carling fjords,

the cud of memory
allayed for once, arbitration
of the feud placated,
imagining those under the hill

disposed like Gunnar
who lay beautiful
inside his burial mound,
though dead by violence

and unavenged.
Men said that he was chanting
verses about honour
and that four lights burned

in corners of the chamber:
Which opened then, as he turned
with a joyful face
and looked at the moon.

There is one pilgrimage that we all, finally, take: the pilgrimage to the site beyond this life. Seamus Heaney writes about the veneration of this final pilgrimage and the way in which the pilgrim, ever nameless and ever faceless, will be you and me. I find this quiet collection of 20 quatrains, offered up in a trinitrine structure, to be both deeply familiar and disturbingly foreign. In section one, the pilgrim is in a domestic space, one that is doused with sacred rituals and Christian symbols to assuage the fears of those attempting to assist the pilgrim on the final leg of his journey. The sectarian violence of the 1972 Bloody Sunday massacre at Belfast haunts my reading of section two, where the pilgrimage gains momentum and is collectively envisioned as one that is triumphant. The processional leaves the domestic site behind and nudges towards the archaic and tribal burial site.

Section three pulls together both worlds of the prehistoric and the contemporary in its conflation of pre-Christian and Christian notions of resurrection. Recently, I took a pilgrimage from the Republic of Ireland up across the Boyne River, which divides the south from the north, past Newgrange in County Meath, then across to County Londonderry to St Mary's Church in Bellaghy, and finally arriving at the grave of Heaney. He had died in August 2013, some 15 years after I had met him. His last words, as it were, are cut low and quiet into his headstone: "Walk on air against your better judgement." Be bold, even in the face of your last pilgrimage.

The pilgrimage in section one of *Funeral Rites* is deeply familiar and domestic. It begins indoors where the role of men and women is divided. The women hover on the periphery as if doubtful, while the men step in and shoulder the burden of assisting the pilgrim to make this ultimate journey from the known to the unknown. This final pilgrimage mobilizes others to make sense of their own narratives and belief systems by imbuing the departing pilgrim with the signatures of faith: "rosary beads ... shroud ... candles ... gleaming crosses." The mourners, whose time has not yet come, are connected to these "dead relations" and yet there is an unease, a disquiet, in those who are left behind. This is conveyed in the paradox of the warm chill between the departing pilgrim and those farewelling: "Dear soapstone masks, / kissing their igloo brows / had to suffice." A pilgrim must make this final pilgrimage alone. It is a singular undertaking to which one surrenders physically and metaphysically. The final pilgrimage from death to the site beyond the known can never be conveyed as anything but a place of violent rupture from the familiar. The final movement of section one conveys this passageway as one filled with foreboding: "the black glacier / of each funeral / pushed away." We have now moved from the preparatory stages of the dead that happens away from the public eye in the quiet domestic sites of family homes to its onward passage.

On Wednesday 2 February, 1972 in Creggan Derry, tens of thousands of people attended the funeral of 11 of the 14 people who were shot by the British Army during Bloody Sunday. Meanwhile 90% of all of Dublin stopped work and 100,000 Dubliners carried 13 empty coffins with black flags to the British Embassy. The whole island of Ireland seemed to stand still on that cold, wet day of mourning. From here we move up to *Brú na Bóinne* or the Valley of Tombs. This Neolithic site contains Newgrange, one of three large passage tombs, as well as 40 or so other smaller tombs. This site is evidence of a highly organized and settled community with its own rituals and ceremonies surrounding the dead. Moreover, this mystical place reveals traces of the sophisticated knowledge of architecture, engineering, astronomy, and art.

Section two takes up this journey across the sectarian violence that still plagues Northern Ireland. This is a place where binaries are tied closely together: "neighbourly murder... blinded home... emptied kitchens." It is because of the very madness of sectarian violence that the mourners "pine for ceremony, / customary rhythms". Consequently, the cortege follows the dead pilgrim on his final pilgrimage not to the Christian icons of the sacred but to the archaic and tribal *Brú na Bóinne*: "Quiet as a serpent / in its grassy boulevard...its head already enters / the megalithic doorway." The snake connotes fertility and rebirth in pre-Christian symbolism, so it is not surprising that the pilgrim's ultimate pilgrimage is to the site of his beginning. What is left behind by the pilgrim is an unseeing emptiness; what is about to be entered is a doorway to a lighted inner chamber.

At this point the place to which the pilgrim goes can only be imagined; thus, section three commences with placing the stone over the mouth of the entrance: a gesture reminiscent of the entombment of Jesus according to the New Testament. Meanwhile, the cortege moves on up into the legends of the Icelandic north "past Strang and Carling fjords". It is as if the whole island of Ireland is in mourning and moves from the south across the border, the fjords signify into the north and beyond. We know that the "cud of memory" will only be placated momentarily; meanwhile, the tribal feud continues. Perhaps this is why the mourners continue the journey despite the pilgrims having reached their final resting place.

Heaney asks us to imagine those buried pilgrims now joining the communion of other unholy souls. They have been made sacred by memories and rites: "imagining those under the hill / disposed like Gunnar / who lay beautiful / inside his burial mound." Gunnar is the great warrior who was loyal to his country and heroic in battle. It is in the final sentence of this poem that the past and the present converge; the burial site of Gunnar becomes that of Jesus, which in turn becomes that of the victims of the Bloody Sunday Massacre and will ultimately be the burial site of all pilgrims. A shaft of light has traveled through this poem to this final epiphany. We realize the poem itself has been a type of roof box that needed time and movement in order to light the final chamber. The pilgrim turns to face the light: "Men said that he was chanting ... and that four lights burned / in corners of the chamber...he turned / with a joyful face / and looked at the moon." Hearsay and supposition predict joy; it is a moment of epiphany made known to the pilgrim as he reaches the destination of his final pilgrimage. I cannot help but recall the last words Heaney spoke, "Noli timere". In all ways *Funeral Rites* leaves us with the same message: do not be afraid.

Pub Pilgrimage by Francie Lynch (2015)

I'm making a pub pilgrimage,
A malted Mecca trip;
I'm leaving all I love at home
Crusading with the Picts.
I'll be alone with all my thoughts,

It's what must needs be done,
To keep the demons off.

Publicans meet me on the steps,
On Sundays by the side;
This trip of three thousand miles
May kill should I survive.

My altar's elbow worn,
The finest oaken wood;
I'll climb the stairs on knees,
Hear bells, raise cups of cheer.

There's games of chance,
Some romance,
With songs and several fools;
It has trappings of Canterbury
In pubs all called O'Tooles.

There's Highland mead,
And broken bread,

With harps from inner rooms,
I'll have dispirited spirits
And revel inside tombs.

My cave awaits on my return,
It's dark and hard and cold;
But I know the light's within my sight,
If I move this granite stone.
I'll bring with me a scapula
To make those visions stop,
The relics that I sought,
Those demons of a sot.

    Francie Lynch is a contemporary poet who immigrated as a child to Ontario, Canada from County Monaghan, Ireland. This free verse poem made up of six stanzas, with the occasional end rhyme but changeable meter, explores the interplay between the sacred and the profane. Lynch marries an everyday icon, the pub, associated with vice and excess with that of the sacred or holy expedition, the pilgrimage. *Pub Pilgrimage* is much more than what one may think at first glance. Throughout the poem, the present participle or present continuous tense as well as the future tense is used to convey what this pilgrim is preparing to do and wishes to happen. In other words, this is a pilgrimage already happening in his imagination but yet to unfold in reality. What is it to long for pilgrimage? Perhaps it is a common desire to long for freedom and solitude that can be found in undertaking a future expedition. A pilgrimage requires persistence and reflection in order to be receptive to the epiphanies along the way. Indeed, at times the pilgrim needs fortitude to reach the ultimate destiny. This pilgrim undertakes a crusade to the place where his own resurrection may take place and where he can face a lack of faith in himself which in the past has held him back.
    Historically, Christian pilgrims moved across Europe on established trade routes to certain sacred sites of worship while others traveled in Crusader packs to the Holy Lands to fight against Islamic inhabitants. These pilgrims looked for hospitality in taverns en route; they need to eat, drink, and bed down for the night. *Pub Pilgrimage* like *The Canterbury Tales*, emerges out of such a setting. Thus, the conflation has long been established of public houses and pilgrims; it is an act of transubstantiation that connects the ordinary with the extraordinary. Throughout *Pub Pilgrimage*, Lynch interplays the codes and symbols of the pub with that of the pilgrimage until all our readerly expectations are completely overturned. We walk out of this poem, a little dishevelled, a little intoxicated by seeing the light after rolling back the stone.
    In stanza one, the pilgrim announces, with alliterative flourish, that he is on a "pub pilgrimage" to a "malted Mecca". These oxymoronic terms sum up the heart of the poem, which is the confirmation of truths found in contradiction. Like all pilgrims, leaving the familiar despite it being the very site of "love", he knows that this is part and parcel of fulfilling the necessary demands of pilgrimage. This modern day pilgrimage takes the pilgrim back to his roots (hence his destiny is to

go "Crusading with the Picts"). The last lines of the first and last stanzas references "demons". The pilgrim argues in the first stanza that he must do this pilgrimage to keep the demons at bay and by the last stanza that these are the demons of a habitual drunkard. The irony of course is that he takes his demons with him to quench their thirst. Every pilgrim knows they too take their demons with them on the pilgrimage, step by step.

Stanzas two, three, and four in *Pub Pilgrimage* offer up an imagined experience of the pilgrim arriving at his destination. In those parishes in Scotland, Wales, and Ireland, where pubs are closed on a Sunday, drinkers can go round to the back entrance to purchase their drinks. This works as a metaphor for how many believers bypass the rules and regulations established by the Church. This pilgrim explains that the "three thousand miles", the distance from Canada to the UK, might nearly kill him if he doesn't get that drink. He can well prove his devotion to the bars venerated by pilgrimage, sacrifice, and commitment: "My altar's elbow worn, / The finest oaken wood." Moreover, he is deeply familiar with the rituals associated with this holy devotion of drinking in pubs: "I'll climb the stairs on knees, / Hear bells, raise cups of cheer." In many ways, Lynch satirizes those pilgrims who make an artifice of the spiritual experience of pilgrimage. In stanza four, the poet is suggesting that every Irish pub has the "trappings of Canterbury". The perennial path of pilgrimage is crowded with the ordinary signatures of life, conveyed in the cumulative listing of "games of chance, / Some romance, / With songs and several fools". We are constantly reminded that the experience of pilgrimage is ordinary.

It is not until the last two stanzas of *Pub Pilgrimage* that we begin to see the merging together of the commonplace and the numinous. Furthermore, the poem becomes more complex and dense in its ambitions. Stanza five opens with the hoped for communion offered to the pilgrim: "Highland mead, / And broken bread." This suggests local pub victuals as well as the consecrated Eucharist. The ordinary everyday pub begins to morph into something more ambiguous. We have the signatures of "harps", the national emblem of Ireland, but this could also be something more transcendental coming from "inner rooms". This pilgrim partakes in "dispirited spirits", suggestive of both alcohol and spiritual enlightenment and the revelling that takes place "inside tombs" could be both the snug of a pub but also the celebration of life beyond what is known.

By stanza six, we have moved from the simple literal idea of someone traveling back to his ancestral roots to arrive at a local pub, to a complex metaphorical notion of what it is to be a pilgrim. The ambiguity between the ordinary and the extraordinary set up in stanza five segues into the unambiguous tomb of Jesus, given to him by Joseph of Arimathea. Here, the poet joins pilgrims throughout the past who have journeyed to this historic site: "My cave awaits on my return, / It's dark and hard and cold; / But I know the light's within my sight, / If I move this granite stone." His faith is absolute and he is without fear in the knowledge that at the end of his pilgrimage, the epiphany of resurrection will be his. What he will bring to that end point are tokens of his belief in the transcendent: "I'll bring with me a scapula / To make those visions stop." In order to cast out those dreams which thwart his redemption he must make his own pilgrimage. This pilgrim knows the true crusade for the sacred lies in acknowledging the "sot" in himself; in other words the broken and profane humanity of oneself.

Pilgrimage by Natasha Trethewey (2006)

Vicksburg, Mississippi

Here, the Mississippi carved
its mud-dark path, a graveyard

for skeletons of sunken riverboats.
Here, the river changed its course,

turning away from the city
as one turns, forgetting, from the past –

the abandoned bluffs, land sloping up
above the river's bend – where now

the Yazoo fills the Mississippi's empty bed.
Here the dead stand up in stone, white

marble, on Confederate Avenue. I stand
on ground once hollowed by a web of caves;

they must have seemed like catacombs,
in 1863, to the woman sitting in her parlour,

candlelit underground. I can see her
listening to shells explode, writing herself

into history, asking *what is to become
of all the living things in this place?*

This whole city is a grave. Every spring –
Pilgrimage – the living come to mingle

with the dead, brush against their cold shoulders
in the long hallways, listen all night

to their silence and indifference, relive
their dying on the green battlefield.

At the museum, we marvel at their clothes –

preserved under glass – so much smaller

than our own, as if those who wore them
were only children. We sleep in their beds,

the old mansions hunkered on the bluffs, draped
in flowers – funereal – a blur

of petals against the river'sgray.
The brochure in my room calls this

living history. The brass plate on the door reads
Prissy's Room. A window frames

the river's crawl toward the Gulf. In my dream,
the ghost of history lies down beside me,

rolls over, pins me beneath a heavy arm.

Pilgrimage by Natasha Trethewey was published in 2016 in her Pulitzer Prize winning collection of poems entitled, *Native Guard*. In 2012, she was named the 19th U.S. Poet Laureate as well as the State Poet Laureate for Mississippi. This is interesting because when she was born in Mississippi in 1966, she was regarded as an illegal because her parents were an interracial couple and miscegenation was a crime. I love the distilled emotion of this poem and the controlled form. This is an elegy to a personal and national history that has been erased. I have been thinking about the way in which pilgrimages are made in order to know oneself. To take this journey back into the nation's self and thus into oneself is a way of understanding roots, purpose, and destiny. Perhaps in contemporary times where religion plays less of a role for Westerners, the desire to walk in the footsteps of those now dead is a way of coming to terms with one's own mortality, identity, and connection to history.

Pilgrimage is made up of 18 unrhymed couplets and one end line. We are immediately positioned in Vicksburg, Mississippi. The expedition to Vicksburg National Military Park, a vast site of 91.4 kilometers squared, commemorating the Civil War Battle and the Siege in 1863, is indeed, a holy journey: a sacred pilgrimage for many. One walks on hallowed ground with over 19,000 killed and buried there. Vicksburg was first occupied by Native Americans, then the French, then the Spanish, then white settlers. It was the strategic node on the great Mississippi River, the lifeblood of America, which connected trade from the north, where cotton from the south had been recycled into transportable textiles and finished goods. During the Civil War, the Mississippi's trade and commerce was effectively blocked at Vicksburg by the Confederates; it was imperative if the north was to regain control over the lower Mississippi that they would need to split the South in two and end vital supplies to the Confederate line. In 1863, despite the erection of artillery batteries by Confederates on the sharp bend of the Mississippi River, where Vicksburg stood on the commanding bluffs, Confederate General Ulysses S. Grant landed tens of thousands of soldiers and commenced the 47-day siege. Citizens, including women and children who had followed their men to this area in order for them to fight, dug tunnels and lived in dirt caves to survive the relentless 100 kilogram mortar shells and 13 kilogram artillery shelling. There were 46,000 casualties. The Confederates were seen as Crusaders leaving home in order to fight the holy war. Their sacrifice was made for the sacred belief in protecting Christian values that were being destroyed by the North.

Trethewey offers us a pilgrim to Vicksburg, Mississippi in modern times. The river runs as a metaphor throughout her poem; it is the force of nature that cannot be stopped or controlled despite humanity's efforts to own it, shape it, and reconfigure a particular history upon its watery skin. I can see the tourist pilgrim arriving at this historical battlefield and pointing out iconic markers. Hence the word "Here" not only begins the poem but repeatedly interrupts the poem as the pilgrim points out the significant and worthy.

The first marker of the pilgrimage is the Mississippi River, which makes its own pilgrimage to the Gulf of Mexico. The river's life-taking force foreshadows the sacred site of Vicksburg: "the Mississippi carved / its mud-dark path, a graveyard / for skeletons." Trethewey's use of meandering enjambment imitates the meandering memories that river through a nation's wounds, forming its identity. The repetition of "Here" occurs in the second sentence where the pilgrim points out how "the river changed its course...as one turns, forgetting, from the past". Vicksburg National Military Park receives tens of thousands of visitors a year. The pilgrim continues to gaze upon the river and its landscape as it turns northwards to the Yazoo River, which flows into the Mississippi Delta.

The third and final repetition of the pilgrim pointing and announcing "Here" moves us from the dead in the Mississippi River to the battlefield itself. The dead are buried beneath the pilgrim's footsteps: "Here the dead stand up in stone, white / marble, on Confederate Avenue." The monumentalizing of the dead keeps them alive and present to the modern day pilgrims. I remember walking this very avenue where monuments declare the loyal allegiance of certain Union or Confederate regiments, and singular soldiers are named and their stories briefly monogramed. After a while, I could not read on. There is no denying that you are walking over a vast cemetery where the horror of brother fighting against brother is just beneath the surface of a "ground once hollowed by a web of caves...like catacombs". This is an allusion to Abraham Lincoln's Gettysburg Address in 1863 where he acknowledges that the blood of the dead, in this Civil War, consecrated the nation and made it holy. In other words, these pilgrims who come to Vicksburg to tour the Park do so because they are making a pilgrimage to the heart of their sacred nation. One formed in blood, hatred, division, and unimaginable brutality.

Mary Ann Webster Loughborough was 27 when she arrived in Vicksburg with her two-year-old daughter; she was following her Confederate soldier husband. Loughborough wrote *My Cave Life in Vicksburg*, a bestseller in both the South and the North. This was her record of survival during the siege, where they were attacked night and day as well as being starved and dehydrated. Their rations were two biscuits, two slices of bacon or mule, and a spoonful of rice and one of peas. Their water came from ditches and mud holes. Her records show how they longed for death. Trethewey imagines these cave dwellers attempting to outlast the siege in a singular woman existing in her "candlelit underground". As we walk alongside the pilgrim in this poem, we too can "see her / listening to shells explode, writing herself / into history, asking *what is to become / of all the living things in this place?"*. Our relationship with the pilgrim and with the dead is personal and intimate. It is as if the floor between the present and past collapses and we make a pilgrimage through this living necropolis: "This whole city is a grave...the living come to mingle / with the dead."

Why do we walk pilgrimages? I wonder if it is because we need to walk in the footsteps of those long dead, on a path that has gravitas and meaning, so that our own print on this earth joins theirs and is immortalized. Despite its intimacy, it is a problematic relationship that the living pilgrim has with the dead: "listen all night / to their silence and indifference, relive / their dying on the green battlefield." Those who have already died do not need the pilgrims; however, those who walk in the footsteps of the dead need to experience the simulacra of dying and being dead. Hence, this sacred site is forever fertile. The pilgrimage takes in the museum, a microscopic commemoration of the mythology of a nation's self-actualization. The Confederates were seen as children of unenlightened times; thus, "we marvel at their clothes...so much smaller / than our own, as if those who wore them / were only children": the real implication being the unforgivable act of a nation killing its own offspring.

We move from the Vicksburg National Military Park to its surroundings where a pilgrim can take rest in the grand antebellum mansions. Bear in mind that the majority of the Confederates were not conscripted from ruling classes who occupied such homes. These grand antebellum homes, icons of the Deep South, were built on the blood, sweat, and tears of the African American slaves. Now they are seen by the modern day pilgrim as tombs of a bygone era: "the old mansions hunkered on the bluffs, draped / in flowers – funereal." We are reminded that this pilgrimage, made in the 21st century, is part and parcel of a tourist route. This intertextual reference to "The brochure in my room" authorizes the site of pilgrimage as *"living history"*. In other words, the schizophrenic feeling of being in both the present and the past, the living and the dead, the physical and the metaphysical, haunts the experience of pilgrimage. We are both at home and estranged, mirrored in the "brass plate on the door / *Prissy's Room*", a nod to Margaret Mitchell's novel, where black bodies lived lives enslaved to homes where they were always estranged.

The final section of the poem looks both outward and inward. Penultimately, it takes us out through the window into the Mississippi River where the poem began and then to the Gulf of Mexico beyond. We are left inside the subaltern's room, trapped beneath the weight of a story that is still to be told. There is something insidious and malevolent in the apprehension of history as a ghost which "lies down beside me, / rolls over, pins me". In all of the chaos, carnage, rape, abuse, and murder of the American Civil War as witnessed here in Vicksburg, the black slaves' narrative remains largely unrecorded and unaccounted. Not only are nations formed in blood but they are shaped by silencing those voices which might profane the hallowed iterations of acceptable history. Pilgrims are challenged to see the whole story of the path they tread. This poem, this "window" into a pilgrimage to Vicksburg, is just the beginning. Maybe that is why we are compelled to travel such pilgrim trails.

4

Poetry with a Divine Will: Numinous Poetry

I came to the sacred via poetry. In fact, I am going to go one step further. I think that without poetry, the aesthetic language of poesies, there can be no transmutable experience of the divine. Poetry gives us the language to make sense of the metaphysical, the knowledge that there is more to life than just matter. I also think that certain poems demonstrate a divine will in that they connect us deliberately and exactingly to what is outside of ourselves, to all that is irreducible. Thus, numinous poetry attempts to resolve that tension between ego and divinity as well as our separateness and God's infinity. As much as poems with a divine will can inspire awe, they can also be profoundly disturbing. The poems I am sharing with you convey both these aspects of the numinous: on the one hand, they draw back the veil, and the luminous grandeur of divine will is revealed, and on the other hand, there's an element of danger and unsettling disquiet in each of these poems.

Australia's Vince Buckley reveals the intense divinity ever present in our own temporality whose persistence is unrelenting until we arrive at the epiphanic last three words of the poem. Les Murray offers us a head trip. His *Poetry and Religion* could proselytize the most cynical as he convinces us that worship of the divine is contingent upon poetry until we see this in the flight of crested pigeons and rosella parrots at the tail end of the poem! Then we come to the magnificent *Magnificat* by Noel Rowe who resists the dominate narratives of Jesus' life and gives voice to a modern day, highly charged evocation of the divine will.

America's Langston Hughes reclaims the defiled, abused, and suffering Christ for the African American people. *Christ in Alabama* remains one of the 20th century's most dangerous and wanted poems. The great Modernist W. H. Auden wrote *For the Time Being* after immigrating to the USA from England: the distance forged a ferocious criticism of the way people experience glorious spiritual vision but pack it away as a calendar event. Howard Nemerov is a Russian Jew who challenges us to consider the betrayal of Jesus by Judas as the greatest act of good. Indeed, *The Historical Judas* leaves us wondering about our own ongoing complicity in the betrayal of all Jesus represents. Then we come to Charles Wright, originally from Tennessee, with his *Last Supper* that quietly invites us to sup at the table of the divine, despite our hesitancy.

England's William Shakespeare conveys the power of the divine in that it shapes our desire to be. Hamlet's numinous soliloquy is about the tensions, doubts, and hungers associated with self-actualisation. The great metaphysical poet, John Donne, reminds us that we need to think about death and rather than fear it, consider the way it offers passage to life eternal. The language of Gerard Manley Hopkins' *God's Grandeur* shimmers with its divine will and yet the notion of the Holy Spirit flies in the face of all orthodoxy, suggesting it is a maternal love. G.K. Chesterton's *The Donkey* shows us what it is to suffer with Christ and yet remain steadfast and loyal to him. And finally, T.S. Eliot's dramatic monologue of the *Journey of the Magi* gives voice to our own indeterminate efforts to make pilgrimages to the most scared but not really to understand the experience.

Day with its Dry Persistence by Vincent Buckley (1966)

In day with its dry persistence
In night with the first star
Down the mid-night passages
Or in the small corners of silence
Or at the bedside hot with death
A restlessness clings and will not
Be rubbed off on paper.

Yet there are some tempos that prefer me,
Some twigs that burst with shaking
Blossom and dew, some lights that are constant,
Some movements of the earth that bring me
In constant pilgrimage to Genesis,
To the bright shapes and the true names,
Oh my Lord.

I love the boldness of this little sonnet. It is so simple and tenacious a statement. Not an argument or a conceit or a burst of wondrous seductive song-lines. Instead it is a laconic statement of fact. Buckley is interested in the way places can open up toward the transcendent. This sonnet is aware of both the solid and fragile world around him. Each time I come back to this particular sonnet of his, I am reminded of the paintings of the Australian artist Russel Drysdale who was making art the same time Buckley was writing poetry. There's something sparse and empty about the imagery in this poem and yet it opens up to a transcendent world immense with possibility. Buckley was keenly aware of the way poetry could mine significant moments, like the watchful death of a beloved parent, and either open up to the transcendent or devolve into a journey around and around the poet's own consciousness. It was with the publication of *Arcady and Other Places*, in which this sonnet was collected, that Buckley began his foray into poetry that reflected the imagination and place that surrounded him. I also think it is interesting to look at the contextual influences around Buckley at the time of writing *Day with its Dry Persistence*, and that is the impact of Vatican II. From 1962 to 1965, the council of over 2000 men met to renew the Catholic Church's rites of liturgy and its connection to the modern world. As the Australian poet Noel Rowe says, it was a time where the vertical and horizontal models of theology wrestled for power and control of God. For Buckley, this triggered his withdrawal from institutionalized Church because it had failed to mediate the spiritual and the sensual. This was better mediated by poetry.

As we enter his sonnet, we see how the incarnation, which permeates Buckley's poetry and this sonnet in particular, in the Church's hands has been envisioned far too dogmatically. In the first stanza, Buckley speaks of the persistence of the incarnation in the external and internal ordinary landscape. In the dry rustle of leaves and the night star in the great southern skies or in the shadowy corners of a room as one keeps vigil alongside the dying, there is something more. This, for the poet, is the surety of immanence. He asserts that there is a restlessness to connect to the wonder of what it is we see and experience but don't ordain. This unquiet unease within us compels us endlessly forward into the mystery. This persistence of the immanence cannot be erased from our own articulated self-narratives. The metaphor assures us that it cannot be erased. Indeed, that combination of plosive and sibilance in the word "persistence" echoes its Latin etymology of continuing steadfastly.

The second stanza opens with what the poet does not "prefer", and that is a cadence at which the day is performed. In contrast to this, he speaks of certain tempos which *do* speak to him. The examples Buckley then offers are fast and slow time, allegro and largo, in "twigs ... shaking / Blossom and dew" and the constancy of "lights". This aural and visual image of bony twigs moving in time with the elements of life, "Blossom and dew" are mimetic of the persistence of the immanent. It is these selected "movements of the earth" that bring one back to the eternal journey. Buckley's sacred expedition is a constant one, driven by the dry persistence of his everyday world: an endless holy search for that which will parch his restlessness and thirst. In many ways, it is a desire to go back to the beginning, to the origin, when all that was taking shape, took shape, as it was named, according to Biblical mythology. The words "bright" and "true" stand out for me. It suggests that the shapes had life because of the light which imbued them, and the names had truth.

The volta occurs in this compact little sonnet between the 13th and 14th lines. It ends the second sentence; indeed, the sonnet is only made up of two sentences! With the drop away final line from the second stanza I can't help but wonder if Buckley is suggesting that not even the immanent can be controlled by any structure or form, we impose. This break-away final line is marooned. It is a line cast adrift. It is a colloquial expression of the exasperated, the frustrated, the wondrous, and the extraordinary. A deliciously ordinary phrase: "O my Lord." It is the epiphany on seeing: that after the restlessness of such dry persistence the ordinary world reveals the Lord.

Poetry and Religion by Les Murray (1987)

Religions are poems. They concert
our daylight and dreaming mind, our
emotions, instinct, breath and native gesture

into the only whole thinking: poetry.
Nothing's said till it's dreamed out in words
and nothing's true that figures in words only.

A poem, compared with an arrayed religion,
may be like a soldier's one short marriage night
to die and live by. But that is a small religion.

Full religion is the large poem in loving repetition;
like any poem, it must be inexhaustible and complete
with turns where we ask Now why did the poet do that?

You can't pray a lie, said Huckleberry Finn;
you can't poe one either. It is the same mirror:
mobile, glancing, we call it poetry,

fixed centrally, we call it religion,
and God is the poetry caught in any religion,
caught, not imprisoned. Caught as in a mirror

that he attracted, being in the world as poetry
is in the poem, a law against its closure.
There'll always be religion around while there is poetry

or a lack of it. Both are given, and intermittent,
as the action of those birds – crested pigeon, rosella parrot –
who fly with wings shut, then beating, and again shut.

    This tight jigsaw of a poem contemplates the relationship between poetry and religion. It is made up of eight tercets and ten sentences, some of which are sharp and abrupt while others use enjambment to propel us into the tercet below. Murray offers a profound and crystallized focus on the way religion is poetry! There is not a word out of place and while the poem's lexical choice seems deceptively accessible, its selection has the precision of a surgeon. It's an interesting conceit, isn't it? That poetry is a religion or that religion is poetry or even that there is a powerful relationship between the two concepts. The structure of the poem takes us down a rabbit hole; we seem to burrow deeper and deeper until we find ourselves in a bright fantastical world that seems utterly convincing.

    The opening sentence of this poem is an assertion that "Religions are poems". Murray doesn't use a simile but an exacting metaphor. What does this assertion mean? Let's first look at what constitutes these two projects. The word "religion" comes from the Latin *religare* and later *religio* and is a bond or reverence for God. This desire to be connected to the sacred translates into rituals and rites governing people's relationship with the metaphysical. Furthermore, religions, not spirituality, emerge out of literate times and are thus contingent on language. As for poetry, it is an artistic form of expression evoked originally in song and oral recitation. It existed well before the literate world. Poetry has a quality of beauty and intensity often with a distinctive style and rhythm. Its subject matter explores everything from the physical to the metaphysical: from the conscious to the subconscious. So, how are religions poems? It would seem that religion is a preoccupation with God whereas poetry's preoccupation is with language. If the metaphor holds true that "Religions are poems", then at the basis of our bonded love for God is the love of language. Put another way, the love of language or poetry is at the heart of religious practice.

The second sentence commences in tercet one and runs on into tercet two. Here, Murray spirals deeper and deeper into this conceit that at the heart of our love of God is the love of poetic language. He is exploring the idea that when religions successfully pull together the many parts of what it is to be human into powerful aesthetics and significant knowledge, it is an act of making humanity complete. Religions are quintessentially poetry: "They concert / our daylight and dreaming mind, our / emotions, instinct, breath and native gesture / into the only whole thinking: poetry." Thus, religions arrange a number of our synapses into an intense and beautiful expression of what it is to be human. The choice of the verb "concert" indicates that harmony and musicality evoked by religions are an evocation of poetry: that religions pull together the known and the unknown, which again is the core business of poetry.

The third sentence is a slip stream of the quixotic theory on language. Murray argues that words come first and indeed, according to Genesis, first there was the Word. This also reverberates in 20th century Saussuran semantic theory where we are reminded that language comes before thought: "Nothing's said till it's dreamed out in words." What this amounts to is the mind-numbing idea that without language there can be no thought. There is no concept existent without words. Language is privileged; its value is heightened above all cognizant capabilities. Thus, the love of language must be at the forefront of the human enterprise and what results is our bond, obligation, and reverence for God. Before we complete tercet two, we are thrown a paradox, just in case the poem hasn't offered sufficient complexity and challenge! Murray introduces a third major concept, the preoccupation of both religions and poetry, and that is truth. Whatever truth is, it is not restricted by language: "nothing's true that can be figured in words only." If this assertion is correct, then neither poetry nor religion can corral truth.

The third tercet explains how poems, when compared to an "arrayed religion", can seem like a single night of passion that sustains the lover for a lifetime. Murray qualifies this comparison as a "small religion" in the final short sentence of the tercet. The fact that he uses the conjunction "but" between the simile and the qualifier indicates that a poem's singular passion, tailored for one, will not manifest into the grand narrative. Here the poem is an intimate, memorable, and intense "short marriage" of minds: the poet's and the reader's. While it offers a single "soldier" reason "to die and live by", it is not enough. Thus poems, or religions, that restrict their audience and eschew the ongoing purpose of offering enlightenment and love to all, are limited and inconsequential.

It is in the 4th tercet that we are confronted with the largesse of poetry. Murray posits that the difference between the limited poem or religion and the "full religion" or "large poem" is "loving repetition". So, it is not a one night marriage but something that lives on richly enfolded between poet and reader, forever. In other words, the great poem is reiterated and ingeminated into our very being so much so that it becomes the complete and whole expression of the sublime. In answer to our questions "Now why did the poet do that?" to the "large poem" we are rewarded with answers both "inexhaustible and complete". Indeed, great poems do keep offering variations of meaning every time a reader asks why this, why that? These sorts of poems, these sorts of religions, are living and thus are "complete / with turns" that continually keep us questioning and wondering. A sign of a masterpiece is that it lives on and breathes through one generation to the next because not only does it demonstrate textual integrity, it has a quality of beauty and meaning that still resonates with us.

Tercet five makes two short assertions: "You can't pray a lie ... you can't poe one either". Mark Twain's fictional character, Huckleberry Finn from the eponymous novel, asserts the first, and Murray's witticism follows up in the second. Both are true. Twain's 13-year-old protagonist knows that the solemn invocation for help from God cannot be an act of dissembling. It is the one relationship that defies dishonesty. Another way of looking at this is that both the practice of religion and poetry requires an honest relationship. What does Murray's riposte add? Edgar Allan Poe's poetry was concerned with the how of language, not the what. Truth is about its effects and thus Poe's poetry, which formed a bridge between Romanticism and Modernism, explores how truth sounds and how it is seen. His cynicism emerges out of America's antebellum years where the subject of truth is not as significant as how it appears. It seems to me that religion and poetry are being asked to contemplate not only truth but how it is seen.

Running through tercet five, six, and seven is the extended metaphor of the mirror. Into poetry and religion, we look to know ourselves. When the mirror's reflection is "mobile" and "glancing, we call it poetry". Put another way, poetry is our "selves" and our worlds caught at angles, a different perspective and while in motion. The truth of what we see reflected is unfixed. Meanwhile, when the reflection is "fixed centrally" it is what we call religion. Thus, religion is unmoving and located at the center. To sum up, poetry is unfixed and perspicacious in its expression of self, whereas religion is fixed. Then we trip on the most simple and complex explanation of the relationship between poetry and religion: "God is the poetry caught in any religion." Rethought, this statement reads that, within religion, the sublime is articulated in poetry. Alternatively, without poetry, there can be no God. Of course, the verb "caught" occurs three times in the final two lines of tercet six: "caught in any religion, / caught, not imprisoned. Caught as in a mirror." It is poetry that captures the divine, not religion; moreover, the arrest of the celestial is not constricted or restrained but rather resultant of the effect of a true presence. The extended metaphor is completed in the 8th sentence when we are reminded that, in poetry, we will always find the presence of God, which will know no end: "a law against its closure."

The penultimate sentence of the poem uses enjambment from tercet seven into eight. Murray argues that religion is dependent on the beauty and knowing that poetry articulates. With poetry, religion can exist meaningfully; a world without poetry would mean religion needs to supply the world with hope and salvation from such suffering: "There will always be a religion around while there is poetry /or a lack of it". It's a circular argument to some degree but it is also indicating the sacred role poetry plays in the development of what it is to be human.

In the last tercet and sentence of this poem, we are left with a comparison of religion and poetry to "the action of birds". Neither the presence of poetry or religion is continuous. Perhaps that is why their value as intense, beautiful, and insightful expressions of humanity's relationship with the physical and metaphysical is so significant. The bird flight of poetry and religion suggests wonder and persistence: "with wings shut, then beating, and again shut." The reference to the "crested pigeon, rosella parrot" is distinctly familiar to an Australian, suggesting that both religion and poetry are living and familiar. Moreover, this analogy implies that poetry and religion are not quite tamed. If poetry and religion are both timorous and euphoric actions, then they move about in the slip stream of our life, forever just beyond our reach.

Poetry and Religion makes endless "turns" when we ask it certain questions. We move from a singular unorthodox assertion, religions are poems, to an array of arguments. These arguments may or may not have convinced you. Ultimately, worship is contingent on language and in particular, poesies. Most convincing is Murray's final truth that the glory and impossibility of bird flight is a divine poetic expression. As such, it is the definitive religion.

Magnificat 5. Resurrection by Noel Rowe (2004)

Yes, Simeon, there was sorrow, but much fun
Too, when he set about making contradiction.

I should have known: for when the glorias first were sung,
It was to celebrate my son, born among the dung.

Ever since I have been hearing heaven's laughter.
Cana's newly-wed, absorbed in what was coming after,

did not even notice how the water changed its mind.
The Pharisees got a holy shock as a man born blind

told them if they didn't get a hold on their desires,
so taken up with Christ, they'd land themselves among his followers.

Sacred irreverence. It is a gift to those found free
In the spirit. Even Zacchaeus found it in himself, up a tree,

and Lazarus, sauntering around in his shroud.
There was a time too when, expecting stones, a crowd

got instead some bread and fish. I heard a thief steal
his way back to paradise. The structure of the real

is mercy. Having seen so many reversals.
I should have known he would test his muscles

on the stone, and walk away from the dazed
grave, leaving its mouth open and amazed.

Noel Rowe was my teacher. We spent many an irreverent hour laughing at a shared love of the ridiculous. He was a good teacher. He was kind and filled with secrets. I went to his funeral not long ago and wondered what had happened; why did he die so young? What sort of life did he actually have? Rowe had a way of seeing the world that was both sacred and ordinary. The word *Magnificat* comes from the Latin and refers to one of the ancient canticles sung by the Blessed Mother. It is written up in the Gospel of Luke 1:46-55. Like Rowe's canticle above, the *Magnificat* in the New Testament is made up of a series of coupled statements that sing the magnificence of the Lord. According to legend, when Mary was pregnant with Jesus, she met her older cousin Elizabeth, who was pregnant with John the Baptist, and both women imbued this ordinary moment with the sacred. Elizabeth addressed Mary with the words contained in the first half of the *Hail Mary*. Mary responded with the *Magnificat*. Luke's infancy narratives contain four promise-fulfilments: Mary's *Magnificat*, Zechariah's *Benedictus*, the angel's *Gloria in Excelsis Deo* and Simeon's *Nunc dimittis*. These are interesting song patterns of synonymous parallelism that reflect Jewish hymnology. Rowe's study of theology allows him to engage deeply with this form and context in order to create an interface between the praise of God and a celebration of the magnificence of Jesus's birth, life, and resurrection.

Like the *Magnificat* in Luke's Gospel, Rowe's poem is made up of couplets that use synonymous parallelism. Here in Rowe's poem, Mary amplifies the beloved nature of her son. She refers to eight separate incidences in the narrative of the life of Jesus: the presentation of Jesus at the Temple, the birth of Jesus in a stable, the wedding at Cana, the restoration of sight to a blind man, Zacchaeus up a tree, Lazarus rising from the dead, the miracle of the loaves and fish, the penitent thief promised entry to heaven, and finally Jesus as the risen Lord. In *Magnificat* by Rowe, Mary addresses her song to Simeon, the just and devout Jew who met Jesus, Joseph, and Mary as they entered the Temple of Jerusalem 40 days after Jesus' birth. According to tradition, Simeon recognized the messiah in Jesus and thus the prophecy was fulfilled that he would see the salvation of Israel before he died. In Luke 2:34-35, Simeon warns Mary that this messianic life to be lived by her son will cause her unimaginable suffering: "This child is destined to cause the falling and rising of many in Israel... And a sword will pierce your own soul too." So, Rowe is offering a contemporary take on this canticle: a hymn of praise to God from Mary but also an articulation of the life they had when lived as mother and son.

"And Mary said..."

In this opening phrase in the *Magnificat* in Luke's Gospel, we know that the young Virgin Mary is speaking her praise of God to her cousin. In Rowe's poem, Mary is in another speaking position; she is no longer the young ignorant girl but rather a woman who has known extraordinary suffering but moreover has been transformed by the act of resurrection, which marks her son as the messiah. In his poem, we start in medias res in Mary's direct address, or apostrophe, to Simeon, not Elizabeth. Rowe's first rhyming couplet is a neatly contained sentence where Mary mentions that, in contrast to the sorrow predicted by Simeon, there was "fun ... when he set about making contradiction". This three lettered word "fun" arrests us. Nowhere have I ever heard or considered the story of Jesus to be "fun". We commence with an unexpected idea that it was amusing or entertaining to witness the impact of Jesus' teachings on the orthodoxies of his day: be it in Judaism or Roman occupation of Judea or rebel movements. Moreover, these "contradictions" Jesus applied to orthodoxies were deliberate and significant. Mary's address, from the start, verges on reproach, as if urging Simeon to see another side to the life of Christ. She seems determined to represent her life not simply as a wound but rather as an ongoing extension of the canticle she once sung over 30 years beforehand.

"My soul magnifies the Lord,
and my spirit rejoices in God my Saviour..."

In this couplet from the Gospel, we see the parallel phrase, "My soul ... my spirit": both metaphysical elements of the self, reflecting and rejoicing the love given to Mary from the Lord. Rowe's response is to draw on another of the four narratives, of which the *Magnificat* is one, the angel's *Gloria in Excelsis Deo*. Of course, Mary "should have known" that her son was the anointed one because she was a devout Jew and as such knew the prophecies of the Old Testament. Moreover, at his birth the angels sung the very song of glory and praise to the birth of the "Lord, King, heavenly God, Father, almighty; Lord, the only-begotten Son, Jesus Christ, and Holy Spirit". The juxtaposition in Rowe's poem is established in setting. While the birth of Jesus is hailed by celestial bodies and the heavens over Bethlehem filled with sublime song, the mother and baby lie in a filthy animal stable: "for when the glorias first were sung, / It was to celebrate my son, born among the dung." We know this infant narrative; we are deeply familiar with its unexpected twists and turns and yet in Rowe's hands it reads fresh and cheeky. Moreover, he is giving the self-effacing devout voiceless Virgin Mother of God a bit of sass.

"...for he has looked on the humble estate of his servant.
For behold, from now on all generations will call me blessed..."

The next couplet from the Gospel makes reference to the lowliness, humility, and servant status of Mary as well as the promise that the God of Israel will *see* and raise up the destitute. Rowe's third couplet contains a one-line sentence followed by the wedding at Cana vignette, which runs on into the following couplet. Mary tells Simeon that "Ever since" the birth of her son she has "been hearing heaven's laughter". The present participle and alliteration of "hearing heaven's laughter" is surprising and unexpected. This laughter, like the fun mentioned in the opening of the poem, suggests joy. I think this is the lightning rod of Rowe's poem. We are not expecting joy and laughter and fun in the narrative of Jesus. We are expecting gravitas and sobriety and solemnity. All of a sudden, Rowe has made the story we know so well completely human but wondrous, at the same time. He has fleshed out the story we know but with a different voice and one we find in all its wit and insouciance, deeply familiar. Mary tells Simeon about the newlyweds "absorbed in what was coming after", the conjugal bliss of their wedding night. Does she wonder what this constitutes, having remained a virgin? It is certainly not how the most sacred feminine is traditionally represented and yet I find her more endearing.

"...for he who is mighty has done great things for me,
and holy is his name..."

This next couplet from Luke's *Magnificat* exclaims the bounty and favor God has bestowed on his people and in particular, Mary. The wedding at Cana, Galilee, was the site of Jesus' first miracle and could be interpreted as an attestation of himself as God. In John's Gospel, Mary lets her son know that the guests have run out of wine and despite his reluctance to act, Mary assumes his compliance, thus Jesus turns water into the best wine of the celebration. At this point, because of this miracle, many of his disciples believed he was the messiah. Having said that, miracles were part of an archaic storytelling trope that offered its listeners enriched meaning beyond the limitations of their prosaic world. Rowe's 4th rhyming couplet completes the reference to the wedding at Cana but with a decided lack of interest in the phenomenon where "water changed its mind". The use of anthropomorphism here conflates the action of Jesus changing his mind with the molecular structure H_2O changing into C_2H_5OH: from water into alcohol. Like a bumpy joy ride, we hit another miraculous reference that is the restoration of sight to a blind man by Jesus: another reminder of the great things he has done. Mary recalls, tongue in cheek, that the Pharisees "got a holy shock" as a result. This separatist group (and strict adherents of the Torah) represents some of the layers of resistance to Jesus.

"...And his mercy is for those who fear him
from generation to generation..."

In the Gospel, Mary sings the belief in a compassionate God: one who will offer tenderness to the miserable and down-trodden and will do so unceasingly. Rowe's 5th couplet engages with this idea of a merciful God, who, with gentleness and charity, offers salvation to a believer. The poem throws us off course by the blind man's impertinence, who from the position of possible outcast is now the temerarious individual who confronts the Pharisees and "told them if they didn't get a hold on their desires ... they'd land themselves among his followers". The irony being that their obsession for Christ would lead to their very own conversion. Thus, the man who was blind and could not see now has insight into the extraordinary power of Jesus. In many ways, this is Mary's account to Simeon of the tension between the naysayers and the believers. Her interest seems to lie outside the domain of orthodoxy as she picks up on the peripheral nuances of her son's story as a way of proving this life journey, she witnessed had its share of the ridiculous. Thus, her story resonates with us.

> "...He has shown strength with his arm;
> he has scattered the proud in the thoughts of their hearts..."

In Luke's *Magnificat*, the synonymous parallelism in "he has shown strength ... he has scattered" indicates the unceasing power of the Lord who is as merciful as he is righteous. Rowe's 6th couplet begins with a fragmented two-word sentence: "Sacred irreverence." This paradox is a contemplation of the Old Testament God to whom Mary revered, who protected the humble and dispersed the proud of heart. Mary goes on to propound her down to earth theology: "It is a gift to those found free / in the spirit." This is an understanding of God that liberates us from atrophying distance to familiar intimacy because here is the messiah whose message is as holy as it is radical. For me, Rowe brings this home again and again in his *Magnificat*, and I am challenged to engage with an account of Jesus that has been hitherto untold. There is a strength in this raw and cheeky account as much as there is a scattering of those hypocrisies that censored, and continue to censor, our relationship with God. In the final line of this couplet, which runs on into the next couplet, we are introduced to Zacchaeus, the tax collector, who found this spirit of freedom "in himself". From a despised traitor collecting money for the occupying Romans, he became hospitality's pinup boy, which led to his own salvation. This event of Jesus calling him down from "a tree" in Jericho had a ripple effect among the onlookers who couldn't believe a prophet would lower himself to insist he eat at the table of the tax collector: an act of sacred irreverence if ever there was one.

> "...he has brought down the mighty from their thrones
> and exalted those of humble estate..."

Again, the Gospel's *Magnificat* uses the juxtaposition of God's action which "brought down the mighty" and "exalted" the humble. Rowe's poem explores this preoccupation with these contrasting manifestations of humanity and God's response to them, through the eyes of his mother. The poem's 7th rhyming couplet mentions the exalted Lazarus "sauntering round in his shroud". The raising of the dead is the catalyst that sent shock waves through the schizophrenic crowd, who a short time later, hailed Jesus as the messiah by laying palms beneath his feet on the road to Jerusalem, only to condemn him to death days later. Restoring Lazarus to life was the ultimate defeat of the enemy, death: "Lazarus, sauntering around in his shroud." It's comical to imagine this beloved friend of Jesus risen from the dead and moseying about with a certain insouciance. Amusing moments, laughter, irony, and fun continue to make their way through Mary's narrative of what their life was like as if the promised agonizing wound of a sword through her heart was not the whole of her story. This couplet takes us into the story of the loaves and fish miracle, or the feeding of the 5000 recorded in all four Gospels. Mary recounts this event in a laconic and piecemeal way: "There was a time." It is as if this wasn't the drama that made its way into all four Gospels but rather a vague memory of a moment: a period in their lives when the fickle crowd was onside.

> "...he has filled the hungry with good things,
> and the rich he has sent away empty..."

Here the Gospel's *Magnificat* sings the ongoing generosity of the Lord in filling "the hungry with good things" while turning the "rich ... away empty". Rowe responds in couplet eight with the story of an unexpected feast. This is a tale where expectations are overturned, the magic becomes the real, and the world never remains the same again. From the expectant "stone" noted in couplet above, the crowd gets "instead some bread and fish". Indeed, the hungry are filled with good things. The stony landscape of Judea around which crowds move, following Jesus and his charismatic brand of teaching, metaphorically translates as some home-brand, local food for thought. What they got instead in their hopes for nourishment was vastly surpassed. Bread is a symbol for quintessential nourishment and fish for the risen Christ. So, the crowds expected the landscape of the known and were fed eternal nourishment of the risen Christ. Mary then, as a type of aside, mentions some hearsay: "I heard a thief steal / his way back to paradise." It is as if the frame of her storytelling to Simeon is haunted by what is to come, despite her efforts to share the titbits of their life which from her perspective were ordinary, yet she always knew her son was extraordinary. In her peripheral vision to this event of the feeding the crowd, she hears the penitential bandit who recognizes Christ at Calvary and so bargains his way to redemption.

"...He has helped his servant Israel,
in remembrance of his mercy..."

In the Gospel, we hear Mary declare that because their people have been faithful to God, he has responded with compassionate love. The 9th rhyming couplet completes the enjambment and responds directly to the Gospel's *Magnificat*: "The structure of the real is mercy." Mercy is not just a specific type of love but a praxis: to stand at the origin of suffering and to remain present and active throughout the suffering, endowing it with a particular direction. Thus, God hears the cry of his suffering people and responds with compassionate kindness and leniency. Therefore, Mary tells Simeon that she has "seen so many reversals". Throughout her life, she has witnessed the reversal of suffering, injustice, and hopelessness. Indeed, the sword through her heart has been overturned by fun, angelic heralding, miracles of wine making, sight and life restoration, and tax collectors and thieves redeemed, not to mention the feeding of five thousand. It is no wonder she adds (rather colloquially and with a certain dash of wit), that it is no wonder her son would "test his muscles" in the final drama of his life.

"...as he spoke to our fathers,
to Abraham and to his offspring forever."

The final couplet of the Gospel's *Magnificat* reminds us that God's truth is to sustain us to the end of the world. Rowe concludes his poem in a 10th couplet where the resurrection fulfils the prophecies and offers salvation to believers. Mary tells Simeon of the shock that people experienced in the wake of the risen Lord. Their reaction is projected onto the canvas of Jesus' burial site and thus works as an objective correlative. The "dazed grave" with its "mouth open and amazed" conjugates, through internal rhyme and anthropomorphism into the utterly unexpected. Which begs the question: why the astonishment? It would seem that despite the fulfilment of prophecy there were still grave doubts or maybe they just couldn't imagine what was taking place. Hadn't his followers, and in particular Mary, by now realized who they were dealing with? Apparently not. It is this truth, told by his mother to Simeon, which disturbs me the most. We are more than two thousand years on, and we are still coming to terms with what it means to have witnessed the birth, life, death, and resurrection of Jesus Christ.

Christ in Alabama by Langston Hughes (1931)

Christ is a Nigger,
Beaten and black –
    Oh, bare your back.

Mary is His mother
    Mammy of the South,
    Silence your Mouth.

God's His father –
    White Master above
    Grant us your love.

Most holy bastard
Of the bleeding mouth:
    Nigger Christ
    On the cross of the South.

Christ in Alabama still cracks like a whip! Whether one reads the 1931 version, which is slightly more confronting than that published in 1967, Langston Hughes' brief riff on the gross injustices of the Scottsboro 9 can be heard loud and clear a century later. The title dislocates us; how is it possible that Christ would be in the Deep South in 1931? If anything, Christ's presence was notably absent. So, I read this tight coil of a poem and wonder where, in fact, is Christ in Alabama? In the travesty of the Scottsboro 9 court case that made legislative history for all of America, there seems to be a complete absence of mercy, justice, and redemption. In 1931, two young white females accused nine African American males, aged 12 to 20, of rape while they were traveling on a train. The case was first heard in Scottsboro, Alabama. Later, the girls testified that they had fabricated the story but despite this an all-white jury found the nine males guilty. The African Americans were given sentences from 75 years to the death penalty and all but two served prison sentences. A number of retrials ensued and, despite convictions overthrown decades later, the lives of all nine African American young men were damaged beyond repair. We know this story in part from Harper Lee's Pulitzer Prize winning *To Kill a Mockingbird*, but there have also been a number of documentaries, plays, and books written about this case, where racism and the right to a fair trial had to be drastically reimagined.

Hughes' strong sense of racial pride as an African American made him one of the most important thinkers and writers of the Harlem Renaissance, a cultural political epoch that commenced in the 1920s. This was a movement of artists, dancers, musicians, writers, poets, and political thinkers who celebrated African American life and culture. Hughes' poetry taps into the African American song tradition from slave ships, plantations, gospel choirs, and Blues and Jazz, as well as those emerging out of the burgeoning civil rights movement. Therefore, his poems have a cadence that is deeply imbued in his people's rhythms and ways of thinking. This poem, *Christ in Alabama*, is no exception. In some ways this poem could be a prayer or a slave song or a poem for civil justice. Indeed, the call and response technique used within the frame of these four stanzas is a nod to the black gospel choirs, who were experiencing their own renaissance.

This is a dangerous poem. It evokes the desperate plight of those people, specifically here as African Americans, who were forgotten and abandoned: forgotten and abandoned by the jurisprudence system, by the constitution, by the abolition of slavery declaration, by human rights and by God himself. I have shared this poem with students over the past three decades and the impact is palpable. People read this poem and respond in such different ways: some are shocked, angry, and outraged while others are offended, cynical, and dismissive. Regardless, I think it is a poem that needs to be heard. No matter how many times I read Hughes' poem, I am left asking: if this is what the place of oppression looks like, and Christ is there, then do we remain fixed in a state of crucifixion?

The opening line of this four stanza poem is so confronting that to this day, there is still debate about whether such a statement can be made. Can the messiah be black? To a White Western mindset steeped in Christian mythology, this is a giant unprecedented leap into a post-colonial perspective. Moreover, can Christ be called a "nigger"? If so, Christian imagination must be reeling with the messiah being represented in the most pejorative and offensive terms. Christ is therefore marginalized, abandoned, and demonized because, as a "nigger", he threatens so called civilised law and order of the hegemony. In the second line of the first stanza is the phrase "Beaten and black". This is a dual reference to the passion of Christ where he was beaten and abused as well as the passion of the African American people who were abused, raped, beaten, and lynched. That Christ in his suffering is conflated with the story of the African American is arresting; that his skin color is named "black" would have been shocking in 1931, 1967, and perhaps even today.

So, the first line of each stanza is the call and the final line or lines, indicated by indention and italics, is the response. I hear the call given by the African American people and the response given by White Christian America. So, to sum up the first stanza: the African American calls out that Christ's suffering is a shared experience with their own; their voice is direct and intimate. This is a political call for social justice and one that dismantles traditional representations of the Christian messiah. Disturbingly, the White Christian American response is for the suffering Christ, the suffering African American, to continue to "bare your back". Therefore, this is a place of purgatory, a place without redemption, while Alabama refuses to concede defeat.

The second stanza opens with an orthodox statement of belief in the African American call.

In saying "Mary is his mother", Hughes takes possession of the familiar Christian narrative for the African American people. Consequently, Mary is the mother of the suffering Christ and the suffering African American. If there is discomfort in this reading, it is that Hughes binds the black Christ, the "nigger" Christ, the African American Christ to Mary. This would make her black or a "nigger" or an African American: a frightening prospect for those in 1931 who were so threatened by miscegenation. The White Christian response here in stanza two undercuts the standardized term "mother" with the white romanticised term "Mammy", first used by Harriet Beecher Stowe to depict the enslaved female looking after the children of the white master. Part of the revisionist history of post-Civil War includes this nostalgic representation of racial and gender essentialism. In this stanza, the call and response of the identity of Christ's mother moves between the mythology of Christianity and that of white supremacy. The imperative to "Silence your mouth" is part of the ongoing control and mastery by White supremacy over the marginalised. This phrase also references the gagging that went on with the Scottsboro 9 and all those who suffered under the Jim Crow laws.

The third stanza commences with another orthodox statement. Hughes insists on reclaiming orthodox Christian beliefs in order to call attention to the atrocities experienced by the African American people. In the first line of this stanza, the belief in the trinity is asserted: "God is His father." In writing that God is the father of the suffering Christ, he is also unequivocally stating that God is the father of the African American people. What is being done unto his son and his people is being done unto him. How would this have impacted those White Americans who were complicit in the ongoing crimes committed against the African Americans? The response of the White Christian America follows: "White Master above." We are under no illusions that God has been imagined as white and commanding, indeed, overlording his minions as a white slave owner might. The added response "Grant us your love" suggests that, despite the ongoing atrocities committed by God-fearing White America, they still demand love from Father God. Interestingly, in Hughes' 1967 version of this poem, the last line changes to "Grant Him your love". It is as if the request for God's love needs to be directly requested for the suffering Christ, the suffering African American. Let's keep in mind that, in 1967, the civil rights movement continues because the Civil Rights Act signed in 1964 is still nascent.

In the final stanza, we open with a two line call from the voice of the African American. Christ is the most sacred of all illegitimate sons; he is without rights and without agency: "Most holy bastard." The suffering Christ, the African American people, are without protection from the law. That word "bastard", in all its pejorative splendor, would have been a hit in the face. Christ is to be read as the lowest of the low, just as the African American people are. This is the Christ "Of the bleeding mouth". This is second reference to the word "mouth" in the poem. The visceral image of the mouth, of Christ bleeding, conveys the notion that his truth must be heard and redress must be given.

The response that follows in the final two italicized and indented lines is calculated to shock. Instead of "Christ is a Nigger" we are confronted by "*Nigger Christ*"; the move from noun to adjective makes the ground beneath our feet shift. Where the noun functions to reclaim the messiah for the African American people, the adjective indicates there is a separate and different deity for the African Americans, and it is one which is lesser, pejorative, and worthy of lynching. In the final line, the response asserts that this lesser God is exactly where he should be: "On the cross of the

South." Thus, we end the poem knowing that the perpetual state of crucifixion is the reality of the Nigger Christ, the Scottsboro 9, and every African American man, woman, and child.

Finally, let's just look back at the call sung by the African Americans on the slave ships, in the plantations, in the gospel choirs, in the Blues, and in the Civil Rights Movement: "Christ is a Nigger, / Beaten and Black / Mary is his mother / God's His father / Most holy bastard / Of the bleeding mouth." It's a dangerous song, right? Let's hear the response from all those complicit in racism: "Oh, bare your back. / Mammy of the South, / Silence your Mouth. / White Master above / Send us your love. / Nigger Christ / On the cross of the South." I find this profoundly disturbing. *Christ is a Nigger* is a call and response poem that was as astonishing then as it is today. The call is courageous in the way it reclaims the defiled, abused, and suffering Christ for the African American people; the response is horrifying because it condones and is complicit in the ongoing acts of crucifixion. This is the gospel according to America at the time of Hughes' writing and rewriting of *Christ is a Nigger*.

For the Time Being: Christmas Oratorio III by W. H. Auden (1942)

Well, so that is that. (1) Now we must dismantle the tree,
Putting the decorations back into their cardboard boxes --
Some have got broken -- and carrying them up to the attic. (2)
The holly and the mistletoe must be taken down and burnt,
And the children got ready for school. (3) There are enough
Left-overs to do, warmed-up, for the rest of the week --
Not that we have much appetite, having drunk such a lot,
Stayed up so late, attempted -- quite unsuccessfully --
To love all of our relatives, and in general
Grossly overestimated our powers. (4) Once again
As in previous years we have seen the actual Vision and failed
To do more than entertain it as an agreeable
Possibility, once again we have sent Him away,
Begging though to remain His disobedient servant,
The promising child who cannot keep His word for long. (5)
The Christmas Feast is already a fading memory,
And already the mind begins to be vaguely aware
Of an unpleasant whiff of apprehension at the thought
Of Lent and Good Friday which cannot, after all, now
Be very far off. (6) But, for the time being, here we all are,
Back in the moderate Aristotelian city
Of darning and the Eight-Fifteen, where Euclid's geometry
And Newton's mechanics would account for our experience,
And the kitchen table exists because I scrub it. (7)
It seems to have shrunk during the holidays. (8) The streets
Are much narrower than we remembered; we had forgotten

The office was as depressing as this. (9) To those who have seen
The Child, however dimly, however incredulously,
The Time Being is, in a sense, the most trying time of all. (10)
For the innocent children who whispered so excitedly
Outside the locked door where they knew the presents to be
Grew up when it opened. (11) Now, recollecting that moment
We can repress the joy, but the guilt remains conscious;
Remembering the stable where for once in our lives
Everything became a You and nothing was an It. (12)
And craving the sensation but ignoring the cause,
We look round for something, no matter what, to inhibit
Our self-reflection, and the obvious thing for that purpose
Would be some great suffering. (13) So, once we have met the Son,
We are tempted ever after to pray to the Father;
"Lead us into temptation and evil for our sake." (14)
They will come, all right, don't worry; probably in a form
That we do not expect, and certainly with a force
More dreadful than we can imagine. (15) In the meantime
There are bills to be paid, machines to keep in repair,
Irregular verbs to learn, the Time Being to redeem
From insignificance. (16) The happy morning is over,
The night of agony still to come; the time is noon:
When the Spirit must practice his scales of rejoicing
Without even a hostile audience, and the Soul endure
A silence that is neither for nor against her faith
That God's Will will be done, That, in spite of her prayers,
God will cheat no one, not even the world of its triumph. (17)

This disturbing narrative poem haunts you long after it is read. Auden uses the word *oratorio* in the title: a delicious Italian word with Latin roots. For some the title is reminiscent of Bach's *Christmas Oratorio*. An oratorio is a large scale narrative, most often a musical work for orchestra and solo voices, typically for a scared theme, performed without costume, scenery, or action. So, I am already thinking about the sacred theme of Christmas, the birth of Christ, and the way in which the poem is Auden-esque in that it is typically unadorned, without costume or scenery and indeed with little action. The long poem threads its way through a narrative that is uncannily familiar. It is a poem orchestrated for the collective. It is performed by all of us in a variety of ways. The oratorio text is more or less dramatic in character. Bach's 1734 composition was made up of six parts, and Auden's poem is indicative of the third part of the oratorio, which is the adoration of the shepherds, when the shepherds bear witness to the birth of Christ. Ironically, according to Auden, our witness is short-lived and superficial. Bach's *Christmas Oratorio* was regarded as highly sophisticated parodic music, and the purpose was threefold: as a serious compositional technique, as a re-use of well-known melody to present new words, and as an intentionally humorous, even mocking of existing musical material. This makes me think about many things but in particular the way this poem parodies the existing sentiments of Christmas while also considering the Christmas period of 1941/1942. Finally, the phrase, "For the time being", precedes the announcement of genre in the title. This is a familiar expression, one that implies for the present or until some other arrangement is made, which suggests that this is a transient tale: one that is still emerging and contingent on the emergence of another possibility. In summary, the title alone suggests a darker satirical reworking of the legendary witness given to the second coming.

This narrative is made up of 17 sentences and, because of the density of the poem, I will look closely at each sentence. The first sentence is sharp and perfunctory: a statement of fact indicating that the business is over. The next 15 sentences trawl over the housekeeping of Christmas day while the last sentences stretches over six and a half lines in an attempt to understand the Soul, Spirit, and God. The second sentence takes us into the time-honoured practice of packing away the tree: acknowledging, by pausing before and after the discovery, that every year there is breakage and erosion of the traditional signatures of Christmas. The third sentence takes us to another short fact: that life proceeds in its infinite ordinariness. The 4th sentence is a nod to the bacchanalia of Christmas with its excess of food and drink and attempts to love. The dry satirical estimation of our "Grossly overestimated" powers is a reminder of our hubris. Then, we are taken to the parodic truth in the 5th sentence of the "Vision" of the messiah being nothing more than "an agreeable possibility" who we send away. In this sentence, we are likened to a child who cannot keep a promise and thus we remain "disobedient servants". In the 6th sentence, the olfactory scents of the feast of Christmas are replaced with "an unpleasant whiff" of Lent and Good Friday. What interests me here is the cyclical nature of the Gregorian calendar that moves from the birth of Christ to his passion, suffering, final death, resurrection, and then back to his birth when December rolls around again, and so the story plays out endlessly. The never ending cycle of birth, death, and birth, the quintessence of the mystery of Christian mythology, must in some ways be recognizable in the perpetual cycle of victories and failures throughout the long haul of World War II. Always at the periphery of this poem is the accusation that giving witness to the messiah is temporary, transient, and unsustainable by the masses; always "a fading memory". Moreover, apprehension is more a reality for those who have survived the Battle of Britain and the London Blitz who were constantly living a Lenten penitence and an ever-present reminder of death.

The 7th sentence brings us to a philosophical musing on "the time being". We have turned our back on Christmas but as yet have not entered Easter; a threshold place. We are all in this place together. Our "Aristotelian city" achieves its highest state in the minutiae of household chores and public transport. Furthermore, "Our experience", for the time being, is reduced to a small set of intuitively appealing truths from which we deduce other propositions, "Euclid's geometry", as well as an understanding that forces will cause motion, ("Newton's mechanics"), is a disturbing and reductionist (but accurate) summary of our ordinary daily thinking behind our ordinary daily lives. We then move into Descartian proof of knowledge in "the kitchen table exists because I scrub it". This suggests that, for all the glory of these great minds, we have nothing but the trivia of our entrapped lives. I love the trope of the short 8th sentence indicating, in its brevity, that the table has seemingly "shrunk". In other words, the site of nourishment has been diminished. Indeed, by the 9th sentence, everything is lesser after the glory of Christmas: the "streets ... narrower" and the "office ... depressing".

It is as if in giving witness to the birth of Christ, our ordinary lives become insignificant. Auden goes on to argue in the 10th sentence that for those "who have seen / The Child" live on as if life is to be endured or suffered. As if on seeing the Child everything else is made more difficult. The metaphor that follows in the 11th sentence explains why we move from innocence to experience. After the locked door is opened, we can never return to the innocence of childhood: "the innocent children... Outside the locked door... Grew up when it opened." The 12th sentence digs into this axiom: that after "remembering the stable" the presence of Christ is intimate and the personal pronoun, "You" is used, not the impersonal and removed "It". This knowledge is a guilty burden as we "repress our joy". Then, in the 13th sentence, Auden speaks to the contemporary conundrum of searching for "some great suffering" to fill our purposeless lives. Auden indicates in the 14th sentence that we are ever "tempted" to pray to be lead into evil: a sure bet for a life of suffering and reflection. The irony is that one glimpse of the Son creates a crisis and leads us to beseech the Father. Indeed, there is a tone of absolute confidence in the 15th sentence, assuring us that we will know evil as it will come to us in a force that will be "More dreadful than we can imagine". Having seen what they had seen in the war, it is not unimaginable that Auden, emerging out of the zeitgeist, would speculate on the evil to end all evil; the atomic bomb was dropped some three and a half years later. This takes us to the penultimate or 16th sentence where we return to the mundanity of the everyday life of paying bills, repairing machines, learning irregular verbs, and ultimately attempting to redeem "the Time Being / From Insignificance." In other words, we have witnessed the birth of Christ with all its glory and hope and yet have chosen lives of quiet and insignificant desperation.

So we arrive at our final 17th sentence. Here we stand somewhere between the "happy morning" which is over and the "night of agony still to come". Auden situates us at high noon. We are reminded of the oratorio where the Spirit is practicing "scales of rejoicing" as if in anticipation of the glory that could be. Meanwhile the Soul, which is feminized, is left alone to anticipate "That God's Will be done". The noun and verb mirror of "will" sits at the center, reminding us that it is all beyond our manipulations. The message in the final line and a half is disturbing because Auden is telling us that this very "Will" "will" not be persuaded or cajoled despite the Soul's petitions. God will not placate the prayerful: "That, in spite of her prayers, / God will cheat no one, not even the world of its triumph." I think about the Germans and English all praying for triumph in 1939, 1940, and 1941: a request that is contingent upon the defeat of their enemy. Auden is telling his audience then and now that none of us will be tricked out of the world's "triumph", but rather we will get what we deserve in the final reckoning. In 53 lines, we are delivered an oratorio of disturbing significance and one that resonates with our own "time being", a phrase that crows three times throughout the body of the poem. This is what it is to have seen but not to have understood; this is what is to have had the experience but have missed the meaning; and this is what is augured when we turn our back on the promise of goodness and take up evil "for our sake". Auden's warning is dire; let us not fail to do something more than treat the vision as an agreeable calendar event.

The Historical Judas by Howard Nemerov (1980)

He too has an eternal part to play,
What did he understand? That good has scope
Only from evil, flowering in filth?
Did he go smiling, kissing, to betray
Out of a fine conviction to his truth,
Or some original wreckage of our hope?

If merely mistaken, at any rate,
He had a talent for the grand mistake,
The necessary one, without which not,
And managed to incur eternal hate
For triggering what destiny had got
Arranged from the beginning for our sake.

Let us consider, then, if not forgive
This most distinguished of our fellow sinners,
Who sponsored our redemption with his sin,
And whose name, more than ours, shall surely live
To make our meanness look like justice in
All histories commissioned by the winners.

I have always been disturbed by the depiction of Judas in literature and art. I thought it was just another excuse for anti-Semitism. The vilification of Judas makes me uneasy. What if he was a devout and holy Jew who needed to put an end to blasphemy and the obscene disregard for orthodoxy? What if he was unsure and miscalculated the effect of giving intelligence over to the ruling occupiers? Moreover, if he had been one of Jesus' disciples then surely, he was loved and trusted by the Lord and was included because of what he brought to this new world that he, along with the other disciples, were proselytizing. So, one mistake, one unholy mess, one moment of lapsed judgement, and he is the world's greatest villain. I mean, you've got to feel sorry for him because isn't he us? Don't we all miscalculate the extent to which our betrayals impact the destiny of others? And of course, legend narrates that Judas did it for silver: what a wonderful grab of teleology to explain away thousands and thousands of years of anti-Semitism. At the heartland of Christian belief is that Judas' act is necessary and instrumental in the messiah fulfilling the prophecy to be the risen Lord. Nemerov's poem is made up of three stanzas each containing a rhyme scheme of a, b, c, a, c, b then d, e, f, d, f, e and finally g, h, i, g, i, h. The first stanza poses the questions about the historical Judas, the second stanza considers a hypothetical about his act of betrayal, and the third and final stanza offers a reason for our need to vilify Judas.

In the first stanza, Nemerov considers four questions about the historical Judas Iscariot, an attempt to understand what motivated his brave act of resistance. The first question is broad: "What did he understand?" Nemerov is asking about the cognitive processes Judas underwent, which is necessary to understand this figure in the Christian legend. Of course, it is a whimsical question because there is no account by the assailant. If Jesus had proclaimed himself the messiah when riding into Jerusalem on the Sunday beforehand then I would think the rubber had definitely hit the road. Perhaps Judas was unable to stay with the charade. Maybe he decided to screw his courage to the sticking point and out this charlatan. Or this could just have been a case of second thoughts, (as if none of us had them)! Let us not forget the stakes are high; on the one hand, you have the hostilities of a Roman Empire occupying Judea, and on the other hand, you have the very orthodoxies of Judaism being eroded. I mean, it is a problem to a law-abiding Jew. Maybe the answer is simply that Judas didn't understand the effect of this betrayal.

The word *betrayal* comes from the Latin *tradere*, to hand over. So, to hand over Jesus to those already hunting him down has gone down in the annals of art and literature as perfidious to the extreme. Did Judas want the fulfilment of the prophecy and so enabled Jesus' death and resurrection? Now here's a philosophical dilemma: can good come from evil? So, are we to consider the importance of evil in the aetiology of good? Because without a doubt in the believers' minds, this act of betrayal led to the greatest good: eternal resurrection. Surely, we would have to concede therefore that this is a "flowering in filth". The subtle connection between the words with the alliterative fricative f reminds us that this was exactly what ensued. The third question Nemerov poses in stanza one is about motivation. Was the passing of intelligence by Judas to the Roman soldiers, who were enforcing law and guarding against possible threats to Roman rule, an act of bravery that emerged from his "fine conviction to his truth"? I would have thought that to go against the tide of radicalized freedom fighters requires extreme bravery. Or was Judas motivated by the fundamental human fault displayed in the Garden of Eden: hopelessness? At the end of the day, is it just too much of a leap of faith to believe in an all-powerful God who loves us individually and intimately? Let's pause and look back over the shoulder of the first stanza and see the words that are linked quietly almost subconsciously by their end rhyme: "play ... betray"; "scope ... hope"; "filth ... truth." Stanza one explores the *play* of the dice in the game of *betrayal*; the *scope* of *hope* can be illusory; and the *truth* of Jesus as messiah is a belief contingent on the *filth* of betrayal.

If we move to the second stanza, we see that it is interested in the hypothetical of Judas' betrayal. This stanza is one complete unit of thought in a six-line sentence. The poet compares the "merely mistaken" to the "grand mistake". To refer to an act of betrayal as a "mistake" reduces it from high crime and treachery, to a blunder. To move from mere to "grand" speaks volumes about Christian history needing that hair trigger to launch into the complex fulfilment of prophecy. In other words, this "grand mistake" was "The necessary one". So, Judas did what was necessary. He alone had the courage to see through what had to be done. What if Judas was the only true believer: the first really committed follower of Christ? What if Judas knew that if he didn't move on this no one else would and then nothing would have been achieved or fulfilled? The phrase "without which not" is a nod to the Latin term *sine qua non*; meaning an indispensable and essential action, condition or ingredient. In other words, without Judas the fulfillment of the prophecy could not happen. There were many other disciples, men and women; there had been crowds of people who had followed Jesus, listening to his words and witnessing his acts; and there had been whole mobs calling out for his recognition as their savior from the occupying foreign force and a somewhat vengeful representation of God. One of their own promising them another way, a liberation from oppression on every level. Yet did they really believe?

Maybe only Judas did and only he had the fearlessness to set the ball rolling. For this singular act of love, he "managed to incur eternal hate". So, this truth gives me pause. Throughout history, we have seen the way marginalized people have been the subject of hate, violence, and unmitigated exclusion, and the Jews are part of that polemic. In some ways, the narrative around Judas, the various depictions of him in art, indicate certain pejorative signatures of the Jew, such as the willingness to betray one of his own, selling loyalty for money, and the lack of conscience with which this was done. Ironically Judas' act ensured that "destiny...Arranged from the beginning" was begotten. Indeed, Nemerov reminds us that Judas did this "for our sake": a chilling prompt for us to reflect on why we vilify him. Shall we look back over our shoulder again this time at the second stanza's end rhyme: "rate ... hate"; "mistake ... sake"; "not ... got." Here we pause to reflect on why we *rate* our *hate* for Judas; this act should be remembered as no *mistake* but something done for our *sake*; and would *not* have *got* what we have in the promise of life everlasting.

The third stanza examines why we need to vilify Judas. By the time we get to the third stanza, we have been forced to ponder the significance of Judas' act and contemplate some of the possible motivations. In this final stanza, we are called to "consider" and "forgive" Judas. It is not until we look into the mirror of our horror and hatred that we recognize this villain. Our proximity to Judas is tantalizingly close, as Nemerov affectionately refers to him as "our fellow sinner". Unlike us, Judas stepped up and "sponsored our redemption", thus his name lives on far "more than ours". In the final two lines, we consider the outcome of being on the side that writes history and the way in which we construct it for our own ends. Judas has always been a type of scapegoat throughout the past two thousand years. Why? What are we so guilty of? What is it that we don't want to see? I wonder whether we actually resent the sponsoring of our redemption. Or do we resent that idea that someone as insignificant as Judas put the wheels in motion for the fulfilment of prophecy.

Judas' name and infamy remain live in order to "make our meanness look like justice in / All histories commissioned by the winners". If our salvation has been secured by Judas' acknowledgment of Jesus as the messiah in the fulfilment of the prophecies, then there is a discrepancy between his actions and his eternal punishment. We need so desperately to shape up the New Testament to fit the prophecies of the Old, including the exact notorious sum of 30 pieces of silver, as prophesized by Zechariah 11:12-13. So, I turn away from the problematic ideological contradictions of the Bible and Christian teachings and focus on the poem. It is in our interests to commission a story that valorizes Jesus and vilifies Judas. Thus, our meanness is justifiable. Our treachery and ongoing marginalization of those who cannot be trusted and those who would sell out their own is validated. A final glance over our shoulder at the third stanza's end rhyme "forgive ... live"; "sinners ... winners"; and "sin ... in." We are left with a bitter taste of these subtly conjoined words. To *forgive* Judas is to resist the ongoing lie and live in the *truth*. Furthermore, the reality is that the *winners* of this history are *sinners*, and this should not be forgotten: whoever is without sin should cast the first stone; and finally, the *sin* for which Judas is remembered allows us to retain a sense self-righteousness *in* the condemnation of certain people.

Last Supper by Charles Wright (2006)

I seem to have come to the end of something, but don't know what,
Full moon blood orange just over the top of the redbud tree.
Maundy Thursday tomorrow,
then Good Friday, then Easter in full drag,
Dogwood blossoms like little crosses
All down the street,
lilies and jonquils bowing their mitred heads.

Perhaps it's a sentimentality about such fey things,
But I don't think so. One knows
There is no end to the other world,
no matter where it is.
In the event, a reliquary evening for sure,
The bones in their tiny boxes, rosettes under glass.

Or maybe it's just the way the snow fell
a couple of days ago,
So white on the white snowdrops.
As our fathers were bold to tell us,
it's either eat or be eaten.
Spring in its starched bib,
Winter's cutlery in its hands. Cold grace. Slice and fork.

    What I love so much about this quiet poem is the proximity of seasons to the uber moment of Christianity. Wright establishes a tension between the present moment and the Christ narrative some 2000 years ago. It is a free verse poem made up of eight sentences of varying lengths shaped into a trinitrine structure of three stanzas: the first contains seven lines, the next six, and the last seven, altogether making a 20-line poem. The title of the poem refers to the final meal shared between Christ and his disciples on the eve of his betrayal by Judas Iscariot to the Roman occupying force of Judea. It is at this moment in the Jesus narrative that the bread and wine undergoes transubstantiation to become the body and blood of Christ: the prototype celebration of the Eucharist. Needless to say, this event in the story before the arrest and torture and final death of Jesus has been continually represented in the arts throughout the past 2000 years. Wright, who calls himself a God-fearing agnostic, is contributing to this suite of creativity. It is no surprise to me that Wright, a contemporary American poet, is interested in the transcendent of the everyday as well as the fusion witnessed between the spiritual and natural world.
    This takes us to a closer look at stanza one where we are disorientated and unsure of our setting.

In many ways, this site of the last supper so bestowed with iconic value reads like a contemporary setting in verdant America: or perhaps it could be the Roman occupied Judea at the end of the Roman Empire. Like the poet himself who commences with the subjunctive mood, "I seem", we are orientated to what is imagined. The opening line continues hesitantly, unsure of what is actually being witnessed: coming "to the end of something, but I don't know what". I find the tentative first steps into this poem strangely reassuring. The opening line is about an awareness of ending and yet the rest of that stanza holds signatures of beginnings: "red bud trees … Dogwood blossoms … lilies and jonquils." This cacophony of spring heralds new life under the "Full moon blood orange". This is not only the visual imagery of a spring evening but symbolic of the risen Lord. The flowers and trees become code for Easter. It is as if the poet finds himself in disarray as he is hurled unprepared into the risen new life: "I seem to have come to the end of something, but I don't know what."

Both the season of spring and the Easter moon announce the passion, death and resurrection of Christ: "Maundy Thursday tomorrow / And Good Friday, then Easter in full drag." The first two calendar events are articulated traditionally. From the Latin *mandatum*, meaning mandated, we arrive at Maundy Thursday which reminds us of the rites and rituals that command our remembrances, such as the washing of feet and the last supper. Good Friday, observed as a holy day, is the moment of arrest, trial, and torture of Christ. It is then that we unexpectedly bump into "Easter in full drag". We could interpret this as 19th century theatre slang: that Easter's skirts are full and drag upon the stage of life. Indeed, Easter is regaled in the northern hemisphere in all its seasonal fecundity. This could well be reflective of the resurrected Christ clothed in newfound light. The season of spring imitates the sacred birth of new life: "blossoms like little crosses … bowing their mitred heads." The simile and anthropomorphism reiterate the belief in life after death. So, by the end of the first stanza we are left stumbling upon the season of new life, Easter but despite it occurring each and every year, we are unprepared.

The first and second stanzas are linked by enjambment that continues the fusing of Easter and spring across seven lines of a 20-line poem. The second stanza stays with that tentative, hesitant mood in its opening word "Perhaps", suggesting the uncertainty of the poet's convictions while being open to possibilities. The poet reflects on the "sentimentality about such fey things": a nostalgic pondering on the vague otherworldliness of Easter in the season of spring. At this point, there is a turn in the poem as the poet asserts that indeed it is not "sentimentality" that drives this consideration of the metaphysical world. Therefore, from "seems" to "perhaps" to "think" we are now placed firmly in the absolute knowledge that "There is no end to the other world / no matter where it is". This could simultaneously refer to the cycle of the seasons, which will come and go perpetually, and the cycle of Easter, with the arrival of the last supper. It is as if the physical world of the seasons and the metaphysical world of Easter perform the same alchemy of life death and resurrection. The last supper becomes "a reliquary evening", a type of container of holy relics. The items of the last supper, the bread and wine, are items venerated in the act of transubstantiation. The fascination with relics extends back to the anthropophagus who would consume *the other* in order to take its power. If consumption is not possible, then the relics of bones or skulls are worshipped for their sacred power. The act of the last supper is all about the consumption of the Christ so that those left behind can absorb some of the power promised by the messiah: a strange and somewhat alienating belief in the 21st century to those who are not believers.

The third stanza sweeps us back into that mood of hesitancy and uncertainty, with the phrase, "Or maybe". We consider snow on "white snowdrops" just a few days prior to the blossoming of spring. The proximity of death, represented in the wintery snow, to life conveyed in the snowdrops of early spring, is not just a reminder of the Christian axiom of resurrection but is nature's revivification and restoration of life after death. Wright's argument is that, faced with nature, we cannot doubt the power of resurrection. He refers to some lessons that have been passed down to us about survival and empowerment: "it's either eat or be eaten." Hence, consuming Christ's body and blood, as well as observing spring as an Easter act, is to witness life devouring death. Indeed, forebears are "bold to tell us" that to eat is the only way in which we can survive; ipso facto, to live eternally we must partake in the last supper. The last three sentences are delightful. A trinitrine moment of acknowledging what it is one is about to digest. The antepenultimate sentence anthropomorphizes spring with a clean white bib holding "Winter's cutlery", in all its bone and blade, ready to eat everlasting life. The penultimate sentence is a fragment, "Cold grace", suggestive of the cool benediction of early spring. The ultimate sentence, another fragment, contains two words of action: "Slice and fork." The poem itself deals with two actions: Easter and spring. The connection between these two verbs is consumption. Therefore, Easter is a consumption of mortal death in its promise of eternal resurrection just as spring is the consumption of wintery death followed by its perpetual capacity to offer new seasonal life. The final three sentences are an invitation to sup at last, regardless of our hesitancy, at the table of our Lord.

To Be or Not to Be by William Shakespeare (1602)

To be, or not to be: that is the question:
Whether 'tis nobler in the mind to suffer
The slings and arrows of outrageous fortune,
Or to take arms against a sea of troubles,
And by opposing end them? (1) To die: to sleep;
No more; and by a sleep to say we end
The heart-ache and the thousand natural shocks
That flesh is heir to. (2) 'Tis a consummation
Devoutly to be wish'd. (3) To die, to sleep;
To sleep: perchance to dream: ay, there's the rub;
For in that sleep of death what dreams may come
When we have shuffled off this mortal coil. (4)
Must give us pause: there's the respect
That makes calamity of so long life. (5)
For who would bear the whips and scorns of time,
The oppressor's wrong, the proud man's contumely,
The pangs of despised love, the law's delay,

The insolence of office and the spurns
That patient merit of the unworthy takes,
When he himself might his quietus make
With a bare bodkin? (6) Who would fardels bear,
To grunt and sweat under a weary life,
But that the dread of something after death,
The undiscover'd country from whose bourn
No traveler returns, puzzles the will
And makes us rather bear those ills we have
Than fly to others that we know not of? (7)
Thus conscience does make cowards of us all;
And thus the native hue of resolution
Is sicklied o'er with the pale cast of thought,
And enterprises of great pith and moment
With this regard their currents turn awry,
And lose the name of action. (8)

    This wonderful, pitch perfect iambic pentameter poem is more about raging against the sufferings and injustices life throws you than it is about giving up to suicidal ideation. This is about the question "who shall I be"? Will I be a person who lives with courage and takes action or a person who lives a coward's 1000 deaths of inaction? This soliloquy is about identity. The verb *to be* is concerned with self-actualization. This is not the self-talk of an indulged philosophical prodigy. Rather, this is about the pep talk one gives oneself before riding into battle. It is the voice of any one of us who, despite facing a world of nay-sayers, knows they must say yes! This 33-line poem is made up of, for ease of our discussion, eight sentences.

    The first sentence runs for four and half lines. To be me or not to be me: to exist as I am or to not exist as I am is the existential question of *Hamlet*. This question he poses, after contemplating the facts of his untenable situation, remains a question for us today, and this is the greatness of Shakespeare. Hamlet ponders on what it is that constitutes nobility of spirit in a man: "to suffer ... Or to take arms ...?" In other words, does one live the highest moral principle by enduring or by going into battle? On some level, it is a bit New Testament versus Old. On another level, it is a consideration for a just war. Let's think about the back story of *Hamlet* for a moment; there is regicide, a court in a state of Bacchus revival and a potential invasion from Norway all of which make for the decimation of the Danish kingdom. These are serious times. Unlike Laertes and Fortinbras, Hamlet draws on his training from Wittgenstein, where to ask the right question is more vital than to arrive at the answer. This opening sentence is layered with rich metaphors: "slings and arrows of outrageous fortune ... arms against a sea of troubles." We are in no two minds about the outcome of the battle: the weapons are no match for the unfixed amorphous enemy. It is a David and Goliath moment where hand weaponry against the largess of the monstrous seems meaningless.

    The second sentence explores the solace and fiat that death will bring. Shakespeare pairs the literary notions of death and sleep, "To die, to sleep", to allow him the poetic pathway to explore the afterlife. Thus, it is this sleep of death that grants respite in the afterlife: "No more...heartache, and the thousand natural shocks / That flesh is heir to." Thus, death is the salve on the wound of life. Christian mythology indicates that we inherit suffering as a result of Original Sin, thus we remain in the wilderness cut off from Eden until we are restored to eternal life. Those sorts of understandings would be imbued in the audience of the time.

The third sentence is short and direct in its edict; this "consummation", this completion or end to the suffering is "Devoutly … wished", as if our whole selves are dedicated devotedly to bring about the end of suffering. Yet it is in the 4th sentence that this thesis of longing to end hardship, which can only be granted by death, hits its straps. The epistrophe of the 2nd and 4th sentences makes a haunting echo in the first half of the poem. Now he considers the aftermath of "To die, to sleep" not so much in terms of ending suffering but rather as an exploration of the afterlife's dream world. The afterlife is problematic because it can only be imagined: "ay, there's the rub." This personal exclamation of assent, archaic in dialect, reminds us that this is an intimate glimpse into the machinations of an individual thrown into absolute discombobulation. The "sleep of death…Must give us pause" because we cannot know what these imaginings may be, and there would be no return. There is something touching in the way Hamlet is everyman who must at some point "shuffle off this mortal coil".

The 5th sentence acts as a type of volta to his reverie. We allow a long life to remain calamitous because the alternative, courage to go into battle, may alarmingly bring about death and its unknown aftermath. Respecting the unknown is something quite different to fearing. The etymology comes from the Latin, *respicere* meaning to look back at and consider. Thus, to consider the site of the unknown, the place from which we emerge and to which we return, is seminal. The 6th sentence poses a powerful question about bearing the list of insufferable injustices: "whips and scorns of time"; "Th' oppressor's wrong"; "the proud man's" insults; "the pangs" of unrequited love; "the law's delay"; "The insolence of office"; and the unworthy person's rejection of your patient goodness. Seven modes of suffering are named, representing a completion of what it is to be vulnerably human. To all of this, Hamlet suggests that the answer is not "his quietus make / With a bare bodkin". Put another way, the unsheathed dagger can offer calm to the unquiet mind because it looks like the readiness of battle without ever having intention of following through. Hamlet is not musing about ending one's life but rather having courage to go into battle against the injustices that plague one's life and are intolerable.

The 7th sentence takes us further into the gyre of what it is to have courage. Hamlet's rhetoric has caught fire, and he asks us who would bear such a burden? Shakespeare offers us graphic aural and visual imagery of the burden of injustice: "To grunt and sweat under a weary life", as if we are nothing more than beasts who endure because we lack the courage to confront the enemy. Again, he argues that we do nothing because of what comes after death; respect now has turned to "dread", a fear of the "undiscovered country, from whose bourn / No traveler returns". This metaphor takes us into the unimaginable place of the afterlife. That it is an "undiscovered country" speaks to the context of Shakespeare's day: the great age of discovery. The navigation into unchartered waters may lead to a place whose boundaries may never release us. Indeed, what the aftermath of death contains "puzzles the will": a phrase suggesting a rational uncovering of what stops us from being all we could be. This conundrum to "bear those ills we have" or "fly to others that we know not of" is at the heart of all decisions where the outcome is unknown. This is about taking the risk to be or remaining not as me.

The final and 8th sentence sums up why the guide within ourselves lies dormant. This a powerful anthropomorphism of thought or resolution not being the vivid color it should be but pale with a sickness of unease because of what is imagined at death's sleep: "thus the native hue of resolution / Is sicklied o'er with the pale cast of thought." So the great undertaking of going into battle despite knowing death is imminent is an "enterprise of great pitch and moment" and one that is ultimately rejected. Hence, the pull and current of resolution "turns awry", from its expected course and loses "the name of action". The final phrase is a sad indictment of all we are not or all we fail to be in our attempts to self-actualize. The Elizabethan audience knew regicide could not go unchecked and a kingdom rank and gross in nature must not remain unweeded. Stability in family, whether played out on a royal chessboard or in our own domestic lives, is contingent on fighting for the right *to be*.

Death Be Not Proud by John Donne (1609)

Death, be not proud, though some have called thee
Mighty and dreadful, for thou art not so;
For those whom thou think'st thou dost overthrow
Die not, poor Death, nor yet canst thou kill me.
From rest and sleep, which but thy pictures be,
Much pleasure; then from thee much more must flow,
And soonest our best men with thee do go,
Rest of their bones, and soul's delivery.
Thou art slave to fate, chance, kings, and desperate men,
And dost with poison, war, and sickness dwell,
And poppy or charms can make us sleep as well
And better than thy stroke; why swell'st thou then?
One short sleep past, we wake eternally
And death shall be no more; Death, thou shalt die.

This wondrous mandala invites meditation. I find its confident voice both reassuring and anxiety generating. The thesis is so determinedly argued that I am nearly but not quite, convinced that death is laughable, ridiculous even. The truth is, as Donne suggests, there is nothing prideful in death. Can one have a proud death? I have been told one can have a good death: surrounded by loved ones, calmly assured of the journey one is about to undertake and all pain gone. Maybe there is such a notion of death being a proud moment for someone: proud that they had the courage to give their life for another or profoundly convinced that they are in possession of a quality that makes their ending valuable. Do we live lives fascinated by death or never thinking of it or very aware it is there but attempting to turn our backs on it? Do people in Renaissance England have more or less fear about death than people of contemporary times? I mean, with all the plagues and wars and everyday possibilities of disaster, reflected in high mortality rates, were people immune to the horror of death or more sensitised to it? Is death a horror?

Maybe that's it ... maybe Donne's desperate bid to out-wit death offers no assurance to those who fear death whatsoever. Perhaps we can all see through this thin veneer of clever playful argument and know that this is a circular argument that really says: you need to think about death! Donne uses the Anglo-Italian sonnet scheme, abba abba cddcee, which in effect offers three quatrains and then a final click of the lock, in the final rhyming couplet. Donne posits a thesis, an antithesis, and then a synthesis. The volta or twist to the story of death occurs between lines 12 and 13 when we are reassured that death will die while we live on. A cop out? I'm not sure. We are certainly focused more on the realities of death throughout this poem, indeed 12 lines worth, rather than the convincing realities of a life resurrected.

To emphasize his subject matter and preoccupation, Donne begins his sonnet by inverting the first iamb. This rhythm catches us out of beat in the first line and makes us feel like we are already running behind: "Death be not proud." The strong stress is unusually placed on "Death" rather than commencing with a weaker stress. This argument is racing ahead with its thesis in the first quatrain. Indeed, by the time we get to the end of the second line, there's a patronizing tone that has emerged to reassure death that it is not the terrible names that "some have called thee". Surely this is the voice of a parent telling its heart broken child that they are not the mean names yelled at him in the schoolyard. So, the apostrophe, or direct and explicit address to Death, in what commenced as high formality has shifted to an informal comforting of Death. We are made aware from the onset that this sonnet is engaged with an array of questions: what is death? What is the nature of death? How should we respond to death? What does death mean to our lives and to the lives of others? Lines three and four take us into the muscularity of Death's thinking: "thou think'st thou dost overthrow." Donne's thesis is of course that life cannot be overthrown by Death. In fact, his sympathies are with "poor Death" who will not be able to end the poet's life because as all poets of great pride know, their mortality is established for all eternity in their poetry.

So, we move to the antithesis of the argument. Here, Death *does* overthrow life, but this is longed for: indeed, death is familiar and pleasurable. He argues that we already know what death looks like. It is not something unknown at all but "pictures" of "rest and sleep". Indeed, for all of us this is the site of "Much pleasure". Ultimately Death will grant "our best men" a passage to respite and "soul's delivery". What interests me here is the agency ascribed to Death. In some ways, Death is a conduit between life and the delivery of one's soul. The verb chosen to describe Death's primary function and action here is "flow". Therefore, Death's function is to move life steadily and continuously in a stream across to another site. Without Death, there can be no passage beyond the physical. Death's pride of place, in the world of metaphysical poetry, is to offer transfer from our elemental selves to our metaphysical self. Curiously, rather than arguing Death's lack of importance in this second quatrain, Donne argues Death's enormous significance.

The final quatrain offers the synthesis of the established thesis: Life cannot be overthrown by Death, and the antithesis is that Death does overthrow Life, but this is pleasurable and serves a greater purpose. These next four lines pull together the argument to suggest that Life uses Death.

Death is not masterful but rather enslaved to whims and follies of humanity. Its usual habitat is the insalubrious and unenviable places of "poison, war, and sickness". We have moved from an initial sympathetic tone in the first quatrain of the sonnet to a chiding tone by the third, but all the while Death is addressed as if it were a child. Donne's purpose here is to *instruct* Death and *delight* us, fulfilling the aim of the poet, according to the Roman poet, Horace. Death has been soothed against profanities and curses; it has been assured its value because it delivers the soul, and finally Death is now to be reproved for its smug self-satisfaction. The rhetoric is heightened, suspending clarity of argument, when Donne asserts that "poppy or charms" are better than the "stroke" of Death. At the end of this quatrain we are given four words: "why swell'st thou then?" This is posed in response to the four-word phrase that commences the sonnet. In other words, why swell with pride when Death has no reason to be proud?

The volta arrives as a psychological inevitability because it is human nature to crave disruption and variation. The twist is that the only death to finally occur will be the death of Death. Now this neat little volta is assisted by internal rhyme in its use of sibilance "sleep past", alliteration "we wake", and the repetition of plosives and sibilance "death shall…death…shalt". Rhyme knits together the value and meaning of those words it couples. So, sleep will pass, we will wake, and death shall be that which we assert it will be. The Shakespearian device of the rhyming couplet is employed at the end of this sonnet. The Nobel Laureate Joseph Brodsky reminds us that this device locks in the truth. A Jacobean ear might have heard the same rhyme in "…ly" and "die". Regardless, a contemporary ear hears this as a near rhyming couplet. In coupling the notion of eternality and dying together, we are confronted with the notion that our metaphysical selves die to eternal wakefulness. If the auditory coupling these days sits less comfortably, perhaps it also reflects our own discomfort with the idea that death offers eternal life. By the time we get to our rhyming couplet, we have considered "sleep" thrice. Like a spell, it has woven itself about the sonnet so much so that we are enthralled by the notion that Death is but a "short sleep" and nothing more.

Finally, from the Latin *prodesse*, meaning to be of value, to the old French *prud*, meaning to be valiant, we come to an understanding of what it is to be proud: to be of value while being valiant. This little symmetrical room of a poem offers an emblem of unity in its meaning and argumentative rigor. Donne's sonnet, in some ways, reflects the original sonnet form, which was a Sicilian love song. This is a parent's love song to its child, Death: soothing Death, assuring Death of its value, chiding Death, and then reminding Death that we are all promised something more beyond the confines of existence. *Death Be Not Proud* is not an elegy to death but a love song to its flawed but wondrous passage to eternal life.

God's Grandeur by Gerard Manley Hopkins (1877)

The world is charged with the grandeur of God.
It will flame out, like shining from shook foil;
It gathers to a greatness, like the ooze of oil
Crushed. Why do men then now not reck his rod?
Generations have trod, have trod, have trod;

And all is seared with trade; bleared, smeared with toil;
And wears man's smudge and shares man's smell: the soil
Is bare now, nor can foot feel, being shod.

And for all this, nature is never spent;
There lives the dearest freshness deep down things;
And though the last lights off the black West went
Oh, morning, at the brown brink eastward, springs —
Because the Holy Ghost over the bent
World broods with warm breast and with ah! bright wings.

The first time I read this poem was in my last year of high school. I am immediately taken back to the boarding school's senior cold and dingy common; I am folded in on myself in one of the unmatched arm chairs reading poetry. I even know the cover of the book from which this poem emerged. Did I understand it back then? Did I understand this cavorting sonnet with its gleeful interplay between tenses? First line present tense, second line future tense, 5th line past tense, and then back to present tense. This intensely hewn sonnet with its action packed promise of where we are and where we can be is profoundly affecting. Indeed, out of the mire of what we have made of nature indicated in the octet, comes the assertion in the sestet, that the sublime, the conflation of nature and the transcendent, will offer succor. This is the alpha and omega of all sonnets in that we begin with the absolute assertion of God's grandeur and end with the Holy Spirit's bright wings. I love the use of enjambment with its energetic feet propelling me further and further into the mystery of this sonnet. But most of all I love the exhalation: "ah!" It is so personal, so intimate, as if it has all just been for this one luminous epiphany of flight. I'm getting ahead of myself, but it is so hard to step slowly through this shock of a sonnet.

The way I see it is that the sonnet is a promise to us: that despite our muddy footprints, our denial of God, and our inability to recognize this place as precious, we will be eternally loved by God. Let's look at the structure of the sonnet: the first octet is made up of three sentences and uses the rhyme scheme of a, b, b, a, a, b, b, a. Indeed, the octet oscillates between the pure vowel sounds of God/rod/shod/trod, constituted by one movement in the mouth and the diphthong of foil/oil/toil/soil, formed by two short vowels run together. Similarly when we head on to the sestet, made up of only one sentence and a rhyme scheme of c, d ,c ,d ,c ,d we are aware of the vowel sounds shifting slightly to play between pure vowel sounds within things/springs/wings and the shift to the pure vowel sounds of spent/went/bent. So all in all, a five sentenced sonnet with its volta classically between the octet and the sestet, in true Elizabethan style. So why this form for Hopkins? It is one of the hardest of all poetic forms to write. It is also the form that takes one idea and rolls it about in your mouth, your ears, and your thoughts. It's a puzzle with a lock. And you know when the key fits this lock when you hear the click of the volta. The volta allows us to see the subject from another perspective or angle which in turn makes the purpose of the sonnet clearer. Here, the subject is of course, God's grandeur. Which connotes patriarchal power and yet the final line is distinctly maternal. Let's look closely at how meaning is shaped.

The exquisite opening sentence at the start of the sonnet tells us, in no uncertain terms, that the world is already suffused and saturated with the resplendent glory. As if our world, like *Frankenstein* only written some 25 years earlier, takes its life force from the electrical currents of God's greatness. From the onset, we are made aware of the excitement and emotion of this tension between us and God. From this moment of being utterly present to the sublime, Hopkins asserts the future in the second sentence, stating that God's grandeur will ignite the world. Hopkins' first simile is both a visual and auditory one of "shining ... shook foil", indicating that God's flame will sound like the shaking of metal leaf imitated in its sibilance. In the second simile, as the alliterative God's grandeur "gathers to a greatness", we are taken to the enjambment of "ooze of oil/ Crushed". Why this? It is an olfactory moment comparing this gathering greatness to the crushed oil of olives releasing their perfume and goodness: oil as both edible and ritualised balm. The third sentence is in fact a sharp question with an ambiguous center: if God's grandeur is so immense and so immanent, then why humanity's reckless abandonment of the scared? The final sentence of the octave is an etching of industrial London; it is a triple utterance of generations who have trod the industrial landscape. It references the workers scorched by trade and the way this purgatorial landscape has left its imprint upon them; moreover, these workers are made dim by the filth of their labor. Thus, man is clothed in the smell and smudge of his rags; he is part of the mechanised world with its implosive dim cloisters. Furthermore, man cannot even be redeemed by plunging his feet into the rich soil because he, like a beast of burden, is shod. So from the dizzy heights of the sonnet's first two sentences, where God's wonder is assured and its extant is imaginable, I am then plunged into the bleak abyss of the last two sentences, where a highly mechanised and labor-intensive world removes me from the sensuous connection with God's grandeur.

The sestet abruptly ends my despair. Nature can never be disempowered. Not only can nature never be used up, but it is there, living within the freshness of things. Hopkins digs in with this truth in the alliterative "dearest ... deep" and "down", suggesting his intimate and emotional relationship with the wonder of nature's freshness. The next two lines offer a painterly moment of the sun falling in the west at the end of the day, to only rise in the east the following morning: the eternal symbol of resurrection of life proceeding death. I'm still inside the frame of an industrial world where lights are turned off, and the world is blackened by soot as much as by nightfall. I love the exclamation in the next line of "Oh" as if the shock of dawn as the sun "springs" up is a miracle in itself. That image of earth as a "brown brink eastwood" reduces our world, compared to the wonder of Nature which cannot be confined to our immediate planet. Why is there dawn? Why resurrection from death of yesterday, in all its unfettered grime and disbelief, to the life of today? We are not to be treated to some scientific paint by numbers explanation. This, after all, is a poem about the grandeur of God. Hopkins explains that dawn is the Holy Ghost, one of the three persons of God, bending over the world and giving suck. It dawns upon us that God's grand gesture to love us is at the warm breast of nature; in other words, nature is the spirit of God. This unexpected image of a mother bent over and covering her infant, thinking deeply about her beloved child, is the very way the Holy Ghost nurtures us. It is moment of enlightenment. So, God's grandeur is made known to us in the maternal nourishment of not only Mother Earth or nature but in God's love. Note how this is not a simile but a metaphor. This mother is both deeply familial and fantastically celestial.

We go from the mother offering a warm breast to her babe, to a shining winged creature. The exhalation, "ah!" is the moment of epiphany when we leap from one moment of vision to the next.

The Donkey by G. K. Chesterton (1927)

When fishes flew and forests walked
And figs grew upon thorn,
Some moment when the moon was blood
Then surely I was born.

With monstrous head and sickening cry
And ears like errant wings,
The devil's walking parody
On all four-footed things.

The tattered outlaw of the earth,
Of ancient crooked will;
Starve, scourge, deride me: I am dumb,
I keep my secret still.

Fools! For I also had my hour;
One far fierce hour and sweet:
There was a shout about my ears,
And palms before my feet.

In 520 B.C., the prophet Zechariah said that the future king of the Jews would ride into Jerusalem on a humble donkey and announce himself as the messiah. In 70 A.D., Luke writes in his Gospel, 19:35, that this prophecy in the Old Testament, Zechariah 9:9, has been fulfilled in Jesus. With this as biblical context, Chesterton turns this fulfilment of prophecy inside out in a way only the prince of paradox can. We have before us a somewhat dainty four quatrain ode to the donkey: a song in praise of the donkey within the Jesus narrative.

The first quatrain takes us into the Phanerozoic Eon, a mere half a billion years back to the evolution of life on earth. A time of pre-determined patterning where the fricative "fishes flew ...forests...And figs" connect the contemporary world to that of time immemorial. The donkey's voice is central from the first quatrain and successfully captures the pre-destiny of its suffering in the rhyme or "thorn" and "born". The donkey is the doppelganger to Jesus in that it too is reborn at the Easter moon: "when the moon was blood." In the Christian calendar, Easter heralds the resurrection of Jesus as the Christ. The donkey is never usually a source of interest in the Jesus narrative, but here, Chesterton places it absolutely central. The donkey disturbs our sense of superiority over animals, and it predicates problems for us in placing a beast of burden as the mirror reflection of the messiah. Furthermore, this is a dramatic monologue written from the perspective of the donkey: the most abject and subaltern of animals.

The second quatrain offers us a description of the donkey: its head, cry, ears and walk parody the aesthetic of the horse. Moreover, the descriptors "monstrous", "sickening", and "errant" all suggest a type of deformity or devilish curse associated with the donkey. This deliberate exaggeration for comic effect is not in the hands of the poet but in the hands of the maker. I am interested here to return to the notion of the doppelgänger. This notion of the shadow self comes to us from a dialogue between the self and its double, a manifestation of unconscious desire. If the donkey is Christ's shadow self then it could be read as an articulation of the hitherto unseen and unsaid. The donkey's perspective therefore, outlines what has been silenced by the rational in the cultural order. This is referred to later in quatrain three as the "secret" kept by the donkey. Orthodoxy speaks to the three-personed God: The Father, Son, and Holy Spirit. The doppelgänger throws out the unified character of Jesus, dependent on ideological assumptions, psychological coherence, and the value of sublimation. It is another way of considering the mystery of Jesus as the messiah, in that in his absence is his presence is.

In quatrain three, the donkey continues to recount its external landscape as well as how it is perceived by itself and others. That it is an animal outside the law, unwilling to be commanded and controlled by authority, and covered in the poorest of the poor's attire. The donkey reflects the Christ of Liberation Theology, remaining focused on the vulnerable, broken, and wounded: he who walks amongst the forsaken. The donkey is notorious for its stubborn disposition and one that displays an "ancient crooked will", a pre-established drive that deviates from the resolve of the usual law givers. The three verbs that follow are in some ways a metonym for the Stations of the Cross: "starve, scourge, deride me." This is an allusion to the torture and torment Christ endured prior to and during his crucifixion: an episode of captivity, deprivation, whipping, and mockery. In other words, the donkey has known Christ's suffering yet, despite this, the donkey is steadfast and true. The double entendre of "I am dumb", without speech and without intellect, allows it to "keep my secret still". The sibilance works as a type of hush around the hitherto undisclosed truth that the donkey carries throughout time. So, what is the donkey's truth and secret? That it has known complete and absolute love in being the poorest of the poor? That is has borne the burden of humanity's greatest crime? That it has always known the Easter resurrection despite its abject state?

The final quatrain reiterates the powerful voice of the donkey. Again, this reminds us that Christ liberates the subaltern, who now can speak. In the opening exclamation, "Fools!" we are positioned as the ignorant ones, dumb and errant parodies of all we should be. The donkey speaks about "my hour / One far fierce hour", as its moment of epiphany. The repletion of hour reminds us that this is a moment repeated over and over in mind while the alliteration of the adjectives never let us forget the intensity and ferocity of this memory. Chesterton then knits "sweet" with "feet" in the final rhyme emphasising the significance of the experiential memory as sensory and vivid. The "shout about my ears / And palms before my feet" reflect the actions of mass hysteria and adoration of the newly proclaimed messiah who enters Jerusalem. The laying of palms is a symbol of victory, peace, and eternal life. The Palm Sunday narrative can never be fully celebrated as a wondrous fulfilment of prophecy because of its dark underbelly, the crucifixion which followed just a few days later.

While there may have been shouts of joy and recognition in the laying of palms, this unruly mob participated in Christ's torture and brutal death. Without the recognition of Jesus as messiah, the prophecy cannot be fulfilled; moreover, without crucifixion there can be no resurrection. In some ways, we are left by the donkey in the eternal moment of prophetic exclamation and kingly adoration. We are eternally within the Easter moment. The lowly are exalted, the voiceless are the truth bearers, and the most humble are made in his image.

Journey of the Magi by T. S. Eliot (1927)

'A cold coming we had of it,
Just the worst time of the year
For a journey, and such a long journey:
The ways deep and the weather sharp,
The very dead of winter.'
And the camels galled, sorefooted, refractory,
Lying down in the melting snow.
There were times we regretted
The summer palaces on slopes, the terraces,
And the silken girls bringing sherbet.
Then the camel men cursing and grumbling
and running away, and wanting their liquor and women,
And the night-fires going out, and the lack of shelters,
And the cities hostile and the towns unfriendly
And the villages dirty and charging high prices:
A hard time we had of it.
At the end we preferred to travel all night,
Sleeping in snatches,
With the voices singing in our ears, saying
That this was all folly.

Then at dawn we came down to a temperate valley,
Wet, below the snow line, smelling of vegetation;
With a running stream and a water-mill beating the darkness,
And three trees on the low sky,
And an old white horse galloped away in the meadow.
Then we came to a tavern with vine-leaves over the lintel,
Six hands at an open door dicing for pieces of silver,
And feet kicking the empty wine-skins.
But there was no information, and so we continued
And arriving at evening, not a moment too soon
Finding the place; it was (you might say) satisfactory.

All this was a long time ago, I remember,
And I would do it again, but set down
This set down
This: were we led all that way for
Birth or Death? There was a Birth, certainly
We had evidence and no doubt. I had seen birth and death,
But had thought they were different; this Birth was
Hard and bitter agony for us, like Death, our death.
We returned to our places, these Kingdoms,
But no longer at ease here, in the old dispensation,
With an alien people clutching their gods.
I should be glad of another death.

    This poem takes us through a vast and changing landscape. We start in the cold winter and move to a desert landscape blasted by grime and heat; then on we push to lush valleys and small townships; until finally we arrive at the landscape of birth and death; only to turn around and make our way back home. It is the journey that fascinates me. The destination is not even described. Instead, this is a reflection on what the magi finally encountered, and yet, it is obscure and unresolved. So, in many ways this poem isn't about the birth of Christ or its ramifications for believers. Perhaps this poem is about the disappointment people experience when they take a risk, a leap of faith, and find it makes no sense. I wonder whether 1927 was a time that could not imagine anything but a purgatorial journey followed by existential angst. Perhaps this was a 1606 reprimand for people coming late to church and complaining about the cold of winter when really, they should have been rejoicing that they were alive. Maybe this poem is about our own lives and how we fail to understand our purpose. *Journey to the Magi* is a far cry from the Christmas carol, *We Three Kings*, sung in its majestic key of E minor. This poem was originally commissioned for a one shilling Christmas card in 1927, but I can't help think it is far too maudlin as a Christmas card!

    The Journey of the Magi is about a journey taken by three members of the priestly caste of ancient Persia who were regarded by some as sorcerers because of their skills in astrology. So, in the corners of this poem lurks the possibility of magic but traipsing about harsh desert landscapes with a grumbling entourage is anything but magical. There is no dignity to these travelers: no pilgrimage of sacred intuition and no kingly gift bestowed upon the Christ. It seems that this journey took years and years to expedite. Did people die along the way? How did they care for the animals? How many were involved in the movement of the magus? Where did they get that sherbet from? Legend, from as far back as 500 A.D. tells us the magus were Balthazar, Caspar, and Melchior. Some sources indicate they were brothers, while others suggest Balthazar was black. Other sources indicate they brought gifts of gold, frankincense, and myrrh. They were wondrous gifts: absurdly impractical (except of course for the gold), and what happened to that gold? Curiously, gold is offered at the birth of Christ and the lesser precious metal, silver, is the price paid for his delivery to death. One can't help but be haunted by a line from another Eliot poem, "In my beginning is my end". *Journey of the Magi* is a dramatic monologue written in free verse made up of 43 lines and has a trinitrine structure of 3 stanzas of unequal length.

The first five lines of stanza one commences with an intertextual reference to Lancelot Andrewes, one of the finest preachers of Jacobean England. Most especially remembered is his *Christmas Day* 1606 sermon, given some seven weeks after the thwarted Gunpowder Plot. In this sermon, Andrewes speaks of a collective purpose in these dark times and the need for greater understanding. He compares the earnest and resilient "people that arrived at Jerusalem on their errand" with the church goers assembled at Whitehall on 25 December, 1606 who are disgruntled by the short distance they had to travel in the dead of winter. In other words, Andrewes is pointing out that the English are reluctant to suffer and endure hardship for their faith. Furthermore, he urges his congregation sitting there with the King to ask: where is Christ? Indeed, Andrewes argues that if we are not prepared to worship Christ "all our seeing, coming, seeking and finding is to no purpose". The day after he delivered this sermon, Shakespeare's players performed *King Lear* for James I: a bleak play concerned with treasonable acts, plotting, invasion, foolish decisions, and a divided nation. This context is reflected in the start of Eliot's poem.

So the opening five lines of Eliot's poem come directly from Andrewes' sermon. I trip immediately, three words in, on the queer transitive verb wedged by alliteration: "A cold coming…" It is all about coming and not going. It is about the coming of the Christ; the coming of the Wise Kings; and the coming of the cold in this instance. I can nearly hear the chattering of the teeth in this opening line. In the first five lines, bound together by the quotation marks, we hear the repetition of the word "journey" and the alliterative use of "ways", "weather", and "winter" as well as "deep" and "dead". This is an articulation of an experience that happened deep in the season of death and dying. Indeed, we remain in this specter until the circle closes at the end of the third stanza with the phrase "another death". Why does Eliot use Andrewes' voice? He is acknowledging that his voice joins those that have gone before him: Andrewes and the Magi. The context of Modernism, Jacobean England, and Arabia some 2000 years ago all collapse into I, experienced here as the reader reads the poem in the 21st century.

When we commence with the magi's dramatic monologue, it is delivered in media res, as if the tale has been going on since time immemorial. This is an existentially familiar story about believers being confronted by hardship, obstacles, and doubt: "And the camels galled, sore footed, refectory, / lying down in the melting snow." The beasts of burden are described as annoyed, limping, and stubborn. Camel riding is all about the smell, the endless army of flies that follow, and the sense of unease because camels bellow and bite at each other and their riders. There is nothing romantic or lyrical about camels. So, if that isn't bad enough, we then come to the qualms: "There were times we regretted / The summer palaces on slopes, the terraces / And the silken girls bringing sherbet." Is this a memory of Persia that plays havoc in their imagination en route? Or is this part and parcel of the actual experience of the journey? Perhaps these are the stop overs where they are waylaid by extra-curricular activities.

The journey is more than just that pilgrimage or scientific pursuit of meaning for the magus; it is an extended metaphor, exploring the journeys of everyman. The exquisite sibilance of "summer", "palaces", "slopes", "terraces", "silken", "girls", and "sherbet" have an Edenic quality that momentarily allows the travelers to recall a time prior to being cast out into the wilderness. Their destiny is the same as those of the diaspora of the Old Testament: to search out and find the messiah in a place where God seems to have abandoned them. The next six lines are a litany of all that is going wrong. Firstly, the handlers are a problem: "camel men cursing...and running away, and wanting their liquor and women." There is something carnival-esque about this whole debauched scene. It is an unholy hot mess. The list continues with the epistrophe of "And". What is recorded is the way they are braced against the cold; the travelers are vulnerable, unwanted, and find no respite in the locations along the way. Fear and unknowing seem to ripple at the body of this motley crew. The final sentence of the first stanza suggests the furtive way in which they got through the gauntlet of suffering and despair: "...voices singing in our ears, saying / That this was all folly." The eerie reference to "voices" puts me in the mind of angelic tricksters, an Ariel creating mischief and havoc for the castaways. Are these the self-same angelic voices that sang Alleluia over the stable?

The second stanza takes us out of a purgatorial landscape into a fecund oasis of a yonic valley. Of course, this is a moment of enlightenment with dawn drawing them "below the snow line". As they leave the winter of their discontent they are confronted with a series of omens: "three trees on the low sky ... an old white horse... and six hands ...dicing for pieces of silver." The first is an augury of the crucifixion at Calvary, traditionally two thieves are crucified alongside Christ; the second is a reference to the *Book of Revelations* indicating the second coming; and the third is a reminder of the betrayal of Christ by Judas Iscariot. These potent symbols tie together the narrative of Christ. All of this is seen by the magus. It is as if their temporality is a conflation of past, present, and future: a warped time portal into which they have stumbled. Perhaps Eliot is implying that we are all living alongside the drama of Christ's birth, death, and resurrection every single day. The final sentence of this second stanza is disjointed and hesitant: "But there was no information, and so we continued / And arrived at evening, not a moment too soon / Finding the place; it was (you might say) satisfactory." We are left with a cliff hanger. We are directly addressed, our presence noted within the drama we observe. If this was cinema, we would see the phrase, *years later* or *time passes* or *decades on* before we roll into the third stanza. We don't get to see the Christ child in the manger with all the trimmings: oxen, donkey, angels singing on high, the lodestar, Mary, Joseph, and shepherds with their sheep. We don't even get to see how those gifts for a King were received by Jews, mere subjects of the Romans.

Was 1927 a time that could not imagine anything but that purgatorial journey and then existential angst? Again, the title is a salient reminder that this is not about the birth of Christ; this is about the journey of those who have perilously navigated themselves toward proof of their faith. The last stanza grapples with the reflection of what it is they witness. The magus speaking is ready, on the one hand, to admit he would undertake the journey all over again, that the journey was worth it and, despite the anguish, offered a level of satisfaction. Yet he hesitates in the act of reflection: "And I would do it again, but set down / This set down / This: were we led all that way for / Birth or Death?" This phrase, used repeatedly by Andrewes in his 1606 Christmas sermon, "to set down", refers in this instance to the act of putting down in writing, to settle into a position on the matter, to come to some rest in his mind. It is a curious meta-poetic moment that makes the immediacy of his question so dramatic. Time has passed and yet still he remains unsure about what it actually was he witnessed. This angst is ours. Moreover, the disturbing proximity of Birth and Death is a central tenet to the Christ narrative. In other words, in Christ's birth, is the promise of his death and resurrection as central to his messianic fulfilment? *Journey of the Magi* deals with the birth and death element of this narrative but not the resurrection component. Thus, the magus refers to being "led all that way" to this paradox: a mystery still troubling the contemporary mind.

We are left with an unresolved argument in the final eight lines of the poem. It is an unsatisfactory ending imitative of the unsatisfactory destination to which the magi were led. The fact is given, unequivocally, of "a" birth they witnessed. It is an unremarkable statement. The indefinite article makes it insignificant. The problem is further explored in that this birth was the same as death and prior to this event he "had thought they were different". What does it mean that birth and death are the same? How can the beginning and the end be similar? This conflation of the physical and the metaphysical, the rational and irrational, is what our minds find so hard to hold together at the one time. The second level of the argument is that this birth was agonising for them "like...our death". So, to witness Christ's birth is to give witness to the whole story; the passion of Christ, his death and resurrection, and in giving witness, we too are reborn. The magi return to the old religious, political, and social system, but they are "no longer at ease...with an alien people clutching at their gods." There is a poignancy here; life can never resume as it was. The magi no longer belong to their own country. They are sovereigns without belonging. Their people appear desperate and foreign. Thus, they are left longing for the end; complete annihilation: "I should be glad of another death." The contexts of the journey of the magi, Lancelot Andrewes' Christmas sermon, Eliot's Modernism, and our own temporalities still resonate with waiting for resurrection. These are times troubled by occupation and suffering and hopelessness: The Roman Empire occupying Judea or the threat of treason in Jacobean England or the existential angst that gripped Modernity. These are not contexts blithely aware of resurrection. Indeed, like Eliot, we are also crippled by preoccupations and moments of despair that distance us from knowing what it is we witness along the journey.

I Walk Through the Valley by Elizabeth Guy (2015)

My father is dying.
Even now, after he is dead, he is dying.
The moment before... the moment afterwards
The months of suffering before... the suffering afterwards...
Dying is a big business.
And grief — a strange country.
Stripping back, humility, endurance, emptiness
Then everything.

Just hours before my father died,
The room was full of shadows and angles,
I had asked him to die.

'It is too much,' I told him, 'too much to bear.'
You have to leave us my whisper catches in the night.
To die.
Into your arms O Lord.
I prayed aloud — frightened by my own voice.
I prayed to the Blessed Mother
Because I am Catholic and a shocking sinner.
I thought it better to bypass the crucified Christ
So, encumbered by his own misfortune.
Into your arms.
Take your son, take him down from this cross.
Hold him to you.
Beloved Son.
I prayed for him to die.
I did.

My father loved children. He was more at ease with children than with grown-ups. It was easier: just teasing and playing as if there would never be a home time. Children loved him.

The nurse comes in and takes my father's pulse. She is ignoring me and addressing most of her commentary to my older sister. My mum lays sleeping on a cot close by. I can hear her snore. The nurse speaks as if my dad is slightly deaf. I want to tell her how he loved women, especially the ones who were a little glamorous, a little edgy, a little playful. She is none of these. So, I wait for her to go, and on her way out, I ask about his pulse because she is annoying me so much.

'Your father's pulse is very strong. It could be days yet.'

She pulls the door quietly behind her, and I watch my father as his shallow and labored breath goes in and out and in and out and in and out and… He lies facing me, and I am holding his hand. My sister continues texting with her back to us. I listen to my mother sleeping near the sliding glass doors. My other siblings are waiting outside in a family room.

Then something happens to me, and I just know. I look at my father and think: *he is going to die, right now*. He breathes in and then out and then in and then out. I wait. I can hear my sister talking quietly on the phone. He is not breathing. I wait a little more. Nothing. I wait. I know he has died, but still I wait. Time slows down and curls unhurriedly around the darkened room, moving softly across his bed and unfurling toward my mother. There is no time, just a room filling up with quiet.

Eventually I surface and say "Mum … come here".

I am surprised because my mother sits straight up in bed. I had been listening to her snore seconds before but now she moves fast — much faster than her 83 years. I get off my seat and make her sit there. I take another seat facing her and my dad. I don't want to tell you about my mother and what she did and said. It's too sad. She is 16 again and drowning in the impossibility of a life without him.

My sister gets off the phone and she leans up against me and then my younger sisters and some of my brothers enter the room. Later, but not too much later, my husband and brother-in-law arrive. My husband tells me afterwards that it felt like he walked into an old Flemish painting: the background dark and deep, very little light and all of us watching the dead. My father doesn't look like himself. I don't know where he is. I think that any moment now my father will walk into the room. He will sit down near my mum and watch on with us. I will look right at him in that unwavering way I can with him, and he will see right into me, and that will probably make us both cry. But I won't be able to help it; I will still look right at him: a painting. Those Flemish masters are my favorite. They would include the detail of everything in that room: the tiniest, faintest slither of light to outline what had previously been unseen. Some of their paintbrushes had only a single hair. That much detail was used because everything mattered, but you already know that.

In the last week before my father died, we say the rosary and other prayers around his bedside; we have priests and nuns come and go. My youngest sister plays *Gabriel's Oboe* from her phone. It is something. My father asks me (about six days before he dies) to promise him we would play *Gabriel's Oboe* at his funeral. He has never referred to his funeral before now.

I say "Of course we will".

"Promise me" he says.

"No" I reply "I don't want to promise you." He looks at me and smiles.

I add, "But I will read a poem at your funeral," I can barely speak, "from me to you." And he repeats "From me to you."

I like irreverence. My father was irreverent. He would catch our eye at rosary after dinner and make us laugh until Mum showed her deep-abiding disappointment. We used to think that this was because, unlike my mother who went to Sacred Heart Primary and then Monte Saint Angelo, my father grew up a pagan, an infidel, a non-Catholic. We used to tease him that he was a 'prodo' and was sent to a public school: no lovely nuns; no angelus at midday to promise you it was time to eat your jam sandwiches; no asphalt playground where boys and girls were separated; and no lessons on the sacraments or what would happen if you died without first getting to confession (if you still had a venial sin on your soul). My father was one of six children and attended Artarmon Public and later Crows Nest High until Year 9 and then off to TAFE to be a carpenter. There it is. On the other hand, my mother could spell any word, name any plant or tree or flower in both Latin and English, and knew her Catechism off by heart. Her parents' dysfunctional marriage led her to the consolation of the liturgy, the Children of Mary on Saturday afternoons and mass most days of the week.

But this is not the story I want to tell you.

I need to go back to just after my father had died, and we are all around his bed. At one point it is just the seven brothers and sisters, with my mum, sitting around my dad. We are a mess of ages. There I am. We are a motley crew. What can you do? Just us and mum. We sit. All of us. Around our father. Our dead father. Quiet. I don't want anyone to say anything that isn't true. Quiet. Quiet. It goes on. And then I start singing a lullaby my mother used to sing to us when we were kids. I don't know why I do this — I am embarrassed, but at the same time, it was kind of trippy.

Over in Killarney many years ago
(my grandmother sang it to my mother, and she sang it to us, and I sang it to my daughter)

my mother sang a song to me in tones so sweet and low
(I am astounded)
just a little ditty
(my brothers and sisters are singing with me)
an Irish lullaby
(my mother sings)
and I'd give the world if you could sing
(my voice falters)
that song to me now
(one brother leans across to tap the rhythm on dad's hand)
to ra loo ra loo ra
(child to parent)
to ra loo ra li
(parent to child)
too ra loo ra loo ra
(my grandparents are in the room)
hush now don't you cry
(long dead)
to ra loo ra loo ra to ra loo ra li
(pause)
too ra loo ra loo ra that's an Irish lullaby.

And I stop, and we all stop. My eyes are filled with the heavy weight of a river to be crossed. We sit still, and I wonder whether my father's eyes have closed and whether he is slumbering somewhere elsewhere, somewhere opalescent. Somewhere.

Time has passed. I visited my mum today. I find being in the house that my father built, where our childhood still roams about in the kitchen and bedrooms and backyard, deeply consoling. My mum doesn't really speak, not yet. She is quiet most often and tired. Terribly tired. I think she gets smaller by the day. I have to talk to her as if she is my father because I was his and I miss him too much. Besides, who would I talk to now he is gone? She is my father and mother now. So probably to her discomfort, but not to her surprise, I talk to her about pretty much everything.

I'm less anxious now when I drive through the Wakehurst Parkway that leads to their home that other people might be there visiting. When my father was immobile, visitors would come all the time and encroach upon my precious time with him. I had no interest in these relatives. I know it's terrible. I know how ghastly I sound because I am. I know as one of the daughters, my role should be to enjoy visits with relatives and their offspring, but I am not so good at small talk. I wanted to talk about poetry with my father and books and ideas. He loved words and we would chat about the etymology of words. He would ask me about the students I taught and about their reception to *Hamlet* or to Yeats or to Heaney. I would ask him about the technicalities of building the house or the clock or the bedside table. Language was our feast. Sometimes I would have essays in my hand bag for marking, and I would give him a bundle, and he would read and mark them with me. He was incorrigible, giving out As, as if there was no tomorrow! He would always talk about what he was reading or what he remembered learning either as a student of wood work or later studying theology under Dr. Woodbury. Then of course there was the book he wrote. He asked me to work with him on an autobiography, and two years later, he had it done. In fact, the only thing he wanted, in the last few weeks of his life, was for me to read aloud from his book. I don't know what that was about. I don't know whether at that late stage, and faced with the certainty of death, all you want to remember is who you were. I don't know.

I loved the story of the house that dad built. I loved the idea of my mum and dad buying property on this goat track between the lake and the ocean, in a time when the suburb had not even a shop. There was no water and no electricity. He built a two room house with wood panelling he had varnished. Not a shack. It was a cottage with a picket fence and a yellow painted door. A kind of cover up really for the appalling state of poverty in which they actually lived. Those stories are full of endurance and resilience. I don't know. I have my doubts. I mean, there were nails in the wall to hang their clothes; I don't think that's OK. There was a sheet that divided the kitchen from the sleeping room. And there were accidents, and I am not talking about my father's; I am speaking about one small boy running through that sheeted door with a knife and sticking that knife through the lower face of the younger brother just missing the jaw bone. Or the boiling water that was pulled off the stove top and left a hideous scar on another brother's shoulder. Was it all like that for everyone back then? I don't really think so... So, the house. My father built the house as the family grew. Meanwhile, as a child, I had a reoccurring dream that my family drove past the house as it was under construction because they didn't recognize it. I am left alone in the front yard: no longer one of nine but rather one of one. In the dream, my parents return and take care of me, but they have left the other siblings elsewhere, and in the delicious rational existence of dreams, we never seem to wonder about where the other children have gone. No rivalry. No forgetting my name or who I am. At last to be me and not have an identity contingent upon the mass identity of a family.

But this is not the moment I want to tell you about. It's dark now outside: velvety black, like the nose of a baby wombat snuffing in the night; bombazine black; jet black for the poor and remembrance. I scoop up my father's love, and it falls like ink down about my head. I scoop him up. He scoops me up. And this is really what I wanted to say.

You see I want to tell you something. In the two nights following my father's death, something happened. On both occasions, I was lying in my bed. I was awake in the dark knowing I couldn't and wouldn't sleep. The first night, Sunday night, it was probably four hours after my father had died, and I lay there listening to my husband sleeping. And then I saw this brilliant phosphorescence of white light on a dark ocean. It was luminescent, warm, and incredibly white. Somehow, I was on that light, and it was deeply relaxing and very, very quiet. Then, like a camera, I moved across it, and then I swung upwards and joined this speed of white light that went up and up and up. I was in this rushing slip stream of white. I was high up in some clouds, and I turned to see someone who I didn't recognize, but he knew me. He was a young man and so incredibly joyful. I wanted to remember who he was and thought at first it might have been my dad when he was young — but I don't know — whoever it was, he certainly knew me. There was so much life everywhere, and this young man's happiness was infectious.

All this time I knew I wasn't asleep, but I didn't want the movement or light that was rushing around me to stop. I stayed and stayed with that light and its warmth for what seemed like hours. It was astonishing and bewildering but somehow deeply familiar.

After a while, I sat up and drank some water, all the time feeling light-headed and strange. And when I laid down, I went straight to sleep.

The next night it happened again. I wasn't sleeping and couldn't sleep and felt very upset about the loss of my father. I was glad to be in my bedroom and in my bed away from everything. I lay there in the dark. Then I saw these beautiful, hard white sheets thwacking up ahead on a white balcony with sundrenched walls and steps nearby. I moved again like a camera and flowed up into the whiteness of the sheets and then pushed past them into more brilliant white. All around me the air was light and warm. Then suddenly I was drawn up and up and up into a vortex of light. It was extraordinary! I was tumbling and rolling and spiralling around spinning, and all the while, I was in this ecstasy of light and brilliance. It was so exhilarating and marvellous and joyful. It was as if I was riding laughter.

Both mornings after these two nights, I told my husband what happened, and he said when I was telling him, I was radiant. I said I didn't know whether I had made this up in my own imagination or whether it had come to me from my father. I really hoped it would happen again and again but it didn't and it never has.

I've thought a great deal about what I saw. I know with absolute certainty my father wanted to show me where he went and what happened to him after he died. Sometimes I think it could have been him that I saw, and other times, I think it was someone else, but I just can't place him. Regardless, that joy I felt was euphoric. It was the most amplified moment of ecstasy I have ever known. I think my father wanted to show me that he was in the arms of absolute love.

5

Troubled Pleasure: The Romantics

The study of the Romantic period, 1790 – 1840, takes us into an extraordinary time in literature but also in Art, Politics, Science and Technology. The poetic works of Wordsworth, Coleridge, Shelley, Byron and Keats establish the cornerstones of how we know ourselves and our worlds. Like all art, understanding the context to these poems is critical and thus I invite you to look closely at the paintings of Delacroix, Gericault, Constable, Turner, Goya, Friedrich, David and Ingres, as well as considering the impact of the Industrial Revolution, the American War of Independence, the French Revolution, the Napoleonic Wars and the British Parliamentary Reform. The Romantic poets changed the way the West imagined nature, the child, the exotic and, most importantly, the ordinary man.

William Wordsworth

from *Prelude* by William Wordsworth (1798)

The mind of Man is fram'd even like the breath
And harmony of music. There is a dark
Invisible workmanship that reconciles
Discordant elements, and makes them move
In one society. Ah me! that all
The terrors, all the early miseries
Regrets, vexations, lassitudes, that all
The thoughts and feelings which have been infus'd
Into my mind, should ever have made up
The calm existence that is mine when I
Am worthy of myself! Praise to the end!
Thanks likewise for the means! But I believe
That Nature, oftentimes, when she would frame

A favor'd Being, from his earliest dawn
Of infancy doth open out the clouds,
As at the touch of lightning, seeking him
With gentlest visitation; not the less,
Though haply aiming at the self-same end,
Does it delight her sometimes to employ
Severer interventions, ministry
More palpable, and so she dealt with me.

One evening (surely I was led by her)
I went alone into a Shepherd's Boat,
A Skiff that to a Willow tree was tied
Within a rocky Cave, its usual home.
'Twas by the shores of Patterdale, a Vale
Wherein I was a Stranger, thither come
A School-boy Traveler, at the Holidays.
Forth rambled from the Village Inn alone
No sooner had I sight of this small Skiff,
Discover'd thus by unexpected chance,
Than I unloos'd her tether and embark'd.
The moon was up, the Lake was shining clear
Among the hoary mountains; from the Shore
I push'd, and struck the oars and struck again
In cadence, and my little Boat mov'd on
Even like a Man who walks with stately step
Though bent on speed. It was an act of stealth
And troubled pleasure; not without the voice
Of mountain-echoes did my Boat move on,
Leaving behind her still on either side
Small circles glittering idly in the moon,
Until they melted all into one track
Of sparkling light. A rocky Steep uprose
Above the Cavern of the Willow tree
And now, as suited one who proudly row'd
With his best skill, I fix'd a steady view
Upon the top of that same craggy ridge,
The bound of the horizon, for behind
Was nothing but the stars and the grey sky.
She was an elfin Pinnace; lustily
I dipp'd my oars into the silent Lake,
And, as I rose upon the stroke, my Boat

Went heaving through the water, like a Swan;
When from behind that craggy Steep, till then
The bound of the horizon, a huge Cliff,
As if with voluntary power instinct,
Uprear'd its head. I struck, and struck again
And, growing still in stature, the huge Cliff
Rose up between me and the stars, and still,
With measur'd motion, like a living thing,
Strode after me. With trembling hands I turn'd,
And through the silent water stole my way
Back to the Cavern of the Willow tree.
There, in her mooring-place, I left my Bark,
And, through the meadows homeward went, with grave
And serious thoughts; and after I had seen
That spectacle, for many days, my brain
Work'd with a dim and undetermin'd sense
Of unknown modes of being; in my thoughts
There was a darkness, call it solitude,
Or blank desertion, no familiar shapes
Of hourly objects, images of trees,
Of sea or sky, no colors of green fields;
But huge and mighty Forms that do not live
Like living men mov'd slowly through the mind
By day and were the trouble of my dreams.

Wisdom and Spirit of the universe!
Thou Soul that art the eternity of thought!
That giv'st to forms and images a breath
And everlasting motion! not in vain,
By day or star-light thus from my first dawn
Of Childhood didst Thou intertwine for me
The passions that build up our human Soul,
Not with the mean and vulgar works of Man,
But with high objects, with enduring things,
With life and nature, purifying thus
The elements of feeling and of thought,
And sanctifying, by such discipline,
Both pain and fear, until we recognize
A grandeur in the beatings of the heart.

I remember sitting in my senior high school English class listening to Sister Ellen read this section of *Prelude* to us. I was watching the rain scoop over the hills of the Lochinvar farmland. I wasn't looking at the print text in front of me because I was transfixed by a young boy rowing away from the shore and the monstrous cliff rising up and up and up into the night sky behind him. The gargantuan spectre seemed to be chasing the boy. I realized that with distance and perspective one could actually see what had always been lurking in the present darkness. So, dwarfed by its sheer presence in the gloaming, the boy decided to make a quick retreat back to safety, even though this meant to turn back to the very belly of the beast! Decades have passed and still I find myself inhabiting a temporality conjured by the Romantic poets. Theirs was a time framed by the first and second French Revolution, the Napoleonic Wars, the Industrial Revolution, the American War of Independence, and British Parliamentary Reform. What an extraordinary time!

Prelude was first written in 1798 when Wordsworth was 28, but throughout his life, he went back to it time and time again. He and Coleridge had grown close and traveled together to Germany, discussing poetry and their emerging philosophy. *Preface to the Lyrical Ballads* defines their self-given mandate, which was to write in the "real language of men" and express in poetry the "spontaneous overflow of feeling…taking its origins from emotion recollected in tranquillity". With this desire to revolutionize poetry, *Prelude* reshapes poetic diction and teases out the role of the poet. The conventional verse of the day was very different to Wordsworth's poem; hence, critics initially dismissed his poetry as insufficiently elevated in tone and subject matter. *Prelude* was always titled for Wordsworth as *Poem to Coleridge* and was made up of 14 books that explored the development of this philosophy concerning nature, society, poetry, and humanity. It was published a few months after Wordsworth's death in 1850. *Prelude* is written in blank verse with unrhymed iambic pentameter; the effect is that it imitates the natural cadences and rhythms of spoken English and is highly accessible and familiar to the ear. This extract begins midway through Book One around about line 340 and finishes at line 415. It is book-ended by Wordsworth's philosophy of nature as guide and teacher, which was central to his childhood.

The boy in *Prelude* comes to us out of a new and emerging notion of childhood. In 1762, Rousseau had published *Emile*, which posited the novel notion that children were innately innocent, rather than born sinful (as previously believed), and should be allowed to develop in nature while following their natural instincts. The Romantics, such as Wordsworth, explored this further and considered the way in which children were closer to God and all that was benevolent. These new experimental ideas took hold of the imagination to such an extent that by the mid-Victorian age, childhood innocence, goodness, frankness, and vision was seen to reinforce the moral wellbeing of adults and society at large. The Romantics also explored the idea of nature as our teacher and guide. This poetic movement reacted against the scientific rationalization of the Enlightenment as well as unchecked pursuit of profits in this age of industrial expansion. The world of the Romantics was tainted by the ever-increasing use of fossil fuels, population growth, overcrowded living conditions, deprivation, and poverty. The Industrial Revolution intensified the division of labor, the impact of time keeping, and rapid mechanization. It is little wonder that people felt spiritually alienated and longed for nature as the site of spiritual renewal. Compellingly, the Romantics explored the idea of the sublime in nature as Janus faced, with terror and beauty, its constituent parts. Terror looked back to the Old Testament notion of awe while the forward looking aesthetic of beauty evinced liberty and hope. Thus, it was not the physical Church that would be the site of the sublime but the cathedral of the universe.

We begin with a tantalizing introduction to an experience that haunted Wordsworth all the days of his life. He philosophizes about the machinations of the mind and the way it has a tendency to pull together all knowledge and experiences: both dark and light. He uses a simile to consider the way the mind is shaped into a coherence, "the breath / And harmony of music", despite being made up of discordant proclivities. The mind pulls together these frictional elements until they "move / In one society". Thus, "miseries / Regrets, vexations, lassitude" make up "The calm existence that is mine when I / Am worthy of myself!".

This is a wonderful and liberating idea: that the darkness can generate light. Indeed, he gives praise and thanks to both the means, allowing oneself to experience the darkness as well as the light and the ends: harmony. The exclamations reflect a self-discovered truth, which is that we are at our most worthy when we have the courage to step into the gloom. This introduction leaves us with Wordsworth's belief about the role of the poet: that the poet has been singled out from his earliest days by nature, who would "open out the clouds…to employ / Severer interventions, ministry / More palpable". It is at this dramatic point that we move into one of the most intense and unnerving experiences hitherto told in poetry.

Like other great tales of dread and trepidation, the school boy traveler is alone moving about undetected in the inky night of the untamed countryside. He is of course supposed to be the young poet himself. The recounted experience is peppered with the details of place to conjure the authenticity of a truthful poet narrator who really did experience what is about to be told. So, along with the boy, we spy "a Shepherd's Boat… to a Willow tree was tied / Within a rocky Cave". This is place specific, "by the shores of Patterdale", and we are reminded of the boy's vulnerability, "Wherein I was a Stranger…alone". What happens next is a result of spontaneous desire, wanton liberty, and hungry adventure: "No sooner had I sight of this small Skiff / Discover'd thus by unexpected chance, / Than I unloos'd her tether and embark'd." The young boy is fearless. Indeed, the rhythm of his rowing is in poetic "cadence" with his surroundings as soon as he pushes off from shore. Up until this point, he is inside a Caspar David Friedrich painting with the moon casting an ethereal light across the lake that is framed by the "hoary mountains": a painterly depiction of the vastness of the universe. The boat moves through the lake's skin of "sparkling light", while the oars, dipping in the water, create "mountain-echoes" and leave prints "glittering idly" behind him. Despite the seemingly pitch perfect visual image, there's a disquiet generated by the acknowledgment that this is "an act of stealth / And troubled pleasure". The boy, in all of this, is simply absorbing the experience, utterly and completely, without hesitancy or apprehension. The world is as it is, and his engagement within it is rightfully placed.

The drama shifts at this point when the boy rows out from the place of mooring. He is obviously chuffed with himself rowing off into the night all alone in a skiff not his and impressed by his rowing prowess: "proudly row'd / With his best skill." Like a magician working his magic, Wordsworth has us enthralled by this scene of innocence and adventure. Meanwhile, something monstrous begins to unfurl: slowly at first and then with increasing speed and largess until the entire canvas of the night is filled with this gargantuan existence. As the boat moves in the opposite direction the rower faces, the young boy begins to see "A rocky Steep uprose / Above", which then morphs into a "craggy ridge...an elfin Pinnacle". His rowing becomes a little more strenuous as he "lustily" attempts to move forward. Yet to no avail because it is at this point that the "craggy Steep" becomes something far more threatening and real: "a huge Cliff, / As if with voluntary power instinct, / Uprear'd its head." No longer is nature the site of bounty but has anthropomorphized into a far more menacing and baleful being. It is no wonder at this point that the young boy "struck, and struck again"! I can see him rise up from the seat with the muscles in his back, shoulders, biceps, and calves straining to row out of reach of this beast. His heart racing as "the huge Cliff / Rose up between me and the stars, and still, / With measur'd motion, like a living thing, / Strode after me". This is the stuff of nightmares. There is no way out except "With trembling hands" to turn the boat around and return to the bark's "mooring-place".

He returns home. Yet as every pilgrim knows who has seen the summit of the sublime, one never returns the same. This young boy is no longer the free and easy child of innocence who regarded nature as his benevolent teacher. The poet ponders this incident for years to come, knowing it was a turning point, and as such that it was an experience that showed him the other face of the sublime: the face of terror. Thus "grave / And serious thoughts" haunted him and addled his brain: "and after I had seen / That spectacle ... my brain / Work'd with a dim and undetermin'd sense / Of unknown modes of being." This is sensation at its finest with its ability to fire the imagination and cause ongoing contemplation. Wordsworth's understanding of the poet's mind is critical because he knows it is not filled with light but rather moments of such darkness. He apprehends that the "mighty Forms" of nature "do not live / Like living men"; indeed, they move "slowly through the mind" and trouble "my dreams". It is interesting to think about nature as such a formidable presence and not just the place of respite from the industrialized city's overcrowded and polluted rat holes. nature, witnessed here, is a power match for any man-made world.

The final stanza of this extract leaves us with a prayer to the universe. The voice of the poet seems to have grown from one who simply recounts the sublime elements of nature, in all its beauty and terror, to one who sees his place in relation to the cosmos. Thus, it is through such experiences as he has just told that the poet learns from the great teacher and guide, nature, about his connectedness to all that exists beyond himself. His prayer is one of praise and adoration: "Wisdom and Spirit of the universe! / Thou Soul that art the eternity of thought!" The poet credits nature and not "the mean and vulgar works of Man", for giving him the very "passions that build up our human Soul". This is a radical departure from the sorts of thinking still gripping the minds of the average person in English society, believing God worked through the hierarchy of the Church in all its man-made splendor. Wordsworth argues that these passions, which make up the human soul, purify "feeling and ... thought" and sanctify "pain and fear". In other words, the sensations of beauty and terror that one experiences form the soul. Furthermore, acknowledging the sacred and profane shapes our souls, "we recognize / A grandeur in the beatings of the heart". Like the young boy out on the lake that night, after reading *Preludes*, I was never the same again.

Elegiac Stanzas Suggested by a Picture of Peele Castle in a Storm, Painted by Sir George Beaumont by William Wordsworth (1806)

I was thy neighbour once, thou rugged Pile!
Four summer weeks I dwelt in sight of thee:
I saw thee every day; and all the while
Thy Form was sleeping on a glassy sea.

So pure the sky, so quiet was the air!
So like, so very like, was day to day!
Whene'er I looked, thy Image still was there;
It trembled, but it never passed away.

How perfect was the calm! it seemed no sleep;
No mood, which season takes away, or brings:
I could have fancied that the mighty Deep
Was even the gentlest of all gentle things.

Ah! then, if mine had been the Painter's hand,
To express what then I saw; and add the gleam,
The light that never was, on sea or land,
The consecration, and the Poet's dream;

I would have planted thee, thou hoary Pile
Amid a world how different from this!
Beside a sea that could not cease to smile;
On tranquil land, beneath a sky of bliss.

Thou shouldst have seemed a treasure-house divine
Of peaceful years; a chronicle of heaven;—
Of all the sunbeams that did ever shine
The very sweetest had to thee been given.

A Picture had it been of lasting ease,
Elysian quiet, without toil or strife;
No motion but the moving tide, a breeze,
Or merely silent Nature's breathing life.

Such, in the fond illusion of my heart,
Such Picture would I at that time have made:
And seen the soul of truth in every part,
A steadfast peace that might not be betrayed.

So once it would have been,—'tis so no more;
I have submitted to a new control:
A power is gone, which nothing can restore;
A deep distress hath humanised my Soul.

Not for a moment could I now behold
A smiling sea, and be what I have been:
The feeling of my loss will ne'er be old;
This, which I know, I speak with mind serene.

Then, Beaumont, Friend! who would have been the Friend,
If he had lived, of Him whom I deplore,
This work of thine I blame not, but commend;
This sea in anger, and that dismal shore.

O 'tis a passionate Work!—yet wise and well,
Well chosen is the spirit that is here;
That Hulk which labors in the deadly swell,
This rueful sky, this pageantry of fear!

And this huge Castle, standing here sublime,
I love to see the look with which it braves,
Cased in the unfeeling armour of old time,
The lightning, the fierce wind, the trampling waves.

Farewell, farewell the heart that lives alone,
Housed in a dream, at distance from the Kind!
Such happiness, wherever it be known,
Is to be pitied; for 'tis surely blind.

But welcome fortitude, and patient cheer,
And frequent sights of what is to be borne!
Such sights, or worse, as are before me here.—
Not without hope we suffer and we mourn.

This 60-line elegy, grouped in 15 quatrains with the rhyme scheme of a b a b is an attempt by Wordsworth to control and express grief. It is an ekphrastic poem composed in 1806 when the poet was staying at Sir George Beaumont's London house. Beaumont, a great admirer of Wordsworth, had a considerable reputation as a landscape painter. Beaumont painted his country property, Peele Castle or Piel Castle also known as Pile of Fouldry, situated on the coast of Lancashire in north-west England where Wordsworth holidayed. It was originally built in the early 14th century by the Abbot of the neighboring Furness Abbey in order to keep an eye on trade in the local harbor and protect against Scottish raids. Sea erosion caused ongoing damage, and despite restoration attempts, its ruination was inevitable. Beaumont's painting suggests elegy, a lament for time passing or nature's requiem and dirge of the mighty. Wordsworth was grieving at the time for the loss of his brother, Captain John Wordsworth of the East India Company, whose ship had foundered off the Bill of Portland. The *Abergavenny*, the ship John Wordsworth captained, was headed to India and China with an estimated value on board of £270,000 in trade, some of this represented an investment by the captain himself. The tragedy is aggravated by the fact that the *Abergavenny* shipwrecked just over two kilometers off the shore of Weymouth in shallow water. By this stage, the litigation over Wordsworth's father's estate and the family's inheritance had been resolved; Wordsworth had married his childhood friend, Mary Hutchinson, and set up a trust fund for his daughter, Caroline, from a previous relationship he had with Annette Vallon in France. Furthermore, Wordsworth had accepted annual patronage from Lord Lonsdale of £100. This is the backdrop from which Wordsworth reflects on the loss of his brother.

I imagine Wordsworth standing in front of Beaumont's oil on canvas, deep in thought. Leaning up close into its drama and then standing back to note the composition filled with tenebrism. Influenced by the picturesque paintings of the Flemish and Dutch, Beaumont's paintings were often exhibited in the Royal Academy. *Peele Castle in a Storm* was hung in Beaumont's Grosvenor Square residence; later, a smaller version was made and sent to Wordsworth to be hung in Dove Cottage.

In the first three quatrains, the poet addresses Peele Castle and discloses his close relationship with it: "I was thy neighbour once… Four summer weeks I dwelt in sight of thee: / I saw thee every day." Wordsworth commences with a familiar and intimate tone of address and makes reference to the castle's moniker, "Pile", which is a visual image of the ruin it already was in the fin de siecle of the 18th century. In many ways, the castle in Wordsworth's memory is more vivid and real than the painterly representation before him, a fanciful notion that forms the backbone of the poem. What is recalled in contemplation is an emotion and sensation that is as real as the actual experience of being there. His castle, prompted by the painting but contained in his mind's eye, is beauteous and benevolent with its sleeping "Form …on a glassy sea. / So pure the sky, so quiet was the air! / So like, so very like, was day to day!" The anaphora of the adverb "so" allows Wordsworth to evoke the extent to which this construction is constant and unchanging.

In many ways, the evocation of the subliminal beauty of Peele Castle and its seascape surrounds, with its personal address of "thy" and "thee", can be read as an address to his own brother. Thus, we start to see John Wordsworth enter the frame of the poet's reverie as he considers unchanging constancy, despite the turbulent surrounds, which was always there and "never passed away". Indeed, it is at this point that his contemplation seems to become troubled by what he "could have fancied… the mighty Deep…the gentlest of all gentle things". In other words, the loss of his brother in a tempestuous shipwreck forced him to face the dark side of nature: terror.

The next five quatrains are a wishful imagining of what could have happened if Wordsworth himself had been the creator. On one level, we are seeing the fanciful desire of painting the castle as he sees it, but on the other hand, it is about wanting to rewrite 5 February, 1805: the moment when the *Abergavenny* met its fate. In quatrain four, Wordsworth begins with an exhalation expressing his hunger to make holy his own heartfelt longing: "Ah! *then*, if mine had been the Painter's hand ...add the...light that never was...The consecration, and the Poet's dream."

Rather than a small pocket of light from the right hand middle ground of the composition, denoting nature's capricious disregard of man's insignificance, Wordsworth would offer "a world...different from this!" His world would be one where the sea "could not cease to smile ... tranquil land ... a sky of bliss". Wordsworth recreates "a treasure-house divine" in which no suffering, lament, or loss would be known.

Over quatrains six and seven, his poem paints an edenic timepiece: "Of peaceful years; a chronicle of heaven... Elysian quiet, without toil or strife." All possibility of a fatal ocean storm is erased and "silent Nature's breathing" gives life. Yet Wordsworth rouses himself and knows the dangers imminent should he stay in this illusion of what he might create "at that time" prior to his brother's death. It is not only a contemplation of an *if only* scenario that we are witnessing, common to most of us in our inability to accept the death of a loved one, but also the realization that art (and in particular poetry) is limited and cannot recreate what is lost forever. It is perhaps this that the poet's emerging sense of worth, significance, and power represented in "steadfast peace", is "betrayed".

The next seven quatrains take us back into the deep dark depths of Wordsworth's reverie, which is Beaumont's representation of *Peele Castle* and the state of grief that seems to be drowning him. Wordsworth acknowledges he has "submitted to a new control" and that "A power is gone, which nothing can restore; / A deep distress hath humanised my Soul." It is because of this altered state of consciousness that he realizes he would be completely unable to look upon the idealized image of the castle that emerges from his summery days of idle: "Not for a moment could I now behold / A smiling sea, and be what I have been." Everything is changed utterly and he will never be the same person he once was prior to the loss of his dearly loved brother. Grief will be forever young within the poet.

He turns once more to the painting before him and addresses Sir George: "Beaumont, Friend! who would have been the Friend, / If he had lived, of Him whom I deplore." The association between the subject of the painting and the nature of his brother's death are interconnected and cannot be prised apart. Wordsworth chides his earlier folly of suggesting he might paint oil on canvas differently and concedes Beaumont has captured the sublime exactly: "I ... commend; / This sea in anger, and that dismal shore... That Hulk which labors in the deadly swell, / This rueful sky, this pageantry of fear!" The spectacle of death's horror plays out again and again before him in the might and power of nature from which man has no succor. The castle now is a synecdoche for the fortified self of the poet who, up until the point of his brother's death, has been "Cased in the unfeeling armour of old time" but now must "brave" the tireless assault of "The lightning, the fierce wind, the trampling waves". In many ways, the castle as seen in his mind's eye, cast in the temperate time of his youth, can no longer exist after witnessing such off shore tragedy.

In the final two quatrains, Wordsworth's elegy farewells his lost brother as well as his own innocence and youth. The one-sided, romanticized notion of nature, where only beauty and not terror was seen, has been smashed. So, no longer is his "heart...Housed in a dream...at a distance" from the true disposition of the sublime in nature. Rather than "happiness", which is blind to calamity and trauma, being the purpose of our pursuits, Wordsworth recommends "fortitude, and patient cheer,

/ And frequent sights of what is to be borne!" In other words, to be of this world facing the series of unfortunate events that leave us bereft and at sea is what is required. We are at the mercy of nature, which has no mercy. The final line of the poem offers an unexpected sentiment of optimism despite the waves of grief and despair: "Not without hope we suffer and we mourn." The elegy is a leave-taking of something greater than just Peele Castle and John Wordsworth; it is a poem that paints the turning point away from the belief that poetry is mere representation. At this dark hour, Wordsworth realizes that the driftwood to which he must cling is poetry.

French Revolution, As It Appeared to Enthusiasts at Its Commencement by William Wordsworth (1805)

> Oh! pleasant exercise of hope and joy!
> For mighty were the auxiliars which then stood
> Upon our side, we who were strong in love!
> Bliss was it in that dawn to be alive,
> But to be young was very heaven!—Oh! times,
> In which the meagre, stale, forbidding ways
> Of custom, law, and statute, took at once
> The attraction of a country in romance!
> When Reason seemed the most to assert her rights,
> When most intent on making of herself
> A prime Enchantress—to assist the work
> Which then was going forward in her name!
> Not favored spots alone, but the whole earth,
> The beauty wore of promise, that which sets
> (As at some moment might not be unfelt
> Among the bowers of paradise itself)
> The budding rose above the rose full blown.
> What temper at the prospect did not wake
> To happiness unthought of? The inert
> Were roused, and lively natures rapt away!
> They who had fed their childhood upon dreams,
> The playfellows of fancy, who had made
> All powers of swiftness, subtilty, and strength
> Their ministers,—who in lordly wise had stirred
> Among the grandest objects of the sense,
> And dealt with whatsoever they found there
> As if they had within some lurking right
> To wield it;—they, too, who, of gentle mood,
> Had watched all gentle motions, and to these
> Had fitted their own thoughts, schemers more wild,

And in the region of their peaceful selves;—
Now was it that both found, the meek and lofty
Did both find, helpers to their heart's desire,
And stuff at hand, plastic as they could wish;
Were called upon to exercise their skill,
Not in Utopia, subterranean fields,
Or some secreted island, Heaven knows where!
But in the very world, which is the world
Of all of us,—the place where in the end
We find our happiness, or not at all!

William Wordsworth crossed the English Channel and arrived in Calais in 1790. Like many of his generation, he was enamoured by the call for *Liberté, Egalité, Fraternité* and found himself caught up in the fervor and excitement of arguably the most significant event to shape the modern West. The radical social changes of the Revolution were based on liberalism and the principles of Enlightenment; it was this that ignited his passionate support. In France, Wordsworth lived in Orleans and Blois, where he not only formed an attachment to Annette Vallon, who would later have their daughter, Caroline, but made significant friendships with soldiers and ardent upholders of the Revolution, such as Captain Michael Beaupuy. The 20-year-old Wordsworth was an eyewitness to the enlistment of volunteers and the proclamation of the Republic. Somewhat bewildered at the start of his stay, Wordsworth left France in December 1792 as a determined revolutionary. The spirit of rebellion and indignation against all social inequities stayed with him for the rest of his life. On return to England, he became disillusioned when the Revolution moved into the Reign of Terror; however, Wordsworth condemned his own King, Regent, and ministry with its ongoing war with France. Influenced by the work of William Godwin, Wordsworth was to turn to the abstract meditation on man and society. Thus, as a young man, Wordsworth had been a liberal, but by his elderly statesman years, he was a Tory.

Just prior to Wordsworth's crossing the channel in 1790, the French Revolution had begun with the storming of the Bastille in 1789 in an attempt to capture gunpowder and weaponry. The citizens began to redesign the country's political landscape by uprooting centuries-old institutions, such as absolute monarchy and the feudal system. Like the American Revolution, the French Revolution was influenced by Enlightenment, particularly the ideas of a popular sovereignty and the inalienable rights of man. The lead up to the Revolution was a powder keg ready to blow. France was near bankruptcy as a result of their involvement in the American Revolution and the unchecked spending of the monarchy. Furthermore, there had been two decades of poor cereal harvests, drought, and cattle disease. Bread prices spiralled as did tax increases until there was widespread unrest. Revolutionary fervor and hysteria swept France in the form of agrarian insurrection, looting, and the exodus. Rumors spread, such as the House of Bourbon was in collapse, and a military coup was imminent. The *Abolition of Feudalism* and the *Declaration of the Rights of Man and Citizen* was signed by the newly formed National Constituent Assembly in August 1789. Not long after, the King was arrested.

Wordsworth left before the execution of Louis XVI, Marie Antoinette et al during the Reign of Terror led by Robespierre, who was himself executed in 1794. Indeed, Wordsworth was well ensconced in England by the time Napoleon dismissed the Directory and declared himself in charge in 1799; by then, England had been at war with France since 1793 and would be until 1815. The French monarchy was not reinstated until the Second French Revolution in July 1830 and lasted until 1848. What the French Revolution had finally achieved was the establishment of a secular and democratic republic. The radical social changes that followed were based on liberalism and the principles of Enlightenment.

Wordsworth's poem *French Revolution*, is an impassioned voice of the French Revolutionary representing the way in which the idealistic and the downtrodden could be caught up in the vortex of change. It is a cry for the secular and democratic promise of salvation here on earth. The voice of this poem is that of an ardent enthusiast and one dedicated to the cause. Its energy builds and builds into a crescendo where in no uncertain terms the poet declares that *this* is the place, here on earth, which we must come to know liberty, equality, and fraternity.

In the first two sentences, the poet declares it was "hope and joy" that in fact assisted the revolutionaries and stood shoulder to shoulder with the ordinary person who was "strong in love". Thus, the sentiments that began the revolution were based on hitherto unrealized aspirations of brotherhood and justice for all. I don't think for one moment Wordsworth has forgotten the power he witnessed in his early 20s. This was the birth of a new age and a new people, and as such, it is imagined in the poem in the third sentence as a "dawn to be alive…to be young". There is a grandeur in *French Revolution*, situated in Book X of *Prelude*. It is by his reckoning, emerging out of what he saw and lived amongst, that the old times "In which the meagre, stale, forbidding ways / Of custom, law, and statute, took at once / The attraction of a country in romance!" In other words, the whole nation was drawn to this beauteous promise of something greater and that the past holding them back could be thrown over for this new world. France was a nation in love with the idea of what it could be, and Wordsworth captures this mesmeric ardor in its first flush of feverish youth.

Reason is personified in sentence five. Like hope and joy who have stood up with the ardent, the spirit of Enlightenment "seemed…to assert her rights…making of herself / A prime Enchantress": a nation captured under the spell of Montesquieu, Voltaire, Rousseau, and Diderot. This undertaking was not just for France but a movement for "the whole earth"! It was as if the world was young and awash with the beauteous promise of a better tomorrow. The symbol he uses to capture the luster and scent of this promise is a "budding rose above the rose full blown". It is the very hint of what it is to be, in all its emerging beauty: a promise of a new existence that cannot even be imagined as yet. This must have been the truth for so many. A world without serfdom, absolute monarchical rule, tyrannical Church laws, and restricted suffrage had never as yet been experienced. The ideas of this zeitgeist were just that, ideas: Enlightenment, the American Revolution, popular sovereignty, constitutionalism, effective governance, the codification and legal protection of natural rights, and anti-clericalism. It must have been an extraordinary time without sign posting or stopping!

By the center of the poem, we are convinced of this time as one that swept up the hopes and dreams of most everyone. By sentence seven, Wordsworth asserts that all were awake "To happiness unthought of". It is this state of wakefulness that is so compelling and extraordinary; moreover, it begins to give life to all sorts of slumbering imaginings. Thus, out of the torpor of the world of the past, the "inert" are "roused". This is now the rising up of the abject and the downtrodden: peasant and urban poor, idealists and thinkers, soldiers and workers, and the bourgeoisie.

We now move to the 9th sentence, and it meanders for 17 lines, describing "the meek and lofty" who rallied to the call of revolution. We first meet the noble and idealistic thinkers, the "lofty...who had fed their childhood upon dreams...who had made / All powers of swiftness, subtlety, and strength / Their ministers... who in lordly wise had stirred / Among the grandest objects of the sense." The realization of the dreams is made possible by their speed, cunning, and fortitude, conveyed in the sibilant "ministers". Furthermore, these "lofty" thinkers agitated grand ideas that they believed they had a "lurking right / To wield". We then meet the patient and long suffering, "the meek" and those "of gentle mood", who began to believe in the wild speculation of what could be. Both the exalted thinkers and the deferential lowly "find" that their "heart's desire" is assisted by this revolution. We are struck by the purity of ambition in the ordinary people behind the revolution.

The sentence ends with the heightened rhetoric of the call to "exercise their skill, / Not in Utopia, subterranean fields, / Or some secreted island, Heaven knows where!" In other words, their knowledge and skills were to be used for a greater purpose and not just for the profit and benefit of superiors. The call of the Church was to suffer and seek solace in heaven, whereas the call of the Revolution was to build a heaven here on earth: "the place where in the end / We find our happiness, or not at all!" How extraordinary must it have seemed to hear this cry and to be swept up in a hope that had never been realized before. Wordsworth's poem captures this momentous enthusiasm.

Lines Composed a Few Miles above Tintern Abbey, On Revisiting the Banks of the Wye during a Tour by William Wordsworth (1798)

Five years have past; five summers, with the length
Of five long winters! and again I hear
These waters, rolling from their mountain-springs
With a soft inland murmur.—Once again
Do I behold these steep and lofty cliffs,
That on a wild secluded scene impress
Thoughts of more deep seclusion; and connect
The landscape with the quiet of the sky.
The day is come when I again repose
Here, under this dark sycamore, and view
These plots of cottage-ground, these orchard-tufts,
Which at this season, with their unripe fruits,
Are clad in one green hue, and lose themselves
'Mid groves and copses. Once again I see
These hedge-rows, hardly hedge-rows, little lines

Of sportive wood run wild: these pastoral farms,
Green to the very door; and wreaths of smoke
Sent up, in silence, from among the trees!
With some uncertain notice, as might seem
Of vagrant dwellers in the houseless woods,
Or of some Hermit's cave, where by his fire
The Hermit sits alone.

      These beauteous forms,
Through a long absence, have not been to me
As is a landscape to a blind man's eye:
But oft, in lonely rooms, and 'mid the din
Of towns and cities, I have owed to them,
In hours of weariness, sensations sweet,
Felt in the blood, and felt along the heart;
And passing even into my purer mind
With tranquil restoration:—feelings too
Of unremembered pleasure: such, perhaps,
As have no slight or trivial influence
On that best portion of a good man's life,
His little, nameless, unremembered, acts
Of kindness and of love. Nor less, I trust,
To them I may have owed another gift,
Of aspect more sublime; that blessed mood,
In which the burthen of the mystery,
In which the heavy and the weary weight
Of all this unintelligible world,
Is lightened:—that serene and blessed mood,
In which the affections gently lead us on,—
Until, the breath of this corporeal frame
And even the motion of our human blood
Almost suspended, we are laid asleep
In body, and become a living soul:
While with an eye made quiet by the power
Of harmony, and the deep power of joy,
We see into the life of things.

        If this
Be but a vain belief, yet, oh! how oft—
In darkness and amid the many shapes
Of joyless daylight; when the fretful stir

Unprofitable, and the fever of the world,
Have hung upon the beatings of my heart—
How oft, in spirit, have I turned to thee,
O sylvan Wye! thou wanderer thro' the woods,
    How often has my spirit turned to thee!

  And now, with gleams of half-extinguished thought,
With many recognitions dim and faint,
And somewhat of a sad perplexity,
The picture of the mind revives again:
While here I stand, not only with the sense
Of present pleasure, but with pleasing thoughts
That in this moment there is life and food
For future years. And so I dare to hope,
Though changed, no doubt, from what I was when first
I came among these hills; when like a roe
I bounded o'er the mountains, by the sides
Of the deep rivers, and the lonely streams,
Wherever nature led: more like a man
Flying from something that he dreads, than one
Who sought the thing he loved. For nature then
(The coarser pleasures of my boyish days
And their glad animal movements all gone by)
To me was all in all.—I cannot paint
What then I was. The sounding cataract
Haunted me like a passion: the tall rock,
The mountain, and the deep and gloomy wood,
Their colors and their forms, were then to me
An appetite; a feeling and a love,
That had no need of a remoter charm,
By thought supplied, not any interest
Unborrowed from the eye.—That time is past,
And all its aching joys are now no more,
And all its dizzy raptures. Not for this
Faint I, nor mourn nor murmur; other gifts
Have followed; for such loss, I would believe,
Abundant recompense. For I have learned
To look on nature, not as in the hour
Of thoughtless youth; but hearing oftentimes
The still sad music of humanity,
Nor harsh nor grating, though of ample power

To chasten and subdue.—And I have felt
A presence that disturbs me with the joy
Of elevated thoughts; a sense sublime
Of something far more deeply interfused,
Whose dwelling is the light of setting suns,
And the round ocean and the living air,
And the blue sky, and in the mind of man:
A motion and a spirit, that impels
All thinking things, all objects of all thought,
And rolls through all things. Therefore am I still
A lover of the meadows and the woods
And mountains; and of all that we behold
From this green earth; of all the mighty world
Of eye, and ear,—both what they half create,
And what perceive; well pleased to recognise
In nature and the language of the sense
The anchor of my purest thoughts, the nurse,
The guide, the guardian of my heart, and soul
Of all my moral being.

                Nor perchance,
If I were not thus taught, should I the more
Suffer my genial spirits to decay:
For thou art with me here upon the banks
Of this fair river; thou my dearest Friend,
My dear, dear Friend; and in thy voice I catch
The language of my former heart, and read
My former pleasures in the shooting lights
Of thy wild eyes. Oh! yet a little while
May I behold in thee what I was once,
My dear, dear Sister! and this prayer I make,
Knowing that Nature never did betray
The heart that loved her; 'tis her privilege,
Through all the years of this our life, to lead
From joy to joy: for she can so inform
The mind that is within us, so impress
With quietness and beauty, and so feed
With lofty thoughts, that neither evil tongues,
Rash judgments, nor the sneers of selfish men,
Nor greetings where no kindness is, nor all
The dreary intercourse of daily life,

Shall e'er prevail against us, or disturb
Our cheerful faith, that all which we behold
Is full of blessings. Therefore let the moon
Shine on thee in thy solitary walk;
And let the misty mountain-winds be free
To blow against thee: and, in after years,
When these wild ecstasies shall be matured
Into a sober pleasure; when thy mind
Shall be a mansion for all lovely forms,
Thy memory be as a dwelling-place
For all sweet sounds and harmonies; oh! then,
If solitude, or fear, or pain, or grief,
Should be thy portion, with what healing thoughts
Of tender joy wilt thou remember me,
And these my exhortations! Nor, perchance—
If I should be where I no more can hear
Thy voice, nor catch from thy wild eyes these gleams
Of past existence—wilt thou then forget
That on the banks of this delightful stream
We stood together; and that I, so long
A worshipper of Nature, hither came
Unwearied in that service: rather say
With warmer love—oh! with far deeper zeal
Of holier love. Nor wilt thou then forget,
That after many wanderings, many years
Of absence, these steep woods and lofty cliffs,
And this green pastoral landscape, were to me
More dear, both for themselves and for thy sake!

We were asked to learn this poem by heart in our last year of high school. Our wildly eccentric English teacher told us we would teach ourselves, learning it by heart. However long it would take to commit to memory would be the time we would need to understand the poem. We were boarders, so it was sink or swim. The English teacher kept her word and never gave lessons on the poem. I had never met a teacher who could move as fast as she could, swathed in the long black habit of the Josephite Sisters. She would whip off her veil, passionately mid-sentence, and re-plait her hair all while reciting Wordsworth or *Hamlet* or *Under Milk Wood*. I remember doing chores on a Saturday morning in the dormitory and everyone everywhere seemed to be carrying the poem, reciting the poem, discussing the poem, and testing friends with the poem. By the end of that term, approximately 120 students had learned *Tintern Abbey* by rote. Did we understand it? It was "felt in the blood and felt along the heart"!

Tintern Abbey, written in 1798, is a fond memory for many, many students of English as well as tourists who have been one of the 70,000 who flock to the Monmouthshire in Wales each year. The Abbey was founded in 1131 by Walter de Clare for the Cistercian order but left in ruins after the Dissolution of Monasteries in the 16th century. The architectural structure at the time was made from pale smooth stone in a pure rational style. The columns, pillars, and windows were at the same base level, generating an architecture of light that would elevate the material to the immaterial. The Cistercian architectural sites offer some of the most beautiful relics of the Middle Ages; often built in remote valleys far from the cities and over-populated areas, they used the ideals of order and utilitarian beauty without superfluous ornament. The ruined Abbey which Wordsworth visits is still haunted by this exquisite symmetry.

Domestic tourism was at its pinnacle in the late 1700s when the war with France problematized the Grand Tour abroad. England's new and improved roads, coupled with such publications like *Observation on the River Wye* by William Gilpin in 1782, added to the allure of places like Tintern Abbey. Indeed, Gilpin piqued interest concerning the picturesque, which was part and parcel of the emerging Romantic sensibility. Unlike the thinkers from the Enlightenment and Rationalism, the Romantics regarded the beautiful and the sublime as non-rational and instinctual. The picturesque became the conduit between these two forces. Beauty, which Burke had unpacked as curvaceous and pleasing, appealed to male sexual desire whereas the sublime horrors appealed to humanity's desire for self-preservation. Therefore, the pursuit of the irregular, the anti-classical and ruins became de rigueur for the leisured classes who could afford to leave the pent up industrialized cities and take refuge in a tour to the countryside. Moreover, the polluted, industrialized, and over-populated cities from which the tourists come remain a stark backdrop to this rural idyll.

The title of this poem, "Lines Composed a Few Miles above Tintern Abbey, On Revisiting the Banks of the Wye during a Tour. July 13, 1798" probably took a while to learn by heart. It speaks to the context of the day. The title positions us "above" Tintern Abbey. So, we, alongside Wordsworth, take up a position in the secluded hills overlooking the ruins and the Wye River that ambles alongside, marking the border between Wales and Gloucestershire England. We are also informed that the poet is "revisiting" this site. This is not a first occasion but rather a visit that is layered with expectations and anticipations established at another time in the poet's life. The poem is a result of "a Tour" and so a pleasure trip that may well have been undertaken in part by train or horseback or walking. It could have taken in a number of other aesthetically worthy stopovers as the tourist develops and reflects on the combination of nature and architecture as a cultural backdrop to their lives. Finally, we are given a specific date: "July 13, 1798": a summer day beside the meandering River Wye, seated on the rolling hillside beneath a sycamore tree.

Only five years before he wrote this poem, Wordsworth had emerged from France and the Reign of Terror, leaving behind his French mistress and their child. He was filled with disquiet about England's war with France; initially, he was a political radical who had two unnoticed poems published. By 1798, the war with France continued as Wordsworth and Coleridge published the first edition of the *Lyrical Ballads*. *Tintern Abbey* is a palimpsest text that is cross hatched by the war with France, Industrialized England, domestic tourism, the picturesque, the Cistercian architecture, and the poet's own personal reflection. Did I know any of this when I committed the entire poem to memory in order to teach myself its mystery? No. The mystery of this poem came slowly to me after days and weeks and months of letting its words and phrases and sentences and stanzas wash over me. Its curvaceous beauty and its reckless sublimity still work its magic. I'm glad I learned the poem this way. It has been mine ever since.

Tintern Abbey is made up of five stanzas and is written in blank verse. Just to remind ourselves, this is unrhymed iambic pentameter where each line contains ten syllables with an unstressed syllable followed by a stressed syllable. Four times in the first stanza Wordsworth tells us that he is here "again" in this place where nature is picturesque, forming a conduit between beauty and the sublime.

In the opening two lines, we are reminded thrice that it has been "Five years…five summers…five long winters" since he has visited "These waters, rolling from their mountain-springs". Indeed, it is on the canvas of nature that he is able to make his poetized meditation: "I behold these steep and lofty cliffs, / That on a wild secluded scene impress / Thoughts of more deep seclusion; and connect / The landscape with the quiet of the sky." The sibilance connects and unifies the "steep…cliffs…a…secluded scene" to his philosophy that fertile places invite the growth and flourish of thinking: "clad in one green hue…Green to the very door." Wordsworth nods to the Cistercian order who once established in the valley surrounding the Abbey orchards, farmlands, and agricultural field work. This has layered the landscape with story. The presence of people is secondary to the power of nature, which seems to curl about and overtake the small and insignificant marks of man: "These hedge-rows, hardly hedge-rows, little lines / Of sportive wood run wild." The alliterative use of the breathless "h" implies the rapacious wildness of nature that can barely be controlled. Wordsworth references the homeless living amongst the ruins of the Abbey at the time of composition. Displacement and vagrancy are resultant of wretched poverty, according to William Gilpin; these indigent people burned charcoal fires along the River Wye sending up "wreaths of smoke…in silence". The opening stanza absorbs all these iterations as it moves instinctively between the present and the past, the personal and the historical, the landscape and the mind, and a burgeoning philosophy and an emerging poem. Thus, we are left with the image of the solitary man lit by a fire.

In stanza two, we come to Wordsworth's central philosophy that the sensations generated by nature are restorative. He establishes a contrast between the reality for most in industrial England: "lonely rooms…'mid the din / Of towns and cities…hours of weariness" and the "beauteous forms" of the English countryside, which would have been enjoyed by few. Nature is a balm that soothes and heals the soul: "Felt in the blood, and felt along the heart; / And passing even into my purer mind / With tranquil restoration." The poet acknowledges this restorative power is "owed" to the beauty of Nature and manifests in the "little, nameless, unremembered, acts / Of kindness and of love" surfacing and offering "unremembered pleasure". Moreover, he reaches further and recognizes that nature relieves "the burthen…the heavy and the weary weight / Of all this unintelligible world, / Is lightened." Nature can restore to such an extent that our corporeal and spiritual selves are fused: "body…become a living soul." In this mediative state, the clarity gained of seeing "into the life of things", results in "the deep power of joy". This is worth sitting back under that sycamore. In a few lines, he has summed up his *weltanschauung* and, as such, has set Romanticism beating. By stanza two, we have a philosophical paradigm for all future English writers.

The brief stanza three that sits in the middle of the poem directly addresses the "sylvan Wye".

Here, Wordsworth takes us back to the cityscape: "In darkness and amid the many shapes / Of joyless daylight; when the fretful stir / Unprofitable, and the fever of the world, / Have hung upon the beatings of my heart." This second reference to the industrialized urban squalor filled with unrelenting exploitation and chaos works in complete contrast to the pastoral idyll of the River Wye. The crisscrossing of time and place makes up the fabric of this poem and suggests the way temporality is dynamic. Nature forms a coherence and unity of experience for the poet because it is here wandering "thro' the woods" that he is restored twice; thus, in this small stanza, the poet exclaims that he has "turned to thee". Thus, nature is the source of immeasurable greatness and succor.

We move now to stanza four where Wordsworth compares his younger self to who he is now. Again, it is nature, as this bucolic pastoral, which is able to unify these two selves and transport him to a state sublime: "The picture of the mind revives again: / While here I stand, not only with the sense / Of present pleasure, but with pleasing thoughts." The image of his present self is conjoined to the sensation of rapturous delight. Indeed, he knows that the sensation will sustain the self he is yet to become: "there is life and food / For future years." His past self is full of raw animal pleasures and instincts: "like a roe / I bounded o'er the mountains...Flying from something that he dreads, than one / Who sought the thing he loved." His boyish self experienced the terror of the sublime visually and thus was limited by this singular sensual apprehension. In other words, he could not transport its incalculable quality of greatness beyond the moment of seeing it: "For nature then...To me was all in all...The sounding cataract...the tall rock, / The mountain, and the deep and gloomy wood, / Their colors and their forms, were then to me / An appetite...not any interest / Unborrowed from the eye." The child imagined here exhibits purity, immediacy and uncultivated vision. This is a development of Rousseau's idea that the child is its own innocent entity.

In contrast, Wordsworth's poet self, who is composing this poem above *Tintern Abbey*, has emerged from the child self and is now seeking to redeem the dying light and joy in his world. This occurs midway through stanza four. There is no regret concerning the loss of his childhood self: "for such loss, I would believe, / Abundant recompense...To look on nature, not as in the hour / Of thoughtless youth." The self, made up of the former, present, and future self, is empowered by the sublime, which is "deeply interfused" with nature. The sublime "rolls through all things...the light of setting suns, / And the round ocean and the living air, / And the blue sky, and in the mind of man." The cumulative listing of sun, ocean, air, sky, and the mind of man intensified by the anaphora of "And" leaves us in no doubt of Wordsworth's philosophy concerning the transformative power of nature. It is this quality of greatness that is both horrific and harmonious, terrifying and beautiful, and compels Wordsworth to be the "lover of the meadows and the woods / And mountains". Our apprehensions are contingent on not only the experience but what we create from that experience. Nature offers us the sublime because it is at the center to all creation and meaning: "the language of the sense / The anchor of my purest thoughts, the nurse, / The guide, the guardian of my heart, and soul / Of all my moral being." This last assertion radicalizes the religious beliefs of his day because Wordsworth audaciously asserts that the sublime can be known outside of Church orthodoxy. Nature is offered as a linguistic footpath, a secure mooring, a caretaker, a mentor, and a protector of the very soul of man.

In this final stanza of *Tintern Abbey*, Wordsworth directly addresses his sister, Dorothy. In a thumbnail sketch of Dorothy, we note that she was born a year after William and was separated from him at the age of 6 until she was 23 due to the death of their mother followed by their father, which meant the five Wordsworth children were divided up between aunts and uncles. Despite their poverty, in 1795, Dorothy and William set up home in Dorset. From then on, they were inseparable. They walked each day, and she traveled with him on all occasions: to Germany in 1789, where Coleridge joined them; to Calais, France in 1802 where Annette Vallon and her child met up with them; to Scotland in 1803 with his new wife Mary Hutchinson; and then to Switzerland in 1820. Dorothy lived another five years after William's death, she herself dying at 84. Although the last 20 years of her life were marked by senility intensified by her addiction to laudanum and opium, she left a life's work of diaries, travelogues, and poems primarily as a result of being a keen naturalist. He refers to her as "my dearest Friend, / My dear, dear Friend". This intensity could well be a reflection of their relationship, but more interestingly for me, this provides another layering to the subject matter of the poem.

Imagined in the last stanza of this poem is nature as benevolent guide who can calm the mind and shape profound thoughts: "lead /From joy to joy…so inform / the mind…With quietness and beauty…so feed / With lofty thoughts." Wordsworth reflects on nature as the metaphysical being receiving prayers to conquer man's hypocrisy: "evil tongues, / Rash judgments…sneers of selfish men…greetings where no kindness is [and] dreary intercourse of daily life." Moreover, nature is proffered as that which inspires awe, veneration, and intimacy: "let the moon / Shine on thee…let the misty mountain-winds be free / To blow against thee." Wordsworth leaves us in no doubt that nature is experiential and transformative. Indeed, this sensation can be revived ever after, and "solitude, or fear, or pain, or grief" will be healed. Of the nine million people in England at the end of the 18th century, most people would have been classified as peasants or working class or laborers or underclass and did not travel out to tourist sites in the countryside, let alone take tours of Europe.

While Wordsworth sat contemplating the sublime in nature most others were living in filth and disease, scraping together the basic necessities for their survival and living in cities where the mortality rates were extremely high. Women had few rights, worked all their lives, or often died in childbirth. Their men lost lives in the many workshop accidents, shipping docks, and construction sites as well as in the forced enlistment for military service. This majority lacked resources and often the means to care for their children who would then become orphans or abandoned. The hostility between classes was fierce. I think it is important to consider this backdrop in order to understand the need to find succor in nature. Finally, Wordsworth calls his sister to hold on to this experience they share together "With warmer love—oh! with far deeper zeal / Of holier love". This poem is a timepiece that lets us see through its kaleidoscope of colors.

Inside of King's College Chapel, Cambridge by William Wordsworth (1822)

Tax not the royal Saint with vain expense,
With ill-matched aims the Architect who planned—
Albeit laboring for a scanty band
Of white-robed Scholars only—this immense

And glorious Work of fine intelligence!
Give all thou canst; high Heaven rejects the lore
Of nicely-calculated less or more;
So deemed the man who fashioned for the sense
These lofty pillars, spread that branching roof
Self-poised, and scooped into ten thousand cells,
Where light and shade repose, where music dwells
Lingering—and wandering on as loth to die;
Like thoughts whose very sweetness yieldeth proof
That they were born for immortality.

It took from 1446 to 1515, over 70 years, for the Kings College Chapel in Cambridge to be built. It was constructed during the War of the Roses and was initially a Roman Catholic chapel but later reconsecrated for the Church of England. It would have dominated the skyline of Cambridge. The impressive flying buttresses of this late Perpendicular Gothic English edifice create an impression of mass, bulk, and power. Inside, it is incomprehensibly weightless and drenched in light. In fact, it is impossible not to look heavenward. The vast fan vaulted ceiling and ornate stained glass windows, with the emphasis on vertical lines, must have been a sublime experience for the people who came to worship. The quality of greatness is manifest threefold in the architectural magnificence, the demonstration of man's capacity to create such art and the symbolic value of God's might. I cannot imagine the effect it must have had in the 16th century to a population overwhelmed at times by uncertainty and suffering. The 26 stained glass windows generate a gravity-defying hall of light and narrate the Christian story from east to west following the rising and setting of the sun.

Henry VI had a vision for this chapel to be unequal in size and beauty. He was 19 when he laid the foundation stone of the chapel in 1446, but it was not until 1515 and several kings later that Henry VIII finalized the build. Cambridge was initially a town situated on a marsh and provided a port for the ingress and egress of goods and services. Henry VI had all existing buildings on the site that would be King's College razed to the ground. Originally only Etonians were to attend King's College, and degrees would be given without examination, but after 400 years, this tradition changed. Wordsworth was a student of Cambridge; in his case, he studied at St. Johns College and was a sizar, receiving financial aid from the college in return for some menial duties. Wordsworth was an undistinguished scholar and received a pass in his studies. This sonnet belongs to a sequence he wrote of 132 ecclesiastical sonnets.

The title of this sonnet indicates that we are sitting alongside Wordsworth in the cool of this chapel. There has been no orientation to the building from an external perspective and no movement from the grassy forecourt outside to the stone floors inside; indeed, it is as if we have always been here ensconced in the quiet and magnificence of the chapel. Wordsworth takes two sentences to convey his message: the artist's intelligence should not be restricted by functionality if great works are to reflect the sublime, which in turn will allow individuals to know eternity is theirs. The opening line begins in high modality with the command to not impose restrictions upon the visionary, Henry VI, who was deemed a "royal Saint". This is intensified in the second line with a parallel argument, asserting that neither should the artist be limited by "ill-matched aims". The monarch and the architect are one; the power vested to the King from God is the same as that given to the artist. In the 3rd and 4th lines of the first sentence, Wordsworth asserts that art should not be constrained by the inadequacy of its audience: "Albeit laboring for a scanty band / Of white-robed Scholars only." In other words, art is greater than the person who commissions or possesses it and should not be restricted by either. The sibilance that holds "scanty" and "Scholars" suggest that words fall short of the glory of art. Finally, in the 5th line, Wordsworth leaves us in no uncertainty that art is a "glorious Work of fine intelligence!" Imagination is capable of transforming contemplation into a work of art.

I love the opening phrase that commences the second sentence: "Give all thou canst." If that is not a motto for life, I don't know what is! It is a phrase stripped back and unadorned. Just like the commencement of the first sentence, this second sentence begins with a verb. Thus, both sentences start with a call to action; the first is not to "Tax", which is in contrast to the positive "give". Wordsworth's plea is to offer all of oneself in the act of creating art: "high Heaven rejects the lore / Of nicely-calculated less or more." There's a wonderful juxtaposition between the quality of greatness expressed in the alliterative "high Heaven", and man's "nicely-calculated" choice of ease over effort. This axiom to give everything one can is obviously the decision of the man who created this sensation in which we sit: the King's Chapel. I like to think about how King's Chapel is an artwork made by people who were oftentimes illiterate, powerless, and insignificant. It is at this point that Wordsworth cites the specificities of this build: "lofty pillars, spread that branching roof / Self-poised, and scooped into ten thousand cells." The towering construction with its vaulted fan ceiling that hangs impossibly above us, with its nests of space, is both the beauty and terror of the sublime. It is here that the very nuance of space and time, contained in the "light and shade", calmly exists. Moreover, "music dwells", both literally and metaphorically, in the everlasting life of this art. This eternal quality is reflected in the present participle of "Lingering—and wandering on".

We are left with a vivid simile suggesting that art can only be an approximation of the sublime experience itself. Wordsworth compares this breath-taking King's Chapel, where we alongside the poet apprehend rapturously, to the sweet realization that we were given life in order to trace the eternal: "Like thoughts whose very sweetness yieldeth proof / That they were born for immortality." Of course, the thoughts are "sweetness" because of the very sensation they savor, and the evidence they offer is that ours is to be born into everlasting light. The sonnet is the celebration of the unlimited and unrestricted imagination that can therefore create art that in turn sends the thoughts of others soaring, unrestricted and unhindered. Thus, art can inspire the greatness in others and their capacity to see the impossible.

Samuel Taylor Coleridge

This Lime-tree Bower my Prison by Samuel Taylor Coleridge (1797)

Well, they are gone, and here must I remain,
This lime-tree bower my prison! I have lost

Beauties and feelings, such as would have been
Most sweet to my remembrance even when age
Had dimm'd mine eyes to blindness! They, meanwhile,
Friends, whom I never more may meet again,
On springy heath, along the hill-top edge,
Wander in gladness, and wind down, perchance,
To that still roaring dell, of which I told;
The roaring dell, o'erwooded, narrow, deep,
And only speckled by the mid-day sun;
Where its slim trunk the ash from rock to rock
Flings arching like a bridge;—that branchless ash,
Unsunn'd and damp, whose few poor yellow leaves
Ne'er tremble in the gale, yet tremble still,
Fann'd by the water-fall! and there my friends
Behold the dark green file of long lank weeds,
That all at once (a most fantastic sight!)
Still nod and drip beneath the dripping edge
Of the blue clay-stone.

Now, my friends emerge
Beneath the wide wide Heaven—and view again
The many-steepled tract magnificent
Of hilly fields and meadows, and the sea,
With some fair bark, perhaps, whose sails light up
The slip of smooth clear blue betwixt two Isles
Of purple shadow! Yes! they wander on
In gladness all; but thou, methinks, most glad,
My gentle-hearted Charles! for thou hast pined
And hunger'd after Nature, many a year,
In the great City pent, winning thy way
With sad yet patient soul, through evil and pain
And strange calamity! Ah! slowly sink
Behind the western ridge, thou glorious Sun!
Shine in the slant beams of the sinking orb,
Ye purple heath-flowers! richlier burn, ye clouds!
Live in the yellow light, ye distant groves!
And kindle, thou blue Ocean! So my friend
Struck with deep joy may stand, as I have stood,
Silent with swimming sense; yea, gazing round
On the wide landscape, gaze till all doth seem
Less gross than bodily; and of such hues

As veil the Almighty Spirit, when yet he makes
Spirits perceive his presence.

A delight
Comes sudden on my heart, and I am glad
As I myself were there! Nor in this bower,
This little lime-tree bower, have I not mark'd
Much that has sooth'd me. Pale beneath the blaze
Hung the transparent foliage; and I watch'd
Some broad and sunny leaf, and lov'd to see
The shadow of the leaf and stem above
Dappling its sunshine! And that walnut-tree
Was richly ting'd, and a deep radiance lay
Full on the ancient ivy, which usurps
Those fronting elms, and now, with blackest mass
Makes their dark branches gleam a lighter hue
Through the late twilight: and though now the bat
Wheels silent by, and not a swallow twitters,
Yet still the solitary humble-bee
Sings in the bean-flower! Henceforth I shall know
That Nature ne'er deserts the wise and pure;
No plot so narrow, be but Nature there,
No waste so vacant, but may well employ
Each faculty of sense, and keep the heart
Awake to Love and Beauty! and sometimes
'Tis well to be bereft of promis'd good,
That we may lift the soul, and contemplate
With lively joy the joys we cannot share.
My gentle-hearted Charles! when the last rook
Beat its straight path along the dusky air
Homewards, I blest it! deeming its black wing
(Now a dim speck, now vanishing in light)
Had cross'd the mighty Orb's dilated glory,
While thou stood'st gazing; or, when all was still,
Flew creeking o'er thy head, and had a charm
For thee, my gentle-hearted Charles, to whom
No sound is dissonant which tells of Life.

Samuel Taylor Coleridge wrote *This Lime Tree Bower my Prison* in 1797 at the age of 25. Two years beforehand he had met Wordsworth and thus began one of the most important friendships in literary history, one that shaped the philosophies of Romanticism. Coleridge had moved to Somersetshire in order to be closer to Wordsworth and they commenced their work on *Lyrical Ballads*. Coleridge had been the youngest of a very large family and seemed to be plagued with feelings of unworthiness and anomie throughout his life; unable to manage his financial affairs, failing to complete various literary projects, trapped in an unhappy marriage, addicted to laudanum and opium. It is difficult to reconcile this image with the man who was central in offering professional advice to Wordsworth and to his friend and poet laureate, Robert Southey. Coleridge seemed to be driven by his poetic and instinctive heart. Earlier, at the age of 22 he had met Southey at Jesus College in Cambridge. Coleridge abandoned his training for priesthood and influenced by pantisocracy he considered moving to the New World with Southey and others to establish this utopia. Instead he married Southey's sister in law, never returned to Cambridge to complete his studies, nor ever knew utopia.

This poem is dedicated to his childhood friend, Charles Lamb, who he had met when attending *Christ's Hospital School*, a charitable institution set up by King Edward VI. Both Coleridge and Lamb survived the brutality of life in this boarding school and remained close throughout their lives. Lamb went on to be a poet, essayist and co-authored *Tales of Shakespeare* with his sister Mary. Lamb suffered from mental ill health from time to time as did his sister but it was Mary who attacked and murdered her mother with a kitchen knife the year before Coleridge published this conversation poem. Toward the center of the poem Coleridge refers to Lamb's current situation as calamitous. In a letter to Coleridge a year before Lamb had written of the "terrible calamities" that had befallen the Lamb family. A peculiar backdrop to a poem that invites mediation on the sublime experience of nature. Retrospectively, the term conversation was given to approximately eight poems by Coleridge where he wrote blank verse in common everyday language in order to express profound poetic images and ideas.

When I lived in Scotland, at the foot of the Trossachs, there was a lime tree bower at the bottom of my rented property. I would walk through it endlessly and my daughter would play there with her friends. Beyond this particular lime tree bower were rolling fields of yellow and brown. Right alongside ran a muddy flatland where highland cattle, with mattered fringes, stomped about showing very little interest in us. While I live in Scotland near my own lime tree bower, I thought often of Coleridge and his friends who had gone ahead of him, rambling. At first, he laments this but then he is so present to their experience that in the end, what did it matter whether he stayed? In fact being alone allowed Coleridge to be everywhere: in his bower alone and contemplative, with his friends trekking the hills and meadows, alongside Lamb a year or so ago in the calamity of his family's city home, and finally standing with Lamb at a point in the future and being awash with the sensation of nature. He dedicates this beautiful ambulant poem to Lamb and speaks of gladness repeatedly. This word, with its roots in Old English, connotes bright and shining. I like to think of Coleridge's friends being filled with bright shining light as they amble throughout the countryside at the poet's insistence. Nature conjures this gladness which is ultimately a sense of blessedness, exuberance and rapture all of which is conveyed in the poem. The poet, unable to follow, imagines the sublime beauty that is experienced not only by his friends out walking, but by himself in the past and his friend Lamb in the future. The bower becomes less of a prison and more of a site of freedom as the poem progresses.

Stanza one begins with a laconic tone indicating the poet's ennui and frustration with the fixity of his situation in contrast to that of his friends: "Well, they are gone, and here must I remain,/ This lime-tree bower my prison!" The juxtaposition of "they" and "I", "gone" and "remain", as well as "lime-tree bower" and "prison" all suggest a situation at odds with itself. It is a pose to establish the poet in a forced state of contemplation and imagination as opposed to those individuals who are experiencing the delight of nature. The poet recounts, with great certainty, that which he has "lost" as a result of his inability to go with his friends: "Beauties and feelings, such as would have been/ Most sweet to my remembrance even when age/ Had dimm'd mine eyes to blindness!" The hyperbole accentuates his regret and piques the reader's interest as to where the expedition was heading and yet surprisingly, we are to discover that it is merely a saunter down a dell and then over a meadow. It is in Coleridge's capacity to imagine the detail that transforms their "Wander in gladness" to something divine. He imagines that they take his advice and descend a cavern: "To that still roaring dell, of which I told;/ The roaring dell, o'erwooded, narrow, deep." The repetition of the onomatopoeia suggests the power, life and animation of nature. The poet, ensconced in the lime-tree bower, offers precise and loving detail of what will be encountered: "the slim trunk of the ash ... yellow leaves ... long lank weeds ... and drip beneath the dripping edge/ Of the blue clay-stone." Nothing goes unnoticed. The stanza ends by witnessing the dripping weeds on the arête of the dell's edge, its ordinariness reborn as wonderment: "Behold ... (a most fantastic sight!)." Coleridge wrote poetry to inspire and inform. He valued personal feelings and believed in the healing power of imagination. In a world of tumultuous change, he believed that creativity could illuminate and transform the world into a coherent vision.

The start of stanza two spiritually regenerates mankind in the landscape of sublime beauty. From this declivity of the dell, fecund with life and yonic sensuality, the friends are reborn: "Now, my friends emerge/ Beneath the wide wide Heaven." This beatitude is expansive and takes in the "tract ... fields ... meadows, and the sea". There is a painterly quality to this scene with the picturesque landfall in the foreground and the background shimmering with color and light: "fair bark... whose sails light up/ The slip of smooth clear blue betwixt two Isles/ Of purple shadow!" It is a Caspar David Friedrich painting! Perhaps *Chalk Cliffs on Rugen* or even *Moonrise over the Sea*. Through this canvas "they wander on/ In gladness". In other words, they are illuminated by what they witness. It is at this point where nature's sublime power offers enlightenment that Coleridge turns directly to his addressee, Charles Lamb. Indeed, the poet removes his dear friend from his metaphorical state of imprisonment, in the "great City ... through evil and pain/ And strange calamity!", and places him here with himself bathed in the light of the sublime.

Coleridge, Lamb, the friends and ourselves gather on this viewpoint overlooking the picturesque sunset. The sibilant soundscape imitates the holy moment we witness: "Ah! slowly sink/ Behind the western ridge, thou glorious Sun!/ Shine in the slant beams of the sinking orb,/ Ye purple heath-flowers! richlier burn, ye clouds!/ Live in the yellow light, ye distant groves!/ And kindle, thou blue Ocean!" This phantasmagoria is breathtaking. While the unhurried sun sets, its beams light up the vegetation until it makes kindling out of the floor and ceiling of this universe. We are here at the very heart of the sublime in nature. Its effect is that we are all "Struck with deep joy...Silent with swimming sense". Again, the quietude of the sibilance suggests this is a sacred moment and one that will sustain us as it enters our very faculties and sense of being. This is apprehended as nature being the embodiment of the divine: "gaze till all doth seem/ Less gross than bodily...As veil the Almighty Spirit, when yet he makes Spirits perceive his presence." We are urged to contemplate nature until it appears less incontrovertible and more an embodiment of the Transcendent.

The bliss and exhilaration experienced in stanza one and two radically alters the poet's state of imprisonment. Now impacted by the sublime in nature the poet can see the sacred beauty all around him. His eyes "dimm'd... to blindness" not so much by age but by inertia, now mark with microscopic detail the universe of his tree-lined chamber: "Some broad and sunny leaf... that walnut-tree...the ancient ivy...Those fronting elms." This foliage is transparent and luminous by twilight. He witnesses nature ever present in the quietude of the "bat" and "humble-bee" as evening comes on. Nature is his teacher and as such offers the unshackled inmate a lesson: "Nature ne'er deserts the wise and pure;/ No plot so narrow, be but Nature there...[thus] keep the heart/ Awake to Love and Beauty!" This axiom, which sits inside the last stanza, is a call to stir oneself to consciousness. At a time in history where everything must have seemed so uncertain, this imperative to "keep the heart/ Awake to Love and Beauty" must have been a clarion call. Furthermore, Coleridge revels that in the state of deprivation the contemplation of joy witnessed in nature, is exultant.

The poet leaves us and his dear "gentle-hearted Charles" with a finale that is just about impossible to forget. It is a fragile etching that grows into a lustrous oil on canvas. The "last rook" flying "Homewards" gets smaller and smaller in the vanishing light: "(Now a dim speck, now vanishing in light)." The spectre is winged by the parenthesis of its diminishing form. The purpose of this infinitesimal speck of nature is to highlight the quality of greatness in the "mighty Orb's dilated glory". I love how we hear the rook "creaking" above our heads as we stand with Lamb and Coleridge. Our conjoining at this moment asserts the truth, that "No sound is dissonant which tells of Life". In nature everything is in harmony, everything is in accord with itself. In this moment, the world seen through the poet's artistry is coherent and unified rather than cacophonous and awry. Thus, in three verses, 80 lines and a short wander, we have come to know sublime majesty and we never left our own bower!

France: An Ode by Samuel Taylor Coleridge (1798)

I
Ye Clouds! that far above me float and pause,
Whose pathless march no mortal may control!
Ye Ocean-Waves! that, wheresoe'er ye roll,
Yield homage only to eternal laws!
Ye Woods! that listen to the night-birds singing,
Midway the smooth and perilous slope reclined.
Save when your own imperious branches swinging,
Have made a solemn music of the wind!
Where, like a man beloved of God,
Through glooms, which never woodman trod,

How oft, pursuing fancies holy,
My moonlight way o'er flowering weeds I wound,
Inspired, beyond the guess of folly,
By each rude shape and wild unconquerable sound!
O ye loud Waves! and O ye Forests high!
And O ye Clouds that far above me soared!
Thou rising Sun! thou blue rejoicing Sky!
Yea, every thing that is and will be free!
Bear witness for me, wheresoe'er ye be,
With what deep worship I have still adored
The spirit of divinest Liberty.

II
When France in wrath her giant-limbs upreared,
And with that oath, which smote air, earth, and sea,
Stamped her strong foot and said she would be free,
Bear witness for me, how I hoped and feared!
With what a joy my lofty gratulation
Unawed I sang, amid a slavish band:
And when to whelm the disenchanted nation,
Like fiends embattled by a wizard's wand,
The Monarchs marched in evil day,
And Britain joined the dire array;
Though dear her shores and circling ocean,
Though many friendships, many youthful loves
Had swoln the patriot emotion
And flung a magic light o'er all her hills and groves;
Yet still my voice, unaltered, sang defeat
To all that braved the tyrant-quelling lance,
And shame too long delayed and vain retreat!
For ne'er, O Liberty! with partial aim
I dimmed thy light or damped thy holy flame;
But blessed the paeans of delivered France,
And hung my head and wept at Britain's name.

III
"And what," I said, "though Blasphemy's loud scream
With that sweet music of deliverance strove!
Though all the fierce and drunken passions wove
A dance more wild than e'er was maniac's dream!
Ye storms, that round the dawning East assembled,

The Sun was rising, though ye hid his light!"
And when, to soothe my soul, that hoped and trembled,
The dissonance ceased, and all seemed calm and bright;
When France her front deep-scarr'd and gory
Concealed with clustering wreaths of glory;
When, insupportably advancing,
Her arm made mockery of the warrior's ramp;
While timid looks of fury glancing,
Domestic treason, crushed beneath her fatal stamp,
Writhed like a wounded dragon in his gore;
Then I reproached my fears that would not flee;
"And soon," I said, "shall Wisdom teach her lore
In the low huts of them that toil and groan!
And, conquering by her happiness alone,
Shall France compel the nations to be free,
Till Love and Joy look round, and call the Earth their own."

IV
Forgive me, Freedom! O forgive those dreams!
I hear thy voice, I hear thy loud lament,
From bleak Helvetia's icy caverns sent—
I hear thy groans upon her blood-stained streams!
Heroes, that for your peaceful country perished,
And ye that, fleeing, spot your mountain-snows
With bleeding wounds; forgive me, that I cherished
One thought that ever blessed your cruel foes!
To scatter rage, and traitorous guilt,
Where Peace her jealous home had built;
A patriot-race to disinherit
Of all that made their stormy wilds so dear;
And with inexpiable spirit
To taint the bloodless freedom of the mountaineer—
O France, that mockest Heaven, adulterous, blind,
And patriot only in pernicious toils!
Are these thy boasts, Champion of human kind?
To mix with Kings in the low lust of sway,
Yell in the hunt, and share the murderous prey;
To insult the shrine of Liberty with spoils
From freemen torn; to tempt and to betray?

V

The Sensual and the Dark rebel in vain,
Slaves by their own compulsion! In mad game
They burst their manacles and wear the name
Of Freedom, graven on a heavier chain!
O Liberty! with profitless endeavour
Have I pursued thee, many a weary hour;
But thou nor swell'st the victor's strain, nor ever
Didst breathe thy soul in forms of human power.
Alike from all, howe'er they praise thee,
(Nor prayer, nor boastful name delays thee)
Alike from Priestcraft's harpy minions,
And factious Blasphemy's obscener slaves,
Thou speedest on thy subtle pinions,
The guide of homeless winds, and playmate of the waves!
And there I felt thee!—on that sea-cliff's verge,
Whose pines, scarce traveled by the breeze above,
Had made one murmur with the distant surge!
Yes, while I stood and gazed, my temples bare,
And shot my being through earth, sea, and air,
Possessing all things with intensest love,
O Liberty! my spirit felt thee there.

Originally this ode was entitled *The Recantation: an Ode* and was published in *The Morning Post*. The editor added a note to the poem indicating it expressed the newspaper's revised attitudes to the French Revolution. This five part poem represents Coleridge's honest self-examination of his initial support for the principles of the Revolution followed by disillusionment. I think it is virtually impossible for us to look back on the French Revolution and consider its virtues without being affected by its bloodbath. Yet for the Romantics and many idealists throughout Europe this was the watershed moment in history that promised equality and rights for all as well as peace with each other and nature. Coleridge is prepared to scrutinise his youthful idealistic beliefs which morphed into mature principled views. Indeed, in his early years he was a political activist and Unitarian, believing God is one entity but ended his days as a conservative and Trinitarian, believing in the three person God. Coleridge supported the Girondist's principles concerning the rights of man and anti-slavery but after the Reign of Terror, and the execution of Girondists and Robespierre, Coleridge privileged stability above all other national pursuits. Indeed, initially, he thought that the Reign of Terror was a result of European powers not allowing the ideals of the French Revolution to grow and flourish; he would later change this view.

Coleridge's position was ultimately revised with France's expansionist tendencies played out in the French Revolutionary Wars 1792 to 1802. While on the one hand the spread of revolutionary ideals led to the end of feudal laws on the other hand the violation of human, local and national rights in these invaded countries were untenable. The invasion of Switzerland by France in January

1798 ended the poet's hostile articles to *The Morning Post* demanding the resignation of Pitt and peace with France. Ultimately, as expressed in this 105 lined poem, the greatest freedom can only be attained with the acceptance of God in nature. The form of *France: An Ode* is worth considering. It offers five sonnets made up of 21 lines apiece. These self-contained sonnets invite meditation and anticipate a shift in argument. Like all odes it addresses a particular subject, in this case, the French Revolution where there has certainly been a volta or shift in the subject matter.

The first sonnet begins with nature, which reflects and inspires liberty. The natural elements of the sky, sea and land offer a blueprint for humanity's pursuit of equality and freedom: "Whose pathless march no mortal may control!... Yield homage only to eternal laws!" The political rhetoric echoing in these lines intensify and heighten the personal experience of nature that goes beyond that of the individual: "How oft...I wound/ Inspired, beyond the guess of folly,/ By each rude shape and wild unconquerable sound!" It is as if the principles of the French Revolution coalesce with that of nature as sublime, this will become a central political paradigm for Romanticism. Thus the first sonnet ends with an exultant manifesto: "Yea, every thing that is and will be free!/ Bear witness for me, wheresoe'er ye be,/ With what deep worship I have still adored/ The spirit of divinest Liberty." The end rhymes link the meanings of the verb *to be* with that of "free" and "liberty"; the penultimate end rhyme "adored" is linked to the verb "soared" in the 5th last line. So, we are under no illusion that the aspiration is that of individual freedom and state sanctioned liberty; in a nutshell to not only decide your actions but to exercise the power to act or speak without restraint.

In Sonnet II we look upon revolutionary France from the beginning. France is gargantuan in her scope and effect: "giant-limbs upreared,/ And with that oath, which smote air, earth, and sea,/ Stamped her strong foot and said she would be free." This reminds me of the Christian construction of the Virgin Mary who crushes the serpent beneath her foot in her fulfilment of Christ's messianic project to grant salvation to all. To Catholic France this is an image of the nation defying the ongoing tyranny of the Bourbons. Coleridge stitches together political and religious thinking to consecrate the early actions of the revolutionaries. Indeed, he personally aligns himself with this early stage: "With what a joy my lofty gratulation/ Unawed I sang." His happiness knows no bounds as he joins with the revolutionary's song of freedom. Coleridge then turns to England which chooses to rise up against France in the First Coalition when the French Revolutionary Wars began: "Like fiends embattled by a wizard's wand,/ The Monarchs marched in evil day,/ And Britain joined the dire array;/ Though dear her shores and circling ocean,/ Though many friendships, many youthful loves." In the simile Coleridge suggests that England was under some sort of spell in its efforts to thwart the spread the revolutionary spirit throughout France and Europe. According to the poet this is counter intuitive because the personified France and England should be affectionate and close. Like Sonnet I, the last four lines of Sonnet II end with a declaration of support and faith in the Revolution but one sharpened by the shame of England's betrayal: "And hung my head and wept at Britain's name." Coleridge courageously shows himself as someone ashamed of his own nation. By the time he is writing this ode he is living in Somerset and keenly aware that invasion is possible and his life, like those around him, is in jeopardy.

At the center of this poem, in Sonnet III, Coleridge pinpoints the Reign of Terror as an event that, at the time, seemed almost justifiable. The madness and blasphemy of this period is contrasted to the aspiration within him. He uses direct speech to represent the young poet who was perhaps beginning to question the means by which freedom and liberty is achieved: "A dance more wild than e'er was maniac's dream... Ye storms ... assembled,/ The Sun was rising ... hid his light." The pathetic fallacy conveys the turbulence and darkness of this period in which all of Europe was enthralled. We move from the juxtaposition of "hoped and feared" in Sonnet II to "hoped and trembled" in this Sonnet III, suggesting the enigmatic nature of the times. Coleridge attempts to reassure himself that "The dissonance ceased, and all seemed calm and bright". The appearance of peace and hope is merely that, an appearance. This speaks to the heart of the poem where the means of the French Revolution fails to justify the ends: "Domestic treason, crushed beneath her fatal stamp,/ Writhed like a wounded dragon in his gore." The vivid imagery conveys the triumph over revolt and yet internal unrest will never die. Again the young poet attempts to assuage his anxiety about the tyranny of the Reign of Terror: "Then I reproached my fears that would not flee./ "And soon," I said, "shall Wisdom teach her lore/In the low huts of them that toil and groan!"" Coleridge's belief in the extraordinary benefits that had hitherto been unknown to the world cannot be underestimated; this was a revolution that offered equality and liberty to every human being. The French Revolution was going to lead to "Love and Joy" uniting "the Earth". It is in understanding this that we can come to consider the enormous sense of disappointment and betrayal that Coleridge felt at the turn of 1798.

By Sonnet IV we see the idealism shattered. France invades Switzerland at the start of 1798 which meant the end of feudalism but also the loss of local democracy and the imposition of taxes and a centralised government. It is now that Coleridge hears the suffering and sees the carnage in such a way that cannot be unheard or unseen: "I hear thy groans upon her blood-stained streams!/ Heroes, that for your peaceful country perished." His support for the invaded is unequivocal and his rage is now palpable in that the proponents of revolution have betrayed the hope of what it could have achieved: "O France, that mockest Heaven, adulterous, blind,/ And patriot only in pernicious toils!/ Are these thy boasts, Champion of human kind?" The country that gave birth to modern democracy now seems to have replaced the chains of feudal law with other wicked despots. France is characterised by being "adulterous" because it has betrayed its marriage to freedom by invading Switzerland, a country that exemplified the sublime in nature. To invade and cause bloodshed is to ultimately "insult the shrine of Liberty".

In the final sonnet we see the paradox of replacing one form of enslavement with another. Moreover, the pursuit of liberty is reduced to a childish contest riddled by chaos: "In mad game/ They burst their manacles and wear the name/ Of Freedom, graven on a heavier chain!" In 1762 Rousseau begins *The Social Contract* with "Man is born free; and everywhere is in chains". This is a call to war against oppression of every kind and yet tragically, and at such enormous cost, some 36 years later it would seem that all has been lost. Coleridge, no longer the young poet but someone who has experienced his own bildungsroman as has France, now laments his advocacy for the "profitless endeavour" of the French Revolution. In many ways his own reputation as a preacher and political activist has unravelled because of his inability to see and hear the treachery and betrayal of the revolutionary's principles. Coleridge is abandoned by his previous aspirations and beliefs. Bereft the poet stands alone feeling the "winds" and overlooking the "waves". At this point he realises that nature will never betray him, like nations have, and thus nature remains the site of true freedom and liberty: "And there I felt thee!—on that sea-cliff's verge...Yes, while I stood and gazed, my temples bare,/ And shot my being through earth, sea, and air ... O Liberty! my spirit felt thee there." This ode is a paean to the newly emerging mature poet but more importantly to the promise of equality, freedom and liberty in his own countryside. The honesty of Coleridge is impressive but the honesty of a poet, in such a public way, is revolutionary.

Dejection: An Ode by Samuel Taylor Coleridge (1802)

Late, late yestreen I saw the new Moon,
With the old Moon in her arms;
And I fear, I fear, my Master dear!
We shall have a deadly storm.
(Ballad of Sir Patrick Spence)

I
Well! If the Bard was weather-wise, who made
    The grand old ballad of Sir Patrick Spence,
    This night, so tranquil now, will not go hence
Unroused by winds, that ply a busier trade
Than those which mould yon cloud in lazy flakes,
Or the dull sobbing draft, that moans and rakes
Upon the strings of this Æolian lute,
    Which better far were mute.
    For lo! the New-moon winter-bright!
    And overspread with phantom light,
    (With swimming phantom light o'erspread
    But rimmed and circled by a silver thread)
I see the old Moon in her lap, foretelling
    The coming-on of rain and squally blast.
And oh! that even now the gust were swelling,
    And the slant night-shower driving loud and fast!
Those sounds which oft have raised me, whilst they awed,
    And sent my soul abroad,
Might now perhaps their wonted impulse give,
Might startle this dull pain, and make it move and live!

II
A grief without a pang, void, dark, and drear,
    A stifled, drowsy, unimpassioned grief,
    Which finds no natural outlet, no relief,

          In word, or sigh, or tear—
O Lady! in this wan and heartless mood,
To other thoughts by yonder throstle woo'd,
     All this long eve, so balmy and serene,
Have I been gazing on the western sky,
     And its peculiar tint of yellow green:
And still I gaze—and with how blank an eye!
And those thin clouds above, in flakes and bars,
That give away their motion to the stars;
Those stars, that glide behind them or between,
Now sparkling, now bedimmed, but always seen:
Yon crescent Moon, as fixed as if it grew
In its own cloudless, starless lake of blue;
I see them all so excellently fair,
I see, not feel, how beautiful they are!

               III
          My genial spirits fail;
          And what can these avail
To lift the smothering weight from off my breast?
          It were a vain endeavour,
          Though I should gaze for ever
On that green light that lingers in the west:
I may not hope from outward forms to win
The passion and the life, whose fountains are within.

               IV
O Lady! we receive but what we give,
And in our life alone does Nature live:
Ours is her wedding garment, ours her shroud!
     And would we aught behold, of higher worth,
Than that inanimate cold world allowed
To the poor loveless ever-anxious crowd,
     Ah! from the soul itself must issue forth
A light, a glory, a fair luminous cloud
          Enveloping the Earth—
And from the soul itself must there be sent
     A sweet and potent voice, of its own birth,
Of all sweet sounds the life and element!

               V

O pure of heart! thou need'st not ask of me
What this strong music in the soul may be!
What, and wherein it doth exist,
This light, this glory, this fair luminous mist,
This beautiful and beauty-making power.
     Joy, virtuous Lady! Joy that ne'er was given,
Save to the pure, and in their purest hour,
Life, and Life's effluence, cloud at once and shower,
Joy, Lady! is the spirit and the power,
Which wedding Nature to us gives in dower
     A new Earth and new Heaven,
Undreamt of by the sensual and the proud—
Joy is the sweet voice, Joy the luminous cloud—
     We in ourselves rejoice!
And thence flows all that charms or ear or sight,
     All melodies the echoes of that voice,
All colors a suffusion from that light.

VI

There was a time when, though my path was rough,
     This joy within me dallied with distress,
And all misfortunes were but as the stuff
     Whence Fancy made me dreams of happiness:
For hope grew round me, like the twining vine,
And fruits, and foliage, not my own, seemed mine.
But now afflictions bow me down to earth:
Nor care I that they rob me of my mirth;
     But oh! each visitation
Suspends what nature gave me at my birth,
     My shaping spirit of Imagination.
For not to think of what I needs must feel,
     But to be still and patient, all I can;
And haply by abstruse research to steal
     From my own nature all the natural man—
     This was my sole resource, my only plan:
Till that which suits a part infects the whole,
And now is almost grown the habit of my soul.

VII

Hence, viper thoughts, that coil around my mind,
     Reality's dark dream!

I turn from you, and listen to the wind,
    Which long has raved unnoticed. What a scream
Of agony by torture lengthened out
That lute sent forth! Thou Wind, that rav'st without,
    Bare crag, or mountain-tairn, or blasted tree,
Or pine-grove whither woodman never clomb,
Or lonely house, long held the witches' home,
    Methinks were fitter instruments for thee,
Mad Lutanist! who in this month of showers,
Of dark-brown gardens, and of peeping flowers,
Mak'st Devils' yule, with worse than wintry song,
The blossoms, buds, and timorous leaves among.
    Thou Actor, perfect in all tragic sounds!
Thou mighty Poet, e'en to frenzy bold!
    What tell'st thou now about?
    'Tis of the rushing of an host in rout,
    With groans, of trampled men, with smarting wounds—
At once they groan with pain, and shudder with the cold!
But hush! there is a pause of deepest silence!
    And all that noise, as of a rushing crowd,
With groans, and tremulous shudderings—all is over—
    It tells another tale, with sounds less deep and loud!
    A tale of less affright,
    And tempered with delight,
As Otway's self had framed the tender lay,—
    'Tis of a little child
    Upon a lonesome wild,
Nor far from home, but she hath lost her way:
And now moans low in bitter grief and fear,
And now screams loud, and hopes to make her mother hear.

VIII

'Tis midnight, but small thoughts have I of sleep:
Full seldom may my friend such vigils keep!
Visit her, gentle Sleep! with wings of healing,
    And may this storm be but a mountain-birth,
May all the stars hang bright above her dwelling,
    Silent as though they watched the sleeping Earth!
    With light heart may she rise,
    Gay fancy, cheerful eyes,
Joy lift her spirit, joy attune her voice;

To her may all things live, from pole to pole,
Their life the eddying of her living soul!
    O simple spirit, guided from above,
Dear Lady! friend devoutest of my choice,
Thus mayest thou ever, evermore rejoice.

Coleridge wrote *Dejection: An Ode* in 1802 and unlike his earlier poetry, here he considers Man and nature as separate entities. Addicted to laudanum which lead to his own erratic decision making, this poem reflects the loss of faith in a world where nature is guide and teacher. It is as if Coleridge realises that only he can save himself. Coleridge seemed on the one hand thwarted by his own incompetence at living responsibly and on the other hand he is buoyed up by his verbal powers which were among the wonders of his age. This tension was magnified by his tendency to lie to others and himself about his addiction while creating poetry that was intensely honest. Odes were written since classical times and Coleridge's form modifies Pindar's, which was established in 500 BC. The ode is used to versify serious and detailed subjects. The 17th century Scottish ballad from which Coleridge quotes at the start of the poem signals his longing for release, not just in its lines but in its form. The ode discloses that the philosophy fuelling his earlier years is fallacious. Indeed, he realises that we are ultimately removed from the sublime potency of nature; it cannot and does not spiritually transform us. The power punch of this ode is the unadorned truth that "we receive…what we give" and nothing will save us but ourselves.

At the time of writing this ode Coleridge was completely indolent, a euphemism at the time for laudanum addiction. His marriage in 1795 to Sarah Fricker, an elegant, emancipated and educated woman was an unhappy arrangement, especially for her. She raised their children, often alone and always without fiscal support. While he went on a walking tour of Germany with Wordsworth she gave birth to their second child and nursed him through a number of illnesses until the baby died the year after in 1799; Coleridge did not rush home but stayed away for another six months. Meanwhile he had become fixated with Sara Hutchinson, Wordsworth's sister-in-law who lived with Wordsworth, his wife and his sister, Dorothy. Coleridge often frequented their home in the Lake's District. This tight knit group of individuals, which did not include Coleridge's wife, spent long hours analysing, commenting and discussing poetry. Whether or not this ode is addressed to Sarah Hutchinson is still under question but by 1804 Coleridge had separated from his wife.

The epigraph is from a 15th century folk ballad where the feminised romantic symbol of the moon morphs into a pathetic fallacy that foretells the trauma of what is to come. There are eight sections to this ode. The first indicates the poet's longing for a storm because he cannot feel and a tempest would shake him out of his torpor. By the 7th section the screaming wind of a storm is upon him and it is this which releases him from his malaise so much so that by the 8th and final section of the poem the poet is able to wish blessing upon the very object of his suffering to whom he addresses: "Lady", the "pure of heart". The poem is both conversational and grave in tone. Most appealing is the notion that all this philosophising about nature and the sublime really offers no respite when it comes to the very human state of suffering, despondency and melancholy. While his spirits are low Coleridge's poem is lively and evocative. He might be posing as the poet who cannot write because of his unhappiness and desolation, but he certainly produces an impressive ode.

In Section I we begin with an intertextual reference to "The grand old ballad of Sir Patrick Spence" and the meta-poetic reference to "the strings of this Æolian lute". Coleridge is arguing for the drama and power of a storm to generate an experience mimetic of the catastrophe of his heart, one that is worth writing about. Up to this point his poetry is nothing but a "dull sobbing draft... better far were mute". His droll honesty is arresting. The poet longs for the portent offered in the epigraph: "lo! the New-moon winter-bright!...the old Moon in her lap, foretelling/ The coming-on of rain and squally blast." Instead what he experiences is merely the desire not the reality of such a tempest; thus he remains unable to "startle this dull pain". Section II of this ode outlines the still emotional state of grief in which he finds himself: "grief without a pang, void, dark, and drear,/ A stifled, drowsy, unimpassioned grief." The palindromic effect of this statement indicates its cyclical control over him. The beauteous impress of nature cannot work a transformative effect on him. It is as if the excess of harmony and beauty precludes the impact of horror and terror and it is the latter qualities that will shudder him into a marked change. The final conclusion of this section is antithetical to the Romantic project: "Those stars... Now sparkling...Yon crescent Moon, as fixed as if it grew/ In its own cloudless, starless lake of blue...I see, not feel, how beautiful they are!" This is a radical departure from the theories he generated with Wordsworth on the powerful restorative effect nature will have on the ordinary man. It would seem here that Coleridge is positing something more about what constitutes the individual: someone who is broken by the vagaries of the heart and in many ways addicted to suffering.

By Section III the poet has drawn some conclusions about his overwhelming sense of loss. What he has lost is unclear; it may well be the love of his Lady or it could be his ability to write but most certainly it is to feel the world that once nurtured and sustained him. Thus, nature which offered respite and empowerment in the past no longer offers him succor. The poet asks what can be done "To lift the smothering weight from off my breast?" and the answer is not to contemplate nature because inspiration is found in the interior self: "It were a vain endeavour,/ Though I should gaze for ever/ On that green light that lingers in the west:/ I may not hope from outward forms to win/ The passion and the life, whose fountains are within." Again, I think this is Coleridge at his most honest and perhaps his most fragile because he knows inspiration is something he must find within himself. Like Section II, here in Section IV he directly addresses the "Lady". In doing so the poet implies the relationship between the lover and the beloved, thus the reader assumes an intimacy. What interests me here is that Coleridge is indicating that we are the creators of our own destiny. Rather than nature or God illuminating our path the poet is suggesting that we are responsible: "we receive but what we give." The Romantics up to this point regarded nature as having the quality of greatness but here it is the human soul that "must issue forth/ A light, a glory, a fair luminous cloud". Indeed, it is from this luminosity that poetry will emerge: "And from the soul itself must there be sent/ A sweet and potent voice."

By Section V Coleridge is on a roll extolling the qualities of luminosity generated by the soul. In his rhetorical flourish the poet says to his beloved that she need not ask what the potent voice may be because the capacity to create beauty is in the very Lady herself: "O pure of heart...Joy that ne'er was given,/ Save to the pure." Furthermore, this experience of joy is manifest in the "spirit" and "power" of nature's dowry which offers "A new Earth and new Heaven". This joy of which he sings is both "sweet" and "luminous" but again comes from within. The magic and power that emanates as a result of this potent voice offers a reconfiguration of all that has been hitherto imagined: "And thence flows all that charms or ear or sight,/ All melodies the echoes of that voice,/ All colors a suffusion from that light." It is hard to believe that dejection is at the forefront of the poet's mind when we complete this section; perhaps the Lady is his muse and as such inspires the poet to believe in the creative process. In Section VI the poet reflects on the way he used joy to ward off distress and misfortune. Moreover, "Fancy made me dream of happiness". The poet now rejects the way in which he used these qualities to guard himself against the slings and arrows of life and ignore "what nature gave me at my birth/ My shaping spirit of Imagination". He has come to realise that it is the power of his own imagination that promises him some sort of release and succor from gloom and despair.

The penultimate Section VII is the most dramatic component of this ode. We have been so whipped up in the poet's "viper thoughts, that coil around" his mind, that no one has noticed the rising storm. He addresses the wind, which generates the operatic and emotionally charged back-stage, saying it is imagination that offers relief from melancholic inertia. The wind is relentless and empowering: "What a scream/ Of agony ... Mad Lutanist! Who ... Mak'st Devils' yule... Thou Actor, perfect in all tragic sounds!/ Thou mighty Poet... What tell'st thou now about?" The wind is personified; it is benevolently and malevolently multi-faceted. Nature's energy releases the poet into a whirling dervish of imagination and creativity. He hears the retreat of embattled armies: "'Tis of the rushing of an host in rout,/ With groans, of trampled men, with smarting wounds." Coleridge is writing this in the depths of the Napoleonic Wars which were vanquishing Europe and resulting in the ongoing conscription of English soldiers. This is a time of fretful uncertainty. He, like all of his contemporaries, were deeply aware of the revolutionary changes both in England and abroad and as such were shaken to the core. This ode is as much about the sense of dispiritedness in the face of *this* zeitgeist as it is about the poet's shambolic personal life filled with addiction.

Another mirror he holds up to his times is the popular drama by Thomas Otway, *The Orphan* (1680), which remained a stock piece on stage until the 19th century. Now the wind is likened to the drama Otway created where the terrifying scene of a child lost in the tempestuous wilderness is "tempered with delight" because her "moans" and "screams" are called forth by the wind; thus they become the sign of "hope" and rescue. The final stanza to this ode, Section VIII, is hushed by the generous sprinkling of sibilance. Here the poet wishes his beloved well and offers up a litany of prayerful requests for her happiness: "Visit her, gentle Sleep! with wings of healing... May all the stars hang bright above her dwelling ... With light heart may she rise... mayest thou ever, evermore rejoice." This is an ode that ends with the unequivocal expression of exuberance and elation. Perhaps it is because the melancholic suffering transforms into the composition of verse. Paradoxically it has been his inertia that brings this roller coaster of a poem before us. A poem that hangs out the shingle of dejection at the start but ends cock-a-hoop in happiness by the final stanza. Without a doubt, Coleridge has shown us a new moon is rising in the arms of the old.

Youth and Age by Samuel Taylor Coleridge (1832)

Verse, a breeze mid blossoms straying,
Where Hope clung feeding, like a bee—
Both were mine! Life went a-maying
With Nature, Hope, and Poesy,
When I was young!

When I was young?—Ah, woful When!
Ah! for the change 'twixt Now and Then!
This breathing house not built with hands,
This body that does me grievous wrong,
O'er aery cliffs and glittering sands,
How lightly then it flashed along:—
Like those trim skiffs, unknown of yore,
On winding lakes and rivers wide,
That ask no aid of sail or oar,
That fear no spite of wind or tide!
Nought cared this body for wind or weather
When Youth and I lived in't together.

Flowers are lovely; Love is flower-like;
Friendship is a sheltering tree;
O! the joys, that came down shower-like,
Of Friendship, Love, and Liberty,
Ere I was old!
Ere I was old? Ah woful Ere,
Which tells me, Youth's no longer here!
O Youth! for years so many and sweet,
'Tis known, that Thou and I were one,
I'll think it but a fond conceit—
It cannot be that Thou art gone!

Thy vesper-bell hath not yet toll'd:—
And thou wert aye a masker bold!
What strange disguise hast now put on,
To make believe, that thou are gone?
I see these locks in silvery slips,
This drooping gait, this altered size:
But Spring-tide blossoms on thy lips,
And tears take sunshine from thine eyes!

Life is but thought: so think I will
That Youth and I are house-mates still.

Dew-drops are the gems of morning,
But the tears of mournful eve!
Where no hope is, life's a warning
That only serves to make us grieve,
When we are old:
That only serves to make us grieve
With oft and tedious taking-leave,
Like some poor nigh-related guest,
That may not rudely be dismist;
Yet hath outstay'd his welcome while,
And tells the jest without the smile.

Coleridge writes this poem in 1832 at the age of 60, two years before he dies. At this point in his life he is living under the supervisory care of physician James Gillman who was committed to controlling the poet's addiction. Throughout his life Coleridge had suffered from anxiety and depression and most possibly was bipolar. The rheumatic fever he had suffered as a child was treated with laudanum hence his life-long addiction. Coleridge had studied and critiqued literature, philosophy, religion and politics. Throughout this time, he wrote extraordinary verse; indeed, to use the phrase he coined, one has to "suspend disbelief" that one man is so capable of so much. *Youth and Age* is a timepiece, not for his time but for all time. It speaks to the good fortune of those who grow old and are able to look back and wonder at the duality of the self as we carry our young self in our old.

The first stanza of *Youth and Age* conveys the bounty of youth in the collision of three tight metaphors. Youth is filled with the ongoing delicious action of the present participle so that the young poet finds verse "straying", hope "feeding" and life "a-maying". I love this last image of life being a dance entwined with "Nature, Hope, and Poesy". There is something fragrantly wholesome and beauteous about the inspiration found in poetry for the young. Even the simile of hope clinging "like a bee" indicates the abundantly fertile state of being a young poet. In stark contrast the second stanza inverts the final line of stanza one into a question: "When I was young?" The poet is now looking back and lamenting the loss of his youth. The excess of exclamation and exhalation creates a soundscape of the poet's grief as he considers the limitations of his aging self: "This breathing house not built with hands,/ This body that does me grievous wrong." The metaphor of being housed within a body that refuses to do as he wills, suggests his control ebbing away. In comparison he uses a simile to recall a time when his body was "Like those trim skiffs"; independent and fearless. Indeed, the landscape of his memory of this time is vividly painted with "glittering sands...winding lakes...rivers wide". The older poet feels that when he was younger, he was more at one with his body: "When Youth and I lived in't together."

In the third stanza the older poet recalls how easy friendship and love were in his youth. The bounty of these relationships nurtured his free spirit: "O! the joys, that came down shower-like,/

Of Friendship, Love, and Liberty." At the center of this stanza he again repeats a line but inverts its meaning by shifting the syntax from exclamation to question mark: "Ere I was old!/ Ere I was old?" You can almost hear the older poet in the first instance being caught up in the remembrances of youthful friendships, love and liberty and then reminding himself that this time has passed. So vivid are the dreams of his youth that it is difficult to reconcile his ageing self with the desires and experiences of his early days. At the heart of this poem is the truth that the youthful and older selves are one and the same: "O Youth! ...Thou and I were one ... It cannot be that Thou art gone!" By the 4th stanza the poet points out that Youth's "vesper-bell hath not yet toll'd". The metaphor indicates that time is not signalling it is drawing to a close. Indeed, the very next line implies that youth has always used disguise and the strangest of these is "To make believe, that thou are gone". He strengthens his argument by suggesting that while on the one hand he may exhibit the physical characteristics of an ageing poet, "locks in silvery slips,/ This drooping gait", on the other hand he is invigorated by nature's youth: "Spring-tide blossoms on thy lips,/ And tears take sunshine from thine eyes!" Hence, ageing is all in the mind: "Life is but thought: so think I will/ That Youth and I are house-mates still."

At the start of stanza five and throughout *Youth and Age*, the poet has privileged the presence and importance of nature. It is this which replenishes his potency to be the creator of poetry. In the opening sentence of this final stanza he suggests that it is all about perspective: "Dew-drops are the gems of morning,/ But the tears of mournful eve!" This metaphor indicates the value of a new day in contrast to the grief of the oncoming darkness. Life lived without hope will only lead to old age filled with regret. We are left with a comparative anecdote of what it is to live a life where one has failed to enjoy hope and a youthful perspective: "Like some poor nigh-related guest,/ That may not rudely be dismist;/ Yet hath outstay'd his welcome while,/ And tells the jest without the smile." The poet ends *Youth and Age* with this rather sanguine lesson that one can avoid being this "poor nigh-related guest" who has "outstay'd his welcome" by holding on to one's youthful perspective which is particularly rejuvenated by nature. Coleridge may well have commenced his poem with the notion that the old poet looks back longingly to his younger self but by the poem's mid-point we are encouraged to reconsider the restorative qualities ever present in nature.

Percy Bysshe Shelley

In 1821, a year before his death, Percy Bysshe Shelley wrote an essay which responded to a witty article written by his friend, Thomas Love Peacock entitled *The Four Ages of Poetry*. Shelley's, *A Defence of Poetry*, articulates a philosophy about poetry and the poet that could only have emerged out of Romanticism. In this treatise Shelley defines reason and imagination, as logical thought and perception. He contends that language shows humanity's "impulse toward order and harmony which leads to an appreciation of unity and beauty". This is the touchstone of Romanticism. Most famously he posits that poets are "the unacknowledged legislators of the world" and that poetry "lifts the veil from the hidden beauty of the world". It is these sorts of contemplative notions that keeps you turning back to his essays. It makes you think about the importance of an art form that requires time and consideration and often just hard work. Shelley works back and 4th through the ages citing the value of various poets and writers for what they have contributed in the making of civilisation. Poets apprehend truth and beauty and as such reflect that which has been hitherto "distorted"; indeed, the poet "is a nightingale, who sits in darkness and sings". I like to think about this and the belief they must have had in themselves and each other. What an age! What a time! These Romantic poets, Wordsworth and Coleridge as well as Shelley's contemporaries, Byron and Keats, must have been shaken to the core by revolutionary thinking and action. A time that demanded the inalienable rights of all men.

So, poetry is a language that is compelled to move towards unity of meaning and coherence. Shelley writes in his essay that poetry "is at once the center and circumference of knowledge...the root and blossom of all other systems of thought". This was a time that required the philosophising of poets and poetry just as much as the muscle of protestors demanded the world be utterly changed. Shelley argues that poetry "makes immortal all that is best and most beautiful in the world"; it curates and holds the dynamic quality of the aesthetic in its power. Poetry "arrests the vanishing apparitions which haunt the interlunations of life"; it articulates the metaphysical and thus "redeems from decay the visitations of the divinity in man". I think this is known instinctively by those of us who find the raison d'être in poetry. Finally, Shelley states that poetry "strips the veil of familiarity from the world and lays bare the naked and sleeping beauty". I think Shelley's meandering heart felt essay emerges out of his context but remains a salient reminder to the twenty first century that poetry is an alchemical art and as such remains profoundly powerful. Moreover, it is a call to arms for any wordsmith to recognise the yearning for coherence, unity, truth and beauty. Without which there could be no civilisation.

So, by the time he had written this essay, at the age of 28, Shelley had already lived a life filled with drama, hardship and financial insecurity. He had endured his traumatic time at Eton and accepted his expulsion from Oxford less than a year after he commenced because of his refusal to retract his publication on atheism. It was his inherited baronetcy that afforded him time and confidence to pursue his practice of writing lyrical poetry and discussing radical politics. He read voraciously, engaged with the intellectual minds and ideas of his time, and pursued love regardless of societal restrictions. His political work impacted the English Chartists, Karl Marx and Leo Tolstoy to name a few. By the time he drowned in the Gulf of Spezia Italy, Shelley had survived the death of three of his children to Mary Wollstonecraft Godwin, his second wife; the suicide of his first wife, Harriet Westbrook; and the suicide of Mary's step sister, Fanny Ismay. To add insult to injury, he had also failed to win custody for his two children after the death of his first wife, as the courts ruled him an unfit parent because of his atheism. The through-lines in Shelley's poetry are a direct result of his social and personal context: restlessness and brooding, rebellion against authorities, yearning for nature, imagining visions and pursuing ideal love and freedom in the untamed spirit.

Let's now turn our attention to *England in 1819* which was written in response to the Peterloo Massacre that occurred in August of that same year. The title of this fateful day was as an ironic salute to the Battle of Waterloo and the defeat of Napoleon just four years earlier. Shelley was responding to the debacle in which England found itself: mad King George III replaced by the licentious Prince Regent, a conservative parliament not responding to the cries of universal suffrage, the protective Corn Laws aggravating widespread famine and chronic unemployment. The charismatic orator, Henry Hunt, was to speak to a crowd on 16 August in St Peter's Field in Manchester. The crowd had been estimated at 8000 men, women and children who came together to demand reform; what they met was the Manchester Yeomanry Calvary, the 15th Hussars, infantrymen and the Royal Horse Artillery unit. Approximately 15 people were killed and 700 people injured. Shelley, like many concerned, believed the laws of England needed revitalisation, such as those concerning Catholics who were not able to vote or sit in parliament or preside over law courts or enter universities. *England in 1819* is a result of the poet's unshakeable belief in the radical thinking emergent of his times. He had read Rousseau, been influenced by his father-in-law William Godwin and remained lifelong friends with the anti-monarchical radical Leigh Hunt, who had been imprisoned for sedition. Shelley longed for a deus ex machina to save his country.

England in 1819 by Percy Bysshe Shelley (1819)

An old, mad, blind, despised, and dying King;
Princes, the dregs of their dull race, who flow
Through public scorn,—mud from a muddy spring;
Rulers who neither see nor feel nor know,
But leechlike to their fainting country cling
Till they drop, blind in blood, without a blow.

A people starved and stabbed in th' untilled field;
An army, whom liberticide and prey
Makes as a two-edged sword to all who wield;
Golden and sanguine laws which tempt and slay;
Religion Christless, Godless—a book sealed;
A senate, Time's worst statute, unrepealed—

Are graves from which a glorious Phantom may
Burst, to illumine our tempestuous day.

This sonnet, with the rhyme scheme of a b a b a b c d c d c c d d manipulates the traditional sonnet form. The two sestets followed by a volta and rhyming couplet suggest a conclusion, even a solution, to the problems outlined in the first 12 lines. The main verb "Are" is delayed until line 13 indicating that the state of England in 1819 is one of postponed actualisation. The first six lines references the Hanoverian line, with its deference to hereditary order, conservativism and ignorance. This is in stark contrast to the drive for democratic principle across the channel in the French Revolution. The second sestet takes note of the people, the military, religion and government, who are responsible for the current political circumstances, including the Peterloo Massacre. The final two lines convey the last vestiges of hope found in the spirit of liberty.

In the first sestet, Shelley profiles King George III who reigned from 1861 to 1820. During his kingship the American colonies were lost in the American War of Independence and England managed to defeat Napoleon at the Battle of Waterloo. George III struggled with mental illness and was replaced in 1810 by his son, the Prince Regent: "An old, mad, blind, despised, and dying King;/ Princes, the dregs of their dull race, who flow/ Through public scorn." The alliterative plosives in "despised" and "dying", aspects of George III, are connected to those of the Prince in "dregs" and "dull". These are the characteristics shared by bloodline and loathed by the general public. They are likened to leeches, who live in a type of quagmire, secreting the life out of the country: "mud from a muddy spring…leechlike to their fainting country cling/ Till they drop, blind in blood, without a blow." The polyptoton of "mud" and "muddy" reflect, I daresay, a realistic early 18th century depiction of life in England but its repetition also reinforces the filth and dirt from which these Royals cogitate. England is seen as victim and this is asserted in the alliterative conjoining of a Kingship sucking the country's life blood. England is weak and unmatched to the pugnacious Royal determination, conveyed in the plosives: "blind in blood … without a blow."

The first sestet is framed by the word "blind", contained in the 1st and 6th line. George III did go blind and the well-known warfare between the Tories and the Whigs seemed blind to the plight of the average person. The great and emerging public art form of satirical cartoons circulated pictorial depictions that could be received, enjoyed and discussed across class. These cartoons were central to the shaping of democracy in England at the time. Following the footsteps of the great satirist, William Hogarth, the two prominent caricaturists were James Gillray and George Cruickshank who represented the Royals, Government and society with biting political wit. Gillray's paired plates *A Voluptuary under the Horrors of Digestion* and *Temperance Enjoying a Frugal Meal* convey the excess of the Prince of Wales and the miserliness of his father. *Plump Pudding in Danger* has Prime Minister Pitt carving the biggest slice of the world. *Two Green Bags* represents the public's disregard for the Prince Regent and his wife. Ludicrous, licentious, ribald and capricious was the depiction by Gillray of the Hanoverian line in this emerging and powerful art form that silenced the hitherto sycophancy of the press toward all things Royal. Meanwhile, the ridiculous fashions and tastes of the upper class continued to be lambasted by Cruikshank.

The second sestet of *England in 1819* focuses on the Peterloo Massacre. The "untilled field" is a reference to St Peter's field where the massacre took place; a croft or open piece of land. The sibilant connection of "starved and stabbed" records the horror of the day as the military "prey" on the defenceless. Consequently, Shelley makes an intertextual reference to Psalm 149 in the Old Testament which is a call to battle: "May the praise of God be in their mouths/ And a double edged sword in their hands … To bind their kings with fetters/ Their nobles with shackles of iron." The double edged sword in the Old Testament has been replaced by a "two-edged sword" wielded here by the military in the post New Testament days of Peterloo. Ironically, instead of the sword being taken up to "bind their kings with fetters" and "Their nobles with shackles of iron" the "army" is committing atrocities such as the destruction of liberty, "liberticide". Furthermore, the people of England have suffered under the Corn Laws, referenced in the "Golden and sanguine laws" and this remains "Time's worst statute, unrepealed". The tariffs and trade restrictions on imported food and grain enforced by the government between 1815 and 1846 resulted in crippling food shortages and high prices. These laws, upheld by the traditional and conservative Tories in power, supported the conservative landholders and were opposed by Whig industrialists and workers. The Corn Laws were not repealed until the commencement of the Irish famine. No wonder the power holders of this nation appeared as hypocrites, espousing Christian values while enforcing laws that seemed nothing but "Christless" and "Godless".

The final rhyming couplet speaks to the hope latent in the zeitgeist of their day. This "glorious Phantom" is the spirit of liberty and one that emerges from the sacrifice others have made, like those victims of the Peterloo Massacre. Liberty "may" emerge from the grave, hence the "Phantom". This lexical choice of "may" is indicative of the hesitancy and uncertainty experienced by England, longing to know the true tenants of democracy. The enjambment from line 13 into 14 is halted after "Burst". This expresses the violent breaking away from the England of the past in all its flabby ineptitude in order to find true enlightenment. This and only this will light the path out of the dark and "tempestuous day" of England in 1819.

Men of England by Percy Bysshe Shelley (1820)

Men of England, wherefore plough
For the lords who lay ye low?
Wherefore weave with toil and care
The rich robes your tyrants wear?

Wherefore feed and clothe and save
From the cradle to the grave
Those ungrateful drones who would
Drain your sweat—nay, drink your blood?

Wherefore, Bees of England, forge
Many a weapon, chain, and scourge,
That these stingless drones may spoil
The forced produce of your toil?

Have ye leisure, comfort, calm,
Shelter, food, love's gentle balm?
Or what is it ye buy so dear
With your pain and with your fear?

The seed ye sow, another reaps;
The wealth ye find, another keeps;
The robes ye weave, another wears;
The arms ye forge, another bears.

Sow seed—but let no tyrant reap:
Find wealth—let no imposter heap:

Weave robes—let not the idle wear:
Forge arms—in your defence to bear.

Shrink to your cellars, holes, and cells—
In hall ye deck another dwells.
Why shake the chains ye wrought? Ye see
The steel ye tempered glance on ye.

With plough and spade and hoe and loom
Trace your grave and build your tomb
And weave your winding-sheet—till fair
England be your Sepulchre.

There is a conversation between the sonnet, *England in 1819* and this famous eight quatrain call to arms, *Men of England*. Both are written while in Italy, which provided a distance to the economic, political and social plight of fellow English countrymen. The poet had deeply held convictions about the values of the French Revolution and how that might be the salvation for England. As a young man expelled from university, Shelley's parents despaired at his views bordering on radical; such as no free thinking intellect could believe in God, that vegetarianism was a spiritual and liberating way of life, sexual freedom should be the right of every man and woman, and the inalienable rights of man were contingent on the entitlement to live in safety, free from oppression. These views intensified throughout his short life. *Men of England* written in 1820 was taken up by the Chartists and Socialists alike and later morphed into the anthem sung by rebel animals in Orwell's *Animal Farm*. The division between classes, the haves and the have nots, remains a central tension within our society; thus, this stirring song, *Men of England*, still offers impact. Shelley's poem is responding to the untenable situation from which the Peterloo Massacre resulted: economic depression, harsh penalties to the Luddites reacting against the mechanization of their ancient trades, Corn Laws, unaffordable prices for basic foods, growing trade unionism, disinterested aristocracy and landholders, limited representation, a conservative Tory government and an unresponsive Royal family.

The power behind *Men of England* is in the use of repetition, whether it is in letters, sounds, syllables, words, clauses, phrases or ideas. The effect is to imprint a message on the listeners' minds; one that is arousing and seductive in its own rhetorical logic. Each quatrain is made up of two rhyming couplets, constituted by the repetition of the consecutive line's end rhyme. This is held together with the mesmeric beat of the trochaic tetrameter, four beats in a line commencing with the stressed syllable. In the first four quatrains we are given a variation of the query, for what reason should people remain enslaved? This is repeated six times. The anaphora of "Wherefore" is an archaic expression suggesting a well-established authority. The poet asks, why toil while they are oppressed by the owners of their production? Shelley considers the farmers, "wherefore plough", the weavers, "Wherefore weave" and the general laborer, "Wherefore feed and clothe and save/ From the cradle to the grave". This synecdoche for the life span of common man is impacted by the tyrannical "lords who lay ye low…Drain your sweat – nay, drink your blood". The rhetoric is arresting and demands the men of England to consider why they refuse to pay the price for liberty: "what it is ye buy so dear? With your pain and with your fear?" Shelley uses cumulative listing in the sarcastic first question of quatrain four: "Have ye leisure, comfort, calm,/ Shelter, food, love's gentle balm?" The worker is left without excuse.

Shelley is scathing in his criticism of the oppressive landowner tyrants, just as he is of the cowardly oppressed who refuse to rise up. This is post the Reign of Terror and still Shelley believes in the principles of the French Revolution. In the first half of the poem the reader is assured of the inequality between the classes in England, the lack of fraternity and the call to liberate oneself from the bonds of oppression. The phrase "Men of England" reconvenes as "Bees of England"; this exergasia amplifies the predicament of a country which is not one of men but of worker bees contributing soullessly to the colony. The metaphor of the English men and women as worker bees is repeated as a polyptoton in the aristocracy as "stingless drones". In the last four quatrains Shelley focuses on the call to liberate oneself from the bonds of oppression. Quatrain six is an inversion of quatrain five as well as an allusion to Isaiah 65:21-22 in the Old Testament: "And they shall build houses and inhabit them; and they shall plant vineyards and eat the fruit of them. They shall not build and another inhabit; they shall not plant and another eat; for as the days of a tree are the days of my people and mine elect shall long enjoy the work of their hands." In other words, in the temporal, the spiritual promises can and should be apprehended. Thus, the mighty are brought low and the lowly empowered. We find that the nouns that assert the truths of quatrain five, "The seed... The wealth...The robes...The arms" are reconfigured as verbs in quatrain six: "Sow seed...Find wealth...Weave robes...Forge arms." The call to action is a forging of arms against the oppressors' wrongs.

The final two quatrains are confrontational. They turn on the men of England and goad them into accepting the status quo. The sibilant congeries of "cellars, holes, and cells" offers a repetition of sound and words, of different meanings but with similar emotional effect, linking the idea of workers cowering in underground sites to the lords who dwell above them in the "hall ye deck" or have made beautiful. The stirring French Revolutionary anthem, *La Marseillaise* composed in 1792 by Captain Claude-Joseph Rouget de Lisle, is referenced in the provocative query: "Why shake the chains ye wrought?" Meanwhile, across the channel the oppressed men of France have risen up and proclaimed to their oppressors, "these vile chains/ These irons been long prepared...To arms, citizens/ Form your battalions/ Let's march, let's march!/ Let an impure blood/ Water our furrows". A far cry from Britain's own anthem, attributed to John Bull written a century and a half earlier, which calls on God to bless and preserve the monarch.

The enjambment between the penultimate and ultimate quatrain of *Men of England* contains the archaic term, "ye", three times, as if Shelley is casting a spell on the worker. He asserts, "Ye see/ The steel ye tempered glance on ye", in other words the workers have forged and shaped the possibility of their arms; moreover, the flash or gleam of light in the term "glance" implies their capacity for visionary enlightenment. All of which is dependent on courage. The traductio of "and" in the final quatrain's first line accentuates the effort of labor that seems only to be used to shape and dig their deaths: "Trace your grave and build your tomb/ And weave your winding-sheet—till fair/ England be your Sepulchre." The synonymia in "grave", "tomb", "winding-sheet" and "Sepulchre" amplify

Shelley's argument that if the workers persist without a revolution, death will be their only reward. This is a song that calls the workers to recognise it is late in the day and something must be done if they want to live their life rather than exist in slavery. If anything, *Men of England* is a rousing song for equality, fraternity and liberty.

Ode to the West Wind by Percy Bysshe Shelley (1819)

I
O wild West Wind, thou breath of Autumn's being,
Thou, from whose unseen presence the leaves dead
Are driven, like ghosts from an enchanter fleeing,

Yellow, and black, and pale, and hectic red,
Pestilence-stricken multitudes: O thou,
Who chariotest to their dark wintry bed

The winged seeds, where they lie cold and low,
Each like a corpse within its grave, until
Thine azure sister of the Spring shall blow

Her clarion o'er the dreaming earth, and fill
(Driving sweet buds like flocks to feed in air)
With living hues and odours plain and hill:

Wild Spirit, which art moving everywhere;
Destroyer and preserver; hear, oh hear!

II
Thou on whose stream, mid the steep sky's commotion,
Loose clouds like earth's decaying leaves are shed,
Shook from the tangled boughs of Heaven and Ocean,

Angels of rain and lightning: there are spread
On the blue surface of thine aëry surge,
Like the bright hair uplifted from the head

Of some fierce Maenad, even from the dim verge
Of the horizon to the zenith's height,
The locks of the approaching storm. Thou dirge

Of the dying year, to which this closing night

Will be the dome of a vast sepulchre,
Vaulted with all thy congregated might

Of vapours, from whose solid atmosphere
Black rain, and fire, and hail will burst: oh hear!

III
Thou who didst waken from his summer dreams
The blue Mediterranean, where he lay,
Lull'd by the coil of his crystalline streams,

Beside a pumice isle in Baiae's bay,
And saw in sleep old palaces and towers
Quivering within the wave's intenser day,

All overgrown with azure moss and flowers
So sweet, the sense faints picturing them! Thou
For whose path the Atlantic's level powers

Cleave themselves into chasms, while far below
The sea-blooms and the oozy woods which wear
The sapless foliage of the ocean, know

Thy voice, and suddenly grow gray with fear,
And tremble and despoil themselves: oh hear!

IV
If I were a dead leaf thou mightest bear;
If I were a swift cloud to fly with thee;
A wave to pant beneath thy power, and share

The impulse of thy strength, only less free
Than thou, O uncontrollable! If even
I were as in my boyhood, and could be

The comrade of thy wanderings over Heaven,
As then, when to outstrip thy skiey speed
Scarce seem'd a vision; I would ne'er have striven

As thus with thee in prayer in my sore need.
Oh, lift me as a wave, a leaf, a cloud!

I fall upon the thorns of life! I bleed!

A heavy weight of hours has chain'd and bow'd
One too like thee: tameless, and swift, and proud.

V
Make me thy lyre, even as the forest is:
What if my leaves are falling like its own!
The tumult of thy mighty harmonies

Will take from both a deep, autumnal tone,
Sweet though in sadness. Be thou, Spirit fierce,
My spirit! Be thou me, impetuous one!

Drive my dead thoughts over the universe
Like wither'd leaves to quicken a new birth!
And, by the incantation of this verse,

Scatter, as from an unextinguish'd hearth
Ashes and sparks, my words among mankind!
Be through my lips to unawaken'd earth

The trumpet of a prophecy! O Wind,
If Winter comes, can Spring be far behind?

It's interesting that Shelley chose such a stylized and controlled form, the ode in terza rima, to pen his apostrophe to the frenzied wild west wind. Instead of being thrown about and whipped into a tempestuous vortex we move through the highly designed passageway of the wind's effects on earth, sky and ocean. It is not until we arrive at Canto IV and V that we realise this is more about the poet than the wind; here, he begs to be the wind and as this is not possible to be the instrument that plays its song. Throughout, the wind is constructed as both life giving and life taking, creator and destroyer, the call to winter and to spring. Contextually, this was written in 1819 while living near Florence. Shelley and his wife, Mary, were grieving for the loss of their daughter, Clara who died in 1818 followed by their son, William in the same year. So perhaps this poem is about the state of grief that blows recklessly into one's life or the winds of revolutionary change howling across the channel. Moreover, this ode could be the emerging nascent role of poet as prophet who declares the dawning of a new age.

For me, *Ode to the West Wind*, is about the power of art and its gargantuan efforts to stay destruction despite the fact that art itself will eventually crumble and disintegrate. The metaphor of the Roman resort as ruins in Canto III, is emblematic of this very point. Moreover, this highly modulated ode made up of five cantos, each containing four terza rimas and one rhyming couplet, takes us to the one question asked in the entire ode: "If Winter comes, can Spring be far behind?" Indeed, this apostrophe to the wind disintegrates into a monologue that expresses the poet's machinations of distracted anxiety and dark uncertainty. This is what is so compelling and keeps us reading *Ode to the West Wind* centuries later. Not because it is another important witness to the political plight of Shelley's day and not because human grief attempts to make sense of loss with language. *Ode to the West Wind* still shakes us because the chaotic power of nature cannot be tamed, despite art's attempts to do so. In fact, its wild fierce spirit can eventually destroy art; hence, we are at its mercy.

Let's take a brief look at all five cantos and the way in which Shelley masterfully controls the uncontrollable, technically, but knows nature will not be tamed and we are slaves to its capricious will. In Canto I the poet addresses the power of the wind as it is witnessed across the earth. The autumnal wind is anthropomorphized and "drives" the "leaves", a word that occurs four times in the ode and is a homonym for both noun and verb. I think this is interesting because in many ways this is about the poet going away from what has been hitherto understood to something new and unsettling, hence his question at the end of the ode, which is a desire for reassurance. Shelley also uses three similes in the first canto to convey the powerful movement of the wind that is invisible: "leaves dead...like ghosts from an enchanter fleeing", "seeds... lie cold and low,/ Each like a corpse within its grave" and "Driving sweet buds like flocks". This interplay between death and life is established at the start because this is a seasonal wind and as such brings winter which can only lead to spring. Thus, the age old paradox is offered that in death there is life is recognised. The wind is the harbinger of action, it is an "enchanter", it moves everywhere and heralds destruction and preservation.

In Canto II we read of the effects of the wind in the "steep sky's commotion". It is one of those wonderful phrases richly aural and visual, suggesting a soaring maelstrom. From here the wind generates its havoc. Shelley takes the action of the autumnal wind driving the leaves in Canto I and moves it into a simile: "Loose clouds like earth's decaying leaves are shed,/ Shook from the tangled boughs of Heaven and Ocean." The pathetic fallacy of rain or dead leaves falling signal the end of what is known. Moreover, it is a force to be reckoned with as it commands the "Angels of rain and lightning." The other powerful simile used in this canto is when the poet compares the rain and lightning to the madwoman's hair: "Like the bright hair uplifted from the head/ Of some fierce Maenad." This reference to Dionysus' frenzied nymphs call to mind the Greek god himself and in particular his attributes of fertility and theatre. In many ways the ritual madness of the west wind every autumn makes the earth fertile for spring to flourish, the theatrical spectacle of this moment is captured in this ode. Finally the wind is heard as a "dirge/ Of the dying year" that will form a "dome" of night; indeed, this dark west wind will be the funereal song across "a vast sepulchre/ Vaulted" with its "vapours" causing "Black rain, and fire, and hail" to "burst"! Shelley's ode is written some 32 years after Coleridge's *Kubla Khan* and I think the influence is palpable.

The third canto is a centerpiece to this ode. In 1823, just a few years after Shelley wrote this poem, J.M.W. Turner exhibited *Bay of Baiae with Apollo and the Sibyl*. It is a luxurious composition that captures the erosion of architect against the undiminished beauty of nature. The narrative behind the painting is that the sibyl asked the god for eternal life, which she was granted but she unfortunately failed to request eternal youth. *Ode to the West Wind* is the same narrative in many ways.

It recounts the destruction of art in the face of the fierce and untameable spirit of nature. The poet retains eternal life in the making of this poem but can never achieve eternal youth, despite his early death. Shelley had met Keats three years earlier in 1816 through their mutual friend, Leigh Hunt, who remained a great advocate for their poetry. Keats wrote his *Ode to May* in the same year as Shelley wrote *Ode to the West Wind* and both poems reference this Romantic site: Baiae. Contained in Shelley's third canto is the ferocity of the wind across the ocean. Here the Mediterranean is aroused and subsumes Baiae, a fashionable coastal resort popular for licentious and hedonist lifestyles at the end of the Roman Empire. The first two and half terzas evoke the wistful, indolent and "Quivering" beauty of this place; a site "So sweet, the sense faints picturing them!" Yet the rest of Canto III conveys the terror and horror nature is capable of, as the wind causes the sea to rise up so that the inhabitants of Baiae "grow gray with fear,/ And tremble and despoil themselves". It was their fate to "know/ Thy voice" and it is ours to hear this outcome. Thus, at the end of Canto I, II and III we are left with a command: "oh hear!" As readers, we crane forward and hear the wind in the power of Shelley's verse.

Canto IV and V move from an apostrophe to a monologue. Shelley begins with hypotheticals of all he cannot be: "If I were a dead leaf... If I were a swift cloud... A wave... and share/ The impulse of thy strength." The closest he ever got to this state of liberty and untamed desire was in his boyhood, where to "outstrip thy skiey speed/ Scarce seem'd a vision" because it seemed possible. In contrast to those heedless days he now strives to reach out and pray in his "sore need". We hear his heart felt prayer: "Oh, lift me as a wave, a leaf, a cloud!/ I fall upon the thorns of life! I bleed!" The poet compares his suffering to the power of the wind, which can enslave us but is also "tameless, and swift, and proud". In Canto V, Shelley requests to be nature's musical instrument, in this way he could convey the beauteous melancholic note of autumn: "Make me thy lyre... Will take from both a deep, autumnal tone,/ Sweet though in sadness." This is a meta-poetic reference to the making of poetry. Then Shelley asserts that the "fierce" spirit of the West Wind is "My spirit! Be thou me". He knows that in being one with the west wind his thoughts, long after he is dead, will be driven "over the universe/ Like wither'd leaves to quicken a new birth!". The verb "quicken" refers to the life giving qualities that will metaphorically ensure the "new birth" of his musings. Versification itself becomes a magic charm that will "Scatter" the burning embers of his thoughts to inspire mankind. Caught up in the frenzy of himself as poet, Shelley's penultimate statement is that his poetry will be "The trumpet of a prophecy" as it awakens the world. To our modern ear it might seem a little fanatical but the importance of the role of the poet had already been laid down by Wordsworth. So why end with a question? The alliterative and assonate rhyme in "Wind" and "Winter" couples these two nouns in close proximity, so that "Spring" seems quite "far behind". We leave this ode hearing that melancholic tone of longing. The poet, like all of us, can only ask nature to be kind and preserve, for as long as possible, art and beauty.

Lines Written in the Bay of Lerici by Percy Bysshe Shelley (1822)

She left me at the silent time
When the moon had ceas'd to climb

The azure path of Heaven's steep,
And like an albatross asleep,
Balanc'd on her wings of light,
Hover'd in the purple night,
Ere she sought her ocean nest
In the chambers of the West. (1)
She left me, and I stay'd alone
Thinking over every tone
Which, though silent to the ear,
The enchanted heart could hear,
Like notes which die when born, but still
Haunt the echoes of the hill;
And feeling ever—oh, too much!— (2)
The soft vibration of her touch,
As if her gentle hand, even now,
Lightly trembled on my brow;
And thus, although she absent were,
Memory gave me all of her
That even Fancy dares to claim:
Her presence had made weak and tame
All passions, and I lived alone
In the time which is our own;
The past and future were forgot,
As they had been, and would be, not. (3)
But soon, the guardian angel gone,
The daemon reassum'd his throne
In my faint heart. I dare not speak (4)
My thoughts, but thus disturb'd and weak
I sat and saw the vessels glide
Over the ocean bright and wide,
Like spirit-winged chariots sent
O'er some serenest element
For ministrations strange and far,
As if to some Elysian star
Sailed for drink to medicine
Such sweet and bitter pain as mine. (5)
And the wind that wing'd their flight
From the land came fresh and light,
And the scent of winged flowers,
And the coolness of the hours
Of dew, and sweet warmth left by day,

Were scatter'd o'er the twinkling bay. (6)

And the fisher with his lamp
And spear about the low rocks damp
Crept, and struck the fish which came
To worship the delusive flame. (7)
Too happy they, whose pleasure sought
Extinguishes all sense and thought
Of the regret that pleasure leaves,
Destroying life alone, not peace! (8)

Maps artificially tame the power of nature. They articulate the utterable horror of wild sea swells and exhausting unconquerable rocky terrain. When you look at the west coast of Italy for example, the Ligurian Sea flattens the differential between the south of France, Monaco, Corsica and Italy. Lean closer and just north-west of Florence you will note La Spezia bay, which is bookended by Lerici and San Terenzo; the landfall is inked pale green in contrast to the map's ocean body of azure blue. La Spezia bay separates the township of Livorno and a small coastal village emerges called Viareggio. So, there it is. Serene colors coding the different shapes of water and land mass with the sites of habitation sprinkled in black print. Order and unity prevail not the madness of sea squalls and storms, nor the grief stricken pacing of shoreline as two women wait for the drowned. One month before his thirtieth birthday, on the 8 July 1822, Shelley was drowned at sea as he sailed home from visiting Lord Byron and Leigh Hunt in Livorno. Shelley, a keen boatman, had set sail that morning from Lerici in calm summer waters with a friend, Edward Williams, and a young English boatman, Charles Vivian. All were lost in the return journey. Mary Shelley and Jane Williams desperately waited for news in the Shelley's home, Casa Magni just outside San Terenzo for ten days. The remains of Shelley, Williams and Vivian were eventually found and a cremation performed on the beach of Viareggio. The Tory newspaper, the *Courier*, ran an obituary: "Shelley the writer of some infidel poetry, has drowned: now he knows whether there is a God or no."

The wide bay of La Spezia became known as the Gulf of the Poets, as artists, writers and composers gravitated to this little edenic enclave. Shelley rented Casa Magni and invited his friends Jane and Edward Williams, whom the Shelleys had stayed with in Pisa, to join them. Shelley envisaged a community of like-minded writers, thinkers and artists living together. At the time the Casa Magni was a dilapidated boat house, crowded and uncomfortable. Mary, just 24, had suffered a dangerous miscarriage in June 1822 and was still weak and depressed. Jane Williams, to whom Shelley wrote 11 poems including this one, became an object of inspiration and obsession. Her musical talents including playing the harp, flute and guitar as well as being an accomplished singer momentarily eclipsed the recuperating Mary. *Lines Written in the Bay of Lerici* is one of the last poems Shelley wrote and, in many ways, cannot be read without the foreshadowing of tragedy in his sudden and youthful death. The lyric is made up of 52 lines in octosyllabic, each line is made up of eight syllables, as well as couplets of iambic tetrameter. This poem is technically rich in enjambment, assonance, metaphor, simile and anaphora. It can be seen as part of a collection of poems

Shelley writes post his creative spurt the year before in Pisa, exploring the thesis expressed in his *To a Skylark*, that "Our sweetest songs are those that tell of saddest thought"; in other words, without tragedy and suffering there can be no great art.

There's a restlessness and brooding in the opening sentence of *Lines Written in the Bay of Lerici*. We commence with the poet abandoned to the plight of solitary contemplation; a state both dreaded and longed for if creativity is to be found. Indeed, the Romantic poet has taught us that the solitary state is necessary for contemplation. The personification of the moon that has "ceas'd to climb" and the sumptuous visual of the "azure path of Heaven's steep" offers us quietude and stillness which is further intensified by the simile in line four. Here the evening's atmosphere is likened to the legendary and fantastical "albatross asleep" while in flight "in the purple night". The stillness of the silence, moon and sleep background the brooding contemplation in which the poet finds himself.

The pursuit of ideal love, another tenet of the Romantic project, is conveyed specifically in the second sentence. The anaphora of "She left me" at the start of the first and second sentence intensifies his solitude. It is in this state that he is able to consider the art of "every tone" that enchants the heart "though silent to the ear". We learn from Greek mythology that the Muses are responsible for teaching Echo to play all manner of musical instruments on Mount Cithaeron. It is their inspiration that ensures the song or poem goes on for all to hear: "Like notes which die when born, but still/ Haunt the echoes of the hill." The muse is the uber ideal love and one who not only is the source of creativity but offers the poet succor and respite, conveyed in the next simile "As if her gentle hand, even now,/ Lightly trembled on my brow". Her power is such that even in her absence the muse is present. She is carried in his memory; thus, she is forever within him. Moreover, the ideal love is contingent on the beloved being absent because while she is present the lover is "weak and tame". Thus, the poet is strong and wild while his muse or beloved is far away.

Sentence three and four in this lyric engages with the Romantic notions of rebellion and non-compliance. Here the poet is locked in a state of solitude where the "past and future" have little effect on him; he lives in the contemplation of the present moment. Rather than be guided by the conventions and belief systems of his contemporaries, the poet rejects the authority of "the guardian angel" and embraces his enthroned "daemon". Indeed, it is in this state of darkness that the poet is able to contemplate his own rebellious heart pulsating faintly.

In *Lines Written in the Bay of Lerici* the power of the visionary imagination is conveyed in the 5th sentence. The poet watches "the vessels glide/ Over the ocean bright and wide". The track left by the passing boats become, in effect, the lines he makes on his page as a poet transcribing his solitary contemplation into a poem. He uses a simile here to compare these tracks made by the gliding vessels to "spirit-winged chariots", offering balm to the suffering. Shelley longs to be made one with the spirit of nature, a Plutonian idea where the tension between the mortal and immortal is resolved in this visionary space of nature. Thus, the vessels are traveling to discover an antidote for the bittersweet pain suffered by the poet. In sentence six, the wind is the cogent promise of change and continues this transition between the real and the magical, between the isolated contemplation and the muse inspired poem, seen in the first direct reference to La Spezia bay as "twinkling".

The final two sentence of *Lines Written in the Bay of Lerici* speak to the Romantic predilection of the untamed spirit in search of freedom. We have a singular presence of someone other than the poet: the fisherman undergoing his time-honoured pursuit of fishing on low rocks in the darkening twilight with a lamp. A solitary and quiet occupation. One that requires contemplation and consideration. In many ways the fisherman is the poet driven by his need and desire despite being vulnerable. Shelley's fancy is that the fish are lured to the light, just as poetic meditations are drawn to the inspiration of the muse. The flame is "delusive" because it leads to the capture and seizure of the free and untamed. Shelley knows that this pursuit of freedom comes at a price: peace and contentment. To be completely absorbed in the task at hand, contemplating nature or writing poetry or catching fish, is to extinguish "all sense and thought/ Of the regret that pleasure leaves". He knows that the pleasure enjoyed when the muse is with him eclipses the pain and regret, he will suffer when she leaves him. Hence the poet exists in a state that is bittersweet.

Lines Written in the Bay of Lerici is haunted by the commiserations of a poet contemplating the abandonment of his muse. Bereft of her inspiration he considers whether his ink will make tracks across his paper to poeticize nature and find medicinal ministrations. It is a poem contemplating the writing process and the price paid for those moments of quiet and pleasurable musing that leads to creativity. That Shelley looks over the very "ocean bright and wide", the site of his grave in less than a month, chills me to the bone. It's uncanny that a poet considers what it is to be bereft of his muse, to have lost all creativity and thus to exist no more, just three weeks prior to his own drowning, in the very sea he contemplates. This poem haunts me and makes me think about what it is to drown in self-doubt and rejection.

John Keats

To Autumn by John Keats (1819)

Season of mists and mellow fruitfulness,
   Close bosom-friend of the maturing sun;
Conspiring with him how to load and bless
   With fruit the vines that round the thatch-eves run;
To bend with apples the moss'd cottage-trees,
   And fill all fruit with ripeness to the core;
     To swell the gourd, and plump the hazel shells
   With a sweet kernel; to set budding more,
And still more, later flowers for the bees,
Until they think warm days will never cease,
     For summer has o'er-brimm'd their clammy cells.

Who hath not seen thee oft amid thy store?
   Sometimes whoever seeks abroad may find
Thee sitting careless on a granary floor,
   Thy hair soft-lifted by the winnowing wind;

Or on a half-reap'd furrow sound asleep,
      Drows'd with the fume of poppies, while thy hook
         Spares the next swath and all its twined flowers:
   And sometimes like a gleaner thou dost keep
      Steady thy laden head across a brook;
      Or by a cyder-press, with patient look,
         Thou watchest the last oozings hours by hours.

   Where are the songs of spring? Ay, Where are they?
      Think not of them, thou hast thy music too,—
   While barred clouds bloom the soft-dying day,
      And touch the stubble-plains with rosy hue;
   Then in a wailful choir the small gnats mourn
      Among the river sallows, borne aloft
         Or sinking as the light wind lives or dies;
   And full-grown lambs loud bleat from hilly bourn;
      Hedge-crickets sing; and now with treble soft
      The red-breast whistles from a garden-croft;
         And gathering swallows twitter in the skies.

What do you make of a poem that is held up as one of the most perfect lyrics in the English language? Academics, poets, students, essayists and journalists have all written eloquently about this poem offering their interpretation and arguing the toss with those who have gone before them. There is so much discussion, so much noise around *To Autumn*. If ever there was a poem in which you should be still and sit and read and listen to the poem itself, it is this one! I listen to others read it, I read it aloud myself, I write out the lines and then start all over again. I often just read one stanza over and over; allowing the soundscape to work its alchemy on me. On the one hand I have nothing to offer but the poem itself, but on the other hand all great art requires our discussion if it is to live. And it *is* a great work of art. It is like standing before Goya's *Third of May* or Picasso's *Guernica*. If you stand still for long enough everything else will drop away and it is you and this colossal masterpiece which was created just for you. Sadly for many, reading *To Autumn* by John Keats is like standing in front of da Vinci's *Mona Lisa* and being jostled from side to side by the selfie snapping crowd while gripping an audio guide where some art critic drones on and on or craning forward and spending more time reading the spiel alongside the painting rather than looking at the artwork itself. I think that great art belongs to everyone. Our challenge is to get inside and take up our own personal and individual residence. I also think that a great poem, like *To Autumn*, can be over scribed which can make you feel that this artwork is not yours and there is no space for you to inhabit. Well this is what I have found: great art will let you in, in fact it needs you to find your place or else eventually it will cease to breathe and to exist. So, lean in to this great poetic masterpiece and take up residence.

To Autumn was written in September 1819 before Keats was diagnosed with tuberculosis. He had trained as a surgeon but gave it up to devote his life to writing poetry. His walks along the River Itchen, while lodging in Winchester through the months of August to October, offered him a canvas upon which he composed this poem. Like many, he had been caught up in the revolutionary fervour associated the Peterloo Massacre of August 1819 which would later boil over into the 1820 trial of its inspiring orator, Henry Hunt. Meanwhile, Keats returned to London in October 1819 and became engaged to Fanny Brawne but continued to be plagued by financial problems. By this stage his beloved brother Tom has died from tuberculosis, in December 1818, and his other brother, George, has sailed for America. Poverty, grief and self-doubt are his bed fellows. Then in the summer of 1820 he was diagnosed with tuberculosis. So, taking the advice of others he traveled to Italy in November rather than attempt to survive another English winter. Finding rooms near the Piazza di Spagna in Rome he was harried by thoughts that he would never be the great poet he wanted to be nor leave an extraordinary legacy of writing. Keats suffered great bouts of doubt and depression while being cared for in Rome by his friend, the young painter, Joseph Severn. Thus, it is less than two years after he writes *To Autumn* that Keats dies. Of course, this poet who was ill, poor and dead at 25, is remembered as one of the great poets of the English language; indeed, in 1853 the renowned critic Matthew Arnold spoke of Keats being in "the school of Shakespeare". Does bio data matter? To understand the meaning of the composer's work, no. To stand in awe before the great masterpiece, possibly. Perhaps the potted biography makes us consider the shock and miracle of this creation, *To Autumn*, written at the age of 23.

In my own long and extensive ramblings, both in the northern and southern hemisphere, I have come to know the meditative quality resultant of being immersed in nature. A straight-forward botanical or geographical description is not enough and a sensory account will also fall frustratingly short of the natural world in which you become immersed. Yet somewhere between the wandering trance and the unfurling imagination is this experience which is singular, private and, without a doubt, sublime. *To Autumn* conveys the ambulatory rhythm of sound. One's pulse and corresponding footsteps correlate to this rhythm, present in the internal rolling sounds of "mists and mellow" as much as it is in the end rhyme of "sun" and "run". So this is a walking poem for me. One that has feet and pulsates in its iambic pentameter. I fill up on the luscious imagery the cornucopia spilling out of the first stanza: "to load and bless/ With fruit the vines ... To bend with apples ... To swell the gourd ... to set budding more." The excess of verbs explodes before your eyes and just when you think it cannot be borne, that the 11 line stanza will burst and drip off the page, Keats turns our eye to a world in miniature: the beehive. We become cognisant of the effect on the honey bees of this seduction of late summer in early autumn: "they think warm days will never cease,/ For summer has o'er-brimm'd their clammy cells." It is an endearing and glorious image that in turn assures us of the bounty of nature. The "fruitfulness" at the start of our rambles in stanza one has been fulfilled and "o'er-brimm'd" by the 11th line.

I am particularly interested in Keats' theory of *Negative Capability* and can see it at work in this poem. This theory suggests that man is capable of staying with uncertainties, mysteries and doubts, thus fact and reason need not be the immediate and instinctive response to experience. So, in stanza two we suspend disbelief and realise that we also have seen autumn in the bounty of her produce: "sitting careless on a granary floor... Or on a half-reap'd furrow sound asleep ... Or by a cyder-press with patient look,/ Thou watchest the last oozings hours by hours." I love this languorous and indolent season. It is not a recount of the facts of autumn but rather an imaginative response to the liminal in-between world of not summer nor winter. Keats argues that poetics is an engagement with the real via the imagination which in turn becomes a moment of transcendence. Indeed, the presence of the transcendent is represented in the autumnal breeze, invisible to the naked eye but utterly seen by the imagination: "Thy hair soft-lifted by the winnowing wind ... Drows'd with the fume of poppies ... like a gleaner thou dost keep/ Steady thy laden head across a brook." This is the aftermath of laboring. The autumnal season transcends exhaustion and offers restoration.

Keats identifies with the experience of autumn and allows it to speak through him. Thus, we hear his voice in the questions that opens stanza three: "Where are the songs of spring? Ay, Where are they?/ Think not of them, thou hast thy music too." While I may blithely say give me the nuanced darkness of an autumnal song over the too busy sounds of spring, I cannot help but note the poignancy in his questions and the tonality of grief, loss and yearning. Curiously, Keats' reassurance to himself, which immediately follows in the line below, requires repression as much as it requires assertion: "Think not of them, thou hast thy music too." I find this answer, just as I find the entire poem, consoling, even though it is being played in the key of some harmonic minor chord. That's how I hear this poem. Achingly beautiful and filled with unresolved intonation. Its echo haunts me long after it is read. This has got nothing to do with Keats' bio data because it has everything to do with the subliminal quality sound has on our emotions. In the final stanza of this lyric we are immersed in a soundscape that fills the very reaches of our soul. The backdrop to this moment is an exquisite John Constable cloud filled sky where the rosy wet sunlight breaks through and sets on the "stubble-plains". It's picture perfect. The musicality of the "choir" swells, it intones the "wailful ... gnats mourn" as much as the "lambs loud bleat". Lean in and hear the "Hedge-crickets sing and now with treble soft/ The red-breast whistles ... And gathering swallows twitter". It's pitch perfect.

I came *To Autumn* after I had already written a PhD on Seamus Heaney, met the man and managed a lifelong love affair with his poetry since my summer days. So, when I first read *To Autumn*, I heard Heaney. He and Keats both represent the natural world that emerges out of instinct and imagination as well as an authentic experiential moment. Heaney writes that he wanted a truthfulness in the life he poeticised, one that was grounded and reliable; thus, even as a young schoolboy he came to love Keats and in particular *To Autumn*. Heaney saw this lyric to be the "ark of the covenant between language and sensation". I think it is true. Keats' *To Autumn* does contain the treasures of God's word and presence. When we amble into his lyric, we witness a dynamic openness between the world and the soul; thus the world and the soul are transformed. It is this transformation which is the truth in Keats' poetry, in all poetry because it is grounded in human experience. Furthermore, beauty in great poetry offers entry to every rambler.

Ode to a Nightingale by John Keats (1819)

My heart aches, and a drowsy numbness pains
    My sense, as though of hemlock I had drunk,
Or emptied some dull opiate to the drains

One minute past, and Lethe-wards had sunk:
'Tis not through envy of thy happy lot,
    But being too happy in thine happiness,—
        That thou, light-winged Dryad of the trees
            In some melodious plot
    Of beechen green, and shadows numberless,
        Singest of summer in full-throated ease.

O, for a draught of vintage! that hath been
        Cool'd a long age in the deep-delved earth,
Tasting of Flora and the country green,
        Dance, and Provençal song, and sunburnt mirth!
O for a beaker full of the warm South,
        Full of the true, the blushful Hippocrene,
            With beaded bubbles winking at the brim,
                And purple-stained mouth;
        That I might drink, and leave the world unseen,
            And with thee fade away into the forest dim:

Fade far away, dissolve, and quite forget
        What thou among the leaves hast never known,
The weariness, the fever, and the fret
        Here, where men sit and hear each other groan;
Where palsy shakes a few, sad, last gray hairs,
        Where youth grows pale, and spectre-thin, and dies;
            Where but to think is to be full of sorrow
                And leaden-eyed despairs,
        Where Beauty cannot keep her lustrous eyes,
            Or new Love pine at them beyond to-morrow.

Away! away! for I will fly to thee,
        Not charioted by Bacchus and his pards,
But on the viewless wings of Poesy,
        Though the dull brain perplexes and retards:
Already with thee! tender is the night,
        And haply the Queen-Moon is on her throne,
            Cluster'd around by all her starry Fays;
                But here there is no light,
    Save what from heaven is with the breezes blown
        Through verdurous glooms and winding mossy ways.

I cannot see what flowers are at my feet,
      Nor what soft incense hangs upon the boughs,
But, in embalmed darkness, guess each sweet
      Wherewith the seasonable month endows
The grass, the thicket, and the fruit-tree wild;
      White hawthorn, and the pastoral eglantine;
          Fast fading violets cover'd up in leaves;
              And mid-May's eldest child,
      The coming musk-rose, full of dewy wine,
          The murmurous haunt of flies on summer eves.

Darkling I listen; and, for many a time
      I have been half in love with easeful Death,
Call'd him soft names in many a mused rhyme,
      To take into the air my quiet breath;
          Now more than ever seems it rich to die,
      To cease upon the midnight with no pain,
          While thou art pouring forth thy soul abroad
              In such an ecstasy!
      Still wouldst thou sing, and I have ears in vain—
          To thy high requiem become a sod.

Thou wast not born for death, immortal Bird!
      No hungry generations tread thee down;
The voice I hear this passing night was heard
      In ancient days by emperor and clown:
Perhaps the self-same song that found a path
      Through the sad heart of Ruth, when, sick for home,
          She stood in tears amid the alien corn;
              The same that oft-times hath
      Charm'd magic casements, opening on the foam
          Of perilous seas, in faery lands forlorn.

Forlorn! the very word is like a bell
      To toll me back from thee to my sole self!
Adieu! the fancy cannot cheat so well
      As she is fam'd to do, deceiving elf.
Adieu! adieu! thy plaintive anthem fades
      Past the near meadows, over the still stream,
          Up the hill-side; and now 'tis buried deep
              In the next valley-glades:

> Was it a vision, or a waking dream?
>   Fled is that music:—Do I wake or sleep?

Keats carries a wooden chair out of the parlour and through to the back garden of Wentworth House in Hampstead. He sits there in the fading spring night and listens to the nightingale in the thicket behind him. As the evening begins to set, he writes his poem. It is late April 1819. The year before, aged 21, he had taken a rambling journey through Scotland with his friend, Charles Armitage Brown. It was his friend's insistence that Keats stays in Hampstead at Brown's home and this is where Keats found himself enthralled by a nightingale's exquisite and complex song. This small, secretive and rarely seen bird has offered up its romantic melody for philosophers, composers and poets throughout time: Aristotle, Homer, Sophocles, Shakespeare, Beethoven and Tchaikovsky to name a few. The nightingale sings day and night throughout his short life, which is no more than three years. From this Keats offers us an odal hymn, a lyric that is stately in its representation of a divine creative power quite separate from the poet but one that the poet wishes to possess. Without a doubt, *Ode to a Nightingale* is a clear demonstration of Keats' capability to embrace doubt and mystery without searching for facts or reason: a Negative Capability tour de force. This poem considers the paradox of the nightingale as both fragile and vulnerable but at the same time immortal. It is the ultimate source of inspiration for the poet. Moreover, the nightingale's song becomes the poem we read. It is as if Keats has carefully transcribed the romantic melody, he experiences one spring evening. These 80 lines before us are the uber troubled pleasure Wordsworth wrote of in *Preludes*; here Keats wishes for his mortal self to die in order for him to become one with the nightingale. Indeed, this is what happened that spring evening. Keats sang his way into immortality.

Perhaps the longevity and textual integrity of *Ode to a Nightingale* is in its paradoxes which remain unresolved and forever rich. In stanza one the song of the nightingale is so acutely experienced it works its pleasurable alchemy as a poison might. The poet repeats three times that his state of happiness is the result of this "hemlock", this "opiate" which ensures "My heart aches, and a drowsy numbness pains/ My sense". The ode begins with the state of suffering rather than the bliss of happiness in witnessing this act of singing "summer in full-throated ease". This speaks to the paradox of longing for darkness in order to know light. The poet cannot achieve this same ease of immortal lyricism while living, thus he declares six stanzas later that he is "half in love with easeful Death". In stanza two he calls for an elixir to quench the thirst he has for immortality: "O, for a draught of vintage! ... O for a beaker full of the warm South." He knows that it is only by drinking deeply from "the blushful Hippocrene/ With beaded bubbles winking at the brim" that he can come alive as conveyed in the plosive power of the springs of Mt Helicon, sacred to the muses and source of poetic inspiration. Paradoxically, in drinking this inspiration and life he can "leave the world unseen, And with thee fade away into the forest dim." To become one with the iconic songbird and remain forever encased in legend is the song of immortality.

The self-abrogation of the poet, contained at the start of stanza three, mirrors how the society erodes the individual in line three: "Fade far away, dissolve, and quite forget ... The weariness, the fever, and the fret/ Here." Keats knows that it is mortality that ends all pleasure; thus, to become the greatest songster of all time would be to overcome the vulnerabilities of what it is to be human.

Stanza three is filled with the groans and "shakes" of the "spectre-thin" human whose very thought is filled with "sorrow...despairs" and the inability to know love "beyond tomorrow". At the start of stanza four, in a moment of grand hope, Keats asserts that in his fading "Away! away!" that he "will fly to thee...on the viewless wings of Poesy". He will become one with the legendary nightingale in the writing of this very ode and in so doing, be immortalised. This poet would, like "tender ... night" bring inspiration and life to the world in darkness but until this happens the poet laments "here there is no light". We are half way through this gorgeous ode where death and immortality is coveted, while nestling in the verdant "beechen green...sunburnt mirth...among the leaves ... and winding mossy ways". This contradiction is at the heart of his poem.

By stanza five we are fully cognisant of the paradoxes afoot in this ode: pleasure and pain, immortality and fragility, fertility and death, bird and poet, and the song of the nightingale and Keats' poem. So, while the poet "cannot see ... in embalmed darkness" he is more than capable of conveying "The grass, the thicket, and the fruit-tree wild;/ White hawthorn...pastoral eglantine...violets... The coming musk-rose, full of dewy wine." A veritable smorgasbord of sensory delight. This is an ode that sings of the promise of life and fecundity. The poet knows that it is only in listening to the darkness, his fears and uncertainties, the palsy that shakes his everyday world, that he can sing a song worthy of his death and immortality. Thus, in stanza six Keats states to that blackness within him: "Darkling I listen." He admits that he has been hitherto seduced by the drowsy promise of giving up this earthly life for immortality: "to cease upon the midnight with no pain." Indeed, such a surrender is possible while he listens to the unearthly beauty of the nightingale's song that pours forth his "soul". This final song from the bird would be the poet's "requiem". This conceptually proficient moment allows us to think about the conflation of the nightingale's divinity and Keats' poesy. They are one and the same.

The last two stanzas offer a final flourish of magnificence followed, like the song of the bird itself, by a gradual diminishing. The opening line of stanza seven can no longer be read as a single statement concerning the nightingale. Rather, it is the epitaph that should have been written on Keats' gravestone some two years later: "Thou wast not born for death, immortal Bird!" As we know his actual epitaph reads, "Here lies one whose name was writ in water". So, we are offered yet another paradox. In life it seemed he was awash with obscurity followed by an early death but in history he remains one of the most remarkable poets of the English language. As in this second last stanza, the meta-poetic reference to the nightingale's song opening the "casements ... on the foam/ Of perilous seas", speaks to the way in which Keats' own verse has the capacity to unlock our hearts. This poignant song is summed up in the last word of stanza seven and repeated as the first word of stanza eight: "forlorn ... Forlorn!" This plaintive cry reverberates in the triple utterance, "Adieu! ... Adieu! adieu!" as the nightingale "fades" away. Like the ghost of Hamlet's father, there is a theatricality in the act of disappearing into nothingness. The poem itself begins to shut down as we hear the nightingale's song diminish and contract: "Past the near meadows, over the still stream/ Up the hill-side; and now 'tis buried deep." We sit with Keats in the darkness of that spring night, trying to make sense of such beauty: "Was it a vision, or a waking dream? ... Do I wake or sleep?" A fitting end to a colossal song.

The Eve of St. Agnes by John Keats (1819)

St. Agnes' Eve—Ah, bitter chill it was!
    The owl, for all his feathers, was a-cold;
    The hare limp'd trembling through the frozen grass,
    And silent was the flock in woolly fold:
    Numb were the Beadsman's fingers, while he told
    His rosary, and while his frosted breath,
    Like pious incense from a censer old,
    Seem'd taking flight for heaven, without a death,
Past the sweet Virgin's picture, while his prayer he saith.

    His prayer he saith, this patient, holy man;
    Then takes his lamp, and riseth from his knees,
    And back returneth, meagre, barefoot, wan,
    Along the chapel aisle by slow degrees:
    The sculptur'd dead, on each side, seem to freeze,
    Emprison'd in black, purgatorial rails:
    Knights, ladies, praying in dumb orat'ries,
    He passeth by; and his weak spirit fails
To think how they may ache in icy hoods and mails.

    Northward he turneth through a little door,
    And scarce three steps, ere Music's golden tongue
    Flatter'd to tears this aged man and poor;
    But no—already had his deathbell rung;
    The joys of all his life were said and sung:
    His was harsh penance on St. Agnes' Eve:
    Another way he went, and soon among
    Rough ashes sat he for his soul's reprieve,
And all night kept awake, for sinners' sake to grieve.

    That ancient Beadsman heard the prelude soft;
    And so it chanc'd, for many a door was wide,
    From hurry to and fro. Soon, up aloft,
    The silver, snarling trumpets 'gan to chide:
    The level chambers, ready with their pride,
    Were glowing to receive a thousand guests:
    The carved angels, ever eager-eyed,
    Star'd, where upon their heads the cornice rests,
With hair blown back, and wings put cross-wise on their breasts.

At length burst in the argent revelry,
With plume, tiara, and all rich array,
Numerous as shadows haunting faerily
The brain, new stuff'd, in youth, with triumphs gay
Of old romance. These let us wish away,
And turn, sole-thoughted, to one Lady there,
Whose heart had brooded, all that wintry day,
On love, and wing'd St. Agnes' saintly care,
As she had heard old dames full many times declare.

They told her how, upon St. Agnes' Eve,
Young virgins might have visions of delight,
And soft adorings from their loves receive
Upon the honey'd middle of the night,
If ceremonies due they did aright;
As, supperless to bed they must retire,
And couch supine their beauties, lily white;
Nor look behind, nor sideways, but require
Of Heaven with upward eyes for all that they desire.

Full of this whim was thoughtful Madeline:
The music, yearning like a God in pain,
She scarcely heard: her maiden eyes divine,
Fix'd on the floor, saw many a sweeping train
Pass by—she heeded not at all: in vain
Came many a tiptoe, amorous cavalier,
And back retir'd; not cool'd by high disdain,
But she saw not: her heart was otherwhere:
She sigh'd for Agnes' dreams, the sweetest of the year.

She danc'd along with vague, regardless eyes,
Anxious her lips, her breathing quick and short:
The hallow'd hour was near at hand: she sighs
Amid the timbrels, and the throng'd resort
Of whisperers in anger, or in sport;
'Mid looks of love, defiance, hate, and scorn,
Hoodwink'd with faery fancy; all amort,
Save to St. Agnes and her lambs unshorn,
And all the bliss to be before to-morrow morn.

      So, purposing each moment to retire,
      She linger'd still. Meantime, across the moors,
      Had come young Porphyro, with heart on fire
      For Madeline. Beside the portal doors,
      Buttress'd from moonlight, stands he, and implores
      All saints to give him sight of Madeline,
      But for one moment in the tedious hours,
      That he might gaze and worship all unseen;
Perchance speak, kneel, touch, kiss—in sooth such things have been.

      He ventures in: let no buzz'd whisper tell:
      All eyes be muffled, or a hundred swords
      Will storm his heart, Love's fev'rous citadel:
      For him, those chambers held barbarian hordes,
      Hyena foemen, and hot-blooded lords,
      Whose very dogs would execrations howl
      Against his lineage: not one breast affords
      Him any mercy, in that mansion foul,
Save one old beldame, weak in body and in soul.

      Ah, happy chance! the aged creature came,
      Shuffling along with ivory-headed wand,
      To where he stood, hid from the torch's flame,
      Behind a broad half-pillar, far beyond
      The sound of merriment and chorus bland:
      He startled her; but soon she knew his face,
      And grasp'd his fingers in her palsied hand,
      Saying, "Mercy, Porphyro! hie thee from this place;
They are all here to-night, the whole blood-thirsty race!

      "Get hence! get hence! there's dwarfish Hildebrand;
      He had a fever late, and in the fit
      He cursed thee and thine, both house and land:
      Then there's that old Lord Maurice, not a whit
      More tame for his gray hairs—Alas me! flit!
      Flit like a ghost away."—"Ah, Gossip dear,
      We're safe enough; here in this arm-chair sit,
      And tell me how"—"Good Saints! not here, not here;
Follow me, child, or else these stones will be thy bier."

      He follow'd through a lowly arched way,

Brushing the cobwebs with his lofty plume,
And as she mutter'd "Well-a—well-a-day!"
He found him in a little moonlight room,
Pale, lattic'd, chill, and silent as a tomb.
"Now tell me where is Madeline," said he,
"O tell me, Angela, by the holy loom
Which none but secret sisterhood may see,
When they St. Agnes' wool are weaving piously."

"St. Agnes! Ah! it is St. Agnes' Eve—
Yet men will murder upon holy days:
Thou must hold water in a witch's sieve,
And be liege-lord of all the Elves and Fays,
To venture so: it fills me with amaze
To see thee, Porphyro!—St. Agnes' Eve!
God's help! my lady fair the conjuror plays
This very night: good angels her deceive!
But let me laugh awhile, I've mickle time to grieve."

Feebly she laugheth in the languid moon,
While Porphyro upon her face doth look,
Like puzzled urchin on an aged crone
Who keepeth clos'd a wond'rous riddle-book,
As spectacled she sits in chimney nook.
But soon his eyes grew brilliant, when she told
His lady's purpose; and he scarce could brook
Tears, at the thought of those enchantments cold,
And Madeline asleep in lap of legends old.

Sudden a thought came like a full-blown rose,
Flushing his brow, and in his pained heart
Made purple riot: then doth he propose
A stratagem, that makes the beldame start:
"A cruel man and impious thou art:
Sweet lady, let her pray, and sleep, and dream
Alone with her good angels, far apart
From wicked men like thee. Go, go!—I deem
Thou canst not surely be the same that thou didst seem."

"I will not harm her, by all saints I swear,"
Quoth Porphyro: "O may I ne'er find grace

When my weak voice shall whisper its last prayer,
   If one of her soft ringlets I displace,
   Or look with ruffian passion in her face:
   Good Angela, believe me by these tears;
   Or I will, even in a moment's space,
   Awake, with horrid shout, my foemen's ears,
And beard them, though they be more fang'd than wolves and bears."

   "Ah! why wilt thou affright a feeble soul?
   A poor, weak, palsy-stricken, churchyard thing,
   Whose passing-bell may ere the midnight toll;
   Whose prayers for thee, each morn and evening,
   Were never miss'd."—Thus plaining, doth she bring
   A gentler speech from burning Porphyro;
   So woful, and of such deep sorrowing,
   That Angela gives promise she will do
Whatever he shall wish, betide her weal or woe.

   Which was, to lead him, in close secrecy,
   Even to Madeline's chamber, and there hide
   Him in a closet, of such privacy
   That he might see her beauty unespy'd,
   And win perhaps that night a peerless bride,
   While legion'd faeries pac'd the coverlet,
   And pale enchantment held her sleepy-ey'd.
   Never on such a night have lovers met,
Since Merlin paid his Demon all the monstrous debt.

   "It shall be as thou wishest," said the Dame:
   "All cates and dainties shall be stored there
   Quickly on this feast-night: by the tambour frame
   Her own lute thou wilt see: no time to spare,
   For I am slow and feeble, and scarce dare
   On such a catering trust my dizzy head.
   Wait here, my child, with patience; kneel in prayer
   The while: Ah! thou must needs the lady wed,
Or may I never leave my grave among the dead."

   So saying, she hobbled off with busy fear.
   The lover's endless minutes slowly pass'd;
   The dame return'd, and whisper'd in his ear

To follow her; with aged eyes aghast
From fright of dim espial. Safe at last,
Through many a dusky gallery, they gain
The maiden's chamber, silken, hush'd, and chaste;
Where Porphyro took covert, pleas'd amain.
His poor guide hurried back with agues in her brain.

Her falt'ring hand upon the balustrade,
Old Angela was feeling for the stair,
When Madeline, St. Agnes' charmed maid,
Rose, like a mission'd spirit, unaware:
With silver taper's light, and pious care,
She turn'd, and down the aged gossip led
To a safe level matting. Now prepare,
Young Porphyro, for gazing on that bed;
She comes, she comes again, like ring-dove fray'd and fled.

Out went the taper as she hurried in;
Its little smoke, in pallid moonshine, died:
She clos'd the door, she panted, all akin
To spirits of the air, and visions wide:
No uttered syllable, or, woe betide!
But to her heart, her heart was voluble,
Paining with eloquence her balmy side;
As though a tongueless nightingale should swell
Her throat in vain, and die, heart-stifled, in her dell.

A casement high and triple-arch'd there was,
All garlanded with carven imag'ries
Of fruits, and flowers, and bunches of knot-grass,
And diamonded with panes of quaint device,
Innumerable of stains and splendid dyes,
As are the tiger-moth's deep-damask'd wings;
And in the midst, 'mong thousand heraldries,
And twilight saints, and dim emblazonings,
A shielded scutcheon blush'd with blood of queens and kings.

Full on this casement shone the wintry moon,
And threw warm gules on Madeline's fair breast,
As down she knelt for heaven's grace and boon;
Rose-bloom fell on her hands, together prest,

      And on her silver cross soft amethyst,
      And on her hair a glory, like a saint:
      She seem'd a splendid angel, newly drest,
      Save wings, for heaven:—Porphyro grew faint:
She knelt, so pure a thing, so free from mortal taint.

      Anon his heart revives: her vespers done,
      Of all its wreathed pearls her hair she frees;
      Unclasps her warmed jewels one by one;
      Loosens her fragrant boddice; by degrees
      Her rich attire creeps rustling to her knees:
      Half-hidden, like a mermaid in sea-weed,
      Pensive awhile she dreams awake, and sees,
      In fancy, fair St. Agnes in her bed,
But dares not look behind, or all the charm is fled.

      Soon, trembling in her soft and chilly nest,
      In sort of wakeful swoon, perplex'd she lay,
      Until the poppied warmth of sleep oppress'd
      Her soothed limbs, and soul fatigued away;
      Flown, like a thought, until the morrow-day;
      Blissfully haven'd both from joy and pain;
      Clasp'd like a missal where swart Paynims pray;
      Blinded alike from sunshine and from rain,
As though a rose should shut, and be a bud again.

      Stol'n to this paradise, and so entranced,
      Porphyro gaz'd upon her empty dress,
      And listen'd to her breathing, if it chanced
      To wake into a slumberous tenderness;
      Which when he heard, that minute did he bless,
      And breath'd himself: then from the closet crept,
      Noiseless as fear in a wide wilderness,
      And over the hush'd carpet, silent, stept,
And 'tween the curtains peep'd, where, lo!—how fast she slept.

      Then by the bed-side, where the faded moon
      Made a dim, silver twilight, soft he set
      A table, and, half anguish'd, threw thereon
      A cloth of woven crimson, gold, and jet:—
      O for some drowsy Morphean amulet!

The boisterous, midnight, festive clarion,
The kettle-drum, and far-heard clarinet,
Affray his ears, though but in dying tone:—
The hall door shuts again, and all the noise is gone.

And still she slept an azure-lidded sleep,
In blanched linen, smooth, and lavender'd,
While he forth from the closet brought a heap
Of candied apple, quince, and plum, and gourd;
With jellies soother than the creamy curd,
And lucent syrops, tinct with cinnamon;
Manna and dates, in argosy transferr'd
From Fez; and spiced dainties, every one,
From silken Samarcand to cedar'd Lebanon.

These delicates he heap'd with glowing hand
On golden dishes and in baskets bright
Of wreathed silver: sumptuous they stand
In the retired quiet of the night,
Filling the chilly room with perfume light.—
"And now, my love, my seraph fair, awake!
Thou art my heaven, and I thine eremite:
Open thine eyes, for meek St. Agnes' sake,
Or I shall drowse beside thee, so my soul doth ache."

Thus whispering, his warm, unnerved arm
Sank in her pillow. Shaded was her dream
By the dusk curtains:—'twas a midnight charm
Impossible to melt as iced stream:
The lustrous salvers in the moonlight gleam;
Broad golden fringe upon the carpet lies:
It seem'd he never, never could redeem
From such a stedfast spell his lady's eyes;
So mus'd awhile, entoil'd in woofed phantasies.

Awakening up, he took her hollow lute,—
Tumultuous,—and, in chords that tenderest be,
He play'd an ancient ditty, long since mute,
In Provence call'd, "La belle dame sans mercy":
Close to her ear touching the melody;—
Wherewith disturb'd, she utter'd a soft moan:

> He ceas'd—she panted quick—and suddenly
> Her blue affrayed eyes wide open shone:
> Upon his knees he sank, pale as smooth-sculptured stone.
>
> Her eyes were open, but she still beheld,
> Now wide awake, the vision of her sleep:
> There was a painful change, that nigh expell'd
> The blisses of her dream so pure and deep
> At which fair Madeline began to weep,
> And moan forth witless words with many a sigh;
> While still her gaze on Porphyro would keep;
> Who knelt, with joined hands and piteous eye,
> Fearing to move or speak, she look'd so dreamingly.
>
> "Ah, Porphyro!" said she, "but even now
> Thy voice was at sweet tremble in mine ear,
> Made tuneable with every sweetest vow;
> And those sad eyes were spiritual and clear:
> How chang'd thou art! how pallid, chill, and drear!
> Give me that voice again, my Porphyro,
> Those looks immortal, those complainings dear!
> Oh leave me not in this eternal woe,
> For if thy diest, my Love, I know not where to go."
>
> Beyond a mortal man impassion'd far
> At these voluptuous accents, he arose
> Ethereal, flush'd, and like a throbbing star
> Seen mid the sapphire heaven's deep repose;
> Into her dream he melted, as the rose
> Blendeth its odour with the violet,—
> Solution sweet: meantime the frost-wind blows
> Like Love's alarum pattering the sharp sleet
> Against the window-panes; St. Agnes' moon hath set.
>
> 'Tis dark: quick pattereth the flaw-blown sleet:
> "This is no dream, my bride, my Madeline!"
> 'Tis dark: the iced gusts still rave and beat:
> "No dream, alas! alas! and woe is mine!
> Porphyro will leave me here to fade and pine.—
> Cruel! what traitor could thee hither bring?
> I curse not, for my heart is lost in thine,

Though thou forsakest a deceived thing;—
A dove forlorn and lost with sick unpruned wing."

"My Madeline! sweet dreamer! lovely bride!
Say, may I be for aye thy vassal blest?
Thy beauty's shield, heart-shap'd and vermeil dyed?
Ah, silver shrine, here will I take my rest
After so many hours of toil and quest,
A famish'd pilgrim,—sav'd by miracle.
Though I have found, I will not rob thy nest
Saving of thy sweet self; if thou think'st well
To trust, fair Madeline, to no rude infidel.

"Hark! 'tis an elfin-storm from faery land,
Of haggard seeming, but a boon indeed:
Arise—arise! the morning is at hand;—
The bloated wassaillers will never heed:—
Let us away, my love, with happy speed;
There are no ears to hear, or eyes to see,—
Drown'd all in Rhenish and the sleepy mead:
Awake! arise! my love, and fearless be,
For o'er the southern moors I have a home for thee."

She hurried at his words, beset with fears,
For there were sleeping dragons all around,
At glaring watch, perhaps, with ready spears—
Down the wide stairs a darkling way they found.—
In all the house was heard no human sound.
A chain-droop'd lamp was flickering by each door;
The arras, rich with horseman, hawk, and hound,
Flutter'd in the besieging wind's uproar;
And the long carpets rose along the gusty floor.

They glide, like phantoms, into the wide hall;
Like phantoms, to the iron porch, they glide;
Where lay the Porter, in uneasy sprawl,
With a huge empty flaggon by his side:
The wakeful bloodhound rose, and shook his hide,
But his sagacious eye an inmate owns:
By one, and one, the bolts full easy slide:—
The chains lie silent on the footworn stones;—

The key turns, and the door upon its hinges groans.

> And they are gone: ay, ages long ago
> These lovers fled away into the storm.
> That night the Baron dreamt of many a woe,
> And all his warrior-guests, with shade and form
> Of witch, and demon, and large coffin-worm,
> Were long be-nightmar'd. Angela the old
> Died palsy-twitch'd, with meagre face deform;
> The Beadsman, after thousand aves told,
> For aye unsought for slept among his ashes cold.

We begin this dramatic ballad in a wintery rocky outcrop, upon which sits a medieval castle keep, with the ferocious black winds smashing against the fortification. The harrowing night offers no respite: we spy a ruffled owl freezing, a hare limping across frozen ground and silent sheep huddling in the icy roar. No one would brave this dark and merciless mid-winter night. We are drawn into the castle to take our own shelter and warmth alongside huge roasting fires with the Baron's kinsmen, knights and ladies. It is the eve of St Agnes and the feasting and dancing is illuminated by candle light. The exuberant crowd is protected from the dire cold, the darkness and the outside. Inside, revelry is made by the friends of the great Baron. Safety is assured because the entrances are bolted and sealed to any intruders. We rub shoulders with the revellers, the Baron, his beautiful daughter Madeline and an old dame.

Below the merriment and carousing, in the basement of the castle, is an old man moving about, out of sight and ear shot. This is the Beadsman. He makes no noise save the soft muffle of his old bare feet, torn tunic and wooden rosary beads that he thumbs as he ambles through the stone chapel. His breath is frosted. In his hungry act of penitence, he stumbles past tombs of the Baron's ancestors. Dust to dust, ashes to ashes. He knows his own death bell tolls. We follow him as he moves up out of the lower ground floor, past the great hall in which the evening is being celebrated. He does not stop. In our peripheral vision we notice that a few doors remain ajar because of all the coming and going of servants and guests. The beadsman has vanished and we are left in the outer hall, quite a distance from the celebrations. Look up. Carved high in the rough walls just beneath the cornices are angels. They seem to be watching over the grand entrance with an eagerness that is both assuring and disturbing. The angels' wings are still across their breasts but their hair is blown back, as if alarmed.

This ballad or narrative poem is written in 42 Spenserian stanzas with the rhyming scheme of a, b, a, b, b, c, b, c, c. The stanzas are nine lines each, the first eight are in iambic pentameter and the 9th is an Alexandrine line in iambic hexameter. This last line is more difficult to write and to hear, because English is a stress timed language and the hexameter relies on the regular timing of phonetic sounds. The title of the poem tells us that this is about heightened anticipation: the eve or night before. It is about the prelude to the grand rhapsody or the antechamber to the mansion. It well may be the orientation and conflict of a narrative but certainly not the dénouement or resolution. Keats poem was written in the wintery January of 1819 while living in Hampstead and is part of a poetic conversation concerned with the proximity between passion and death; as seen in Spenser's *The Faerie Queen*, Shakespeare's *Romeo and Juliet* and Coleridge's *Christabel*. *The Eve of Saint Agnes* was then taken up by the Pre Raphaelites and became a subject of painting and etching by Millais, Holman Hunt and Siddal.

The closeness between death and erotica, or simply the fully lived moment of passion that promises both love and suffering, becomes highly charged when experienced by the young. The fascination with this coupling of erotica and death is there in the story of St Agnes, Madeline and Fanny Brawne. The Italian Saint Agnes a third century virgin was raped, tortured and killed because of her passionate desire to be a bride of Christ and not that of the Roman Prefect's son. She was 13. Madeline, who we meet in Keats' poem, is swept up in the folklore concerning the eve of St Agnes, which occurs on the 20 January. A maiden could dream her lover to her on this night if she fasted, lay naked upon her bed, placed her hands behind her pillow and looked heavenward. If the ritual was followed, he would appear, offer her a feast, kiss her and promise marriage. What wasn't mentioned to poor Madeline was that this passionate vision would also result in the threat of death as her lover's mortal enemy is her kinsmen and their escape leads them into the grip of this deadly storm. Hence, the denouement and resolution aren't looking too good!

Finally, folded into this poetic fascination of erotica and death is Keats' own longing and object of desire, Fanny Brawne. They had met a few months before, in 1818, and Keats had already declared his undying love. That Fanny chose proximity to the tubercular ridden and poverty stricken Keats family, where the prospect of death was more realistic than that of a consummated marriage, makes their tale of love as emotionally charged as that of Madeline and Porphyro or Agnes and her Christ. In many ways *The Eve of St Agnes* is an examination of the high risks associated with desire. Indeed, the coming together of opposites can have troubling consequences: St Agnes and Christ, Madeline and Porphyro, Fanny and Keats, the eve of anticipation and the morning of acknowledgement, the Baron and his foe, the winter night outside and the warm illumination inside, Paganism and Christianity, virginity and conjugal knowledge, the beadsman and the old dame, witches and angels, love and war, outsider and insider, and erotica and death.

Let's look closer at *The Eve of St Agnes*. This ballad is a rich nest of character tales that sit one within the next. So, we commence with the Beadsman; sitting inside his tale is that of the Beldame; within her tale is the Baron's; within his story nests that of Porphyro; inside Porphyro's narrative is Madeline's; and held inside Madeline's tale is St Agnes. The beadsman represents the contrite heart and frames the entire narrative; the opening four stanzas are focused on his travails and the last two lines at the very end of the poem leaves us with his death. Typical of the medieval religious practices, the Beadsman was employed to do penance for the Baron and his family: "Rough ashes sat he for his soul's reprieve,/ And all night kept awake, for sinners' sake to grieve." In this act of suffering he and those he prays for will know great love. He keeps vigil within the deadly cold of the castle's crypt: "The sculptur'd dead, on each side, seem to freeze,/ Emprison'd in black, purgatorial rails." In many ways it can be assumed that these deceased ancestors are part of a dark and hellish past and do not yet know salvation. The purpose of the Beadsman is to give witness to transgression and to pray for salvation. Long after this infamous eve of St Agnes the Beadsman is found at the end of the poem "among his ashes cold". In other words, gone is the holy man who will keep vigil and gone is penitence for acts of transgressions. From the start, the presence of the Beadsman alerts us to a past and present riddled by transgression and greatly in need of redemption.

Nestled immediately within the Beadsman's tale is that of the Beldame. She is the old woman, the aged creature, the Gossip, the crone: "weak in body and in soul." Curiously, she is named after the angels, "Angela", despite violating her duty of care to the maiden, Madeline. She is lively, fearless and her role it is to illuminate the reader of the existing conflict between the lover and the beloved: "Mercy, Porphyro! Hie thee from this place;/ They are all here tonight, the whole bloodthirsty race!" This age old tale is brought back to life by Angela who is swept up in Porphyro's reckless passion: "Thou must hold water in a witch's sieve,/ And be liege-lord of all the Elves and Fays/ To venture so: it fills me with amaze." Paganism crosshatches this tale concerned with Christian penitence and vigils. Angela considers Porphyro's courage to be the result of something other worldly, impossible and not altogether benevolent. Rather than warn the Baron or even Madeline of Porphyro's intrusion the Beldame considers how the "good angels" are about to play a trick upon the maiden who is "asleep in lap of legends old".

So, the Beldame aids and abets this invader to the young virgin's bedchamber. Despite narrating herself as "A poor, weak, palsy-stricken, churchyard-thing,/ Whose passing-bell may ere the midnight toll", Angela is less concerned about conducting herself as a God fearing Christian and more concerned with doing "Whatever he shall wish, betide her weal or woe". Angela's tale constitutes nearly half the poem: she dominates and drives the plot from stanzas 11 to 22 and appears again in the final stanza. In fact, in the 4th and 3rd last line of the poem we read that "Angela the old/ Died palsy-twitch'd, with meagre face deform". Thus, she is punished for the role she played in this narrative. Do we assume Porphyro met a similar end because he is the archetypal intruder, voyeur, seducer and abductor? Somehow, I think not.

The Baron's tale, nestled within Angela's story, is one of woe. He fails to protect his precious daughter; he fails to keep out his mortal enemy and he fails to find redemptive peace. The Baron makes possible the revelry on St Agnes' Eve, as well as employing a Beadsman to conduct penitential prayer for his family. His beneficiary goodness ensures the livelihood of those within just as his malevolent relationship with his existing enemy endangers his own flesh and blood. According to his enemy's perception, the Baron's court is made up of "barbarian hordes,/ Hyena foemen, and hot-blooded lords". Thus, they are regarded as uncivilised, brutish and animalistic. While on the one hand the Baron's court is filled with "many a tiptoe, amorous cavalier" on the other hand we hear of vengeance: "dwarfish Hildebrand;/ He had a fever late, and in that fit/ He cursed thee and thine." The Baron's very castle is a site of transgression: hospitality and vengeance, chivalry and violence, and protection and rebellion. In the final stanza of the poem, where these key players come to rest, we read of the Baron's disturbing vision: "That night the Baron dreamt of many a woe,/ And all his warrior-guests, with shade and form/ Of witch, and demon, and large coffin-worm,/ Were long be-nightmar'd." Surrounded by the spectres of his once mighty stronghold, the Baron's future is a promise of ongoing misery and eternal damnation. Is this his punishment because he failed to erase discord and transgression?

Porphyro's tale is nestled within the Baron's. He exists as an outsider and enemy. Porphyro roams actively beyond and within the narrative that embowers Madeline, who of course is object and therefore passive to his decisive actions. He comes from "across the moors" to either fulfil Madeline's prayerful ritual or violate her maidenhood, depending on your perspective. We read that he bears a "heart on fire"; moreover, this heart of Porphyro is "Love's fev'rous citadel". So, in effect, Porphyro's heart is a microcosm of the Baron's mighty castle. Porphyro transgresses all rules and warnings because he is driven by this visceral desire pumping through his body: "Flushing his brow, and in his pained heart,/ Made purple riot." He hides within her bedchamber in a closet and watches as Madeline slowly strips. Despite growing "faint", he recovers sufficiently to watch the maiden who obediently follows the rituals on St Agnes' eve. Is this an act of deception or trickery or love? Keeping in mind that he is *other* and from "across the moors", it is not surprising that Porphyro lays out a feast with eastern excess and exotica: "Manna and dates, in argosy transferr'd/ From Fez; and spiced dainties, every one/ From silken Samarcand to cedar'd Lebanon."

Porphyro violates the codes of chivalry and does so with disturbing calm: "his warm, unnerved arm,/ Sank in her pillow." He allows himself to become "entiol'd in woofed phantasies". This refers to his ravenous appetite and lust which will inevitably end in the death of Madeline's maidenhead. By stanza 36 the deed is done in that the proximity between erotica and death is narrowed in the consummation of Poryphro's conscious desire and Madeline's dream: "like a throbbing star…Into her dream he melted, as the rose/ Blendeth its odour with the violet." Of course, Love's alarm sounds with the "frost-wind … pattering the sharp sleet/ Against the window-panes". Now time is of the essence: "St Agnes' moon hath set." Despite calling her his "bride", Porphyro works hard to calm Madeline. He assures her he is "A famish'd pilgrim, - saved by a miracle", technically this is incorrect because her violation was not made possible by divine intervention but rather by his deliberate intrusion. He insists they flee the castle and leave behind all she has known. They venture out into the dark and bitter cold of night. We read in the final stanza that Porphyro has made the impossible happen when he takes his beloved from the castle of his enemy into the unknown and tempestuous future: "These lovers fled away into the storm." So, it would seem that his tale does not end well.

It makes sense that Madeline's story nestles inside that of Porphyro. The virtues that Spenser spins his allegory around in *The Faerie Queen* are holiness, temperance, chastity, justice and courtesy. His epic poem gives witness to the efforts of some who attempt to transgress the rites and rituals of a righteous world. Keats' poem on the other hand is less sure of the battle between good and evil. Madeline seems to want too much of the world in which she lives. Her own imagination and salacious desires supersede the flattery and courtship of the knights at her father's castle. While her "maiden eyes divine,/ Fix'd on the floor" her hunger for the "honey'd middle of the night" leaves "her breathing quick and short". Madeline is a product of both Paganism and Christianity: she is both "hoodwink'd by faery fancy" while remaining "St Agnes' charmed maid". Is Keats suggesting there is a close proximity between Paganism and Christianity?

Madeline is talked about, but she says little. Madeline is likened to both a saint and a mermaid: in stanza 25 she kneels with a silver cross with her hair about her "like a saint". One stanza later she slowly strips nearly causing Porphyro to pass out: "Loosens her fragrant bodice; by degrees/ Her rich attire creeps rustling to her knees:/ Half hidden like a mermaid in sea-weed." We can smell her, hear her and see her. Keats places us in the closet with Porphyro and like him, we want more.

Madeline has become the uber object of desire. Out of 42 stanzas Madeline speaks only in stanza 35 and then again in 37. In the first instance she thinks she is still dreaming and frets for Porphyro's happiness; in the second instance she is awake to the transgression that has occurred and bemoans the death of her dream to be married. She is whisked away by the resourceful Porphyro with neither her consent nor her resistance despite the fact that she is "beset with fears".

At the heart of all this drama and trauma lies the story of St Agnes. This martyr knew only too well of the transgressions of others and died for her passionate conviction to be none other than the bride of Christ. Everybody's fate is somehow tied to St Agnes: the Beadsman must do "harsh penance on St Agnes Eve", the Beldame knows "it is St Agnes' Eve-/ Yet men will murder upon holy days", the Baron of course is haunted by the visitations of the dead on this holy eve, Porphyro calls upon Madeline to open her eyes "for meek St Agnes' sake" and Madeline herself thinks she sees "fair St Agnes in her bed". Therefore, at the heart of all these tales, experienced by various characters, is the abuse and death of a 13 year old girl, who is ironically venerated as an object of love. Indeed, Keats' *The Eve of St Agnes* explores what happens when sacred love becomes a hotbed of desire. Not even the deadly cold of a night in mid-January could cool that heat.

When I have fears that I may cease to be by John Keats (1815)

> When I have fears that I may cease to be
> Before my pen has gleaned my teeming brain,
> Before high-pilèd books, in denicer,
> Hold like rich garners the full ripened grain;
> When I behold, upon the night's starred face,
> Huge cloudy symbols of a high romance,
> And think that I may never live to trace
> Their shadows with the magic hand of chance;
> And when I feel, fair creature of an hour,
> That I shall never look upon thee more,
> Never have relish in the faery power
> Of unreflecting love—then on the shore
> Of the wide world I stand alone, and think
> Till love and fame to nothingness do sink.

The 22 year old who wrote this sonnet was stocky, healthy and athletic. He had passed his surgeon examinations 18 months beforehand and had not yet set eyes on Fanny Brawne. At the time of composition, he was living with his two brothers and developing a passion for reading and writing verse. His small circle of supporters and influencers included: Leigh Hunt, Charles Lamb, William Hazlitt, Percy Shelley, Charles Wentworth Dilke and Charles Cowden Clarke. This sonnet *cannot* be read as a lament for a life made altogether short by grief and tuberculosis and the longing for Fanny Brawne. At this point in time, Keats is neither frail, defeated nor consumptive. Granted that his indigent state effected every move he made, at the same time it is important to consider his tenacity, ambition and self-belief as a poet. I don't read this sonnet to be about death, his brother Tom was still alive, nor do I think he is referring to Brawne, as he had not yet met her. Moreover, when he wrote this sonnet, he had not shown any symptoms of tuberculosis. Reading poetry against the composer's bio data has never been my interest. Rather I read this sonnet as a contemplation of the verb *to be*. Like many 22 year olds, Keats is envisaging what and who he will be. This is about life, not death. It is about that wonderful egotistical self confidence that so many of us know in our early twenties. Keats believes the world is his and furthermore, he is called to make his mark upon it. He is chomping at the bit to be that great writer he feels he can be; someone who will be forever read and known. There is so much to say that he can hardly contain himself. This sonnet unequivocally articulates a young man's belief in his talent and purpose, not to mention his absolute faith in fulfilling his destiny as a poet.

This little pocket rocket has a lot more going on than first meets the eye. Keats follows the Elizabethan sonnet form; using iambic pentameter with three quatrains and a final couplet, all with the rhyme scheme of a, b, a, b, c, d, c, d, e, f, e, f, g, g. Expectedly, the octet sets up the conundrum which the sestet attempts to solve. Unexpectedly, this Elizabethan sonnet, in the hands of a young Romantic poet, contains not one but two voltas. It is written as one continuous sentence and thus this is one continuous unit of thought. Keats meditates on his "fears" that he "may cease to be" himself, but after the second volta he realises that it is precisely because he stands "alone" and thinks, that his undiluted true self will outlive careless love and idle fame. The one undivided unit of thought is that Keats is a singular undivided self. He knows that to be true to his talent and purpose is his only choice and destiny. In the first quatrain he explodes the pastoral metaphor of writing being an act of harvest: "Before my pen has gleaned my teeming brain,/ Before high-pilèd books, in denicer,/ Hold like rich garners the full ripened grain." His identity is contingent on the act of writing which is an idealised gathering of thoughts and sensations from his mind, ripening with imagination. These thoughts will be stored in a library of books which is likened to a granary after a rich harvest. You have to love him! He is 22 and has published some verse to negative review. Yet he is surrounded by believers! This was the age for young bloods and Keats is fearless, this is exactly why he can pose this hypothetical in the opening line and close it down by the second last line of the sonnet.

The second quatrain offers us the symbol of romance and changeability in the moon. Here he wonders what life would be like if he never got to poeticize the darkness and light of love's face: "I behold... night's starred face,/ Huge cloudy symbols of a high romance,/ And think that I may never live to trace/ Their shadows." The paired inversions of the darkness of the night and the light of stars, as well the moon and the darkness of cloud, all reflect Keats' ambition to gather and reap all that's beneath and above him; his immediate world and that of the universe will be his harvest. This is a sonnet written by a poet who desires to understand life, just as those did in Plato's *Allegory of the Cave*. The poet "traces" the reality as he believes it to be; hence he reads his own capabilities as "the magic hand of chance". So, the octet suggests he needs to be vigilant to the threats of not fulfilling his true identity. He must glean from his imagination and trace with his pen the darkness and light of life and love. At the ripe age of 22 he knows that a life where one's talent and purpose remain dormant, is a life not worth living.

His mediation continues in the sestet. Here he has two distinctly different people enter the sonnet as a way of disrupting his train of thought, the first one nearly derails him completely while the second reinforces his belief that the solitary cogent life of a poet, is a life that will outlive all others. The first entrant walks in midway through line nine and is the "fair creature of an hour", the second entrant walks in midway line 12 and is himself. In the first three and half lines of the sestet Keats contemplates the experience of unrequited love, the quixotic elixir of the poet: "I shall never look upon thee more,/ Never have relish in the faery power,/ Of unreflecting love." To suffer for the object of love will allow him to write poetry which will become "high-piled books". Therefore, the lover who has arrived in the middle of line nine morphs into the poet himself. Thus, the object of desire remains a means to an end because without a muse there can be no poet. Hence the em-dash in the middle of line 12 which in effect points to himself. In other words, all that has come before is the making of the poet. It is in this way that Keats intends never to cease.

As a final comment to this chapter it is obvious but important to note that reason cannot explain everything. The Romantic poets knew this as did other artists and thinkers of their time. Hegel teaches us that we make the most progress when we allow ourselves to create opposites and then attempt to combine them into a synthesis. In this sonnet we ponder on the one hand the idea of ceasing to be and on the other hand being alive to one's capabilities and drive. These two different ideas appear as binaries. In this one sentence sonnet Keats' offers a synthesis of these contrary ideas in suggesting that if he thinks and contemplates in solitude, while standing "on the shore/ Of the wide world", he will never cease *to be* but rather always remain himself. Keats believed it was his destiny to write poetry formed by solitary contemplation, sensation fueled imagination and heart felt engagement with his immediate world. The final rhyming couplet locks in Keats' truth: the poet's voice will live on, while "love and fame to nothingness do sink". Without a doubt this is a sonnet about one's full blown confidence, at 22, to be all one is destined to be. Thus, this is a sonnet about life!

6

A Singularness of Heart: Pre-Raphaelite Poetry

What *were* those Victorians up to? This chapter explores the poetry of the mid- to late-Victorian age and in particular the poetry of the Pre-Raphaelites. In the drawing room of John Millais' parents in 1848, the so called "Brotherhood" was formed by some painters, sculptors, and writers, young bloods of the Arts, including Dante Gabriel Rossetti, William Holman Hunt, and John Everett Millais. Their declarations included a number of things: to have genuine ideas, study nature attentively, to sympathize with what is direct, serious, and heartfelt in previous paintings, and to create *good* art. The Pre-Raphaelites and their followers pledged themselves against old brown paintings or art that was not aesthetically vivid, high modal, and engaged with the other worldly. They applied techniques of hyperrealism, a flattening of perspective, sharp outlines, bright colors, and close attention to detail, all of which strained the conventions of symmetry and proportions. Later, others would join them, including George Meredith, William Morris, Edward Burne-Jones, and George Swinburne. Their work focused on atmosphere, mood, and altered states of consciousness. Theirs was the generation of artists who picked up Theophile Gautier's 1835 phrase "l'art pour l'art", art for art's sake, and used it as their Bohemian creed, distancing themselves from the didactic and utilitarian functionality of their predecessors. In order to modernize art, they argued for the return to simplicity and sincerity. The Pre-Raphaelites poets were inspired by certain poems and the Bible, medieval romances, Arthurian legends, Ovid, Chaucer, and Shakespeare.

Was there a Pre-Raphaelite Sisterhood? Christina Rossetti and Lizzie Siddal offer their poetry to this artistic milieu of youthful rebels preoccupied with themselves and the creative process. The women in the Pre-Raphaelite circle were crucial to the work of the Brotherhood: as photographers (Julia Margaret Cameron), painters (Rosa Brett, Barbara Leigh Smith, Anna Mary Howitt, and Marie Spartali Stillman), and muses (Annie Miller, Fanny Cornforth, Jane Morris, and Marie

Zambaco). *The Germ*, a magazine published by the Pre-Raphaelites, pulled together experimentation with form as well as the collective efforts of these women and men. They believed in looking back beyond Raphael in order to revive art and create a future. The art critic of the Victorian era, John Ruskin, offered patronage and critical support to the work of these revolutionaries. To this day, the value of the Pre-Raphaelites is debated: were these poets, painters, illustrators, and designers forward thinking or retrogressive? Why do they continue to enthral and trouble us? They left behind an intensely rich tapestry of knights, goblins, female beauty, sexual yearning, and legends about artists' models such as Siddal lying in a bath of Thames water as Millais painted her while outside the February snow covered the city. The Pre-Raphaelites followed a zeitgeist that went against the grain of conformity, which was prized by the Victorian sensibility. Two great poetic influences on the Pre-Raphaelite poetry are *La Belle Dame sans Merci* by John Keats and *Lady of Shallot* by Lord Alfred Tennyson. Let's have a brief look at both.

La Belle Dame sans Merci by John Keats (1819)

O what can ail thee, knight-at-arms,
    Alone and palely loitering?
The sedge has withered from the lake,
    And no birds sing.

O what can ail thee, knight-at-arms,
    So haggard and so woe-begone?
The squirrel's granary is full,
    And the harvest's done.

I see a lily on thy brow,
    With anguish moist and fever-dew,
And on thy cheeks a fading rose
    Fast withereth too.

I met a lady in the meads,
    Full beautiful—a faery's child,
Her hair was long, her foot was light,
    And her eyes were wild.

I made a garland for her head,
    And bracelets too, and fragrant zone;
She looked at me as she did love,
    And made sweet moan.

I set her on my pacing steed,

And nothing else saw all day long,
For sidelong would she bend, and sing
    A faery's song.

She found me roots of relish sweet,
    And honey wild, and manna-dew,
And sure in language strange she said—
    'I love thee true'.

She took me to her Elfin grot,
    And there she wept and sighed full sore,
And there I shut her wild eyes
    With kisses four.

And there she lulled me asleep,
    And there I dreamed—Ah! Woe betide! —
The latest dream I ever dreamt
    On the cold hill side.

I saw pale kings and princes too,
    Pale warriors, death-pale were they all;
They cried—'La Belle Dame sans Merci
    Thee hath in thrall!'

I saw their starved lips in the gloam,
    With horrid warning gaped wide,
And I awoke and found me here,
    On the cold hill's side.

And this is why I sojourn here,
    Alone and palely loitering,
Though the sedge is withered from the lake,
    And no birds sing.

John Keats is writing this mesmeric ballad, made up of a dozen quatrains, in Wentworth Place, Hampstead. Fanny Brawne and her family have moved into a part of Wentworth Place, but Keats has already met her the year before while he nursed his brother Tom who was dying of tuberculosis. In 1819, Keats becomes unofficially engaged to Fanny after he completes *La Belle*, months afterwards he experiences his first signs of tuberculosis. Somewhere between his first and second serious haemorrhages, his engagement to Fanny is made official, and she nurses him until he decides to go to Italy in September 1820 to take up residence near the Piazza di Spagna in Rome; by February

1821, he is dead. He is 24 when he writes *La Belle* and 26 when he dies. Just imagine what poetry we would have had if Keats had lived to the ripe old age of 80, like Wordsworth (whom Keats met two years prior to writing *La Belle* at the immortal Dinner Party hosted by the painter Benjamin Haydon). I think about the young Keats sitting next to the stately Wordsworth, momentarily ignoring Haydon's painting *Christ Entry into Jerusalem* and discussing Coleridge's *Rime of the Ancient Mariner*. Why were they talking about this poem? Perhaps Charles Lamb, sitting opposite, had mentioned Coleridge's capacity to cast a spell. Keats meets Coleridge around about the time he writes *La Belle*. Professor of Anatomy at the Royal College of Surgeons in London, Joseph Henry Green introduced Keats to Coleridge for a meeting that lasted approximately two hours and was diarized by both poets. Coleridge resided at Highgate Hill, on the other side of Hampstead Heath. Keats and Coleridge took a walk where they discussed many things: poetry, sensation, metaphysics, dreams, consciousness, will, volition, monsters, and ghosts. Keats is veritably haunted by Coleridge's voice after that one encounter.

La Belle emerges out of the Romantic era during the Regency period, some 20 years prior to the birth of the Victorians and 30 years before the Pre-Raphaelites declare their intentions. *La Belle* considers what happens when one surrenders freedom, a heartfelt prize of the Romantics; moreover, it does this while exploring the medieval canvas of knights-at-arms, supernatural powers, and a creative integrity reflected in the observations declared by the observer and the observed. In many ways, I cannot read *La Belle* without thinking Keats is simply offering a condensed version of *Rime of the Ancient Mariner*. The unsuspecting Wedding Guest in *Rime* has been replaced by the poet in the first three quatrains of *La Belle*; the poet (who is also the reader) asks the questions of the knight-at-arms that we long to ask. Of course, the grey-beard loon, the ancient mariner, is the knight himself who recounts his cautionary tale as a way of explaining his loitering. Both the mariner and the knight are outriders. Their fate is to be hunted and to retell the tale for younger and unsuspecting passers-by. Both *Rime* and *La Belle* take place in nature. Here the sublime, in all its terror and beauty, is ever present, and sensation trumps reason. At the heart of this ballad is the femme fatale.

The first three quatrains of *La Belle* is the poet asking the knight what has caused this lifelessness. This archaic word "ail" and the chivalric role "knight-at-arms" immediately places us in a temporality that could well commence: a long, long time ago, in a land far away. In other words, it belongs to a collective Western imagination of battles against evil and champions of good that populated the Arthurian legends. In the first three quatrains, the all observing poet considers the symptoms of the knight's ailment: "Alone and palely loitering... lily on thy brow, / With anguish moist and fever-dew." One can't forget Tom, Keats' brother, who had died of tuberculosis just five months prior to writing this poem. Consumptives appeared pale, fever ridden, and sweat drenched while desperately hungry for breath. The backdrop to this young male in the grip of deathly longing is a landscape that prepares for the onset of winter: the season of death: "The sedge has withered from the lake, / And no birds sing." Here the poet notes that the rose of the young man's cheek is "fading" because his very life "withereth". Rather than imitate the busy squirrel who prepares for the leanness of winter, this knight has squandered his summer and has gone away with suffering: "woe-begone."

The next nine quatrains involve the knight-at-arms fixing us with his glittering eye as he recounts a tale fantastical. This is an ancient tale of desire and terror, one where the femme fatale uses her sexual allure to drag a man to his demise. Why? For the sheer pleasure that she can. This struggle between good and evil, between man and woman, between the real and the imagined, is at the heartland of all great stories. She is of course "a lady ... Full beautiful—a faery's child". Any woman with her hair out, living in nature, and with a certain untamed wildness to her very being is a dangerous threat. We are in effect wedding guests to this chilling marriage between the knight and the lady. In quatrain five, we read the seduction scene instigated by the knight: "I made a garland for her head, / And bracelets too...She looked at me as she did love, / And made sweet moan." I mean seriously, what was he thinking? How was this going to end well? I love the way the young knight assumes that the jewellery he makes for her from nature, manacled about her wrists and crowned upon her head, will result in declarations of love: a look and then a moan. La Belle is all freedom and sensation. His obsession with her is all consuming as he places her on his "pacing steed" which they rode "all day long". Such is his appetite, one that cannot be satiated, that he eats the fruit of her denic haven: "roots of relish sweet, / And honey wild, and manna-dew." This faery food offers sweet spiritual nourishment (at least that's what he thinks). What do we hear from La Belle? Nothing, other than she sings a faery song and speaks in a strange language, one where he assumes she says: "I love thee true." This ballad is not about *her* voice it is about *his* desire and its rampant unchecked increase of appetite.

By quatrain eight, we have moved from the phallic steed, riding to the yonic entry and then into her "Elfin grot". In other words, the knight is completely disarmed; he is ensnared in her enchanted declivity. Once again, he wrongly assumes that he has comforted her and shut down her weeping and sighing with his passionate kisses. Rather than La Belle sleeping, we find in the very next quatrain that she has "lulled" *him* asleep.

It is here that we have in triplicate the outcome of the knight's encounter with the femme fatale. The first result is a haunted dream: "pale kings and princes... Pale warriors, death-pale... their starved lips in the gloom, / With horrid warning gaped wide." These ghoulish creatures are forever cursed by their insatiable appetite for La Belle. These once great men of command and stature are now reduced to resemble the ghastly crew that steered the ancient mariner's vessel back home. These apparitions announce "La Belle Dame sans Merci / Thee hath in thrall!" The calque reminds us that this encounter is beyond the familiar and known to the erotic and exotic. The second result of his encounter with her is when the knight awakens it is in juxtaposition to all that La Belle seems to initially promise: "I awoke...On the cold hill's side." The ballad's circularity offers closure to the tale and a rhetorical conclusion to why the knight remains forever haunted, awaiting her return; hence, she is without mercy. This takes us to the third and final outcome of his encounter with her, a response that is reminiscent of the Ancient Mariner: "this is why I sojourn here, / Alone and palely loitering." The Pre-Raphaelites responded to what they considered in *La Belle* as direct, serious, and heartfelt in the knight's cautionary tale about his faery femme fatale.

The Lady of Shalott by Alfred Lord Tennyson (1843)

Part I
On either side the river lie

Long fields of barley and of rye,
That clothe the wold and meet the sky;
And thro' the field the road runs by
    To many-tower'd Camelot;
And up and down the people go,
Gazing where the lilies blow
Round an island there below,
    The island of Shalott.

Willows whiten, aspens quiver,
Little breezes dusk and shiver
Thro' the wave that runs for ever
By the island in the river
    Flowing down to Camelot.
Four gray walls, and four gray towers,
Overlook a space of flowers,
And the silent isle imbowers
    The Lady of Shalott.

By the margin, willow veil'd,
Slide the heavy barges trail'd
By slow horses; and unhail'd
The shallop flitteth silken-sail'd
    Skimming down to Camelot:
But who hath seen her wave her hand?
Or at the casement seen her stand?
Or is she known in all the land,
    The Lady of Shalott?

Only reapers, reaping early
In among the bearded barley,
Hear a song that echoes cheerly
From the river winding clearly,
    Down to tower'd Camelot:
And by the moon the reaper weary,
Piling sheaves in uplands airy,
Listening, whispers " 'Tis the fairy
    Lady of Shalott."

Part II
There she weaves by night and day

A magic web with colors gay.
She has heard a whisper say,
A curse is on her if she stay
    To look down to Camelot.
She knows not what the curse may be,
And so she weaveth steadily,
And little other care hath she,
    The Lady of Shalott.

And moving thro' a mirror clear
That hangs before her all the year,
Shadows of the world appear.
There she sees the highway near
    Winding down to Camelot:
There the river eddy whirls,
And there the surly village-churls,
And the red cloaks of market girls,
    Pass onward from Shalott.

Sometimes a troop of damsels glad,
An abbot on an ambling pad,
Sometimes a curly shepherd-lad,
Or long-hair'd page in crimson clad,
    Goes by to tower'd Camelot;
And sometimes thro' the mirror blue
The knights come riding two and two:
She hath no loyal knight and true,
    The Lady of Shalott.

But in her web she still delights
To weave the mirror's magic sights,
For often thro' the silent nights
A funeral, with plumes and lights
    And music, went to Camelot:
Or when the moon was overhead,
Came two young lovers lately wed:
"I am half sick of shadows," said
    The Lady of Shalott.

Part III
A bow-shot from her bower-eaves,

He rode between the barley-sheaves,
The sun came dazzling thro' the leaves,
And flamed upon the brazen greaves
    Of bold Sir Lancelot.
A red-cross knight for ever kneel'd
To a lady in his shield,
That sparkled on the yellow field,
    Beside remote Shalott.

The gemmy bridle glitter'd free,
Like to some branch of stars we see
Hung in the golden Galaxy.
The bridle bells rang merrily
    As he rode down to Camelot:
And from his blazon'd baldric slung
A mighty silver bugle hung,
And as he rode his armour rung,
    Beside remote Shalott.

All in the blue unclouded weather
Thick-jewell'd shone the saddle-leather,
The helmet and the helmet-feather
Burn'd like one burning flame together,
    As he rode down to Camelot.
As often thro' the purple night,
Below the starry clusters bright,
Some bearded meteor, trailing light,
    Moves over still Shalott.

His broad clear brow in sunlight glow'd;
On burnish'd hooves his war-horse trode;
From underneath his helmet flow'd
His coal-black curls as on he rode,
    As he rode down to Camelot.
From the bank and from the river
He flash'd into the crystal mirror,
"Tirra lirra," by the river
    Sang Sir Lancelot.

She left the web, she left the loom,
She made three paces thro' the room,

She saw the water-lily bloom,
She saw the helmet and the plume,
    She look'd down to Camelot.
Out flew the web and floated wide;
The mirror crack'd from side to side;
"The curse is come upon me," cried
    The Lady of Shalott.

Part IV
In the stormy east-wind straining,
The pale yellow woods were waning,
The broad stream in his banks complaining,
Heavily the low sky raining
    Over tower'd Camelot;
Down she came and found a boat
Beneath a willow left afloat,
And round about the prow she wrote
    The Lady of Shalott.

And down the river's dim expanse
Like some bold seër in a trance,
Seeing all his own mischance—
With a glassy countenance
    Did she look to Camelot.
And at the closing of the day
She loosed the chain, and down she lay;
The broad stream bore her far away,
    The Lady of Shalott.

Lying, robed in snowy white
That loosely flew to left and right—
The leaves upon her falling light—
Thro' the noises of the night
    She floated down to Camelot:
And as the boat-head wound along
The willowy hills and fields among,
They heard her singing her last song,
    The Lady of Shalott.

Heard a carol, mournful, holy,
Chanted loudly, chanted lowly,

Till her blood was frozen slowly,
And her eyes were darken'd wholly,
    Turn'd to tower'd Camelot.
For ere she reach'd upon the tide
The first house by the water-side,
Singing in her song she died,
    The Lady of Shalott.

Under tower and balcony,
By garden-wall and gallery,
A gleaming shape she floated by,
Dead-pale between the houses high,
    Silent into Camelot.
Out upon the wharfs they came,
Knight and burgher, lord and dame,
And round the prow they read her name,
    The Lady of Shalott.

Who is this? and what is here?
And in the lighted palace near
Died the sound of royal cheer;
And they cross'd themselves for fear,
    All the knights at Camelot:
But Lancelot mused a little space;
He said, "She has a lovely face;
God in his mercy lend her grace,
    The Lady of Shalott."

This wonderful 170-line narrative poem is made up of 19 stanzas. Part I offers us a setting: one that is steeped in the mythology of the rural idyll surrounding Camelot where, beyond the protection of the citadel, magic and mayhem persist. Part II explains how the Lady of Shalott is imprisoned in the tower and not allowed to look past the tapestry she weaves; ingeniously she does observe the heavy traffic that moves to and fro out of Camelot via a mirror. In Part III, she sees the utterly fabulous Sir Lancelot, but the mirror reflection is not enough, so she defies her restrictions and looks directly at him. Of course, the curse is activated. In the final Part IV she finds a boat, casts off, sings her death song, and eventually dies as she drifts into Camelot. The 1832 version was revised by Tennyson and this version was released in 1843. Each stanza is made up of nine lines with the rhyme scheme of a a a a b c c c b. Tennyson uses iambic tetrameter; for example, "On either side the river lie / Long fields of barley and of rye" and trochaic tetrameter "willows whiten, aspens quiver, / Little breezes dusk and shiver". Written approximately 15 years on from Keats' *La Belle*, this narrative conveys what needs to happen to dangerous women whose heartfelt longing is so extreme that they will deliberately disobey societal strictures. Lady Shalott's fate is already fixed, and her death is in stark contrast to the pathetic palely loitering knight-at-arms. Indeed, here Sir Lancelot acknowledges her loveliness all too late.

Tennyson's poem was popular among the Victorians generally and in particular the Pre-Raphaelites. His poem is loosely based on Elaine of Astolat in the Arthurian legends. Tennyson captured the interest of the Pre-Raphaelites with his bright palette of precise details. John William Waterhouse painted three separate episodes from this poem: *The Lady of Shallot* (1888), *The Lady of Shallot looking at Lancelot* (1894), and *I am Half Sick of Shadows* (1916). In amongst this obsession with Tennyson's poem, he also painted *La Belle Dame sans Merci* in 1893. Other Pre-Raphaelites and their followers, such as Siddall, Rossetti, and Millais, were also inspired to paint Tennyson's *Lady of Shalott*, but my preference would have to be William Holman Hunt's version. I love the way her representation fills up the compositional space. She is terrifying, handsome, and deliberately wilful. Her hair rises wildly, her face is determined, and she is active in her destruction. I mean, if you are going to go down, go down fighting!

While *La Belle* is the femme fatale, the *Lady of Shallot* is trapped and restricted in a man-made domesticated space: one that disallows her any access to the real world. As in keeping with the Cult of Domesticity of the 1830s, the *Lady of Shallot* is resultant of the axiom: let home be now your empire, your world. Both *La Belle* and *The Lady of Shallot* are cautionary tales. They speak to the fear, in the imagination of men, of woman as object of desire. In many ways, Tennyson's poem is the sequel to Keats' poem. One could suppose that the Lady of Shallot is cursed for having once been the beautiful merciless woman; instead of being able to roam the countryside somewhere in the liminal space of the real and the imagined, she is now on the outskirts of patriarchal rule, Camelot. Her threat to unsuspecting knights-at-arms has been reduced. Yet she is still referred to, in whispers, as "the fairy"; in other words, she, like La Belle, is regarded with fascination and fear. Both poems use the pastoral setting, the rural idyll that is idealized, as the backdrop. We also see Edmund Spencer's *Faerie Queene* at work in Tennyson's poem in the trope of the mirror as the instrument to awaken love as well as the Red Cross Knight, representative of the attributes of valor and chivalry. Tennyson doesn't mobilize the Spenserian stanza of eight iambic pentameter lines, followed by an alexandrine or iambic hexameter line but writes his stanzas in nine lines nonetheless. There are traces of William Shakespeare's *A Winter's Tale* when Lancelot is heard singing "Tirra Lirra" and Percy Shelley's closet drama *Prometheus Unbound* in the defiance against the gods.

Two points of fascination for the Pre-Raphaelites were "woman trapped" and "woman dying" or "artist trapped" and "artist dying." Entrapment happens on a number of levels. The Lady of Shalott is trapped by a curse, within the web she weaves, within the "Four gray walls, and four gray towers" in which she resides, within an island that "imbowers" her, within a river surrounded by "fields of barley and of rye", and within the precinct of the "many-towered Camelot". That's some fortification! If we lean closer, we hear she "heard a whisper say, / A curse is on her" but by whom and why she has no idea. The entrapment continues as "she weaves by night and day / A magic web … the mirror's magic sights". We could see this as the Lady of Shalott being complicit with her own entrapment; alternatively, she undermines her capture by vicariously observing the outside world and recreating this via the tapestry. Indeed, the passing traffic of Camelot is entrapped within her web.

This is where I begin to consider the Lady of Shalott as the quintessential Pre-Raphaelite artist. She is isolated and makes art with "colors gay". It is only the observation of "two young lovers" that triggers this artist to want more. And she gets more. After four stanzas of closely and meticulously observing and representing Sir Lancelot in her tapestry, she has captured a spectacular moment of high art. Caught in her web of desire and creativity he is the something more that all great artists await. This is the pinnacle of her oeuvre. Perhaps this is why she chooses to deliberately and most intentionally see through the end game.

The fascination with woman or artist dying has nothing to do with morbidity and everything to do with signing off on a life's work. The use of pathetic fallacy at the very start of Part IV is Tennyson at full theatrical throttle: "In the stormy east-wind straining, / The pale yellow woods were waning, / The broad stream in his banks complaining, / Heavily the low sky raining." It is the world in chaos in Biblical proportions: wind howling, darkness closing, the river swelling, and the heavens opening, and rain pouring. Nature irrupts as a result of the curse being activated. The Lady of Shalott, in death, is majestic and performative. Just prior to the commencement of Part IV, she deliberately and intentionally executes her destiny: "She left the web, she left the loom, / She made three paces…She saw the water lily bloom, / She saw the helmet…She looked down on Camelot." In the space of five lines and six verbs she decides her destiny, her death. It is calculated and absolute.

From this point she descends from her prison and finds a boat and most interestingly "round about the prow she wrote / The Lady of Shalott". In effect she is signing out or signing off her masterpiece. We, like the people of Camelot, are made aware of this formidable moment not only by the storm but also by the haunting self-iterations of the Lady of Shalott "singing her last song". In this 1842 version, Lancelot has the last word and acknowledges her beauty, her right to the Christian ritual of prayer, and her identity. It is a recognition of her value. This vivid ballad enthralled many Pre-Raphaelites and their followers perhaps because they saw themselves in Lady Shalott. Tennyson's poem is a mirror which captures the artist compelled to create and to create more and more until the pinnacle achievement is reached, followed by the signing off by the artist and the public recognition of its value.

O Silent Wood by Elizabeth Eleanor Siddal (1857)

O silent wood, I enter thee
With a heart so full of misery
For all the voices from the trees
And the ferns that cling about my knees.

In thy darkest shadow let me sit
When the grey owls about thee flit;
There will I ask of thee a boon,
That I may not faint or die or swoon.

Gazing through the gloom like one

Whose life and hopes are also done,
Frozen like a thing of stone
I sit in thy shadow – but not alone.

Can God bring back the day when we two stood
Beneath the clinging trees in that dark wood?

This quiet sonnet, written around 1857, is in many ways a contemplation of the wilfulness of the heart. Legend has it that when Siddal was a young adolescent, working class and ill-educated, she read an extract of a Tennyson poem printed on a newspaper scrap that wrapped a pat of butter. Enamoured by poetry, she moved beyond the confines of her background and work as a milliner, to ascend the heady path of muse to the Pre-Raphaelites and then artist and poet in her own right. Whether our image of Lizzie Siddal is Millais' drowned Ophelia, or Deverell's androgynous Viola, or Holman Hunt's rescued Sylvia, or Rossetti's highly articulated Regina Cordium, or Siddal's own luminous self-portrait, her body of work is extensive. Much has been romanticized about Siddal: the woman who became Rossetti's monomania, or Siddal the model who contracted pneumonia then tuberculosis from lying too long in that bath of cold Thames water, or Siddal the muse who inspired the Cult of Beauty for the Pre-Raphaelites. What I find fascinating is the way the poetry that emerges from the Pre-Raphaelites and their followers put in writing what was being captured in painting: the etherealized sensations, deliberately displacing the subject from the logical context, and disrupting the expected relationship with the external world. All of this is here in the poetry that emerges from this movement. *O Silent Wood* idealizes the sensory, heightens symbolism, allows the physical state to be superseded by the mental state, and reveals the self-contained world of the poet.

This English sonnet is made up of three quatrains and a final rhyming couplet. Indeed, the entire sonnet uses seven rhyming couplets, which is salient considering it is the lover yearning to be coupled with the beloved. The first quatrain begins with the exhalation "O" as the lover addresses the "silent wood". This use of the apostrophe allows Siddal to expose and explore the psychological state of the lover. The lover, of course, is active and traditionally male, thus he easily enters this dark and unpredictable place of desire and longing. It is curious that Siddal chooses to write in the active voice of lover; she defies poetic convention and societal expectations of her day. The trees and ferns are elaborately personified: "voices from the trees / And the ferns that cling about my knees." It is as if nature itself mirrors the very suffering and misery experienced by lovers the world over, and it is this which she brings into the silent wood: the dark contemplative forested place. This wretchedness cleaves to her. It is in the second quatrain that we discover why she has come: "In thy darkest shadow let me sit." In other words, she seeks solace, a place of respite and reprieve from the misery that clings to her. It is in the cool darkness of shadows and quiet that she directly asks nature for "a boon / That I may not faint or die or swoon". Nature is a place of powerful restorative effect.

The final quatrain expresses the crescendo of her despair. She uses two similes to convey the fixity of her emotional and psychological state. Firstly, she is gazing "like one / Whose life and hopes are also done". The implication is that this trance state gives her the look of someone suicidal. Secondly, she indicates she is "Frozen like a thing of stone"; the visual image suggests her heart has hardened and she is no longer capable of feeling her suffering. Yet it is because in the "shadow" of this wood she knows she is "not alone", and it is this which offers a fragment of hope. Moreover, the volta arrives in the final rhyming couplet, when she poses the question that up until this point, she has been unable to even contemplate: "Can God bring back the day when we two stood...in that dark wood?" We realize the wood had been a place in the past that belonged to them both: perhaps the site of their secret assignations or loving rendezvous or clandestine tryst. The references to shadow, gloom, and darkness conjure covert and stolen moments of love. The dual reference to "cling" in quatrain one and then "clinging" in the final line reminds us of the desperate hold this passion has had on her. The sonnet is a bold articulation of the wilfulness of the heart even in such heightened anxiety and uncertainty. The fact that we are left with a question in the silent wood suggests to me that there is no answer to her longing.

Worn Out by Elizabeth Eleanor Siddal (1858)

Thy strong arms are around me, love
My head is on thy breast;
Low words of comfort come from thee
Yet my soul has no rest.

For I am but a startled thing
Nor can I ever be
Aught save a bird whose broken wing
Must fly away from thee.

I cannot give to thee the love
I gave so long ago,
The love that turned and struck me down
Amid the blinding snow.

I can but give a failing heart
And weary eyes of pain,
A faded mouth that cannot smile
And may not laugh again.

Yet keep thine arms around me, love,
Until I fall to sleep;
Then leave me, saying no goodbye
Lest I might wake, and weep.

This is a really fascinating poem. She writes this in 1858, two years before Dante Gabriel Rossetti finally concedes to marry her. By this stage, they have been lovers for about a decade, despite his dalliances with other women. Siddal pursues her writing and art but agrees to Rossetti's request to only model for him; he in turn makes over 1,000 drawings and paintings of her. John Ruskin is her devoted patron and pays her 150 pounds a year for anything she writes or draws or paints. Ruskin urges Rossetti to ignore his family's wishes (to reject her because of her lowly birth) and marry her. At this point, she is addicted to laudanum and has endured the many breakups of their relationship. What I find most compelling is that here she begins her five quatrain poem with the delicious imagery of the intimacy of lovers and seemingly ends the same; but look closer, and we see in the final quatrain that it is the lover offering comfort to the beloved as she dies. This trope of the site of lovemaking as the site of death is well established in literature. Yet it would be wrong to think this is a lament of love gone wrong that leads ultimately to the beloved's demise and death. I read this poem as the beloved's assertive re-evaluation of the love she will give and indeed a clear expression of her desire to leave him if it were possible.

Siddal's poems are not renditions of self-pity; they are more complex. She articulates their love as having other possibilities, even if only imagined. I think it is important to remember the times in which she was writing and the Victorian society that was so restrictive. Here is a woman who has come from nothing and received no education; it was through her sheer tenacity and will that she became the sought after model. When the influential Ruskin backed her with annual financial support, there were few women of her day who could boast the same. She developed her skills to draw and paint with Rossetti's help and developed her capacity to think and write as an autodidact. Regardless, her poems are tightly sprung and offer unexpected insight into a self that is slightly haunted by the temporality in which she finds herself and thus ever struggling to emerge. Moreover, the tension between entrapment and escape is ever present from the beginning to end. From the start, the lover folds her in his embrace, and we could assume we have been taken into the site of the most intimate and personal: "Thy strong arms are around me, love / My head is on thy breast." It is not until the 3rd and 4th lines of the opening quatrain that we are made aware of the disquiet in this classic pose of lovemaking. Here, the beloved's "soul has no rest" despite the "Low words of comfort" from the lover. Our assumptions have been disrupted. This is not the site of ecstatic love but rather a scene of distress.

The second and third quatrains, offering explanation and backstory, are tied together with the exquisite metaphor of the beloved as a bird. The strong arms around her take on a more sinister meaning in that the beloved sees herself as a "startled" bird "whose broken wing" stops her from flying "away from thee". While she imagines herself as a creature of flight and freedom, she also knows she is damaged. In quatrain three, we learn that her early love, perhaps one full of flight and freedom, became her undoing. In being vulnerable to love which she "gave long ago", she was blown off course into an unseen cold: "The love that turned and struck me down / Amid the blinding snow." This is a cautionary tale about the many ways in which the human heart can dangerously trust in another. As a consequence, we see her in quatrain three articulating what it is that she is now prepared to give: "a failing heart / And weary eyes of pain, / A faded mouth that cannot smile." No more will she offer the sort of intense pure love she was once so willing to give. This former expression of love is sickly, tired, and bereft of all color. This is the outcome of entrapment. This is what love looks like when it has been caged, wings broken, and blinded by the cold. In the final quatrain, the tension between entrapment and the natural desire to escape comes to a head. Here, the beloved asserts that the lover should "keep" his arms about her "Until I fall to sleep; / Then leave me." The sleep eternal is what she desires, as there can be no escape from the state that love has rendered her. Life without this freedom is regarded by the beloved to be untenable. She asks for no possible disruptions from her course of action, not even a farewell from the strong armed lover, "Lest I might wake, and weep". To choose death over a life of entrapment is an unexpected and a somewhat courageous outcome.

The Defence of Guinevere by William Morris (1858)

But, knowing now that they would have her speak,
She threw her wet hair backward from her brow,
Her hand close to her mouth touching her cheek,

As though she had had there a shameful blow,
And feeling it shameful to feel ought but shame
All through her heart, yet felt her cheek burned so,

She must a little touch it; like one lame
She walked away from Gauwaine, with her head
Still lifted up; and on her cheek of flame

William Morris wrote this dramatic monologue when he was 24 in 1858. The Victorians invented the dramatic monologue, and it was Robert Browning's use of this form that had the deepest impact on the Pre-Raphaelites. Morris takes an extract of Sir Thomas Malory's *Morte d'Arthur* and in approximately 292 lines writes 97 terza rimas in aba, bcb, cdc rhyme. Morris composes a stirring and, at times, bewildering, defence delivered by Queen Guinevere as she stands trial for betraying her king. If found guilty, the punishment will be death by fire. Gauwaine accuses her of adultery, and legend has it, she is guilty. In Morris' poem, she is unparalleled in her rhetoric and unfaltering in her argument, which is that she is sincere. The backstory reveals that she was trapped by a passion so powerful and overwhelming that all moral conventions dissolved; besides, a loveless marriage to Arthur was the bleak alternative. I see her surrounded by the knights, all jostling to see her condemned, she who has caused so much havoc. Indeed, she will continue to be the source of mayhem and destruction until the rule of Camelot is finished: all for a love of a woman with fabled beauty. Now where have we heard that before? We begin this epic poem media res with the Queen burning with the slap of accusation: "Her hand close to her mouth touching her cheek." Morris offers us a painterly image of her shame, in the simile, "As though she had had there a shameful blow".

To be clear, no one had slapped Guinevere, but slapped she feels after the public humiliation of being accused of adultery. Throughout the entire poem runs the hot ambiguity of shame and passion: "to feel ought but shame / All through her heart, yet felt her cheek burned so." She knows that she ought to feel guilty, but the physiological reaction of blushing is a response to the act of desire she has committed. She then offers an analogy to her accusers so they may feel the trap she finds herself within, one that offers no moral pointers. Guinevere asks the knights to suppose they were at the point of death and God's angel asked them to choose one of two cloths symbolizing heaven and hell.

"And one of these strange choosing cloths was blue,
Wavy and long, and one cut short and red;
No man could tell the better of the two.

"After a shivering half-hour you said:
'God help! heaven's color, the blue;' and he said, 'hell.'
Perhaps you then would roll upon your bed,

"And cry to all good men that loved you well,
'Ah Christ! if only I had known, known, known;'
Launcelot went away, then I could tell,

"Like wisest man how all things would be, moan,
And roll and hurt myself, and long to die,
And yet fear much to die for what was sown.

"Nevertheless you, O Sir Gauwaine, lie,
Whatever may have happened through these years,
God knows I speak truth, saying that you lie."

Her voice was low at first, being full of tears,
But as it cleared, it grew full loud and shrill,
Growing a windy shriek in all men's ears,

    Guinevere likens her impossible scenario of being asked to respond to the accusations of adultery in such a way to win over the sympathy of her listeners, and indeed, it is impossible to not see the wicked trick played upon her. Fate is whimsical. Of course, no faithful queen when confronted with a test of her moral character, and asked to choose the red or the blue cloth, would choose red with its symbolic value of passion. She chooses blue, "heaven's color", yet there is no rhyme or reason that the blue cloth symbolizes hell. The dice was loaded from the start. The interlinking of the terza rimas highlight what was made "known", suggesting carnal knowledge, to the "moan" of Guinevere and ultimately what was "sown". It is this sort of ambiguity that weighs this poem with understandings of not only the conundrum of the medieval period but that of the Victorians when it comes to the battle between passion and the morally reprehensible.

Here, we also see Guinevere's first accusation, as if she is the prosecutor herself, against her accuser, Sir Gauwaine: "Whatever may have happened through these years, / God knows I speak truth, saying that you lie." I love the audacity of this woman. She is Helen, Eve, Bathsheba, and Joan of Arc: formidable and unflinching even as the kindling is being gathered. This phrase is repeated later in the poem because she names Gauwaine's crime of hypocrisy and insincerity as greater than her crime of adultery. Her fault could only be that of a sincere heart. Her sincerity should be evidence of her goodness. This is the truth of passion. Guinevere's articulation is heard variously as acceptably feminine "low at first, being full of tears", then as unacceptably feminine, "grew full loud and shrill / Growing a windy shriek in all men's ears". The scene Morris creates for this tryst to take place is a tour de force. Here is the beautiful fecund but innocent queen married to "Arthur's great name and his little love". She is young and lonely; meanwhile, the seasons weave their magic on her readiness. Enter Lancelot:

"Came Launcelot walking; this is true, the kiss
Wherewith we kissed in meeting that spring day,
I scarce dare talk of the remember'd bliss,

"When both our mouths went wandering in one way,
And aching sorely, met among the leaves;
Our hands being left behind strained far away.

"Never within a yard of my bright sleeves
Had Launcelot come before: and now so nigh!
After that day why is it Guinevere grieves?

"Nevertheless you, O Sir Gauwaine, lie,
Whatever happened on through all those years,
God knows I speak truth, saying that you lie.

"Being such a lady could I weep these tears
If this were true? A great queen such as I
Having sinn'd this way, straight her conscience sears;

"And afterwards she liveth hatefully,
Slaying and poisoning, certes never weeps:
Gauwaine be friends now, speak me lovingly.

Firstly, she offers an erotic account of meeting Lancelot in the walled garden in spring: a setting loaded with the symbolism of virginity and desire. Then she again accuses Gauwaine of lying and deceit which is in stark comparison to her sincerity. Finally, she offers proof of her honesty in that being a lady and of royal blood she can do nothing but be true and sincere. The "kiss" is what she dares not speak of because it still generates such "bliss". In other words, the retelling of this indiscretion offers her, as well as her listeners, a frisson of desire. Indeed, the terza rima that follows offers pure erotica: "both our mouths went wandering in one way, / And aching sorely." Here, passion is the longing to be completely satisfied. Central to this ecstatic sexual encounter is the restraint they placed on themselves, "Our hands being left behind strained far away". Their kissing is entwined with the fertility of nature: "leaves … spring day." Obviously, there is much more to the story that Guinevere is not revealing, hence the refrain: "Whatever happened on through all those years." This suggests that the kissing in that particular garden on that particular day was not so much a one off but a representation of the way in which the variables around them, such as nature, her loveless marriage to Arthur, and happenstance colluded to actualize their transgression.

Her tears are testament to her sincerity: "Being such a lady could I weep these tears / If this were true?" The rhetorical question connected to referencing herself as "a lady" eschews doubt of her value and worth. This is reinforced by intensifying her subject position as "A great queen". Here she is fighting for her life, and what does it ultimately boil down to? Her reputation. Everything rests on whether her reputation as queen can outweigh the accusation of her being unfaithful. She mobilizes Christian sentiment and reveals that she has "sinn'd", which scorched her conscience: "And afterwards she liveth hatefully." In the final line of this terza rima, she appeals with final flourish to Gauwaine to "be friends now, speak me lovingly." As if all could be brushed aside because her rhetoric has proven her demonstrable grief. Yet Gauwaine does not show pity. Thus, Guinevere changes tactics as a great strategist must:

I pray you pity! let me not scream out
For ever after, when the shrill winds blow

"Through half your castle-locks! let me not shout
For ever after in the winter night
When you ride out alone! in battle-rout

"Let not my rusting tears make your sword light!
Ah! God of mercy, how he turns away!
So, ever must I dress me to the fight,

"So: let God's justice work! Gauwaine, I say,
See me hew down your proofs…

Here Guinevere evokes prayer, the threat of screaming and the promise to cut down every shred of evidence against her brought to the Royal court by Gauwaine. The great queen initially prays for Gauwaine's "pity", as well as "God of mercy", and "God's justice". Curiously, the plea for clemency comes before that of fairness. The entire drama, from Guinevere's perspective, swings between these two different pleas of judgement: clemency suggests her guilt and a fair trial suggests her innocence. This ambivalence in the queen about herself, let alone the view others may have of her, generates further tension. The queen also threatens to cry out in such a way that would haunt the waterways and night surrounding the castle. Guinevere pronounces that her sorrow will eat away at the hearts of the knights in such a way that would render their strength in battle impotent: "Let not my rusting tears make your sword light … So, ever must I dress me to the fight." Indeed, she argues that it is this very display of distress that will fortify her in battle against the injustice brought against her. This will be her strength not her weakness. It is in this way that Guinevere will "hew down your proofs". It's a wonderful example of Guinevere's deft manoeuvring of argument and rhetoric. Legend has it that she was buying time for Lancelot to arrive and rescue her. Or perhaps she was having way too much fun with the cut, thrust and parry of debate.

"You, Gauwaine, held his word without a flaw,
This Mellyagraunce saw blood upon my bed:
Whose blood then pray you? is there any law

"To make a queen say why some spots of red
Lie on her coverlet? or will you say:
'Your hands are white, lady, as when you wed,

"'Where did you bleed?' and must I stammer out, 'Nay,
I blush indeed, fair lord, only to rend
My sleeve up to my shoulder, where there lay

"'A knife-point last night': so must I defend
The honour of the Lady Guinevere?
Not so, fair lords, even if the world should end

"This very day, and you were judges here
Instead of God…

    Later Guinevere recalls the bitter day in Fausse Garden when, to her horror, her bedsheets were found with spots of blood by Mellyagraunce. The implication, despite being married to Arthur for some time, is that she has been deflowered by Lancelot. Guinevere at first is so distraught by having to explain why there are blood spots on her bedsheets to the men before her that she covers her face in shame: "must I stammer out, 'Nay, / I blush indeed, fair lord, only to rend / My sleeve up to my shoulder." The unsaid is of course that it could well be menstrual blood; however, the queen gathers herself together and explains that she slept with a knife in her bed, and this is what pierced her and caused the blood stains. At the end of this strange explanation, she insists that she will not explain and defend herself even if the knights were God himself. The poem moves on with Guinevere recalling the battle between Lancelot and Mellyagraunce, the latter of course was slain by the hero. It is at this point that she offers her next argument which is that she is beautiful and thus incapable of wickedness: "say no rash word / Against me, being so beautiful; my eyes." Furthermore, her suffering fortifies her and makes her a warrior and a match to these accusing knights: "my eyes / Wept all away to grey, may bring some sword / To drown you in your blood." Indeed, she asks the knights to look at her "long throat", "mouth", "hand", and long "tresses" and ask themselves if such a beauty would lie. Guinevere believes to doubt this would be abominable: "To say this thing is vile?" So, at this point we would think the knights are stymied as she has hammered them with proof of her sincerity, beauty, and good breeding. Their case seems lost except for a small piece of the puzzle.

'But in your chamber Launcelot was found':
Is there a good knight then would stand aloof,

"When a queen says with gentle queenly sound:
'O true as steel come now and talk with me,
I love to see your step upon the ground

"'Unwavering, also well I love to see
That gracious smile light up your face, and hear
Your wonderful words, that all mean verily

"'The thing they seem to mean: good friend, so dear
To me in everything, come here to-night,
Or else the hours will pass most dull and drear;

"'If you come not, I fear this time I might
Get thinking over much of times gone by,
When I was young, and green hope was in sight:

"'For no man cares now to know why I sigh;
And no man comes to sing me pleasant songs,
Nor any brings me the sweet flowers that lie

"'So thick in the gardens; therefore one so longs
To see you, Launcelot; that we may be
Like children once again, free from all wrongs

"'Just for one night.' Did he not come to me?
What thing could keep true Launcelot away
If I said, 'Come'?

At this point in the argument, Guinevere beautifully sidesteps the proof of being found alone in bed with Lancelot. Here, her argument is simply that she asked him to keep her company. As Lancelot is good and pure, he agreed. She is undaunted and explains that "When a queen says with gentle queenly sound: / 'O true as steel come" then of course he would oblige. Her authority as queen is absolute, and her requests could never be heard as lurid or wanton but "queenly". Lancelot is given the iconic naming of "O true as steel" suggesting his strength and potency. Moreover, he is "Unwavering" and "gracious" as his very words "all mean verily / The thing they seem to mean". In other words, there is nothing but integrity about this greatly esteemed knight favored above all others by the king. The queen explains that she commanded Lancelot to come to her at night simply to pass the time away in conversation, "Or else the hours will pass most dull and drear". Furthermore, she was worried that she would be beset by the hopes and dreams of the past: "I fear this time I might / Get thinking over much of times gone by, / When I was young, and green hope was in sight." The desires she once had, rich and fertile in her young feminine imagination, had not come to fruition, hence she longed for distraction. Of course, this might be regarded as cause for adultery.

In offering proof of her innocence, she leaves behind traces of her guilt. So, Lancelot obliges because he can do nothing but concede to his queen. Besides, the queen has assured him of the innocence of this encounter: "we may be / Like children once again, free from all wrongs." Guinevere concludes the defence with a summation of her power: "Did he not come to me? / What thing could keep true Launcelot away / If I said, 'Come'?" In many ways this begins to sound like the defence of Lancelot as she continues on with Lancelot crying when he realizes they have fallen asleep because it may seem improper. Guinevere is declaring her power again and again before the knights and Gauwaine who would dare accuse the queen of the most heinous of all crimes: treason. In the ante penultimate terza rima the queen declares, "All I have said is truth, by Christ's dear tears". So, there she leaves her defence and swears by it as someone true of faith. The narrator gives us the final scene:

She would not speak another word, but stood
Turn'd sideways; listening...
    ...
Her cheek grew crimson, as the headlong speed
Of the roan charger drew all men to see,
The knight who came was Launcelot at good need.

So, the defence of Guinevere is delivered finally by a knight on a "roan charger"; Sir Lancelot to the rescue. What do we make of this ending? It is in keeping with the legend. We have a woman who is abducted and eventually brings a kingdom to its knees. Miller offers us the tale as we know it, and yet, the Guinevere he has given us has rallied against the limitations of her times and has defended herself for more than 290 lines in tera rima! This is a formidable and modern woman who can engage in the legal argument and in fact turn her accusers into salacious leering dishonest henchmen who besmirch the name of the Royal house as well as the king's noble knight. Miller traces the tension generated by the ambiguous figure she cuts: both innocent and guilty. She is both innocent of transgressing the mores of her rigid and unimaginative society and guilty of sincerely wanting more.

Goblin Market by Christina Rossetti (1862)

Morning and evening
Maids heard the goblins cry:
"Come buy our orchard fruits,
Come buy, come buy:
Apples and quinces,
Lemons and oranges,
Plump unpeck'd cherries,
Melons and raspberries,
Bloom-down-cheek'd peaches,
Swart-headed mulberries,
Wild free-born cranberries,
Crab-apples, dewberries,
Pine-apples, blackberries,
Apricots, strawberries;—
All ripe together
In summer weather,—
Morns that pass by,
Fair eves that fly;
Come buy, come buy:
Our grapes fresh from the vine,
Pomegranates full and fine,
Dates and sharp bullaces,
Rare pears and greengages,
Damsons and bilberries,
Taste them and try:
Currants and gooseberries,
Bright-fire-like barberries,
Figs to fill your mouth,
Citrons from the South,
Sweet to tongue and sound to eye;
Come buy, come buy."

Evening by evening
Among the brookside rushes,
Laura bow'd her head to hear,
Lizzie veil'd her blushes:

Crouching close together
In the cooling weather,
With clasping arms and cautioning lips,
With tingling cheeks and finger tips.
"Lie close," Laura said,
Pricking up her golden head:
"We must not look at goblin men,
We must not buy their fruits:
Who knows upon what soil they fed
Their hungry thirsty roots?"
"Come buy," call the goblins
Hobbling down the glen.

"Oh," cried Lizzie, "Laura, Laura,
You should not peep at goblin men."
Lizzie cover'd up her eyes,
Cover'd close lest they should look;
Laura rear'd her glossy head,
And whisper'd like the restless brook:
"Look, Lizzie, look, Lizzie,
Down the glen tramp little men.
One hauls a basket,
One bears a plate,
One lugs a golden dish
Of many pounds weight.
How fair the vine must grow
Whose grapes are so luscious;
How warm the wind must blow
Through those fruit bushes."
"No," said Lizzie, "No, no, no;
Their offers should not charm us,
Their evil gifts would harm us."
She thrust a dimpled finger
In each ear, shut eyes and ran:
Curious Laura chose to linger
Wondering at each merchant man.
One had a cat's face,
One whisk'd a tail,
One tramp'd at a rat's pace,
One crawl'd like a snail,
One like a wombat prowl'd obtuse and furry,

One like a ratel tumbled hurry skurry.
She heard a voice like voice of doves
Cooing all together:
They sounded kind and full of loves
In the pleasant weather.
Laura stretch'd her gleaming neck
Like a rush-imbedded swan,
Like a lily from the beck,
Like a moonlit poplar branch,
Like a vessel at the launch
When its last restraint is gone.

Backwards up the mossy glen
Turn'd and troop'd the goblin men,
With their shrill repeated cry,
"Come buy, come buy."
When they reach'd where Laura was
They stood stock still upon the moss,
Leering at each other,
Brother with queer brother;
Signalling each other,
Brother with sly brother.
One set his basket down,
One rear'd his plate;
One began to weave a crown
Of tendrils, leaves, and rough nuts brown
(Men sell not such in any town);
One heav'd the golden weight
Of dish and fruit to offer her:
"Come buy, come buy," was still their cry.
Laura stared but did not stir,
Long'd but had no money:
The whisk-tail'd merchant bade her taste
In tones as smooth as honey,
The cat-faced purr'd,
The rat-faced spoke a word
Of welcome, and the snail-paced even was heard;
One parrot-voiced and jolly
Cried "Pretty Goblin" still for "Pretty Polly;"—
One whistled like a bird.

But sweet-tooth Laura spoke in haste:
"Good folk, I have no coin;
To take were to purloin:
I have no copper in my purse,
I have no silver either,
And all my gold is on the furze
That shakes in windy weather
Above the rusty heather."
"You have much gold upon your head,"
They answer'd all together:
"Buy from us with a golden curl."
She clipp'd a precious golden lock,
She dropp'd a tear more rare than pearl,
Then suck'd their fruit globes fair or red:
Sweeter than honey from the rock,
Stronger than man-rejoicing wine,
Clearer than water flow'd that juice;
She never tasted such before,
How should it cloy with length of use?
She suck'd and suck'd and suck'd the more
Fruits which that unknown orchard bore;
She suck'd until her lips were sore;
Then flung the emptied rinds away
But gather'd up one kernel stone,
And knew not was it night or day
As she turn'd home alone.

Lizzie met her at the gate
Full of wise upbraidings:
"Dear, you should not stay so late,
Twilight is not good for maidens;
Should not loiter in the glen
In the haunts of goblin men.
Do you not remember Jeanie,
How she met them in the moonlight,
Took their gifts both choice and many,
Ate their fruits and wore their flowers
Pluck'd from bowers
Where summer ripens at all hours?
But ever in the moonlight
She pined and pined away;

Sought them by night and day,
Found them no more, but dwindled and grew grey;
Then fell with the first snow,
While to this day no grass will grow
Where she lies low:
I planted daisies there a year ago
That never blow.
You should not loiter so."
"Nay, hush," said Laura:
"Nay, hush, my sister:
I ate and ate my fill,
Yet my mouth waters still;
To-morrow night I will
Buy more;" and kiss'd her:
"Have done with sorrow;
I'll bring you plums to-morrow
Fresh on their mother twigs,
Cherries worth getting;
You cannot think what figs
My teeth have met in,
What melons icy-cold
Piled on a dish of gold
Too huge for me to hold,
What peaches with a velvet nap,
Pellucid grapes without one seed:
Odorous indeed must be the mead
Whereon they grow, and pure the wave they drink
With lilies at the brink,
And sugar-sweet their sap."

Golden head by golden head,
Like two pigeons in one nest
Folded in each other's wings,
They lay down in their curtain'd bed:
Like two blossoms on one stem,
Like two flakes of new-fall'n snow,
Like two wands of ivory
Tipp'd with gold for awful kings.
Moon and stars gaz'd in at them,
Wind sang to them lullaby,
Lumbering owls forbore to fly,

Not a bat flapp'd to and fro
Round their rest:
Cheek to cheek and breast to breast
Lock'd together in one nest.

Early in the morning
When the first cock crow'd his warning,
Neat like bees, as sweet and busy,
Laura rose with Lizzie:
Fetch'd in honey, milk'd the cows,
Air'd and set to rights the house,
Kneaded cakes of whitest wheat,
Cakes for dainty mouths to eat,
Next churn'd butter, whipp'd up cream,
Fed their poultry, sat and sew'd;
Talk'd as modest maidens should:
Lizzie with an open heart,
Laura in an absent dream,
One content, one sick in part;
One warbling for the mere bright day's delight,
One longing for the night.

At length slow evening came:
They went with pitchers to the reedy brook;
Lizzie most placid in her look,
Laura most like a leaping flame.
They drew the gurgling water from its deep;
Lizzie pluck'd purple and rich golden flags,
Then turning homeward said: "The sunset flushes
Those furthest loftiest crags;
Come, Laura, not another maiden lags.
No wilful squirrel wags,
The beasts and birds are fast asleep."
But Laura loiter'd still among the rushes
And said the bank was steep.

And said the hour was early still
The dew not fall'n, the wind not chill;
Listening ever, but not catching
The customary cry,
"Come buy, come buy,"

With its iterated jingle
Of sugar-baited words:
Not for all her watching
Once discerning even one goblin
Racing, whisking, tumbling, hobbling;
Let alone the herds
That used to tramp along the glen,
In groups or single,
Of brisk fruit-merchant men.

Till Lizzie urged, "O Laura, come;
I hear the fruit-call but I dare not look:
You should not loiter longer at this brook:
Come with me home.
The stars rise, the moon bends her arc,
Each glowworm winks her spark,
Let us get home before the night grows dark:
For clouds may gather
Though this is summer weather,
Put out the lights and drench us through;
Then if we lost our way what should we do?"

Laura turn'd cold as stone
To find her sister heard that cry alone,
That goblin cry,
"Come buy our fruits, come buy."
Must she then buy no more such dainty fruit?
Must she no more such succors pasture find,
Gone deaf and blind?
Her tree of life droop'd from the root:
She said not one word in her heart's sore ache;
But peering thro' the dimness, nought discerning,
Trudg'd home, her pitcher dripping all the way;
So crept to bed, and lay
Silent till Lizzie slept;
Then sat up in a passionate yearning,
And gnash'd her teeth for baulk'd desire, and wept
As if her heart would break.

Day after day, night after night,
Laura kept watch in vain

In sullen silence of exceeding pain.
She never caught again the goblin cry:
"Come buy, come buy;"—
She never spied the goblin men
Hawking their fruits along the glen:
But when the noon wax'd bright
Her hair grew thin and grey;
She dwindled, as the fair full moon doth turn
To swift decay and burn
Her fire away.

One day remembering her kernel-stone
She set it by a wall that faced the south;
Dew'd it with tears, hoped for a root,
Watch'd for a waxing shoot,
But there came none;
It never saw the sun,
It never felt the trickling moisture run:
While with sunk eyes and faded mouth
She dream'd of melons, as a traveler sees
False waves in desert drouth
With shade of leaf-crown'd trees,
And burns the thirstier in the sandful breeze.

She no more swept the house,
Tended the fowls or cows,
Fetch'd honey, kneaded cakes of wheat,
Brought water from the brook:
But sat down listless in the chimney-nook
And would not eat.

Tender Lizzie could not bear
To watch her sister's cankerous care
Yet not to share.
She night and morning
Caught the goblins' cry:
"Come buy our orchard fruits,
Come buy, come buy;"—
Beside the brook, along the glen,
She heard the tramp of goblin men,
The yoke and stir

Poor Laura could not hear;
Long'd to buy fruit to comfort her,
But fear'd to pay too dear.
She thought of Jeanie in her grave,
Who should have been a bride;
But who for joys brides hope to have
Fell sick and died
In her gay prime,
In earliest winter time
With the first glazing rime,
With the first snow-fall of crisp winter time.

Till Laura dwindling
Seem'd knocking at Death's door:
Then Lizzie weigh'd no more
Better and worse;
But put a silver penny in her purse,
Kiss'd Laura, cross'd the heath with clumps of furze
At twilight, halted by the brook:
And for the first time in her life
Began to listen and look.

Laugh'd every goblin
When they spied her peeping:
Came towards her hobbling,
Flying, running, leaping,
Puffing and blowing,
Chuckling, clapping, crowing,
Clucking and gobbling,
Mopping and mowing,
Full of airs and graces,
Pulling wry faces,
Demure grimaces,
Cat-like and rat-like,
Ratel- and wombat-like,
Snail-paced in a hurry,
Parrot-voiced and whistler,
Helter skelter, hurry skurry,
Chattering like magpies,
Fluttering like pigeons,
Gliding like fishes,—

Hugg'd her and kiss'd her:
Squeez'd and caress'd her:
Stretch'd up their dishes,
Panniers, and plates:
"Look at our apples
Russet and dun,
Bob at our cherries,
Bite at our peaches,
Citrons and dates,
Grapes for the asking,
Pears red with basking
Out in the sun,
Plums on their twigs;
Pluck them and suck them,
Pomegranates, figs."—

"Good folk," said Lizzie,
Mindful of Jeanie:
"Give me much and many: —
Held out her apron,
Toss'd them her penny.
"Nay, take a seat with us,
Honour and eat with us,"
They answer'd grinning:
"Our feast is but beginning.
Night yet is early,
Warm and dew-pearly,
Wakeful and starry:
Such fruits as these
No man can carry:
Half their bloom would fly,
Half their dew would dry,
Half their flavour would pass by.
Sit down and feast with us,
Be welcome guest with us,
Cheer you and rest with us."—
"Thank you," said Lizzie: "But one waits
At home alone for me:
So without further parleying,
If you will not sell me any
Of your fruits though much and many,

Give me back my silver penny
I toss'd you for a fee."—
They began to scratch their pates,
No longer wagging, purring,
But visibly demurring,
Grunting and snarling.
One call'd her proud,
Cross-grain'd, uncivil;
Their tones wax'd loud,
Their looks were evil.
Lashing their tails
They trod and hustled her,
Elbow'd and jostled her,
Claw'd with their nails,
Barking, mewing, hissing, mocking,
Tore her gown and soil'd her stocking,
Twitch'd her hair out by the roots,
Stamp'd upon her tender feet,
Held her hands and squeez'd their fruits
Against her mouth to make her eat.

White and golden Lizzie stood,
Like a lily in a flood,—
Like a rock of blue-vein'd stone
Lash'd by tides obstreperously,—
Like a beacon left alone
In a hoary roaring sea,
Sending up a golden fire,—
Like a fruit-crown'd orange-tree
White with blossoms honey-sweet
Sore beset by wasp and bee,—
Like a royal virgin town
Topp'd with gilded dome and spire
Close beleaguer'd by a fleet
Mad to tug her standard down.

One may lead a horse to water,
Twenty cannot make him drink.
Though the goblins cuff'd and caught her,
Coax'd and fought her,
Bullied and besought her,

Scratch'd her, pinch'd her black as ink,
Kick'd and knock'd her,
Maul'd and mock'd her,
Lizzie utter'd not a word;
Would not open lip from lip
Lest they should cram a mouthful in:
But laugh'd in heart to feel the drip
Of juice that syrupp'd all her face,
And lodg'd in dimples of her chin,
And streak'd her neck which quaked like curd.
At last the evil people,
Worn out by her resistance,
Flung back her penny, kick'd their fruit
Along whichever road they took,
Not leaving root or stone or shoot;
Some writh'd into the ground,
Some div'd into the brook
With ring and ripple,
Some scudded on the gale without a sound,
Some vanish'd in the distance.

In a smart, ache, tingle,
Lizzie went her way;
Knew not was it night or day;
Sprang up the bank, tore thro' the furze,
Threaded copse and dingle,
And heard her penny jingle
Bouncing in her purse,—
Its bounce was music to her ear.
She ran and ran
As if she fear'd some goblin man
Dogg'd her with gibe or curse
Or something worse:
But not one goblin scurried after,
Nor was she prick'd by fear;
The kind heart made her windy-paced
That urged her home quite out of breath with haste
And inward laughter.

She cried, "Laura," up the garden,
"Did you miss me?

Come and kiss me.
Never mind my bruises,
Hug me, kiss me, suck my juices
Squeez'd from goblin fruits for you,
Goblin pulp and goblin dew.
Eat me, drink me, love me;
Laura, make much of me;
For your sake I have braved the glen
And had to do with goblin merchant men."

Laura started from her chair,
Flung her arms up in the air,
Clutch'd her hair:
"Lizzie, Lizzie, have you tasted
For my sake the fruit forbidden?
Must your light like mine be hidden,
Your young life like mine be wasted,
Undone in mine undoing,
And ruin'd in my ruin,
Thirsty, canker'd, goblin-ridden?"—
She clung about her sister,
Kiss'd and kiss'd and kiss'd her:
Tears once again
Refresh'd her shrunken eyes,
Dropping like rain
After long sultry drouth;
Shaking with aguish fear, and pain,
She kiss'd and kiss'd her with a hungry mouth.

Her lips began to scorch,
That juice was wormwood to her tongue,
She loath'd the feast:
Writhing as one possess'd she leap'd and sung,
Rent all her robe, and wrung
Her hands in lamentable haste,
And beat her breast.
Her locks stream'd like the torch
Borne by a racer at full speed,
Or like the mane of horses in their flight,
Or like an eagle when she stems the light
Straight toward the sun,

Or like a caged thing freed,
Or like a flying flag when armies run.

Swift fire spread through her veins, knock'd at her heart,
Met the fire smouldering there
And overbore its lesser flame;
She gorged on bitterness without a name:
Ah! fool, to choose such part
Of soul-consuming care!
Sense fail'd in the mortal strife:
Like the watch-tower of a town
Which an earthquake shatters down,
Like a lightning-stricken mast,
Like a wind-uprooted tree
Spun about,
Like a foam-topp'd waterspout
Cast down headlong in the sea,
She fell at last;
Pleasure past and anguish past,
Is it death or is it life?

Life out of death.
That night long Lizzie watch'd by her,
Counted her pulse's flagging stir,
Felt for her breath,
Held water to her lips, and cool'd her face
With tears and fanning leaves:
But when the first birds chirp'd about their eaves,
And early reapers plodded to the place
Of golden sheaves,
And dew-wet grass
Bow'd in the morning winds so brisk to pass,
And new buds with new day
Open'd of cup-like lilies on the stream,
Laura awoke as from a dream,
Laugh'd in the innocent old way,
Hugg'd Lizzie but not twice or thrice;
Her gleaming locks show'd not one thread of grey,
Her breath was sweet as May
And light danced in her eyes.

Days, weeks, months, years
Afterwards, when both were wives
With children of their own;
Their mother-hearts beset with fears,
Their lives bound up in tender lives;
Laura would call the little ones
And tell them of her early prime,
Those pleasant days long gone
Of not-returning time:
Would talk about the haunted glen,
The wicked, quaint fruit-merchant men,
Their fruits like honey to the throat
But poison in the blood;
(Men sell not such in any town):
Would tell them how her sister stood
In deadly peril to do her good,
And win the fiery antidote:
Then joining hands to little hands
Would bid them cling together,
"For there is no friend like a sister
In calm or stormy weather;
To cheer one on the tedious way,
To fetch one if one goes astray,
To lift one if one totters down,
To strengthen whilst one stands."

In 1862, when Christina Rossetti writes this ballad at the age of 32, she is more or less mid-way through her life. By 1894, she is dead of breast cancer. Is this poem at this juncture in her life a children's narrative or a cautionary tale for young women or a rewrite of the Garden of Eden tale or an exploration of lesbian love or a treatise on woman as exchangeable goods or a monogram on the solidarity of sisters or an allegory about the forbidden fruit of nuptial pleasures to unwed maidens? The longevity of her poem speaks to the fact that its meaning is very much in the eye of the beholder. Indeed, at different points in my life, I have read this poem and known irrevocably what it is saying only to find that a few years on the poem's meaning has morphed into something else. Most certainly this ballad is about the delicious and dangerous consequences of transgression. Going against the grain was inherently a Pre-Raphaelite undertaking. Rossetti was the daughter of an exiled Italian poet and scholar who came to live in England where he married and had four children: all of whom made their own mark in the world of the arts or scholarship. Her poetry offered detailed attention to Nature while exploring transgressions concerned with morality, constancy, humility, and divine love. At this time in literary history, Christina Rossetti and Elizabeth Barrett Browning were regarded as the great female poets of the Victorian age. Indeed, Rossetti would have followed Alfred Lord Tennyson as Poet Laureate if she hadn't died at the point when she did. Rossetti's poem, *Goblin Market,* was an immediate success and hailed for its original voice, simplicity of form, and fresh approach to age old preoccupations, such as, exploring the consequences when one pursues desire over and above devotion, whether to one's duties, social expectations, or religious strictures. This ballad is made up of 29 stanzas of unequal length and altogether constitutes 567 lines. Yet the use of inclusive rhyme, frequent end rhyme, and inversion of the first iamb, so that it starts with a strong rather than a weak stress, make this poem a roller coaster to read. Once you start, you cannot stop!

Goblins are incongruous to a rational world. Moreover, European folk tales about these grotesque mischievous demi devils from the medieval past should be kept for dark nights around a hearth. These goblins in Rossetti's ballad are sensational. They are always present in the minds of the maidens. They are legion and multiply in their desirous attempts to sell their fruit, press the consumer to taste, and then join them to sup. Whatever it is that they have, Laura wants it more than the other option of her daily tedium of chores. I think it's interesting that what Laura wants will preclude her from being a bride, as it did to poor old Jeanie, and yet she still wants it. She knows her own hunger will be her undoing and yet pursue it she must. The fact that she devours Lizzie soaked in the juices of the forbidden fruit is simply further evidence of Laura's drive to satiate her hunger. Women and appetites are not a comfortable conjoining: not then and not now. I love Laura's appetite. I love her sheer abandonment of propriety as she tastes that which is on offer. That she begins to disintegrate and diminish when she doesn't feed her appetite is proof that women need to consume what is their choice. Even the cautionary tale Laura offers her own children years later is double edged, as she recalls what happened when she went astray from her destined "tedious way". Let's have a specific look at goblins and women's appetites.

It seems to me that the goblins, like seasonal or itinerate workers, are plying their trade where and when they can: "Morning and evening / Maids heard the goblins cry: / "Come buy our orchard fruits, / Come buy, come buy." The delightful interplay between alliterative rhyme, "Morning...Maids", and anaphora, "Come buy...Come buy, come buy", as well as inclusive assonant rhyme, "goblins...orchard", create a soundscape that rivals the visual imagery of the cornucopia for sale. Fruit, of course, is laden with warning from the Garden of Eden to Germanic fairy tales. Yet, for an Industrialized Victorian England where overcrowding, poor sanitation, and a basic diet of bread, gruel, and broth was the plight of the average person, the seduction of fresh fruit is inestimable: "Figs to fill your mouth, / Citrons from the South, / Sweet to tongue and sound to eye; / Come buy, come buy." Surely the goblins are little more than street vendors and merchants, foreign perhaps to the familiar Victorian landscape but at the same time, very real to the imagination and hungry Victorian people. The goblins' code of commerce and values of hospitality are very different to Victorian women as represented by Lizzie. The goblins call: "Taste them and try." The use of the alveolar "t", pronounced with the tip of the tongue or near its ridge, has a tantalizing effect on the ear of the listener. As commercially enterprising travelers, these goblins marshal fast for a possible sale: "Came towards her hobbling, / Flying, running, leaping, / Puffing and blowing, / Chuckling, clapping, crowing, / Clucking and gobbling, / Mopping and mowing." The excess of present participle verbs crowds the ballad with rhythm and rhyme in a frenetic response to please the customer.

Their foreignness is zoomorphic: "Cat-like and rat-like, / Ratel- and wombat-like, / Snail-paced in a hurry, / Parrot-voiced ... Chattering like magpies, / Fluttering like pigeons, / Gliding like fishes." This reflects the suspicion and resistance to the other by the Victorians.

The goblins emerge here in this 1860 ballad as a result of the systematic fearmongering associated with the costermonger. These were colorful street sellers, *coster* was a medieval apple and *monger* denoted seller, who were regarded as both unsavoury and alluring. Their disregard of authority, love of gambling, lack of education, and disdain for marriage was seen, particularly by the Commissioner of Police in 1860, as a blight on Victorian society. They threatened regulated commerce and obstructed street traffic. Yet, their cultural signatures were fascinating: colorful attire; back and rhyming slang that generated a type of secret language as well as sales patter; and poems and chants to attract customers. Indeed, they provided rapid food distribution in locations away from the fixed market places, which was highly desirous for the working class as well as for those unable to move freely across the public sector such as women in Victorian England. The goblins' banter is hospitable and encouraging: "take a seat with us, / Honour and eat with us...Be welcome guest with us, / Cheer you and rest with us." The diacope of "us" conveys the feeling of hospitality and collusion between the giving and taking of welcomed food. The goblins are understandably bewildered, then frustrated and then irate when Lizzie, unlike Laura, refuses to accept the terms and conditions they have established: "They began to scratch their pates ... demurring, / Grunting and snarling... Barking, mewing, hissing, mocking." The secret language of these costermongers can well be understood probably because it is represented as animalistic. The consequences of flaunting the conventions of commerce peculiar to the day (and let's face it Lizzie wants the fruit but not at the ultimate cost required) are confronting: "cuff'd and caught ... Coax'd ... Scratch'd ... pinch'd ... Kick'd and knock'd ... Maul'd and mock'd her." The interplay between the guttural "c" and the alveolar "d" become onomatopoeic of the battering Lizzie receives. The goblins are a force to be reckoned with and demonstrate little regard for the niceties of Victorian times.

Transgressing further niceties of society in 1860 England would have to be the representation of women's appetite. Laura is hungry. From the onset we see that she "bow'd her head to hear" the call to buy the fresh fruit, whereas Lizzie "veil'd her blushes". What Laura responds to is the opportunity to experience what she desires; what Lizzie responds to is the shame of imagining what she desires. It is a really interesting moment of contrast between the two sisters. They are surely the Janus face of the Victorian woman: Lizzie the Victorian woman and Laura the Pre-Raphaelite sister. I love the way that Lizzie "cover'd up her eyes" after instructing her sister not to look at the goblin men. In stark contrast "Laura rear'd her glossy head, / And whisper'd like the restless brook: / "Look, Lizzie, look"". This divergence is compelling. Laura has her lustrous hair uncovered, a signature of sexual allure and also a Pre-Raphaelite signature of the sexually liberated woman. Furthermore, Laura's desire to be more than a mirror self to Lizzie is conveyed in her restless meandering spirit, which will not be silenced, hence she speaks to Lizzie with high modal command, to open her eyes to the possibilities of what could be. *Reverie* by Dante Rossetti had not yet been painted but when Laura "stretch'd her gleaming neck" this is what I see. It is the feminine straining forward in her desire to have; it is the most beauteous and elegant depiction of yearning, "When its last restraint is gone."

The abandonment of strictures and controls surely is the most dangerous of all transgressions that any woman at any time could commit.

Laura's hunger comes at a price, but one she is willing to pay. When "sweet-tooth Laura" hurriedly acknowledges she has no money she quickly accedes to the goblin's alternate currency option, a lock of her hair. This has various symbolic values in Victorian times. On the one hand, it is a token of betrothed love from a beloved to the lover; it is also a symbol of eternal life as a lock of hair was kept as a memento mori by Victorian and more curiously it was regarded as a talisman for spells. Laura pays the price: "She clipp'd a precious golden lock. / She dropp'd a tear more rare than pearl, /Then suck'd their fruit globes fair or red." Her simple actions in "clipp'd", "dropp'd" and "suck'd" indicate how the barriers to satiate her desires are illusory. Indeed, the pleasure and satisfaction she achieves in fulfilling her hunger is mesmerizing because we usually do not see women devouring and consuming with such abandon as we do with Laura: "She suck'd and suck'd and suck'd the more … She suck'd until her lips were sore." This is a taboo.

Such appetites shake the very bedrock of society because women's appetites are to be dictated by men; otherwise, they could become dangerous. Laura is no longer content in restricted drudgery: "Fetch'd in honey, milk'd the cows, / Air'd and set to rights the house, / Kneaded cakes of whitest wheat, / Cakes for dainty mouths to eat, / Next churn'd butter, whipp'd up cream, / Fed their poultry, sat and sew'd." The listing of chores would harden the heart of any inmate. Here, desire is to be met with purity, "whitest wheat", made only for delicate and petite appetites: "dainty mouths".

No wonder Laura longed for "the night" with all its promise of hidden pleasures. Of course, women with appetites beyond the confines of their small sheltered lives cannot be allowed to flourish; they need to be punished to warn other small sheltered lives not to pursue the dangerous call of desire. Yet to this day *Goblin Market* is a ballad that tastes delicious because of the transgressive proclivities it conveys.

Modern Love by George Meredith (1862)

I
By this he knew she wept with waking eyes:
That, at his hand's light quiver by her head,
The strange low sobs that shook their common bed
Were called into her with a sharp surprise,
And strangled mute, like little gaping snakes,
Dreadfully venomous to him. She lay
Stone-still, and the long darkness flowed away
With muffled pulses. Then, as midnight makes
Her giant heart of Memory and Tears
Drink the pale drug of silence, and so beat
Sleep's heavy measure, they from head to feet
Were moveless, looking through their dead black years,
By vain regret scrawled over the blank wall.

Like sculptured effigies they might be seen
Upon their marriage-tomb, the sword between;
Each wishing for the sword that severs all.

II
It ended, and the morrow brought the task.
Her eyes were guilty gates, that let him in
By shutting all too zealous for their sin:
Each sucked a secret, and each wore a mask.
But, oh, the bitter taste her beauty had!
He sickened as at breath of poison-flowers:
A languid humour stole among the hours,
And if their smiles encountered, he went mad,
And raged deep inward, till the light was brown
Before his vision, and the world forgot,
Looked wicked as some old dull murder-spot.
A star with lurid beams, she seemed to crown
The pit of infamy: and then again
He fained on his vengefulness, and strove
To ape the magnanimity of love,
And smote himself, a shuddering heap of pain.

...
XVI
In our old shipwrecked days there was an hour
When, in the firelight steadily aglow,
Joined slackly, we beheld the red chasm grow
Among the clicking coals. Our library-bower
That eve was left to us; and hushed we sat
As lovers to whom Time is whispering.
From sudden-opened doors we heard them sing;
The nodding elders mixed good wine with chat.
Well knew we that Life's greatest treasure lay
With us, and of it was our talk. "Ah, yes!
Love dies!" I said; I never thought it less.
She yearned to me that sentence to unsay.
Then when the fire domed blackening, I found
Her cheek was salt against my kiss, and swift
Up the sharp scale of sobs her breast did lift –
Now am I haunted by that taste! that sound.

XVII
At dinner, she is hostess, I am host.
Went the feast ever cheerfuller? She keeps
The Topic over intellectual deeps
In buoyancy afloat. They see no ghost.
With sparkling surface-eyes we ply the ball:
It is in truth a most contagious game:
HIDING THE SKELETON, shall be its name.
Such play as this the devils might appall!
But here's the greater wonder; in that we,
Enamoured of an acting naught can tire,
Each other, like true hypocrites, admire;
Warm-lighted looks, love's ephemerae,
Shoot gaily o'er the dishes and the wine.
We waken envy of our happy lot.
Fast, sweet and golden shows the marriage-knot.
Dear guests, you now have seen love's corpse-light shine.

...

XXXIX
She yields: my Lady in her noblest mood
Has yielded: she, my golden-crownèd rose!
The bride of every sense! more sweet than those
Who breathe the violet breath of maidenhood.
O visage of still music in the sky!
Soft moon! I feel thy song, my fairest friend!
True harmony within can apprehend
Dumb harmony without. And hark! 'tis nigh!
Belief has struck the note of sound: a gleam
Of living silver shows me where she shook
Her long white fingers down the shadowy brook,
That sings her song, half waking, half in dream.
What two come here to mar this heavenly tune?
A man is one: the woman bears my name,
And honour. Their hands touch! Am I still tame?
God, what a dancing spectre seems the moon!

XL
I bade my Lady think what she might mean.
Know I my meaning, I? Can I love one,
And yet be jealous of another? None

Commits such folly. Terrible Love, I ween,
Has might, even dead, half sighing to upheave
The lightless seas of selfishness amain:
Seas that in a man's heart have no rain
To fall and still them. Peace can I achieve
By turning to this fountain-source of woe,
This woman, who's to Love as fire to wood?
She breathed the violet breath of maidenhood
Against my kisses once! but I say, No!
The thing is mocked at! Helplessly afloat,
I know not what I do, whereto I strive,
The dread that my old love may be alive,
Has seized my nursling new love by the throat.

...

XLIX
He found her by the ocean's moaning verge,
Nor any wicked change in her discerned;
And she believed his old love had returned,
Which was her exultation, and her scourge.
She took his hand, and walked with him, and seemed
The wife he sought, though shadow-like and dry.
She had one terror, lest her heart should sigh,
And tell her loudly she no longer dreamed.
She dared not say, 'This is my breast: look in.'
But there's a strength to help the desperate weak.
That night he learned how silence best can speak
The awful things when Pity pleads for Sin.
About the middle of the night her call
Was heard, and he came wondering to the bed.
'Now kiss me, dear! it may be, now!' she said.
Lethe had passed those lips, and he knew all.

L
Thus piteously Love closed what he begat:
The union of this ever-diverse pair!
These two were rapid falcons in a snare,
Condemned to do the flitting of the bat.
Lovers beneath the singing sky of May,
They wandered once; clear as the dew on flowers:
But they fed not on the advancing hours:

Their hearts held cravings for the buried day.
Then each applied to each that fatal knife,
Deep questioning, which probes to endless dole.
Ah, what a dusty answer gets the soul
When hot for certainties in this our life! —
In tragic hints here see what evermore
Moves dark as yonder midnight ocean's force,
Thundering like ramping hosts of warrior horse,
To throw that fain thin line upon the shore!

George Meredith's 1862 sonnet sequence, *Modern Love*, is made up of 50 sonnets each written in 16 lines and without the volta, so are they even sonnets? Well, they invite meditation, are symmetrical in form, and pursue a singular topic, and so maybe they are sonnets. Even to contemporary readers of today, *Modern Love* is a disturbingly honest portrayal of marriage: the unspeakable pain, the leveling of punishment, the grief of love lost, the secrecy of illicit love found, the fixity of one's life, the awareness of escape, and the ragged back and forth before the termination of love.

Meredith was accused of indecency when *Modern Love* was first published, and it was not reprinted until 1892. At the time, the intimate relationship between a husband and wife was not considered an appropriate subject matter and this was further antagonised by critical reception suggesting *Modern Love* was a biographical poem depicting the end of Meredith's marriage to Mary Peacock Nicolls. This sonnet sequence speaks of the breakdown of love in a marriage, infidelity, hypocrisy, despair, bewilderment, and unhappiness. Locked in a marriage that does not satiate her desire or her sense of fulfilment, the wife in *Modern Love* troubled the very foundations of what was acceptable and indeed, permissible. Meredith was responding to a context where the permanency of certain values was under scrutiny: such as marriage and the place of women. Himself-as-poet, the wife, the wife's lover, and the poet's own mistress populate the pages of this sequence. At all times we are offered only the poet's point of view, and it is no surprise that he blames the wife entirely for the irreparable breakdown of their marriage; yet in the last ten sonnets, he seems to realize that he is also responsible. Knowledge that is too little too late as his wife takes poison and dies. Meredith's first marriage was tumultuous when he married Mary Ellen Peacock Nicholls seven years his senior, widowed and with a daughter. She left him and their son for the Pre-Raphaelite artist, Henry Wallis. This was in 1856, the same year Wallis exhibited *The Death of Chatterton* to critical success; ironically, George Meredith had been the model. Wallis' painting depicts the young struggling artist Thomas Chatterton, a Romantic poet who poisoned himself in 1770.

Sonnet I places us in the marriage bed. This site is one of hidden truths, distress, longing for another, and a lack of connection. It commences media res with the husband waking to hear his wife weeping, which she stifles once she is aware he is awake: "By this he knew she wept with waking eyes: / That, at his hand's light quiver by her head, / The strange low sobs that shook their common bed / Were called into her with a sharp surprise, / And strangled mute." Immediately we are in a drama that disrupts our expectations. Instead of the wife being consoled and the sorrow being righted, the husband can only offer a trembling gesture, an action that lacks virility and consolation. Their bed is "common", suggesting a site that is shared or mutual and yet her lament is "strangled mute", indicating that this is very much her own secret and private experience. Moreover, she then lays "stone still" until they both are "looking through their dead black years". They have become the hard and cold marble "effigies" of a church's crypt. We are left with no doubt that their martial bed is "their marriage-tomb". This idea, of the lovers' bed as their tomb, is wrapped up in the Janus faced understanding of desire. Desire is made up of Eros and Thanatos, erotic pleasure and suffering death: "Each wishing for the sword that severs all." There is certainly something slightly erotic in the voyeuristic opportunity given to the reader to look into the most intimate of spaces, the bedroom: a compelling opening to a portrait of modern love.

Sonnet II takes us into the dark machinations of the husband and wife who both harbor lies and deceit: "Each sucked a secret, and each wore a mask." The sibilant phrase, "sucked a secret", suggests a delicious enjoyment of their falsehoods. The drama compounds in this sonnet when the husband suggests his torture is caused by his wife's "beauty". Her beauty infects his mouth with a "bitter taste" and as a result he is "sickened". Yet he cannot resist being susceptible to her charms and so when "their smiles encountered, he went mad, / And raged deep inward, till the light was brown / Before his vision, and the world forgot, / Looked wicked as some old dull murder-spot." His anger generates a murderous vision.

Meredith's metaphor that the wife is a "star" that crowns "The pit of infamy" sanctions the polarization of women being either Madonnas or whores. In this case, his wife is the Madonna of all whores; she has made holy and sacrosanct the most detestable evil. Yet the husband becomes what he condemns; in acting on his "vengefulness" he "strove / To ape the magnanimity of love". In other words, the hypocrisy he identifies in his wife he is also guilty of. Indeed, his duality is more contemptible than hers because he is disguising his revenge as love, whereas she is nothing more than a product of his judgement, imagination, and patriarchal Victorian context.

In sonnet XVI, a memory of intimacy surfaces. It is a deeply affecting moment in the sonnet sequence because it speaks to the way in which love is a hot mess. The husband needs to frame this memory with qualifiers that indicate it was merely a passing moment (nothing more), and yet, the setting and detailed account suggests something far more poignant and meaningful. The memory bobs out of the "shipwrecked" debris of their flailing relationship, where they were "Joined slackly" or loosely. Yet the setting he cannot help but reveal is one recalled in distinct and intimate detail. Together they sit in loving companionship in front of the burning fire, a symbol of their passion. He refers to their "bower" nestled in the heart of infinite stories of their "library" and in ear shot of the warm and lubricated chat of others. Indeed, the simile he uses to describe themselves is one of "lovers". Moreover, he acknowledges that "Life's greatest treasure lay / With us, and of it was our talk". This was the truth of their relationship and the truth often of the breakdown of love: that in the midst of trauma and catastrophe, memories of intimacy exist. It is the husband, not the vilified wife, who poisoned this moment: "Ah, yes! / Love dies!" I said...She yearned to me that sentence to unsay." So, despite the fact that they have been discussing the love that lay within them, represented in the metaphor of "Life's greatest treasure", despite the warm bower in which they enjoy the burning fire, despite enjoying themselves as lovers, the husband obliterates the moment with a callous remark. While he might be "haunted" by the salty taste of the tears on her cheek, he is also oddly aroused by the impact his lamentable comment has on his wife, recalling his "kiss" while her sobs lifts "her breast". Malice and arousal seem close bedfellows.

It is no surprise that sonnet XVII explores the hypocritical nature of modern marital love. This sonnet reads in direct contrast to the connection he felt in his wife in sonnet XVI, and yet, it captures the on again off again turbulence of love ending. Here, Meredith uses the extended metaphor of a game to convey the way in which the husband and wife play at married love in front of their guests at a dinner party: "we ply the ball...a most contagious game...Such play as this." She is the perfect hostess who keeps the conversation intellectual and buoyantly "afloat". He is also performing the role of the perfect host and in fact recognizes "the greater wonder" of the gracious hospitality that they "Each ... admire".

I love the way that they are seduced by their own deception. Of course, the game within the game is actually that of hiding their innermost secret, that their love is dead: "HIDING THE SKELETON." Ironically, this is written in upper case as if to affect shouting but in reality, conveying the truth. Meredith extends this metaphor so the guests "see no ghost" while they sup with this perfect couple; hence, they must be directly addressed by the husband: "Dear guests, you now have seen love's corpse-light shine." This phantom light that lures travelers from their designated path has been identified, and thus, these guests have been lured off into a fantasy act of a perfect marriage. Beneath the surface their "marriage-knot" is neither secure nor "sweet" nor "golden". What we, the guests, and the married couple have been privy to is "love's ephemerae": an ancient Greek term that suggests the life span of love is only one day. Love is transient and impermanent.

By the time sonnet XXXIX emerges, the husband has deliberately taken a mistress to combat his wife's *alleged* infidelity. The first 12 lines represent the husband's obsession with not only his Lady but also the signifiers of romantic love. There is no obstruction to his conquest: "She yields... Has yielded." Thus, the mistress is the antonym to his wife who has resisted giving him the love he requires but has offered it elsewhere. Here with his mistress, he is the unassailed conqueror who claims the mistress' romantic attributes in lyrical ecstasy: "my golden-crownèd rose! / The bride of every sense! more sweet than those / Who breathe the violet breath of maidenhood." The mistress is both the signature of the erotic and pure woman. The yonic symbol of the rose suggests the promise of carnal bliss. Furthermore, the mistress is also in her bridal state and offers the violet blush of a virgin.

Still, this is not enough; the husband must crescendo into the dizzy heights of exclaiming the feminized beauty of the moon, which casts its light about their enchanted rendezvous: "O visage of still music in the sky! / Soft moon! / I feel thy song ... Her long white fingers down the shadowy brook, / That sings her song." It's positively Keatsian! So enamoured is he that he works himself up into a swoon: "half waking, half in dream." It is at this point that we move into the last four lines of the sonnet with its abrupt change of tone signalling the arrival of his wife and her lover. Rage and mayhem eschew as the poet husband sees "Their hands touch! Am I still tame? / God, what a dancing spectre seems the moon!" No longer is the moon drenching his new found affair in the song of romance; rather, its changeable nature is now an untamed madness haunting the cuckolded husband.

Sonnet XL takes us mid-stream into an argument between the husband and his mistress. The perfect husband plummets from ecstasy to misery as his mistress asks the obvious: does he still love his wife? I am afraid he doth protest too much when he answers with two emotionally charged rhetorical questions: "Know I my meaning, I? Can I love one, / And yet be jealous of another?" The husband does not know himself well and is profoundly jealous of the new love his wife has found, despite his claims to the contrary. What then follows is an analysis of "Terrible Love". So, the husband does have some awareness of the spell he is under and recognizes the hold it has on him. He proffers his opinion, inserting the archaic term "ween" meaning to be of the opinion. The husband acknowledges that "even dead" this terrible love has great power over him: "half sighing to upheave / The lightless seas of selfishness amain: / Seas that in a man's heart have no rain / To fall and still them." The metaphor of this appalling love lifting up the dark ocean of desire until it surges with such force, indicated by the archaic term "amain", that it cannot be subdued, suggests how completely he is drowning in love for his wife. He then asks how can peace be achieved by turning to his wife: "this fountain-source of woe, / This woman, who's to Love as fire to wood?"

Firstly, the metaphor indicates that while she is the source of inspiration, the wife is a grotesque muse generating endless anguish. Secondly, the parallelism indicates that she is completely and utterly destructive. Thus, peace cannot be achieved while his obsessive love for her continues. This is a man in the throes of torment and extreme distress. The husband recalls her blush of purity once: "She breathed the violet breath of maidenhood / Against my kisses once! but I say, No!" He sees himself shipwrecked on this dark sea of desire, "Helplessly afloat". He is without bearings and cannot navigate his way to safety. He knows that it is this which is strangling his fledging new found love with his mistress: "The dread that my old love may be alive, / Has seized my nursling new love by the throat." He is damned.

The penultimate sonnet XLIX takes us to his wife's suicide. The husband finds his wife thwarted by the sea of dark desire: "He found her by the ocean's moaning verge." So strong is his love that it has become her triumph and her curse. In a dreamlike state, she walks upon the shore of this surreal ocean of love as the "wife he sought, though shadow-like and dry". It is as if his inability to let her go has made her a lesser version of herself. Therefore, she refuses to look inward: "She dared not say, 'This is my breast: look in.'" In her heart she knew she had returned to him, a broken thing. In this piteous state, she "pleads" for "Sin". So, he responds, because he is her "Sin", and goes to her in "the middle of the night". It is as if she requires him to seal the deal, which will once again lead her to asphyxiation: "'Now kiss me, dear! it may be, now!' she said. / Lethe had passed those lips, and he knew all." The river in Hades, the ancient underworld, took its passengers to oblivion and forgetfulness. This is her only balm. So, is this the only outcome for a modern woman to return to the husband and have sex even though she is locked in a loveless marriage?

The dénouement of this opera of modern love is sonnet L. Here the poet husband offers up the zoomorphic metaphor of his wife and self being carrion birds of prey, forced to live the feverish life: "These two were rapid falcons in a snare, / Condemned to do the flitting of the bat." The lives of the poet husband and the wife have become a travesty. Despite the sibilant assurances of spring in all its fertility, they are lovers who hunger for the darkness: "Lovers beneath the singing sky of May…Their hearts held cravings for the buried day." To each other they offer nothing but pain and suffering; in the endless interrogation and accusatory rhetoric which make up their world: "Then each applied to each that fatal knife / Deep questioning, which probes to endless dole." The paradox is that our "hot" cravings for "certainties" are met in the end with the profoundly unsatisfying "dusty answer". This is modern love. The final four lines of the sonnet sequence suggest that this is a tale that needs to be heard. Indeed, the "tragic hints here" are a drop in the ocean of the dark, surging passion ever present in the Victorian world. Meredith finalizes this sonnet sequence by completing one of the extended metaphors that has worked its way throughout *Modern Love*: the dark ocean as forbidden love: "dark as yonder midnight ocean's force ... To throw that fain thin line upon the shore!" No wonder this poem was banned!

At a Month's End by Algernon Charles Swinburne (1866)

The night last night was strange and shaken:
More strange the change of you and me.
Once more, for the old love's love forsaken,
We went out once more toward the sea.

For the old love's love-sake dead and buried,
One last time, one more and no more,
We watched the waves set in, the serried
Spears of the tide storming the shore.

Hardly we saw the high moon hanging,
Heard hardly through the windy night
Far waters ringing, low reefs clanging,
Under wan skies and waste white light.

With chafe and change of surges chiming,
The clashing channels rocked and rang
Large music, wave to wild wave timing,
And all the choral water sang.

Faint lights fell this way, that way floated,
Quick sparks of sea-fire keen like eyes
From the rolled surf that flashed, and noted
Shores and faint cliffs and bays and skies.

The ghost of sea that shrank up sighing
At the sand's edge, a short sad breath
Trembling to touch the goal, and dying
With weak heart heaved up once in death —

The rustling sand and shingle shaken

With light sweet touches and small sound —
These could not move us, could not waken
Hearts to look forth, eyes to look round.

Silent we went an hour together,
Under grey skies by waters white.
Our hearts were full of windy weather,
Clouds and blown stars and broken light.

Full of cold clouds and moonbeams drifted
And streaming storms and straying fires,
Our souls in us were stirred and shifted
By doubts and dreams and foiled desires.

Across, aslant, a scudding sea-mew
Swam, dipped, and dropped, and grazed the sea:
And one with me I could not dream you;
And one with you I could not be

As the white wing the white wave's fringes
Touched and slid over and flashed past —
As a pale cloud a pale flame tinges
From the moon's lowest light and last —

As a star feels the sun and falters,
Touched to death by diviner eyes —
As on the old gods' untended altars
The old fire of withered worship dies —

(Once only, once the shrine relighted
Sees the last fiery shadow shine,
Last shadow of flame and faith benighted,
Sees falter and flutter and fail the shrine)

So once with fiery breath and flying
Your winged heart touched mine and went,
And the swift spirits kissed, and sighing,
Sundered and smiled and were content.

That only touch, that feeling only,
Enough we found, we found too much;
For the unlit shrine is hardly lonely
As one the old fire forgets to touch.

Slight as the sea's sight of the sea-mew,
Slight as the sun's sight of the star:
Enough to show one must not deem you
For love's sake other than you are.

Who snares and tames with fear and danger
A bright beast of a fiery kin,
Only to mar, only to change her
Sleek supple soul and splendid skin?

Easy with blows to mar and maim her,
Easy with bonds to bind and bruise;
What profit, if she yield her tamer
The limbs to mar, the soul to lose?

Best leave or take the perfect creature,
Take all she is or leave complete;
Transmute you will not form or feature,
Change feet for wings or wings for feet.

Strange eyes, new limbs, can no man give her;
Sweet is the sweet thing as it is.
No soul she hath, we see, to outlive her;
Hath she for that no lips to kiss?

So may one read his weird, and reason,
And with vain drugs assuage no pain.
For each man in his loving season
Fools and is fooled of these in vain.

Charms that allay not any longing,
Spells that appease not any grief,
Time brings us all by handfuls, wronging
All hurts with nothing of relief.

Ah, too soon shot, the fool's bolt misses!
What help? the world is full of loves;
Night after night of running kisses,
Chirp after chirp of changing doves.

Should Love disown or disesteem you
For loving one man more or less?

You could not tame your light white sea-mew,
Nor I my sleek black pantheress.

For a new soul let whoso please pray,
We are what life made us, and shall be.
For you the jungle and me the sea-spray,

And south for you and north for me.

But this one broken foam-white feather
I throw you off the hither wing,
Splashed stiff with sea-scurf and salt weather,
This song for sleep to learn and sing —

Sing in your ear when, daytime over,
You, couched at long length on hot sand
With some sleek sun-discolored lover,
Wince from his breath as from a brand:

Till the acrid hour aches out and ceases,
And the sheathed eyeball sleepier swims,
The deep flank smoothes its dimpling creases.
And passion loosens all the limbs:

Till dreams of sharp grey north-sea weather
Fall faint upon your fiery sleep,
As on strange sands a strayed bird's feather
The wind may choose to lose or keep.

But I, who leave my queen of panthers,
As a tired honey-heavy bee
Gilt with sweet dust from gold-grained anthers
Leaves the rose-chalice, what for me?

From the ardours of the chaliced center,
From the amorous anthers' golden grime,
That scorch and smutch all wings that enter,
I fly forth hot from honey-time.

But as to a bee's gilt thighs and winglets
The flower-dust with flower-smell clings;
As a snake's mobile rampant ringlets
Leave the sand marked with print of rings;

So to my soul in surer fashion
Your savage stamp and savour hangs;
The print and perfume of old passion,
The wild-beast mark of panther's fangs.

This magnificent poem tells the story of two estranged lovers who have been abandoned by love. The sea, sky, and shoreline become the theatre, conveying the hopelessness of lovers doomed. Algernon Charles Swinburne, diminutive in stature, was a giant of talent. In this poem, he demonstrates his formidable capabilities in 132 lines constituted by 33 quatrains. Swinburne's poem creates a poetic landscape in vivid colors, high modal emotion, and intense other-worldliness. *At a Months End*, published in 1866, conveys the powerful palette of the Brotherhood, and in a way, offers another perspective to Morris' *Modern Love* sonnet sequence. Let's consider the title of this poem, "At a Month's End". The poet has completed all transactions and drawn up all accounts of these two lovers who initially stepped out on the darkling stage with the squall of their love life about them. These two players begin to see themselves in wild untethered creatures who know that their forsaken love can no longer create a landscape in which they can co-habit.

The first seven quatrains represent the wild windswept seascape, witnessed at night by the two lovers who have chosen, "for the old love's love forsaken", to walk out toward the sea, "once more". The internal rhyme, repetition, and alliteration create a mesmeric read. There is an eerie strangeness with the lovers suggesting something fatalistic and foreboding. The stage is set in these first seven quatrains with the soundscape that swells from the orchestra pit: the amplified sibilance of the sea "serried / Spears of the tide storming the shore"; the alliterative wash of "We watched the waves"; the sibilant fricative of "chafe and change ... chiming, / The clashing channels"; and the uvular "rocked and rang". Anticipation rises as the players step out on to center stage.

Quatrains eight and nine tell us that they are not awakened to this soundscape because they bear their own tempestuous land and sea scape within: "Our hearts were full of windy weather, / Clouds and blown stars and broken light. / Full of cold clouds and moonbeams drifted / And streaming storms and straying fires." This site where love has abandoned them is without light or protection; it is an ominous and dangerous place. The next seven quatrains follow the extended metaphor of the lover as a sea bird. Swinburne imagines this is how the beloved sees the lover: as a free and powerful bird completely one with the external landscape. In quatrain ten, they gaze upon the "sea-mew" and are momentarily distracted from the "doubts and dreams and foiled desires" that articulate their forsaken love. This bird plummets with acrobatic delight, which is captured in the assonant verbs: "Across, aslant ... scudding ... Swam, dipped, and dropped, and grazed." Both watch on but remain separate and private in their musings. The next three quatrains begin the build-up of similes of the lover as sea bird: free, pure, pale, bright, and faithful. This culminates in the 14th quatrain where the lover imagines the beloved as "flying / Your winged heart touched mine." At this point, the beloved realizes the dangers of imagining the lover as something other than what he is.

From quatrains 17 to 25, we leave the metaphor of sea birds to something far more exotic. The lover imagines the beloved as his captured "black pantheress". Throughout these particular quatrains, the poet explores the human desire to capture, tame, and ultimately change the nature of the wild being one has targeted: "Who snares and tames ... Only to mar, only to change her / Sleek supple soul and splendid skin?" He is adamant in his knowledge that her soul will be lost should the hunter use "blows... bonds to bind and bruise." Swinburne's own sadomasochistic peccadillos in real life heighten the plosive frenzy of the hunt, here in the poem, thus we are forced to linger over the suffering inflicted and received in the name of love. The lover is aware that his destiny, expressed in the archaic use of "weird", and his "reason" cannot be eased by drugs, charms, or spells. Yet, he knows that all lovers are fools and he attempts to capture her: "Ah, too soon shot, the fool's bolt misses!" At last, with a sober reflection matching the beloved's, the lover concludes that "You could not tame your light white sea-mew, / Nor I my sleek black pantheress."

I think it is interesting that the lover imagines himself as a "sea-mew" (the archaic term for sea gull, the large coastal bird that is ground nesting and opportunistic but monogamous). He imagines his beloved as a "black pantheress", which I would have thought were few and far between in Victorian England. The black leopard is large, fierce, and considered all body and no soul. Both animals are carnivores but without a doubt she is the life-threatening, unpredictable variable in their landscape of forsaken love. Thus, they are incompatible and belong in different worlds: "you the jungle and me the sea-spray, / And south for you and north for me."

In the last eight quatrains of this poem, the lover sends a talisman of himself into the air. He breaks a "foam-white feather" from his "wing", which floats towards the sun-drenched sand where his beloved reclines. The feather carries his potent song, which will distract her while she is copulating with "some sleek sun-discolored lover". As a consequence, she will recoil as if burned from her new lover's intimacies: "Wince from his breath as from a brand / Till the acrid hour aches out and ceases, / And the sheathed eyeball sleepier swims." The forsaken "old love" thus takes his revenge so that the beloved must forfeit all love and dream only of him: "Till dreams of sharp grey north-sea weather."

In the last four quatrains of the poem, the lover leaves "my queen of panthers" as "a tired honey-heavy bee". With pedantic detail, he considers the departure he is making from the beloved and her yonic "rose-chalice"; indeed, their own lovemaking has been a fiery descent from which he flies forth, burned and marked "hot from honey-time". He leaves the beloved and the poem with the build-up of two similes that culminate in a parallelism: "as to a bee's gilt thighs ... flower-smell clings; / As a snake's mobile rampant ringlets / Leave the sand marked with print of rings; / So to my soul ... Your savage stamp and savour hangs." In other words, the beloved has left her mark on the lover. This imprint of herself is nonetheless violent and brutal. Meanwhile, his soul bears the "wild-beast mark of panther's fangs", which ultimately has allowed the lover to create a poem of such bite.

Willowwood 1 by Gabriel Dante Rossetti (1869)

I sat with Love upon a woodside well,
Leaning across the water, I and he;
Nor ever did he speak nor looked at me,

But touched his lute wherein was audible
The certain secret thing he had to tell:
Only our mirrored eyes met silently
In the low wave; and that sound came to be
The passionate voice I knew; and my tears fell.
And at their fall, his eyes beneath grew hers;
And with his foot and with his wing-feathers
He swept the spring that watered my heart's drouth.
Then the dark ripples spread to waving hair,
And as I stooped, her own lips rising there
Bubbled with brimming kisses at my mouth.

In 1869, Dante Gabriel Rossetti published his sonnet sequence, *Willowwood*. This is a local place name given to an area in Somerset, where his sister, Christina, and mother had lived. Rossetti was one of the founding members of the Brotherhood and galvanized the Pre-Raphaelites to create and live out their artistic enterprises. Rossetti himself suffered from self-doubt, obsessions, self-reproach, melancholia, paranoia, and a range of other problems. Although gifted as both an artist and poet, Rossetti had grave concerns about his abilities and seemed to need the exclusive access to firstly Elizabeth Siddal then Jane Morris as infatuated objects of desire. He was drawn to women who were withdrawn, oftentimes sick, and melancholic. Rossetti's sonnet sequence can be read as a turning away from his painting of wife and former muse, Siddal to the obsessive depiction of his next muse and lover, Morris. Rossetti married Siddal in 1860, and she was dead less than two years later. Her ethereal tragic beauty seemed to haunt Rossetti long after she was dead.

Prior to his marriage to Siddal, Rossetti had met Jane Burden in 1857; she quickly became his model. Jane married William Morris in 1859 after Rossetti introduced them. Rossetti and Jane Morris remained companions and lovers on and off until Rossetti's death from blood poisoning. The two paintings in particular that frame this sonnet sequence are Rossetti's representation of Dante's great muse, Siddal as Beatrice in *Beata Beatrix* (1863) completed a year after his wife's death, and his portrayal of Jane Morris in *Water Willow* (1871). The sonnets represent the lover bereft and desirous for the beloved, and yet, she is absent. The beloved is the muse to the poet or lover, but she is also nothing more than the flux and fluidity of an image in the water. Let's have a closer look at each sonnet.

In *Willowwood I*, the lover sits in close proximity to "Love", otherwise known as Eros. Hesiod wrote about Eros in 700 B.C. as one of the four primordial gods: the others being Chaos, Gaia or Earth, and Tartarus or the Underworld. Later, Greek Mythology depicted Eros as the handsome son of Aphrodite in full command of his sexual powers and a master artist. The Roman mythology depicted Eros as Cupid, a blindfolded chubby child. Thus, Eros is the god who inflicts the delicious wound upon the unsuspecting beloved. The beloved is always passive and the lover, active. The beloved is object and the lover subject.

In Rossetti's first sonnet, the lover is seemingly impotent but desirous of the potency Eros can generate. Eros and the lover sit "upon a woodside well / Leaning across the water". This well is the

19th century equivalent of Helicon's sacred springs associated with the muses. The muses embodied inspiration for poetry, songs, and myths, so it is no surprise that the lover is longing for the beloved (who was once his muse). The sonnet's octet, with the rhyming scheme of a b b a a b b a, sets up the conundrum of the lover bereft of his beloved as muse; the sestet c d d e e d offers a seductive solution.

Eros takes up his lute and plays; his music transforms into the "passionate voice" of the beloved. The lover weeps, and his tears alter the watery reflection of the beloved: "at their fall, his eyes beneath grew hers." Eros then moves his "wing-feathers" across the spring so that the "dark ripples spread to waving hair". The lover leans in and "her own lips rising there / Bubbled with brimming kisses at my mouth". The lover remains suspended in this position of yearning until sonnet four. The lover is in a freeze-frame. Forever bent over the well of his desire with his lips closed over the beloved's, who remains nothing but a reflection. The act of kissing is also the act of drinking in her loveliness and ending the lover's drought. Thus, in this first sonnet, we see the way in which Eros is a shapeshifter who toys with the lover. There is something reminiscent here of Ovid's Narcissus, where the beauteous young man gazes lovingly into the reflection of himself. Is the lover really yearning for the beloved, or is he wanting inspiration from the muse? Is the desire to create ultimately an act of self-love? What we see is that the poet's drought has been broken because sonnet one has just appeared.

Willowwood 2 by Gabriel Dante Rossetti (1869)

And now Love sang: but his was such a song,
So meshed with half-remembrance hard to free,
As souls disused in death's sterility
May sing when the new birthday tarries long.
And I was made aware of a dumb throng
That stood aloof, one form by every tree,
All mournful forms, for each was I or she,
The shades of those our days that had no tongue.
They looked on us, and knew us and were known;
While fast together, alive from the abyss,
Clung the soul-wrung implacable close kiss;
And pity of self through all made broken moan
Which said, 'For once, for once, for once alone!'
And still Love sang, and what he sang was this:--

In the octet of the second sonnet, the lover is carried along in a desolate and doleful atmosphere, evoked by Eros' plaintive song. This extreme yearning is conveyed in the parallelism: "As souls disused in death's sterility / May sing when the new birthday tarries long." Put another way, just as souls which are abandoned in the "sterility" of death yearn for the anniversary of birth's newness, so is the longing evoked by Eros' song. The lover becomes aware of the shades in the wooded setting who are "mournful forms" and then notices that "each was I or she". The lover and beloved as doppelganger is part of the Gothic mythology and pertains to the myth of Narcissus whereby a malevolent likeness or double walker not only offers a virtual reality but also one's death.

Rossetti's painting *How They Met Themselves*, initially painted on his honeymoon with Siddal and then later completed in 1864, captures his obsession with this concept of duality and reflection. Awash with the spectral presence of all they were in the past, it foregrounds the fate of the lover and his beloved as a result of dwelling in the shadow of death rather than ascending to the divine sphere. The volta takes us into the sestet where we see the doppelgangers of the lover and the beloved ratchet up calamity. They move in close together and are vividly "alive" in the underworld with the "implacable close kiss". The doppelgangers of the lover and beloved declare in "broken moan... / For once, for once, for once alone!", perhaps suggesting that this can be their only way of reuniting once more. We leave sonnet two on a cliffhanger with Eros about to launch into the actual song that has conjured the shades, the doppelgangers, and the lover's wretchedness.

Willowwood 3 by Gabriel Dante Rossetti (1869)

'O ye, all ye that walk in Willowwood,
That walk with hollow faces burning white;
What fathom-depth of soul-struck widowhood,
What long, what longer hours, one lifelong night,
Ere ye again, who so in vain have wooed
Your last hope lost, who so in vain invite
Your lips to that their unforgotten food,
Ere ye, ere ye again shall see the light!
Alas! the bitter banks in Willowwood,
With tear-spurge wan, with blood-wort burning red:
Alas! if ever such a pillow could
Steep deep the soul in sleep till she were dead,
Better all life forget her than this thing,
That Willowwood should hold her wandering!'

Here, Eros' song is one of hope edged with caution. With the melodious interplay of "w" and "l", the octet sings of the soul's dark suffering as it remains in a place of deprivation and loss. Eros addresses all who are gathered at Willowwood in the archaic plural term "ye": shades, doppelgangers, and the lover himself (who with "hollow faces burning white" hunger for the "unforgotten food"). At the end of the octet, Eros makes a promise: "Ere ye, ere ye again shall see the light!" Therefore, before long, redemption from this night of the soul will end.

The volta takes us into the sestet where we look closely at what is growing close by the banks of Willowwood: herbaceous plants that are the objective correlative of the weeping and suffering of the haunted: "tear-spurge wan, with blood-wort burning red." Indeed, it is this very landscape that will ensure the soul's descent: "if ever such a pillow could / Steep deep the soul in sleep till she were dead." How right the poets got it, from Homer to Virgil to Dante and Rossetti; grief is the place that will destroy you if you choose to stay there. One's heartache will nurture the descent into complete and utter self-annihilation. Finally, Eros sings that it is "Better all life forget her than this thing / That Willowwood should hold her wandering!" It is better to live a life without the beloved than to be trapped in mourning and haunted by the spectre of her.

Willowwood 4 by Gabriel Dante Rossetti (1869)

> So sang he: and as meeting rose and rose
> Together cling through the wind's wellaway
> Nor change at once, yet near the end of day
> The leaves drop loosened where the heart-stain glows,--
> So when the song died did the kiss unclose;
> And her face fell back drowned, and was as grey
> As its grey eyes; and if it ever may
> Meet mine again I know not if Love knows.
> Only I know that I leaned low and drank
> A long draught from the water where she sank,
> Her breath and all her tears and all her soul:
> And as I leaned, I know I felt Love's face
> Pressed on my neck with moan of pity and grace,
> Till both our heads were in his aureole.

The lover is no longer frozen in time, his lips pressed against the water. Here scoops up to his lips the replenishing spring of inspiration, which is the beloved, which is the muse: "meeting rose and rose / Together cling." All the while, Eros has been singing, time has been passing, and this is played out in the musical score of the wind's lament and the fall of leaves: "the wind's wellaway … near the end of day / The leaves drop." Thus, the lover, transfixed by the watery kiss of the beloved, understood that their union, like Eros' song, would have to come to an end: "So when the song died did the kiss unclose." For a kiss to open means that the lover's thirsty lips are no longer pursed but disconnected from that of the beloved's. Consequently, she falls back into the well, and her image begins to drown. One cannot help but think of Siddal at 20 posing for Millais' drowned *Ophelia*. This painting, with its botanical specificity and faithful rendering, was regarded by the Victorians as quintessential Pre-Raphaelite. The intensity of subject matter and method was regarded as new and shocking. All of this can be seen in such poems as Rossetti's sonnet sequence here. In the sestet, we edge towards the conclusion of this drama. The lover admits that he drinks long and deep from the beloved's sorrow and soul. Thus, the beloved as muse has entered him. The great shapeshifter Eros now pushes up against the lover's neck so that both the beloved and lover are encased in light; they are made holy: "I felt Love's face / Pressed on my neck with moan of pity and grace, / Till both our heads were in his aureole."

As a final note to this chapter, it is interesting to consider that the Pre-Raphaelite painters rejected working on a canvas prepared with black paint; rather, they prepared their canvases with white paint and even at times wet white paint to generate luminosity, a radical notion at the time. I think the same primer was applied to Pre-Raphaelite poetry. Moreover, the division between poetry and painting was retracted. They went forward poet and painter alike with John Ruskin's axiom to represent with a singularness of heart. The Pre-Raphaelites did not prize conformity but rather created a world that still excites our eye and mind to this day.

7

As We See Ourselves: Australian Poetry

Recently I taught a course that offered a survey of the way we see ourselves in Australian poetry. This mirror reflected a multi-faceted Australian self: humorous yet deeply thoughtful, challenged and filled with self-doubt, honest but seductive and so on. National identity is built on a range of preoccupations and poetry is the crystalized voice of who we are. Poetry provides a glass through which we look to see ourselves, then and now. It pins down the core of what matters. Poetry preserves the transient and beautiful. It is the media through which we can come to know ourselves. The unexpected responses are important to contemplate because we need these if we are to grow into our full engagement with how we see ourselves as Australians and as a nation. In this chapter I would like to pair two poets together and listen to the dialectic. I ask myself: Do women and men write poetry differently? Are they preoccupied with the same sorts of subject matter? Can art provide entry points or aftermath pathways to the poems we read? What do you think?

I remember at Sydney University Professor Elizabeth Webby teaching the Australian 19th century poets and writers. I had lived and worked in a remote mining town as well as traveled extensively through the outback of Australia before I got to Sydney University, so in some ways I was interested to see whether there were representations of the tension I had experienced between city and country life. In Kalgoorlie, the world of academic argument, fashion trends and political correctness were, for the most part, irrelevant. When traveling the Canning Stock Route and the Gunbarrel Highway or when exploring the Mitchell Plateau and the Kimberley, I began to see the ways in which landscape outside of the city was intensely meaningful. It had its own body and psyche. Placed within that landscape I too seemed to become a different person; someone without radio static because the dial had now located the exact station of who I was. The exact station: I am washing my two year old daughter by moonlight on the other side of the old Toyota High lux. It's late in the evening but warm. No one tells you about desert skies. Thick and primeval; the desert night sky is enormous and bedecked with stars of such luminosity! My daughter stands in a small plastic container and I douse her in warm water, chatting and giggling. Then behind me, down the sand dunes a herd of wild camels charge. I stand up and she presses into my leg. The smell and sight and sound of these huge animals is stunning. They come as one and weave their way with such grace and beauty that I don't speak. I don't call out. I don't move. There is moonlight above them and it is the most incredible spectacle I have ever witnessed. Their power. Their nonchalance. Their noisy quiet. They veer to the left and run past where we stand. On and on they run but slower now until we cannot see or hear or smell them. At this moment my daughter says: "Camels."

Reverie by Louisa Lawson (1895)

I am sitting by the river,
And I while an hour away,
Watching circles start and widen
In their momentary play.

Here a stronger whelms a weaker
As its ring expanding flies,
There one rises to the surface,
As another fades and dies.

And I solemn grow with thinking,
For just now it would me seem,
That each life is like a circle -
On time's deep, impellant stream.

Do we not upon its bosom
Linger for a little day,
Making faint and fleeting impress,
Then forever fade away.

While the strong unresting river
Toward Eternity doth glide,
All regardless of the circles
That have pulsed upon its tide.

Louisa Lawson writes *Reverie* in 1895 and publishes it in *The Dawn*. This was the journal she established and employed an all-female staff, bringing down upon her the ire of Trade Unions. Lawson was born on a station out of Mudgee New South Wales and was one of 12. When she married Norwegian born Niels Larson they Anglicized their name to Lawson. She moved on from the life of being married to a mining prospector and arrived in Sydney as a single mother with four children. Here she ran boarding houses and established her own journal, *The Dawn*, which was a success for 17 years. An articulate suffragette and feminist, Lawson argued for women's right to vote, to hold public office, to be educated, to have legal and economic rights, to have union protection and to be free from domestic violence. When New South Wales' white women gained the vote in 1902, Lawson was introduced to Parliament as the *Mother of Suffrage*. Sadly, in old age Lawson suffered from loneliness, impoverished circumstances and loss of memory and was admitted to *Gladesville Hospital for the Insane*. When she died at 72 in 1920 she had seen enormous change and constitutional development. Her world had been charged by energy, debate and self-improvement;

Reverie is made up of five quatrains where lines two and four rhyme. The river is the extended metaphor for the way in which our thinking and our actions make a momentary impression on life. Rather than see this as a depressing realisation that our life basically amounts to nothing, Lawson suggests that it is these very thoughts and actions which move us all towards eternity. A view in accord with the spiritual thinking of her day. As for Lawson herself I can't see her at any point having the time or the peace of mind to sit by a river and whittle away the hours in contemplation. I see that more as a male poet's prerogative as well as a first world contemporary option. Although a promising academic student she, like many women before and after her, left school in her third year of high-school to look after her siblings. Married at 18 and mother of four children, she remained hard working and resourceful without financial support from her children's father throughout her adult life. Sitting by the river and pondering the mysteries of life is a poetic subject matter that offered the reader certain expectations. Just like the Romantic poets one 100 years before her, Lawson understood nature to be the guide, teacher and source of inspiration. Moreover, our connection with the sublime could be experienced in the meditation of the natural landscape.

In the first quatrain Lawson connects the endless playfulness of widening circles in the river with whiling away time: "I am sitting by the river,/ And I while an hour away." Her audience is primarily *The Dawn* readership; so white women, sufficiently educated and progressive thinkers. She wanted to not only appeal to middle class women but to the working class so she kept the price of the journal low enough for working class women to afford. The subject matter reflected her deeply religious ideas of pedagogical writing but also it was a salient reminder that Lawson, under her pseudonym Dora Falconer, had working class roots in the Australian outback. Furthermore, *The Dawn* was in direct opposition to *The Bulletin* published solely for men and representing women as vain, conniving and bent on entrapment. Here in her poem Lawson constructs a woman emancipated from the domestic, situated in the great expanse of nature and musing the wonders of eternity. Indeed, she writes a poem that explores thinking about thinking. The second quatrain, like the first, considers the endless cycle of ever changing patterns on the river's skin: "Here a stronger whelms a weaker... There one rises to the surface." It is full of clarity and could be read symbolically as the way thoughts and actions sometimes make deeper marks, whereas at other times they might be subsumed into the thoughts and actions of others. Both quatrains draw us on, with their rhythmic cadence, to a realisation that we are part of a national consciousness because our thoughts and actions are absorbed by the landscape of our country.

Lawson spells out the point of comparison for us here in the third quatrain. She contemplates: "That each life is like a circle -/ On time's deep, impellant stream." Today the adjectival phrase would be "impelling stream" but either way it generates the idea that our lives offer a completion to time passing, no matter how small and insignificant. The river of time can do nothing but flow on and yet it is shaped momentarily by what our lives contribute. It is a gentle and tender message to readers of her day. The 4th quatrain continues this idea of lingering upon the "bosom" of the river of time. This in turn suggests that time nurtures and suckles sufficiently to make "faint and fleeting impress". The repetitious use of the alliterative "f" in this quatrain's 3rd and 4th line, links together "faint", "fleeting", "forever" and "fade". This is the ephemeral nature of our mark on time. The soundscape of these words imitates the soft undulation of the river and thus assure us that this is in keeping with the natural order of the universe. The final quatrain takes us beyond the poem's lyrical beginnings of sitting alongside a river contemplating our thoughts and actions as well as that of time. Lawson offers us reassurance that while the river of time is "unresting" it glides "Toward Eternity". There is nothing turbulent or tempestuous about this force of nature as it makes its way to time without end. Thus the "circles" we have made also go to this site of perpetuity. Our thoughts and actions have "pulsed upon its tide", offering a life beat, no matter how small, to Eternity.

What a beautiful soft reverie to offer a calamitous world, one that remains filled with doubt, hardship and suffering. I do think we still see ourselves as a nation that finds the landscape both life taking and life giving. Here, Lawson, is asking us to take time in companionable quiet with the Australian landscape in order to revitalise and send our thoughts, aspirations and concerns into the belly of eternity.

In Defence of the Bush by Banjo Patterson (1892)

So you're back from up the country, Mister Lawson, where you went,
And you're cursing all the business in a bitter discontent;
Well, we grieve to disappoint you, and it makes us sad to hear
That it wasn't cool and shady -- and there wasn't plenty beer,
And the loony bullock snorted when you first came into view;
Well, you know it's not so often that he sees a swell like you;
And the roads were hot and dusty, and the plains were burnt and brown,
And no doubt you're better suited drinking lemon-squash in town.

Yet, perchance, if you should journey down the very track you went
In a month or two at furthest you would wonder what it meant,
Where the sunbaked earth was gasping like a creature in its pain
You would find the grasses waving like a field of summer grain,
And the miles of thirsty gutters blocked with sand and choked with mud,
You would find them mighty rivers with a turbid, sweeping flood;
For the rain and drought and sunshine make no changes in the street,
In the sullen line of buildings and the ceaseless tramp of feet;
But the bush hath moods and changes, as the seasons rise and fall,
And the men who know the bush-land -- they are loyal through it all.

But you found the bush was dismal and a land of no delight,

Did you chance to hear a chorus in the shearers' huts at night?
Did they "rise up, William Riley" by the camp-fire's cheery blaze?
Did they rise him as we rose him in the good old droving days?
And the women of the homesteads and the men you chanced to meet --
Were their faces sour and saddened like the "faces in the street",
And the "shy selector children" -- were they better now or worse
Than the little city urchins who would greet you with a curse?
Is not such a life much better than the squalid street and square
Where the fallen women flaunt it in the fierce electric glare,
Where the sempstress plies her sewing till her eyes are sore and red
In a filthy, dirty attic toiling on for daily bread?
Did you hear no sweeter voices in the music of the bush
Than the roar of trams and 'buses, and the war-whoop of "the push"?
Did the magpies rouse your slumbers with their carol sweet and strange?
Did you hear the silver chiming of the bell-birds on the range?
But, perchance, the wild birds' music by your senses was despised,
For you say you'll stay in townships till the bush is civilised.
Would you make it a tea-garden and on Sundays have a band
Where the "blokes" might take their "donahs", with a "public" close at hand?
You had better stick to Sydney and make merry with the "push",
For the bush will never suit you, and you'll never suit the bush.

Can you imagine a high profile Australian magazine today publishing poetry in a number of consecutive issues as a way of shaping a national identity? Here we have two of the most prominent poets of this country locking horns, kind of playfully, about what it means to be Australian. *The Bulletin* was established in 1880 as a fiercely nationalistic, pro Labor and pro Republican publication. It was a place in which aspiring writers could test their mettle. *The Bulletin* offered a mix of political commentary, Australian Literature and sensationalist news. In 1886 it changed its banner from "Australia for Australians" to "Australians for White People". The iconic bush poets emerged from this backdrop. Andrew Parton 'Banjo' Paterson, 1864 – 1941, was born near Orange and grew up in Bingalong, near the Menindee Lakes, and then Yass until he was sent to Sydney Grammar School. Banjo was the name of his favorite horse and he called himself this when he began writing. He trained as a solicitor then worked as a war correspondent during the Boer War and Boxer Rebellion. For Paterson, the national character was the tough independent heroic underdog. It was Henry Lawson, 1867 – 1922, who got his editor of *The Bulletin* to pay for his trip to the bush in 1892 to investigate the way in which the drought had impacted on the country and the people. Unlike Paterson, Lawson had no romantic illusions about the rural idyll. Indeed, it was his writing which eventually led to Australian realism: dryly laconic, passionately egalitarian and deeply humane writing.

Who is invited to articulate an imagined nation space? At this point in time it was mostly white educated men. The poet Mary Gilmore was not part of this highly stylized contretemps, despite her being on *The Bulletin's* writing staff. The Indigenous contribution to the representation of how this nation was to be imagined was, needless to say, certainly not part of this engagement. How relevant was this well humoured interaction between poets bantering for a national identity to the Australian non-educated workers? I hardly think it meant a great deal. Regardless, over six months in 1892, Banjo Paterson and Henry Lawson were the high profile poets using poetry to argue the validity of a national identity that was either rural or urban orientated. Sales for *The Bulletin* increased as a result. Lawson had initiated this idea with Paterson. It began with Lawson's poem on 9 July 1892 and ran until 20 October 1892 with Paterson having the last poetic word. *In Defence of the Bush* was actually written in response to Lawson's *Borderland*. The other poets involved were Edward Dryson and Francis Kenna.

In Defence of the Bush is written in rhyming couplets and made up of three stanzas of varying lengths. The first line of the poem names Paterson's rival "Mister Lawson" and continues with multiple references to the second person personal pronoun, reminding the reader that this is a direct attack. As a Sydney girl I am tripped by the "back from up the country" but then I remember that this is published in Melbourne and therefore from that perspective it does look back over its shoulder up the map of Australia in order to see itself. Paterson peppers the first stanza with the emotional pejorative: "Cursing...bitter discontent...grieve to disappoint...sad to hear." He makes a dig at Lawson for being such a "swell" that even "the loony bullock snorted" at him with great disdain. The irony of "the roads were hot and dusty, and the plains were burnt and brown" suggest that the beauty of the nation is in the eye of the beholder. Dorothy Mackeller would publish her poem expressing her love of a sunburnt country a dozen years later. The final insult from Paterson to Lawson is of course that he is "better suited drinking lemon-squash in town". The bush is a hard drinking man's world.

In stanza two Paterson moves from landscape of Australia's rural idyll to "the men who know the bush-land". He writes of the way in which this canvas changes according to the seasons: moving from "sunbaked earth ... gasping like a creature" and "thirsty gutters" to "a field of summer grain" and "mighty rivers with a turbid, sweeping flood". The use of contrast works to reinforce the polarised positions Lawson and Paterson's have set up as devotees of either the city or the country. At the tail end of stanza two Paterson criticizes Lawson's urban world that does not respond to the changes in the weather, it is not a living thing, unlike rural or outback Australia. The metamorphosis of the Australian landscape is represented as deeply powerful in its unpredictability and those who abide by its elements "are loyal through it all".

The third stanza randomly steps through 11 provocative statements or questions designed to discredit Paterson's pugnacious poetic partner. The implication is always that Lawson has missed the salient points of beauty in the Australian bush: "Did you...hear a chorus in the shearer's hut...Did they [sing] by camp-fire's cheery blaze?" This segues into Paterson asking if Lawson heard the old Irish ballad: "Rise up, William Riley." This bittersweet ballad emerged in the second decade of the 19th century and sings of the false arrest, imprisonment and threat of transportation, all in the name of love. Riley's colleen turns out to be the very lady from whom he is accused of stealing; all is righted in the end as he is acquitted and goes forth to live the life of Riley. This is a meta-poetic reference from Paterson to remind his listeners that it is the power of song and poetry that will remember a history and offer hope for a future. The 3rd, 4th, 5th and 6th rhyming couplets compare the people of the bush to those in the city. Paterson asks whether Lawson's "haggard women" and their "husbands gone a-droving" are in fact more "sour and saddened" than the men and women of the city; he asks whether the shyness of the children in the outback is a characteristic more tolerable than that of "city urchins" cursing; Paterson asks whether the outback is a better life when the city offers the spectacle of the prostitute under "the fierce electric glare"; and finally he asks if a seamstress can do better than "sewing till her eyes are sore and read/ In a filthy, dirty attic". This banter is not about an aesthetic preference, this is a fierce debate about moral certitude.

The final section of stanza three takes up Paterson's meta-poetic reference to bird song, in the 7th, 8th and 9th couplet. The song of the bush is this poem, one that would "rouse your slumbers". In other words, *In Defence of the Bush* is a wakeup call to a nation to recognise the heroism, resilience and grandeur of the bush. This bush ballad is in opposition to the "roar of trams and 'buses, and the war-whoop of the push". Paterson compares the natural beauty of life with the violence and calamity of man-made artificiality. The *Push* of course, were groups of criminals who roamed the city streets in gangs, picking fights and robbing unsuspecting passer-by's. The non-sanitised unpublished version of *Bastard from the Bush* by Lawson is well worth a glance and certainly does not vilify these treacherous gangs. Thus, it is with irony that Paterson concedes Lawson must remain in the city till the "bush is civilised". The penultimate rhyming couplet asks whether Lawson would make the bush "a tea-garden and on Sundays have a band"; these niceties are set aside for the feminine sensibility in the 1890s. Therefore, Paterson takes a swipe at Lawson's manliness; indeed, he ridicules Lawson's hope for the bush to be civilised by inserting the terms "blokes" and "donahs", bush argot, in these vignettes of genteel past times. Paterson slyly asks would Lawson insert "a "public" close at hand?" suggesting that city life is variously dirty, morally reprehensible and intemperate. The bush accordingly is everything in contrast to the city.

Finally, Paterson asserts that Lawson had "better stick to Sydney". This is the first time the specific city is named. Paterson leaves us and Lawson with a chiasmus: "For the bush will never suit you, and you'll never suit the bush." The effect is that the listener thinks they have heard the entire argument and is lead to favor one side. In this case, it is that those not willing to romanticize the bush should think long and hard about what their national inheritance will be. Curiously, for Lawson it meant that he was replaced by Paterson on the ten dollar bill in 1993. It is not fashionable to teach Australian bush ballads in schools at the moment. This imagining of place and people is not in the psyche of contemporary Australians. I think we do see ourselves as a country that embraces the debate. What I like is the rigor and muscularity of this argument Paterson and Lawson establish, where sentimentality has a role to play in generating a love of country.

Five Bells by Kenneth Slessor (1939)

Time that is moved by little fidget wheels
Is not my Time, the flood that does not flow.
Between the double and the single bell
Of a ship's hour, between a round of bells
From the dark warship riding there below,

I have lived many lives, and this one life
Of Joe, long dead, who lives between five bells.

Deep and dissolving verticals of light
Ferry the falls of moonshine down. Five bells
Coldly rung out in a machine's voice. Night and water
Pour to one rip of darkness, the Harbour floats
In air, the Cross hangs upside-down in water.

Why do I think of you, dead man, why thieve
These profitless lodgings from the flukes of thought
Anchored in Time? You have gone from earth,
Gone even from the meaning of a name.
Yet something's there, yet something forms its lips
And hits and cries against the ports of space,
Beating their sides to make its fury heard.

Are you shouting at me, dead man, squeezing your face
In agonies of speech on speechless panes?
Cry louder, beat the windows, bawl, your name!

But I hear nothing, nothing ... only bells,
Five bells, the bumpkin calculus of Time.
Your echoes die, your voice is dowsed by Life,
There's not a mouth can fly the pygmy strait -
Nothing except the memory of some bones
Long shoved away, and sucked away, in mud;
And unimportant things you might have done,
Or once I thought you did; but you forgot,
And all have now forgotten - looks and words
And slops of beer; your coat with buttons off,
Your gaunt chin and pricked eye, and raging tales
Of Irish kings and English perfidy,
And dirtier perfidy of publicans
Groaning to God from Darlinghurst.

Five bells

Then I saw the road, I heard the thunder
Tumble, and felt the talons of the rain
The night we came to Moorebank in slab-dark,
So dark you bore no body, had no face,

But a sheer voice that rattled out of air
(As now you'd cry if I could break the glass),
A voice that spoke beside me in the bush,
Loud for a breath or bitten off by wind,
Of Milton, melons, and the Rights of Man,
And blowing flutes, and how Tahitian girls
Are brown and angry-tongued, and Sydney girls
Are white and angry-tongued, or so you'd found.
But all I heard was words that didn't join
So Milton became melons, melons girls,
And fifty mouths, it seemed, were out that night,
And in each tree an Ear was bending down,
Or something had just run, gone behind grass,
When, blank and bone-white, like a maniac's thought,
The naphtha-flash of lightning slit the sky,
Knifing the dark with deathly photographs.
There's not so many with so poor a purse,
Or fierce a need, must fare by night like that,
Five miles in darkness on a country track,
But when you do, that's what you think.

Five bells

In Melbourne, your appetite had gone,
Your angers too; they had been leeched away
By the soft archery of summer rains
And the sponge-paws of wetness. The slow damp
That stuck the leaves of living, snailed the mind,
And showed your bones, that had been sharp with
The sodden ecstasies of rectitude.
I thought of what you'd written in faint ink,
Your journal with the sawn-off lock, that stayed behind
With other things you left, all without use,
All without meaning now, except a sign
That someone had been living who now was dead:
'At Labassa. Room 6 x 8
On top of the tower; because of this, very dark
And cold in winter. Everything has been stowed
Into this room - 500 books all shapes
And colors, dealt across the floor
And over sills and on the laps of chairs;

Guns, photoes of many differant things
And different curioes that I obtained....'

In Sydney, by the spent aquarium-flare
Of penny gaslight on pink wallpaper,
We argued about blowing up the world,
But you were living backward, so each night
You crept a moment closer to the breast,
And they were living, all of them, those frames
And shapes of flesh that had perplexed your youth,
And most your father, the old man gone blind,
With fingers always round a fiddle's neck,
That graveyard mason whose fair monuments
And tablets cut with dreams of piety
Rest on the bosoms of a thousand men
Staked bone by bone, in quiet astonishment
At cargoes they had never thought to bear,
These funeral-cakes of sweet and sculptured stone.

Where have you gone? The tide is over you,
The turn of midnight water's over you,
As Time is over you, and mystery,
And memory, the flood that does not flow.
You have no suburb, like those easier dead
In private berths of dissolution laid -
The tide goes over, the waves ride over you
And let their shadows down like shining hair,
But they are Water; and the sea-pinks bend
Like lilies in your teeth, but they are Weed;
And you are only part of an Idea.
I felt the wet push its black thumb-balls in,
The night you died, I felt your eardrums crack,
And the short agony, the longer dream,
The Nothing that was neither long nor short;
But I was bound, and could not go that way,
But I was blind, and could not feel your hand.
If I could find an answer, could only find
Your meaning, or could say why you were here
Who now are gone, what purpose gave you breath
Or seized it back, might I not hear your voice?

I looked out of my window in the dark

At waves with diamond quills and combs of light
That arched their mackerel-backs and smacked the sand
In the moon's drench, that straight enormous glaze,
And ships far off asleep, and Harbour-buoys
Tossing their fireballs wearily each to each,
And tried to hear your voice, but all I heard
Was a boat's whistle, and the scraping squeal
Of seabirds' voices far away, and bells,
Five bells. Five bells coldly ringing out.

Five Bells.

A few decades after Slessor wrote this wondrous poem to the littoral, the threshold space that shapes time, he penned these words about his beloved city in his 1970 selected prose publication *Bread & Wine*: "The character and life of Sydney are shaped continually and imperceptibly by the fingers of the Harbour...the water dyed a whole paint-box's armoury of color with every breath of air, every shift of light or shade, according to the tide, the clock, the weather, and the state of the moon. The water is like silk, like pewter, like blood, like a leopard skin, and occasionally merely like water...the Sydney ferry-boats...take the place of trains and trams...built by practical men to pay practical dividends." I love the way in which he, like many Australians, are preoccupied with that zone where land meets the sea. Australians cling tenaciously around the circumference of this country and in so doing remain in a landscape that is in a constant state of flux and change. We know that the littoral is a site that is both life giving and life taking. A fecund ever-ever, never-never place, where consciousness meets unconsciousness and the rational meets the irrational. John Olsen was inspired to not only paint this poem but to then create a mural; both works capture the rhythms of the city throbbing alongside the great cell of the harbour. It is here, in this littoral site, that Slessor considers the plasticity of time.

I don't see *Five Bells* as an elegy to the cavalier larrikin, Joseph Young Lynch. I think this loose blank verse poem, without rhyme and using iambic pentameter, is a consideration of Bergsonian time. The French philosopher Henri Bergson explained that the moment we measure time it evades us because we assess time as an immobile complete line and yet it is mobile and forever incomplete. Individuals experience time variously; slowly paced, quickly paced, moderately paced and so on but Science reads time as a measurement that is constant and the same. Here in *Five Bells* memory cannot find purchase in the separation of past and present nor in the great signatures of the tolling bell. The motif of the nautical measurement of time, in particular "five bells" runs throughout the poem but not in a tight precise way but rather expanding and contracting as does the irregularity of time. Unlike the tolling of a civil clock which numerates the hour, the ship's timekeeping indicates the four hour watch broken up precisely by the tolling of eight bells for each half hour. Nautical bells shape the working life of the ship: it signals danger in fog, calls alarm with enemy approaching, notes the end of the four hour watch, as well as the end of a sailor's life. Thus, *Five Bells* is an exploration of the plasticity of time and the way in which the dead stay with us.

This blank verse is made up of ten stanzas of various lengths. Five out of the ten stanzas are written in 1937, the other five stanzas are set some ten years beforehand. The first stanza is in italics. It is the trigger that starts this reverie. On hearing the five bells toll Slessor is inexplicably transported to one of the dark edges of his time. In the opening sentence Slessor argues that his "Time" is not denoted by the mechanics of a clock but "the flood that does not flow". From the onset we are placed somewhere both abstract and representational: somewhere between time and water. The second sentence introduces this threshold space where Slessor exists, as perhaps we all do as Australians: "Between the double and the single bell/ Of a ship's hour, between a round of bells/ From the dark warship". Therefore, Slessor's existence, his time, has been flanked by the shoreline of clear representations and the wash of abstract memories. This is the site of the littoral. Most interestingly his time has been lived out as "many lives" one of which is that "Of Joe, long dead, who lives between five bells". Joe Lynch disappeared off the ferry going from Circular Quay to Mosman at 7:45pm on 14 May 1927. Lynch fought off his would be rescuer and drowned, his body was never recovered.

In stanza two we move to the haunting images of light, water and darkness imagined as the place of death for Lynch. Here representation is unfixed and inverted: "Harbour floats/ In air" while its anchor becomes "the Cross [that] hangs upside down in water". The world is turned upside down in the moment of man overboard. Stanza three moves us back to 1937 with Slessor pondering the random enigma of why the dead return to haunt the living. I am caught on the three words "why", "gone" and "something", all are repeated three times. Indeed, Slessor's angst can be summed up in these three words: *why* has this other self *gone* and left him with *something* that "hits and cries" and beats against the opening of space "to make its fury heard". I like this idea, that trapped within us remains the dead; that our time is plagued by the raging of these once living selves. In stanza four Slessor calls out to Lynch through the window "pane" of water; a metaphor for memory, self and the fluidity of time. Meanwhile, Lynch's clamorous anguish cannot be heard: "shouting at me...agonies of speech on speechless panes". Slessor urges Lynch to "Cry louder, beat the windows, bawl your name!" Somewhere in this littoral space of life and death, survival and drowning, land and sea is a place of belonging.

In stanza five Slessor laments that rather than catch Lynch's voice he hears "nothing, nothing...only bells/ Five bells". The repetition imitates the meaningless marking of time. Hourglasses, watches and clocks with their precisely uniform alarms, bells and ticking are simple and unsophisticated measurements of time. Yet one's time is in the vagaries of memory shards. Lynch is enigmatic, represented as ephemeral and not of this world: "voice...dowsed by Life...some bones/ Long shoved away, and sucked away, in mud...unimportant things you might have done." He is also deeply familiar and ever present: "slops of beer; your coat with buttons off,/ Your gaunt chin and pricked eye." To trouble this further, Lynch's narration of self is folded into tales of "Irish kings and English perfidy,/ And dirtier perfidy of publicans...from Darlinghurst". The chorus of "Five bells", suggests memory shards. Stanza five has Lynch in and around Sydney Harbour, stanza six in Moorebank, stanza seven Melbourne, and stanza eight Gladesville. All four stanzas keep us in the mid-1920s.

So, stanza six takes us out past Liverpool to the unsealed five mile road leading into Harley

Matthew's Riverside vineyard in Moorebank. It reads like a staccato scene of King Lear out in the wild and benighted storm tossed heath. I love the dependence on hearing in this stanza because seeing is rendered impossible in the "slab-dark"; except for "The naphtha-flash of lightning slit the sky,/ Knifing the dark with deathly photograph". This sizzling image disrupts the drunken gambolling of "I" and "you" where random non sequiturs are heard but are unclear, uncertain and unfixed. Beleaguered by thunder, lightning, wind, tree branches and things scurrying underfoot their thirst drives them on, "poor a purse/ Or fierce a need". The chorus "Five Bells" randomly forms a break between Moorebank and Melbourne.

Stanza seven puts us in Melbourne in the mid-twenties, a time when both Slessor and Lynch worked for *Punch* magazine. *Five Bells* explores the vicissitudes that make up the palimpsest text of one's time. This stanza offers a contrasting self to what has gone before, "your appetite had gone/ Your angers too...leeched away/ By the soft archery of summer rains". Here Slessor refers to a used notebook given him by Lynch while living in a boarding house in Melbourne, imagined here as *Lambassa*, a former grand establishment that deteriorated into a boarding house. It, like the battered Moroccan bound notebook, are talismans of Lynch's time. Slessor does this in order to simulate a direct quotation from Lynch's journal with its misspellings generating a sense of authenticity and truth. Stanza eight completes the 1927 sequence of vignettes. We move to Gladesville where Lynch lived with his family. This is about the self always moving backward, creeping a little "closer to the breast". These are images of gas lit arguments and headstones cut piously by Lynch's father: "funeral-cakes of sweet and sculptured stone." Monumentalising the dead in order to nourish the living.

Stanza nine and ten consider the act writing *Five Bells*, some ten years after the death of Lynch. The poignancy of stanza nine builds and builds. Slessor is ultimately mourning the way in which we cannot make sense of our time, our existence, our sense of self. It is the dead self to whom Slessor addresses his many questions; believing that if he could just know where Lynch has gone, why Lynch was here and what purpose he served, all would be resolved. Slessor describes his own dying on that fateful night back in May 1927: "I felt the wet push its black thumb-balls in...I felt your eardrums crack,/ And the short agony." Most heartbreaking is the way Slessor is unable to hold on to this other self, be it Lynch or the young Slessor: "But I was bound, and could not go that way,/ But I was blind, and could not feel your hand." The last stanza reminds us that the overarching canvas of this poem takes place in the littoral; somewhere "between" land and water. This is simultaneously concerned about the present moment and the past; the center self and the peripheral; the living and the dead; the rational and the irrational. I am sure you can hear echoes of Eliot's *Prufrock* not only in the repetition of "between" in stanza one and the phrase "each to each" in stanza two but in the overarching theme of meaninglessness dogging the Modernist imagination. The meta-poetic reference to the "waves with diamond quills" reminds us that all that really exists is the poem by Slessor; not the watery past or the elusive self. Like Slessor, forever keening to hear Lynch's voice, we too long for high resolution. Instead we are left with the death knoll in the phrase "five bells". *Five Bells* is a shoreline where the resolution of death offers no resolution. This threshold space where land and sea converge is existence: time that cannot be fixed by measurement. I think this is how we see ourselves as Australians; cohabiters of the land and the sea but not quite getting purchase in either of these sites of belonging.

Show me the order of the world by Gwen Harwood (1990)

Show me the order of the world,
the hard-edge light of this-is-so
prior to all experience
and common to both world and thought,
no model, but the truth itself.

Language is not a perfect game,
and if it were, how could we play?
The world's more than the sum of things
like moon, sky, center, body, bed,
as all the singing masters know.

Picture two lovers side by side
who sleep and dream and wake to hold
the real and imagined world
body by body, word by word
in the wild halo of their thought.

    Here in this sonnet we are invited to meditate upon the inadequacy of language. A wonderful conceit when considering Harwood's successful rendition of this sonnet. Yet it is more than just the inadequacy of language with which we live our lives. It is about the hunger to get closer and closer to the truth or essence of things. Moreover, it is about the way in which we do experience that quintessence in language of intimacy. Why a sonnet? It invites mediation, it examines a singular subject, it offers symmetry in its rendering and there is a shift or volta in the argument between the second and third stanza. I love the way this sonnet is so unapologetic. Harwood is demanding to see the impossible as a way of exposing the proximal. This in turn is presented not as a short coming but rather the greatest and most familiar mystery. Let me backtrack. Harwood situates her poems in a context that seems to offer us purchase. While some of the settings she may use are not part of our own lives there is something always there that is deeply familiar and reassuring. Her language is exact and exacting. Indeed, some might classify her as an imagist because her word choice and placement is so precise and so often without fat. Whenever I read her poetry, I have a great sense of an unadorned world and one very purpose driven.
    In the first stanza Harwood asks the ultimate question, the question of all questions: "Show me the order of the world." In other words, allow me to see the divine pattern that connects all living and non-living beings. To whom is the imperative aimed? Is it me, her audience? Is it God or some other divine presence? Is it society at large who formulated signifiers in order for there to be connection and understanding? Or perhaps it is a rhetorical device that allows Harwood to

present her argument. Whatever your interpretation it is an arresting commencement to the sonnet. As proof that our language is merely an approximation, a limited representation, she offers a metaphor: "order of the world." If all language is a metaphor for the thing itself then when we talk about metaphors in writing what are we really considering? It's strange to think about signs being a representation of the thing itself and thus a metaphor. The mere fact that it takes many many words to attempt to describe this very phenomenon is in itself more proof that language fails us.

I like that second line with its crisp image of "hard-edge light" and dental plosives of d and t that in turn lead us into the sibilance of "this-is-so". Harwood's conjoined words expose the way in which we need the elasticity of language in a constant attempt to articulate our world. Harwood asks to know the divine pattern that connects all living and non-living beings but to know it before she can express it: "prior to all experience." To know the core rather than the periphery. She asks for this knowledge to directly connect the thing itself to that which formulates language; so that there is no gap between the sign and the signified. Therefore, she argues that not only would it be "common to both world and thought", and not a version or "model" of the thing itself but rather "the truth". She asks the impossible. She asks for a language that is not an approximation, not a representation, not a metaphor of the thing itself. She asks for this in order to see the divine pattern. So, by the end of the first stanza we are made profoundly aware that we need to be circumspect in our management of expression because in every way our language falls short. Indeed, the stanza ends with a bold and unambiguous assertion that unless we are shown "the order of the world", we cannot find truth. Therefore, truth is not in the proximal.

The second stanza reinforces the argument set up in the first. We are offered a rhetorical question to seal the deal: "Language is not a perfect game." While the rules of expression might place strictures upon us so that we might achieve accuracy, the rules can never be absolute and complete. Moreover, not only is language dynamic and ever changing, the ways in which it can be interpreted is legion. This takes us back to the start of the sonnet because if language was "perfect" we would know the divine; hence "how could we play?" Indeed, to know the world, the divine pattern that connects all living and non-living beings, is to know the connection and intimacy between its parts. Harwood asserts the holistic concept that the efficacy and significance of a group of things "like moon, sky, center, body, bed" interacting with one another, is greater than their value when acting in isolation from one another. It is this interaction or connection or intimacy that holds the key to how we understand "this-is-so". The "singing masters know" is a phrase that suggests there is an interplay between lyrics, musical accompaniment, timing, breathing and modulation. I wonder whether Harwood is suggesting that it is actually in the creative arts such as the language of song, and poetry as the uber song, that we get close to seeing "the order of the world". I think so.

From this deeply complex argument, which is underscored by post structuralist language theories, the sonnet takes a turn in stanza three. The volta offers us a singular sentence. We are now no longer located in the cerebral but the visceral, the flesh and bone of the mystery. Like the sonnet form itself we are given a perfectly balanced snapshot. Harwood's words are precise and unadorned and as such allow each one of us to imagine, unencumbered by adjectives or adverbs. These two lovers are "side by side...body by body, word by word". It is a pas de deux of exquisite beauty. The bony language gives us space. This is the powerful way in which the space created by language actually allows us to recognise the divine pattern that connects us to our world. The image of the lovers holding "the real and imagined world...in the wild halo of their thought" indicates that they have been shown the order of the world, hence their divine radiance.

Harwood had a lifelong love affair with the philosophical writings of the Austrian Ludwig Wittgenstein. As I read her poem Wittgenstein's comments enter my thinking: "The limits of my language mean the limits of my world ... whereof one cannot speak thereof one must be silent." Thus, in summary, I think her sonnet contemplates the hunger in us all to know and understand the divine pattern that connects all living and non-living beings. This is what drives us to keep expressing in our proximal fashion what we know and experience, in an attempt to get closer to the mystery. Meanwhile we are stymied by language. Ironically it is this very inadequacy that keeps the mystery sacred. Finally, and most significantly, it is the intimacy with another that we come to an ecstasy and a divinity of knowing. Thus, we are left with the haunting spectre of the last line of the sonnet. What a powerhouse sonnet! I would like to think that as Australians we see ourselves caught up in this wild cerebral interplay with Wittgenstein, post structuralist theory, body to body raw connection and the desire to know the divine mystery. I like to think that as Harwood washed up the dishes from the meal she made her sons and husband, with the cold dark rolling in from the Tasman Sea, at the same time teaching herself German grammar and vocabulary from a propped up text book at the sink, that we would be reading her sonnet decades later and be absolutely blown out of the water.

A Poet Thinking Beyond Facts by Les Murray (2004)

Why write poetry?
For the prospect of high-prestige unemployment and proud penury.
For the trance in which all artistic work is done.
For the joy of working always slightly beyond your intelligence.
For the experience of fusing the three minds we all possess,
which are called Waking Consciousness,
Dream (including Daydreaming or Reverie)
and the Body, and experiencing them in tense harmony.
For the way this fusion persists in the work we make, but not in ourselves,
so that we have to create it again and again.
For the way poetry makes us work out our pain and our tragedies
while dancing in rhythm with a book balanced on our head.
For not needing to rise socially and betray the poor in order to write it.
For a degree of fame less devouring than stardom or celebrity.
For the way poetry models all creative thinking,
and the way ideas which scorn it or never acquire it look briefly triumphant but soon vanish.
For the way all art gives a stillness to the matter it raises,
so that they have sufficient life and need not be enacted, perhaps horribly, in the real world.
Hitler could not make a poem of his obsessions.

For the way poetry at once confers meaning and fractures it,
pointing it towards further and greater depths
and so preventing it from imprisoning our spirit.
For the shame and even archaic fear poetry provokes in those who want to dismiss it.
For the fact that you can't lie in a poem or a prayer.
The reasons for reading poetry are all versions of the above.

When I was a young teenager, one Sunday out of the blue my father and I caught a bus into the city to Poet's Corner in Hyde Park. Just me and him. I had been writing poetry for as long as I could remember and somehow I found myself holding a poem or two when we arrived. My father had found out that Les Murray would be conducting a poetry reading and asking people to come forward and read their poems. By then I had already read Murray's *Spring Hail* and *Absolutely Ordinary Rainbow*. I remember thinking when I saw him that he was nothing like I had imagined. I can't remember the poems he read but I remember finding it harder and harder to breathe when I realised his reading was coming to an end and my father was expecting me to go forward and read one of my own poems. I was mortified but also exhilarated. Other people shot forward as soon as Murray was done and he sort of watched on with slight disinterest. I don't know how long it was before I stepped forward but I did of course, I was filled with my father's love. There was nothing I couldn't do and so I read a poem, maybe I read two, then I came back and sat down next to my father. By that stage it was over and budding poets were crowding about Murray and so my dad and I moseyed on by. Somehow in the fray Murray caught my eye and turned to me and said: "Don't stop." I was flustered and embarrassed but deeply pleased. Later, on the bus ride home, my father asked me what I wanted to do with my life and I said *poetry*.

In *A Poet Thinking Beyond Facts*, Murray poses a question and then offers 13 optional answers as to why a poet should write poetry, finishing his poem with a statement indicating that, in fact, all options are the answer. I find this manifesto deeply reassuring. It is a creed, an anthem, a proclamation that there will be no surrender. That poets should not stop! Poetry is a secret and ancient language that holds all truth. It is the alpha and the omega of all human expression. It is the art form which is simultaneously implosive as it is explosive. A nation without poetry cannot have a civilisation; a people without poetry cannot have a soul. I live in a world that may seem to be forgetting this and so when I read Murray's poem I am filled with a sense of optimism and joy. It is as if he is saying here are the reasons why we are on earth, for this and this only.

In the first optional answer to the question "Why write poetry?" he answers by coupling the unexpected together, "high-prestige unemployment and proud penury", its contrast generating a sardonic self-mocking tone; something peculiarly Australian. The second and third reasons offer "trance" and "joy" as raison d'etre for the poet to get out of bed in the morning and get on with his work which is always just slightly beyond his reach. The 4th and 5th reasons explore the "fusion" of "Consciousness, Dream…and the Body" manifest in poetry but "not in ourselves", hence the drive to create again and again. I'm particularly fond of the 6th reason. I like to think about how art is the attempt to capture that which is ephemeral and elusive. Furthermore, my life's pursuit which is the study of poetry, has shown me that great poetry can often emerge out of suffering, expressed with precision while keeping a close eye on the poetic tradition: "work out our pain and our tragedies while dancing in rhythm with a book balanced on our head."

The 7th and 8th reasons Murray offers, as to why he writes poetry, speak to his politics and the way in which the Western contemporary world considers this art of little value. In the 9th option he posits that "poetry models all creative thinking". Poetry is the condensed nature of thought; everything is reduced to its absolute essence in order to fly beyond itself. The 10th and 11th reasons as to why poets write poetry offer deeply complex and layered understandings of the value of poetry as art. Here he states it "gives a stillness to the matter it raises". I love this idea of the spinning world being forced to stop by the sheer force and power of a poem. That in all the frenetic noise and movement of our lives poetry offers stillness; not calm, not motionlessness but stillness. Poetry also "confers meaning and fractures it" so that it becomes elusive. Indeed, it is this just out of reach quality that keeps a great poem alive to us every time we go to it; reading it as if it is the first time, every time. The 12th and 13th optional answers of why write poetry are about being responsive to the metaphysical. It is a vocation, a dedication of one's life to something greater than the poet him/herself. Thus, the dismissal of poetry will incite "shame and even archaic fear" and the attempt to "lie in a poem" is impossible. He offers the alchemy of poetry as "fact" which not only flies in the face of rational argument but responds comfortably to the title of the poem which is to think beyond the facts. Here, without a doubt is an Australian 20th century *Defence of Poetry*.

South of my Days by Judith Wright (1956)

South of my days' circle, part of my blood's country,
rises that tableland, high delicate outline
of bony slopes wincing under the winter,
low trees, blue-leaved and olive, outcropping granite-
clean, lean, hungry country. The creek's leaf-silenced,
willow choked, the slope a tangle of medlar and crabapple
branching over and under, blotched with a green lichen;
and the old cottage lurches in for shelter.

O cold the black-frost night. The walls draw in to the warmth
and the old roof cracks its joints; the slung kettle
hisses a leak on the fire. Hardly to be believed that summer will turn up again some day in a wave of rambler-roses,
thrust its hot face in here to tell another yarn-
a story old Dan can spin into a blanket against the winter.
Seventy years of stories he clutches round his bones.
Seventy years are hived in him like old honey.

Droving that year, Charleville to the Hunter,
nineteen-one it was, and the drought beginning;

sixty head left at the McIntyre, the mud round them
hardened like iron; and the yellow boy died
in the sulky ahead with the gear, but the horse went on,
stopped at Sandy Camp and waited in the evening.
It was the flies we seen first, swarming like bees.
Came to the Hunter, three hundred head of a thousand-
cruel to keep them alive - and the river was dust.

Or mustering up in the Bogongs in the autumn
when the blizzards came early. Brought them down; we
brought them down, what aren't there yet. Or driving for Cobb's on the run
up from Tamworth-Thunderbolt at the top of Hungry Hill,
and I give him a wink. I wouldn't wait long, Fred,
not if I was you. The troopers are just behind,
coming for that job at the Hillgrove. He went like a luney, him on his big black horse.

Oh, they slide and they vanish
as he shuffles the years like a pack of conjuror's cards.
True or not, it's all the same; and the frost on the roof
cracks like a whip, and the back-log break into ash.
Wake, old man. This is winter, and the yarns are over.
No-one is listening
South of my days' circle
I know it dark against the stars, the high lean country
full of old stories that still go walking in my sleep.

    I have never been a great fan of Judith Wright. I can't remember why exactly. She was taught to us at school and I resisted her representations of sensuality and mothering and intimacy. I found it suffocating. Later I would think the frequent split infinitive just made it too hard going. Now I actually realise she is an acquired taste. In a nut shell you need to grow older in order to hear her. I don't think, for me anyway, she was a poet for anyone in their twenties let alone their teens. Now, I must say that *South of my Days* is classic and beautiful, the title alone is worth stopping to contemplate. This phrase has a delicious ambiguity. To me I like to think about it being an expression of the end point of one's life or as Shakespeare would put it, the winter of our life. Wright offers us a narrative poem about the nation space that formed and sheltered her identity, to which she circles back in the final stage of her life. Indeed, the wintery lean landscape in which we find ourselves is in fact the objective correlative of her later years, underscored by such tales as those told by old Dan.
    Wright narrates an Australia that may not be familiar to our experience but it is to our mythology; moreover, it becomes the vehicle by which she drives her own examination of self-identity. An Australia that is life taking and life giving. Wright's emotional engagement with the landscape re-

flects her poignant consideration of her own life as it nears the end, haunted by apprehensions that perhaps no one is listening. The five stanza poem made up of approximately eight lines apiece tells us on one level, about the inter-relationship between man, survival, animal, landscape and weather; and on another level our eye takes in the panoramic vision of a stark, lean and arid country. At all times this is a narration about identity. The identity of self, of nation, of old age, of the end game, of the post-colonial and of the subaltern. This narration intrinsically tells the story of "my blood's country", one that I now find deeply moving.

The first stanza begins with a dramatic pan shot of her landscape taking in the reach of the background then foreground, followed by a close up of specific foliage with just a glimpse at a shelter in the periphery. I like the enigmatic first two lines of the poem; at the end of her days she circles in on the country of her heart. This is her visceral place of belonging. What rises up from this desire, is the mountain range that has framed her: "of bony slopes wincing under the winter." This exquisite interplay between assonance and alliteration generates an image that will haunt the narration of self throughout this poem. This first stanza introduces us immediately to this "clean, lean, hungry country". The assonance working an image of sparsity that generates desire. With microscopic care Wright reveals waterways that are "leaf-silences,/ willow chocked" and the under-bush a "tangle of medlar and crabapple". It is a landscape of excess wildness. Beneath seven lines of wild bush landscape we discover the "old cottage" which "lurches in for shelter". The use of personification here intensifies the human habitation as frail and temporary in amongst the Australian landscape.

The second stanza takes us indoors. Here, inside the old cottage, we huddle away from the "black-frost night" and take shelter in narration. The cottage is a body within the body of the landscape; just as we are a body within the nation's body. Therefore, the cottage is personified when its "walls draw in to the warmth/ and the old roof cracks its joints". The place of belonging is a tired and aged self, one who seeks comfort and a way to make sense of life. This is done by remembering the period of youth and vitality, manifested as summer: "summer will turn up again...to tell another yarn." From these vignettes of resilience and adversity one can shore up against the oncoming cold and wintery approach of death: "old Dan can spin into a blanket against the winter." Old Dan could be an archetype of the seasonal storyteller, he could be everyman of the 19th century fin de siecle of Australia who carved out a nation, and he could be the self who still strives to understand what it is that life offers. The repetition of "Seventy years" is indicative of a lifetime of narratives which in turn busily occupy Dan and draw others to him.

We are then offered three narratives by old Dan. This intertextual device draws us close as we try to see ourselves somewhere in the stories. The first yarn is set in south western Queensland and we follow the droving down from Charleville to the Hunter Region in New South Wales. Some 1,226 kilometers are covered by the stockmen moving their livestock in the severe drought of 1891. This time in Australian pastoral history was a tough one, with a number of years of below average rainfall leading to animals perishing. Indeed, cattle fell by 40% and sheep by 50%. We follow the drovers down to the McIntyre, one of the border rivers between Queensland and New South Wales and then on to Sandy Camp some 200 and 50 kilometers further before making our way finally into the Hunter Region. The third stanza is peppered with the signatures of a particular temporality: "Charleville to the Hunter", "the McIntyre", "the yellow boy", "the sulky" and "Sandy Camp." It is the poetry of the postcolonial in elevating the vernacular of their daily life to something worth telling. The story is tragic and macabre with the young boy's death not becoming known until some 200 kilometers later and indicated by "the flies we seen first, swarming like bees". There is also a tragic loss of livestock on a journey where the cattle were led to "the river that was dust". It is a story well known in the efforts to make Australia a pastoral nation. Imitative of oral history with its grammatical errors and implication that the listener is familiar, the yarn also reflects the voice of the subaltern, the drover whose stories are now scattered, lost and forgotten.

The next two narratives are found in the 4th stanza. Old Dan recalls the hazardous and difficult job of mustering or rounding up livestock on the Victorian Alps, the "Bogongs". Yet all for naught: "the blizzards came early. Brought them down; we/ brought them down." The plosives and repetition speak to the dangers and devastations which impacted on man and beast. Dan then segues into the final anecdote of meeting Captain Thunderbolt, Frederick Wordsworth Ward, the bushranger who remained at large for over six and half years in the New England area. Again, we have temporal signatures that are uniquely Australian, such as old Dan working for *Cobb & Co*, the principle means of transport in the eastern colonies; and place names such as Tamworth, Hungry Hill and Hillgrove, which remain markers along today's *Thunderbolt's Way*. In keeping with the mythologies of the larrikin and the alliance forged with the underdog or anti-authority rebel, Old Dan gives Thunderbolt "a wink", uses his first name "Fred" and warns him of the approaching "troopers". Rather than see Thunderbolt as a felon and escaped prisoner we see hilarity in this legendary bushranger racing off "a luney…on his big black horse". We want to identify with this wiry old story teller who has had so many lives in one and lived alongside legends that have made our history colorful.

There is a shift in tone when we arrive at the final stanza. No longer are we seeing ourselves in the legendary yarns of Old Dan. We note that the narratives have been nothing but a magician's game: "they slide and they vanish/ as he shuffles the years like a pack of conjuror's cards./ True or not, it's all the same." This is an arresting development to the seduction of storytelling. Like the poem itself, the narratives have been simply a device to tell the story of self, to provide a way of understanding one's identity in situ. Time passes and we are reminded of the cottage in which we sit. Time passes… Wright's imperative slices the reverie: "Wake, old man. This is winter, and the yarns are over./ No-one is listening." There is an urgency here and a sense that it has all been for nothing. I wonder whether grave doubts about the value of what one has contributed is simply par for the course. Wright speaks with absolute certainty when she names that her end is near: "South of my day's circle/ I know it dark against the stars." It is here that I find hope. In her deepest knowing of self, situated within her blood's country, she can see the shape of who she has been because of the darkness. There is a beautiful poignancy in the "high lean country" image. It is one of cattle struggling through drought and it is one of horsemen who have lived a life of great hardship. Wright has shown us that our imagination holds the "old stories", which will sustain us in our dreaming. I still think this is how we see ourselves.

Ladybird by David Malouf (2014)

Childhood visitors,

the surprise of
their presence a kind of grace.
Kindest of all the ladybird,
neither lady
(unless like so much else
in those days disguised
in a witch's spell) nor
bird but an amber-beadlike
jewel that pinned itself
to our breast; a reward for
some good deed we did not
know we'd done, or earnest
of a good world's good will
towards us. Ladybird, ladybird,
fly away home, we sang,
our full hearts lifted
by all that was best
in us, pity for what
like us was small (but why
was her house on fire?), and sped her
on her way with the same breath
we used to snuff out birthdays
on a cake, the break and flare
of her wings the flame that leapt
from the match, snug
in its box, snug in our fist under the house
that out of hand went sprinting
up stairwells, and stamped and roared
about us. Ladybird,
mother, quick, fly
home! The house, our hair, everything close
and dear, even the air,
is burning! In our hands
(we had no warning
of this) the world is alive and dangerous.

This is a little poetic gem. Malouf writes a beautiful magical ode that captures the ladybird beetle, the *Coccinellidae*, then releases it into our blazing imagination. It is quintessentially Malouf. So exact and familiar and yet so dazzlingly unexpected. What a gorgeous 36 line ode consisting of six sentences and three addendums in parenthesis. Even the symmetry speaks to Malouf's meticulous care. There is something about the Ladybird that stills us momentarily ... it makes us bow down quietly ... and feel grateful that it trusted us long enough to let us wonder. There are over 6,000 species of the *Coccinellidae* worldwide; their size can vary from 0.8 to 18mm while their color ranges from yellow to orange and red with black or sometimes white spots. Their Latin name was given because, as you can probably guess, *coccineus* denotes the color scarlet. Common parlance originally called these little sprites *Our Lady's Bird* because the Virgin Mary was depicted wearing a scarlet cloak. The nursery rhyme that you might remember dates back to 1744, *Tommy Thumb's Pretty Songbook Volume Two*, but there are a number of versions including the grimmest: "Ladybird, Ladybird fly away home/ Your house is on fire/ Your children are burned." Malouf is representing the way childhood teaches us that there is a fine line between the realities narrated by responsible adults and those promised to us in nursery rhymes.

Let's take a closer look. The first short sentence is made up of three lines and is filled with poise and charm with words like "visitors", "surprise", "presence" and "grace". So, these miniature insects are transient and unexpected, offering us momentary awe. So even in the first line we can see that this ode is *fairytalesque* and promises us magic and truths along with a cautionary tale. The second sentence takes us meandering through 12 lines of the ladybird's features, perplexities, connotations and description until finally we are left with a metaphor. So, this insect is "kindest of all", "neither lady...nor bird", "unless...disguised in a witch's spell"; moreover, it is an "amber-beadlike/ jewel that pinned itself/ to our breast". This sentence expands with the excess and enthusiasm of childish sentiment. While the metaphor of the ladybird as medal for some good deed is heart-warming, we cannot fail to notice, tucked away inside the parenthesis, the reminder that childhood was filled with salient tales disguised as benevolent only to reveal their malevolence. The unanticipated is a Malouf speciality.

The ode now erupts into calamity and impatience. We recognise the intertextual reference to the nursery rhyme in the third sentence. Initially the ladybird is sung with "our full hearts lifted/ by all that was best/ in us, pity for what/ like us was small". In other words, there is an identification with the vulnerability of another and a recognition of the feeling of grace in ourselves as children as we ensure the safety egress of the ladybird. And yet the presence of another parenthesis warns us that there is a subconscious awareness of threat and danger to that very self in miniature: "(but why was her house on fire?)" It is at this point that the ode takes on an urgency spurned on by the fire. It is the breath of innocence that "sped her/ on her way". We are all familiar with the cautionary narrative told to small vulnerable beings. I think what sits at the center of fear for most of us is that idea that home is no longer safe. It is to this dark anxiety that the nursery rhyme sings. Note that the same breath that speeds the ladybird home is that which "we used to snuff out birthdays/ on a cake"; a constant reminder that life is finite and fragile. The power of association is made between the naked candle flame and the ladybird: "the break and flare/ of her wings the flame that leapt/ from the match." This quickening flash of the ladybird's wings is the match fire. This is reinforced in the ode when the match is "snug/ in its box", just as the ladybird is "snug in our fist". So, what is being said here? That within small vulnerable selves is carried the bead of its own destruction. That in the iridescence of one's creation is the potential for one's destruction. By the end of this third sentence we have the disturbing image of destruction and havoc: "went sprinting/ up stairwells, and stampeded and roared/ about us." Is this the children's doing? Is this what innocence can release? Or rather this is the horror, latent within each one of us, that we have the potential to unleash.

The tail end of the ode spins implosively through the 4th, 5th and 6th sentences. A type of Morse code of warning, a staccato imperative: "Ladybird,/ mother, quick, fly/ home!" She is now the maternal in miniature. She is the keeper of the hearth and to whom we turn for nurture and succor. The magnitude of the catastrophe is conveyed in a list of the unimaginable: "The house, our hair...even the air/ is burning!" I can imagine the frenetic child's play morphing into such hysterical imaginings. What happens next is the cold realisation that "In our hands...the world is alive and dangerous". Let's think about this for a minute. Destruction is in our hands. The ruin of home is potentially our doing. The protection of the vulnerable, albeit in humanity or the eco system, is our purview. More literally, the ladybird in our hands is the shock of life, wild and untamed, nestling right there; meanwhile, its vulnerability makes it not only beautiful and familiar but also precarious. As children we had no idea that life could be so terrifying, "(we had no warning/ of this)"; thus, we have been given our third and final aside, which only becomes too true in adulthood. Perhaps this is why we read nursery rhymes with such trust. We connect to the *small us* in each tale and somehow understand that the brute reality threatening the vulnerable is a message to us to beware and not roam to far from home, should fires be started that could reduce it to ashes.

I think this poem explores the mythology we create around our childhood place of belonging. Malouf is suggesting the natural world offers insight into the threats and dangers ever present to a seemingly fairy-tale idyll. Finally, through his poem we come to see ourselves as cradling the wondrous and thus we need to consider its fragility.

The Whistler by Dorothy Hewitt (2001)

Has the man next door
buried his wife in the garden?
she doesn't whistle the hits of the 40s
anymore at the kitchen window
I can't even see her shadow against the blind
there is something ominous about that silent window
the immaculate garden shaved and vacuumed
within an inch of its life

perhaps she has left him
or died in the local hospital
I never heard her speak
or saw her walking
only her voice in the still air
like a bird caught in a cage
trilling to be let out

how he must have hated that whistle
enough to strangle her
chocked off at mid-note
their shadows wrestling silently
against her venetian blind
if he dug her grave at midnight
the spade would scrape
on the sandstone bottom
if he planted a rose over her
red as blood it would flourish

whatever method was used
she has gone at last
freed from her pottering lord
shaking his fist at the currawong's whistle
as he savagely hacks off the roses

every autumn the leaves fall
and the fog forms a curtain
to smother our secret lives.

Dorothy Hewitt was a prolific writer and her oeuvre covers drama, novels, poetry and collaborations with musical theatre. I like to imagine that this particular poem happens during her life in Falconbridge, the lower Blue Mountains, where she lived with her third husband and two daughters. It was published a year before her death in 2001 in a collection of poems. I like the ordinariness of her subject matter where menace seems to lurk on the periphery. Here is a simple free verse poem about "The Whistler": a woman without a name or occupation or life or so it would seem, someone who could very well be dead. Yet her presence is everywhere throughout this poem, she haunts both the taciturn husband as well as the poet. What does it mean for a woman to whistle? Not hum or sing but whistle. Does it suggest that there is something independent about her, something precocious and unrestrained? Isn't it a public display of the fact that her mind is her own and not deeply concerned with what is around her? Is whistling synonymous with freedom? Whistling is music that comes out of the human body without an instrument; just about everyone can whistle. It can be used to signal enthusiasm but also disapprobation. Thus, I like to think of whistling as a double edged sword that is wielded by the independent.

In the opening stanza Hewitt proffers a question about her neighbour. It is an Australian Gothic but it is also reminiscent of Hitchcock's *Rear Window* in the rarefied air of suburban living: "Has the man next door/ buried his wife in the garden?" This woman is a spectre and known as "The Whistler", "his wife" and "shadow" and the ominous suggestion of her disappearance is in "the immaculate garden shaved and vacuumed/ within an inch of its life". The overwrought efforts to control nature is a projection of the control placed on women, relegating them into domesticity "within an inch of life". The poem is situated in the mid-20th century, a time where women began to rebel against the expectations placed on them as domestic slaves restricted to the marital home. In the second stanza we consider a number of scenarios, as if we are Jimmy Stewart and Grace Kelly, momentarily distracted from our own sites of domestic confinement: "perhaps she has left him/ or died in the local hospital." The dramatic outcomes are in sharp contrast to the banality of a nameless faceless woman in the kitchen window condemned to voicelessness. Except for the song of her whistle, so despite her being stationary and inarticulate, the fixity of her life is disrupted by "her voice in the still air". Maybe this is an act of defiance or protest against all that has confined her. Hewitt uses the simile of her being like a caged bird which resonates with Maya Angelou's *I Know Why the Caged Bird Sings*, a feminist triumph published some 30 years previous. Hewitt offers us a voice "trilling to be let out" because the purpose of the woman's song is freedom.

In the third stanza the marital tension is intensified. Both he and she are represented as "shadows wrestling silently/ against her venetian blind". The struggle is faceless and voiceless thus their struggle remains invisible to the outside world. In some ways this makes it all the more insidious. Inconspicuousness and secrecy begin to represent the struggle between men and women in the domestic space as imagined by the poet. The repetition of the word "blind" in stanza one and three as noun, also triggers its verbal meaning. What are the sorts of atrocities we are blind to in our own society? Perhaps the entrapment of women in domestic roles. In true Hitchcockian storytelling we now have a possible motive and method of murder, "he must have hated that whistle/ enough to strangle her" as well as clues to the disposal of the body: "he dug her grave at midnight... he planted a rose over her." For poetic effect Hewitt makes her rose "red as blood", replacing the 1954 *Rear Window* yellow roses beneath which Thorwald's wife was buried. Certainly, Hewitt vilifies the husband. He is the whistler's "pottering lord/ shaking his fist at the currawong's whistle/ as he savagely hacks off the roses". His domain is the exterior landscape and hers interior, his actions aggressive, hers passive, his intention is to control and hers to escape. It's funny too. In many ways he is a caricature of a man because he represents all autocratic overlords who enslave and command.

I find the ending a curiosity. We have time passing with the reference to the cyclical nature of what occurs "every autumn" and, despite this or maybe because of it, these "secret lives" simply go on behind the veil of anonymity. It begs the question why? Hewitt says "the fog forms a curtain". I would suggest the constituent parts of the fog are apathy, a lack of compassion, a desire not to be involved, a retainment of the status quo and a wariness of complexity. Finally, twice the word "window" has been used in this poem and three more times it has been implied because of the reference to blinds or curtains. Thus, we are left with the notion of a portal, a viewing point, a site of egress and ingress. Moreover, this poem suggests that one can escape and or remain caged. I think that for the most part the life of suburban banality is the way we see ourselves, if we are honest. A life riddled by the fascination with and speculation about the neighbour but certainly not sufficiently spurned on to do anything more than dispassionately observe, as if through a rear window. I think Hewitt is telling a few home truths, hence our sense of discomfort.

Terra Australis by James McAuley (1942)

Voyage within you, on the fabled ocean,
And you will find that Southern Continent,
Quiros' vision – his hidalgo heart,
And mythical Australia, where reside
All things in their imagined counterpart.

It is your land of similes: the wattle
Scatters its pollen on the doubting heart
The flowers are wide awake; their air gives ease.
There you come home, the magpies call you Jack
And whistle like larrikins at you from the trees.

There too the angophora preaches to you on the hillsides
With gestures of Moses, and the white cockatoo,
Perched on his limbs, screams with demoniac pain;
And who shall say on what errand the insolent emu
Walks between morning and night on the edge of the plain?

But northward in the valleys of the fiery Goat
Where the sun like a centaur vertically shoots
His raging arrows with unerring aim,
Stand the solitary ecstatic pyres
Of unknown lovers, featureless with flame.

James McAuley takes four quintets to sing his love song to this great southern land. The magic of his poem begins in the first two lines because he asserts that this beloved country is within you. The Southern Continent is not external to you but indelibly etched into your psyche, your heart, your imagination, your longing and your wonder. Perhaps this is true for all homelands and yet the considerations and constructions around *Terra Australis* are legend. The Latin term denotes the hypothetical continent appearing in maps as early as those documented by Macrobius in the 5th century. Earlier than this Aristotle speculated that the northern hemisphere's land mass must be balanced by land in the southern hemisphere. So, the desire for this country has obsessed the European imagination. As for its Indigenous inhabitants, McAuley makes no reference. It is definitely a white European enterprise as represented here in the poem.

The poem opens with the quest, journey and pursuit. The goal is to discover this country within oneself: "Voyage within you, on the fabled ocean,/ And you will find that Southern Continent." The country of one's belonging is more accurately within one's own mind; it is in the memories of seasons and landscapes, in the aromas and flavours of plucked fruit and childhood meals, in the touch of hot sand and icy mountain fronds. Moreover, the imagined country is in the relationships unique to all of us and deeply located in the place we call our own. It is as if we have always been in pursuit of the "fabled ocean" that needs to be faced and forged if we are to find "that" legendary place of home. In the first quintet words like "fabled", "mythical" and "imagined" shimmer and remind us of the way in which belonging is complex, romanticised and made more valuable. The 16th century Portuguese navigator is referenced with an "hidalgo heart", as if the pursuit for colonies emerged out of passion and heart felt longing, rather than greed. Australia is the illusory binary to the known world of Europe. McAuley suggests that this nation contains all things "counterpart": space, freedom, newness, natural riches and potential subjects.

Our terms of references are initially forged from our homeland. Thus, "It is your land of similes". Perhaps that is why it is imbued in our thinking because we have learnt the world according to how it compares and contrasts to Australia, as our first known country. Any hesitancy or resistance is removed because we are seeded to the landscape: "the wattle/ Scatters its pollen on the doubting heart". Hence, we are always home. The familiarity of the call of butcher birds jettisons any sense of estrangement that we may feel at different points in our life: "the magpies call you Jack/ And whistle like larrikins at you." Our native birdlife is raucous and disarming but at the same time deeply reassuring that we belong. In quintet three McAuley brings the gravitas of the Old Testament to the Australian bush. Here "the angophora preaches to you on the hillsides/ With gestures of Moses". The personification of the flowering tree, endemic to Australia, becomes the *Promised Land* for God's chosen people. The screaming white cockatoo and "insolent" emu complete this haven, that is paradise, with a touch of the demonic. The poem ends dramatically with country as the burial site for those who have loved her, under the canopy of constellations.

It is here under the southern skies of *Capricornus* and *Centaurus*, where we are shot through with the sun's rays. The final quintet takes us "northward in the valleys of the fiery Goat/ Where the sun like a centaur vertically shoots / His raging arrows with unerring aim". In other words, we know ourselves to be stardust and forever of this earth. Hence our love affair with *Terra Australis* doesn't end with our death but rather our ecstatic love burns on in our final return to this country. Written in the middle of World War Two this poem, with its iambic pentameter and rhyme of the 3rd and 5th lines, can also be read as a patriotic love song for those young men who would need to carry their homeland within them as they set forth for foreign shores to fight. Indeed, these very men became part of the war's graveyard and remain "unknown" and "featureless" but burn forever bright for those who will remember them. Lest we forget, this is as we see ourselves.

Detail from an Annunciation by Crivelli by Rosemary Dobson (1951)

My sisters played beyond the doorway,
My mother bade me hush and go,
I did not think that any saw me
I went so still on tip of toe.

My sisters played beneath the olives
They called like birds from tree to tree;
I climbed the stairs and through the archway
Looked where no one else could see.

My hair hung straight beneath my cap,
My dress hung down in fold on fold,
And when the painter filled it in
He edged it round with strokes of gold.

My mother thought I played without,
My sisters thought I played within,
Only the painter saw me hide –
The brush stroke held upwards to begin.

I saw the Dove, I saw the Lady
Cross her hands upon her breast,
I heard a music, and a shining
Came upon my eyes to rest.

I am twelve, but I was eight then:
No one listens when I tell –
Least of all my little sisters –
What I saw and what befell.

Look upon the painter's picture,
See, he shows you where I hid,
What I saw and how I listened –
You believe me that I did?

Ekphrastic poetry is more than the sum of its parts and *Detail from an Annunciation by Crivelli* by Rosemary Dobson is no exception. Poetry written in response to art brings that artwork to life in such a way that it hasn't been hitherto imagined; the artwork on the other hand makes possible the poetry. As lyrics are to music, ekphrastic poetry is to art. Basically the world is a richer place because of this subgenre. To be honest I looked long and hard before I saw the little girl to the left of the painting who tightly grips the balustrade to lean around and observe that which everyone else seems to be oblivious; the seminal moment unfolding between the Virgin Mary and the Holy Spirit. So hard was she to find that I thought I had the wrong painting and then I saw her and everything made sense! I love the idea that crowded in by the business of late 15th century Italian politics and commerce is a mere child, a female one at that, who is the only one who bears witness to the ontological nuances of Christian faith.

I think about those worshippers who would have knelt beneath this altarpiece commissioned by the Franciscan convent of Ascoli Piceno in Italy in celebration of *libertas ecclesiastica*, inscribed at the base of the painting, meaning self-government. Were their eyes fixated on the Virgin? Or were they distracted by the model of their town carried in the hands of Emidius, their patron saint, as he waits outside the barred window with the archangel Gabriel. I wonder if some of the prominent townsfolk were painted in to the upper middle ground and background; busily important in their new found civic autonomy. Or were they tricked by the trompe l'oeil at the front of the pictorial space where the gourd and apple placed over the inscription blur the division between the sacred and the temporal scene. Dobson did not travel to the Italian region of Marche to find this Renaissance town with its exquisite altar piece, rather she would have gone to visit the *National Gallery in London* when she lived in the late 1960s, where this altarpiece now resides. Worshippers in galleries replace those in chapels.

There is such an exuberant femininity to this ekphrastic poem made up of seven quatrains. From the onset we are aware of what is within the frame and what is beyond. Most pleasurably Dobson use a tone of intimate inclusivity in the way she conveys the young girl leaning in to tell us the whole picture. The simple diction and use of rhyme represent an innocence and wonder from the child's perspective which infectiously becomes ours. This is a tale about quietude and women and watchfulness: "My sisters played...My mother bade me...I went so still on tip of toe." It is a child centric world where the all observing is overlooked, not only by her distaff, but initially by us. I love the way her insignificance is summed up in her own mind: "I did not think that any saw me." Why would they? She is the lowest of the low. She is emblematic of the innocent female: the Virgin Mary. Like any child remaining in a secret space she is deeply aware of where she is supposed to be: "My sisters played beneath the olives/ They called like birds from tree to tree." Distraction gives her licence and allows her to look "where no one else could see". Even the gorgeous archangel, messenger of God, and Emidius look at each other as if discussing whether or not they should approach the barred window dividing the Virgin's private chamber from the barrier. This little sprite of a girl not only dares to look but sees what no one else can. Her audacity is triumphant.

The next two quatrains deliberately take us into the hand of Venetian painter Carlo Crivelli. So, her hair, cap and dress are described in a meta-art moment by revealing the composer's act of creation: "And when the painter filled it in/ He edged it round with strokes of gold." The use of gold normally depicts the sacred because gold leaf used in art works was the most expensive of all colors. Is she tinged with the sacred because of what she witnesses? Moreover, the credibility of the annunciation as a scene that truly happened is conveyed when "Only the painter saw me hide –/ The brush stroke held upwards to begin". The syntactical em dash suggests that the discovery of her hiding arrests the painter's hand momentarily. The mother and sisters are mentioned again, reinforcing the way the girl daringly breaks from the familiar to witness an emerging new world. Unlike them she is in frame, although perilously close to the left border, she is part of the drama unfolding. The 5th and antepenultimate quatrain unequivocally reveals her epiphany but from a child's perspective and thus lacking knowledge about what it was that she saw: "I saw the Dove, I saw the Lady/ Cross her hands upon her breast." The dove is symbolic of the Holy Spirit and the Lady, the Virgin Mary. The cross is indicative of the incarnation and death of the messiah; the Virgin Mary's joy, sorrow and mystery. Moreover, the child hears "music, and a shining/ Came upon my eyes to rest." Really this is the end of the poem for all intents and purposes. Although she doesn't have the capacity to fully apprehend what it is she sees, the child, in her innocence, does recognise the moment and as a consequence is imbued with the Holy Spirit. This stays with her. It is an enlightenment that infuses her with insight.

The penultimate and ultimate quatrains are curious. We are out of the painting, an exemplar of High Renaissance art, and in the place of faith and belief. Time has passed and this is no longer a contemporary site where the witness of Christ's conception takes place: "I am twelve, but I was eight then:/ No one listens when I tell." In fact, those most familiar and ever present are doubtful of the sacred and extraordinary witnessed in the secular world and ordinary. We are left with a final quatrain that in many ways is a poetic trompe l'oeil. We are given the imperatives "Look" and "See". Thus, with high modality, we are told to go back to the painting and give witness, just as she did. The trick of argument here is we are invited to agree that she "saw and ...listened". Indeed, "the painter's picture" cannot be interpreted any other way; therefore, we concede that she did see and hear, she did witness the Annunciation. Put another way, we have just admitted the Annunciation occurred. It is a spirited and delightful poem. So alive and dynamic is her artless and unguarded voice that we can hardly resist a belief in her and all she came to know. I like to see ourselves as Australians who are culturally connected to High Renaissance as much as to any movement in the arts. These great movements are not nation specific in that what was created belongs to each and every one of us. I think Dobson is making claim of this fact and asserting that what we give witness to belongs just as much to us. It's just a matter of believing.

Soup and Jelly by Fay Zwicky (1990)

"Feed Fred and sit with him
and mind he doesn't walk about.
He falls. Tell him his ute is safe
back home. Thinks someone's pinched it,
peers around the carpark all the time.
His family brought him in it and
he thinks it's gone.
He was a farmer once . . ."

I take the tray. The ice-cream's almost
melted round the crumbled orange jelly
and the soup's too hot. I know
I'll have to blow on it.

Hunched, trapped behind a tray,
he glances sideways, face as brown
and caverned as the land itself,
long thin lips droop ironic
at the corners, gaunt nose.
The blue and white pajamas cage

the restless rangy legs.
In and out they go, the feet
in cotton socks feeling for the ground.

"Are you a foreigner?"
"Not exactly. Just a little sunburnt,"
and I put the jelly down. I musn't feel
a thing: my smile has come unstuck.
I place a paper napkin on his lap. He winces.
"You're a foreigner all right," he says.
"OK," I say. What's one displacement more or less,
wishing I were a hearty flat-faced Fenian
with a perm and nothing doing in the belfry.
Someone like his mother. Or a wife who
spared him the sorrow of himself.
Now he grabs the spoon. "I'll do it."
"Right," I say, "You go ahead. Just ask me
if you want some help." The tone's not right.
I watch the trembling progress of the spoon
for what seems years, paralysed with pity
for his pride.

How does a dark-faced woman give a man called Fred
who cropped a farm and drove a battered ute
a meal of soup and jelly?

Outside the window, clouds are swelling
into growing darkness and there's a man
hard on his knees planting something in the rain.

I like the stark resonance of this poem. It stays with me. I like the way it is a conversation and then something a whole lot more. It begins as something so ordinary. A caregiver receiving instructions about one of the elderly men to whom she is about to offer lunch. He is predictably truculent and obstreperous. She is patient and watchful. Then it seems to morph into another thing entirely. I think I like the way that this subject is worthy of poetry. Here we have an elderly man in some sort of nursing home or convalescent facility having lunch fed to him. This is a poem about transformation. He is transformed from his former self as a strong and capable farmer. She is transformed from the caregiver to someone who is rendered unnecessary. The setting itself is transformed from a closed space separated from the outside world to a Biblical narrative shaping a national iconography. When I was an undergrad at Macquarie University, Zwicky was the poet in residence. I remember her understated manner, or so it seemed, and the way she would be surprised at the fact we had read and wanted to talk about her poetry. I think I even got her to sign my copy of one of her collections. Funny to think about that now. I remember her reading from *Kaddish*. I was mesmerised by the calque of Hebrew and the muscular construction of her father in Melbourne. When I came across *Soup and Jelly*, I was immediately enamoured by the title. I found it bold and defiant to write a poem about the absolutely ordinary. I am a sucker for the octogenarian male, even the septuagenarian can wheedle his way into my heart. There's something about that age that just seems to say damn it why not flirt the hell out of everything and everyone. I love the sass and the quick come back. Fred, in Zwicky's poem, has sass all tied up. Admittedly his one liners are limited but behind that ferocity and fear I am drawn to his imprisoned humanity.

This free verse poem commences media res with Zwicky as care giver being instructed by someone more experienced and knowledgeable about the incorrigible Fred. His name is synonymous with a bygone era where men and women lived separate lives in the harsh Australian rural world. Our introduction to this central character is summed up in a few iconic codes: his name, his ute, his family and his identity as a farmer. Therefore, we are positioned to read him as hardened, tough and taciturn; a type of backbone to the Australian mythology of itself. What interests me the most about this first stanza is the reference to the family bringing Fred in the ute to this place. I'm thinking something like a six cylinder, column shift *Ford Falcon XW* ute with a front bench seat. Who drives? The son? Pregnant daughter in law in the middle, Fred on the left with the window down and no one daring to tell him to wind it up as they motor down the freeway to the big smoke. A nine and five year old in the back, laying under the tarp, itchy blankets beneath them. Oh, and a Kelpie back there in the tray. It's 1973 after all. I am thinking about the attachment men have to their cars, particularly Australian men in outback rural settings. A vehicle means independence, freedom and the ability to work. Without one you are going nowhere fast. It is no wonder Fred frets: "Thinks someone's pinched it,/ peers around the carpark all the time." This idea of entrapment, imprisonment and detention is a through line throughout this poem.

In stanza two our eyes move briefly to what is carried in to Fred's room. Food that is for the inactive, easily digested and most probably bland. Food not as fuel for the engine's body but rather to comfort. The expectation of this cosy food is disrupted: "ice-cream almost/ melted…and the soup's too hot." It has the traces of a fairy tale… intruder tastes the food and tries the furniture of Papa, Muma and Baby Bear. There's a discomfort in her knowledge that she will need to cool the soup for him: "I know/ I'll have to blow on it." It is as if she is already on a collision course where the intimate act of feeding food to a fully-fledged adult is underscored by an infantile dependency. In stanza three the camera swings back to Fred. He is described as "face as brown/ and caverned as the land itself,/ long thin lips…gaunt nose". The topography of his face is the weather ridden landscape of sheep or cattle country in rural Australia. It is hardened by a harsh climate and unrelenting worry of drought and unpaid bills. Fred is "Hunched, trapped" and the striped pyjama bottoms appear as a "cage". I think this is the most poignant moment in the narrative. Indeed, his cantankerous and racist commentary surfaces as a result of his entrapment. His legs are "restless, rangy…in and out they go, the feet/ in cotton socks feeling for the ground". This is powerfully emblematic of the way Fred has come in from the wide open plains to a sanitised interior scape where shoes are not required because there is no movement, no work and no escape.

Fred's voice erupts in stanza three. Querulous, demanding and exacting. Wary of that which is not familiar, which speaks to half a century and more of remaining in a small microcosm of sameness. The homogeneity of rural wheat country is legend but I also think it is anyone of us, because at the end of the day we all seem to surround ourselves with same. In this strange surreal interior scape of institutionalised living there would be very few familiar references to which Fred could clutch. The phrase "foreigner" is repeated twice, once as a question and then as an assertion; Zwicky reinforces her otherness by not engaging. Rather she appears flippant "Just a little sunburnt" and conceding "OK". Yet what rages beneath becomes resentment, dressed up as self-pity, "What's one displacement more or less". She then matches this with her own scathing racism: "wishing I were a hearty flat-faced Fenian/ with a perm and nothing doing in the belfry." Zwicky's identity as an Australian with European Jewish heritage is at the heart of understanding this empathy for those trapped in another place and time. I like the way this admirable sentiment is conveyed in the human mess of racist slurs and fear felt by both Fred and Zwicky. She mentally slights both his mother and his wife "who/ spared him the sorrow of himself." She is caustic and there is nothing to redeem her attack, hidden though it is, from his vulnerable confined self, except that she is self-aware: "I mustn't feel/ a thing...The tone's not right." What transforms her is Fred's tenacity to be free of dependency: "Now he grabs the spoon. "I'll do it."...I watch the trembling progress of the spoon/for what seems years." The adverbial phrase "trembling progress" is deeply moving. It represents the exposed and unsteady way forward that is his life now in this place filled with the unfamiliar.

The penultimate stanza poses the existential question of how did we all get where we are, at any given point in time. It also asks, how is it possible that such people cross our paths? Again, self-consciously aware of her otherness Zwicky refers to herself as a "dark-faced woman". Fred on the other hand is summed up as someone driven in the past by the action of outdoor work: "cropped a farm and drove a battered ute." Most tellingly, the paucity of the food offered, "soup and jelly", on the one hand mocks the man who was once a highly capable outdoor man but on the other hand indicates a ritual of giving and receiving. For most of us, the meal seems soul destroying. The question posed seems to indicate she is at a loss to understand let alone answer. Rather Zwicky offers the 6th and final stanza as a type of symbolic response. The last three lines of this poem are infused with tender pathos with maybe something verging on hope. We are taken beyond the confines that imprison him and her, no longer trapped in a struggle of dependency and care, to that which is "Outside the window". Unlike the drought wrenched landscape of Fred's past, we are aware of the heaven's opening and an impending deluge: "clouds are swelling/ into growing darkness." It is the promise of the sublime in nature. Dwarfed by this but vitally a part of it is "a man/ hard on his knees". The anonymity of this figure is representative of every man and woman who is ultimately bowed before the unstoppable force of nature and time. It is something more though, because this infinitesimal nondescript figure is "planting something in the rain", in other words come what may here is a gesture of hope, of a belief in tomorrow. Here is the metaphorical hour of one's death, where the resurrection of the self and life everlasting, is believed. I am left hoping that this final image is how we see ourselves.

Next to Nothing by Noel Rowe (2004)

My sister's staying   things are not
where I'm used   to finding them
my bachelor hands   often doing double takes
after saucepans rice   and cutting knives
even god help me whiskey glasses   this time
I tell myself it doesn't matter   tell myself I'm glad
to have the inconvenience   night after night
I've heard her cough   day after day
watched her hunched shoulders just ahead of me
getting off the 380 bus at Darlinghurst
where the wind   scrapes its fingernails
against the locked doors   of the Sacred Heart Church
if she's afraid she doesn't say   taking each day as it comes
heading to the Clinic where   she'll write her name and time
in a book that faces a door   with a sign above it saying
"Radiation in Use"

My mother's here as well   she wants to help
she always does   can't help herself
was given kids to raise   when she was only four
living in the bush above Taylor's Arm
no windows in the house   only old sugar bags
that sometimes in the pitch black night would start to move
mostly just the wind but once   she was sure
there was someone there   she's still afraid at night
and lonely always lonely   death for her
will be difficult   when she finds she can't work her way around it
for the moment though   she's cleaning out kitchen cupboards
ironing tablecloths sweeping up camellias trimming ferns making meals
from next to nothing   just relax I say
I can't she says as long as I can keep moving   the pain is not so bad
her bones shrinking   her skin too easily bruised (just the cortisone?)
she too coughs at night   and when she sleeps
you hear her mouth   hungry at the air
she says she can no longer pray   wonders if she should
worry about this   I'd like to say it isn't words
that constitute prayer but can't   when it comes to god
these days my tongue   cracks open

others of the family stay   in Macksville everyone asking them

what's happening   the priest has put my sister in the parish bulletin
they're saying prayers   for her recovery
(please god they're not putting too much emphasis on *thy will be done*)
this makes it worse   for them up there they're in the dark
at least down here we see   her body won't give up
its place to circling dust motes   her walk still asks of earth
equal return of strength   she's learning how to live
with death inside her   where it's always been

My other sister   so we're told isn't coping well
taking it hard instead of being as she should be strong
she starts to scream when across the phone she hears *the news
isn't good lymphoma cancer they'll have to operate*
perhaps she's tougher than we think   sees what even now I try to block
her sister's body cut from sternum down   open at the middle
so doesn't care whether or not   her cardigan's on straight
later on she too comes to help   ironing tablecloths and making meals
from next to nothing each day the two of them
walk around the block   one day they get as far as the video store
this is getting dangerous   they're almost back to normal
soon they'll settle in   we'll all be watching *Charmed*
and eating jelly babies   months later in the freezer I find
the apples that she stewed   and eat them remembering her
when she was young   we were all bred
on disappointment   eventually it tells

My youngest brother who's deaf   and never learned
to socialise   or do his maths
too much trouble   his teacher later said to justify
putting him   in a corner down the back
now runs music shows   on radio 2NVR
rehearses in the bath then   with nothing written down
touches the controls and lets   his thick-tongued troubles
turn to song   but when his sister asks
to speak with him   he won't take the phone
don't talk to me about that   no doubt remembering year after year
in Sydney operations on his ears   he had a dog once Charlie
so keen to be in everything   one day he jumped the fence
still wearing his lead   and hung there choking on love

Middle brother also stays at home   to keep an eye on things

living on the edge   of what was once the family farm
(now cut in half)   he looks across the valley where
the Nambucca makes   each day the same
search for ocean   while the Star Hotel packs away
another dozen tales   the locals tell
because I was gone from home   before his stories
had a chance to grow   I sometimes find it hard
to know   what to say to him
one night he took his telescope   and touched
the shoulder of the dark
it turned and looked back galaxies
too long in the city   I'd forgotten how clean-cut
the stars   can be

my older brother   on the morning of her operation
drives us all to hospital   easier than a train cheaper than a taxi
a little later in the day   he gets his thanks
an accident on Parramatta Road   a drunken driver rams the car behind him
and suddenly the family Sigma has   damages that total more than fifty taxi trips
the drunken driver hasn't got a license or a visa but he gets out
laughing because he's rich   the woman in the car between
is trapped screaming   she has to be cut free and is too afraid
to let my brother hold her hand   later in the day he asks
why good intentions always bring   so much bad luck
it's a family theme   his life divides
from when he left   his father on the farm
to go to the city   where he lived in a boarding houses full of cockroaches
as we grow older it seems   more necessary to recall
being young   and playing in the swamp
between the farm and the hill   he was Phantom Ghost Who Walks
I was Bantar Pygmy Warrior   don't laugh
better that than playing baddies   in childhood's moral scheme
it's the baddies who   are dying all the time

he gave me once   one of the old wire strainers we used
putting up fences with our father   to get the tension right
I hold it now   to feel the way
its weight   takes up my hand.

Noel Rowe writes poetry with a tough-minded tenderness. I like the way he sees the world. In this instance, writing about family is complex and troubling. He wrote this poem some three years before his own early death from cancer in 2007. By this stage I had lost touch with him. He had been such a significant teacher to me when I returned from Chile to take up post graduate studies at Sydney University. He had that ability to connect one on one with people in a way that made you feel you were the only one in the room. I remember visiting him in his house in the inner west and the calm of that domestic space. It was filled with quiet shadows and dark furniture, or so I remember. There were Buddhist icons and nothing Catholic despite his former years in the priesthood. We had a very honest relationship, or did we? I recall talking to him about my trip wires, poor mistakes and ongoing anxieties. I asked about him being gay and how that rolled out in the seminary. He seemed to listen a lot and laugh a great deal with me but I am not sure if he ever revealed too much. Noel was kind in a way that mattered. My girlfriend had also been taught by him but had since been in a terrible life threatening accident, while traveling in Peru. She nearly died. When eventually she could be brought back to Australia with severe brain damage, we realised her *Masters in Australian Literature*, gained under Noel's tutelage, was shockingly redundant because she could hardly speak let alone read or write. Noel steadily worked with her over the years and she found her way back into the world of language and actually worked with him to achieve a *Masters of Letters*. We still talk about him.

Here we have a long private conversational poem to us from Rowe about his family. They are representative of the complex psychology that underpins all human tribal networks. In a fragmented stream of consciousness Rowe narrates the impact of his sister's lymphoma cancer on him and his family. Indeed, his three brothers, two sisters, mother and self are at the heart of this slow burn drama. The backdrop is inner city Sydney with the occasional telescoping back out to Macksville, where Rowe grew up, then finally we glimpse the outer galaxies. The eight stanzas that make up this free verse, contain a center space margin. A backbone space that splits the lines in half. The syntax is sparse with only one full stop in the entire poem. There is something deceptively simple and easy about his style, as if he is just telling us something that is running through his mind. Yet if you look closer you can see that the separation is in him as he observes and removes himself. So, the non-standardised center margin represents this distance within himself towards those he loves. Indeed, the final image of Rowe holding "old wire strainers we used/ putting up fences with our father", ensuring its "weight takes up my hand", is an apt final reminder that Rowe fences himself away from the tribe of his family as a way of dealing with the tension. What appeals to me enormously is the way Rowe gets straight to the center of the matter: identifying the psychosis in one's family, recognising the uselessness of frenetic activity in the face of oncoming death and the methods of coping.

This is every tribe, be it family or close friendships or colleagues or nations, who are struggling to make sense of a world they can't control. The fragmentation of his seemingly transparent chat about the nuances of human interaction sum up the way in which Rowe is broken, incomplete and in a state of disintegration because all ideologies are rendered useless now. The first stanza is about immediate disorientation. The familiar placement of things has been rejigged as a direct result of "My sister's staying". Yet, while he cannot find "saucepans rice and cutting knives/ even god help me whiskey glasses" in his own home, the location codes outside the home are specific and identifiable: "380 bus at Darlinghurst...the Sacred Heart Church." It is as if public place beyond the private and intimate domestic space is the only way the internal drama can be navigated. Moreover, home truths are useless now. Rowe comes to naming his sister's illness slowly: a "cough", "hunched shoulders", "if she's afraid she doesn't say", "Clinic" and then "Radiation in Use." This imitates the reluctance with which the facts of his sister's imminent death is faced.

Stanza two introduces the next family member, his mother. She brings her own suffering such as loneliness, an inability to be still and her loss of faith. We get some backstory here to his mother's life up at *Taylor's Arm*, some 20 odd kilometers from Macksville. Her life has been one of taking care of children, poverty and fear. The frenetic activity of "ironing tablecloths...making meals/ from next to nothing" is repeated in stanza four when his other sister comes to stay. Like all tribes, there are salient prejudices, pathologies and pejoratives that underscore their mentality. The importance of scraping together a shared meal, a communion of sorts, from hardly anything is one such belief. Later, in stanza three, Rowe writes "we were all bred/ on disappointment" and still later in stanza seven "why good intentions always bring so much bad luck". These belief statements are important to consider when trying to make sense of why people in certain tribes play out dramas in the way they do. One's expectations forged in the collective mindset determines our capacity to accept the inevitable, especially what we cannot change.

In stanza three we move on up to Macksville on the Nambucca River and to the locale of the family's Catholic parish. Rowe contrasts his mother's inability to pray: "the priest has put my sister in the parish bulletin/ they're saying prayers for her recovery/ (please god they're not putting too much emphasis on *thy will be done*)." The dark aside from Rowe is pitch perfect in its irony. The unbroken line of this aside suggests the prayer Rowe sends forth is not a fragmentation but rather a complete and whole thought. Meanwhile his sister is "learning how to live/ with death inside her where it's always been". A brutal and poignant line suggesting that death has been ever present as it is to us all. Stanza four opens the door to "My other sister...isn't coping...starts to scream". All these different reactions are accepted and taken into the family's stride. While death seems impossible to control or stop, accepting each other's reactions and responses is easier, a method of getting to the final point of acceptance. In this stanza Rowe uses an outer garment to visualises the impending operation in which his "sister's body cut from sternum down open at the middle/ so doesn't care whether or not her cardigan's on straight". The 5th stanza allows us to meet Rowe's deaf brother who seems to have risen above the tragedies of his own life to work for the community radio station in Nambucca valley: "on radio 2NVR...his thick-tongued troubles/ turn to song." We learn of the injustices his youngest brother endured while attending school and even of the beloved dog who "one day jumped the fence/ still wearing his lead and hung there choking on love". It is these traces of memory that make up the iterations of self, remembered fondly with distance by other members of the tribe.

The antepenultimate and the penultimate stanzas recall Rowe's other two brothers. The "Middle brother stays at home...of what was once the family farm/ (now cut in half)...I sometimes find it hard/ to know what to say to him". This sense of estrangement experienced in the familiar is troubling but not atypical. The distance between the brothers, geographically and symbolically, is played out in a singular memory of coming together to share a "telescope...it turned and looked back galaxies". A memory of seeing the same, of being eye to eye on something. Rowe's "older brother...drives us all to the hospital" but then ironically is caught in an accident where a woman "is trapped screaming" while the assailant "the drunken driver hasn't got a licence or a visa but he get's out/ laughing because he's rich". Once again, we see the trademark of injustice as seen through the retelling of family lore.

Overwhelmingly, this poem reads as a family tale of bad luck, of misfortune and of poor timing. Yet despite this or maybe because of it we see the threads of tenderness that stitch these people together. Indeed, Rowe ruminates on the axiom that "as we grow older it seems more necessary to recall/ being young". The layering of binaries persists, it is here where opposites come together that an impossible synthesis is found. So, Rowe recalls games of heroes and exotica: "he was Phantom Ghost Who Walks/ I was Bantar Pygmy Warrior don't laugh." His intimate conversational tone draws us into the fabric of his tribe until we too feel the thick romance and familiarity of it all. The ultimate stanza is short. Its focus is not on what happened to his sister but rather the shadowy figure of his dead father. To me it has resonances with Heaney's poem, *Digging*, which recalls how his father's spade for digging out bog, becomes his pen. Rowe leaves us with wire strainers which are used to join and strain wire, particularly for building or mending fences along farm paddocks. At the end of this poem he writes: "I hold it now to feel the way/ its weight takes up my hand." It is a powerful end to a tribal tale that has no ending. In many ways this poem has linked and pulled together the tensions of the family's separate and shared wires. In other ways this poem has helped create a way to fence oneself off from the unresolved suffering of others to whom one can offer little. A quiet and broken poem about what it is to be family. For what it is worth I so see ourselves as a nation, like this broken and tender family. Rowe just makes it all the more familiar.

8

A Terrible Beauty is Born: Irish Poetry

The Hermitage by Anonymous (9th Century)
Translated by Frank O'Connor

Grant me sweet Christ the grace to find -
Son of the Living God! -
A small hut in a lonesome spot
To make it my abode.

A little pool but very clear
To stand beside the place
Where all men's sins are washed away
By sanctifying grace.

A pleasant woodland all about
To shield it from the wind,
And make a home for singing birds
Before it and behind.

A southern aspect for the heat,
A stream along its foot,
A smooth green lawn with rich top soil
Propitious to all fruit.

My choice of men to live with me
And pray to god as well;

Quiet men of humble mind -
Their number I shall tell.

Four files of three or three of four
To give the psalter forth;
Six to pray by the south church wall
And six along the north.

Two by two my dozen friends -
To tell the number right -
Praying with me to move the king
Who gives the sun its light.

A lovely church, a home for God,
Bedecked with linen fine,
Where over the white Gospel page
The Gospel candles shine.

A little house where all may dwell
And body's care be sought,
Where none shows lust or arrogance,
None thinks an evil thoughts

And all I ask for housekeeping
I get and pay no fees,
Leeks from the garden, poultry, game,
Salmon and trout and bees.

My share of clothing and of food
From the king of fairest face,
And I to sit at times alone
And pray in every place.

What would compel a person to want to renounce all worldly goods and comforts in the pursuit of an ascetic life? Hermits live in seclusion from the world and a hermitage is the settlement where a small group of these hermits might live together religiously and as ascetics. Hermits or ascetic solitaries were common in early Middle Ages Ireland. The etymology of hermit comes from the Greek *eremia* for desert and is a reference to the Desert Fathers of the 4th century and indicates the solitary life. The most determined hermits sought their desert on the islands on the sea. In the 9th century there was a group of articulate and highly persuasive monks who referred to themselves as companions of God and as such revitalised the hermitage tradition. Why did hermits feel this compunction? Monasteries had in the earlier 6th to 8th centuries made strong alliances with the rich and wealthy families of Ireland; thus, the monastic and the secular were increasingly indistinguishable with wealthy landlords becoming abbots and then passing this rule on to their sons. Meanwhile, monks also fought in wars and often turned to their Kings rather than their fellow churchmen for support. So, the culdees or revivalists of the monastic life in the 9th century encouraged hermits to retire to a secluded spot and pray, study and work the land for their providence. So, it is about withdrawing from the world and contemplating God. This poem speaks to the cenobite as opposed to the eremite; to the hermit living in community as opposed to the hermit living alone and in seclusion. Finally, the hermits of the 9th century Ireland would have practised *Lectio Divina* or the four lessons of God: *Lectio*, reading Scripture, *Mediatio*, reflecting on the Scripture, *Oratio*, praying and *Contemplatio*, deep reflective thought.

These 11 quatrains translated by O'Connor sing of such joy in the hope of this life! Indeed, it is a type of *Oratio*. I am baffled and intrigued but I am also cautious. It's the 9th century Ireland: ongoing Viking raids, unrelenting hunger and cold, followed by horrific deaths make for a hard life. Why make it harder? Here are men wishing to live together in seclusion. A small group of men who might all worship Christ. This is a poem that sings of the aching bodily desire to have everything in having nothing. Yet it is not *nothing* because what the poet actually wishes to find is detailed and delightful. It is an *oratio* with a considerable shopping list. At the onset the poet is asking for the "grace to find". To discover abundance because of the free and unmerited favor of God; to reach out for divinely given bounty. A part of me can't help but think that every man woman and child of Ireland in the Early Middle Ages would have wished for the same: "A small hut...A little pool...A pleasant woodland... My choice of men...A lovely church...A little house where all may dwell." This beautiful *oratio*, full of lustre and hope, is an apostrophe in that it addresses "sweet Christ...Son of the living God". Indeed, the Almighty is invoked half a dozen times in this song of request.

To request seclusion in order to reflect upon the glory of God is something imbued in the hermit's life. The removal of outside influences is central to the contemplative life. The poet calls for a "small hut in a lonesome spot". Many of these hermitages were built on islands and their lives would have been carved out by squalling tempests, ferocious winters and blinding darkness every single evening. He moves from this request to a site from where sins may be washed away and fellow believers reborn in Christ: "A little pool...where all men's sins are washed away." From this all else may follow. In other words, to be initiated into the sect allows the poet a type of licence to request items for their ongoing advancement as a community. So, the hut is to be surrounded by a woodland, to "shield it from the wind" and placed in a "southern aspect for the heat". This sounds like good real estate. There are birds in the woods offering up a timorous soundscape and a "rich top soil...Propitious to all fruit". This is edenic. So, the garden of bounty is demanded for a community already baptised into this cenobite life. The next three quatrains focus on the poet's desire to hand pick his men: "My choice of men to live with me." It is surprising to hear the pragmatic request from the poet to select those whom he decrees will offer advantage to the community: "Quiet men ...Their number I shall tell." The number he repeats three times: "Four files of three or three of four" or "Six to pray ...And six along the north" or "my dozen friends". This number is a Biblical allusion to the

12 tribes of Israel, the protected people of God. The *oratio* which the selected 12 will conduct is "to move the King". It is as if their psalter and ongoing prayer will beseech God to offer them more.

The poet requests for a Church in which *Lectio* and *Mediatio* can be conducted. The church, in keeping with religious ideas of the day, would indeed be "a home for God". So, the request to find a little hut for the poet, then a home for God and later, a little house for his men, speaks to the desire to find shelter. This is poignant in that it must have surely been terrible times to live and so difficult to achieve safety let alone inner peace and thus insight. Here in this "lovely Church" we see traces of wealth within poverty: "linen fine...white Gospel page...candles shine." These signatures of Mass, including the taking of the Eucharist, was central to the hermit's life. Here is an indicator of the connection with a church practice beyond themselves and maybe even to the alliance with a greater monastic order. The last three quatrains sing a request for the housing of his fellow hermits, to form the final aspects of the hermitage. It is in this housing for the collective that "body's care be sought". Although he goes on to qualify that this is without "lust or arrogance [or] ....evil thought". In this representation the body's needs are childlike and innocent. Again, it would certainly form an enormous contrast to the backdrop of violence, chaos and trauma of everyday living in Ireland. The poet then lists what he hopes to find without a fee: "Leeks from the garden, poultry, game,/ Salmon and trout and bees." Even to the untrained gourmet's eye this looks pretty tempting: fresh fruit and vegetables, free range poultry and game, highly valued fresh water fish, and the sweetness of honey from which mead may be made. It is around this point that I am wondering why anyone would choose to stay in mainstream society. This bounty would be shared equitably, as noted in the last quatrain, given from the beautiful benevolent face of God. And if this isn't enough the poet seeks to find momentary solitude to *Contemplatio*: "at times alone/ And pray in every place."

This song, constructed in the subjunctive mood, is so full of wishful optimism. It could nearly be a recruitment pamphlet for eremitism. It is no wonder that 9th century Ireland saw a revitalisation of the ascetic solitaries in the Catholic struggle to engage with *metanoia*, the process of changing one's life by submitting to God in all ways. For some it was obvious that the ongoing and frequent threat of invaders meant that shelter from such adversaries was in vain without the protection of a greater power: "Except the Lord build the house they labor in vain that build it; except the Lord keep the city, the watchman waketh but in vain." To this day you can take a small boat out to *Skellig Michael* and clamber about its impossible craggy parapets where the cenobites once lived. Their bee hive ruins offer no shelter from the driving wind and rain, despite it being summer, the only time these boats will take you out there. There is something outrageous and mad in this site of spiritual contemplation. When the sun breaks through the war torn sky, bruised, battered and bleeding with Irish weather, it points to the skelligs: sheer volcanic eruptions pausing momentarily in their violence. It is a leap of faith that any sane person would believe one could actually reach the skelligs and survive the journey, let alone live one's whole life there in communion with God. What a God it must have been back then!

Lightenings viii by Seamus Heaney (1991)

The annals say: when the monks of Clonmacnoise

Were all at prayers inside the oratory
A ship appeared above them in the air.

The anchor dragged along behind so deep
It hooked itself into the altar rails
And then, as the big hull rocked to a standstill,

A crewman shinned and grappled down the rope
And struggled to release it. But in vain.
'This man can't bear our life here and will drown,'

The abbot said, 'unless we help him'. So
They did, the freed ship sailed, and the man climbed back
Out of the marvellous as he had known it.

    I go back to this gorgeous little sonnet time and time again. Whenever I read it I feel I am in a cinema: all dark and quiet and full of anticipatory excitement. I watch the screen up ahead and there it is: a ship hovering just meters away from me, suspended in disbelief and wonder. I love how there are traces of this imagined moment that hooks itself into my world and anchors itself there. Right there. Just above me. What am I to do? Then out of this spectacle a sailor shimmies down the rope in a vain effort to unhook the anchor wedged deep against the altar rails. Still I do nothing. I love how I am awoken from my stupor by the abbot with an instruction to help the young sailor. Most disturbingly is the fact that the sailor will drown if he stays here in *my* world and that's when I realise: I am in the sea, I am in the fathomless dark of the ocean – not him, not this magical realist moment of ship with crewman hovering mid-air. So, help him we did. Then everything is possible: the anchor is unhooked, the ship is freed, the sailor shimmies back up the rope and the ship sails off. All this movement in one line despite the fact that all the other lines had this ship still, stuck, silent. A part of me wants to call out to the ship: *Wait! Take me with you!* Such is my longing for the magic of adventure. I don't want to be abandoned, left in that quiet oratory, in the dark sea of worship. Yet, it is at this point, the poet reminds me that all is possible in the dark fathomless sea of my imagination. It is here that liberation occurs. The poet knows that the marvellous is my world; that my world is metaphysical and wondrous; and beauty can be unbearable for some.

    This is a legend contained in an old musty smelling tome somewhere... This is a record of what happened a long time ago... once upon a time. This is a Seamus Heaney sonnet. It is an explosion of delight every single time I read it! Clonmacnoise means meadows of the sons of Nós and can be found in the mid-way point between Dublin and Galway in County Offaly on the River Shannon. This monastery was founded in the 6th century and was a centripetal force of religion, learning, craftsmanship and trade. Kings of Ireland and scholars of Europe all visited. Beneath the oratory in which the monks were praying lies the body of Saint Ciaran. He was the founding member of this community and built the first church along with the help of Diarmait Ui Cerbaill, the first Christian High King of Ireland. According to legend when St Columba visited the monastery, he claimed he saw angels. During the 8th and 12th centuries the monastery was invaded at least 80 times by the English and the Vikings. In the 11th century the population grew from ten men to two thousand. During this time artisans made some of the most beautiful and enduring artworks in metal and stone as well as the creation of a vellum manuscript. The English garrison of Athlone destroyed and looted Clonmacnoise one last time in 1552, leaving it in the ruins that we see today. The original annals of Clonmacnoise, now lost, recorded the events of Ireland from pre-history to 1408.

Recently, I traveled out to Clonmacnoise. A Sunday morning, grey watercolors soggy above and verdant cold green mush below. The River Shannon bending with lazy insouciance this way and that. It rained, of course. I think it must have been June, so summer and it rained and rained and rained. Beyond the actual monastery ruins, grazing on the banks of the river, were heavy cows moving about their business. Uninterested in the growing number of tourists pouring into the ruins. Every so often the showers would increase in velocity and tourists would scamper about to take shelter. I had just walked some of the *Camino* in France so muck and mud and a bit of weather was no deterrent. Anyway, I searched about until I came to the oratory. A tiny doorway leading into an even smaller space, despite there being no roof or windows. I walked about touching the walls and thinking about Heaney and the monks and the crewman who nearly got stuck in our world. If you press your ear to the stone you can almost hear the struggle. And then the oratory grew expansive and the sun literally came out from behind the clouds and ran lines of *Naples Yellow* and *Burnt Sienna* through the gothic windows. It was a glory to behold! Later that day as we sat around my dear friend's dinner table on her farm close by, with her two young laborers, we talked about what we had seen and Heaney's sonnet. One of the young men recited the poem just off the cuff, between his baked dinner and a slab of brown bread. My country, my mother's country, my grandfather's country all the way back to the diaspora of the Great Famine.

Swineherd by Eiléan Ní Chuilleanáin (1977)

When all this is over, said the swineherd,
I mean to retire, where
Nobody will have heard about my special skills
And conversation is mainly about the weather.

I intend to learn how to make coffee, as least as well
As the Portuguese lay-sister in the kitchen
And polish the brass fenders every day.
I want to lie awake at night
Listening to cream crawling to the top of the jug
And the water lying soft in the cistern.

I want to see an orchard where the trees grow in straight lines
And the yellow fox finds shelter between the navy-blue trunks,

Where it gets dark early in summer
And the apple-blossom is allowed to wither on the bough.

I've always found this marvellous sonnet enchanting. The swineherd surfaces in Homer, the Bible and in Hans Christian Anderson: a best friend, a prodigal son and a disguised prince. An occupation that would be slightly insalubrious, with the mud and sharp teeth of a pig as a daily occupational hazard. Indeed, a lowly livelihood. This sonnet considers the ambitions and hopes of this keeper of swine. Here we have a dramatic monologue by the swineherd recording all that he wants to achieve in retirement: "When all this is over...I mean to retire." When all what is over? The herding of pigs? Working for someone else? We are not to know but rather invited to imagine. The structure is first stanza of four lines, second stanza of six lines and third stanza of four lines. The first and the last stanza offer more questions than answers. It is the swineherd's heartfelt wish that his "special skills" go unnoticed. Whether those skills are hospitality, humility, integrity or simply herding swine, he is in need of another life. One where "conversation is mainly about the weather" and thus in the first stanza of the sonnet we have the swineherd's hope to dissolve into the landscape of the ordinary, the mundane, the everyday. This makes me wonder at the marvellous as he had known it, prior to retirement. Was it a time of the great Odysseus' heroic return to Ithaca or the loving father's discovery of the wayward son or the prince's rejection of his princesses' gratitude? It makes me recalibrate my understanding of swineherd as a lowly position. Perhaps Ní Chuilleanáin is playing to that very prejudice. Perhaps the swineherd has been deeply underestimated time and time again.

The second stanza offers a glorious list of what the swineherd hopes to learn. The list is surprisingly commonplace: "how to make coffee...polish the brass fenders." We have a glimpse into his temporality. Here there are "Portuguese lay-sister in the kitchen" and a cold enough climate to want to keep an open hearth. Out of what medieval story book has he just stepped? It's illustrated as a genre piece with pots, pans, canisters, ladles, knives, bowls and mugs. I see the quasi-religious order bustling about preparing meals for those on the estate; the workers rough, ready and hungry for their turn to eat and drink and sit down. The swineherd may wish for new skills, those in keeping with indoor laboring away from the persistent snorkel of the pig and early morning rising. A new life where he can afford to "lie awake at night/ Listening to cream crawling to the top of the jug/ And the water lying soft in the cistern." This imagined sound of the "cream crawling to the top of the jug" stands in for the imagined visual, demonstrating just how keenly felt is this desire. This is a mouth-watering yearning for the rich glut of cream at the top of settled milk. This is the sound of water in the tank works as an easy reassurance that all is as it should be throughout the night.

The final four lines, the last sentence of the sonnet, intensifies this astonishing world the swineherd longs to see. Here we have a "yellow fox" and "navy blue trunks" of orchard trees, a place that "gets dark early in summer" and excess replaces frugality. It's a veritable Van Gogh painting where a lurid palette is so arresting and glorious you suspend disbelief and see the buttery yellow fox move swiftly to the left of a cobalt tree trunk. The sky above is an eddying swirl of indigo, cerulean and lime tenebrism, despite the fact that harvest is at its peak and the orchard heavy with summer fruit. We are in a world where all is inverted. The swineherd moves from outdoor laboring to indoor chores, visual imagining is replaced with auditory sensations of desire, and the real is replaced with the surreal in a landscape that is strangely familiar. This is about the way in which the marvellous is deeply imminent in the ordinary. It is a reminder that no one should be underestimated because it is in their ambitions and dreams that we can see their true selves. The South American writers teach us that magical realism is an inadequate term; what they are witnessing is realism...there is nothing magical about it because the world is made up of the physical as much as it is made up of the metaphysical. The extraordinary, remarkable, exceptional and marvellous are well and truly here, in Ní Chuilleanáin's *Swineherd* in our very own world.

Second Coming by W. B. Yeats (1919)

Turning and turning in the widening gyre
The falcon cannot hear the falconer;
Things fall apart; the center cannot hold;
Mere anarchy is loosed upon the world,
The blood-dimmed tide is loosed, and everywhere
The ceremony of innocence is drowned;
The best lack all conviction, while the worst
Are full of passionate intensity.

Surely some revelation is at hand;
Surely the Second Coming is at hand.
The Second Coming! Hardly are those words out
When a vast image out of *Spiritus Mundi*
Troubles my sight: somewhere in sands of the desert
A shape with lion body and the head of a man,
A gaze blank and pitiless as the sun,
Is moving its slow thighs, while all about it
Reel shadows of the indignant desert birds.
The darkness drops again; but now I know
That twenty centuries of stony sleep
Were vexed to nightmare by a rocking cradle,
And what rough beast, its hour come round at last,
Slouches towards Bethlehem to be born?

Inside the *State Russian Museum* in St Petersburg is Bryullov's enormously beautiful and terrifying masterpiece, *The Last Day of Pompeii*. This 466 by 651 centimeter oil on canvas has a magnetic and shocking effect. I have returned again and again to see Bryullov's apocalyptic vision. What astounds me is the way in which eschatology is captured in a way that transcends time and place; whether it be in ancient rock art, classical Roman epistles, Russian paintings or Irish poetry it seems to be human nature that we consider the catastrophic end. Three years before publishing *Second Coming* in the *Dial*, Yeats had already published his 1916 poem, *Easter Uprising*. In this earlier poem three times he choruses "A terrible beauty is born" to articulate the Janus face of desire: beauty and terror. By 1919, World War 1 has come to an end, the Russian Revolution has morphed into the Russian Civil War and the Easter Uprising has given way to the Irish War of Independence. Modernism is nascent but believing utterly that God is dead and the paradigms that had governed the lives of those in Europe prior to the war are now completely redundant. Old values of the Church and State had been derived from a mindset that no longer believed that order would triumph over chaos. Like the remarkable depiction of the people in *The Last Day of Pompeii* looking skywards to the unimaginable horror that was about to descend upon them, the Modern Western world seemed to quake at the beast they had unleashed that could not be stopped.

Second Coming is made up of two stanzas and the first is one sentence. In an eight line sentence there is approximately 11 verbs. Here is a poem that throws us into intense action. This is not a slow burn meditative poem but rather a head spinning frenzy that whirling dervishes you into another reality. This must have been exactly what it felt like in the center of the zeitgeist when Yeats was writing. He knew people arrested and killed after the Easter Uprising, he knew the political polarities passionately fighting their corners which led to the Civil War in Ireland and he knew the ways of thinking emerging out of the transcendental movement all of which created an unprecedented historical political canvas. The first stanza lets us feel the gyre of turbulence. We are positioned in the unfixed center where we witness anarchy and the drowning of innocence. We open media res inside the present participle of the verb "turning" repeated to revolve around and around in the "widening gyre"; an inverted vortex that acts as a tornado across the prairies of our imagining.

Falconry no longer orchestrates the taming of a wild bird to catch prey; indeed, the hitherto trained wild bird of prey can no longer hear the commands of the master to kill and return with carnage. Disorder, lawlessness and mayhem ensue. I can see the machine of society thrumming so intensely that it begins to disintegrate and send its contingent parts flying. It is this spectacle that is "loosed upon the world" and further clarification is offered along the axis of this stanza: "Mere anarchy is loosed." The past participle of the verb tells us that this has already occurred, there is no clawing back. Moreover, at the center of the stanza, like the center of this world, we are reminded of unfixed anarchy. The Latin origins of "Mere" suggests the undiluted, which only intensifies the chaos further. Not just is "innocence...drowned" but the worship of innocence is drowned, suggesting that we have no ritual to celebrate the blameless, virtuous and worthy. Without ritual we are without civilisation; without innocence we are without a beginning. We have only the apocalyptic end. The final two lines of this stanza reminds me of Yeats' *Easter Uprising* in that I can't help but feel this statement emerges out of his own very real temporality: "The best lack all conviction, while the worst/ Are full of passionate intensity." The known individuals either lack faith in their principles or are driven on and on by hatred.

The second stanza begins with the adverb "Surely" which indicates Yeats' dogged assurance that divine disclosure is imminent. The anaphora of "Indeed" is the poet reassuring himself that these portents and auguries have meaning and purpose. The second stanza is focused on the promise of the "Second Coming". This Christian concept of the return of the Christ is found in canonical gospels. Messianic prophecies are central to eschatological narratives where it is believed, as cited in Mark's Gospel, that "He will come again in glory to judge the living and the dead, and his kingdom will have no end". The promise of the Second Coming is repeated thrice in the poem as if Yeats is placating himself, and us, that chaos is a precursor to the arrival of the messiah. Yet the messiah that emerges out of the second stanza is far more disturbing than the chaos itself. Yeats then takes six and a half lines to describe the emerging messiah: "a vast image ... somewhere in the sands of the desert/ A shape with lion body and the head of a man/ A blank gaze ... moving its slow thighs." This description always reminds me of Shelley's "colossal wreck", *Ozymandias*, that is both "boundless and bare" and it too seems to emerge from the "lone and level sands stretch[ed] far away". This image haunts and disturbs. Yeats refers once again to his own metaphysical framework in citing the Latin term "Spiritus Mundi" to describe the collective soul of the universe containing the memories of all time. He believed that it was from this source that all poets gained their inspiration. In other words, it is the world spirit that offers all images and symbols and even a collective unconscious.

It is from this place that the second coming emerges and its impact is palpable with flights of "indignant desert birds" casting wheeling shadows in its wake. This disturbance is already picked up by the poet who says that it "Troubles my sight". The lumbering heaviness, the relentless moving forwards and the "gaze blank and pitiless as the sun" are features that deeply unsettle us. Here is the long awaited messiah and yet the merciless visage is out of keeping with the Christian mythologies of the messiah's compassion and omniscient love. The last five lines of the poem takes us back into that canvas of eschatological horror, the objective correlative of the last days of judgement: "darkness drops." Yeats then inserts himself clearly with "now I know/ That twenty centuries of stony sleep/ Were vexed to nightmare by a rocking cradle". What is being said here? Is Yeats suggesting that for the last two thousand years we have been locked in a "stony sleep" and thus resistant to the message of the Christ, completely immune to his teachings which offered salvation? Moreover, this resistance and immutability to the birth of Christ, the ever present "rocking cradle", has in fact troubled us into this "nightmare" witnessed by Yeats' contemporaries. Therefore, if the birth of Christ, with all its promise of redemption, was heeded, would the world have been in the mess it found itself in when 1919 rolled around? The poem ends with a question. The answer is located in the title. Yet we are dislocated by the reference to the Second Coming as a "rough beast". This is more like a satanic image, the enemy to God. Is this to be the Second Coming? This violent brutal depraved cruel four-footed animal that moves slowly, lazily and slovenly towards the iconic site of the Christ's nascent beginnings? It is unstoppable. It is destiny and one that we have ensured. So when Yeats asks: "And what rough beast, its hour come round at last,/ Slouches towards Bethlehem to be born?" the answer has got to be, the Second Coming we deserve.

Anseo by Paul Muldoon (1980)

When the Master was calling the roll
At the primary school in Collegelands,
You were meant to call back *Anseo*
And raise your hand
As your name occurred.

Anseo, meaning here, here and now,
All present and correct,
Was the first word of Irish I spoke.
The last name on the ledger
Belonged to Joseph Mary Plunkett Ward
And was followed, as often as not,
By silence, knowing looks,
A nod and a wink, the Master's droll
'And where's our little Ward-of-court?'

I remember the first time he came back
The Master had sent him out
Along the hedges
To weigh up for himself and cut
A stick with which he would be beaten.
After a while, nothing was spoken;
He would arrive as a matter of course
With an ash-plant, a salley-rod.
Or, finally, the hazel-wand
He had whittled down to a whip-lash,
Its twist of red and yellow lacquers
Sanded and polished,
And altogether so delicately wrought
That he had engraved his initials on it.

I last met Joseph Mary Plunkett Ward
In a pub just over the Irish border.
He was living in the open,
In a secret camp
On the other side of the mountain.
He was fighting for Ireland,
Making things happen.
And he told me, Joe Ward,
Of how he had risen through the ranks
To Quartermaster, Commandant:
How every morning at parade
His volunteers would call back *Anseo*
And raise their hands
As their names occurred.

Muldoon's three stanzas made up of 14 lines apiece is clean and compelling. Indeed, each stanza could be read as a self-contained sonnet and each of these 14 line stanzas have a volta, invite meditation and offer a symmetry. I read this poem before I ever read poems by Joseph Mary Plunkett. That Muldoon offers this autobiographical teasing intensifies our engagement with the fate of this young boy. *Anseo* means here, at this present point. It's this temporality that interests me. When I did come to read Joseph Mary Plunkett I wanted to think that Muldoon's poem is autobiographical and this recalcitrant misunderstood school boy turns out to be one of the signatories of the *Proclamation of Independence* and subsequently one of the Martyrs of 1916. Yet this cannot be. Plunkett would have been at school at the fin de siecle. Muldoon would have been at school some 60 years later. So, it's a sleight of hand imagining. Why does Muldoon need to see that boy as one of the adults who were instrumental in the Easter Uprising? Perhaps we are looking at a history that never ends. A story that constantly repeats itself. This is a beautiful first person lyric that considers a childhood and the makings of a man, both Plunkett and Muldoon. I like the even quality of the poem. These stanzas, use the occasional end rhymes and play with short lines to accentuate key moments, offer balance and symmetry. The word *Anseo* occurs four times. So, I guess I am thinking about the way in which Muldoon is saying how present he is to this unremarkable incident that on reflection is a bildungsroman moment. Of course, I can see the way in which violence begets violence. The way institutionalisation of children's education contains irrelevance and, in some ways, a sadistic inevitability of punishment in response to adults simply not understanding.

Stanza one places us at roll call in Collegelands, County Armagh, named as such because it was formerly a branch of Trinity College Dublin. We begin with expectations, power imbalance and accountability. The calque disrupts us momentarily but we sidle in beside Muldoon as he explains easily and reassuringly that "*Anseo*, meaning here, here and now,/ All present and correct,/ Was the first word of Irish I spoke." So, readers, not bilingual, can rest assured that they are in the company of same. From this primary schooler's perspective, we see the importance of the "Master" in all his sarcastic and sadistic splendour. Here are the rules of engagement clearly marked: "You were meant to call back Anseo." Muldoon contrasts this first Irish word for him with the last word on the roll. Hence, we arrive at Joseph Mary Plunket Ward. Muldoon employs autobiographical teasing. This is at once the name that encapsulates nationalist commitment, romantic tragedy and martyrdom. The addition of "Ward" signifies a few ideas: firstly, that this is a descendent from the bardic north, or a common surname of Irish travelers or finally an insolent reference to being a ward of the court, a term given to those mentally incapable of being able to handle their own affairs. Indeed, the Masters "silence, knowing looks,/ A nod and a wink" forces the onlooking primary students to be complicit with the victimisation of this young truant. This first stanza gives us pause. The raising of the hand, a singular action indicating complicity with the expectations of the majority to a particular tribal ritual, is in contrast to the action of the collective silence and acknowledgment that the non-compliant is the outsider.

Each stanza begins media res, heightening the sense of drama. The first memory the poet shares of actually seeing Ward is when he returns from the task of selecting his instrument of punishment: "To weigh up for himself and cut/ A stick with which he would be beaten." This weighing up or evaluation of what is to occur threads together Joseph Mary Plunkett and Ward and Muldoon. It is the bildungsroman of the Ireland. This has occurred time and time again to young Ward because we hear of the various whipping sticks he has chosen in the past: "With an ash-plant, a salley-rod… the hazel-wand." The ash-plant and hazel-wand are imbibed with allusions to Heaney and Yeats but there is nothing but vulnerability and disgust at the alliterative description of "hazel-wand…whittled down to a whip-lash". The hyphenating of these items places the noun first and its potential action in quick succession, therefore the ash, salley, hazel and whip are variously plant, rod, wand and lash. The last four lines of this second stanza offers with deft precision a stunning visual of the craftsmanship gone into the stick selected by Ward. The hazel-wand's gloss is "Sanded and polished/ And altogether so delicately wrought/ That he engraved his initials on it". This defiance against authority even in the face of brutal corporal punishment suggests the single mindedness of Ward and his courage. What I linger on in this stanza are the two shorter lines: "Along the hedges…Sanded and polished." In some ways this is emblematic of the terrible beauty that can be born. Weaponry lovingly crafted from the very landscape that offers both complicit belonging and deliberate exclusion.

Time has passed and as adults Muldoon and Ward meet once more in this third and final stanza. The trinitrine structure of this poem offers a completion of their bildungsroman. Here, as in stanza one, Joseph Mary Plunkett Ward is named in full; this shape changer makes us consider the effects of time passing. The border between the Republic of Ireland and the United Kingdom takes us into a variation of the world of their youth. This sectarian divide replaces the Masters with an army presence, the movement of troops and an emotionally charged fight. Ward is now "living in the open/ In a secret camp…fighting for Ireland". This suggests Ward is part of Irish mythology, a *Fianna* or young landless Irish warrior who is "Making things happen". The last sentence of the stanza places us in both Plunkett and Ward's world. One that is militarised and disciplined and very much part of a tribal response to the politics of exclusion and inclusion that dictates Irish lives. The Irish Volunteers were formed in 1913 as a direct response to the formation of the Ulster Volunteers. It was the Irish Volunteers who drove the Easter Uprising and followed the military plans worked out for them by Joseph Mary Plunkett. Therefore, in this conflation of time and place "His volunteers would call back *Anseo*/ And raise their hands/ As their names occurred". The accountability of the assembled is an ironic salute to the primary school roll call. Indeed, the final two lines of the poem repeats the same phrase from stanza one. Sandwiched between stanza one of the primary school roll call and stanza three of the Irish Volunteers roll call is stanza two's shaping of a weapon. Here is the call to be present, to stand and be counted and to indicate that you are here in this place: *Anseo*. A place where violence begets violence, where history repeats itself, and all tribal warfare commences from the cradle to the grave. Muldoon's poem is an Anseo, a call in response to the terrible beauty that was born.

I see his blood upon the rose by Joseph Mary Plunkett (1911)

I see his blood upon the rose
And in the stars the glory of his eyes,
His body gleams amid eternal snows,
His tears fall from the skies.

I see his face in every flower;
The thunder and the singing of the birds
Are but his voice—and carven by his power
Rocks are his written words.

All pathways by his feet are worn,
His strong heart stirs the ever-beating sea,
His crown of thorns is twined with every thorn,
His cross is every tree.

This sonnet pulls together a number of preoccupations of Joseph Mary Plunkett. Here we are invited to contemplate romance, crucifixion and liberation. In fact, why not listen to the achingly beautiful song *Grace*, written to remember the marriage to Grace Gifford on the eve of his execution. This song has stayed with me ever since the first time I heard it. In many ways the poetry, heroism and martyrdom of Plunkett is heightened by the fact that he marries his beloved the night before his execution. The Catholicism of his day, his Jesuit training at Stonyhurst College, his family backing as well as his tubercular illness all made him the man he was. At 23 he writes this sonnet some five years before the Easter Uprising. His love of the Incarnate Word and its connection to all created things allowed Plunkett to be the visionary and poet he was. Indeed, in the company of his friends and signatories, Pearse and McDonagh, the Uprising was masterminded by writers with a literary bent. From the GPO he was arrested and taken to Kilmainham jail. His last words expressed his resolve to die for his beliefs, like Christ, knowing that this would result in joy. The joy is a long time coming.

Plunkett sees the presence of Christ, his suffering, death and resurrection, in all of nature. The blood of Christ shed for his beliefs in a better world is there for Plunkett in the beauteous rose: "I see His blood upon the rose." No longer just a yonic symbol of love, the rose is the texture and palette of the passion of Christ. Herein is the Eros and Thanatos of the messiah's passion. Indeed, Christ's omniscience, "the glory of his eyes" is in the canopy of stars and his body white and pure "gleams amid eternal snows". Even his compassion for us is in the rain from the heavens. This is more than pathetic fallacy this is the ongoing unrelenting extended metaphor of Christ as the natural landscape known to Plunkett. This is Christ as universal, writ both macroscopically and microscopically. It is a litany that romances the suffering, death and resurrection of Christ as Ireland. Christ's visage is "every flower". The absolutism of Christ as everything and ever present begins to gain fever pitch. Christ's voice is both the "thunder and singing of the birds" and his power has carved a language on the rocks. This is the inescapable sublime. It is reminiscent of the Romantic poets whose imagination wrought a divine vision. The last quatrain of this sonnet acknowledges the ever present risen Christ. One could argue that this very sonnet is the translation of Christ's written word across Ireland. It certainly is, according to Plunkett, one steeped in Catholic mythology.

The final quatrain contains the volta of this sonnet. We shift from the poet as subject to Christ as subject. This resolution at the poem's end, is consoling. Whatever the way forward for Plunkett,

Christ has already trodden there. The "pathways by his feet are worn", thus the poet is reassured that his is the way of the Lord. The radicalisation of a Jesuit education cannot be underestimated. Moreover, the Catholicism of Ireland at this point was such that nationalism and republicanism were central to the sense of a liberated future. The island of Ireland, ever vulnerable to the marauding invaders, has at its core "His strong heart...ever-beating sea". This suffering Christ of Ireland is pre resurrection and as such shares their state of anguish and travail. This agony is their crown. Consequently, "His cross is every tree". The synecdoche of Christ's crucifix as the tree, and in this case specifically the tree in Ireland, comes to be the lens through which we see the ever present pain of the Irish national. Indeed, this was a vision for 23 year old Plunkett who was, a few years later, going to see the battle at the GPO followed by the execution of many of his friends not to mention himself who died for an Irish republic. Perhaps the poem develops another layer of meaning in that "his blood upon the rose" is young 27 year old Plunkett's blood on the fair rose of Grace Gifford, who was his bride of no more than 12 hours but never married again.

The Mother by Patrick Pearse (1916)

I do not grudge them: Lord, I do not grudge
My two strong sons that I have seen go out
To break their strength and die, they and a few,
In bloody protest for a glorious thing,
They shall be spoken of among their people,
The generations shall remember them,
And call them blessed;
But I will speak their names to my own heart
In the long nights;
The little names that were familiar once
Round my dead hearth.
Lord, thou art hard on mothers:
We suffer in their coming and their going;
And tho' I grudge them not, I weary, weary
Of the long sorrow-And yet I have my joy:
My sons were faithful, and they fought.

On 3 May 1916, Patrick Pearse wrote to his mother and sent with the letter this poem. It was a few days before his execution for treason in leading the rebellion at the GPO in Dublin. In the letter Pearse writes: "you asked me to write a little poem which would seem to be said by you about me." A strange request, if ever it was made, by a mother to her son in Kilmainham Prison. Margaret Pearse eventually became an Irish politician and died in 1932. The Pearse family were politically active in the pursuit of Irish nationalism and republicanism. Pearse himself believed he went to the firing squad to die a soldier's death for Ireland and for freedom. He said: "We have done right. People will say hard thinks of us now, but later on they will praise us. Do not grieve for all this but think of it as a sacrifice which God has asked of me and of you." The day after Pearse's execution his younger brother was executed, not for being a leader of the rebellion but for being Pearse's brother.

Pearse developed his love if Irish history, language and literature when he was first at school. Authentic Gaelic was largely spoken in Connaught, a region severely affected by the Great Famine. Pearse wanted Irish history and culture taught in schools and believed the Catholic colleges were not doing enough in the spread of Irish nationalism. He founded St Enda's, a school that offered Irish history, language and literature and as it said in Irish on the prospectus: "where young people should spend their lives working hard and zealously for their fatherland and, if it should ever be necessary, to die for it." *Sin Fein* and other republican movements had far more impact than Pearse who was regarded as a maverick with a sense of romanticism, literature and emerging belief in martyrdom. Prior to the outbreak of World War 1 he was becoming increasingly fanatical and went about raising funds for the Irish Volunteers, the public face of the outlawed Irish Republican Brotherhood. The Home Rule Bill was suspended when World War 1 broke out but Pearse believed that the time was ripe to overthrow the British rule of Ireland. Pearse had failed to recognise that many people of Ireland, including those in Dublin, relied on the British for work. Hence the Easter Uprising of 1916 was a minority uprising with no uprisings occurring elsewhere. During the rebellion Pearse said, "When we are all wiped out, people will blame us for everything, condemn us...but in a few years they will see the meaning of what we tried to do". In this he was right. Pearse was captured and charged with treason and on 16 May 1916 he was executed, along with 14 other rebel leaders. It was after death that Pearse found real fame. In death he was known as the "First President of Ireland" and Irish history and culture became part of the education system after 1922.

This sonnet, *The Mother*, is written by Pearse from the perspective of his mother. I think about the way in which men, whether they be idealistic, fanatical, violent, misunderstood, alienated, broken, damaged or visionary sons, dress up their actions for nationalism in the guise of mother love. Indeed, nation and the feminine are conflated in our imagination. Mother Ireland is mythologised with her curvaceous and fecund landscape; with her history of rape and gag by invaders; and with her songs to Irish men to defend her dream of a future without oppression. So, I really do see this sonnet as Pearse's insistence to justify his life contracted by fanaticism and eventually violence. The mother's voice opens the sonnet with a plaintive statement that indicates she has no resentment to either her sons or to the Lord. The repetition in the opening line of "I do not grudge" could in many ways be heard as a subconscious moment of guilt from the male poet's perspective. Without the women's compliance in the fight for Ireland and republicanism there could be no battle. Here Pearse is speaking for all mothers in effect and setting out a lionised version of what "The" mother of Ireland would say. Hence all mothers that follow would step in line, needless to say that in 1981 during the Long Kesh Hunger Strike, Paddy Quinn's mother did not. Pearse's mother, on the other hand, states that her "two strong sons" leave her to be broken and to die "In bloody protest for a glorious thing". Willie and Patrick were part of the rebellion and did die for the cause protesting the ongoing English occupation of Ireland. The next three lines have a religious overtone suggesting that these sons of Ireland have fought for her freedom: "shall be spoken of among their people,/The generations shall remember them,/And call them blessed." This sacrifice begins to take on messianic proportions. There is a Biblical tone to their remembrance. In many ways this is Pearse writing his obituary. Here is the heroism outlined by the hitherto hero.

On the one hand it is the widow Margaret Pearse who speaks and indicates that all she has now are "long nights" and a "dead hearth" around which she will remember the names of her sacrificed sons. On the other hand, this is Mother Ireland who speaks for a suffering nation who will never forget the fallen: "I will speak their names to my own heart." Their names have been spoken for over 100 years and they have not been forgotten. The tenderness by which the sons of Ireland are remembered is contained in the phrase: "little names that were familiar once." The hearth and heart are poetically interchangeable. Both terms are used to indicate the pulsating center of love, nurture and care. Both are connected to fire and passion. Both indicate a type of shelter from the world and place of belonging. Her own heart now will replace the "dead hearth" and it is in this heart that she will keep her sons alive by naming them and never forgetting. At the start of the last sentence of the stanza the Lord is invoked again: "Lord, thou art hard on mothers." The drama has been heightened now as we consider that it is God himself who asks this sacrifice of the sons of Ireland. In other words, this is a God given request to free themselves from the yoke of English oppression. The mother speaks for the collective: "We suffer." This is in keeping with Catholic mythology about the mother of Christ suffering. Mother suffering has been entrenched in Catholicism for centuries. Again, we are assured, now for the third time that Mother Ireland "grudge them not". Rather, she is tired and drained by "the long sorrow" but not indefatigable because "I have my joy". Here is the greatest strain on my imagination, her joy is that her sons kept the faith, fought and died.

This sonnet is riddled with so many issues and problems. Here we have a man condemned to his death writing a poem about his heroism and his future iconic status. Here we have a man writing to his yet to be declared nation about the way in which the crucifixion of Christ is being played out on Irish soil. Ireland is the mother of the crucified Christ, aka Patrick. Resurrection and Republicanism are somewhat the same in this context. Here is a man writing in a woman's voice in way that is not even thinly veiled but deeply imbued with Catholic notions of the suffering mother. The poets and writers that participated in the Easter Uprising as well as those like Yeats who wrote to immortalise it as an heroic moment in Irish history make me think about the importance of mythology in galvanising revolution. Auden wrote on the death of Yeats and the cusp of World War II, some 17 years in to a divided Ireland: "Mad Ireland hurt you into poetry./ Now Ireland has her madness and her weather still, / For poetry makes nothing happen." Ireland definitely hurt Pearse into poetry and into the romanticisation of an independent homeland. I also think there is a madness here that I cannot judge because I wasn't there and I am wholly ensconced in a different temporality and culture. Did poetry make nothing happen? When I read this sonnet of Pearse, and consider his ongoing legend and symbolic value, I would have to disagree with Auden.

Kathleen Ni-Houlahan by Anonymous (18th Century)
Translated by James Clarence Mangah

Long they pine in weary woe, the nobles of our land,
Long they wander to and fro, proscribed, alas! and banned;

Feastless, houseless, altarless, they bear the exile's brand,
But their hope is in the coming-to of Kathleen-Ni-Houla-han!

Think her not a ghastly hag, too hideous to be seen,
Call her not unseemly names, our matchless Kathleen;
Young is she, and fair she is, and would be crowned a queen,
Were the King's son at home here with Kathleen-Ni-Houla-han!

Sweet and mild would look her face, O none so sweet and mild,
Could she crush her foes by whom her beauty is reviled;
Woollen plaids would grace herself and robes of silk her child,
If the king's son were living here with Kathleen-Ni-Houla-han!

Sore disgrace it is to see the Arbitress of Thrones
Vassal to a Saxoneen of cold and sapless bones!
Bitter anguish wrings our souls – with heavy sighs and groans
We wait the Young Deliverer of Kathleen-Ni-Houla-han!

Let us pray to Him who holds Life's issues in his hands –
Him who formed the mighty globe, with all its thousand lands;
Girding them with seas and mountain, rivers deep, and stands,
To case a look of pity upon Kathleen-Ni-Houla-han!

He, who over sands and waves led Israel along –
He, who fed, with heavenly bread, that chosen tribe and throng –
He, who stood by Moses, when his foes were fierce and strong –
May He show forth His might in saving Kathleen-Ni-Houla-han!

Kathleen, daughter of Houlahan, is a mythical figure who has become an emblem for Irish Nationalism. There are many appellations of Kathleen but all of them require the sacrifice of the sons of Erin. Oftentimes she has appeared as an old woman begging the young men to free Ireland from colonial rule which ultimately leads to their martyrdom and her rejuvenation into a young beautiful queenly figure. From the 1789 Irish Rebellion to the 1919 Irish War of Independence; from the formation of the Irish Republican Army to the 1981 Hunger Strikes, Kathleen was invoked. This mythological creature represents the need for blood sacrifice in order to redeem and rejuvenate Ireland. The young men are rewarded for their martyrdom by being remembered for ever. Like the seasonal rejuvenation and the sacrificial aspects of Christianity in the resurrection of the crucified Christ, Kathleen promises an end to Irish oppression. Indeed, the Irish diaspora during the 19th century, caused by the Irish Potato Famine, was a time where the nostalgia and longing for Ireland was at its zenith hence the legend of Kathleen became the personification of Ireland. In the early 20th century Irish people felt a great sympathy for both Kathleen and Deidre's tragic experiences and misfortunes. W. B. Yeats plays on both these feminine figures of mythology and helped revive Irish national consciousness in the fin de siècle.

This six quatrain poem sings of the time when Kathleen will be saved by Ireland's men who have been hitherto denied their rightful Kindship. The first quatrain laments they who "pine in weary woe...wander to and fro...Feastless, houseless, altarless". These exiles are emotively conjured and can only expect salvation through the intervention of Kathleen. Some obdurate law has "proscribed...and banned" these men branded as landless. Landlessness amounts to being without sustenance, shelter or communion with their God; it is if their body and soul was contingent upon Irish soil. The second quatrain engages with the myth of Kathleen herself. The poet dismisses the illusion of her as "ghastly hag, too hideous to be seen" offers instead the vision of "matchless Kathleen;/ Young she is, and fair she is". Obviously, beauty and youth are worth saving. Moreover, she "would be crowned a queen/ Were the king's son at home". This is the beginning of the reference to the king's son which we hear of throughout the poem. In many ways the king's son is the son of the greatest king of all in Christian mythology, Jesus. Thus, the sons of Ireland who are willing to die for Kathleen in order to restore sovereignty are in fact to be the new Christ, the second coming, Ireland's messiah. The chorus that ends each quatrain tracks the coming of the Lord to save Kathleen.

In many ways by the third quatrain Kathleen is conflated with not only Mother Ireland but also Mary the Mother of Christ. Here she is both beautiful and terrifying. Like the statues of Mary that adorn Irish churches of old she is "sweet and mild" but fiercely crushes an open mouthed serpent underfoot. Curiously in this quatrain she is swathed in the traditional blanket, "plaid", of Ireland while "robes of silk" signal the kingly power of "her child". This is a promise to the young men prepared to be her martyrs that they will be held in her arms and transmogrify into the Redeemer of faithful Ireland. Until this takes place Kathleen remains in a state of dishonour and abuse. Quatrain four gives witness to the "Sore disgrace it is to see the Arbitress of thrones,/ Vassal to a Saxoneen of cold and sapless bones!". It is anathema to the Irish national psyche that the Virgin sovereign, displaced and in need of rescue, is subordinate to the English. Indeed, the contrast between Kathleen who would determine the kingship of her land and Kathleen as slave to the taciturn and dry Saxons inspires the national Irish male imagination to suffer "Bitter anguish ...heavy sighs and groans". In Luke's Gospel, chapter 5 verses 16 to 21, Jesus states that he is the anointed one who has been sent by God, prophesised in Isaiah chapter 61 verses 1 to 3, to deliver the believers from suffering into a crown of beauty from blindness into sight and from captivity into liberty. Isaiah foretells that the oaks of righteousness, who have been planted by the Lord, will seek vengeance for oppression. The English rule of Ireland is the story of the Hebrews under the rule of Ancient Egypt, just as it is the story of Jews under the rule of Roman Empire.

The last two quatrains are a call by the poet to us to "pray to Him" who is the all-seeing God, the one who has promised delivery. The majesty of God is described in the 5th quatrain: "Him who formed the mighty globe, with all its thousand lands;/ Girdling them with seas and mountains, rivers deep, and strands." What is outflowing from the young Redeemer is landfall. This is Ireland as much as it is the body of Kathleen in her fecund allure. The 6th quatrain is an allusion to the exodus of the Hebrews out of Egypt. It was this Redeemer who led his oppressed people across "sands and waves", fed them on "heavenly bread" and chose them as the tribes of Israel who will lead Ireland. Their God "stood by Moses when his foes were fierce and strong". This is a call to every young man of Ireland to rise up and save beloved Kathleen from the foe no matter how ferocious and mighty. This is a national anthem. Like all imaginings of a nation this one is steeped in the blood of its young men in their efforts to rejuvenate the beauteous crown, mythologised as both Mother and Virgin.

It is song made by men for men and has very little to do with the feminine. For me it is sad more than it is heroic and that it was revitalised as a subject matter throughout times of intense oppression in Ireland makes it even more poignant. This iconic female continues to cause hurt and be hurt.

Bomb Disposal by Ciaran Carson (1987)

Is it just like picking a lock
With the slow deliberation of a funeral
Hesitating through a darkened nave
Until you find an answer?

Listening to the malevolent tick
Of its heart,
The message of the threaded veins
Like print, its body chart?

The city is a map of the city
Its forbidden areas changing daily.
I find myself in a crowded taxi
Making deviations from the known route.

Ending in a cul-de-sac
Where everyone breaks out suddenly
In whispers, noting the boarded windows,
The drawn blinds.

Ciaran Carson: Belfast born, Irish speaking, Catholic first name, Protestant surname, musician, novelist, poet, taught by Heaney at Queens University, narrowly escaped death when a bullet missed him in a taxi going down Falls Road, a survivor. His poetry spirals inward: within Ireland is Northern Ireland, within Northern Ireland is Belfast, within Belfast, the Falls Road, within the Falls Road his childhood home remembered as Clann Mhic Carrain, a household with its own laws, customs and language. Carson offers up a steady four quatrain poem that unpacks the violent streetscape of the city of Belfast. The title refers to the defusing or removal and detonating of unexploded and delayed action bombs. Understandably this was a hazardous occupation for the

Ammunition Technicians of the Royal Logistic Corps, RAOC, who dealt with the bombs planted by the *Provisional IRA, PIRA*, and other groups. These bombs ranged from simple pipe bombs to sophisticated victim triggered devices and infra-red switches. Road side bombs were primarily used by PIRA during *The Troubles* as well as improvised mortars in parked cars with self-destruct mechanisms. *The Troubles* is the term given to the Irish suffering under the occupation of British Armed Forces, *Operation Banner*, from August 1969 to July 2007. The role of the British Army was to support the Unionist Government of Northern Ireland and specifically the Royal Ulster Constabulary in their assertion of authority of British rule in Northern Ireland. At the peak of *The Troubles* 21,000 British troops were deployed. *Falls Curfew*, 1970, *Operation Demetrius*, 1971, and *Bloody Sunday*, 1972, were some of the incidents that generated Catholic hostility toward British military deployment. This deployment offered threefold support: routine protecting of the local constabulary to carry out normal policing duties, additional deployment of assets for observation posts and border control, and specialists such as bomb disposals.

The first two quatrains are shaped into two questions; the final two quatrains offer a singular short answer of sorts followed by a personal example posed by the poet to prove his point. Carson asks the first question in the opening quatrain. The question is posed as a simile: "Is it just like picking a lock...Until you find an answer?" The subject of the question is likened to the "picking of a lock". This is a surreptitious activity and one that is undertaken often in stealth and by someone seeking trespass leading to the violation of property or person. On the other hand, finding "an answer" suggests that the assailant genuinely seeks clarity and is driven to undertake any level of danger in order to discover the truth. If whatever is being unpicked in order to arrive at an answer is a type of bomb disposal, as the metaphor of the title indicates, then what is being undertaken is to offer life instead of death. We must ask ourselves what is the real question coded behind the similes and metaphors. Is it: How is it living in Belfast? Or, why do you persist in staying? Or, What do you hope to achieve? Carson places in the center of this question the image of picking the lock or fuse of a bomb. He uses a metaphor of "the slow deliberation of a funeral/ Hesitating through a darkened nave". This scene where death is ritualised is imitative of the ways in which we must come to understand *The Troubles*.

The second question posed in the second quatrain asks whether you can read the message of the bomb at the same time as you seek to diffuse it. At the heart of the question is the act of "Listening to the malevolent tick/ of its heart". It is as if one has to really hear deeply and profoundly to what is wicked and violent in order to understand. It is the sound of blood pumping through the veins of a city imbued with battle that needs to be interpreted, analysed and responded. The arteries of this message spread under the corporeal body of the city of Belfast. The bloodline tracks across this landscape to form "its body chart". The poet is the surgeon holding up the scan to be able to decipher the disease, the cancer and the infested cells in order to ascertain if it is inoperable. So in this second quatrain two metaphors hold the question together: one concerned with the bomb as the ticking heart and the other as the blood or message it pumps through the body, of the city and the individual. The first two lines of quatrain three are curious. Here is an answer of sorts: "The city is a map of the city." The place of belonging is in fact a replica or version of itself; a copy of copy. The living breathing community is an image of what it considers itself to be or how it has been imagined. The quixotic reality of "its forbidden areas changing daily". There is something unfathomable and ridiculous in this simulacra of a city. It is an unfixed and therefore unnavigable world of disease, corruption and violence; thus, bomb disposal becomes impossible.

The final sentence of the poem begins midway through quatrain three and into quatrain four. It is another sort of answer and one where the poet travels through these veins of his city and steps out on to its blood path. It begins with the "crowded taxi" ride through deviations and derivations until he is spat out into a dead end. What has been "known" is abandoned and improvisation is the only way to deal with a cityscape apprehended by violence and anxiety. The destination has unexpectedly changed and he is inadvertently swept up in this journey: "I find myself." His discovery of self is therefore contingent on his discovery of this very landscape in which he plays out his life. A place riddled by the unanticipated and the somewhat bewildering. In this site of belonging, dislocation is central, represented in the calque of "cul-de-sac". A street with one inlet and outlet works to slow down and protect but also to entrap and ambush. Dead end streets were used intentionally in Antiquity for defence purposes. Aristotle pointed out the impact during war of the dead end street, included in the *Hippodamian* grid, suggesting that foreign troops would find it difficult to discover their way out when under attack.

It is disturbing to consider this place is inhabited by both the local and the foreign troops. From this "crowded taxi ... everyone breaks out suddenly/ in whispers". The fear is palpable and is equal measure knowing and unknowing. They are sitting targets. Tellingly, this nightmare moment has its eyes shut to whatever pending explosion is likely to occur: "the boarded windows,/ the drawn blinds." Powerfully we are also abandoned by the pen of the poet. We sit there with the crowd in the taxi and wait. Have we done sufficient good? Have our lives amounted to anything? Have we defused the violence running through our own veins?

The Strand at Lough Beg by Seamus Heaney (1979)
In Memory of Colum McCartney

All round this little island, on the strand
Far down below there, where the breakers strive
Grow the tall rushes from the oozy sand.
--Dante, Purgatorio, I, 100-3

Leaving the white glow of filling stations
And a few lonely streetlamps among fields
You climbed the hills toward Newtownhamilton
Past the Fews Forest, out beneath the stars--
Along the road, a high, bare pilgrim's track
Where Sweeney fled before the bloodied heads,
Goat-beards and dogs' eyes in a demon pack
Blazing out of the ground, snapping and squealing.
What blazed ahead of you? A faked road block?

The red lamp swung, the sudden brakes and stalling
Engine, voices, heads hooded and the cold-nosed gun?
Or in your driving mirror, tailing headlights
That pulled out suddenly and flagged you down
Where you weren't known and far from what you knew:
The lowland clays and waters of Lough Beg,
Church Island's spire, its soft tree line of yew.

There you used hear guns fired behind the house
Long before rising time, when duck shooters
Haunted the marigolds and bulrushes,
But still were scared to find spent cartridges,
Acrid, brassy, genital, ejected,
On your way across the strand to fetch the cows.
For you and yours and yours and mine fought shy,
Spoke an old language of conspirators
And could not crack the whip or seize the day:
Big-voiced scullions, herders, feelers round
Haycocks and hindquarters, talkers in byres,
Slow arbitrators of the burial ground.

Across that strand of yours the cattle graze
Up to their bellies in an early mist
And now they turn their unbewildered gaze
To where we work our way through squeaking sedge
Drowning in dew. Like a dull blade with its edge
Honed bright, Lough Beg half shines under the haze.
I turn because the sweeping of your feet
Has stopped behind me, to find you on your knees
With blood and roadside muck in your hair and eyes,
Then kneel in front of you in brimming grass
And gather up cold handfuls of the dew
To wash you, cousin. I dab you clean with moss
Fine as the drizzle out of a low cloud.
I lift you under the arms and lay you flat.
With rushes that shoot green again, I plait
Green scapulars to wear over your shroud.

In his writing Heaney creates a poetic nation state. This site of belonging includes the whole island of Ireland. This is the place where memory will not fail. Indeed, memory cleanses and heals, as Heaney recreates the death of his cousin Colum McCartney. The land contains these stories which in turn anoints the whole island of Ireland into nationhood. Heaney's poetry comes out of the muck and mire of the bog-side, the dark peat of violence and remembering, and the thick juicy fen of his beginnings. It is a landscape that is all devouring and thus is imagined as a terrible beauty. Colonialism's panopticism cripples people into a restricted debate between republicanism versus unionism, rather than examining a nation space beyond these bifurcations. Here we read a beautiful elegy in memory of Colum McCartney who was stopped on his way home from Dublin after attending a sports event in 1975. He and his mate were flagged down, abducted and shot. The *Protestant Action Force* claimed responsibility. McCartney was 22 years old. The epigraph from Dante at the start of the poem places us in the landscape of mourning. Perhaps this is an elegy to a nation, a dirge for a place of belonging that offers succor to no one. The title of the elegy locates us in the place where McCartney was known and grew up. It is a site of verdant farmland around the opaque blue-green lough. All three stanzas return McCartney, to whom the poem addresses, back to the strand at Lough Beg. Indeed, this stand, this shoreline, is a liminal space where we are waiting to move out of a purgatorial state. Written in a trinitrine structure, we move through the Father, Son and Holy Ghost of a nation, which has made a religion out of violence.

In the first stanza we are orientated into the ceaseless sectarian violence that is sacred to Northern Ireland, particularly in the 1970s. It is a seductive orientation, one that moves through the ordinary signatures of a road trip with its "filling stations", "lonely streetlamps", "fields" and "hills". Heaney names the burgeoning town of "Newtownhamilton" and the "Fews Forest" national park. In doing this he brings his and McCartney's world to us, as if we are familial. From here we move out into the mythologies of Irish King Sweeney who roamed his homeland starving, naked and eventually driven mad by those who pursued him: "bloodied heads/ Goat-beards and dogs' eyes in a demon pack." At this point we start to become wary of the trail we are on and wonder if this works as some sort of augury up ahead. Indeed, the Middle Ages folklore and the road block in *The Troubles* are linked by the blaze of danger. The alliterative demon dogs morph into the *UVF*, who often wore disguises, such as the uniforms of the *UDR*, and set up phoney checkpoints in order to capture victims. Heaney asks McCartney if it was in fact a "faked road block" or the "tailing headlights/ That pulled out suddenly and flagged you down" which ended in his demise. The unknowing is poignant, it speaks to the anonymity of "heads hooded and the cold-nosed gun". More centrally it zooms in on McCartney's abandonment to the elements of this night and nation. This is a place "Where you weren't known and far from what you knew". What is it to be of a nation but without citizenship? To be murdered because you are not of this locale but rather one that is some 55 minutes away. The last two lines offer a tender water color of the place that McCartney knew and was known: "lowland clays", "water", church "spire" and "soft tree line of yew", an Elysium.

Guns connect the first and the second stanza. From the *UVF* firearms we move to duck shooters behind McCartney's house on Lough Beg. In the landscape of McCartney's death, and that of his childhood, lurks the threat of violence and division. Here in this edenic landscape of Lough Beg, Heaney reminds his dead cousin that gunshot "Haunted ... the bulrushes", a nod to Dante. Ironically this victim of violence was too "scared to find spent cartridges,/ Acrid, brassy, genital, ejected". The accumulation of the shell's characteristics suggests something sinister and malevolent; as if there remained a latent threat or omen of what was to come. In stark contrast, McCartney walks a bucolic setting "across the strand to fetch the cows". This division in the landscape underwrites this elegy. McCartney and Heaney's people were Catholics, Nationalists and farmers in the north. In the second sentence of stanza two we are offered the insouciant characteristics of his people: "For you and yours and yours and mine fought shy,/ Spoke an old language of conspirators/ And could not crack the whip or seize the day". The sing song use of the second person pronoun and possessive, lulls us into an empathy with those unwilling to act politically. Their ancestors were kitchen workers and farm hands, "Big-voiced" but "Slow arbitrators". We see inadequacy and fumbling, not paramilitary precision and strategic ambush.

The final stanza raises up the spectre of McCartney. Here the stain of fratricide is washed clean by the natural landscape of Lough Beg. We follow Heaney and McCartney trampling through the other worldly beauty of this landscape. We are in the present tense. Gone is the landscape containing childhood memories traced with the sharp olfactory of gunshot; gone too is the nocturnal landscape of violent apprehension and murder. In its place we walk an Elysian field made sacred by the innocence and quietude of a victim. Heaney pulls the image together with alliterative coupling: "graze/gaze", "bellies/unbewildered", "where we work our way", "squeaking sedge" and "Drowning/dew". This is classic Heaney and confirms the undulating musicality of his poetry. Mesmerised by such an incantation of place we look upon this "stand of yours", and consider the simile he uses: "like a dull blade with its edge/ Honed bright." Here is a landscape that promises illumination on the ongoing violence. The elegy ends with the transformation of both Heaney's dead cousin and nation, sprawled in its own blood: "I turn because the sweeping of your feet/ Has stopped behind me, to find you on your knees/ With blood and roadside muck in your hair and eyes." On one hand, the ghost of the dead stops so the poet looks back, on another hand, the nation is fixed on its axis of violence hence the poet is forced to reposition.

The Strand at Lough Beg is about a young victim reduced to supplicating himself before the national travesty of violence, a long way from his home. This is not a hero's mythologised death, a martyrdom for the cause, but rather the filthy detail of an execution. Without a doubt, Heaney transforms this moment into something sacred. It is the natural landscape, not the political, that restores the dead to resurrected life. The natural landscape is fecund and "brimming", its dew works to cleanse and make pure that which is barbaric, offensive and recidivist. The intimate action of kneeling and then gathering dew "To wash you, cousin", is heart breaking. It is a pieta: "I lift you under the arms and lay you flat." Here is the ancient ritual of taking down the dead from its place of crucifixion and preparing it for burial. The promise of everlasting life in the liminal purgatory, captured here in both Heaney and Dante, leaves us with hope. Dante's rushes "shoot green again" thus the violated body of both the victim and the nation regrow. The color "green", signalling Ireland as well as verdant life, is repeated in the last line as these slender water-side plants become the funerary shroud. Catching his cousin in this elegy is really catching himself, his nation and his reader. For Heaney this is about intimacy, tactility and familiarity.

Cliona by Catherine Twomey (2008)

You are letting her go

from you slowly
so gently she hardly
knows.
She unties you like
an apron,
puts you on again.
Watching her grow
is catching yourself
after years, hearing
your own voice.

In sunlight
she returns to you
from her swim
to be dried.

Little fish.
You remember the bowl
of your womb, the ocean
that held her where
you felt her swim.

You are letting her out
now, loosening
like a kite's string
seeing her for the first
time in her own orbit
in the drive, cycling.

I am enamored by this petite ode of love. It is tender and sure footed. Most powerfully it suggests that in loving another, we catch a reflection of who we truly are. In many ways the terrible beauty born is the emerging knowledge that separation from one's child is central to the child's bildungsroman and formation of self. Twomey's ode is an address to the mother and it is intimately written in the second person. This ode could also be read as an address to Mother Ireland as she begins to disentangle herself from a nation hitherto formed by tribal strife allowing the whole island of Ireland to come of age. The title of this ode, *Cliona*, is the name of Ireland's principal goddess. There are many legends about her, commencing from the early Middle Ages. Most interestingly she is associated with the sea; its wrecks, perils, drownings and treasure trove. One legend indicates that she herself fell asleep by the sea which waiting for her lover, Ciabhán, and was washed out by a giant tidal wave. Ciabhán lets her go ultimately to be transformed into the goddess of love and beauty. This is a drama played out slowly, calmly and without calamity. It suggests that all is as it should be.

In the first stanza Twomey uses that direct address of "You" so that we are immediately aware we are mid action. The decision is ours to relinquish possession of "her" but it is suggested we do so "slowly" and "gently". What interests me is that the knowledge of this is all ours, not hers. She is not requesting freedom and release but it is something we already know to be her destiny. The second sentence offers a familiar domestic image as "She unties you like/ an apron". The simile suggests the relationship with Cliona is maternal in that the apron indicates care and nourishment associated with the familial relationships. The end of the second sentence is curious as Cliona takes you off and then "puts you on again". The emergence of Cliona as an independent and separate self is not immediate, it is inconsistent and transient. Perhaps indicating that the desire for complete self-actualisation is hampered by desire for comfort. The final sentence of this stanza is imbued with your action: "Watching...catching...hearing." Again, the present participles remind us that this is a continuous, ongoing and progressive feat; moreover, it takes time. It is in letting her go that she is able to grow. This doesn't erase you, rather "your own voice" is found in her. I think this does catch you unawares when it happens, indeed, it can take your breath away when you hear yourself made more beautiful, more whole and more exquisite in her.

The next two small stanzas play with the origins of the name, Cliona. She is the treasure trove that is washed back from the sea. She returns more beautiful than before: sunlit and wanting you. The sea is literal, mythological and embryonic. Her emergence is one of an ever growing independent self but it is also a rebirthing of the Irish goddess Clíodhna as well as a new Ireland. The zoomorphic metaphor of "Little fish" asserts Cliona's other worldliness. The poet reminds you of "the bowl/ of your womb, the ocean/ that held her where/ you felt her swim". Now you start to see that her potential to be herself began in you, in your own sea of desire. The image of the womb as a curvaceous, deep concave is a metaphor for the embryonic and mythological ocean in which she originally swam. I love the fancy of considering she has always been coming towards you; whether beloved, child, mythologised goddess of love and beauty or a newly emerging nation. I like to think about being a mere care taker for an infinitesimally small moment in Cliona's glorious new life. Yet it is in this new life that you catch yourself.

The last stanza is a thin long sentence like the "kite string" itself, which is let out in order for flight. In "loosening" our grip we are "seeing her for the first/ time". Here is the idea of distance offering perspective; therefore, you are assured of the benefits of standing back and letting go. Moreover, as a result of your action, she fulfils her own trajectory. She is now capable of turning circles on her bicycle in the drive, such fierce independence, who knows the extent of what she can accomplish! In some ways this is the story of the future when one is able to free another from the past. This is an ode to you about what you already know or at least suspect. It addresses the mythologies we made of the past; these mythologies hanker to morph into something more. Their release will be our release.

A Prayer for Old Age by W. B. Yeats (1934)

God guard me from those thoughts men think
In the mind alone;

He that sings a lasting song
Thinks in a marrow-bone;

From all that makes a wise old man
That can be praised of all;
O what am I that I should not seem
For the song's sake a fool?

I pray -- for fashion's word is out
And prayer comes round again --
That I may seem, though I die old,
A foolish, passionate man.

    Here we have a sonnet. Written in 1934 when Yeats was nearly 70 and only five years before he died. When Yeats entered the Irish writing scene, he found that poetry was either sentimental or patriotic. It was in a time when artistic, political and social lives were interconnected. Yeats sought illumination in translations of Irish mythologies, visionary poetry such as that of Blake and Shelley, fairy tales heard in his Sligo childhood, transcendentalism and philosophy. He created his own meta thinking as *Anima Mundi*, a type of collective soul from which all images emerge. Yeats favored images of extravagance, immeasurability and triumph in a world that seemed deformed, incomplete and perishable. In his maturity he sought divinity less in the objective correlative of landscape and more in himself. By 1934 the imaginative life had returned to Yeats in the form of younger female lovers. His appetite knew no bounds. In the same year he wrote this little sonnet he underwent the *Steinach Rejuvenation* operation, a vasectomy that was supposed to restore sexual potency. After this operation Yeats produced passionate poetical effusions, as well as a sexual swagger. Yeats was human. He was flawed and wonderfully talented; he was selfish and inspiring; he was a master of cadence and driven by passion. He created images in his poetry that not only reflected his age but illuminated, for many of us, the way in which we have come to know ourselves.

    When I read the opening quatrain of this sonnet, I am an absolute believer. Yeats often has this effect on me. This prayer bursts out of the blocks with a guttural plosive: "God guard me." Indeed, it is an imperative. His entreaty is unequivocal and unapologetic: he seeks protection from his cerebral contemplations but not from his visceral desires because it is his visceral desires which will ensure his eternal life. Immortality is in "He that sings a lasting song". In other words, passionate thoughts of the blood will mean this sonnet, and Yeats' oeuvre, will last forever. The phrase "Thinks in the marrow-bone" is poetry condensed to its essence. To ruminate and exist in the organic tissue of the bone, under the skin, in the cell of all life. This is what it is to be a poet.

    The next quatrain continues with the plea to God to guard him. He asks God to protect him from "all that makes a wise old man...be praised". Admired and extolled in septuagenarians, octogenarians and nonagenarian are qualities such as sagacity, judiciousness and prudence not to mention a penchant for metaphysical cogitation. While the repetition of "all" is a sober reminder that the visceral, mercurial and instinct are not on the menu for the old aged; Yeats' exclamatory "O" is filled with longing. Thus, he ends his prayer with a rhetorical question. Yeats is making the point that "For the song's sake", in order to write poetry that stands the test of time, there is no other choice but to have the identity of "a fool". In other words, he must surrender the appetites of the spiritual and embrace those of the body, even though at his age he won't be praised for doing so, if he is to write the poetry he must write. He will be the archetypal "fool", the truth teller, and with irreverence, impudence and sass articulate the way of the world. Yeats' request here is not so much about being irrational, silly and thoughtless but rather being left alone to play out the most fearless role: that of the poet.

The final quatrain begins curiously. Instead of the immediate request to God to safeguard him in the decisions he is compelled to make, Yeats moves to the more impersonal poetic flourish of "I pray". It is an announcement of sorts: "for fashion's word is out/ And prayer comes round again." What does he want us to see here? I believe he is making a comment about the vainglorious self whose decisions are driven by what is *a la mode*. The volta occurs in the final two lines of this sonnet. It is in the marrow of the word "seem". Yeats concludes his prayer that he "may seem...A foolish, passionate man" when he dies. What is it to seem? To give the impression, to appear, to indicate the signs of, but not necessarily be that in essence. Yeats uses verbs disruptively in many of his poems, it is a small trip wire that dislocates you long after you have left the poem. So, is his request to look as if he is the wise old man, who enjoys the visceral, but also knows wisdom? I keep looking at the phrase in the penultimate line, "I die". The phrase is not "when I have died" but rather it is written in the present tense. I can't help but wonder is this a tongue in cheek reference to *la petite morte*? Surely Yeats is playfully reminding us that even though he is old, he is utterly and viscerally connected to life and enjoying every moment of it! This is one heady prayer

Ireland by John Hewitt (1932)

We Irish pride ourselves as patriots
and tell the beadroll of the valiant ones
since Clontarf's sunset saw the Norsemen broken...
Aye and before that too we had our heroes;
but they were mighty fighters and victorious.
The later men got nothing save defeat,
hard transatlantic sidewalks or the scaffold...

We Irish, vainer than tense Lucifer,
are yet content with half-a-dozen turf,
and cry our adoration for a bog,
rejoicing in the rain that never ceases,
and happy to stride over the sterile acres,
or stony hills that scarcely feed a sheep.
But we are fools, I say, are ignorant fools
to waste the spirit's warmth in this cold air,

to spend our wit and love and poetry
on half-a-dozen peat and a black bog.

We are not native here or anywhere.
We were the keltic wave that broke over Europe,
and ran up this bleak beach among these stones;
but when the tide ebbed, were left stranded here
in crevices, and ledge-protected pools
that have grown salter with the drying up
of the great common flow that kept us sweet
with fresh cold draughts from deep down in the ocean.

So we are bitter and are dying out
in terrible harshness in this lonely place,
and what we think is love for usual rock,
or old affection for our customary ledge,
is but forgotten longing for the sea
that cries far out and calls us to partake
in this great tidal movements round the earth.

Hewitt is a 20th century Belfast poet detailing Yeats' poetics; which is that Ireland gives birth to a fanatic heart. Yeats writes "great hatred, little room, maimed us from the start". I see both the "great" and the "little" here in Hewitt's poem. I am drawn to the desolation and honesty of this keening. The keen is a poetic form in Ireland that goes as far back as the 7th century AD. Its poetic elements include: listing the deceased, praising the deceased, and recognising the genealogy of those left behind. It is a vocal lament and one that was often used as the voice of protest. Hewitt's four stanzas sum up a history of arrival, possession and ongoing protection. It is tribalism at its most basic. Stripped of sentimentality and patriotic fervour it is profoundly uncomfortable with contemporary tribalism.

Let's look at the first stanza. The collective pronoun and the highly charged assertion of the first line in the poem articulates a national consciousness: "We Irish pride ourselves as patriots." Patriotism is a tricky business. Western imagination has had a troubled relationship with this concept, while poetry in particular has exposed its multifaceted nature. The voice is imitative of a proud nationalist's recount of the battles fought and the heroism demonstrated in forging a nation. Indeed, patriotism is contingent on the telling and retelling of those who have given their lives in the pursuit of Irish independence: "tell the beadroll of the valiant ones." In the first instance Hewitt refers to the defeat of the Danes at the *Battle of Clontarf* in 1014; he then laconically indicates "Aye and before that too we had our heroes; /but they were mighty fighters and victorious". It is as if we are sitting in the snug of a pub in Dublin, rain outside and the hum of voices within, drinking glasses of warm Guinness and leaning in to hear a story, told and retold tirelessly. The description of the heroes, who existed in the past, is one of admiration. Yet before we complete the first stanza we are aware that heroism is something of yesteryear because since then Irish men have experienced nothing but "defeat/ heard transatlantic sidewalks or the scaffold". In other words, this is now a nation that has been overthrown, its people deported or handed down a death sentence for their sins.

The tone shifts dramatically in the second stanza. It is full of irony and vitriol. This is not a nation emerging out of the mythologies of St Patrick and sainthood but rather one that is "vainer than tense Lucifer". Hewitt imagines his people as the beloved angel who was cast out of heaven for his vanity. Thus, it is suggested that the pint we were having around the crackling fire in stanza one was a moment of mere vanity and self-congratulatory pride. Instead, what has been inherited is a nation that failed to follow through and protect what it had fought to gain. Here now is Ireland "content" with pathetic land holds, crying out "adoration" just because it secured a marshland, "rejoicing" in inclement weather and "happy" with a landscape that is infertile, impotent and unproductive. This list of responses is sobering. It makes a mockery out of the national past time of sentimental and patriotic storytelling. We hear Hewitt's voice in the middle of this stanza, with his anguished repetition: "But we are fools, I say, are ignorant fools." A wiser nation of people would not linger in Ireland's literal and metaphorical "cold" climate nor would it waste its mind, heart and art on the formation of nation. Hewitt's preoccupation with the bleak unrelenting landscape of stony outcrops and bogs continues on until his death in the late 1980s. Most telling is that when he wrote this poem, he was a 25 year old Belfast man, educated at Queens University, who turned his back upon the mythologies that would sustain Ireland in its pursuit of independence.

The third stanza is constituted by two sentences. The first is a short and direct assertion that the Irish are not "native" to their own country. The second sentence runs on for seven lines outlining their own invasion of Ireland. The opening sentence of stanza three sets up a counter point to the opening sentence of stanza one, indicating the long and complex relationship of nation building. Patriotism asserts the right of possession to one's landscape; whereas diasporic wanderings suggests a rootlessness. Hence, Hewitt uses the extended metaphor of an ocean to articulate this ebb and flow of human movement across time and place: "the Keltic wave", "this bleak beach", "tide ebbed", "ledge-protected pools", "salter", "common flow" and "cold draughts from deep down in the ocean". It is as if the Celts marauding across Europe, washed up unexpectedly on the Irish coastline and ironically were abandoned there by unpredictable tides. Thus, nationhood is formed variously through acts of calculated aggression and unpredicted acts of nature. Hewitt narrates "We...ran up this bleak beach...but...were left stranded". The ironic image works in contrast to stanza one where heroes, larger than life, strode upon the national imagination of what it was to be Irish.

We find ourselves washed up in the final sentence contained in the final stanza. It is the endpoint of the poem's argument. The collective pronoun "we" has been invoked eight times and the possessive "ourselves", "our" and "us" used half a dozen times, reinforcing rigorously that this is the true Ireland. In stanza four no longer are "we" imagined as mighty and victorious but rather "bitter" and "dying out". The Irish are, therefore, without a future. Rather than keening for the loss of what Ireland could have been, Hewitt argues that the lament is generated by the Celts' yearning for the sea to come and take them back to their legendary place of belonging of central Europe. This alien and isolated island on which the Celts have found themselves, is a place of "terrible harshness". This is not a landscape worthy of plundering let alone protecting. The invasion and taking of Ireland along with the constant defence of its borders, has been a mistake. Indeed, "what we think is love for usual rock, /or old affection for our customary ledge" has been nothing but a "yearning" to go home. What a dangerous keening to the Irish people about their beloved nation. What a courageous and insightful voice to replace the fervour that maimed Ireland from the start. Ireland is reduced to the "usual rock" and "customary ledge", a little room, a land already deeply inscribed by traditional and habitual iconography that in reality amounts to insignificance. Moreover, it is upon this precipice that the Irish cling. It is in the last two lines of the poem that Hewitt makes us hear the sea crying and lamenting as the people of Ireland to join the ongoing "great tidal movements" of the Irish diaspora "around the earth".

A Warning to Conquerors by Donagh Macdonald (1968)

This is the country of the Norman tower
The graceless keep, the bleak and slitted eye
Where fear drove comfort out; straw on the floor
Was price of conquering security.

They came and won, and then for centuries
Stood to their arms; the face grew bleak and lengthened
In the night vigil, while their foes at ease
Sang of the strangers and the towers they strengthened.

Ragweed and thistle hold the Norman field
And cows the hall where Gaelic never rang
Melodiously to harp or spinning-wheel.
Their songs are spent now with the voice that sang;

And lost their conquest. This soft land quietly
Engulfed them like the Saxon and the Dane
But kept the jutted brow, the slitted eye-
Only the faces and the names remain.

The son of one of the leaders of the Easter Uprising, publishes this poem in 1968. The title stands alone from the poem made up of four quatrains. While the poem tells a potted history of the most recent invader, the title suggests that this should be heard as a cautionary tale to any prospective aggressors. He writes this poem at the start of *The Troubles* where terrorist acts invaded the contemporary psyche of Ireland. The poem is overshadowed from beginning to end by the presence of the "Norman tower". This fortified keep, built within the castle stronghold or motte-and-bailey, was both a military protectorate and a political statement. It was the hallmark of Norman penetration and conquest. With their military superiority, program of castle building, lack of unified opposition from the Irish, support from Henry II and the Pope, the Norman Conquest succeeded in stages from 1066 onwards. Thus, began the ongoing assault and counteroffensive that has taken us to contemporary times. The keep itself was not introduced into Ireland until 1170 but became the face of the invader. It was constructed as a four-sided tower approximately four stories high, a little like our poem at hand.

The first quatrain juxtaposes Ireland and the invaders: "This is the country of the Norman tower." So, from the opening line we are situated in a landscape of otherness; a place that is alienated by its signposting of its own history. The tower is then personified as "graceless" with "bleak and slitted eye". This is an unwelcoming maladroit harbinger of nationhood. It is one that watches on and yet is in many ways the last refuge, should the outer stronghold fall to a new adversary. The first quatrain ends with this unease toward the new usurper; one riddled by dread and a sense of the temporary: "Where fear drove comfort out; straw on the floor/ Was price of conquering security." Thus, the place of belonging for the Normans was one that would never know relief. The second quatrain continues this idea of a hollow victory for the conquerors. Unlike the usual construction of the Normans as restless, reckless, self-confident and adaptable survivors, MacDonagh imagines the invaders forever vigilant against further counter offensives. Their faces are synonymous with the face of the keep: the "bleak …eye" of the first quatrain's keep is interchanged seamlessly with the Norman soldier's "face grew bleak" in the second quatrain. Thus, the keep is a synecdoche for the helmeted face of the Norman invader. Moreover, this readiness for battle remains the Norman's burden for "centuries" while the Irish are "at ease" within their occupied country. This is an unusual perspective to have of an occupying force. The tone is nearly insouciant suggesting that the Irish will outlive this most recent of all conquerors. The people of Ireland referred to the Normans as grey foreigners and for centuries sung "of the strangers and the towers they strengthened". MacDonagh himself joins the ranks of poets and songwriters who have committed, to Irish memory and imagination, the outsider as foe.

This meta-poetic reference is continued in quatrain three when we read that conquerors' fields and halls were bereft of such song and melody. In its place "Ragweed and thistle hold the Norman field/ And cows the hall". Theirs is a derelict site, and in the projected shortness of time, reduced to the ruins of today. The strong oral tradition of the Gaels, indeed the oldest vernacular literature in Western Europe, serves an aesthetic and functional purpose. Moreover, it is a record of a truth. The enjambment used at the end of the third quatrain into the fourth, mimics the ongoing purpose of the song despite the claim that "Their songs are spent…with the voice that sang". This same candid song intones the loss and failure of the Irish "conquest". The last sentence of the poem speaks of Ireland as a "soft land", a fecund burial ground that has entombed raiders throughout time: "Engulfed them like the Saxon and the Dane." The Saxon Vikings, from what is now Germany, began attacks on Ireland from 684 AD and the Danish Viking from 795 AD onwards. MacDonagh's warning to conquerors is clear: the country itself will overwhelm you, it will consume your flesh and soul. The conquerors' remains will be spat out on the landscape; hence, the skeletal remains of these Norman towers: "the jutted brow, the slitted eye." It is fit and keeping that the son of the poet and political activist, Thomas MacDonagh, should write a poem that threatens those who wish to become conquerors of Ireland.

Requiem for the Croppies by Seamus Heaney (1969)

> The pockets of our greatcoats full of barley -
> No kitchens on the run, no striking camp -
> We moved quick and sudden in our own country.
> The priest lay behind ditches with the tramp.
> A people hardly marching - on the hike -
> We found new tactics happening each day:
> We'd cut through reins and rider with the pike
> And stampede cattle into infantry,
> Then retreat through hedges where cavalry must be thrown.
> Until, on Vinegar Hill, the final conclave.
> Terraced thousands died, shaking scythes at cannon.
> The hillside blushed, soaked in our broken wave.
> They buried us without shroud or coffin
> And in August... the barley grew up out of our grave.

This powerful sonnet was written at a time when other poets were versifying the 1916 Easter Uprising. Heaney's sonnet commemorates the 1789 Irish Rebellion against English domination. The event signals non-sectarian Irish solidarity and nationalist tactics. Twenty thousand Irish awaited their fate on Vinegar Hill, County Wexford where they were encircled and slaughtered by superior English artillery. Heaney captures the tribe's sense of the common enemy which planted the seeds of hatred and violence, suffering and sacrifice, germinating in later generations such as the 1916 Easter Rising and *The Troubles*: "The pockets of our greatcoats full of barley...We moved quick and sudden in our own country./ The priest lay behind ditches with the tramp...We found new tactics happening each day:/ We'd cut through reins and rider with the pike/ And stampede cattle into infantry." Heaney offers this power punch of a sonnet to deliver history. Roused by the theft of their land and inspired by the non-sectarian leadership of the United Irishmen and the French Revolutionaries, they gave themselves the name "Croppies" because of their short hair styles in imitation of the French Revolution Republicans. Nevertheless, Irish farmhands and laborers seemed pathetic against the English uniformed militia. Heaney identifies with this bedraggled, ineffective and failed tribal group, as he repeatedly uses the collective pronoun: "We moved quick...We found new tactics...We'd cut through." This is further intensified by the repetition of the collective possessive pronoun: "our greatcoats...our own country...our broken wave."

The nation space of northern Ireland is made up of many cultural repertoires. In this sonnet Heaney conveys the sadness of being "on the run" in his own country as a national condition. The "croppies" symbolise the ongoing movement for freedom but also a continuous diaspora which remains seminal to being Irish. This double consciousness of longing for home while being in it, surfaces throughout Heaney's poetry. It signals his sense of displacement, of living in a partitioned and occupied country and his desire for sovereignty. Heaney suggests that the divisions so easily and popularly drawn, Catholic-Republican versus Protestant-Unionist, cannot be maintained in the face of a shared Irish history. In other words, Ireland has a longer tradition of identifying as one group against invasion, than it has of existing as a divided nation. This ethnic conflict provokes poets like Heaney to offer his sonnet as a protest for an imagined community recognised by all of Ireland: "Until, on Vinegar Hill, the final conclave. / Terraced thousands died, shaking scythes at cannon./ The hillside blushed, soaked in our broken wave."

The Catholic idea of resurrection is present in the hopes of republicanism: out of chaos and death will come order and new life. The oppressor, regarded here as England, believes they will pacify, intimidate and bribe the oppressed, Ireland. The English watch-dog cannot see the sacrifices of the *Fenian* dead, which only strengthens Irish resolve to fight until there is complete freedom, and ironically, until Ireland is a mass grave. Ireland has had a long history of politically motivated violence prior to partition and yet the battles of 1916, an event led and inspired by poets, was fought by Catholic and Protestant, Unionist and Republican, side by side. Heaney's northern Ireland is a place constructed by the discourse of various ethnic communities or, as Heaney might put it, tribes.

Advent by Patrick Kavanagh (2004)

We have tested and tasted too much, lover-
Through a chink too wide there comes in no wonder.
But here in the Advent-darkened room
Where the dry black bread and the sugarless tea
Of penance will charm back the luxury
Of a child's soul, we'll return to Doom
The knowledge we stole but could not use.

And the newness that was in every stale thing
When we looked at it as children: the spirit-shocking
Wonder in a black slanting Ulster hill
Or the prophetic astonishment in the tedious talking
Of an old fool will awake for us and bring
You and me to the yard gate to watch the whins
And the bog-holes, cart-tracks, old stables where Time begins.

O after Christmas we'll have no need to go searching
For the difference that sets an old phrase burning-
We'll hear it in the whispered argument of a churning
Or in the streets where the village boys are lurching.
And we'll hear it among decent men too
Who barrow dung in gardens under trees,
Wherever life pours ordinary plenty.
Won't we be rich, my love and I, and please
God we shall not ask for reason's payment,

The why of heart-breaking strangeness in dreeping hedges
Nor analyse God's breath in common statement.
We have thrown into the dust-bin the clay-minted wages
Of pleasure, knowledge and the conscious hour-
And Christ comes with a January flower.

Kavanagh makes you feel like you are in safe hands. There is something deeply uncompromising about his poetry. When I read Kavanagh, I feel connected to a world where we are at the essence of things; possessions, occupations, ambitions are all a little superfluous really. This wonderful lyric examines, in two seven line stanzas, Advent the time before Christmas; while the final 14 line stanza reveals the aftermath of Christmas. Perhaps stanza one and two combine to form a sonnet; just as the third stanza could be read as a stand-alone sonnet. The first two stanzas reference childhood and the preparatory time of Advent which includes looking ahead for Christ, repenting and doing penance. The final stanza is a celebration of the Christ child discovered in the new year's flower. There is a matter of fact-ness about a Kavanagh poem. I find *Advent* reassuring, despite its complex and subtle indicators that we are flawed and broken in our ability to respond to epiphany.

The first stanza is made up of two sentences. In the first the poet addresses his beloved and asserts "We have tested and tasted too much". They are hampered by the excess of this life; it cloys and hinders their ability to be open to the real "wonder". Ironically by devouring life "Through a chink too wide" they are unable to really taste what it is that they consume. This is contrasted by the long sentence that follows which imitates the lengthy drawn out time of penance practiced during the four weeks leading up to Christmas in preparation for the arrival of Christ. The imagery is monastic in the "Advent-darkened room" with "dry black bread and the sugarless tea". Indeed, the act of penance is to change one's life in harmony with the change of heart. The ascetic intake of coarse rye bread and tea without sugar is so ordinary, so undemonstrative of a penitent heart, that it reveals the authenticity of their efforts. This is done in order to "charm back the ... child's soul". Again, the simplicity of their faith is touching. It is conveyed without qualification and can only be received without judgement. All this in order for the edenic moment to be reversed momentarily: "we'll return to Doom/ The knowledge we stole but could not use." So here we are at the threshold of the real issue. The poet may be speaking to his beloved, his Muse, his Eve; indeed, they maybe one and the same, his own holy trinity. This knowledge is an allusion to the forbidden fruit taken from the tree of knowledge. Here is a desire to restore the original relationship that, was once severed, between man and God. While this is in keeping with the abstemious climate of Advent, for the poet to be prepared to hand back that knowledge, the inspiration of the taboo, leaves us slightly sceptical.

If stanza one and two combine to form a sonnet then there are a few structural factors we need to examine. Firstly, the sonnet invites meditation on a singular subject. The combination of stanza one and two invites our mediation on the austere and contrite steps that need to be taken in order to reorientate one's life in the first season of the Church year, Advent. Secondly, the sonnet contains a volta or turning point. The first stanza outlines the way in which repentance is to be practiced should equanimity between God and his children be restored. The second stanza demonstrates this turning point where the poet reimagines the childlike state of looking out over God's kingdom. Thirdly the sonnet considers a subject that is worthy of one of the most complex forms of poetry. In this case we consider the upcoming birth of Christ; therefore, stanza one and two may be regarded as two parts of one sonnet, the break in between asserting its volta. Consequently, in stanza two Kavanagh names what it is to experience restoration as God's children: "the newness... the spirit-shocking/ Wonder... the prophetic astonishment." It is a powerful and tempting new reality. Here Eden is named in the seemingly insignificant: "a black slanting Ulster hill...whins...bog-holes, cart-tracks, old stables." These signatures of home are seen anew. It is here that "Time begins." There is something deeply assuring and familiar about his phrase that may resonate with all of us. It is in the landscape of our childhood, in all its insignificant shrubs, pathways and nameless hills that we know the world is filled with life. A preternatural Eden.

Kavanagh is not the first to use this trinitrine structure to lead up to and away from the arrival of Christ without giving actual witness to the birth itself; glance back at Eliot's *Journey of the Magi*. Neither is he alone in recounting the way in which the Christmas miracle ultimately has little effect on those awaiting the messiah; consider Auden's *Christmas Oration*. What Kavanagh does, is offer a tenderness towards a flawed humanity. As if this is the broken, errant child that remains exclusively lovable in God's eyes. It is a different rendering of having the experience but missing the meaning. This stand-alone sonnet of stanza three is structured in four sentences. Like all sonnets its symmetry reflects the measure and precision of the subject considered. Here we contemplate the way in which "after Christmas we'll have no need to go searching". This sums up the human condition, as if the great clarity and cleansing achieved at Advent cannot be maintained. In the first sentence Kavanagh refers to the sacred and ancient phrase. It is knowing that Jesus is messiah that sets our hearts "burning"; and yet that very truth later becomes a blasphemy that permeates the everyday: "whispered argument of a churning/ Or in the streets where the village boys are lurching." The world is back to what it always was, with its daily tasks of churning butter and cursing school boys. This in not regarded insidiously but rather as the ongoing machinations of life: "we'll hear it among decent men too/ Who barrow dung." There is no vitriol or condemnation in the way Kavanagh represents how these ordinary folk invert the sacred; rather, here is the evidence that Jesus Christ is present daily in the "ordinary plenty".

The penultimate sentence is poignant. The poet begins in the subjunctive mood as he speaks of himself and his love: "Won't we be rich." In this way he expresses his attitude to the sublime experienced in the ordinary. Reason is not to be the way in which he and his love will apprehend the "heart-breaking strangeness in dreeping hedges/ Nor analyse God's breath in common statement". The coined word "dreeping", which may be a combination of deep and dripping or a nod to the Scottish *dree* meaning enduring, suggests the presence of Christ in their own familiar Eden. The last sentence is full of promise and hope, notwithstanding the dark wintery landscape of a flawed and broken humanity. Here Kavanagh asserts that we have "thrown into the dust-bin" earth's payment of "pleasure, knowledge" and the present moment. In other words, we have cast aside the physical apprehension of this world as being solely sufficient in order to make room for the experience of the metaphysical. The sonnet's volta occurs in the final line: "And Christ comes with a January flower."

The unexpected arrival of a flower in the heart of winter is imitative of the startling realisation that Christ has resurrected from the dead. *Advent* allows an excess of light into our own deeply flawed humanity. Rather than be left exposed and found wanting we are warmed and inspired by the arrival of Christ, ever present in our ordinary and familiar landscape.

A Woman without a Country by Eavan Boland (2013)

> As dawn breaks he enters
> A room with the odor of acid.
> He lays the copper plate on the table.
> And reaches for the shaft of the burin.
> Dublin wakes to horses and rain.
> Street hawkers call.
> All the news is famine and famine.
> The flat graver, the round graver,
> The angle tint tool wait for him.
> He bends to his work and begins.
> He starts with the head, cutting in
> To the line of the cheek, finding
> The slope of the skull, incising
> The shape of a face that becomes
> A foundry of shadows, rendering —
> With a deeper cut into copper —
> The whole woman as a skeleton,
> The rags of her skirt, her wrist
> In a bony line forever
>   severing
> Her body from its native air until
> She is ready for the page,
> For the street vendor, for
> A new inventory which now
> To loss and to *laissez-faire* adds
> The odor of acid and the little,
> Pitiless tragedy of being imagined.
> He puts his tools away,
> One by one; lays them out carefully
> On the deal table, his work done.

It is 1850 and my great great grandparents and their children take the road from Limerick to Cork. They hire a trap from the local smithy. Here at the Cork docks they say farewell to four of their five children. Three go to America and one to Australia. When my great great grandparents return home to Limerick with their youngest daughter, their neighbours have arranged a small wake. The grieving for the children who left never, ever ends. The Gorta Mor, the Great Famine 1845 to 1852, has been a cavernous yaw over Ireland for the past seven years. This was a time of mass starvation, disease and emigration. It made an indelible mark in the consciousness of a nation; impacting on not only the demography but on the political and cultural landscape of Ireland. It was a watershed as it entered folk memory and rallied nationalist sentiment. The relations between the English occupying force and the Irish, frayed. The potato blight was aggravated by English absentee landlords, English land acquisition of Ireland and the English Corn Laws now effective in Ireland.

Meanwhile, *The Illustrated London News*, *The Cork Examiner*, *Punch*, the *Pictorial Times* and *Harper's Weekly* all carried images of the Great Famine made by engravers. These disturbing visuals record a history that is hard to forget: the discovery of the potato blight, exterior and interior cottage depictions, outdoor scenes, begging, landlords and ejection, food riots and attacks, workhouses, relief, funerals, embarkation, the voyage, disembarkation, and life elsewhere. When I sift through these remarkable art pieces depicting the savagery of Irish reality, I pause at Bridget O'Donnel and children. My great grandmother's name was also, Bridget. In this etching the planes of her forehead and cheekbones are wide; her cheeks and eyes hollow with the engraver's scratching. She is Fames in Ovid's *Metamorphoses*; both desirable and terrifying.

It is 2013 and Eavan Boland writes *A Woman Without a Country*; a gaunt poem that watches a man watch a woman emerge. The engraver is nameless just as the engraved woman is nameless. He is intensely engaged in the creation and production of both art and historical record. She is the object of his gaze and as such remains an *émigré*, still awaiting citizenship in her nation state. I like the bony brittle feel of this poem. There is not wads of flesh or veins of visceral emotion. Rather a sharp dextrous rendering of Ireland as both ravenous and ravishing. The first four lines of the poem show with precision, the certainty of the engraver's movements: "he enters/ A room with the odor of acid./ He lays the copper plate on the table./ And reaches for the shaft of the burin." Note the short staccato sentences. Here is a man who knows what he's about. These are the rituals of daybreak where he is engaged in meaningful work. Here are the *dailiness*, as Boland says, of the ordinary common lives: the smell of acid that will bite down on the intaglio, the engraved design, already marked by the steel tool. The importance of the engraver's skills is manifest in the mass produced and distributed broadsheets that connect the literate and illiterate world. Indeed, the next three sharp short sentences take us out to the streets of Dublin and in ear shot of the paper boys calling out headlines in order to sell the very news the engraver is representing. The repetition in "All the news is famine and famine" suggests an unrelenting weariness with the Gorta Mor and its ongoing tragedy. Back to the scene in the engraver's workshop the next three lines, focus on the specific tools that await him: "flat graver...round graver...angle tint tool." All is in readiness. Indeed, there is something sacred and quiet in the way he "bends to his work".

At this point, we leave the short sharp sentences and the engraver preparing with precision and surety. We move beyond his work space; the city is waking up and getting ready for its day framed by ongoing suffering. What follows is a single sentence made up of 17 lines. Throughout this entire sentence the engraver is bowed over his art making. It is Pygmalionesque. By the time we reach the end of the sentence the object of his adoration has come to life. Our eye follows the burin as it shapes out "the head...the cheek...The slope of the skull". So far, the image is unsexed. It is not until the incision of the shape of the face with its "foundry of shadows", created by "a deeper cut into copper", that we see her emerge. Boland's foundry metaphor reminds us that we are looking at a construct, an image, a representation made at the hands of a skilled artisan. Then "The whole woman" emerges "as" a corpse. The Ireland that cannot feed its children. Her "bony line", chiselled by the engraver, separates her from the possibility of life. Indeed, in the spirit of art imitating life, Boland maroons the word "severing" on its own indented line, scoring its effect into our mind's eye. This victim of the Great Famine is cut off from that which oxygenates her and gives her life. Yet note the qualifier: "severing/ Her body from its native air until." Until? Until she is given life on "the page" via the "street vendor". Is Boland taking stock of the way a national calamity can be bought and sold? Without a doubt, this engraving and this poem, "adds" the acidic bite of what is "being imagined".

The last three lines of Boland's poem makes up the final sentence. It is one of downing tools. In keeping with the spirit of the poem that looks closely at the trappings of art making we watch the way in which the engraver "lays" out his tools, "One by one", with careful indifference. It is only with the meticulous accuracy can an image be truly rendered. When the engraver's work is done so is Boland's. Both have created art; both have given witness. We are awash in the inky truth of their art not to mention that of Fames. She has staggered across many a landscape be it that of Greek mythology, Roman imaginings, Ireland's Gorta Mor or contemporary feminist representations of woman without country. For the most part she is a troubled construct of desire and terror. Boland's title haunts the reading of this poem. If Ireland had been its own country, rather than an occupied one, the aggravation caused by English laws and practices may have led to a different outcome. One where the Bridgets of Ireland could have known succor instead of starvation and grief. But this woman had no country.

The Skylight by Seamus Heaney (1991)

You were the one for skylights. I opposed
Cutting into the seasoned tongue-and-groove
Of pitch pine. I liked it low and closed,
Its claustrophobic, nest-up-in-the-roof
Effect. I liked the snuff-dry feeling,
The perfect, trunk-lid fit of the old ceiling.
Under there, it was all hutch and hatch.
The blue slates kept the heat like midnight thatch.

But when the slates came off, extravagant
Sky entered and held surprise wide open.
For days I felt like an inhabitant
Of that house where the man sick of the palsy

Was lowered through the roof, had his sins forgiven,
Was healed, took up his bed and walked away.

    I love this poem. I love the way it speaks of you and me. The way it outlines clearly *my* resistance to cutting a hole into the snug space that keeps us all dry and safe, if a little lightless. I love the way Heaney concedes at the start that it was *you* who wanted more light. Like all great sonnets there is a turn, a volta, which is at the break in the sonnet and in pours extravagant space. Being a carpenter's daughter I love the attention to detail, the tongue-and-groove of pitch pine, and the way these words dovetail into each other to mimic perfection. Within this ordinary moment of an everyday life the poet gives witness to that miracle of light: enlightenment.

    Every day I want the light to stream in. My life's task is to build that skylight. If there is ever resistance to creating the skylight perhaps it's because the snuff-dry feeling is so delicious and safe; perhaps the nest-up-in-the-roof effect of the familiar is too fondly retained. Having said this I know that without the skylight there can be no wide open surprise. I love how this light will heal and forgive past transgressions; how even I will be made whole in this miracle of enlightenment and be able to walk away from all that confines me. This sonnet is a palimpsest text with the traces of so many other stories. I believe the world is made better, made more whole, because of what we are doing in carving out this skylight.

    Let extravagant sky enter.

    The last time I was in Ireland the sky was soggy, at times, alarmingly so. Of course, it was summer which made no difference because every so often the sky would send sharp slanting needles of rain, from which no Gortex jacket could shield me. The day we drove out to Bellaghy was a Sunday morning. Grey mattered clouds, icy rain and grey pebble dash houses leaning right in on the road. Initially, we went out to Lough Beg to watch its slow meander and we leaned over the rail on the fishing boat siding and talked about Heaney and his cousin and his poetry. Later, around mid-morning, we drove into the car park of St Mary's Catholic Church. There was no one about and so we had the whole grave yard to ourselves. It was easy to find, Heaney's gravestone. It was large and clean with the epitaph: *Walk on air, against your better judgement.* I guess that's exactly what he is doing. I asked one of my students recently what she thought it meant after she saw it on my business card; immediately she answered: *be bold!* How perfect. A leap of faith … a jump off the cliff … into the breach even in the face of annihilation. Yes, this poet has taught me that very truth. Finally, I persuaded himself, who is a God-fearing agnostic, to come into the huge blue stone church and look around. This all went well but very quickly and nearly without us noticing it began to fill up with Church goers. We decided to leave before the Mass began and exited to the car park. Our car was wedged in the center of a sea of cars parked seemingly without rhyme or reason. In other words, there was no getting out of Mass. We returned and shuffled back into what seats remained. On a final note, I have never sat through a sermon where the priest not only began by quoting a poet but continued throughout his address reflecting on the wisdom and challenge generated by some of the greatest poets of his nation; including Patrick Kavanagh and Seamus Heaney. I was in heaven and walked on air!

Vale Heaney.

9

A Life Worth Living: The Russian Silver Age

Anna Akhmatova

I wrung my hands under my dark veil by Anna Akhmatova (1911)

Translated by Stanley Kunitz

I wrung my hands under my dark veil...
"Why are you pale, what makes you reckless?"
-- Because I have made my loved one drunk
with an astringent sadness.

I'll never forget. He went out, reeling;
his mouth was twisted, desolate...
I ran downstairs, not touching the banisters,
and followed him as far as the gate.

And shouted, choking: "I meant it all
in fun. Don't leave me, or I'll die of pain."
He smiled at me -- oh so calmly, terribly --
and said: "Why don't you get out of the rain?"

When I first moved out of home, I lived in a small one bedroom apartment close to the city. It was on the top floor, no lift. On the right there was the bedroom with bathroom and on the left the kitchen. It must have been built in the 1920s. On the kitchen wall, I had written out something from the life of a poet called Anna Akhmatova. Where had I found this scrap of information? I don't know. Why was it on the wall? I don't know. What was so compelling that I would recall it decades and decades later? Have a look: *"During the frightening years of the Yezhov terror, I spent 17 months waiting in prison queues in Leningrad. One day, somehow, someone picked me out. It was the woman standing behind me, her lips blue with cold. Jolted out of the torpor characteristic of all of us, she said into my ear (everyone whispered there): "Could one ever describe this?" And I answered: "I can.""* At the time I didn't know anything about Akhmatova, nothing about her poetry or her place in Russian history and so I wonder, how did that scrap of her life come to be in that tiny rundown apartment when I was only 20?

The Yezhov terror meant little to me but I knew this must have been during the Stalin era and so I worked out that she was waiting to see someone, someone she loved, how else could she have survived Russian winters outside this prison. Some 30 years on I have visited Russia a number of times and always in winter. I have gone often to Akhmatova's apartment. Like a pilgrim, quiet and unsteady. I think now about her granite city of Leningrad and the bone breaking cold that comes up through your feet and shins and thighs and into your hips and pelvis, then up your spine and into the base of your neck. I know how your lips go blue with cold. I think about the way in which your body goes quiet and slow and begins to shut down when you are forced to wait, even momentarily, outside. I think about the intimidation of this city on steroids. This is the mighty city built by Peter the Great on a swamp. It was his vision to create a window to Europe. Europe one way, Asia the other, the East below, God above and Russia at the very center. This city where Akhmatova walked and wrote and loved and grieved and petitioned the release of her son, survived the Siege of Leningrad in World War 2. This was not a country of surrender this is a country that would kill its own sons and daughters rather than relinquish Mother Russia. This is a place where one's voice needs to be careful; hence the whisper. So, I think about the need to bear witness. Even back then in my rented apartment I remember the controlled anguish of those words from the woman standing behind Akhmatova. The desperate need to have some sort of record of what it was they were living; the need to know that somewhere somehow this would matter to others. To bear witness. To come out of the torpor. Otherwise who other than God would see and care? Akhmatova's words "I can" never ever left me. There is something profoundly courageous in that short phrase. It remained with me for decades: this imperative to bear witness, this courage to do what you can, this message that a life cannot go unrecorded.

Anna Akhmatova, the great poet from Russia's Silver Age, a Renaissance for the Arts from 1880 to 1920, spent time between 1938 and 1956 in the prison queues visiting her son Lev Gumilyov. Lev was imprisoned off and on between these years because the secret police had arrested and executed his father in 1921. The Yezhovschina or Yezhov phenomenon was referred to later as the Great Purge or the Great Terror. Eight million people in Russia were arrested, this constituted about 6% of the population at the time. Of those arrested it is estimated that 1.2 million were killed. Yezhov was the head of the Secret Police, NKVD, and carried out these arrests and executions for Stalin between 1936 and 1938. Two thousand of these arrests were artists, writers and the intelligentsia; of which 1,500 died. At one point the papers for Akhmatova's arrest were in place, unbeknownst to her. At this time, she was once again petitioning for the release of her son Lev and wrote a dithyramb to Stalin to secure Lev's release. This made no difference to her son's release but did however mean her own arrest and imprisonment was not acted upon. Lev's father, Nikolay Gumilyov, was a poet and arrested and executed by the secret police in 1921. So, this is a little of the backdrop. Meanwhile, I have loved Akhmatova's sparse style; she is made of bone and fearlessness which seems to make the drama of her poetry even more startling.

I wrung my hands under my dark veil is a haunting unequivocal poem. A cold foreign familiar setting that moves from the downward turbulence of an interior space to a darkling exterior landscape. A woman tells her story of a lover who left. We are the audience on the edge of our seat; calling out the questions that are all wrong because even in their answers we still don't understand what it is we comprehend instinctively. A narrative that delivers passion, Eros and Thanatos, not quietly but in all its trauma. A story that goes on and on and is every story that has ever happened of love gone wrong, promises misfired, actions misjudged. A tale shot through with the primordial need to not be forsaken. It is cinema at its best. It is Russian poetry at its summit.

I wrung my hands under my dark veil is an early Akhmatova poem. I find it deeply moving. We begin with anguish in the twisting of her hands and the wearing of a "dark veil". Is she in mourning? Is she in hiding? The emotions are not concealed but rather revealed in the concise step by step of her ravaging torment. This is such a cinematic moment. She is all consuming. Her veiled body and face is undisclosed to us and yet her distress is so apparent. This gesture of wringing one's hands is surely about having absolutely no idea what to do with oneself. You will go mad with the uncontrollable emotion surging through you. She is not alone because a voice asks her: "Why are you pale, what makes you reckless?" I'm not so sure it is the lover asking. I think we are asking. I think we are so transfixed by her anguish that we call out our question. I see now her white face from behind her dark veil. She is a spectre of suffering. Yet she is not victim. The second question contained in that second line suggests she is assailant. She takes full and complete responsibility in her answer in the final two lines of the quatrain: "I have made my loved one drunk/ with an astringent sadness." The beloved intoxicates the lover usually with inspiration and ecstasy and insatiable hunger; not typically with a caustic wretchedness. Unless of course it is not equally requited. What haunts me is, if this is a result of her deliberate actions then why the hand wringing at the start of the poem? It is high drama at its best with the tension imploding her into a state of dark transformation.

The next two quatrains are the cinematic flashbacks. We lead in with "I'll never forget"; and indeed, when this poem is read, one never seems to forget the drama that unfolds. The lovers must have been indoors prior to the flashback commencing because we begin with the lover rushing away and out to a more public, more harrowing, exterior landscape. Away from the domestic space of private intimate passion, boundaries shift and the lovers' fragility intersect. What is said indoors cannot be reigned back in a public landscape where the options to escape are endless. The lover charges out and at that moment the drama is spinning out of control and there is no winding it back: "He went out, reeling...mouth twisted, desolate." This is not the action or description of anyone other than victim. This lover comes hurtling out of the site of love with rejection or disbelief or incomprehensible pain written across his body. The mouth, a place of kissing, of tender words and impossible promises, is not usually apprehended as distorted and disconsolate. We are at the apex of this drama as she flies down the stairs after him. There is an extreme urgency in "I ran downstairs, not touching the bannisters". This is a beloved who must get to the lover before he reaches the outside, but too late as she stops at "the gate". Is the world too public, too uncertain as a landscape, for the two of them to survive? The public world is not for private dramas. It is not for the amplification of the heart.

Yet here the beloved shouts and chokes. Here at the gate, at the threshold between the world of the familiar and the world of the outside, she takes her last chance. Her desperation is palpable. And yet what comes out is queer and poignant and too sad: "I meant it all/ in fun. Don't leave me, or I'll die of pain." The danger house of fun; the trip wires of the ludic. What had been said or done in fun? Why wasn't it received this way or is the beloved rewriting history? I am struck by the intensity of so much pain in the lover, in response to this misinterpreted fun. Where does fun really take place between lovers? There are rules and regulations; a little match fixing and a lot of care taking. There are unbreakable principles, sniffed out early by the lovers. Why is there a gap between her meaning and his reaction? I think the plaintive cry to her lover not to abandon her is the cry of the newborn cast into the world. It is every man and woman's cry. To not be abandoned, to not be left alone, to not be forsaken. This is her cry. She knows with absolute certainty that she will die of the pain. There is no other outcome for her. This is her last desperate plea. His response is a complete reversal of how we first saw him at the start of this cinematic poem because now he is smiling and he is calm. This is a shock for us; to see the public face, the visage for the world beyond their intimate lives.

I see exactly where this is taking place. They are three flights up and their apartment is dark and its only door open in wide mouth surprise at the impossibly quick change of events. The banisters are dark wood and the floorboards down the stairs and on the landing are worn and tired. When she tears outside through the singular heavy door of the apartment block it is the cusp of nightfall and it has been softly raining all this time but neither of them had realised. The rain begins to get heavier as she reaches the gate a few meters away; the gate that takes them out to the public thoroughfare leading into town. How could all of this have happened in such a maddeningly short time? It seems one moment they were in the apartment with its wireless playing in the background as they prepared the evening meal and the next moment, they are here in the cold wet oncoming darkness. How could this be possible? I don't know about these enigmatic words he speaks to finish off the poem: "Why don't you get out of the rain?" I don't think for a minute this comes from a lover who wants reconciliation and is demonstrating care for the beloved's well-being. As if the two of them are about to turn back together and climb back up those steps and talk it all out carefully and wrap their bodies into each other and recognise that everything is salvageable because of their love. I don't think so. How could it be thus when the first quatrain tells us about a future devoid of the lover and the beloved in the garb of mourning and in physical distress. These strangely cool words the lover says are something else. It is as if he is immune to the distraught horror of his beloved; he is immune to the pathetic fallacy that veils this moment. He has had enough. He is done. He is about to turn and leave and needs her to return to the domestic private space, the one riddled with the memory of him and their love and their rupture. Go back to the eschatological site of their story, return to past tense. His way is forward not backward. There is no reply to his question because there is none to give, there is nothing more to say. What's done is done.

Lot's Wife by Anna Akhmatova (1922)

Translated by Stanley Kunitz

And the just man trailed God's shining agent,
over a black mountain, in his giant track,
while a restless voice kept harrying his woman:
'It's not too late, you can still look back

at the red towers of your native Sodom,
the square where once you sang, the spinning-shed,
at the empty windows set in the tall house
where sons and daughters blessed your marriage-bed.'
A single glance: a sudden dart of pain
stitching her eyes before she made a sound...
Her body flaked into transparent salt,
and her swift legs rooted to the ground.

Who will grieve for this woman? Does she not seem
too insignificant for our concern?
Yet in my heart I never will deny her,
who suffered death because she chose to turn.

In Genesis, Chapter 19 of the Old Testament, we read of the story of Lot and his wife. A subject that has captured the imagination of artists and poets and theologians over the centuries. The story in Genesis tells us about Lot begging the angels who were going to pass by his door to come in and spend the night in his home. He offers them food and washes their feet in keeping with the obligations of hospitality. Before long the mob turns up, bangs on Lot's door and demands he relinquish his guests to them. Lot refuses and offers his two virgin daughters to the mob instead. The mob refuses the offer and attempts to take Lot's home by storm and get hold of the guests. The angels rise up and smite the mob with blindness so that they eventually give up and leave. As per the instruction of the angels Lot then goes to his son in laws' homes and conveys the angels' warning that they need to go with Lot to escape the imminent destruction of Sodom by the Lord. The sons in laws think Lot is joking and do not heed the warning. When morning comes Lot himself lingers and he has to be pushed out of Sodom. Lot tarries again on the exit route and begs that instead of crossing the great plain and getting to the mountain as per the angelic instruction he be allowed to make cover in the nearest village, Zoar. The angels concede. Just as he gets there dawn is breaking and God lets rain, fire and brimstone pour down on Sodom and Gomorrah; needless to say everything is destroyed. Lot's wife looks back and is turned to a pillar of salt. Lot and his two daughters move up into the mountains behind Zoar where they are later impregnated by their father.

It's August 1930. Akhmatova's poetry is banned in Russia. She has survived World War 1, the overthrow of the Tsarist rule, the Russian Civil War, the rise of Stalin and the Great Terror. Cramped in living quarters in St Petersburg she lives with Punin, her third husband, his first wife, her daughter and parents and later when Akhmatova ends her relationship with Punin his third wife moves in to that same confined space. In this place of belonging she writes *Lot's Wife*. Is this poem about the Genesis story in the bible or about the nameless women who live lives of frugal despair or about a landscape that is beyond redemption? Yet against the backdrop of this biblical tale Akhmatova casts her lot. Before us is a tale blighted by every character. Here is a man, Lot, who is prepared to let the mob take and rape this daughters so that the angelic guests are left in peace; here is a man who is resistant to leave Sodom and needs endless prompting to get a move on; here is a man who was not in despair for the other daughters, their husbands and children who were left behind in Sodom; here is a man who shows no response to the metamorphosis of his wife into a pillar of tears; and here is a man who later impregnates his remaining daughters. It's not good. At this point I am starting to suspect that the real story behind this poem is the unrelenting canvas of Akhmatova's temporality and the way in which it offers no succor.

Let's follow the movement of this poem. In the opening line of the opening stanza we have Lot straggling behind the angel. Not striding or running but ambling in a way that indicates hesitancy or reluctance, or uncertainty. Despite this he and the angel are definitely the double act here. Heroes both: "the just man trailed God's shining agent." So, Lot is even handed, dependable, rational and fair while the angel, of course, is magnificent. This unlikely pairing leads us out of danger and into the Promised Land, well at least into the backstory of the tribes that will inhabit the Promised Land. It's strange because from the onset I am unsettled. While we have shining justice up ahead it seems unforgivable that little care is taken for those further on down the ranks. The movement continues in the "restless voice...harrying" Lot's wife. Of course, she would be agitated and harassed, she is leaving behind her other daughters, she is not in command of this expedition, and she is voiceless and nameless. What is ahead? What is about to happen to the two daughters she has managed to be with, considering her husband was about to give them up to the mob at the door the night before? The future looks bleak. She seems plagued with doubt about the so called promise of redemption. I wonder about this restless voice; is it a voice of another "shining agent"? Or is it one of her daughters or a loyal household servant or a devil wandering the Black Mountain Plains or is it her own voice, at last, come to speak for the first and last time because what does she have to lose?

The voice begins at the end of the first stanza and in a run on line it moves us into the second stanza. Thus, we move from the two lead male actors out front on the prairie crossing, well actually the more mortal of the two is dragging his heels, with women folk coming up behind. One of the insignificant nameless females, the one who will not found the tribes of Israel with Lot, hears a voice over. This voice seems to be accompanied by a slow flickering reel of the family home movie: "red towers ...the square...spinning-shed...empty windows...tall house...marriage bed." Every time I read this poem, and in particular this section, I am spiralled back to the red towers of the Kremlin, Stalin's city, Red Square. Why look back on this place of impenitent sin. Why not look forward and flee? In many ways this speaks to the pathology of love for the mother land and nothing could be more real and prescient of this than the love for Mother Russia. This is a land that has suckled its people at a breast that is both possessive and indifferent. Look at the reel again: we are taken from towers in the distance to a midrange look at the square, then a closer shot of the shed, then the camera swings up to the house window and zooms in on the marital bed. It's a brief record of one's life.

A gesture to a time of former happiness: "where once you sang...where sons and daughters blessed." Momentarily we are not in the hurried black plains beyond her hometown, rushing blindly toward an unknown destiny. We are still and quiet. This doesn't look like a place of vice and illicit sex; this looks like home.

Is the home movie a distraction, is it an illusion or is it the only truth? We move on into the drama we already know will happen. The inevitability of fate; a Russian sensibility. I also think about the women and men who did not leave their homeland during the various battles raging throughout Russia at this point. Many would perish badly. Thus, the landscape of home and redemption is in the eye of the beholder. The twist in the second part of stanza two reminds us that at one level this narrative is about the test of obedience by the all-powerful over its minions. Perhaps Lot's wife was welded into a pillar to remind the world of the phalanx of power or perhaps her tears of grief replaced her living self. Akhmatova takes us slowly through the metamorphosis of Lot's wife's in a way that no earlier record bothered to do because Lot's wife did not really matter other than being a symbol of there-for-the-grace-of-God go I. She takes a "single glance", that's all it is, hardly worthy of comment or criticism but autocratic regimes cannot afford the slightest infraction; certainly not from a possible enemy of the state. For her sedition she is immediately and swiftly punished: "sudden dart of pain/ stitched her eyes before she made her sound..." The sightlessness and soundlessness of the torture is disturbingly familiar for those who survived Stalin Russia. We can see through her, as if the pillar of salt is a type of dithyramb to an untamed, savage despotic dictatorial God: "her body flaked into transparent salt." This is the only form in which the enemy of the state can be immobilised: "legs rooted to the ground."

The final stanza contains the direct voice of the poet to us. It begs us to consider two questions: "Who will grieve" and "Does she not seem too insignificant...?" In some ways these questions are the same because it comes from a place that knows she is not worthy of lament or an outpouring of weeping, because Lot's wife is faceless, nameless and voiceless. She belongs to a desert story that has no relevance to our world. Then, women were possessions and without rights. Hers is a role to play; that of wife, mother and follower. If she deviates from this path then she will be punished. As she was. This makes me think about standing in the Leningrad Siege Museum one Christmas day, the cold so tough that the River Neva just meters away was one roiling angry mass of frozen grey. Inside we walked through the museum that seemed more of a bunker with various warrens. I think about the photos of people frozen to death on the streets of St Petersburg, what was then Leningrad, September 1941 to January 1944. I think about the lists and lists of the dead recorded in some official book. I think about the faces and faces and faces of those who perished. Nine hundred days they waited to die; 900 days. Hitler wanted them dead in 30 days. Cut off from the world. Cut off from the rest of Mother Russia. No running water, no heat, no food, nothing. A menagerie of before and after photographs. There was one photo: an 80 year old woman kisses her 83 year old husband good bye as he takes up a position of defence on the barricades beyond the city limits. He carries a spade. I had to look away. Unbearable. Is it better to remain just a little detached all your life so that in the end it is bearable? I move on and see another photograph of two women pulling a small sled down Nevsky Prospect. When I look closer, I see a small child's body swathed in a sheet; dead. Too much. Too much. So, is Lot's Wife just one of the millions who are meant to die, unrecorded, uncared for, and unmourned? Akhmatova's ferocious reply is unassailable: "I never will deny her". And indeed, she proves her politics by this very elegiac poem. Akhmatova gives witness to those voiceless, nameless and faceless victims, who with great courage, "chose to turn".

Requiem by Anna Akhmatova (1935 to 1961)

Translated by Stanley Kunitz

I
You were taken away at dawn. I followed you
As one does when a corpse is being removed.
Children were crying in the darkened house.
A candle flared, illuminating the Mother of God. . .
The cold of an icon was on your lips, a death-cold sweat
On your brow - I will never forget this; I will gather
To wail with the wives of the murdered streltsy
Inconsolably, beneath the Kremlin towers.

II
Silent flows the river Don
A yellow moon looks quietly on
Swanking about, with cap askew
It sees through the window a shadow of you
Gravely ill, all alone
The moon sees a woman lying at home
Her son is in jail, her husband is dead
Say a prayer for her instead.

III
It isn't me, someone else is suffering. I couldn't.
Not like this. Everything that has happened,
Cover it with a black cloth,
Then let the torches be removed. . .
Night.

IV
Giggling, poking fun, everyone's darling,
The carefree sinner of Tsarskoye Selo
If only you could have foreseen

What life would do with you -
That you would stand, parcel in hand,
Beneath the Crosses, three hundredth in line,
Burning the new year's ice
With your hot tears.
Back and forth the prison poplar sways
With not a sound - how many innocent
Blameless lives are being taken away...

V
For seventeen months I have been screaming,
Calling you home.
I've thrown myself at the feet of butchers
For you, my son and my horror.
Everything has become muddled forever -
I can no longer distinguish
Who is an animal, who a person, and how long
The wait can be for an execution.
There are now only dusty flowers,
The chinking of the thurible,
Tracks from somewhere into nowhere
And, staring me in the face
And threatening me with swift annihilation,
An enormous star.

VI
Weeks fly lightly by. Even so,
I cannot understand what has arisen,
How, my son, into your prison
White nights stare so brilliantly.
Now once more they burn,
Eyes that focus like a hawk,
And, upon your cross, the talk
Is again of death.

VII
The word landed with a stony thud
Onto my still-beating breast.

Nevermind, I was prepared,
I will manage with the rest.

I have a lot of work to do today;
I need to slaughter memory,
Turn my living soul to stone
Then teach myself to live again...

But how. The hot summer rustles
Like a carnival outside my window;
I have long had this premonition
Of a bright day and a deserted house.

VIII
You will come anyway - so why not now?
I wait for you; things have become too hard.
I have turned out the lights and opened the door
For you, so simple and so wonderful.
Assume whatever shape you wish. Burst in
Like a shell of noxious gas. Creep up on me
Like a practised bandit with a heavy weapon.
Poison me, if you want, with a typhoid exhalation,
Or, with a simple tale prepared by you
(And known by all to the point of nausea), take me
Before the commander of the blue caps and let me glimpse
The house administrator's terrified white face.
I don't care anymore. The river Yenisey
Swirls on. The Pole star blazes.
The blue sparks of those much-loved eyes
Close over and cover the final horror.

IX
Madness with its wings
Has covered half my soul
It feeds me fiery wine
And lures me into the abyss.

That's when I understood

While listening to my alien delirium
That I must hand the victory
To it.

However much I nag
However much I beg
It will not let me take
One single thing away:

Not my son's frightening eyes -
A suffering set in stone,
Or prison visiting hours
Or days that end in storms

Nor the sweet coolness of a hand
The anxious shade of lime trees
Nor the light distant sound
Of final comforting words.

X
Weep not for me, mother.
I am alive in my grave.

1.
A choir of angels glorified the greatest hour,
The heavens melted into flames.
To his father he said, 'Why hast thou forsaken me!'
But to his mother, 'Weep not for me. . .'

2.
Magdalena smote herself and wept,
The favorite disciple turned to stone,
But there, where the mother stood silent,
Not one person dared to look.

A requiem is a mass for the dead, a ritual to remember. The word requiem comes from the Latin, meaning to rest. I think about this. The dead are already at rest, I suspect the requiem is for the restless grief of those left behind. The requiem is to give respite to those in mourning; it's a ritual in which we can lay down our grief and burden and take rest. I want to just look at ten moments of this mighty poem; ten Stations of the Cross. I've stripped back the prologue and the epilogue.

Consider what is left is a small door opening to unspeakable suffering. Akhmatova wrote *Requiem* between 1935 and 1961. It was published in Munich in 1963 but not in Russia until 1987. There are ten numbered poems within this sequence; the first poem is dedicated to her third husband, Nikolay Punin, who was arrested and eventually died in prison, while the other nine poems are her song of despair for her son, Lev Gumilyov, who was arrested in 1933 at the age of 21, then in 1935, 1938 until 1943, and again in 1949 until 1959.

Ironically, *Poem 1* begins at the end: "You were taken away at dawn." In the spirit of Russian fatalism, we begin with the separation of the beloved from the lover, not at dusk or nightfall, but rather in the moment of daybreak when everything is visible and exposed. Thus, at the beginning we have the end. The scene is likened to a scene of execution, with the beloved following: "a corpse is being removed/ Children crying." The religious iconography is a consolation: "candle flared, illuminating Mother of God.../an icon." Mother God and Mother Russia are conflated, not only here in this poem but in the imagination of the Russian people. Therefore, the consolation of the iconography is a consolation given by a nation. Akhmatova's relationship with this moment is personal and intimate because this is the taking away of her husband: "The cold...was on your lips, a death-cold/ sweat/ On your brow." Two decades later Punin dies in the gulag during Stalin's final years. Akhmatova's desolate lament for Punin becomes a dirge for Russia: "I will gather/ To wail with the wives of the murdered streltsy/ Inconsolably, beneath the Kremlin towers." In joining the wives of the streltsy, the executed rebels against Peter the Great in 1698, Akhmatova ensures the lament against autocratic despotic rule cannot go unwitnessed. *Poem 1* is written in 1935 when Punin and his step son Lev were arrested for supporting Mandelstam's anti Stalin verse.

The Don River moves us into *Poem II, III* and *IV* composed in 1938 when Akhmatova mourns for Lev who was arrested in this year for plotting to kill the Leningrad Communist Party leader Andrey Zhdanov. Initially sentenced to be shot he was then sent to the Baltic Canal labor camp on the White Sea, a long way from the Don River. This river connects the Black Sea to the Caspian when it meets the Volga. The Volga River, the longest river in Europe and known as the national river of Russia, forms a backbone from north to south and connects to lakes and other rivers that eventually reach out to the White Sea and then across to the Baltic. In Poem II we have the all-seeing moon watching with a certain indifference over both son and mother: "Swanking about, with cap askew." The personification of the moon's jaunty swagger is in stark contrast to the "shadow of you/ Gravely ill" and "woman lying at home". This is a place of darkness and silence; a time of unspeakable carelessness and isolation. This poem is the song of all Russian women who grieve for their sons and husbands; thus, we are implored to "Say a prayer" for "her". Poem III reinforces the idea that Akhmatova is every Russian woman singing this requiem: "It isn't me, someone else is suffering." In her direct way Akhmatova calls for light to be extinguished and the insufferable acts of the past to be covered in mourning cloth; her Russia is in a state of "Night". In Poem IV we are presented with a before and after revolutionary image of life. The "carefree sinner of Tsarskoye Selo" was "everyone's darling"; this was the site of Akhmatova's childhood and reflected the emerging world of liberating ideas and experimental artistic practices in Russia. She wonders how the former life could have been adequate preparation for the life ahead. Post revolution is a time of atrocity. "You would stand, parcel in hand/ Beneath the Crosses"; she along with hundreds of other wives, mothers and daughters line up to visit political prisoners in Leningrad's infamous prison, the Crosses, in the hard cold of "the new year's ice". Laughter and playfulness have been replaced with "hot tears". Silence is reinforced once again. From 1925 to 1940 all Akhmatova's publications were officially banned; hence *Requiem* was passed word of mouth to some of her closest friends. This poem gives witness to those times and asks the most dangerous question: "how many innocent / Blameless lives are being taken away..."

In 1939 Lev's sentence was reconsidered and he was sent to the gulag in Norilsk in the far north of Siberia for five years. What follows in *Poem V, VI, VII* and *VIII* is the incoherent grief of a mother in a purgatory not knowing her son's final fate. These four poems powerfully convey her uncertainty. She becomes the state of unknowing. There is a type of madness here as winter gives way to spring then summer; leaving her holed up in her apartment atrophied by worry and in the end asking death to end it for her. In *Poem V* Akhmatova clearly names the Communist state as that which "threatens me with swift annihilation". The "enormous star", the red pentangle is a symbol for revolution, the proletariat, peasantry, agriculture and international solidarity, but is also the reason for Russia's suffering. Her embodiment of this suffering is unequivocal: "For seventeen months I have been screaming,/Calling you home./ I've thrown myself at the feet of butchers." Her poetry is so personal so filled with giving witness to that which cannot be spoken that it is no wonder this could only be preserved through word of mouth. Her apartment was frequently searched, she was threatened repeatedly with arrest and recording devices monitored her life within her apartment. This constant state of anguish, doubt and fear leaves her to trust nothing: Lev is both "my son and my horror" and she cannot "distinguish/ Who is an animal, who a person". Time passes with no hope: "dusty flowers ... the talk/ is again of death." *Poem VI* offers an invigilation that is ceaseless: "nights stare...Eyes...focus like a hawk". A conflation of her vigil and that of the guards.

In *Poem VII*, when the verdict comes down of Lev's removal to Norilsk, Siberia Akhmatova realises that personal memory can have no place in a world that generates a State memory: "I need to slaughter memory,/ Turn my living soul to stone." The new year's cold has thawed and the poplars that fill the communal garden in front of her apartment, indicative of the arrival of summer, "rustles/ Like a carnival outside my window". Ironically it is this traditional symbol of life and hope that prompts her to recall: "I have long had this premonition/ Of a bright day and a deserted house." It would not be surprising, considering the fate that has befallen so many Russians that Akhmatova would have lived waiting for the worst to come; moreover, as the son of a counter revolutionary, ideological adversary and internal émigré, Lev had little chance of a different destiny. *Poem VIII* is an apostrophe to Death. Here Lev is conveyed to the artic of Norilsk in Siberia by the NKVD, "blue caps". This reached its maximum horror in the year Lev arrived where political prisoners were forced to mine nickel and copper which was then transported down the Yenisey River. Lenin's re-education of class enemies had been swapped for hard labor. Stalin had effected a terror state. Here an estimated 200 000 prisoners died of starvation and exposure to the elements. For 280 days a year this is a place of winter where its peak temperatures can plummet to 58 degrees below zero. To this hell Lev was sent. A death sentence. So Akhmatova invites Death to enter rather than endure the torturous wait. Death is "so simple and so wonderful", she leaves her door open to this guest such is her certainty that Death will come to her son and thus to her. She is unperturbed by how Death will manifest; whether as a weapon of war "a shell of noxious gas", or an unknown assassin "a practised bandit with a heavy weapon", or an infectious deadly disease "a typhoid exhalation", or the perfidious alternate truths "a simple tale prepared by you" that will condemn her to death in a gulag. Like the river Don, the river Yenisey is a current that pulls life on.

Poem IX is recorded in 1940 some nine months later and Lev has survived his first winter in Norilsk. This time for Akhmatova remains a chamber of torment. She believes "Madness with its wings/ Has covered half my soul". While it teases her to the brink of suicidal hopelessness: "It feeds me fiery wine/ And lures me into the abyss." Its triumph is cruel as she is left with personal intimate memories that will not be erased. She is left to recall both "my son's frightening eyes" and "the sweet coolness of a hand". Memory is central to a requiem. Ritualising the dead and generating solace for both the dead and the mourners requires an authentic remembering. It was at this point that Akhmatova is evacuated from her apartment in Leningrad to Kazakhstan during some of the Siege of Leningrad. It was here that she composes her final station of the cross: *Poem X*. Lev is the crucified Christ the moments before his death and resurrection who directly addresses his father and mother: "Weep not for me, mother./ I am alive in my grave... To his father he said, 'Why hast thou forsaken me!'/ But to his mother, 'Weep not for me. . .'" The conflation of Lev as Christ, Gumilyov as Father God, and Akhmatova, as Mary the Mother of God, does not stray far from the Russian imagination of regarding the narrative of Christ as somehow personally theirs to make sense of their own iconic suffering. The twist, of course, is that Lev is buried alive in the Siberian labor camp and there is no solace or help forthcoming from any God be it transcendental, parental or State. The outlook is apocryphal: "The heavens melted into flames." The drama below the ongoing unending crucifixion of innocence in Stalin Russia is played out by three most beloved characters: the Magdala, John and his Mother. They are the witnesses to his suffering and as such suffer in turn: "Magdalena smote herself and wept,/The favorite disciple turned to stone...the mother stood silent,/Not one person dared to look." I am haunted by this final line. Nothing could mirror suffering more precisely.

Requiem is the living monument, to not only the imprisonment of her son, but to the millions of Russians who suffered under Stalin's state of terror. The largest of Akhmatova cannot be contained here where we glance momentarily into the Silver Age of Russian poetry. Here is an extract of the epilogue to *Requiem*: "Everywhere, forever and always,/ I will never forget one single thing...If someone someday in this country/ Decides to raise a memorial to me...Build it here where I stood for three hundred hours/ And no-one slid open the bolt... and an old woman Howled like a wounded beast./ Let the thawing ice flow like tears/ From my immovable bronze eyelids/ And let the prison dove coo in the distance/ While ships sail quietly along the river."

I leave you with my own diary extract of when I last visited Akhmatova's apartment in St Petersburg, where she lived for over 40 years:

On one of my visits to Akhmatova's Fountain House

I'm really cold walking through the communal garden into her apartment block. I walk up the three flights of steps and nothing looks like it has ever been any different. I look upwards and trudge on, thinking about her. How many times did she walk up these stairs? And the others who climbed these steps to take away her son and husband. And more.

I move from the stairs into the shallow entrance of her apartment. Punin's overcoat still hangs on the hat stand waiting for his return. It is loose and large. Hanging slightly open. Of course, I start thinking about Gogol and the desire for little other than home. I want to touch Punin's long brown overcoat but I also don't want to; it is tired and old and empty. But I know she touched it again and again and again. Waiting for him to come home.

I move into a corridor that runs behind the bedrooms and sitting rooms into the kitchen. There's an old stove and a rudimentary tap above a deep sink. Overhead, on a short cord diagonally across the stove, hang dishcloths and the like. I walk on further down the corridor to her son's makeshift bedroom of books, a light and a chair. There is no bed.

I think about her in this apartment. A tentative dweller. Not able to take up too much space, inhabiting the edges of people's lives; the corners of kindness. A woman's life. What is that like? To live so carefully on nothing.

I come around to the front of the apartment now and look in on Punin's room, where he and she slept. Just there on a wide couch. His desk, his art and his books. Their friends would come into this room and talk, read poetry, argue. Early on Punin was a supporter of the Revolution. Not later. Not when Mandelstam came and read his anti-Stalin poem right here to a small intimate group of friends. Punin, Lev and Mandelstam were arrested for this very act and imprisoned. A friend must have been the informer. The authorities came for Punin in this very room.

Then on to a sitting room where they also took their meals. A table laid out in readiness surrounded by photos. I sit down. Punin, his first wife, her father, a grandmother, Punin's daughter and son in law, Akhmatova, Lev, then Punin's third wife. What is that expression? Necessity/adversity/misery makes strange bedfellows. Here in Fountain House in Leningrad in Russia in the Stalin reign of Terror, all three nouns exactly articulate the reality I watch over.

I move into a small room which became her room when she and Punin fell out and his next wife arrived to stay. I am struck by the nothingness of this room. The childlike cell. There's a small backless couch, a desk and a window. I look at the photos and see one of a young boy. A son of the neighbouring family who moved into the room next to hers during the war. I remember a fragment of a poem she wrote to him when she heard later, he had died in the Siege of Leningrad. Meanwhile the gulags took Punin, Lev, Punin's son in law and his father in law.

In the last sitting room, the one that was converted into the room for the neighbours, there hangs Modigliani's drawing of Akhmatova. Up against the opposite wall is a large chair and desk where she and Isaiah Berlin talked into the night, this ultimately led her to be declared a non-person and all her writings suppressed. I turn my back on all this and look out the window.

So much suffering. And cold. And quiet. Small. Little lives. A big intellectual life but silent, apart from the distilled poems. I step out the front door and a small window from an alcove I hadn't seen in the kitchen looks out on to the landing where the front door is already closing. I am told that this was where people would look out to see who had rang the doorbell. Unexpected visitors were dangerous. All I can think as I walk down the three flights of stairs was - that was a life. That was it. Game over.

Osip Mandelstam

On the pale-blue enamel by Osip Mandelstam (1909)
Translated by A. S. Kline

On the pale-blue enamel,
that April can bring,
birch branches' imperceptible
sway, slipped towards evening.

A network of finely etched lines,
is the pattern's finished state,
the carefully-made design,
like that on a porcelain plate,

the thoughtful artist set,
on the glazed firmament,
oblivious to sad death,
knowing ephemeral strength.

When Mandelstam writes this poem, he is 18. He has moved from Warsaw to St Petersburg. He studies at the Sorbonne, the University of Heidelberg and then the University of St Petersburg, leaving without a completed degree. He marries, writes poetry, gets arrested, exiled, is given a reprieve but then arrested again. He is dead at 48. In this span of time from 1909 to 1938, despite being ostracized by the Bolsheviks then hounded during Stalin's reign, his poetry fires a shot across the bow to his oppressors. His poetry is both fearless and achingly vulnerable. I cannot imagine living through these times in which he lived. He must have wondered if Art was dead because God certainly was. Mandelstam said: "Only in Russia is poetry respected, it gets people killed. Is there anywhere else where poetry is so common a motive for murder?" His wife, Nadezhda, committed to memory his entire opus with the goal of eventual publication. She wrote *Hope Against Hope* and *Hope Abandoned* to give testament to the literary heritage her husband evinced. If we go back to the start of Mandelstam's poetry and then continue forward, we will see the change of subject matter but not his seminal ability to hold what is fragile.

On the pale-blue enamel is a little gem of a poem! The extended metaphor of glazing enamel runs through the three stanzas. The artistry of the ceramicist is imitative of the artistry of all creativity including that of the poet. Even in the first stanza we have this collision of the ceramic, creation and poetry. It is the month of Spring that coats the sky in the lighted palette offsetting the slip and sway of birch trees. The visual is beautiful with a stand of slender white arms of the birch reaching the sky; their movement faint and indiscernible. The second stanza reminds us of the close relationship between creation and the decorative arts, which in turn becomes the poetic arts. The movement of the branches becomes "the pattern's finished state/ the carefully-made design" but it has also become "lines", magnificently drawn. This moment in Spring, this vignette, is arresting because it is perceived as deliberate and not random. The pattern is "carefully-made" by the moving birches and likened to "a porcelain plate/ the thoughtful artist set". This run on line into stanza three is the first time we find a reference to the ceramicist/creator of nature/poet. The surface, of art and life, is sealed with the everlasting movement of trees swaying imperceptibly against a Spring sky. In other words, art seals the beauty of eternal movement. The artist, be it the ceramicist or poet or Nature, is "oblivious to sad death"; therefore, the inevitability of all life leading to death is not captured here but rather "ephemeral strength". This celebration of the transient and fleeting makes its heart-breaking beauty all the more exquisite. At 18 Mandelstam sees permanency as weakness whereas the ephemeral is worthy of immortal poetry.

A flame is in my blood by Osip Mandelstam (1913)
Translated by A. S. Kline

A flame is in my blood
burning dry life, to the bone.
I do not sing of stone,
now, I sing of wood.
It is light and coarse:
made of a single spar,
the oak's deep heart,
and the fisherman's oar.
Drive them deep, the piles:
hammer them in tight,
around wooden Paradise,
where everything is light.

This petite odic sonnet invites meditation. Mandelstam bids us to enter his poetic self in order to understand his passion and pursuit. The fire in him is visceral and corporeal. It is all consuming and renders to ashes life that is not fertile and alive to the poetic genius: "A flame is in my blood/ burning dry life, to the bone." His song "now" is to "wood" not of "stone". If this sonnet is a song to the immediate burning drive in Mandelstam to create poetry, about nature as well as man-made tools of trade both equally beautiful and worthy, then it is a song in relationship to other songs, in other times and places. Out another way, his poetry belongs to a wider and deeper songbook.

The next four lines is a poetic dedication to the nature of wood. Like the flame that has made kindling out of dry life, poetry blazes and offers enlightenment to those who will be warmed by its true "coarse" or rustic nature. From its "single spar" verse of finite and exquisite beauty, is created "the oak's deep heart,/ and the fisherman's oar". His tight, economical and minimalist sonnet is an intuitive and perspicacious manifesto of the art and practice of composing poems. In citing nature and man-made objects, both hard and fast things of the real world, Mandelstam aligns himself with the preoccupations of the Acmeist. These were a group of poets who rejected the Symbolists last two decades dominance of Russian poetry where intellectual and linguistic haze was privileged. The oak and the fisherman's oar work well as metaphors for the poetic enterprise as they are suggestive of timelessness and tirelessness, respectively.

In the final lines of Mandelstam's sonnet, the tone seems to intensify with the imperative: "Drive them deep...hammer them in tight." It is as if the art and practice of poetry must set the foundations to society's paradise. Two points here as we pause: one is that it is poetry not religion or politics that will create a glorious utopia and second it is culturally specific. The "wooden Paradise" seems to be a nod to these remarkable 17th century church structures built in the north west of Russia that stand like giant weathered tomes of poetry, articulating hope, beauty and salvation from suffering. Hence, paradise itself is borne out of wood. In the final line we are promised that it is here in this art and practice of poetry that "everything is light". These early poems are so tender and full of the promise of a better future. Tragically, what follows is World War 1, Revolution and Civil War. The aftermath is worse: Stalin's Reign of Terror constituted by upheaval, loss of property and work, poverty, fear, sickness, homelessness, hunger, censorship, surveillance, repression, arrest, torture and death. Despite all this, Mandelstam's flame still burns.

This night is irredeemable by Osip Mandelstam (1916)
Translated by A. S. Kline

This night is irredeemable.
Where you are, it is still bright.
At the gates of Jerusalem,
a black sun is alight.
The yellow sun is hurting,
sleep, baby, sleep.
The Jews in the Temple's burning
buried my mother deep.
Without rabbi, without blessing,
over her ashes, there,
the Jews in the Temple's burning
chanted the prayer.
Over this mother,
Israel's voice was sung.
I woke in a glittering cradle,
lit by a black sun.

This 16 line lyric has a mesmeric quality that haunts you long after you have finished reading. In Russia to grieve for mother is to grieve for a loss of one's connection to nationhood. The mother here in this poem may well be triggered by memories of his own mother who died of heart failure at this point in his life but it brings to the surface a lament for Mother Russia, both are loves forged from birth. The place of his belonging is no longer one of peace. Jerusalem, etymologically the city of peace, is now "lit by a black sun". The world as he has known it is now vanquished. This poem offers an apocalyptic vision of the new world; one that is deeply disturbed at the edges by the anxious attempt to keep innocence asleep. We are thrust into this lyric with the unequivocal truth that "night is irredeemable". Thus, we are immediately confronted by the unalterable nature of darkness, or ignorance, or suffering. The second sentence of the lyric creates another reality, another temporality, one that is filled with hope and life and wisdom: "Where you are, it is still bright." This not only sets up the dichotomy between the reality of this here and you there but also between the connotations of "night" and that of "bright". Mandelstam is writing this poem deep in the mid-way point of World War 1, his mother has died and he is separated from his beloved Nadezhda. Moreover, Russia is on the brink of a revolution that will topple the Tsarist autocracy. It is no wonder that Mandelstam felt he stood on the threshold where "a black sun is alight".

It is in this moment of history, straining with conflict and contradictions, that Mandelstam is able to use an image that clearly represents this paradox. In the next four lines we have both babe and mother in the throes of different types of sleep: that of innocence and that of the dead. But the repetition of "sleep, baby, sleep" suggests a certain apprehension as if the sleep of innocence is on the cusp of ending. This is framed by the auguries of the suffering sun and the burning Temple. "The yellow sun is hurting" could be read as those suffering under the Zionist flag or it could be that life itself is heartbroken at the atrocities witnessed in war. There is little consolation as the night goes on "Without rabbi, without blessing", indicating that the world is bereft of ritual and the solemnisation of the death of loved ones and innocence. The repetition of "the Temple's burning" is an ongoing image of desecration and destruction. The suffering endured in the anti-Semitic pogroms in Russia as well as that experienced in World War 1, cannot be overrepresented. The conflation of the personal and historical suffering is a hallmark of this lyric. Throughout, we are brutally aware that there is no solace. The final four lines make a powerful punch. The lyric becomes a dirge: "Over this mother,/ Israel's voice was sung." The personal "my mother" has become "this mother", suggesting that loss is collective and immediate. The awakening is disturbing: "I woke in a glittering cradle,/lit by a black sun." The age of innocence is over and the poet's very foundations are illuminated by the glory and horror of dazzling darkness. The black sun is a conceit. It speaks to life drawing to an end and freedom being extinguished. The lyric is both sinister and eschatological; it is different to what we have read prior to the War and the pending Revolution. For Mandelstam, his world was shifting exponentially.

Tristia by Osip Mandelstam (1922)
Translated by A. S. Kline

I have studied the Science of departures,
in night's sorrows, when a woman's hair falls down.
The oxen chew, there's the waiting, pure,
in the last hours of vigil in the town,
and I reverence night's ritual cock-crowing,
when reddened eyes lift sorrow's load and choose
to stare at distance, and a woman's crying

is mingled with the singing of the Muse.

Who knows, when the word 'departure' is spoken
what kind of separation is at hand,
or of what that cock-crow is a token,
when a fire on the Acropolis lights the ground,
and why at the dawning of a new life,
when the ox chews lazily in its stall,
the cock, the herald of the new life,
flaps his wings on the city wall?

I like the monotony of spinning,
the shuttle moves to and fro,
the spindle hums. Look, barefoot Delia's running
to meet you, like swansdown on the road!
How threadbare the language of joy's game,
how meagre the foundation of our life!
Everything was, and is repeated again:
it's the flash of recognition brings delight.

So be it: on a dish of clean earthenware,
like a flattened squirrel's pelt, a shape,
forms a small, transparent figure, where
a girl's face bends to gaze at the wax's fate.
Not for us to prophesy, Erebus, Brother of Night:
Wax is for women: Bronze is for men.
Our fate is only given in fight,
to die by divination is given to them.

By 1922 Russia was in no doubt about the power of the Bolsheviks post Revolution. From 1917 to 1922 the country had undergone a radical transformation from autocratic Tsarist rule to proletarian self-determination. This period gave witness to Lenin's Red Terror, where the Communist secret police liquidated over 250,000 opponents to the Bolsheviks; the Russian Civil War, where the Red and White Army fought to capture the impossible length and breadth of Russia; and the Crisis Year of 1921, where six million peasants died of starvation along with 30% of the population of St Petersburg, and 50% of Moscow. Moreover, the increasing control wielded by the Bolsheviks on the type of art created by artists placed more and more pressure on poets like Mandelstam. Yet instead of writing about the masses and comradeship he deliberately chose to write about the individual, a decision that sealed his fate. *Tristia*, a nod to Ovid's poems of the same name, is in many ways an exhalation of Mandelstam's own commencement of exile. In taking this stand to write about love, the individual, the personal and the intimate. Mandelstam is cutting himself adrift. Perhaps Mandelstam saw very early on, that this brave new world was not the Russia he knew and to be castaway from its bold new shores, was the most courageous act he could make. He is 23.

This elegy of love from the *Tristia* collection has a powerfully 21st century voice, despite the backdrop of oxen chewing the cud and cocks crowing. These act as literary tropes indicating time passing. What we have in this beautiful collection of four octaves is the moment when a lover realises that the farewell to a beloved is deeply familiar and has been performed by him and by the Ancients and will be repeated again and again for time immemorial. The farewell, the sorrow, the elegy is also utterly connected to the welcome, the joy and the love-song to the beloved. This is what it is to be passionate. To know love is to know Eros and Thanatos. At the center of this departure is a pragmatic understatement that this has happened before. I love the opening sentence: "I have studied the Science of departures,/ in night's sorrows, when a woman's hair falls down." It's a delicious moment to start at the end. I can see the lover watching his beloved sleep, with her hair tumbling across the sheet, all the while knowing he is to leave her. Time passes with the cinematic eye panning to the window and the nocturnal rituals beyond. It is in this somewhat melancholic but slightly objective state that the lover realises this is the inspiration for every artist: "when reddened eyes lift sorrow's load and choose/ to stare at distance, and a woman's crying/ is mingled with the singing of the Muse." To look, allows the poet to write four exquisite octaves.

In the second octave the lover considers the way in which departure morphs into welcome, and the cycle of love continues. Mandelstam recalls the moment when Xerxes ordered the burning of the Parthenon and Athens, causing the people's exile from their own city and place of worship. Thus "that cock-crow is a token,/ when a fire on the Acropolis lights the ground", and it is a given that this very same harbinger of the departure of day will celebrate the dawning of the morning: "the cock, the herald of the new life,/ flaps his wings on the city wall?" Mandelstam is asking why fret when a love affair ends because it offers inspiration for art. Indeed, the poet lover openly admits at the start of the third octave that "I like the monotony of spinning,/ the shuttle moves to and fro,/ the spindle hums." The metaphor clearly tells us that this back and forth from departure of love to arrival of love is the thread from which he can weave his poetry. Indeed, Augustan Tibullus' beloved Delia, with naked feet and long hair runs to meet the lover: "Look, barefoot Delia's running/ to meet you, like swansdown on the road!" Like the great Roman poets, Mandelstam knows that the first and most central subject for the elegy, is love. Thus, he considers the paradox of departure and welcome; death of love and the arrival of love; Thanatos and Eros: "Everything was, and is repeated again:/ it's the flash of recognition brings delight." This recognition of the familiar pattern of the back and forth movement between elegy and love, known only too well for Tibullus, is jouissance according to Mandelstam.

The final octave pulls together Mandelstam's references to the Classics and secures his own poetic enterprise within that same company. We commence with an assertion that accepts the fate of love as elegy, "So be it" and move into the poem's own temple of divination that predicts the outcome of the cycle of love's departure and arrival. Unequivocally the outcome is death for the lover and the beloved. Here is the scene of young girls melting candle wax on the surface of a shallow dish of water to form shapes that can be read as predictions of what is to come: "on a dish of clean earthenware,/ like a flattened squirrel's pelt, a shape,/ forms a small, transparent figure, where/ a girl's face bends to gaze at the wax's fate." This is a secretive, powerful and dangerous ritual. Mandelstam reminds Erebus, from Greek mythology, that prophesy is women's business. It is worth pausing here to consider another layer to the departure/arrival cycle. Erebus the god of shadows and his sister Nyx, the goddess of Night, are parents to Hemera, the goddess of day, who pushes her parents aside in order to shed light across the world. Here is a primordial tale from the Greeks that capture this exact same poetic moment of dark loss and bright love. The lover poet declares that it is "Not for us to prophesy, Erebus, Brother of Night:/ Wax is for women: Bronze is for men". In these times in which Mandelstam lived, there was one destiny for men and that was to fight. The mention of "Bronze" is a nod once again to Tibullus who states the same. Yet it is the final two lines that resound inexorably: "Our fate is only given in fight,/ to die by divination is given to them." We are not to forget that this is an elegy. That despite the profound delight of recognising that departures always lead to arrivals, it is death that will have the final say. This will be the truth for Mandelstam and for Russia as he had known her.

Night Piece by Osip Mandelstam (1931)
Translated by A. S. Kline

Come love let us sit together
In the cramped kitchen breathing kerosene.

There's fuel enough to forget the weather,
The knife is ours and the bread is clean.

Come love let us play the game
Of what to take and when to run,

O come with me and come what may
And holding hands to hold off the sun.

By the time Mandelstam wrote this exquisite little poem the Stalin repression was a terrifying reality. Mandelstam was physically and mentally exhausted by the constraints placed on writers and the entire society. After writing no more than 20 poems in the last decade Mandelstam began writing again in the early 1930s. In returning to poetry he knew he was fated to die at the hands of the cruel and terrifying regime. Up until this point Nikolay Bukharin, who was part of Stalin's ruling circle, had supported Mandelstam and his wife. Mandelstam's close friends and contemporaries had all been affected by the Stalin Terror: Gumilyov had been shot, Pasternak stopped writing poetry, Akhmatova withdrew all work from publication, and Mayakovsky and Tsvetaeva both committed suicide. This shaped the psychological landscape of Mandelstam's existence. Which makes the beauty of this poem all the more precious. I see this scene with absolute clarity. A narrow kitchen that sits at the start of a corridor running behind bedrooms that are made up as sitting rooms during the day, dining room, maybe a study. The couple's space would not have been solely their own.

Housing was in crisis and the Mandelstams were living on the hospitality of his brother in Moscow, there could have been other families who lived there too. The kitchen is a thin thoroughfare with a sink and one tap, a small range and a few enamel plates, pans and utensils. It's sparse. The small table at which they sit is old. The chairs don't match. There is some washing still hanging over the range. It's quite late and someone climbs the stairs past their apartment to the floor above.

This is a love song to a moment that needs to be held forever. It is so ordinary a scene that at first one thinks it is just capturing the true things in love that make life worth living; such as talking together late at night in a kitchen. It is written in four unrhymed couplets and the translator has used end rhymes to link the couplets from one to another: a,b,a,b,c,d,c,d. The couplet mirrors the connection of the lover and his beloved. He says "Come love let us sit together", it is an invitation for intimacy, and one that is deeply familiar. What follows is the unexpected: "In the cramped kitchen breathing kerosene." The kitchen with its functionality and public bustle is not the site we would have imagined for a lovers' rendezvous. Moreover, it is insalubrious with its confined space and stench of paraffin. Then we saunter into the next couplet and realise that not only is it night, indicated by the title, but it is cold outside: "There's fuel enough to forget the weather." The weather is God in Russia. It dictates whether you live or die, eat or starve, exist or perish. The couple have bread that "is clean" and a knife that "is ours". On the one hand I am still thinking this is just about the communion of lovers late at night keeping warm and taking in the sustenance of each other and food, but on the other hand my suspicions are rising. Is the bread not normally clean? Does the knife mean more than a knife to cut this bread? And at the back of my mind I am wondering whether you can die from inhaling the fumes of kerosene.

The first line of the third couplet is a slight variation to the first line of the first couplet: "Come love let us play the game." The invitation again to the beloved and at first glance we are led to believe it might be an amusing activity in which the lovers engage; a distraction to the long cold nights. Alternatively, it could be the lover entreating the beloved to go along with what has been asked of them. To me it is the lover asking her to be willing to face the imminent challenge of playing the game "Of what to take and when to run". Here is a life lived on the threshold of annihilation. The third couplet is nearly laconic in the way it discloses the transience of their lives. The two questions for them tell us they are ever vigilant and must move swiftly to save their lives, taking perhaps only what they can carry. The question of where they will go is not relevant; getting out before it is too late is the imperative. The third couplet ends with a run on line to the 4th couplet suggesting the lover's sense of urgency and hope in the beloved granting him his final request: "O come with me and come what may/ And holding hands to hold off the sun." The poem needs to resist becoming an aubade, here in the darkness the lovers may possibly remain safe and have each other; whereas in the harsh light of day and with the full light of knowledge, their world may become dangerously impermanent. I find this poem both daring and sad. I think about them there in the cold and quiet moment, knowing that they were all they had. I think about how real that moment was, across from each other in the familiar smells of the kitchen with the kerosene burning and the sounds of others sleeping just beyond the kitchen passageway. Neither of them could have imagined what was to happen next.

Stalin Epigram by Osip Mandelstam (1933)

Translated by A. S. Kline

Our lives no longer feel ground under them.
At ten paces you can't hear our words.

But whenever there's a snatch of talk
it turns to the Kremlin mountaineer,

the ten thick worms his fingers,
his words like measures of weight,

the huge laughing cockroaches on his top lip,
the glitter of his boot-rims.

Ringed with a scum of chicken-necked bosses
he toys with the tributes of half-men.

One whistles, another meows, a third snivels.
He pokes out his finger and he alone goes boom.

He forges decrees in a line like horseshoes,
One for the groin, one the forehead, temple, eye.

He rolls the executions on his tongue like berries.
He wishes he could hug them like big friends from home.

    Here is the Russian *David and Goliath story*. It is a tale of a wily and vulnerable poverty smacked poet who slung a poem, like a sharp deadly stone, into the eye of the monstrous demagogue. The stone remains. It has become in some ways legend. It is a witty quip made up of eight unrhymed couplets that became Mandelstam's death sentence. David hit the target but Goliath stood standing for another 20 years. Mandelstam read *Stalin Epigram* to ten friends, two of whom reported it to the Cheka, the secret police, but it was some six months later that Mandelstam was arrested and the poem was deemed counter-revolutionary. Mandelstam was tortured physically and psychologically. Akhmatova asked Pasternak for help who in turn asked Bukharin, who once again intervened and probably saved Mandelstam from execution. Mandelstam was then exiled to Cherdyn in the Urals. Pasternak was greatly admired by Stalin and this was the key to Bukharin's success in getting the sentence reduced from Cherdyn to Voronezh, south west of Moscow. Throughout this time of exile Nadezhda was permitted to be with him but they lived a hand to mouth existence. Without his wife's vigilance and care he would never have survived the suicide attempts and the hardship of the next several years.

The first half of this poem holds a mirror up to the people and to Stalin; the second half of the poem reveals the sycophants who propped up Stalin. It is direct and blunt in the way the poet stands in front of a country in ferment and says: *enough!* The unutterable becomes immortalised in this poem. Tens of millions have died and the nation is savagely maimed, wrecked and broken hearted. If a poet has no courage to stand up before one of the greatest giants of oppression, then who? In the opening lines we hear of psychological instability that pursued people's lives: "Our lives no longer feel ground under them./At ten paces you can't hear our words." By the second couplet the poem becomes the biting satire of infamy with the "snatch of talk" invariably being about "the Kremlin mountaineer". The climb to the top of the complex and fortified hub of power by Stalin was a result of ruthless strategy and cunning ambition. The description of this dictatorial potentate is one associated with surrealist horror: "the ten thick worms his fingers… the huge laughing cockroaches on his top lip." This is something subhuman. It is a hybridization of human and invertebrates. The Romanovs were replaced by the cult figure of Lenin who then morphed into something Kafkaesque. Moreover, the power and horror this creature wields is exact: "his words like measures of weight…the glitter of his boot-rims."

The next half of the poem suggests that those men around this autocrat were both toadies and minions. Indeed, Stalin "toys with the tributes" of this "scum of chicken-necked bosses… half-men", implying the way he might casually turn upon one of his own. Like the tyrant, these flatterers are not fully human but rather versions of something much more ridiculous and pathetic: "One whistles, another meows, a third snivels." Stalin's power in contrast is unparalleled: "He pokes out his finger and he alone goes boom." That his commands are reduced to a sound made by an inanimate object is telling. The repetition of the personal pronoun "he" followed by a verb six times in this second half indicates he is a man of action. Stalin is variously a mountaineer, a surrealist monster and now a blacksmith as he "He forges decrees in a line like horseshoes,/ One for the groin, one the forehead, temple, eye." These rulings emanate from him in the furnace of his own hell. They are deadly in their aim at the vulnerable victim. There is a wilful playfulness in Stalin's actions as if he takes delight in the torture and killing of the so called State's victims. In the last couplet Stalin becomes the executioner who savours the taste of another's pain and blood. Indeed, Stalin has a quasi-erotic response to the dying and dead: "He rolls the executions on his tongue like berries. He wishes he could hug them like big friends from home." Mandelstam's direct and personal attack on Stalin in this poem sealed his fate. I wonder about that person who would stand before a tank or a soldier with a loaded weapon or a dictator who was arguably the most heinous of all time. I wonder about those ten friends gathered in Punin's apartment one cold autumn night in St Petersburg to hear this poem that even Nadezhda had not heard before. I wonder about those two whose minds peeled off and took this scene with its poem seared in their brains, to the Cheka. Akhmatova says this was the beginning of Mandelstam's passport to immortality. What courage it must have taken to set forth.

Alone I stare into the frost's white face by Osip Mandelstam (1937)

Translated by A. S. Kline

Alone I stare into the frost's white face.
It's going nowhere, and I—from nowhere.
Everything ironed flat, pleated without a wrinkle:
Miraculous, the breathing plain.

Meanwhile the sun squints at this starched poverty—
The squint itself consoled, at ease . . .
The ten-fold forest almost the same . . .
And snow crunches in the eyes, innocent, like clean bread.

Just over a year after he was to write this brief poem Mandelstam would be sentenced to five years in a labor camp. So, this poem is written while living in exile in Voronezh, where he was friendless, poverty stricken and without hope. It resounds in melancholic despair and dispassionate acceptance. In the first stanza he meditates on the seemingly permanent state of the frost. In fact, he sees himself as this frost who is immobilised by the dead of winter. The frost and the poet are "ironed flat, pleated without a wrinkle". As if both are no more than their outward appearance of self. There is nothing within, nothing but this thin veneer of life. Indeed, that there is evidence of life is astounding: "Miraculous, the breathing plain." Regardless, the wintery landscape is a pathetic fallacy.

In the second stanza "the sun squints" down upon Mandelstam's world. What can be observed is "this starched poverty" where all life is laundered out of the poet living in a state of dire need. The irony that Mandelstam is imprisoned in poverty while the natural world around him is in bounty speaks to a fatalistic acceptance that there is no salvation for him. The final line of the poem is a poignant collision of senses. The look and sound of the crunch of snow connotes the look and sound of crunchy "clean bread". The mention of the bread being clean is a reminder of his life of poverty and the failed harvests and suffering most endured throughout these years. The promise of bread and the look of a deadly winter is symbolic of the yearning to end ubiquitous hunger. This poem is a quiet and honest stage whisper, murmured just off in the wings. Mandelstam's death was coming and he knew it.

Yet to die. Unalone still **by Osip Mandelstam (1937)**

Translated by A. S. Kline

Yet to die. Unalone still.
For now your pauper-friend is with you.
Together you delight in the grandeur of the plains,
And the dark, the cold, the storms of snow.

Live quiet and consoled
In gaudy poverty, in powerful destitution.
Blessed are those days and nights.
The work of this sweet voice is without sin.

Misery is he whom, like a shadow,
A dog's barking frightens, the wind cuts down.
Poor is he who, half-alive himself
Begs his shade for pittance.

The drama of Mandelstam's impending death played on his mind. This last poem, made up of three stanzas, examines the way the mind explores his surrounds and the people in it through the lens of death. He begins with a moribund axiom, that up until this point he is still to pass through death. The next short sentence that follows indicates life around him continues and that he is not isolated. When Mandelstam had been sentenced into exile, Stalin had apparently given instruction that he was to be isolated but preserved. In Voronezh he was always with Nadezhda, and the comings and goings of very few others. During this time, he wrote up to 90 poems. He was without support from a wider group of family and friends and literary society; he was cast off from being acceptable and thus could not find employment.

The first stanza begins with two fragmented sentences: "Yet to die. Unalone still." The first is about his ongoing preservation and the second is about his seemingly non isolation. There is something humbling about the way in which Nadezhda is represented with her "pauper-friend" delighting in "the grandeur of the plains/ And the dark, the cold, the storms of snow". It is as if Mandelstam watches all this from a distance and despite his surprise that he is neither dead nor alone, the world around him goes on. Unlike him others seem to take pleasure and see the beauty in their world: "Live quiet and consoled/ In gaudy poverty, in powerful destitution." Extravagant poverty and destitution are the absolute signatures of their life and despite this or maybe even because of it Mandelstam counsels himself to accept it is enough. So we move from the stark agony of the opening two fragmented sentences to a beatitude: "Blessed are those days and nights." What I find so moving is the last line of this second stanza, where with reverence and love Mandelstam recognises that this life, is "without sin". This life is about "The work of this sweet voice". It is a call to find in himself, contentment and fulfilment. It is a courageous poem.

In his poetry Mandelstam reflected the incongruity of living in a Soviet Russia. On the one hand the State represented the people but on the other it denied individual consciousness. What was it to live, if you were denied your own individuality? Perhaps this is only a question for the post 20th century mind but nevertheless it is not a question limited to the West. What is it to have the State deliver peace, land and bread after the nation has hauled out of the Romanov's Byzantine administration, if one cannot be master of one's own mind? In May 1938 Mandelstam had been charged, once again, with counter-revolutionary activity and sentenced to a gulag for five years in Kolyma, Siberia. In a transit camp near Vladivostok on 27 December 1938 he was found dead. While the official record said heart failure, witnesses say he succumbed to insanity while others say typhus. The

Russian Nobel Laureate Joseph Brodsky says Mandelstam was "a voice trembling like a match burning in a high wind yet utterly inextinguishable". Without this voice, how would we have known?

Marina Tsvetaeva

For the most part, I think about Tsvetaeva's life as a life of tragedy but maybe it was just a Russian life. Indeed, compared to those not of her class she probably lived at least some of her life in comfort and support. Her father was the Professor of Fine Arts at Moscow University and her mother, a concert pianist. As a child she traveled and lived abroad with her family. She married Sergei Efron and had two daughters and a son. She had affairs with Osip Mandelstam and Sofia Parnok, corresponded with Boris Pasternak and admired Anna Akhmatova as well as Alexander Blok. Tsvetaeva rejected the Russian Revolution and when her husband joined the White Army she found herself trapped in Moscow for five years where she was forced to place both her daughters in an orphanage, her youngest died. Tsvetaeva left Russia for Paris, Berlin and Prague in 1922 and did not return until 1939. During this time and perhaps because of her husband's work for NKVD or perhaps because of her somewhat lukewarm criticism of Soviet Russia, she was not accepted in the Russian émigré community. With her son, she returned to Russia months after her husband and daughter. Efron and his daughter were arrested for espionage, he was shot and the daughter served 16 years in various labor camps. Tsvetaeva and her son were evacuated to Yelabuga in 1941 where she committed suicide. In her adult life she seemed plagued by ostracism and grief. Like Pasternak and Akhmatova, Tsvetaeva wrote a number of poems dedicated to the Russian symbolist poet, Alexander Blok.

from *Poems for Blok* by Marina Tsvetaeva (1915)
Translated by Ilya Kaminsky & Jean Valentine

Your name is a—bird in my hand,
a piece of ice on my tongue.
The lips' quick opening.
Your name—four letters.
A ball caught in flight,
a silver bell in my mouth.

A stone thrown into a silent lake
is—the sound of your name.
The light click of hooves at night
—your name.
Your name at my temple
—sharp click of a cocked gun.

Your name—impossible—

kiss on my eyes,
the chill of closed eyelids.
Your name—a kiss of snow.
Blue gulp of icy spring water.
With your name—sleep deepens.

When I read this light, playful and ingenious poem I consider Tsvetaeva at 24. Despite the atrocities of the war and the burgeoning ruination caused by the Tsarist rule, here is joy and adoration towards Blok and the art of poetry. This poem made up of three stanzas of sestets is a young woman's flirtation with language, concepts and Blok himself, an established poet. It is a sensual delight. The first sestet explores the taste of his name in her mouth and on her tongue and lips; the second sestet considers the sound of his name as stone, hooves and a cocked gun; and the third sestet unpacks the delicious possibility of touching his name with a kiss. Tsvetaeva uses the em dash as part of this informal and intimate love poem. The em dash may represent missing words in which case one is left to wonder what could be the several unsaid words throughout this poem that she wishes only Block to hear; perhaps a fancy but one in keeping with the frolic of this poem.

The first sestet places Blok's name on her hand then on her tongue: "Your name is a—bird in my hand,/ a piece of ice on my tongue." It is a soft, quick, wild heartbeat of a name and something that cannot be tasted too long. Tsvetaeva ponders the way her lips open to say his name. While he has a name of only "four letters", it is "A ball caught in flight,/ a silver bell in my mouth." The sestet is a ludic game of catch followed by the quick taste of his name. The second sestet moves up the drama of this flirtation. Here Blok's name is a sound: "A stone thrown into a silent lake...The light click of hooves at night." Both these images suggest the background quiet in order for us to hear the name. As if we need to be open and receptive. The landscape is one of isolation and night-time, connoting perhaps the rendezvous of lovers. The final image of this sestet is heady and intoxicating in the eruption of such violent desire: "Your name at my temple/—sharp click of a cocked gun." Signifying the sorts of risk and powerlessness associated with passion. The final sestet is the culmination of desire and filtration, moving the drama from taste and sound to touch. Despite the forbidden nature of what it is she desires, Tsvetaeva closes her eyes and lifts her face to the "impossible—/ kiss on my eyes...Your name—a kiss of snow." This is a vicarious love poem, one that is seemingly unrequited but nevertheless assertively executed. The touch of his name is a spring of inspiration, one that enters her, so that her "sleep deepens", redolent of the aftermath of full consummation. It's hard to fathom why Blok never met Tsvetaeva.

Bound for Hell by Marina Tsvetaeva (1916)
Translated by Stephan Edgar

Hell, my ardent sisters, be assured,
Is where we're bound; we'll drink the pitch of hell—
We, who have sung the praises of the lord
With every fibre in us, every cell.

We, who did not manage to devote
Our nights to spinning, did not bend and sway
Above a cradle—in a flimsy boat,
Wrapped in a mantle, we're now borne away.

Every morning, every day, we'd rise
And have the finest Chinese silks to wear;
And we'd strike up the songs of paradise
Around the campfire of a robbers' lair,

We, careless seamstresses (our seams all ran,
Whether we sewed or not)—yet we have been
Such dancers, we have played the pipes of Pan:
The world was ours, each one of us a queen.

First, scarcely draped in tatters, and dishevelled,
Then plaited with a starry diadem;
We've been in jails, at banquets we have revelled:
But the rewards of heaven, we're lost to them,

Lost in nights of starlight, in the garden
Where apple trees from paradise are found.
No, be assured, my gentle girls, my ardent
And lovely sisters, hell is where we're bound.

This poem is a song to the women who dared. It is a bacchanalian tribute to the women who had the courage to live their lives as they saw fit. I'm not sure if it would be attributable to the majority of Russian peasant women desperate to make ends meet, still reeling from World War 1 where their menfolk were taken to fight and then the uprisings in St Petersburg that led to the two revolutions and the overthrow of the Tsar. This was the second decade of the 20th century and Russia, as they had known it, was being reborn in their very lifetime. Tsvetaeva married to Efron, had an affair with Osip Mandelstam and then Sofia Parnok. She was not restricted by the conventions and conduct that controlled others in society. There is a jaunty tone in this poem, one that indicates she is without regret. In this translation the poem is structured into six quatrains, with an a, b, a, b rhyming scheme. It is this as much as the imagery that gives the poem a sing song quality; encouraging one to swing a pint of beer in a seedy tavern and recite the lines at full throttle.

The opening quatrain establishes a juxtaposition between where the sisters are headed and from where they have come: "Hell, my ardent sisters, be assured,/ Is where we're bound…We, who have sung the praises of the lord." Straight away we get the impression that this is a song to passionate, fervent and zealous women. This is not for the faint hearted or those with little ardour and pale love. It's a rousing celebration of a life not restricted by gender roles of carer or motherhood: "We, who did not manage to devote/ Our nights to spinning, did not bend and sway/Above a cradle." It is only in the fairy tales that women spin or sew as a talisman of their waiting for the hero to rescue them. In Tsvetaeva's Russia there is no hero coming. There is no night to be wasted in that fantasy. The image of watching over a sleeping child is part of the restrictions placed on women, an act of waiting. I would suspect that in these times there would have been such urgency for life because they would have witnessed the impermanent nature of life all around them. Indeed, the symbolism of the "flimsy boat" bearing these women away is a gesture to the shortness of life and the fact that they are caught up in a national drama that is of seismic scope.

The third quatrain suggests that the loves of these women who dared be unconventional were deliberately other to what was expected. The sensuality of wearing "Chinese silks" and singing "songs of paradise/ Around the campfire of a robbers' lair" cast Tsvetaeva and her sisters as creatures belonging to a world of love and adventure. Indeed, the next quatrain recalls these exotic moments nostalgically. She refers to this group of women, herself included, as "careless seamstresses" playing "the pipes of Pan...each one of us a queen". There's a laconic, licentious element to their characterisation. The singular phrase that seems to sum up the reason for Tsvetaeva and her sisters being bound for hell is: "The world was ours." On the one hand this is exactly what it must have felt like! The old world gone and a new world emerging. Or more emphatically, a time of surety evaporated and one of uncertainty and mayhem taking its place.

The last two quatrains take us across the temporalities of these hell-raising women. They have come from poverty and have gone to a place, illuminated by the stars. The transition from being a woman bound for heaven to a woman bound for hell is captured in the backdrop of poverty and imprisonment: "draped in tatters, and dishevelled...We've been in jails." Is it no wonder they chose "a starry diadem [and] banquets"? In taking the rewards of earth they are precluded from "the rewards of heaven". Orthodoxy is dead. The axioms of the past fade. The last quatrain hints at the languorous appetite associated with temptation and "my gentle girls, my ardent/ And lovely sisters". Perhaps it is in that very phrase that one suspects Tsvetaeva is referring to forbidden and transgressive love: lesbian love. Regardless, these women who dared are lost in a darkness lit only by paradisiacal enticement.

The fin de siecle in Russia meant many things but not so much the open practice of homosexuality. This love was anathema to all Russian radical revolutionary thinking. For poets to write about their homosexual or homoerotic passions was not tolerated and was considered irrelevant to the political concerns of the day. Sofia Parnok ran counter to this and she and Tsvetaeva, rather than being part of the hidden population, openly flaunted their love affair. Indeed, between 1915 and 1916 they were the talk of Moscow literary society. They lived together in a summer house in the poet's colony in Koktebel where Osip Mandelstam was a guest and became Parnok's rival for Tsvetaeva.

I am happy living simply by Marina Tsvetaeva (1919)
Translated by Ilya Kaminsky & Jean Valentine

I am happy living simply:
like a clock, or a calendar.
Worldly pilgrim, thin,
wise—as any creature. To know

the spirit is my beloved. To come to things—swift
as a ray of light, or a look.
To live as I write: spare—the way
God asks me—and friends do not.

It's 1919 in Russia. The catastrophic losses of World War 1 are incalculable for Russia. The Civil War has begun and the Red Army battle at various fronts with the White. Russian against Russian. By the end of 1919 the country is devastated in every way. Famine has ravaged whole towns and many are reduced to cannibalism. It would take years to sort out the madness and the mischief that had led to mass genocide. This was the beginning of the collectivisation of consciousness and the emergence of the avant-garde poets, writers, musicians and artists whose style invoked Constructivism or Productionism. This was a time where old artistic genres were abandoned in lieu of objective and impersonal art. Writers and artists attempted to strip away description and narrative so that their work was devoid of spiritual or metaphysical trappings. This new society required new expressions; indeed, many believed that these poets, writers, artists and musicians could create a new human being. Tsvetaeva was not one of them. Between 1918 and 1920 her poetry was in praise of the White Army. In 1919 her youngest daughter dies of starvation in an orphanage; so to read "I am happy living simply" leaves me with a disquiet that goes straight to my bones.

This petite and intimate poem is made up of two stanzas. Tsvetaeva's desire to live simply is compared to lifeless time pieces. It is as if her desire is to be alive only in the measurement of minutes and hours and days and months and years. As if there is no other purpose. The word "happy" is a tripwire. It is a choice, a decision. She uses the metaphor or a "Worldly pilgrim"; a wayfarer, a believer both "thin" and "wise". Where has she traveled metaphorically to come to know the sacred or that which could sustain her metaphysically? Wherever it has been, her body is spare and marked by the ravages of that journey, yet her mind is enlightened. The run on line from the end of stanza one to two connects the narrative of herself and her experience to what it is that she has discovered: "To know/ the spirit is my beloved." If the spirit is her beloved then she is the lover, the active agent in the pursuit of love. In this second stanza is an interior life of precipitous and perspicuous movement. It is because of the beloved that her access to the interior world is alive and vivid: "To come to things—swift/ as a ray of light, or a look." Now the point of comparison is an intimate epiphany. The final two lines are indicative of the way in which writing and living are conflated for Tsvetaeva; they are one and the same. Perhaps writing makes living bearable or living makes writing essential. Regardless, her writing and living are defined by her times and as such they are "spare—the way/ God asks me—and friends do not." This makes me think about a monastic life, empty of worldly luxuries and comforts. This is a woman down to her bare bones; it is no wonder that she believes her writerly practice emerges from her beloved spirit.

Wires by Marina Tsvetaeva (1923)
Translated by A. S. Kline

> *Heart's wave would not have foamed*
> *So high, and turned to Spirit,*
> *If it were not that the ancient mute*
> *Rock of Fate so opposed it.*
> Hölderlin

A singing line of posts,
Holding up the sky,
Sending you my share
Of earthly dust.
The alley
Sighs – wire to pole –
Telegraph: love – you – ou –ou...
Beg you... (No printed form,
Can hold it! Simpler by wire!)
These – pillars, Atlases, that
Send celestial tracts
Racing...
Across telegraph
Posts: Fa – are – well...
Do you hear? The last severance,
Of ruined mouths: fo – or – give...
This – rigging, on seas of fields,
A calm Atlantic voyage:
Further, further – and fu – use...
With Ariadne: Re – ee – eturn
Turn back! Hospitals, gifts,
Doleful: don't go!
These – wires of steel,
Wires – Aida singing
Receding...far off,
I conjure: Re – egret...
Pity! (In this chorus, how
Distinguish?) In the fading cry,
Reluctant passion –
Eurydice's breath:
Over the thresh – h – hold

Evridiki: al – a – as,
Not – a –

So, it's 1923 and Tsvetaeva has left Russia with her surviving daughter, Ariadne, for Berlin where she is reunited with her husband, Efron. The small family move on to Prague later in 1922, where Efron studies at the university, and she works, writes and conducts a passionate affair with a military officer, Konstantin Rodzevitch. In 1925 the family move to Paris, Tsvetaeva gives birth to her son and for the next 14 years the family remain in France before returning to Russia. Here, in this 1923 slim whip of a poem, she reveals the anguish of longing. Her poem is made up of 33 lines many of which fragment and disintegrate. In effect it is an ode to the telegraph wires that bring and send messages of hope, love, sorrow and regret; the ingredients of a passionate love affair gone wrong. The poem is prefaced with a few lines from the German Romantic poet, Friedrich Holderlin. It's a wonderful metaphor for the way in which obstacles to love merely make the passion more intense, more immortal. Embarking on love affairs is a difficult ocean to navigate. Living inside one's heart and mind, keeping check on the secrets, being vigilant to not reveal in body or words the doppelganger within is just the beginning of the turbulence. The tempest swells and swells until drowning looks like salvation. The intertextual references to Greek mythology, from Atlas to Ariadne to Eurydice, puts us in the mind-frame of fatalistic tragedy. Here is a site where the sky may fall down, mazes may consume and the thresholds may pull you back to the Underworld.

I love the way the poem begins with the "singing line" of telegraph poles. The song can be variously a love song, a dirge, a lament, a ditty. The idea that they are "Holding up the sky" suggests that communication to her lover is the only thing keeping catastrophe at bay; in keeping with this is the belief that this very communication will ultimately turn to "dust". From the start there is a fatalism that attaches itself to the upkeep of love. From singing we move to sighing, in keeping with the sorrow of such a love song: "The alley/ Sighs – wire to pole –/ Telegraph: love – you – ou –ou.../ Beg you..." The visual image of the parallel lines of the telegraph poles stretching on into the distance connotes forever and always. The making and breaking of electrical connections, the telegraph, is in itself a metaphor for this very experience of clandestine love. Not only does the metaphor represent the drama at the core of this poem but the form itself begins to imitate content; with the actual messages to the lover connecting, disconnecting and ultimately falling away to dust. She indicates in an aside, caught in the parenthesis, that print cannot capture the disintegration of love in all its fragmentation.

The telegraph poles are posts, alley ways and now pillars. She calls them "Atlases" to conjure the weight and burden they bear. Moreover, across their shoulders' sprints heart quickening love in the fragments of "Fa – are – well..." and "fo – or – give..." The telegraph poles now become "rigging, on the seas of fields". Here we pick up Holderlin as we sweep into the Atlantic ocean and then "Further, further – and fu - " until we are washed up in the archipelago of Classical Greece. Ariadne helps the lover, Thesus, escape the maze but what happens to Ariadne? We hear her cry: "Re – ee – eturn/ Turn back!" Now "These – wires of steel" sing like the soprano in Verdi's great opera, Aida, who was an enslaved Nubian princess dying in the arms of her forbidden lover in the vault of the Underworld. Bereft of her lover and life she conjures "Re – egret.../ Pity! (In this chorus ...)". Her life has become a tragic opera. Indeed, the drama at this point is so heightened that in Aida's "fading cry", we sense the end. The orphic song of love and passion is now a dirge. It has looked back and seen love return to the Underworld: "Eurydice's breath:/ Over the thresh – h – hold/ *Evridiki*: al – a – as,/ Not – a - " What an intense operatic lyric, overbrimming with allusion and awash with the excess of emotion. As readers we are drawn on and on into this descent of longing from which one may never return. A poem that takes you down to the wire.

from *An Attempt at Jealousy* by Marina Tsvetaeva (1924)
Translated by Ilya Kaminsky & Jean Valentine

How is your life with that other one?
Simpler, is it? A stroke of the oars
and a long coastline—
and the memory of me

is soon a drifting island
(not in the ocean—in the sky!)
Souls—you will be sisters—
sisters, not lovers.

How is your life with an *ordinary*
woman? without the god inside her?
The queen supplanted—

How do you breathe now?
Flinch, waking up?
What do you do, poor man?

"Hysterics and interruptions—
enough! I'll rent my own house!"
How *is* your life with that other,
you, my own.

Is the breakfast delicious?
(If you get sick, don't blame me!)
How is it, living with a postcard?
You who stood on Sinai.

How's your life with a tourist
on Earth? Her rib (*do* you love her?)
is it to your liking?

How's life? Do you cough?
Do you hum to drown out the mice in your mind?

How do you live with cheap goods: is the market rising?
How's kissing plaster-dust?

Are you bored with her new body?
How's it going, with an earthly woman,
with no sixth sense?
                        Are you happy?
No? In a shallow pit—how is your life,
my beloved? Hard as mine
with another man?

It's 1924 and Tsvetaeva has been living in France in exile for at least two years. Her affair with Rodzevitch is over. Efron is suffering from tuberculosis and so the small family has moved to Paris. This hard and sharp poem begins at the high note. There is no compromising in her poetry, at least we see none here. Here is a poem made up of 11 uneven stanzas. It is a bumpy irregular road of anger, despair and spite without end, resolution or finale. Indeed, there are 23 questions that make up the vitriol that Tsvetaeva throws at her former lover. You get the distinct feeling that the lover ended it with her, not the other way around. There is one moment when she addresses the subject as "poor man"; thus, I am reading this as an address to the lover. The poem opens with two questions and they are direct and confronting: "How is your life with that other one? Simpler, is it?" We begin in the middle of a jealous fueled struggle. This is followed by an image that takes us into the next stanza, a movement across the waterway. The "memory of me" is a metaphor of "a drifting island". So, the poet has become irrelevant, an unanchored and mobile land mass that is not in the streamline of her lover. She curses the lover: "—you will be sisters—/ sisters, not lovers." The emasculation she wishes upon him is high opera and her frenzy builds. Tsvetaeva doesn't see herself as an "ordinary/ woman"; hence she asks: "How is your life ... without the god inside her?" Contained here is Tsvetaeva's identity as both the devastated self and the self of immeasurable grandeur. Unlike the Russian sensibility of ambivalence, Tsvetaeva is utterly without doubt about the intimate and personal. Stanza four is filled with questions demanding to know what reality could be life for him now he is without Tsvetaeva: "How do you breathe...poor man?" His very capacity to function and live is under threat.

The middle of the poem is intersected by the direct speech of the former lover, a memory shard she spits back at him: "Hysterics and interruptions—/ enough! I'll rent my own house!" Here we have the only moment his voice interrupts her didactic spleen. Although it is reference to a former flash in their past it could well be the same message he would give her now, standing before the unravelling of her pique in this very poem. **Tsvetaeva** is larger than life, more than what can be handled by him, and she is on the highest volume possible. That's the very power of the poem. This voice will not be shushed or spoken over or told to calm down or speak rationally or silenced in any way. This voice, is not done. She refers to him as "my own"; at once tender and full of passion. A harsh reminder of what was. The next stanza asks and answers: "How is it, living with a postcard?/ You who stood on Sinai." This is a momentary pause on the hurling of dishes. The metaphor of the new beloved being nothing more than a diminutive image of the real thing. How can anything be the true landscape of love now that Tsvetaeva is gone?

The following five stanzas are a relentless cross examination. There is no time or space in which he may reply. Tsvetaeva refers to the one who has replaced her, as "a tourist/ on Earth", doomed to walk the landscape to which she will never truly belong. We catch the scorned woman's longing, a whispered ache, an incredulous pining: "(*do* you love her?)" I find this powerfully moving because in the full operatic persistence of this poem we come to see that Tsvetaeva is attempting to convince herself that his is a life bereft of her, not vice versa. And yet...and yet. So she races on with more questions at high pitch in the 8th and 9th stanzas accusing him, on the one hand, of ignoring the memory of them and, on the other hand, filling his mind with the minutiae of the ordinary: "Do you hum to drown out the mice in your mind?... How's kissing plaster-dust?" In the penultimate stanza she reminds him again and again that he has gone from someone who is more than the sum of all that is earthly, to someone who is less than. In the final stanza we move to the last note: "Are you happy?... my beloved?" Again, this gentle exquisite term of affection. We have turned to the heart of the poem. In answer to that quintessential questions she offers an answer of her own: "Hard as mine/ with another." The fever pitch is broken. Suffering goes on for both of them. Perhaps that's why this poem is entitled "An Attempt...". Tsvetaeva is making an effort, she is trying to conjure up the tempest of all jealousies, but in the end, all they are both left with is hardship.

from *Poems to Czechoslovakia* by Marina Tsvetaeva (1939)
Translated by Elaine Feinstein

They took quickly, they took hugely,
took the mountains and their entrails.
They took our coal, and took our steel
from us, lead they took also and crystal.

They took the sugar, and they took the clover
they took the North and took the West.
They took the hive, and took the haystack
they took the South from us, and took the East.

Vary, they took, and Tatras they took
they took the near at hand and far away.
But worse than taking paradise on earth from us
they won the battle for our native land.

Bullets they took from us, they took our rifles
minerals they took, and comrades too:
But while our mouths have spittle in them
The whole country is still armed.

At the time of Tsvetaeva's exile, 1922 to 1939, the Russian émigré aristocracy lived in Paris; the Russian émigré intelligentsia lived in Berlin; and the Russian émigré writers and scholars lived in Prague. The new republic of Czechoslovakia, due to its anti-Bolshevik sentiment, provided Russian émigrés with asylum and financial support. During Tsvetaeva's time of exile in Czechoslovakia she was immensely productive. Indeed, she was assured publication in the *Will of Russia* literary journal. In 1939 Tsvetaeva returned to Russia and in that same year Nazi Germany invaded Czechoslovakia; hence we have *Poems to Czechoslovakia*. This extract of poem IV offers four quatrains of intense imagery. The poet represents Nazi Germany as a machine that eats its way through the nation of Czechoslovakia; it is ravenous and cannot be stopped. Its appetite knows no bounds. The verb "took" occurs 20 times in these 16 lines. The energy of this extract is palpable because of this powerful image of grasping, seizing, capturing, robbing, stealing, procuring, grabbing, appropriating and removing.

The four quatrains begin by suggesting that the taking was done with such ferocious haste. The repetition of the verb "took" starts to read like a chant of the terrifying loss of one's country. The mineral boon is described as the "entrails" of the mountains and this is stolen and stripped away from the body. The plunder is listed "coal...steel...lead...crystal" it is an inventory that cannot be forgotten. Most compelling is the use of the collective pronoun "us" and its possessive "our". Tsvetaeva identifies with the suffering people of Czechoslovakia. In the next quatrain she considers the contraband taken forcibly from this nation into Germany; from the specific: "They took the sugar...the clover...the hive...the haystack" to the abstract: "they took the North...the West...the South...the East." This contrast is arresting and makes us see that there is nothing too insignificant nor too colossal that cannot be confiscated by this terrible ravenous force.

In the third quatrain the booty includes the Carpathian Mountains that borders Poland and "worse than taking paradise on earth from us/ they won the battle for our native land". The glory of the Tartars, in all their immensity, become a leitmotif for the love and grief of a nation ravished and taken. The final quatrain indicates the defencelessness of the Czechoslovakian people in the face of the *Munich Pact* as well as the reality of the invasion: "Bullets they took from us, they took our rifles...and comrades too." So, we are left with the penultimate image of a people vulnerable, powerless and immobilized by poverty after the invaders have plundered their nation. Yet the final two lines are a victory cry: "But while our mouths have spittle in them/ The whole country is still armed." Here is the belief in the mightiest weapon of all: the voice that will not be silenced. This is why Tsvetaeva joins her voice with her Czechoslovakian confreres.

And there's no Grave by Marina Tsvetaeva (1941)
Translated by Yevgeny Bonver

And there's no grave! No separation, ending!
The table's un-spelled, the house – wakened up.
Like Death – on a gay dinner after a wedding,
I'm Life, arrived on the last evening, sup!

In 1941 her husband Efron was executed for espionage, her daughter sentenced to 16 years of imprisonment and Tsvetaeva was evacuated to Yelabuga. Here she struggled as an isolate with no means of support. On 31 August she committed suicide. I read everywhere that no one came to her funeral. Maybe it is a salient reminder that so much of Tsvetaeva was just too much: her open support for the White Army, her choice to go into exile, her inability to connect politically or philosophically with any of the émigré communities in which she lived, her tempestuous love affairs, the marriage to Efron and his espionage and the death of her first daughter in the orphanage and the imprisonment of the second. Then there is her poetry that is so uncompromising. So, we come to this four line quatrain which says too much and not enough.

It is clarity at sheer velocity. With astonishing surety Tsvetaeva knows there is "no grave! No separation, ending!" She begins at the end. An eschatological truth or premonition. The opening line reads as a bursting shout! As if she is roused from the relentless grief and mourning of her adult life. Tsvetaeva tells us that there is no liminal space between the dead and the living but that we are all together. The table has been broken from its spell of quiet functionality and what is conjured in its place is the heartland of home: "the house – wakened up." This is no longer a place of bereavement, loss and ending but rather a place of insight, dynamism and beginnings. It is as if death has conjured a life affirming community. Death is indeed likened to the feast that follows a wedding. It is bountiful, nourishing and worthy of celebration: "Like Death – on a gay dinner after a wedding." Moreover, it exists in the proximity of love. So, what has happened? Has too much happened? No longer do the old tropes work when it comes to ascribing meaning to death, as she knows it. Is death so ever present that it is now welcomed? Does death, in the end, offer the promise of life because nothing else will? Tsvetaeva writes herself into this last line, of her last quatrain, in the last few weeks of her life and metaphorically her last evening. She asserts that she is "Life" and like death she is taking her place to "sup!" For me it is a final acceptance of the paradoxes of her time that ravaged her family and her friends and her country. Here she knows that life sits down to eat with death; that they are perhaps one and the same creature.

Boris Pasternak

For as long as I can remember a copy of *Dr Zhivago* has been in my father's library. I have it now on my desk. The pages are thick and stained in the way that old books grow old. My father treasured this book and I love that he loved it. The photo of Boris Pasternak on the back cover is brooding and disconnected. I remember being taken to see the film with Omar Sharif and Julie Christie when I was young. I don't know who I was more in love with: Zhivago or Lara. I certainly wanted to be her; she does survive after all. So, it was a long time later that I realised Pasternak was a poet as well as a novelist; indeed he was first and foremost the one of the greatest poets of the Silver

Age. Pasternak was awarded the Nobel Laureate in 1958, an honour he was compelled to decline. His legendary novel was banned in Russia until the late 1980s but it had been smuggled out to Milan decades earlier. He was born into a highly talented Jewish family in the Ukraine and he could have been a painter or a musician. He chose poetry. Pasternak had an uncanny ability to remain just out of reach of Stalin's ruthless tyranny. His friendship gave succor to Mandelstam, Akhmatova and Tsvetaeva. He was married twice but what I remember most is the story about his mistress who was arrested by the KGB, tortured and imprisoned. She miscarried but refused to say anything incriminating about Pasternak. She was then sentenced to ten years in the gulag. I think about this woman: Olga Ivinskava. She was already a single mother when Pasternak met her so she risked her own child for him not to mention her unborn baby. His poetry is moving and unforgettable. There is something deeply romantic and personal in his work. Perhaps it was all this that made Ivinskava decide to sacrifice so much. Or perhaps this had nothing to do with her decision.

February by Boris Pasternak (1912)
Translated by Andrey Kneller

Oh, February. To get ink and sob!
To weep about it, spilling ink,
While raging sleet is burning hot
Like in the blackness of the spring.

To rent a buggy. For six grivnas,
Amidst the church-bells, clanking wheels,
To steer it where a shower drizzles
Much louder than ink or tears.

Where thousands of rooks fall fast,
Like charcoaled pears to their demise
And as they hit the puddles, cast
Dry sadness to depths of eyes.

Beneath – thawed patches now appear,
The wind is furrowed by the yelling.
New poems are composed in tears,
The more unplanned, the more compelling.

This is such a lovely quiet poem about writing and sadness and a Russian winter. This translator has used the occasional end rhyme, particularly in the last quatrain, to lock in a truth about the harrowing effects of nature and poetry. Let's start with February in Russia: zero winter. Moscow in February is bitterly cold. It hurts to be outside no matter what you wear. It is hard work to move about, to push yourself, to make a life. Living as much as possible in interior spaces with claustrophobia, depression and a desperate need for fresh air, not to mention the constant concern about fuel for heating and provisions. All of this dominates one's thinking. In the first quatrain we begin with a fragmented sentence, an exhalation and an address: "Oh, February." From the start there is a tone of lament, frustration and despair. The conflation of writing and tears begins in the very first line and is ever present throughout the four quatrains. This is the poetics of anguish. It is as if the weeping becomes the very ink the poet uses: "To get ink and sob!/ To weep about it, spilling ink." This statement is palindromic and foregrounds the art of writing poetry. Beyond the interior space of writing Pasternak contemplates the paradox of "raging sleet…burning hot" and the way that this ultimately is thawed by spring.

The second quatrain offers a suggestion, an end to the state of being entrapped by misery: "rent a buggy." For a small sum of money, the poet is transported to the outside landscape with its cacophony of sounds: "church-bells, clanking wheels." Life and energy are restorative and rejuvenating. Indeed, the breaking of the bitter winter and the promise of spring is suggested in this quatrain: "where a shower drizzles/ Much louder than ink or tears." In other words, the signatures of an impending break to a February winter, resonates more loudly than the lamentations of the poet at his work. The conceit of course is that this is a poem about writing a poem. The wintery world always gives way to life in spring. As spring nudges its way into the landscape of the poet's writing, an entirely different poem is born. In the third quatrain we have this startling image: "thousands of rooks fall fast…they hit the puddles." It's a lyrical landscape with the birds signalling the start of spring.

Just as in Savrasov's *Rooks* in Tretyakov Gallery, this is a painterly moment still wet and unpredictable with soggy skies and landfall shadowed in puddles. This is a plein air of the poet's melancholia. In the last quatrain more indicators of spring break apart the unrelenting winter; there is a thawing of the snow and frost and sleet even the howl of the wind makes inroads into the impenetrable wintertime. And Pasternak asserts that it is the spontaneous "poems … composed in tears" that are "the more compelling". It is this delightful landscape of wintery poetics, made possible because of the misery of endless cold and excessive darkness that leaves us captivated.

Storm, Instantaneous Forever by Boris Pasternak (1919)
Translated by Jon Stallworthy and Peter France

Then summer took leave of the platform
and waiting room. Rising his cap,
the storm at night for souvenir
took snap after dazzling snap.

The lilac darkened. And the storm
came bounding in from the meadows
with a sheaf of lightning flashes
to light the office windows.

And when malicious delight ran

down corrugated iron in torrents,
and like charcoal on a drawing
the downpour crashed against the fence,

the avalanche of consciousness began
to glimmer: light, it seemed, would soon
flood even those corners of reason
where now it is bright as noon.

Unlike many of his contemporaries Pasternak decided not to emigrate after the October 1917 Revolution. Instead he stayed living in or near Moscow believing Russia was his only home and country. This poem to a summer storm is a powerful contemplation of the unexpected; the tension between creation and destruction; as well as the excessive moment of enlightenment. It is another demonstration of Pasternak's delicate attention to detail in nature and the way weather and landscape are so inextricably linked to the poet's psyche. We begin with summer leaving and so are positioned in that liminal space of "the platform", a place of anticipation and the endless activity of arrivals and departures. Each season pulls in to the platform but remains ever watchful of the next incoming season. I love the way the night storm that arrives unexpectedly in this summery season is personified: "Rising his cap,/ the storm at night for souvenir/ took snap after dazzling snap." It is a salutation, a greeting that demands our response. Perhaps because of the storm's unpredictable arrival keepsakes are snatched to immortalise this moment. The repetition of "snap" becomes the camera shutter capturing the souvenir, the sudden quickness of the storm and the onomatopoeia of the tempestuous squall.

The next three quatrains deal with the sound and fury of the lightning and thunder. Even the most beloved lilac of Russia is mentioned. This hardy little flower that blooms in spring and offers renewed hope throughout summer with its vitality, freshness and fragrance seems to grow gloomy and watchful. The energy in the storm is anthropomorphized: "the storm/ came bounding in from the meadows/ with a sheaf of lightning flashes." In its very clutches is the mischief of high voltage electrical discharge. I pause to think about the current charging through Russian history in the summer of 1919. Russia was in the horror of its own Civil war with unimaginable atrocities committed by the Red and White Army, including the execution of 1600 peasants on the Adrianovki Station in the Transbaikal region. These acts of inhumanity to men, women and children were known as part of the growing landscape of post-Revolutionary Russia. In the last line of the second quatrain we are told "lightning flashes/ to light the office windows." A powerful image of the effects of nature or a metaphor for the havoc caused by the current political storm. Either way we are deeply aware of the significance of light and the way it physically illuminates one's world, so much so, that it cannot be ignored.

The deluge that occurs as a result of this summer tempest is paradoxical. It is described as "malicious delight". Akhmatova, Mandelstam, Pasternak and many artists and writers of the time welcomed the Revolution as the dawning of a new age for Russia. Moreover, the fervour of these times was intoxicating, for a short period. The aftermath of terror, carnage and suffering would become their lives for the next 60 years. Quatrain three and four uses enjambment; indicating the unceasing downpour of rain. This torrential storm is both an auditory and visual spectacle. The sound of rain running "down corrugated iron in torrents" is deafening. Yet what it does is effect an "avalanche of consciousness". It is as if, at this point in time, one's awareness and understanding of the summer storm makes one feel destabilised. Indeed, enlightenment evokes enlightenment or insight follows insight or perception generates more perception to the point that the violence of the deluge is replaced by light: "light, it seemed, would soon/ flood even those corners of reason/ where now it is bright as noon." Is this a salient reminder that all seasonal changes will pass? This is a poem about a sudden summer storm but it is also so much more because it is a poem about Russia's revolutionary and civil war context. It is a poem that believes that truth will out and light will challenge even the darkest night.

> from *In Memory of Marina Tsvetaeva* by Boris Pasternak (1943)
> Translated by Robert Chandler
>
> It's as hard to image
> you don't exist
> as to imagine you are a miser-millionaire
> among starving sisters.
>
> What can I do for you? Say.
> There's a quiet reproach
> in the way
>
> you've gone your way.
> Losses are riddles. In vain
> I try to find
> an answer.
> Death has no outline.
>
> Half-words, tongue-slips, delusion –
> and only
> faith in resurrection
> by way of direction.
>
> Winter makes a splendid memorial:
> a glimpse of twilight,
> add currants, pour wine
> – and there's your remembrance meal!
>
> An apple tree in a drift, the town

wrapped in snow,
seemed all year long
to be your grave, your headstone.

Facing God, you reach out
toward him, from earth,
just as before
your days had reached their final count.

This moving elegy to Tsvetaeva speaks to Pasternak's belief that he had let her down, in the final hour, when she needed him most. It is written two years after her suicide. They had had an extraordinary epistolary relationship for many years. Pasternak and Tsvetaeva wrote to each other over 13 years and for a brief moment of time that also included Rilke. The great Bohemian-Austrian poet had identified Pasternak as a significant poet in the early 1920s and Pasternak began his correspondence with Rilke and later introduced him to Tsvetaeva. Rilke died of leukaemia in 1926 and never met with Pasternak or Tsvetaeva as hoped. Pasternak would continue an epistolary love affair with Tsvetaeva until their meeting in 1935 in Paris. This meeting was an experience of bitter disappointment. While Tsvetaeva spoke longing of her return from exile to Russia, Pasternak spoke sarcastically of what Russia had turned into. Despite this their correspondence demonstrated their love of Germany, their similar experiences of having grown up in Moscow, both having had a professorial father and a concert pianist as a mother, as well as their shared sense of desolation. Although Pasternak did try to intervene for Tsvetaeva when her husband and daughter were arrested in 1939, there was nothing he could do. They had been significant to each other in encouraging the creation of poetry and not surrendering to their shared sense of displacement.

These seven quatrains sing a song of grief. It is not an ululation or even a lament but a song of grief. It is shaped in the hard bones of regret and loss. The etymology of grief comes from Old French, *grever*; to burden. Pasternak's poem evoked the burden felt in the death of someone once loved. When Tsvetaeva committed suicide in Yelabuga we are told no one attended the funeral. A note that makes the burden for those left behind even heavier to bear. The first two lines articulate Pasternak's bewilderment: "It's as hard to image/ you don't exist." So much of Pasternak's relationship with Tsvetaeva had been about imagination; their exchange of poetry and letters had created an entire imaginary landscape where love on many different levels could be played out.

The poignancy of Pasternak's question cuts right to the heart of the elegy. He asks: "What can I do for you?" The imperative to just "Say" implies that all will be done, he would do anything. As a result of Tsvetaeva's long exile but also because of the times in which they were living, she was to remain an outsider until her death. The final step of taking her life distances her even more, in a time when so many were desperately trying to survive. The short sharp paradox works as a maxim for this poem: "Losses are riddles." The next few images demonstrate the unsatisfactory nature of proximal responses: "Death has no outline./ Half-words, tongue-slips, delusion… faith." In other words, the eschatological investigation leads to few clues: no outline of the dead body, no deliberate, conscious and complete articulations; just the unknown and knowable. Hence, all losses are riddles.

In the antepenultimate and penultimate quatrains, we move to a landscape of grief. Of course, it is winter and twilight, both symbolic; the former of death the latter of liminal space: "Winter makes a splendid memorial:/ a glimpse of twilight." From this painterly backdrop emerges the vigil kept by those left behind. The piquant black berry that thrives in Russia's cold damp fertile soil offers sweetness and the wine, ritual sustenance. Indeed, her "remembrance meal" is both a visual and epicurean feast. Pasternak gives us the whiteness of winter, the fractured light of twilight, sharp sweetness of rich dark currents and the liquid balm of wine. Tsvetaeva's site of burial is imagined as a landscape denuded of humanity. The snow covers the memory like a blanket of silence. It covers everything and seems "to be your grave, your headstone". It is upon this canvas that Pasternak is compelled to write her eulogy. The inevitability of Tsvetaeva's fate is inscribed in the final quatrain. In death Tsvetaeva is represented as formidable: facing her God. This is not a coward's death but the death of someone who had enormous courage "just as before". She is in death, how she was in life. It was the inevitability of her lot, she knew it, God knew it and Pasternak knew it: "your days had reached their final count." Pasternak's poem is a finite and everlasting invigilation to Tsvetaeva, a great poet and one of Pasternak's great loves.

Hamlet by Boris Pasternak (1946)
Translated by Robert Chandler

The hum dies down; alone on stage,
my back against the wall, I try
to sense within a distant echo
the twists and turns of destiny.

A thousand glinting opera glasses
focus the dark into my eyes.
O Father, should it be possible –
allow this cup to pass me by.

I like your stubborn, bold design,
and I've agreed to play this part.
But other forces are at play now –
this once, please count me out…

The acts cannot be rearranged
and there's no turning from the road.
Alone, a sea of cant all round me:
Life is not a walk across a field.

One of the most compelling productions of *Hamlet* I saw was where a young woman played the Prince of Denmark. She was svelte and peterpanesque, with her blonde frayed hair and body, a coil of intensity. The stage was dark for most of the production and I seemed to remember the sound of the surf outside the small theatre, crashing and roaring in the dark. A beast on the edges that wanted to come in. The decision to cast Hamlet as a woman enraged some critics but for me, for the first time in all the years of reading and teaching and watching productions of *Hamlet*, it felt right.

Again, the tight form of 16 lines generating four quatrains. We commence media rez, a classic Homeric poetic technique: "The hum dies down; alone on stage." We are in a thrilling liminal space where the anticipation of the drama about to unfold, is palpable. There is an inevitability about this narrative, the Hamlet and Jesus stories are already told and known. Yet still we lean forward in our seats to hear and see what happens next. For the player he is caught in our eye line, in the anticipation, in the procrastination, in the horror of knowing what is to befall him. He is isolated and trapped in the mythology of what will be told again and again for time immemorial: "alone on stage,/ my back against the wall." This is about entrapment and there is nothing to be done except to accept the fate that has been handed to you; the narrative has already been written. Just as much as we are straining forward, the player on stage is also attempting to hear the faintest "distant echo" of what is to unfold. While the destiny is inevitable the "twists and turns" before reaching his eschatological end is terrifyingly unknown.

This is not just a poem of intimacy between the player and me but rather a relationship between the poet and his vast audience. The audience is in darkness and watches silently. It heightens its ability to see with "opera glasses" to ensure that a singular movement does not go unwitnessed. This audience is a body of anticipation and hungry reception. The poet is deeply aware of his audience and it is because of this that he is able to look into the darkness. We can now decipher the stage is in fact the olive trees in the shadowy gloom of the garden of Gethsemane. We lean a little closer and see the player is not alone but to his right, in what initially seemed nothing but an old acacia bush, is two or three people asleep on stage. The player is quiet and wraps his right hand about the left side of his neck. He stands very still. Center stage: "O Father, should it be possible –/ allow this cup to pass me by." His words are hardly audible but we hear them with perfect precision. These are words that were always coming to us. Is he crying? Do we see tears or sweat or shivering? Nothing. Just stillness, a knowing and a need to use words even though he has no hope that they will be heard.

Hamlet now speaks, Jesus now speaks, the player now speaks, and the poet now speaks. More curiously it sounds like I am speaking because of the pre dominance of the personal pronoun: "I like your stubborn, bold design,/ and I've agreed to play this part." The tenacious pattern marked out for me can only be admired. There is something brave and unapologetic about the life I am designed to live. Shakespeare has already taught me that the world is a stage but here Pasternak is adding that I have consented to perform my role. Great theatre will do that to you. It will transport you from the dark anonymity of the stalls to the stage itself. It will make you cry out, laugh aloud and go down dying for a cause. Great poetry will fearlessly engage in the untouchable narratives of what has gone before us. Somewhat like a girl playing Hamlet. I am thrown back to Pasternak who tells me "other forces are at play now –/ this once, please count me out." I wonder if a life of surviving as poet in Russia has just about taken its toll on 56 year old Pasternak. He has never left the epic apocalyptic production played out on Russia's stage: 1905 Russian Revolution, World War 1, February and October 1917 Revolution, 1918 Civil War and death of the final Tsar, 1921 Russian Famine, 1922 creation of the USSR, 1924 onwards the establishment of the Gulags, Collectivisation, Stalin's Years of Terror, World War 2, the Siege of Leningrad and so on. And while this has been playing out, the poet has refused to surrender.

The final quatrain returns us to the quietness of the final act. It has all been played out a long time ago. Hamlet knew it, Jesus knew it, Pasternak knew it and the player whom we watch knows it: "The acts cannot be rearranged/ and there's no turning from the road." There is only one way forward and this must be followed. The final act five with all its promised dénouement and resolution cannot be replaced by act one with the introduction of setting and characters and the establishment of conflict. It is in act five that we have arrived. It is drawing to a close and although the narrative is deeply familiar and we know how it ends there is a part of us that remains on the edge of our seat hoping against hope that some Deus Ex Machina will drive us someplace hitherto unrealised. Then we notice, despite our own immobility, we have arrived back where we began. The player is alone and the beast of the sea pounding relentlessly just beyond the theatre in the nightly wings sounds like "a sea of cant"; it is in fact the restless sanctimonious murmurings of the hypocritical faithful. This is the soundscape of the unweeded garden in which Pasternak had tried to live, where things rank and gross in nature flourished. The great Russian poet leaves us with a proverb from his land: *"Life is not a walk across a field."* Is this the truth for Hamlet? For Jesus? For the Pasternak? For the player? Is it the truth for Russians? It is my truth made manifest in the restless longing to hear poetry.

10

Poetry that Saves a Nation: Nobel Laureates

What is poetry that does not save
Nations or people? Milosz

The Prize...

Here is a handful of Poet Nobel Laureates who have been lauded as the voice of their nation. As recipients of the Nobel Prize these poets are internationally recognised as voices of their nations. Their imaginations both replicate and undermine geo-political boundaries. On the one hand their poetics reflect the notion of imagined communities with their localised and idiomatic use of language and culture, but on the other hand their worlds demonstrate the pressure of living within a geopolitical environment. Their nation states are the embodiment of ravenous wants, forever in a state of incompletion. In exposing their nation space as a site of belonging and nurture, these poets are exposing a hungry body. In 1895 Alfred Nobel left his considerable wealth and fortune from the invention of dynamite to the founding of the Nobel Prize. This international prize is awarded to the highest achievement in the field of Physics, Chemistry, Physiology or Medicine, Literature and Peace. Nobel Laureates are thus heralded as offering the greatest benefit to mankind in their field.

And the Winner is...

1963 Giorgos Seferis "for his eminent lyrical writing, inspired by a deep feeling for the Hellenic world of culture".

Seferis was 63 when he went to Stockholm to receive this accolade. He had been born in 1900 in Urla, Asia Minor and given the name Georgios Seferiades, by the time he died aged 71, Urla had become Izmir, Turkey. Exiled from the country of his birth, Seferis studied at the Sorbonne and then became a career diplomat for most of his life. Being forever in a state of foreignness and permanently evicted from his birth country, is a stamp on the passport of his poetry. At the start of the 20th century Greece was still recovering from the Greco-Turkish war and the series of bankruptcies that followed. In the first and second decade of the 20th century Greece remained embroiled in the Macedonian Struggle and then World War 1; it was also intent on taking back Macedonia, Epirus, Crete and finally Asia Minor. By 1922 more than a million Orthodox Greeks were traded for 400,000 Muslim Turks in the destruction of Asia Minor. This created a wound that could not be healed. Displaced Greeks desperate for homes and economic security became the diaspora of the mid 20th century. In April 1941 Greece fell to Nazi Germany and this led to the destruction of ancient sites, large scale executions and the extermination of the Jewish communities in Athens, Thessaloniki and Rhodes. Civil war from 1944 to 1949 ensued after Germany left Greece. The Royalists enjoyed US support and eventually defeated the Communists. From 1949 onwards Greece remained unstable politically and financially until the establishment of the Junta, supported again by the US, in 1967. The Junta remained in power for seven years despite social rebellion. By 1974 Greece had a new constitution and by 1981 it had joined the European Union. This thumb nail sketch gives some perspective to Seferis' life and concerns articulated in his poetry. The Nobel Prize committee acknowledge him to be representative of the Hellenic poets and as such forever in a state of wandering exile. Let's have a brief look at four poems: *The Return of the Exile*, *Denial*, *Helen* and *Mythistorema*. Our purview is to note Seferis' empathy for Hellenic culture as well as the way in which his nation space is lyrically rendered for his compatriots.

The Return of the Exile by Giorgos Seferis (1931)

Translated Edmund Keeley

'My old friend, what are you looking for?
After years abroad you've come back
with images you've nourished
under foreign skies
far from you own country.'

'I'm looking for my old garden;
the trees come to my waist
and the hills resemble terraces
yet as a child
I used to play on the grass
under great shadows
and I would run for hours
breathless over the slopes.'

'My old friend, rest,

you'll get used to it little by little;
together we will climb
the paths you once knew,
we will sit together
under the plane trees' dome.
They'll come back to you little by little,
your garden and your slopes.'

'I'm looking for my old house,
the tall windows
darkened by ivy;
I'm looking for the ancient column
known to sailors.
How can I get into this coop?
The roof comes to my shoulders
and however far I look
I see men on their knees
as though saying their prayers.'

'My old friend, don't you hear me?
You'll get used to it little by little.
Your house is the one you see
and soon friends and relatives
will come knocking at the door
to welcome you back tenderly.'

'Why is your voice so distant?
Raise your head a little
so that I understand you.
As you speak you grow
gradually smaller
as though you're sinking into the ground.'

'My old friend, stop a moment and think:
you'll get used to it little by little.
Your nostalgia has created
a non-existent country, with laws
alien to earth and man.'

'Now I can't hear a sound.
My last friend has sunk.

Strange how from time to time
they level everything down.
Here a thousand scythe-bearing chariots go past
and mow everything down.'

    I find this beautiful call and response lyric quite heart felt in its simplicity. It could be two countrymen speaking; one asking the initial question and the other replying, one having stayed behind and the other having roamed. Or it could be the country speaking to the returned exile. Either way the relationship between the two is significant. They are old friends and their call and response travels the length of eight stanzas; commencing with the country asking the question of the returned exile but ending with the returned exile asking a question of his country. Despite a deep and abiding history and tenderness between the two, neither is capable of satisfying the other with an answer. Indeed, it is as if they do not share the same language. The first voice asks in the opening line: "My old friend, what are you looking for? ...with images you've nourished/ under foreign skies." This speaks immediately to the preoccupation of nostalgia which permeates the original literary score of Greece: Homer's *Odyssey*. Steeped in Seferis' and the Hellenic world's imagination is the expeditious tale of yearning for home while resisting return. *Nostalgia* is a Homeric word denoting homecoming and pain; indeed, by the 17th century it was regarded as a medical condition. The returned exile's imaginings have been fed by distance and dislocation thus he says: "I'm looking for my old garden." The returned exile's voice is the self and thus I wonder whether it is *all* our plight to enter the world longing to return; in other words, is our existence haunted by the wistful desire for that once beheld edenic embryonic paradise? According to the returned exile the landscape nostalgically longed for is of grand proportions and makes the child within him, "breathless".

    The 3rd and 4th stanza talk through what the returned exile is seeking. The first voice is conciliatory and asks his "old friend" to "rest/ you'll get used to it little by little". This is a curious piece of advice that occurs four times in the poem. On the one hand the first voice is suggesting that the exile begins to feel familiar with this homeland once again and in time it will not be seemingly so unusual. On the other hand, the first voice is suggesting that this is the particular state of affairs and one is powerless to its inevitability. There is a complicity offered by the country to the exile, one where "together we will climb...we will sit together" so that "your garden and your slopes" will come back. Can that sense of home only be restored by trusting a relationship between the landscape and the returnee? The returned exile seeks a place of belonging that is steeped in the past: "I'm looking for my old house." The image he has sustained, while under foreign skies, is one that nurtures, shelters and offers continuity with the past: "I'm looking for the ancient column." This is an Hellenic world known to the sea faring imagination of the West. Contrastingly what the returned exile finds is a "coop" or a confined cage that has "men on their knees/ as though saying their prayers." He has returned to a defeated subservient people not to countrymen of legend and conquest. In many ways, returning home is contingent on the returned exile accepting the inevitable: "You'll get used to it little by little."

    The 6th stanza is the turning point. While the call and response continues the returned exile now asks his country a question: "Why is your voice so distant?" The national voice is detached and withdrawn. Ironically the country itself has become exiled to itself. It is unrecognizable, it offers shelter or connection to its past. Rather than writ large in the beloved imagination of the returned exile it is growing "gradually smaller...sinking into the ground". The country in stanza seven confirms itself as "a non-existent country, with laws/ alien to earth and man". The returned exile confronts a homeland that either never existed or no longer exists. Again, the refrain for complicit complacency: "you'll get used to it little by little." I can't help but hear from the country a menacing threat to accept this rediscovered place of belonging as it is, or to turn away and remain forever in a state of exile. This is offered in the amiable terms of friendship: "My old friend." In the final stanza the exile is deaf to the country's pleas. The exile asserts that "My last friend has sunk", in other words his country as ship in an Hellenic seafaring world, has capsized and all are drowned. We are left with an image of his country being completely erased by offensive war machines: "Here a thousand scythe-bearing chariots go past/ and mow everything down." The Hoplites, Greek infantry, were mowed down by war chariots with scythe blades mounted on either side. The exiled self is bereft of country even though he has returned. This unresolved longing for a place of belonging, as well as the continuity of the past and present, is seminal to Seferis' poetic project.

Denial by Giorgos Seferis (1931)

Translated Edmund Keeley

On the secret seashore
white like a pigeon
we thirsted at noon;
but the water was brackish.

On the golden sand
we wrote her name;
but the sea-breeze blew
and the writing vanished.

With what spirit, what heart,
what desire and passion
we lived our life; a mistake!
So we changed our life.

Forty years after Seferis writes this poem it is sung by tens of thousands of Greeks as they follow his coffin. Since the Homeric Age, Greece has known ongoing occupation and the shifting of its watery boundaries. From 1914 to 1950 Seferis is in exile; he returns to Greece after ten years of foreign military occupation is concluded. This time of occupation, followed by civil war led to economic devastation, mass population displacement and severe political polarisation that would impact the next 30 years. The mid 20th century for Greece was a time of terror, famine and poverty where much of the power of the state had been transferred to the military. In 1967 the coup overthrew King Constantine II and a junta headed by the Regime of Colonels, Papadopoulos, Makarezos and Pattakos, established a repressive right wing rule until 1974. During this time civil rights were suspended, political repression intensified, human rights abused, torture was rampant and free political expression stifled. Seferis issued a statement to BBC World Service in 1969 calling for this totalitarian rule to end; he then went into voluntary house arrest. *Denial* was banned but became the anthem for the resistance to the regime.

The poem, in many ways, is a foreshadowing of this social consciousness that rose up against the tyranny after decades of repression in the 20th century. This lyric is the song of a nation; it sings of a national psyche. This nation space is realised as "the secret seashore...the golden sand". It is legendary; water bound but clandestine. It is a place where "we thirsted" and "the writing vanished". Seferis is a symbolist so he is not describing but evoking. This place is one where the water is "brackish" and unclean to drink. Moreover, this is a place where the collective yearning to create a national identity is swept away: "we wrote her name/ but the sea-breeze blew." Despite the paradisiacal archipelago and rich literary history, Greece is not nourishing the soul of its people. The last quatrain demands resistance from the people if they are to fight repressive regimes.

Let's look closely at the anaphora in triplicate: "what spirit, what heart/ what desire and passion." Here are the visceral characteristics of Greece living life. This is what the homeland is despite the decades of brutal oppression. Seferis concludes this exclamatory sentence with situational irony: "a mistake!" These expressions of aspirations, have amounted to nothing. The last line suggests that because of the enormous chasm, between what was hoped for and what was granted, "we changed our life". How this change was constituted in the heart of the poet in 1931, the resistance fighters in 1970 and readers of today, can only be interpreted variously. Did the Greeks change their lives by modifying their passion for freedom? Did the Greeks change their lives by ensuring the chasm between hope and achievement was reduced? Or did the Greeks change their lives to become part of the wandering odyssey? These are the enigmatic thoughts that trouble us long after the poem is read.

Helen by Giorgos Seferis (1953)

Translated Edmund Keeley

> *Teucer: ...in sea-girt Cyprus, where it was decreed*
> *By Apollo that I should live, giving the city*
> *The name of Salamis in memory of my island home.*
> *Helen: I never went to Troy; it was a phantom.*
> *Servant: What? You mean it was only for a cloud that we struggled so much?*
> Euripides

'The nightingales won't let you sleep in Platres.'

Shy nightingale, in the breathing of the leaves,
you who bestow the forest's musical coolness
on the sundered bodies, on the souls
of those who know they will not return.
Blind voice, you who grope in the darkness of memory
for footsteps and gestures — I wouldn't dare say kisses —
and the bitter raving of the frenzied slave-woman.

'The nightingales won't let you sleep in Platres.'

Platres: where is Platres? And this island: who knows it?
I've lived my life hearing names I've never heard before:
new countries, new idiocies of men
or of the gods;
my fate, which wavers
between the last sword of some Ajax
and another Salamis,
brought me here, to this shore.
The moon
rose from the sea like Aphrodite,
covered the Archer's stars, now moves to find
the heart of Scorpio, and alters everything.
Truth, where's the truth?
I too was an archer in the war;
my fate: that of a man who missed his target.

Lyric nightingale,
on a night like this, by the shore of Proteus,
the Spartan slave-girls heard you and began their lament,
and among them — who would have believed it? — Helen!
She whom we hunted so many years by the banks of the Scamander.
She was there, at the desert's lip; I touched her; she spoke to me:
'It isn't true, it isn't true,' she cried.
'I didn't board the blue bowed ship.
I never went to valiant Troy.'

Breasts girded high, the sun in her hair, and that stature
shadows and smiles everywhere,
on shoulders, thighs and knees;
the skin alive, and her eyes

with the large eyelids,
she was there, on the banks of a Delta.
And at Troy?
At Troy, nothing: just a phantom image.
That's how the gods wanted it.
And Paris, Paris lay with a shadow as though it were a solid being;
and for ten whole years we slaughtered ourselves for Helen.

Great suffering had desolated Greece.
So many bodies thrown
into the jaws of the sea, the jaws of the earth
so many souls
fed to the millstones like grain.
And the rivers swelling, blood in their silt,
all for a linen undulation, a filmy cloud,
a butterfly's flicker, a wisp of swan's down,
an empty tunic — all for a Helen.
And my brother?
Nightingale nightingale nightingale,
what is a god? What is not a god? And what is there in between them?

'The nightingales won't let you sleep in Platres.'

Tearful bird,
on sea-kissed Cyprus
consecrated to remind me of my country,
I moored alone with this fable,
if it's true that it is a fable,
if it's true that mortals will not again take up
the old deceit of the gods;
if it's true
that in future years some other Teucer,
or some Ajax or Priam or Hecuba,
or someone unknown and nameless who nevertheless saw
a Scamander overflow with corpses,
isn't fated to hear
messengers coming to tell him
that so much suffering, so much life,
went into the abyss
all for an empty tunic, all for a Helen.

The Greek Tragedian, Euripides, writes his play *Helen* some 200 years after Homer authored the *Iliad* and the *Odyssey*. Yet the fascination with Helen does not stop there; hers is the name synonymous with the ultimate femme fatale who led men to their sticky end. She is the uber woman who cannot be trusted and her fetishized value ensures the ongoing slaughter and chaos committed in her name. What fascinates me is the fact that she is entirely the figment of male imagination. There is something in her allure and objectification that men need to constantly reinvent in order to remind themselves of the dangers associated with woman. Ten long years of war supposedly fought over Helen. Ironically, according to Euripides and to Herodotus and Seferis, she actually wasn't even taken to Troy. Her eidolon was taken but the real Helen was in Egypt. Seferis picks up this obsession with Helen, a synecdoche of territorial greed, in his eponymously entitled poem. The very epigraph by Euripides that announces the legendary and literary world at war that has led to Teucer's banishment and exile to the "sea-grit Cyprus" is completely undermined by Helen's voice indicating she "never went to Troy". In other words, it was all folly and completely fallacious. A delirious message about the inanity of war.

Here we have Seferis' conceit of the Hellenistic past and present playing out simultaneously. He uses a call and response between the Greek chorus and Teucer. Despite Teucer's familial connections to Troy on his mother's side he fought with the Greeks as a great archer but failed to kill his cousin, Hector. Later, Teucer seized Cyprus and named its fair city after his homeland, the island of Salamis, from which he was banished. In this five stanza poem of free verse we hear the Greek chorus calling thrice: "The nightingales won't let you sleep in Platres." Like a modern day insomniac Seferis, as Teucer, considers the convictions and price paid for a phantom cause. This man, in a state of exile, suffers the loss of his country. It is impossible to tell the real Helen from the counterfeit or the real body from the tunic. The nightingale, referenced eight times throughout the poem, laments the price paid in the ongoing dispute around the acquisition of territory that marked the Hellenistic world then and now. The nightingale is the embodiment of female suffering and mourning in Greek tragedy.

The first stanza is framed by the Greek chorus lamenting the call of the nightingales which "won't let you sleep in Platres". Seferis had stayed in this town in Cyprus and suggested, tongue in cheek, that the song of these birds affected his insomnia. More interestingly is to imagine Seferis as Teucer relentlessly awakened to a personal state of exile, displacement and dispossession. The present is haunted by the past and so the plaintive song moves across "sundered bodies, on the souls/ of those who know they will not return". The Hellenic world is a watery place of the real and the phantom; the enslaved and the invader. The synaesthesia of the "Blind voice" of the nightingale suggests a sensory collision impacting "the frenzied slave-woman". In the second stanza Seferis, as Teucer, wonders about the trustworthy nature of naming. On the one hand those exiled from their place of belonging seek anchorage in the past but on the other hand the real or phantom nature of these longed for places is questionable: "Platres: where is Platres? And this island: who knows it?...Truth, where's the truth?" There is no sure ground upon which he can place his feet and call home. Indeed, the wander's life happens in the threshold space: "my fate...wavers/ between the last sword of some Ajax/ and another Salamis." It is an existence that is caught somewhere between legend and underwhelming ordinariness. It is a world waxing and waning: "The moon/ rose from the sea like Aphrodite/ covered the Archer's stars, now moves to find/ the heart of Scorpio, and alters everything." The celestial Hellenic skies track the very notion of inconstancy played out by the gods over the fate of Paris, Helen and the entire Greek and Trojan population. Teucer's final line in this stanza is the existential angst spoken by every man in the modern age: "my fate: that of a man who missed his target." This is Seferis at his best.

Throughout the third stanza the Greek chorus, sung by slave women and Helen, reminds us that at the heart of nation making is catastrophe brought about by illusion. Helen is the illusion. She never existed or at least only as a figment of the imagination of men. She is what is needed for men to writhe and roil in the name of territorial disputes. Helen is whatever man, the warrior, the poet, the critic wants her to be. So when her voice cuts across this third stanza it merely disrupts an epic tale that has generated story telling from that point hence: "'It isn't true, it isn't true,' she cried./ 'I didn't board the blue bowed ship./ I never went to valiant Troy.'" The legend is unsure whether Helen was raped and abducted or whether she went willingly; this is because she has become all things to all men. Perhaps she was not in Troy; thus "She whom we hunted" was an excuse for their own orgasmic war rush. While Teucer asks the whereabouts of truth in stanza two, in stanza three Helen answers not here. Not only is home unstable but the realities upon which it is built is without foundation. In stanza three Teucer is unable to reconcile the fact that despite her being "a phantom image...for ten whole years we slaughtered ourselves for Helen". This is the heart of the poetic dilemma. Great destruction comes about as a result of what is created in the imagination of men. The voluptuous and salacious lingering on the fetishized body parts of Helen in this stanza perfectly articulate the dilemma man has made for man: "Breasts girded high, the sun in her hair...on shoulders, thighs and knees;/ the skin alive, and her eyes/ with the large eyelids." Yet an illusion it always was and is: "Paris lay with a shadow as though it were a solid being."

The 4th and 5th stanzas intensifies the tragedy of the Hellenic world past and present. Teucer's voice is a 20th century invocation to acknowledge the carnage and grief caused by illusive desire: "Great suffering had desolated Greece... for a linen undulation, a filmy cloud,/ a butterfly's flicker, a wisp of swan's down,/ an empty tunic." Helen is a nothingness. A whimsy, an invention and most definitely a folly. As we segue into the 5th stanza we know that while the Hellenic world remains forever awake to the lamentations of the "Tearful bird" that "won't let you sleep", it paradoxically "isn't fated" to be heard. History repeating itself is central to Seferis' imagined community, as it creates and destroys itself endlessly. It is the collision between the past and the present that generates a tidal ebb and flow across the archipelago of legendary truths.

We have come the full circle from the "sea-girt Cyprus" to the "sea-kissed Cyprus"; an island encircled by enchantment and augury in the name of Helen. The modern day poet Teucer is "moored alone with this fable" and as such is an isolate and forever dispossessed of a secure foothold on the truth. The anaphora of "if it's true that it is a fable,/ if it's true that mortals ... if it's true/ that in future years" indicates a persistent desire to know what is the truth because the coda that has generated the Hellenic homeland has been hitherto deceptive. We are left with the foreshadowing that "some other Teucer,/ or some Ajax or Priam or Hecuba,/ or someone unknown and nameless...isn't fated to hear...that so much suffering, so much life,/ went into the abyss". It was all for nothing: "all for an empty tunic, all for a Helen." I think this is a wonderful poem that speaks to the way in which we nostalgically yearn for the past and for the place of belonging that we believe is rightfully ours. I think it also is a chilling reminder that the traumas of the 20th century and onwards, with its world wars and civil wars, as well as the ongoing countless atrocities associated with occupation. The Trojan war that form the legendary underlay to all Western storytelling and imagination resurfaces in modern warfare. Moreover, the name of Helen remains an aide-mémoire for us to reflect upon the emptiness behind man's desire to have all that is not his to have.

Mythistorema by Giorgos Seferis (1935)

Translated Edmund Keeley

Argonauts

And a soul
if it is to know itself
must look
into its own soul:
the stranger and enemy, we've seen him in the mirror.

They were good, the companions, they didn't complain
about the work or the thirst or the frost,
they had the bearing of trees and waves
that accept the wind and the rain
accept the night and the sun
without changing in the midst of change.
They were fine, whole days
they sweated at the oars with lowered eyes
breathing in rhythm
and their blood reddened a submissive skin.
Sometimes they sang, with lowered eyes
as we were passing the deserted island with the Barbary figs
to the west, beyond the cape of the dogs
that bark.
If it is to know itself, they said
it must look into its own soul, they said
and the oar's struck the sea's gold
in the sunset.
We went past many capes many islands the sea
leading to another sea, gulls and seals.
Sometimes disconsolate women wept
lamenting their lost children

and others frantic sought Alexander the Great
and glories buried in the depths of Asia.

We moored on shores full of night-scenes,
the birds singing, with waters that left on the hands
the memory of a great happiness.
But the voyages did not end.
Their souls became one with the oars and the oarlocks
with the solemn face of the prow
with the rudder's wake
with the water that shattered their image.
The companions died one by one,
with lowered eyes. Their oars
mark the place where they sleep on the shore.

No one remembers them. Justice

    This is the 4th poem in a cycle of 24 free verse poems. The Greek word *mythistorema* was coined in the 19th century and it is used to describe myth, history and story. This cycle of poems was a pioneering poetic composition, resultant of Modernism and influenced by T.S.Eliot's *The Wasteland*. In *Mythistorema* Seferis explores the continuous parallels between the contemporary world and that of antiquity; the way in which suffering is neither unique nor modern; and the impossibilities of returning home. In poem four of the cycle the Argonauts, the companions to Odysseus, work hard to return the wanderer home but know that history, memory and imagination will fail them. Indeed, the ten year odyssey to Ithaca from Troy after the completion of the war, is only made possible because of the legendary sailors of the Argo. As an interesting aside, Jason and the Argonauts predates Homer by 70 years. This 4th poem in *Mythistorema* is in many ways the heartland of Seferis' poetics. Throughout stanza one, two and three there are prophecies and auguries; both offering blessing and foreboding. Not only do all three stanzas offer a way of looking ahead but simultaneously they offer an opportunity of looking back.
    In this poem there are three stanzas of unequal length, book ended by fragmented sentences. The opening fragment is "Argonauts"; suggesting that legend not only gives witness to the exilic self but can offer insights and sage advice. The axiom that follows in the first stanza, haunts poem four: "a soul/ if it is to know itself/ must look/ into its own soul." This palindromic truth appears in the second stanza and then comes to a sticky resolution in the final stanza. Here are the legendary sea men of Greek mythology, accompanying the uber wanderer and offering philosophical guidance. Have the journeys of their past equipped them with this knowledge? Is the journey to the homeland a metaphor to discover one's identity? The Argonauts' truth indicates that the spiritual or immaterial part of the self is found by looking inward; not by searching outwardly. There is some degree of comfort in this for the diaspora or person in exile, if homeland, as it once was, is forever denied. Surely Odysseus must have thought that he would never reach home as he met challenge after

challenge on his way back to love. The Argonauts warn us about what type of looking is required; looking into one's "own soul" not into the "mirror". The separation between the physical and the metaphysical is absolute. Indeed, we are reminded that looking into our own reflection will result in seeing "the stranger and enemy". I like to think about this idea, that our material and physical selves do not show us our metaphysical selves; for that we must look elsewhere.

The second stanza offers a laudation of the Argonauts. We learn that they were "good...companions" and "didn't complain". Seferis uses metaphors from the grand narrative of nature to convey the Argonauts' strength: "they had the bearing of trees and waves/ that accept the wind and rain/ accept the night and the sun." Indeed, when all around them is changing they are stalwart and indefatigable. The Argonauts "sweated at the oars with lowered eyes/ breathing in rhythm/ and their blood reddened a submissive skin". This heroic and legendary support given to Odysseus is a physical commitment and mental submission to the trials and tribulations visited upon those who wander. The phrase "with lowered eyes" is repeated when the Argonauts "were passing the deserted island with the Barbary figs...beyond the cape of the dogs/ that bark". Their submission is also their souls' protection from temptation. This cape, south of Athens, is Cape Skyllaion also known as the Cape of Dogs, and is so named after Ovid's tale of Scylla whose hungry heart led to her tragic demise. In other words, the channel of Poros through which they rowed was narrow and dangerous because of the call of its lure. Like a chant they cite the axiom "to know itself...it must look into its own soul" in order to steer themselves and Odysseus beyond these waters. Their commitment is rewarded because their "oars struck the sea's gold/ in the sunset". We are reminded that this journey to find one's homeland and therefore one's self and soul, is haunted by perils of the heart where the "disconsolate women wept/ lamenting their lost children".

The third stanza simultaneously offers hope and despair and then ultimately culminates in "Justice", which ironically is that "No one remembers them". To reach homeland, and thus to know oneself and one's soul, cannot be achieved. What they have instead are traces of life in all its anticipatory joy in the "shores full of night-scenes/ the birds singing...memory of great happiness" and traces of desolation in the death of the Argonauts: "The companions died one by one/ with lowered eyes. Their oars/ mark the place where they sleep on the shore." This is the unexpected because Homeric legend does ensure Odysseus' return; what Seferis offers is a contemporary tale of his Hellenic world where the wanderer in search of his homeland, his identity and soul cannot in fact succeed. The journey of the exiled self is plagued by centrifugal and centripetal forces: of diasporic wandering away and nostalgic yearning to return. This pull push movement on the watery archipelago "shattered their image". Thus, the ongoing voyage in the Hellenic world, which simultaneously occurs in antiquity and in the present, is one fated to never find landfall in one's homeland. Why? The Hellenic hero of yesterday and today has allowed this exilic state to become his soul: "Their souls became one with the oars and the oarlocks."

And the Winner is...

Pablo Neruda 1971 "for a poetry that with the action of an elemental force brings alive a continent's destiny and dreams"

Pablo Neruda was born Ricardo Eliecer Neftali Reyes Basoalto in 1904. During his life he was a Chilean consul, Communist, Senator, fugitive, close advisor to President Allende, murdered victim of the Pinochet regime in 1973 but above else a poet for his nation. During the first three decades of Neruda's life Chile was caught in a cultural struggle where new social groups agitated for political rights. The Catholic Church's stranglehold on Latin American life was being challenged by the rising groups of nationalists, anarchists, communists and fascists. There was little balance between political unity and ethnic or regional diversity. Neruda was preoccupied with national identity and he, like many artists, was given a major role in society and enjoyed a moral power and public status unparalleled in Europe. Neruda's poetry reflects the Modernist's distrust of rhyme and meter, replacing it oftentimes with rupture, discontinuity and alienation and the occasional evocation of everyday speech. Neruda's time away from Chile in the consulate from 1925 to 1935 was formative; and this was intensified when he was forced underground from 1948 to 1952. His nostalgia for home, while abroad and in hiding, would trouble his writing for the rest of his life. Neruda's poetry galvanised workers to continue to fight for justice and the basic human rights denied them; his poetry contributed to a socialist government's reimagining of a nation; his poetry rethought Latin American history. Neruda died some two weeks after the 11th September 1973 coup. He was suffering from prostate cancer but was killed by an injection of Staphylococcus aureus bacterium, a highly toxic poison, authorised by Pinochet. Despite curfews and military surveillance thousands of people walked behind his cortege to the general cemetery singing the national anthem of Chile and the Internationale.

I moved to live in Chile during the early 90s. I was then in my late twenties and my daughter was only three at the time. I taught at one of the colleges and had a passionate affair with everything Chilean. I visited Neruda's museums in some of the homes he lived. I learnt Spanish and traveled north and south of Chile; I also holidayed in different parts of Latin America during this time. The father of my best friend there in Chile had been a fellow poet and so much of her childhood was spent visiting Neruda in his home at Isla Negra. She had photos of Neruda spinning her and her sister about in an old wooden barrel along the flat sandy beach. I met lots of people who knew him, as well as many people who had lost loved ones during the coup in the 70s. Even when I lived in Chile there were tanks in the street, armed soldiers stopping you in your vehicle and a military presence ever vigilant around Santiago where I lived. When I eventually returned to Sydney, I decided to write a PhD on the way in which Neruda, along with two other poets, wrote poetry to create a place of belonging for the people of his nation. The geo political nation state had failed them so seriously that his poetry would be their salvation.

Central America by Pablo Neruda (1950)
Translated by Elizabeth Guy

Land slender as a whip,
brewing like a storm,
your passage in Honduras,

>   your blood in Santo Domingo,
>   at night,
>   your eyes from Nicaragua
>   touch me, call me, entreat me,
>   and throughout the American land
>   I touch doors to speak
>   I touch bound tongues
>   Raise curtains, plunge
>   My hand into blood:
>   O my suffering
>   Land, O death gasp
>   Of the great silence established
>   O nations of long agony
>   O weeping waistline.

In South America the earth was seen to be nurturing and abundant like a mother figure; the Mayas believed they were fashioned out of maize and thus buried their newborn's umbilical cord and placenta in the earth. On the third voyage to the Americas, Columbus explained that the difference in measurements in the newly discovered sky convinced him that the earth was not spherical as he had believed but was shaped in the form of a woman's breast, with the nipple high up near the sky, and for this reason ships could rise on a gentle incline. On this lovely nipple of land, Columbus situated Paradise. To feminise South America in this way was an uncanny anticipation of the rape and violation that was to occur in the name of colonisation. The continent as desecrated and dishonoured is taken up by many South American poets who wrote in the wake of the Conquistador nightmare. Neruda wanted to avenge this homeland and so in the *Canto General* from which this poem is taken, he refers to the Conquistadors as those who rape, violate, spoil, outrage, torture and all but destroy the original America

The words "slender", "blood" and "eyes"; the line "touch me, call me, entreat me"; and the final image "weeping waistline" are tell-tale signs of Neruda's love affair with his feminised homeland formed by misery and suffering, oppression and hunger. His nation space is both greater than and less than the geo-political nation state of Chile. It is Central and all of South America but it is also the immediate locale of his beloved's body or the salt mines in Antofagasta or the port town of Valparaiso that falls down into the sea. Published in his formidable, epic and Whitmanesque *Canto General* in 1950, Neruda is certainly reading this nation space as one exploited throughout history while still in a state of trauma. As a poet he sees the importance of offering political representation: "I touch doors to speak/ I touch bound tongues/ Raise curtains,/ plunge/ My hand into blood."

To be the voice of a nation is to experience firsthand what the subaltern endures: doors are closed, tongues are bound and curtains are shut. So, the poet touches, raises and plunges in order to reach into the heart of his nation. At the end of this poem there is a repeated apostrophe to his homeland: "O my suffering/ Land, O death gasp/ Of the great silence established/ O nations of long agony/ O weeping waistline." This direct address to an imagined and poetic nation space is palpably tender and heartfelt. The exhalation in the anaphora "O" becomes a litany of suffering that cannot be forgotten. In many ways, nations are imagined as the feminine to be seduced. They are dark mysteries to be raped, plundered and unravelled. Neruda's entire oeuvre is a love song, filled with yearning and pain, for a nation space that needs to be rescued from the brutality of its past and present.

Pequena America by Pablo Neruda (1952)
Translated Elizabeth Guy

When I look at the shape
of America on the map,
love, it is you I see:
the heights of copper on your head,
your breasts, wheat and snow,
your slender waist,
racing rivers that palpitate, sweet
hills and meadows
and in the cold of the south your feet end
its geography duplicated in gold
...
And the red thickness
of the bush where
thirst and hunger lie in wait.
And here my expansive country receives me
...
Still more, when I see you lying down
I see your skin, the color of wild oats,
the nationality of my affection.
Because from your shoulders
the cane cutter
of blazing Cuba
looks at me, covered with dark sweat,
and from your throat
fishermen who tremble
in the damp houses of the shore
sing to me their secret.

Neruda's formative landscape is feminine. His poetics capture the feminine as the primordial site of belonging. Here in this poem the geo-politically defined nation state is usurped by the beloved: "When I look at the shape / of America on the map,/ love, it is you I see." She is a cartographic body of desire, the nation space. Racing down her body, from her head to her toes, Neruda tracks the valuable resources of his nation space: "copper...wheat...rivers...meadows." The nation space will sustain and nurture him and his people. The metaphor of the naked woman's body as site of belonging suggests intimacy; on the one hand a longing by the lover or citizen and on the other hand a hunger for penetration: "my expansive country receives me."

Not only does the citizen want the site of belonging but the site of belonging wants the citizen. Thus, the nation space as constructed here by Neruda subverts the hierarchies in the body politic. Within the body of the beloved nation is "the cane cutter/ of blazing Cuba" and the "fishermen who tremble/ in the damp houses". These are the people of his nation who look to him and "sing" to him. Neruda translates their song into poetry because the body of the beloved, his nation space, has enabled him to do so. She is "the nationality of his affection".

The Fugitive III by Pablo Neruda (1950)
Translated Elizabeth Guy

And I, amid street after street of silence
through the tyrant's soiled city.
Ah! I was the essence of silence
seeing how much love upon love fell
from my eyes on my breast.
Because that street and the other and the snowy
night's threshold, and the nocturnal
solitude of beings, of my people,
submerged, dark, in the slum corpses,
everything, the last window
with its little bouquet of false light,
the crammed black coral
of room after room, my country's
never-spent wind,
everything was mine, everything
raised to me in the silence
a loving mouth filled with kisses.

With his commitment to the fall of fascism in Spain and the rise of the International Communist Party, Neruda's notoriety increased. He could not escape the eyes of the world. During the 1940s and 1950s, as the international power brokers demanded people choose between the left or right, Neruda came under constant surveillance. When communism was outlawed in 1948 by President Videla and Neruda delivered his *I Accuse* speech in parliament a warrant for his arrest was issued. In this infamous speech Neruda reads the names of the miners and their families who are been held in concentration camps. Afterwards he went underground, living in exile, hiding from the ever-watchful government. These years of clandestine living from 1948 to 1952 allowed Neruda to gaze back into the intimate world of his oppressed people.

Here, in this poem the poet gazes in upon the lives of the slum dwelling Chileans: "street after street of silence/ through the tyrant's soiled city." In banning communism many leftist supporters like Neruda believed that the ordinary people would remain silenced and invisible. The exiled poet is given sanctuary by the all-seeing partisan poor who hide him from the authority's myopic surveillance: "Ah! I was the essence of silence/ seeing how much love upon love fell/ from my eyes on my breast." The exhalation, the sibilance and the repetition of "love" expresses the intimacy found between poet and partisan. Here are his people who need championing and rescue: "my people,/ submerged, dark, in the slum corpses." Yet these very people who seek his voice to represent them, give him everything: "everything was mine, everything/ raised to me in the silence." Thus, the exchange between the poet and partisans is "a loving mouth filled with kisses". Neruda's poetry shaped and reshaped histories, brought to the fore what had previously been discarded and challenged the people of Chile to take command of their own destinies.

The Fable of the Siren and the Drunks by Pablo Neruda (1958)
Translated Elizabeth Guy

All these men were there inside
when she entered completely naked
they had been drinking and began to spit on her
she understood nothing as she had recently come from the river
she was a siren that had lost her way
the insults ran over her glistening flesh
...
She did not know tears so she did not cry
she did not know clothes so she did not dress
they tattooed her cigarette ends and burnt corks
and they fell down on the tavern floor with laughter
she did not speak because she did not known speech
her eyes are the color of faraway love,
her arms of topaz gems
her lips carved in the light of coral
...
And by and by she left by the tavern door
...
And without looking back she swam again
she swam towards nothing, she swam to die.

Chile is a high tension tight rope between the subaltern and the powerful. This poem captures the disturbing experience of the thin and sinuous body of the siren being abused and ridiculed by the drunks at the tavern. She represents the powerless and the language-less, in contrast to the dominant and potent. The siren's entrance evokes an aggressive response and she is branded by the drunks' cruelty, rejection and lack of understanding. The siren simply appears at the tavern, she irrupts into the world of excess and commotion, babble and rioting. She is hunger, she is desire, slithering into and disturbing men. The siren doesn't cry because "she did not know tears" and "she did not speak because she did not know speech". Indeed, she is exposed and naked to the condemnation of this drunken court.

She is without language. She is both desirable and terrifying and thus elicits fear. She is the Janus face of hunger because she is both the incarnation and victim of lack: her lack of language and their lack of sympathy. In leaving the tavern she turns and without looking back swims into the mirror of the river. Her return is a gesture towards self-annihilation. She has been excluded from the site of excess, language and power, represented by the tavern and the culture therein. This exclusion starves her into a state of nothingness and eventual death. Neruda's poem captures the tremulous consciousness of the subaltern, she who cannot speak, in a nation space suffering from the psychosis of starvation.

Ode to Salt by Pablo Neruda (1954)
Translated by Elizabeth Guy

This salt
in the saltcellar
I once saw in the mines.
I know
you won't
believe me,
but
it sings,
salt sings, the skin
of the salt mines,
sings
with a mouth smothered
by the earth.
I shuddered in those
solitudes
when I heard
the voice
of
the salt
in the desert.
Near Antofagasta
all
the nitrous pampas
dreams:

a
broken
voice,
an injurious
song.

Then in its caves
the salt jewels, mountains
of buried light,
transparent cathedral,
crystal of the sea, oblivion
of the waves.
And then on every table
in this world,
salt,
your substance
nimble
sprinkling
the vital light
upon
our food. Preserver
of the ancient
holds of ships,
discoverer
on
the high seas,
matter
moving forward
into the unknown, shifting
tracks of foam.
Dust of the sea, in you
the tongue
receives a kiss
from the ocean night:
your ocean is the taste in every
seasoned dish
and here the smallest,
miniature
wave from the saltcellar
reveals to us

not only domestic whiteness,
but the taste of infinitude.

Hunger is preserved as a national inheritance in this ode. Here Neruda celebrates salt which ignites the taste, increases appetite and preserves food that will sustain his nation. Surrounding the idea of salt in this piquant ode is an entreaty to ordinary workers to own not just the means of production but also the history out of which they have emerged. Neruda opens with an intimate voice convincing the reader that the salt he saw in the salt mines "sings/ salt sings, the skin/ of the salt mines,/ sings". The song of salt is politically invigorating; whether it is the song of tonnes of mined salt pouring from the funnels onto the nitrate mounds below, or the relentless shrill of the salt miner's drill, or the workers' song. It is sung "with a mouth smothered" and "a/ broken/ voice" because it is "an injurious song" from the nitrate mines of Antofagasta, the wasteland of the north. It is a "voice" of the mines and of the deserts, but also of laboring solidarity and proletarian recognition. Indeed, it is an ode that sings as a descant to the Communist Internationale. In hearing the song of salt, we are in the ravaged lands of Chile's exploited workers and mined northern regions; we are present to the voice that has been smothered and silenced by a life of oppression and non-representation. In listening we are empowered by the song, just like those who sing.

Neruda then brings together salt's commonplace associations. So salt is "mountains/ of buried light,/ translucent cathedral,/ crystal of the sea, oblivion/ of the waves". Salt illuminates because it conveys knowledge, mystery and beauty. Indeed, it is everywhere: land, sea and sky. Salt is the grain of the nation space, the substance of the sacred. Salt is gritty and ethereal, like the salt of the earth: the workers. Salt is used by everyone, irrespective of class. It is a democratic substance because it is "on every table/ in this world", its power "sprinkling/ the vital light/ upon/ our food". It is central to Neruda's philosophy and politics that in the infinitesimal is the infinite. Neruda's salty ode ignites the tastebuds and increases the appetite of his readers. In the act of remembering, the descendants of exploitation can break the cycle of oppression. Therefore, salt is the "Preserver/ of the ancient/ holds of ships" where food and dreams were transported from Spain to South America. The ode also suggests the middle passage bringing the history of slavery to Latin America. Salt will "discover/ on/ the high seas,/ matter/ moving forward/ into the unknown, shifting/ tracks of foam". Salt represents the ongoing exploitation because salt mines in South America are now owned by first world companies. To taste discovery and adventure the earliest sailor, an old salt, roamed the watery highways to lands brimming with hitherto unplundered treasures. Indeed, the nation space of Chile, captured in the glittering images of treasure "caves", "salt jewels", "mountains/ of buried light" and "translucent cathedrals" would have crystallised an old salt's dreams.

Here the nation space of Neruda's poetics is the beloved body of the sea as it promises to reveal all the mysteries of its elusive marine night: "Dust of the sea, in you/ the tongue/ receives a kiss/ from the ocean night." Chile is day and night, land and sea, sky and earth, exploitation and discovery, cry and silence. Like salt, Neruda's verse sprinkles desire and hunger over the food already offered at the table. It whets the appetite and stimulates the miners to demand more than their thin destinies of poverty. His poetry preserves what will sustain his people. In the holds of his books, the story of his people will be transported to a new and reimagined nation space. His verse is a national song of solidarity, one that can be exported to the world.

And the Winner is...

1992 Derek Walcott "for a poetic oeuvre of great luminosity, sustained by a historical vision, the outcome of a multicultural commitment"

Walcott's nation space of St Lucia in the Caribbean has been colonised over 14 times by different European invaders. This Nobel Laureate imagines St Lucia as female and inscribes on her body enormous hunger where enough is never enough. The ambiguity of this site is that while it is a coveted beauty commodified as paradise for the tourist, it is also objectified as a black Helen for whom men will lay down their lives. Walcott writes his epic *Omeros,* a word that means Homer in Greek, where St Lucia is a microcosm of world history with its great movements of migrants and refugees. Walcott often compares Helen to the island itself: she passes from man to man as the island passes from ruler to ruler but like the island, she has a beauty and individuality that defies ownership.

The name Helen is a variation of Lucy and thus the lush black beauty of Helen in *Omeros,* and elsewhere in his poetry, provides an axis about which the horned island and its elemental men rotate. His nation space is one that has known and experienced the history of lusting for the other by the self. Thus, Walcott imagines his nation space as one of excess, a cultural meta-archipelago without limits and without centers, a creolization, a restless mutation and a history of mythology. Thus, Walcott gorges on Greek mythology, the Old Testament and the Caribbean. He chooses to write his epic poem in terza rima, the form used by Dante in *The Divine Comedy*. A difficult form to sustain. *Omeros* follows the trials and tribulations of two fishermen, Achille and Philloctete, whose sufferings take on the heroic proportions of those in exile; the 300 page poem also navigates the history of the Caribbean across the narratives of exploitation, slavery and battles. In this section below we examine the way in which Helen is not solely the object of desire but subject of her odyssey. Her interaction with the retired British army officer, Major Plunkett, sets up the timeless connection between the gaze, patriarchy and colonisation.

Omeros: Book Two Chapter Eighteen by Derek Walcott (1990)

The bracelet coiled like a snake. He heard it hissing:
Her housebound slavery could be your salvation.
You can pervert God's grace and adapt His blessing

to your advantage and dare His indignation
at a second Eden with its golden apple,
henceforth her shadow will glide on every mirror

in this house, and however that fear may appal,

go to the glass and see original error
in the lust you deny, all History's appeal

lies in this Judith from a different people,
whose long arm is a sword, who has turned your head
back to her past, her tribe; you live in terror

of age before beauty, the way that an elder
longer for Helen on the parapets, or that bed.
Like an elder trembling for Susanna, naked.

He murmured to the mirror: No. my thoughts are pure.
They're meant to help her people, ignorant and poor.
But these, smiled the bracelet, are the vows of empire.

Black maid or blackmail, her presence in the stone house
was oblique but magnetic. Every hour of the day
even poking around the pigs, he knew where she was;

he could see her shadow through the sheets of laundry,
and since she and her shadow were the same, the sun
behind her often made their bent silhouette seem

naked, or sometimes, carrying a clean basin
of water to the bleaching stones, she wore the same
smile that made a drama out of every passing.

Helen not only represents conquest but the island itself. In so doing, she is the object of beauty, temptation and a new found Eden. Helen emerges out of the narratives of Homer, the Old Testament, slavery, colonialism and tourism. Thus, Walcott constructs and deconstructs the post-colonial subjectivity of his nation space. We take up this epic poem at the point where Helen has seized a bracelet from the jewelry box of Plunkett's wife and therefore takes control of both the manacles that originally enslaved her people and the representation of her as Eve, the ultimate femme fatale. The wonderful onomatopoeia of the "hissing" snake indicates temptation is close at hand along with the perversion and adaptation of the divine plan. While on the one hand this gives licence to Plunkett on the other, he sees Helen as both "this Judith" capable of beheading the once great commander, Holofernes, and "Susanna, naked" ready to outwit the drooling elderly voyeurs. No doubt this gives him pause.

Plunkett vacillates between justifying his desire to conquer and responding to the oath of imperialism: "He murmured to the mirror: No. My thoughts are pure./ they're meant to help her people, ignorant and poor./ But these, smiled the bracelet, are the vows of empire." The lust he denies stalks the last three terza rimas of this section as Helen moves about his peripheral vision. She is a "shadow", an insubstantial self, a darkness, the other and a menace that cannot be caught. The oppressed are constructed as needing salvation from their endless state of ignorance and poverty and yet Plunkett becomes more and more aware that the post-colonial subject is all powerful now that the "Black maid" mobilises "blackmail". Here Helen is in control and this is seen in the way "she wore the same/ smile that made a drama out of every passing." Her self-awareness troubles the narrative of Helen as conquerable object. Walcott considers the elusive goal of the conqueror as well as the powerhouse Helen has become, in the post-colonial narrative.

Omeros is an epic poem of eight thousand lines, 64 chapters, seven books and 25 characters. The narrator is Omeros, Homeric grand narrator and blind bard, but he is also vagrant or wandering poet and thus, by default, Walcott himself. Walcott is not simply reworking Homer's story in the Caribbean, but is interested in the failures of mythical structures and lines of tradition to represent the multifarious tensions of his own Caribbean culture. Many characters have names from Greek mythology but keep in mind that African slaves were often given such names. Thus, Walcott captures the ordinary people of his island in their own legendary aura. The sea itself is part and parcel of the nation of the Caribbean. Walcott mashes together ancient and modern histories and mythologies. Like Virgil guiding Dante through hell, Omeros guides the reader through the suffering inflicted on his people via slavery and colonialization. Walcott's nation space offers little succor, provides less protection and is without closure; it is perpetually self-reproducing. This site of belonging is ambiguous. *Omeros* is the struggle to create and reflect the freedom and sovereignty of language.

The Spoiler's Return by Derek Walcott (1981)

The Spoiler's Return is a 200 and 18 line satire in heroic couplets and dedicated to Earl Lovelace. This poem plays to an audience who is casual about commitment, ashamed of their speech and moved only by the farcical or tragi-comic. Walcott argues that the last thing his people need is an idealisation of poverty. *The Spoiler's Return* comes out of the theatre of poverty and degeneracy where everything is possible: sex, obscenity, absolutism and freedom. It is a poem that investigates movement and stillness, as Spoiler returns from the dead with the message of salvation. In this case Spoiler goes "back down" because the limers "pass[ed] him straight"; they were deaf to his message. This lengthy poem targets censorship, political violence, urban rot, lawlessness and insularity. Despite this, art and language are celebrated and renewal and redemption lurk in the shadows. *The Spoiler's Return* exposes the Caribbean as the site of non-paradise created by colonialism and capitalism, which translates into modern corporations controlling natural resources and tourism. Truth, calypso, carnival and satire are the four strands that work continuously throughout this poem but for now let's just examine truth and calypso.

> I sit high on this bridge in Laventille,
> watching that city where I left no will
> but my own conscience and rum eaten wit,

and limers passing see me where I sit,
ghost in brown gabardine, bones in a sack,
and bawl: "Ay, Spoiler, boy! When you come back?"
And those who bold don't feel they out of place
to peel my limeskin back, and see a face
with eyes as cold as a dead macajuel,
and if they still can talk, I answer: "Hell".

The trickster, Spoiler, arrives from Hell on a two week ticket of leave to cast his contempt upon the limers of Laventille, Trinidad. The term "limers" is given to the idle in the Caribbean. The image is one of fascinating horror where the decomposing corpse of Spoiler harangues the limers "to peel my limeskin back, and see a face/ with eyes as cold as a dead macajuel", so that in their apathetic dead lives, the Trinidadians can come face to face with the deadly vision of their redemption. *The Spoiler's Return* tells the truth, just for fun. Overlooking the Caribbean from "high on the bridge" the dead addresses the graveyard of Caribbean apathy, corruption and hunger.

The calypso is an improvised song or ballad composed and sung by West Indians on festive and public occasions. To sing calypso, with its deliberately outrageous word games, is designed to emphasise the singer's self-appointed role as public spokesperson. Calypsonians sing in a fearless manner about any subject. They sound out inequality, injustice, loss, fear, isolation, bigotry and abuse. Calypso is polyphonic and uses a range of instruments to create the music of the West Indian struggle. As a calypso *The Spoiler's Return* exploits the creolization of language and sharp satiric wit or picong. Spoiler's soul is lost already to the underworld but he resurfaces in Laventille, the socially and economically depressed area of Port-of-Spain. He calls to the limers to "tell Desperadoes", a typical name given to the calypsonian steel bands, that he cannot be silenced. Metaphoric brilliance and cadences of the folk language exemplify calypso:

Tell Desperadoes when you reach the hill,
I decompose buy I composing still
...
Is crab climbing crab-back, in a crab-quarrel,
and going round and round in the same barrel,
is sharks with shirt-jacs, sharks with well-pressed fins,
ripping we small-fry off with razor grins
...
So crown and mitre me Bedbug the First –
the gift of mockery with which I'm cursed
is just a insect biting Fame behind,
a vermin swimming in a glass of wine,
that, dipped out with a finger, bound to bite
its saving host, ungrateful parasite,
whose sting, between the cleft arse and its seat,

reminds Authority that man is just meat,
a moralist as mordant as the louse
that the good husband brings from the whorehouse

The bug which bites is the bite of picong and everyone is potentially a victim. Moreover, goodness and morality are relative. Walcott uses original compositions sung by Trinidadian calypsonians and traditional patois such as appropriating the term "boy" which once denoted servitude and inferiority but now affection and familiarity. Walcott also refers to "limers" for friends passing the time of day, "hot boy" for Satan, "Caiso" for calypso, "bohbohl" for bribery and "picong" for biting satiric wit. The Caribbean Walcott knows is the hotbed of every tongue, the infamous Babel:

Arnold's Phoenician trader reach this far,
selling you half-dead batteries for your car;
the children of Tagore, in funeral shroud,
curry favor and chicken from the crowd;
as for Creoles, check their house, and look,
you bust your brain before you find a book
...
and hear, drumming across the Caroni Plain,
the table of the Indian half hour
when twilight fills the mud huts of the poor,
to hear the tattered flags of drying corn
rattle a sky from which all the gods gone,
their bleached flags of distress waving to me
from shacks, adrift like rafts on a green sea,
"Things ain't go change, they ain't go change at all",
to my chorus: "Lord, I want to bawl."

The island of Trinidad, is the island of St Lucia which is every Caribbean island, the site of every diaspora, the place of every remembering, the moment of every forgetting that "must bawl". Thus, this is the home of the Lebanese trader, the indentured Indian and the descendant of African slaves. In this calypso Walcott sings of a homeland that moves across the plains and seas of various languages and sites that signal wreckage in a sea of nations. This idea of the ubiquitous island is as politically fragile and as powerfully subversive as hearing the "drumming across the Caroni Plain". The Indian table drum and the red prayer flag signal religious and national identity replicated thousands of kilometers from the original homeland. In using calypsonian song Walcott is naming the island as a seductive site of picong, performance and creole. Its calypsonian song lures the wanderer with its theatre of poverty and degradation. Thus, *The Spoiler's Return* challenges prevailing ideologies of knowledge; whether that is political authority or the intellectual truths of the Western exclusivity of English Literature and language. These notions of home, satire and carnival create and reflect Walcott's nation space.

The Light of the World by Derek Walcott (1985)

>   *Kaya now, got to have kaya now*
>   *Got to have kaya now*
>   *For the rain is falling*

Marley was rocking on the transport's stereo
and the beauty was humming the choruses quietly.
I could see where the lights on the planes of her cheek
streaked and defined them; if this were a portrait
you'd leave the highlights for last, these lights
silkened her black skin; I'd have put in an earring,
something simple, in good gold, for contrast, but she
wore no jewellery. I'm imagined a powerful and sweet
odour coming from her, as from a still panther,
and the head was nothing else but heraldic.
When she looked at me, then away from me politely
because any staring at strangers is impolite,
it was like a statue, a black Delacroix's
Liberty Leading the People, the gently bulging
whites of her eyes, the carved ebony mouth
the heft of the torso solid, and a woman's,
but gradually even that was going in the dusk,
except the line of her profile, and the highlight cheek,
and I thought, O Beauty, you are the light of the world!

It was not the only time I would think of that phrase
in the sixteen-eater transport that hummed between
Gros-Islet and the Market, with its grit of charcoal
and the litter of vegetables after Saturday's sales,
and the roaring rim shops, outside whose bright doors
you saw drunk women on pavements, the saddest of all things,
winding up their week, winding down their week.
The Market, as it closed on this Saturday night,
remembered a childhood of wandering gas lanterns
hung on poles at street corners, and the old roar
of vendors and traffic, when the lamplighter climbed,
hooked the lantern on its pole and moved on to another,
and the children turned their faces to its moth, their
eyes white as their nighties; the Market
itself was closed in tis involved darkness

and the shadows quarrelled for bread in the shops,
or quarrelled for the formal custom of quarrelling
in the electric rum shops. I remember the shadows.

The van was slowly filling in the darkening depot.
I sat in the front seat, I had no need for time.
I looked at two girls, one in a yellow bodice
and yellow shorts, with a flower in her hair
and lusted in peace, the other less interesting.
That evening I had walked the streets of the town
where I was born and grew up, thinking of my mother
with her white hair tinted by the dyeing dusk,
and the tilting box houses that seemed perverse
in their cramp; I had peered into parlours
with half-closed jalousies, at the dim furniture,
Morris chairs, a center table with wax flowers
and the lithograph of Christ of the Sacred Heart,
vendors still selling to the empty streets-
sweets, nuts, sodden chocolates, nut cakes, mints.

An old woman with a straw hat over her headkerchief
hobbled towards us with a basket; somewhere,
some distance off, was a heavier basket
that she couldn't carry. She was in a panic.
She said to the driver: "Pas quittez moi a terre"
which is, in her patois: "Don't leave me stranded,"
which is, in her history and that of her people:
"Don't leave me on earth," or, by a shift of stress:
"Don't leave me the earth" (for an inheritance);
"Pas quittez moi a terre, Heavenly transport
Don't leave me on earth, I've had enough of it."
The bus filled in the dark with heavy shadows
That would not be left on earth; no, that would be left
on the earth, and would have to make out.
Abandonment was something they had grown used to.

And I had abandoned them, I knew that there
sitting in the transport, in the sea-quiet dusk,
with men hunched in canoes, and the orange lights
from the Vigie headland, black boats on the water;
I, who could never solidify my shadow

to be one of their shadows, had left them their earth,
their white rum quarrels, and their coal bags,
their hatred of corporals, of all authority.
I was deeply in love with the woman by the window.
I wanted to be going home with her this evening.
I wanted her to have the key to our small house
by the beach at Gros-Islet; I wanted her to change
into a smooth white nightie that would pour like water
over the black rocks of her breasts, to lie
simply beside her by the ring of a brass lamp
with a kerosene wick, and tell her in silence
that her hair was like a hill forest at night,
that a trickle of rivers was in her armpits,
that I would buy her Benin if she wanted it,
and never leave her on earth. But the others, too.

Because I felt a great love that could bring me to tears,
and a pity that pricked my eyes like a nettle,
I was afraid I might suddenly start sobbing
on the public transport with the Marley going,
and a small boy peering over the shoulders
of the driver and me at the lights coming,
at the rush of the road in the country darkness,
with lamps in the houses on the small hills,
and thickets of stars; I had abandoned them,
I had left them on earth, I left them to sing
Marley's songs of a sadness as real as the smell
of rain on dry earth, of the smell of damp sand,
and the bus felt warm with their neighbourliness,
their consideration, and the polite partings

in the light of its headlamps. In the blare,
in the thud-sobbing music, the claiming scent
that came from their bodies. I wanted the transport
to continue forever, for no one to descend
and say a good night in the beams of the lamps
and take the crooked path up to the lit door,
guided by fireflies; I wanted her beauty
to come into the warmth of considerate wood,
to the relieved rattling of enamel plates
in the kitchen, and the tree in the yard,

but I came to my stop. Outside the Halcyon Hotel.
The lounge would be full of transients like myself.
Then I would walk with the surf up the beach.
I got off the van without saying good night.
Good night would be full of inexpressible love.
They went on in their transport, they left me the earth.

Then a few yards ahead the van stopped. A man
shouted my name from the transport window.
I walked up towards him. He held out something.
A pack of cigarettes had dropped from my pocket.
He gave it to me. I turned, hiding my tears.
There was nothing they wanted, nothing I could give them
but this thing I have called "The Light of the World".

This loose blank verse in iambic pentameter is made up of eight stanzas of uneven length. It's a beauty. I love the interplay between the title, "Light of the World" which we associate with salvation and deliverance dating back to the hymn created by Charles Wesley and George Elderkin in the mid 18th century, and this Caribbean creolization. In the Wesley hymn Jesus is the light of the world, an adaptation of the statement from the New Testament, John 12:46 "I have come into the world as a light, so that no one who believes in me should stay in darkness". Here in Walcott's poem the light of the world is "this thing", this testament, this poem that sings the song of his nation, peopled by the nameless and ordinary.

Like the "black Delacroix's/ Liberty Leading the People" the woman he sees across from him in the transport is glorified and iconised as "the beauty...humming the chorus quietly", she is his light of the world. Yet it is more than this, it is also the "old woman with a straw hat over her head kerchief" who allows Walcott to meditate and conjugate what it is to belong to this nation space that has left its people behind: "She said to the driver: "Pas quittez moi a terre"/ which is, in her patois: "Don't leave me stranded," ... Abandonment was something they had grown used to." Furthermore, the light of the world is the man who handed back the poet's dropped cigarettes because "there was nothing they wanted, nothing I could give them". In other words, here are his people offering him the light of their world. The poem's title works in contrast to the darkness that the poet is abandoned to, when he is dropped "Outside the Halcyon Hotel./ The lounge ...full of transients like myself". Walcott is doomed as transient and forever existing on the fringes of the nostalgic idyll of his past.

The poem commences with the laid back, laid bare tones of Bob Marley singing in Jamaican slang for a transportation to happiness. This opening rocks Walcott into a febrile obsession with "Beauty" that lasts the length of 19 lines in the first stanza. She is more than just an object of desire because she is the island writ large. Moreover, she is claiming back the island's post-colonial sovereignty in that she is the iconic declaration of revolution leading her people through the battlements of slavery and colonialism. We move along in that "sixteen-seater transport" into stanza two where we watch the packing up of the Gros-Islet Market. This moves Walcott to nostalgically consider his childhood where "the lamplighter climbed,/ hooked the lantern on its pole and moved on to another,/ and the children turned their faces to its moth". Throughout the poem we see light and shadows. The metaphor of turning to this "moth", this illumination within one's childhood memories, both haunts and nurtures Walcott. It is because of this luminescence that "the shadows" can be remembered. Without a doubt this poem is a song of that landscape of nostalgia, lived out in the present moment. The third stanza is about the poet as flâneur: "That evening I had walked the streets of the town/ where I was born...I had peered into parlours/ with half-closed jalousies, at the dim furniture,/ Morris chairs, a center table with wax flowers,/ and the lithograph of Christ of the Sacred Heart." Here is a world that is peppered with its colonial past; filled with the objects that articulate identity and represent memories, hopes and belief systems.

The narrative complication occurs in stanza five: "I had abandoned them, I knew that ... I, who could never solidify my shadow/ to be one of their shadows, had left them their earth." What's interesting here is the positive connotations associated with "shadow". Has their story been just a spectre in the story of slavery and colonialism? Has his people lived like shades in a Dantesque hell? Plagued all his life by neither being black enough nor white enough, Walcott writes about his hybrid identity. Moreover, he chose to leave St Lucia in order to pursue his career as poet and academic. He had relinquished his obligations to his own people and this is what keeps him separate from them. Meanwhile, darkness has descended outside transforming their local bus into "Heavenly transport". In many ways this leads Walcott to want the impossible: to "solidify" his shadow with those of his people. His only consolation is to fantasize about the iconic Beauty on the transport: "to lie/ simply beside her by the ring of a brass lamp." He longs to be one with his island because at the end of this stanza he vows he would never "leave her on earth. But the others, too." The journey in this transport, which flickers between light and dark, is an extended metaphor for his longing to be completely connected with his nation space.

Walcott parallels "Marley's songs of sadness" to his own grief in stanza six. This "great love" for his people, whom he "had abandoned", plays havoc with his own identity and sense of belonging. Nostalgia plays tricks with the imagination in determining what is real and what is salient. The post-colonial self, as represented by Walcott, stands on shifting ground. The meaning of their very language varies and fluctuates, as demonstrated in stanza six; moreover, the interplay of their landscape in darkness occasionally relieved by light suggests the ever-changing: "a small boy peering...at the lights coming...in the country darkness." The songs on the stereo are "as real as the smell/ of rain on dry earth"; the simile suggests that authenticity is somewhere located in sensory engagement. The poet's grief is about a world that cannot be preserved but rather remains just out of reach. The penultimate stanza builds to a crescendo of anxiety as the poet prepares to leave the transport, fully aware that whatever he "wanted ... the transport [would] continue forever [and] her beauty" would not be for him. Rather, his fate or inheritance is to be abandoned to grief: "full of inexpressible love...they left me on earth." The final stanza confirms his suspicions that his people want nothing from him: except this poem which "I have called, "The Light of the World"". Even in that moment Walcott reassigns the 18th century European hymn to the 20th century Caribbean poem. We are left with canticles of salvation that could transport one to happiness.

And the Winner is...

1995 Seamus Heaney "for works of lyrical beauty and ethical depth, which exalt everyday miracles and the living past".

Seamus Heaney left Belfast in 1972 when he could not endure The Troubles any more. A Catholic Nationalist, he writes of an Ireland invoked by two different systems of naming. The border that divides Britain's Ireland and Ireland's Ireland symbolises the fixed distance between these two political nation states. So, Heaney's nation space is the whole island of Ireland and is not yet named but alive in the imaginations of many. His poetry moves about in the divisions exploring Unionist and Republican realities and challenging Ireland imaginatively to re-enter an undivided self. Heaney's poetry gives testimony to transitional history, conceptual indeterminacy, cultural temporality and a wavering between vocabularies. Growing up a descendant of farmers and being privy to the sectarian apartheid conventions that denied him equal opportunities in schooling, health and housing, was to exist in a type of Catholic defeatism. The civil rights movement in the 1960s, The Troubles, and the Bloody Sunday Massacre in Derry had a profound impact on Heaney's poetry. Family becomes Heaney's ur-manuscript and works as a metaphor to understand Ireland's ongoing civil war. His poetry is informed by the landscape of his past and present; the domestic certainties of childhood, the familiar and familial, the ordinary and commonplace, the violence and the suffering. Finally, Heaney writes about exile and in so doing names a nation space in waiting, a site of belonging still yet to offer a sense of home. Exile means the curse of suffering, being hunted and abandoned, but it also means the miracle of escape and flight into an hitherto un-languaged world.

Station Island IX by Seamus Heaney (1984)

"My brain dried like spread turf, my stomach
Shrank to a cinder and tightened and cracked.
Often I was dogs on my own track
Of blood on wet grass that I could have licked.
Under the prison blanket, an ambush
Stillness I felt safe in settled round me.
Street lights came on in small towns, the bomb flash
Came before the sound, I saw country
I knew from Glenshane down to Toome
And heard a car I could make out years away
With me in the back of it like a white faced groom,
A hit-man on the brink, emptied and deadly.
When the police yielded my coffin, I was light
As my head when I took aim."

                              This voice from the blight
And hunger died through the black dorm:
There he was, laid out with a drift of mass cards
At his shrouded feet. Then the firing party's
Volley in the yard. I saw woodworm
In gate posts and door jambs, smelt mildew
From the byre loft where he watched and hid
From fields his draped coffin would raft through.
Unquiet soul, they should have buried you
In the bog where you threw your first grenade,
Where only helicopters and curlews
Make their maimed music, and sphagnum moss
Could teach you its medicinal repose
Until, when the weasel whistles on its tail,
No other weasel will obey its call.

I dreamt and drifted. All seemed to run to waste
As down a swirl of mucky, glittering flood
Strange polyp floated like a huge corrupt
Magnolia bloom, surreal as a shed breast,
My softly awash and blanching self-disgust.
And I cried among night waters, "I repent
My unweaned life that kept me competent
To sleepwalk with connivance and mistrust."
Then, like a pistil growing from the polyp,
A lighted candle rose and steadied up
Until the whole bright-mastered thing retrieved
A course and the currents it had gone with
Were what it rode and showed. No more adrift,
My feet touched bottom and my heart revived.

Then something round and clear
And mildly turbulent, like a bubbleskin
Or a moon in smoothly rippled lough water
Rose in a cobwebbed space: the molten
Inside-sheen of an instrument
Revolved its polished convexes full
Upon me, so close and brilliant
I pitched backward in a headlong fall.
And then it was the clarity of waking
To sunlight and a bell and gushing taps

In the next cubicle. Still there for the taking!
The old brass trumpet with its valves and stops
I found once in loft thatch, a mystery
I shied from then for I thought such trove beyond me.

"I hate how quick I was to know my place.
I hate where I was born, hate everything
That made me biddable and unforthcoming."
I mouthed at my half composed face
In the shaving mirror, like somebody
Drink in the bathroom during a party,
Lulled and repelled by his own reflection.
As if the cairnstone could define the cairn.
As if the eddy could reform the pool.
As if a stone swirled under a cascade.
Eroded and eroding in its bed,
Could grind itself down to a different core.
Then I thought of the tribe whose dances never fail
For they keep dancing till they sight deer.

Station Island IX is made up of five sonnets where a hunger striker from H-Block, Long Kesh in 1981 gives voice to a nation fasting for primal shelter. Station Island is in Lough Derg, County Donegal. It is an island known as St Patrick's Purgatory with its penitential vigil of fasting and praying that still constitutes the basis of a three day pilgrimage. I was there recently and the lough was grey, hard and cold. So many people were arriving to take their place as pilgrims. Young and old they joyously boarded the ferry in order to commence their penitence over on the island; fasting, walking about barefoot and praying at the various different stations which are early remains of medieval monastic cells. The myth of hunger striking has formed Ireland. The notion of self-denial is central to Irish Catholicism and a sense of endurance and sacrifice is at the heart of militant Irish nationalism. The tradition of troscud, taking injurious action against oneself for which another is held responsible, was favored in pagan and Catholic Ireland. Troscud was a medieval legal procedure where a creditor could fast against a debtor or a victim against a perpetrator. Troscud was taken up against a superior because there was no other recourse under Irish law. So, fasting took place on the threshold of the evil perpetrator in an attempt to atone for the sins of oppression and greed. In Christian mythology, fasters are seen as Lenten bodies in preparation for resurrection. So, Bobby Sands and his hunger strikers of Long Kesh in the early 80s come from a long history of fasting.

In sonnet one Heaney begins with the "voice from blight/ And hunger", the voice of Francis Hughes, to open this five part sonnet sequence. Hughes came from the same area as Heaney and was the second hunger striker to die at Long Kesh in 1981. His words are the contraband of a nation under siege. Indeed, the smuggled communications between isolated prisoner and national cause became the food for a community famishing for justice. From the outset the sonnet's voice is schizophrenic because the prisoner is a split self, both the hunter and the hunted: "I was dogs on my own track." Looking down on himself he watches his body disintegrate and become part of the earth: "My brain dried like spread turf, my stomach/ Shrank to a cinder and tightened and cracked." Heaney's nation space suffers from this same deadly preoccupation of maintaining a divided self, a split nation, an unwell schizophrenic state. Disintegrating and detaching oneself from one's environment is the result of living within an historical, political and psychological schism. *Station Island IX* articulates a fasting state of protest that must detach from its environment in order to survive.

As Hughes stares down at his own fasting body he fuses the starving subject and the observed object. The faster's natural disintegration is hounded by his own rampant and violent dog hunger. The hunger strike at Long Kesh began because Republicans demanded civilian clothes to denote their political, rather than criminal, status. This was denied so they wore their prison blankets instead of prison clothes, hence the phrase "Under the prison blanket". The blanket is both a prison and a protection. The last eight lines of the first sonnet demonstrates a reality full of hallucinations. In the grip of starvation Hughes has a vivid recollection of himself "emptied and deadly", as both hunger striker of the present and terrorist of the past. The real and the familiar "Street lights, small towns, country/ I knew from Glenshare down to Toome" figure now as the nightmare of "bomb-flash". The striker, both "hit-man" and victim, watches the vehicle become his coffin. The "white-faced groom" is both assassin and victim, he has been romanced by and wedded to terrorism and sedition. It is in this state of fasting that Hughes comes to see the full horror of the world in which he lived and created.

In the second sonnet we see a nation space in a state of decay. The Republican search for identity is conducted in the theatre of violence against the Unionists. Decay and corruption seep into the dark chamber of H-Block "the black dorm" so that death can be smelt in the "woodworm/ In gate posts" and "in mildew/ From the byre loft". Death can also be heard in the sounds of the pitch and practice of grenade throwing, the "maimed music" of "helicopters" and the piercing betrayal of "weasel whistl[ing] on its tail". Heaney addresses the faster and terrorist, Hughes, and suggests that he should have been buried "In the bog where you threw your first grenade". The bog is the preserved history of violence and suffering while those buried there rejuvenate into martyrs. There is something disturbing in the way the dead hunger striker is sanctified in the ritual of death: "There he was laid out with a drift of mass cards/ At his shrouded feet." Meanwhile, Heaney will not let us forget that this is the martyrdom of an "Unquiet soul".

In the third sonnet sequence the faster is in a purgatorial in-between world, and the images that depict it are hallucinatory and dreamlike. This is a place that has "run to waste", it is "mucky" with "Strange polyp" and "huge corrupt/ Magnolia" is like a "shed breast". We are in the debris of horror where fasters like Hughes sacrificed themselves to save Mother Ireland. Heaney's nation space is troubled by the geo-political demarcation of nation states be it the north/south, Catholic/Protestant, Republican/Unionist divide. This is a result of living within an historical moment profoundly layered by bifurcations and bloodshed. As Hughes' corpse disintegrates in sonnet three we hear his haunting voice: "I repent/ My unweaned life that kept me competent/ To sleepwalk with connivance and mistrust." This confessional insight brings about his swift passage out of this Dantesque descent. Redemption is now possible for this unquiet soul, with the life-bearing metaphors of "a pistil growing from the polyp" and "a lighted candle" offering him another path: "No more adrift/ My feet touched bottom and my heart revived."

This epiphany continues in sonnet four where the dead faster comes face to face with the making of his own death: "the molten/ Inside-sheen of an instrument/ Revolved its polished convexes full/ Upon me, so close and brilliant/ I seemed to pitch back in a headlong fall." Live by the sword, die by the sword or as Heaney writes, Hughes becomes his shot victim which brings about insight: "the clarity of waking/ To sunlight and a bell." The faster regretfully recalls his life lived with a litany of hatred against the socio-economic, political and historical destinies that divided his community: "I hate how quick I was to know my place./ I hate where I was born, hate everything/ that made me biddable and unforthcoming." The faster is both "biddable", obedient to the cause, and "unforthcoming, recalcitrant". Indeed, intoxicated by the horror and beauty of hunger striking, the faster is "Lulled and repelled by his own reflection".

Towards the end of *Station Island IX* the poet considers the inheritance of living in a nation space riddled with schisms and ambiguities. He considers the ineffectual efforts to change what already exists: "As if a stone swirled under a cascade./ Eroded and eroding in its bed,/ Could grind itself down to a different core." The fanatic heart, the stone, remains unflinching in the face of change, the trembling stream. It is this level of steadfastness, resisting the motion of everyday living that is demanded from the politically committed, if the flux of life is to be transformed into the constancy of history. Such beauty is terrible because it requires a cold inhuman persistence that tolerates no afterthought and no reconsiderations. The final lines of the last sonnet gestures to a primitive hunger that drives Heaney's nation: "Then I thought of the tribe whose dances never fail/ For they keep dancing till they sight deer." As the tribe inscribes itself upon its landscape until its prey is captured, so do the fasters inscribe their hunger upon the world's imagination until a just place of belonging is theirs. Heaney's nation space is cut off, isolated and caught in the strange rites of religion, superstition and nationalism.

Punishment by Seamus Heaney (1992)

I can feel the tug
of the halter at the nape
of her neck, the wind
on her naked front.

It blows her nipples
to amber beads,
it shakes frail rigging
of her ribs.

I can see her drowned
body in the bog,

the weighing stone,
the floating rods and boughs,

Under which at first
she was barked sapling
that is dug up
oak-bone, brain-firkin:

her shaved head
like stubble of black corn,
her blindfold a soiled bandage,
her noose a ring

to store
the memories of love.
Little adulteress,
before they punished you

you were flaxen-haired,
undernourished, and your
tar-black face was beautiful.
My poor scapegoat,

I almost love you
but would have cast, I know,
the stones of silence.
I am the artful voyeur

of your brain's exposed
and darkened combs,
your muscles' webbing
and all your numbered bones:

I who have stood dumb
when your betraying sisters,
cauled in tar,
wept by the railings,

who would connive
in civilised outrage
yet understand the exact

and tribal, intimate revenge.

Punishment is one of the half dozen poems inspired by P. V. Glob's *The Bog People* and Heaney's visit to Jutland to view the corpses of these preserved victims of sacrifice and crime. *Punishment* is inspired by the discovery of the Windeby Girl, found two years after the Tollund Man. She was approximately 14 years old, stripped almost naked, shaved, blindfolded and drowned in 50 centimeters of water in a peat bog. The body had been weighed down with a stone and birch branches. Glob's work allowed Heaney to look at the layers of myth behind the Republican ethos and the feminisation of Ireland which demands augury and sacrifice. *Punishment* is preoccupied with starving and staring, as it examines nation building that demands sacrifice, reverence and preservation. The staring girl-child is starved of justice, a name, representation, a recorded history, food, nourishment and love; moreover, she is stared upon by Iron Age man, archaeologist, Professor Glob, poet and reader. She has the status of faster as she appears "undernourished", her nakedness exposed to the gaze: "your brain's exposed/ and darkened combs,/ your muscles' webbing,/ and all your numbered bones." Her fragility is captured in "the frail rigging/ of her ribs". She is the scapegoat, the bearer of Ireland's sins, famine and fast. The use of the female victim reinforces the idea that sacrifice and suffering gives birth to a nation.

The title of the poem signals the sorts of religious, moral and political penalties associated with the Catholic Church, the Provisional Irish Republican Army, the Ulster Volunteer Force and the English government. Retribution exacted by a tribe, a gender, a society, an era, the Bible and the ancient Nordics, washes over into contemporary Irish society. In mobilising the discourse of crime and punishment Heaney portrays an Ireland caught between two worlds, that of the sovereign state and the modern nation state. The sovereign state controls its subject with visible displays of power, such as torture, punishment and death: "I can feel the tug/ of the halter at the nape/ of her neck ... I can see her drowned/ body in the bog,/ the weighing stone ... her shaved head/ like stubble of black corn,/ her blindfold a soiled ... undernourished...cauled in tar." In *Punishment* the subject is controlled by punitive head shaving, blindfolding, undernourishment, hanging and then drowning in bog. She comes to represent Ireland and the way tribal warfare punishes primitively. What is the crime of this female child? Adultery, indifference, sexual expression, youth, vulnerability, economic dependence, fear, being female and a victim of sexual abuse? Yet whatever the crime, the punishment is excessive. For Heaney and for the reader she is "My poor scapegoat" but one needed for the "exact/ and tribal intimate revenge".

According to this discourse of crime and punishment she is the victim of ancient Nordic law, Biblical reckoning and contemporary Ireland. She is hung for adultery then drowned in a sea of bog, weighed down by stones, branches and time. The Old Testament's punishment for adultery was stoning: "I ... would have cast, I know,/ the stones of silence." Heaney uses this to castigate political life. The punishment of shaving a woman's head because she made choices with her body that are not in keeping with the patriarchal laws of the society, has been used throughout the world: "her shaved head,/ like a stubble of black corn,/ her blindfold a soiled bandage." Tacitus observed that Germanic tribes would shave the heads of adulterous women, scourge them and drive them out of the village. Head shaving is also a signature of disease, performed during outbreaks of lice and other infectious plagues, and a casting off of feminine beauty. Heaney likens the bog girl's shaved head to a stubble of "black corn", the fodder that might fuel the imagination of a nation in famine. Ironically, her "blindfold a soiled bandage" offers some protection from the hungry gaze of the voyeurs. Moreover, her eyes and thus her perspective, are the wound that must be covered. Therefore, the unnamed girl is not the one on trial, but Heaney and Ireland, and by default the reader, in our complicit silence and inaction: "I who have stood dumb/ when your betraying sisters,/ cauled in tar,/ wept by the railings." Here Heaney refers to the punishment of tarring and feathering Irish women who have sexual relations with the enemy: English soldiers. The use of the word "cauled" with its suggestion of birthing and the vulnerability of a foetus is particularly poignant in the formation of a nation. In all of Heaney's bog people poems he links the bog person with a baby or foetus: "unswaddled the wet fern of her hair" in *Strange Fruit*, "And his rusted hair ... as a foetus" in *The Grauballe Man* and "The plait of my hair,/ a slimy birth-cord" in *Bog Queen*.

The use of near binaries in civilised/ outrage, exact/ tribal, intimate/ revenge demonstrates the disturbing back-to-back experience of living intimately with violence and death: "I ... who would connive/ in civilised outrage/ yet understand the exact/ and tribal, intimate revenge." Ireland is a war zone where language remains inadequate. "Tribe" and "connive" become the cairn stones for Heaney's poetics. His nation space is made up of tribal groupings, imagined communities and primitive clusters and it is out of these sites of belonging that certain ways of responding are induced and contrived. *Punishment* indicates that fear is the greatest law and the modern state is yet to be realised. This poem is a love song, a play of seduction and scopophilia that lures the reader into a state of culpability. The sensuous experience of being privy to intimate knowledge is conveyed in the employment of first person. This all seeing eye stares at the naked and vulnerable body of the girl: "the tug ... at the nape/ of her neck" and "the wind on her naked front" as it "blows her nipples/ to amber beads". She is the beloved, preserved in the black sea of bog. She has been mummified in the shroud of nation-forming memory and encrusted in amber, the jewel of the underworld. Indeed, when she is dug up, she is "oak-bone, brain firkin". This is reminiscent of ancient funeral practices that would extract the brain of the dead and place it in a cask beside the corpse.

The "I" sees "her drowned/ body" and celebrates her beauty as one with nature: she is young and fertile, "a barked sapling", transformed into the earth. The noose is not only the weapon of her murder, but also "a ring/ to store/ the memories of love". This love knot, her wedding ring, is worn around her neck. Thus, her love is her death, her wedding day her execution. She is "little", "mine" and "flaxen-haired" with a "face [that] was beautiful". The poet desires her and therefore it is he who commits, or longs to commit, adultery. The poet and the reader are the perpetrators of her punishment for a crime which is more ours than it ever was hers. The poet declares a qualified adoration of the victim, "I almost love you" and identifies himself as the perpetrator by admitting "I am the artful voyeur". This love song is about beauty and horror. Heaney's warning against a reverence for such a spectacle is strangely compelling. The bog preserves and freezes. The body of the nation, symbolised in the preserved bodies of the bog people and the hunger striker in *Station Island IX* is caught in the act of troscud; starving on the threshold of sovereignty for justice. The body of the nation imagined as female, devours the sacrificed sons of Ireland in order to offer a rich harvest.

The bog is a black frozen sea that holds the layering of time in order to deliver a nation, centuries later, still in that moment of troscud.

Cassandra by Seamus Heaney (1996)

No such thing
as innocent
bystanding.

Her soiled vest,
her little breasts,
her clipped, devast-

ated, scabbed
punk head,
the char-eyed

famine gawk –
she looked
camp-fucked

and simple.
People
could feel

a missed
trueness in them
focus,

a homecoming
in her dropped-wing,
half-calculating

bewilderment.
No such thing
as innocent.

Old King Cock-
of-the-Walk
was back,

King Kill-
The-Child-
and-Take-

What-Comes
King Agamem-
non's drum-

balled, old buck's
stride was back.
And then her Greek

words came,
a lamb
at lambing time,

bleat of clair-
voyant dread,
the gene-hammer

and tread
of the roused god.
And a result-

ant shock desire
in bystanders
to do it to her

there and then.
Little rent
cunt of their guilt:

in she went
to the knife,
to the killer wife,

to the net over
her and her slaver,
the Troy reaver,

saying, "A wipe

of the sponge,
that's it.

The shadow-hinge
swings unpredict-
ably and the light's

blanked out."

Situated within *Mycenae Lookout*, *Cassandra* is one of five poems that interweave the Trojan War and the troubles of Northern Ireland with the dramatic threads of prophecy and augury. King Agamemnon, on the pretence of avenging Menelaus' loss, wages a war across the Aegean for ten long years but the war continues for as long as the Homeric tale is told and sectarian hatred divides Ireland. The mythologizing of Helen as the most coveted woman in the world, parallels Ireland as the fair country desired by the English invading forces. In *Cassandra* Heaney uses prophecy as a means of promoting a vision beyond the horror and degradation of war. Cassandra, who is a sibyl to the Greeks, is synonymous with prophecies of doom. Prophecy is resultant of second sight, premonition, augury and the inward and outward gaze. Cassandra imparts her visions to the unfocused Athenians.

Thus, prophecy woven into the legends and mythology of ancient Greece is recycled into the fabric of Heaney's nation space. Consequently, Cassandra foresees, the bystanders gawk, the narrator gazes, the Greeks observe, the poet looks, the reader reads and modern day Ireland keeps watch. Most interestingly we are told throughout Heaney's oeuvre that there is "No such thing/ as innocent/ bystanding". To watch is to be guilty; this is central to Heaney's poetics. Therefore, the reader is both dislocated by and responsible for Cassandra's prophecy of doom. During the 1960s and 1970s many Irish poets were asked to declare which side of the political divide they stood. The publication of Heaney's poetry to date had indicated that Heaney despised foreign occupation of Northern Ireland but at the same time he condemned the acts of terror committed by the IRA and the UVF in the name of ethnic or tribal loyalties. Indeed, Cassandra's prophecy casts Athenian royalty in blood and darkness: "in she went ... saying, "A wipe/ of the sponge,/ that's it./ The shadow-hinge/ swings unpredict-/ ably and the light's/ blanked out." Cassandra's prediction of Agamemnon's murder by Clytemnestra at the end of the Trojan War signals the uncanny parallel of Ireland's contemporary slaughter initiated by England's invading forces and perpetuated by Ireland's own lunacy. Heaney's poem is an elegy to history, and yet he is wary not to beautify what is execrable and unspeakable.

Cassandra is a thin wail of hysteria. The poem's typography reflects the fasted site of Heaney's nation space. Cassandra is a slave to Agamemnon, to the horror of her inner vision and to the gaze of the guilty bystanders: "Her soiled vest,/ her little breasts, her clipped, devast-/ ated, scabbed/ punk head,/ the char-eyed/ famine gawk." She is both desirable and filthy, a disease-ridden beauty, conveyed in the adjectives "soiled", "scabbed" and "char". Her own eye/I is famished into a "famine gawk". She is the victim and the incarceration of hunger. The reference to her "clipped ... punk head" transports the Homeric legend into the contemporary urban streets. Like *Punishment*, Cassandra is about woman as scapegoat. Heaney explores the other face of desire in the discourse of slavery where the object of one's hunger becomes the object of one's abuse: "she looked/ camp-fucked/ and simple ... a desire/ in bystanders/ to do it to her/ there and then./ Little rent/ cunt of their guilt." Cassandra is a slave to the history she harbours and to the prophecy that classified her as hysterical, mad and the bearer of ill-omens.

Thus, her abuse, according to those standing by, is justified. The quarrel between Agamemnon and Achilles over their slaves, Chryseis and Briseis, and the war between Ithaca and Troy over Helen are disputes concerning the value of certain commodities in the market. Iphigenia, the daughter whom Agamemnon sacrifices in order to appease the goddess Diana, is simply one more female whose value is determined by this masculine drama and whose identity is named only in relation to the father: "King Kill-/ The-Child-/ and-Take-/ What-Comes/ King Agamem-/ non." Heaney's poetics is concerned with how the woman surrenders herself in the patriarchal society and becomes the empty vessel, the space on which a nation is built. When Cassandra strides towards her death, the nightwatchman refers to her destiny as slavery and sacrifice: "in she went/ to the knife,/ to the killer wife, / to the net over/ her and her slaver,/ the Troy reaver." Female vision and individual agency are sacrificed to form a nation. Athenian, Trojan, Ithacan and Irish women bear the sacrifice in their names, Helen, Cassandra, Iphigenia or Mother Ireland. The nation space imagined by Heaney is stained and cleansed by terror and beauty and thus remains a place of belonging baptised in blood.

And the Winner is...

1996 Wislawa Szymborska "for poetry that with ironic precision allows the historical and biological context to come to light in fragments of human reality"

Wislawa Szymborska was born in 1923 in Western Poland, Kornik, and died in 2012 after living most of her life in Krakow; around the time she was born Poland had free elections and would not return to this Western style liberal democratic political system until some 70 years later in the early 1990s. Szymborska had lived a life in a nation that was struggling to survive between vicious cycles of repression and reform. She completed her education underground during the outbreak of World War II and then worked as a railroad employee, managing to avoid the German labor camps despite ongoing occupation of Poland by the Nazis for the entirety of the war. In 1945 she commenced her studies in Polish Literature and Sociology at Jagiellonian University, one of the oldest surviving universities in the world, but did not complete her degree due to financial difficulties. Poland remained a Soviet satellite state for most of the 20th century. Szymborska's first book of poetry failed to be published in 1949 because it did not meet socialist requirements.

In the early 1950s Szymborska signed a public condemnation of the Polish religious who were on trial for treason, one of the many Stalinesque show trials. She did this as a mark of her support for the Polish Socialist Party. Szymborska then became the poetry editor and columnist for the *Krakow Literary Weekly*, a position she held between 1953 and 1981. Throughout this time Poland experienced enormous economic and political suffering as it struggled to achieve a united and independent Poland. The election of Karol Wojtyla as Pope John Paul II in 1978 and the founding of Solidarity, the independent trade union led by Lech Walesa were two pivotal points in her lifetime that left Poland's ruling party both sidelined and highlighted. The world's first Polish pope emerging out of an oppressive Socialist regime as well as the union between workers and the intelligentsia led, eventually, to the 1991 first entirely free elections where Walesa became Poland's new president.

The Joy of Writing by Wislawa Szymborska (1967)
Translated by S. Baranczak & C. Cavanagh

Why does this written doe bound through these written woods?
For a drink of written water from a spring
whose surface will Xerox her soft muzzle?
Why does she lift her head; does she hear something?
Perched on four slim legs borrowed from the truth,
she pricks up her ears beneath my fingertips.
Silence – this world also rustles across the page
and parts the boughs
that have sprouted from the word "woods".

Lying in wait, set to pounce on the blank page,
are letters up to no good,
clutches of clauses so subordinate
they'll never let her get away.

Each drop of ink contains a fair supply
of hunters, equipped with squinting eyes behind their sights,
prepared to swarm the sloping pen at any moment,
surround the doe, and slowly aim their guns.

They forget that what's here isn't life.
Other laws, black on white, obtain.
The twinkling of an eye will take as long as I say,
and will, if I wish, divide into tiny eternities,
full of bullets stopped in mid-flight.
Not a thing will ever happen unless I say so.
Without my blessing, not a leaf will fall,
not a blade of grass will bend beneath that little hoof's full stop.

Is there then a world
where I rule absolutely on fate?
A time I bind with chains of signs?

An existence become endless at my bidding?

The joy of writing.
The power of preserving.
Revenge of a mortal hand.

I have loved Szymborska for a long time and my love affair began with this very poem. It is a poem that delights the heart. It is playful, clever and defiant. I wonder whether the title of the poem is misleading because it is also very much a poem that forces us to look back on ourselves and consider the joy of reading; and in particular reading poetry. This poem made up of six uneven stanzas written in free verse, asks us to step away from the seduction of reading and consider the mechanics behind the seduction. Ironically this is done with such precision and sleight of hand that we are completely, once again, seduced. In others words the breaking down and examination of the mechanics of poetics in order to understand the seduction is, by its very nature, seductive. Her poem commences with "Why" not "How". To the question, how does the doe bound, the answer must be because the writer writes it so. To the question why does the doe bound, the answer is because we the reader anticipate it to be so or we desire it to be so or we cannot live in a world where it is not so. The reader's yearning drives the writer's craft. In the first three lines Szymborska repeats "written" thrice and indicates that the water's surface "will Xerox" the doe. In every way we are made aware of the signified not being the thing itself. What is being written and read is representation. And yet…and yet…by the 4th line we are alert to the danger of her erasure: "Why does she lift her head… she pricks up her ears." Despite being reminded that her "four slim legs" are "borrowed from the truth" we are immediately aware of her vulnerability; despite her instincts being aroused "beneath my fingertips" we too sit on the edge of our seats wondering – is this the moment where the predator enters?!

Like a David Attenborough documentary we despair to read in the second brief stanza that there "are letters up to no good" getting ready to "pounce", indeed "they'll never let her get away". Cleverly we are reminded of the villainy in the alliterative "clutches of clauses so subordinate" all of which will lead to the inevitable doe's demise. So, here are groups of words that contain a verb dependent on the main clause; subordinate clauses contain additional information but need the main clause to finish the thought. In other words, a subordinate clause cannot stand alone. This is a moment worthy of pause; to my mind this suggests that the main clause representing the doe begs the accompanying subordinate clauses to hide close by, ready to attack. In our reading of the doe at the spring we are already building into that imaginary landscape the predator. The third stanza, made up similarly to the second with four lines, gives names to the predator: "hunters, equipped with squinting eyes behind their sights,/ prepared to swarm the sloping pen at any moment,/ surround the doe, and slowly aim their guns." Our anticipation has been fulfilled and the poet will give us what we already imagined. In many ways our yearning for the fulfilment of the drama surrounding the doe's transient beauty and vulnerability is in the predicted hunters. The poet assures us that we will not be disappointed as her pen "contains a fair supply…of ink". Without a doubt, from one perspective this is a delightful poem about the seduction of writing and in particular poetry; but on a darker perspective this is a consideration of the way in which we imagine a world before it is crafted. That indeed, this imagined world brings about what it is we anticipate; whether it's the lithe beauty of freedom or its annihilation.

The 4th stanza speaks directly to the power of imagination. Not only do the predators not recognise that the doe "isn't life" but rather "black on white"; the poet herself sees only her own omniscient power: "Not a thing will ever happen unless I say so." The power of the imagination is seductive; moreover, it fulfils the desire of readers regardless of their temporalities. The poet is aware of the readers' desires to paradoxically have the thrill of anticipated threat while being assured of the benevolence of the writer: "Without my blessing, not a leaf will fall,/ not a blade of grass will bend beneath that little hoof's full stop." Szymborska, like poets before her, conflate the power of the gun and pen and in so doing suggest the way in which writing can effect change; whether that is for the commonweal or no. At all times we are made aware of the defencelessness of the prey and that her end point is in our hand. The penultimate short stanza asks three questions all of which consider the overarching thesis of the poem, which is, that what we imagine we create. Our desire for the benevolent or the malevolent drama of life is a self-fulfilling prophecy. We are left with three statements in the final stanza; the holy trinity of the writerly purpose. Writing is done for "joy", for the act of "preserving" and for "Revenge". Moreover, if writing is the articulation of that which we imagine, then it also emerges as a result of what the readers anticipate. This masterful poem is not just a summery dappled postcard of deer in the wild; this is a deeply complex reading on the powerful double edged heart of desire.

Nothing Twice by Wislawa Szymborska (1957)
Translated by S. Baranczak & C. Cavanagh

Nothing can ever happen twice.
In consequence, the sorry fact is
that we arrive here improvised
and leave without the chance to practice.

Even if there is no one dumber,
if you're the planet's biggest dunce,
you can't repeat the class in summer:
this course is only offered once.

No day copies yesterday,
no two nights will teach what bliss is
in precisely the same way,
with precisely the same kisses.

One day, perhaps some idle tongue
mentions your name by accident:

I feel as if a rose were flung
Into the room, all hue and scent.

The next day, though you're here with me,
I can't help looking at the clock:
A rose? A rose? What could that be?
Is it a flower or a rock?

Why do we treat the fleeting day
With so much needless fear and sorrow?
It's in its nature not to stay:
Today is always gone tomorrow.

With smiles and kisses, we prefer
to seek accord beneath our star,
although we're different (we concur)
just as two drops of water are.

This is rather a beautiful lyric made up of seven quatrains with the rhyme scheme of a b a b. In Ancient Greece a lyric was a poem sung to the accompaniment of a lyre. The lyric is used to convey the poet's emotions and state of mind. Szymborska's lyric has a melodic quality. It was taken up by Andrzej Munkowski and written into a song which Lucja Prus first performed in 1965. Later Kora would make a punk rock version and more recently it was choreographed into a contemporary ballet, by Roberto Campanella and Robert Glumbek. This speaks to the poem's longevity and to Szymborska's relevance beyond her own temporality. *Nothing Twice* offers a different perspective on pain and loss experienced in the present moment. While it is a contemplation of time passing and of the tragedies that exist within one's life it is, more importantly, a promise that these sufferings will pass. Szymborska is suggesting that it is the very transient nature of life that makes it so beautiful. Life is not a copy of a copy nor is it an experience for which any one of us is prepared. There is something shared and democratic in her representation of living; it is at once familiar and surprising. You walk away from this poem reminded that everything matters; every moment, every person, every experience. We are also reassured that it is the acts of spontaneity and improvisation that make it so rich and bountiful.

The first line of *Nothing Twice* is axiomatic: "Nothing can ever happen twice." Its high modality makes us confront the way in which we invariably disregard the unique never to be repeated, experience of the present moment. The first quatrain asserts the truth that life is unrepeatable, there is no rehearsal but rather a great deal of makeshift spontaneity: "we arrive here improvised/ and leave without the chance to practice." This throws our cautious attempts at prescriptive living to the wind. It also suggests that we are amateurs and not masters of this trade called living. From this thesis we move to quatrain two where we are supplied with the proof in childhood and then in quatrain three, the proof in adulthood. We are initially located in the schoolroom learning the lessons that are supposed to prepare us for life but we are told "you can't repeat the class in summer:/ this course is only offered once". The metaphor of life being a course that is not repeated suggests that the pedagogical approach of childhood learning is redundant. I like her bold playfulness in suggesting that even the "biggest dunce" will have no second chance. The third quatrain takes us into the lessons we should have learnt in adulthood; that "no two nights will teach what bliss is" even if we are in receipt of "the same kisses". The unsaid of course is that if we weren't such dunces, we would already know this and be fully alive to the wonder of a life that is without repetition.

In the 4th and 5th quatrains. Szymborska considers the way we long for the beloved but then when the beloved is with us, we disregard the moment. Stanza four mentions the quickening heart that happens "One day" at the mention of "your name…as if a rose were flung/ into the room, all hue and scent". The simile catapults the beloved into the symbol of romance. Yet the heart and what it holds dear is fickle because "The next day" when the beloved is actually physically there, the lover is impatient to be elsewhere and the symbol of romance is replaced with that of an impediment: "I can't help looking at the clock…Is it a flower or a rock?" Is it human nature that we cannot seem to hold on to the wonder and desire? This lyric is such a salient reminder of what we must treasure. In the last two quatrains Szymborska explores the way in which time passing is a salve on the wounds of our lives: "Why do we treat the fleeting day/ With so much needless fear and sorrow?/ It's in its nature not to stay." If the present moment has no purchase on our daily lives then it behoves us to relinquish the emotions that hold us back. The last quatrain tells us that we are as unique as each day. Not only will nothing ever happen twice but nobody will either. Szymborska is suggesting that it is in our nature to prefer "With smiles and kisses…to seek accord to seek accord", in other words to conform and erase our singularity. The poem demands we see ourselves as precious and as irreplaceable as the present moment: "we're different…just as two drops of water." This point of comparison renders the individual and time as transient and precious. A lyric well worth the reading!

Love at First Sight by Wislawa Szymborska (1958)
Translated by S. Baranczak & C. Cavanagh

They're both convinced
that a sudden passion joined them.
Such certainty is beautiful,
but uncertainty is more beautiful still.

Since they'd never met before, they're sure
that there'd been nothing between them.
But what's the word from the streets, staircases, hallways –
perhaps they've passed by each other a million times?

I want to ask them
if they don't remember –
a moment face to face

in some revolving door?
Perhaps a "sorry" muttered in a crowd?
A curt "wrong number" caught in the receiver?
But I know the answer.
No, they don't remember.

They'd be amazed to hear
that Chance has been toying with them
now for years.

Not quite ready yet
to become their Destiny,
it pushed them close, drove them apart,
it barred their path,
stifling a laugh,
and then leaped aside.

There were signs and signals,
even if they couldn't read them yet.
Perhaps three years ago
or just last Tuesday
a certain leaf fluttered
from one shoulder to another?
Something was dropped and then picked up.
Who knows, maybe the ball that vanished
into childhood's thicket?

There were doorknobs and doorbells
where one touch had covered another
beforehand.
Suitcases checked and standing side by side.
One night, perhaps, the same dream,
grown hazy by morning.

Every beginning
is only a sequel, after all,
and the book of events
is always open halfway through

What's there not to love in this eight stanza free verse poem that explores the capricious nature of love? It explores the high modality of newly found love despite the suggestion that it was always lurking somewhere in the wings. The poem suggests that it is more about our own readiness to see and receive love than whether or not love is present to us. I love the way in which Szymborska considers our own temporalities as being imprinted by the presence of awaiting love. It is all just a matter of time. Oh and belief in the fact that love is there for you, patiently waiting until you are ready to turn and greet it with such certainty. The poem sets up the speaking position of the all-seeing narrator, the "I" who observes, across time and place, the lovers. Let's have a closer look. The opening thesis is that the beauty of passion is constituted not so much by its certainty but its uncertainty: "a sudden passion joined them./ Such certainty is beautiful,/ but uncertainty is more beautiful still." The absolute confidence and conviction of the lovers that they have been conjoined by a force beyond their power sits inside the myths of romantic love. These myths come down to us throughout the ages from Greek mythology where passionate love was the result of cupid's arrow piercing the inadvertent and unsuspecting. Oftentimes, the aim went awry and mismatched or unrequited lovers were borne. Regardless there was a sense that our fate of loving and being loved was always in the hands of the gods. Some were lucky in love and others were not. Hence the "sudden passion" that seizes our lovers in *Love at First Sight*. Yet from the onset the poem asserts that it is the unpredictable nature of love that is the most compelling beauty we have.

The next seven stanzas undermine the rational assertions articulated by the lovers in stanza one. Nothing rational can be said about the visceral experience of passion; the cerebral has definitely left the building when Eros comes knocking. In the second stanza the lovers are contradicted by the "word from the streets, staircases, hallways" which indicates that they have in fact met a "million times" before but, for a plethora of reasons, were not ready to see each other. I like the idea of a cityscape being imprinted by our traces; that our paths crisscross tirelessly again and again. I like the fancy of near misses and the way in which a landscape looks on, waiting for us to look up. It is in stanza three that the narrator emerges. A bold voice and one that is gently provocative: "I want to ask them...a moment face to face/ in some revolving door?/ Perhaps a "sorry" muttered in a crowd?/ A curt "wrong number" caught in the receiver?" The interrogation by the narrator is deliciously specific and would have the lovers considering momentarily the hitherto unimaginable. The fact that we have direct speech offered as evidence to the lovers that they might have indeed spoken to each other, prior to the arrival of the "sudden passion", cleverly undermines the "certainty" that they had never met previously.

Undaunted the poet continues in stanza four and five discussing the curve balls of "Chance" and "Destiny" that have been thrown to us since Ancient Greek Mythology. The goddess of chance was, of course, Tyche who was the daughter of Aphrodite and Zeus. She governed fortune and destiny. I like the way that despite our perception that we are modern contemporary beings we seem to be a hair's breath away from the superstitions and pagan appellations of the Classical period. Here we have two lovers sure footed and positive that they have never met before but are new in the eyes of each other. Yet we read that "Chance has been toying with them/ now for years" it was just that they were "Not quite ready yet/ to become their Destiny." The lovers have been played with, toyed with as "Destiny...pushed them...drove them...barred their path...then leaped aside". It would seem that the deities of love, chance and luck have been more proactive than the lovers themselves. Is this how we still conduct ourselves in the modern world? Are we still waiting for love to be thrown in our path which we have been hitherto blind to see?

In stanza six and seven Szymborska names the "signs and signals" that had been there all along. Our witless lovers were simply ignorant when it came to their interpretation. The signs are random and seemingly insignificant: "a certain leaf fluttered/from one shoulder to another…Something was dropped and then picked up." The poet tells us that this could have happened at any point in time. She even posits the eerie memory shard of a lost ball in the "childhood's thicket" as evidence that the other was present, prior to the recognition of each other as lover. In the penultimate stanza the idea of the lovers coming together before they were "convinced" that love had found them is contained in three mischievous romantic signatures: touching the same "doorknobs and doorbells", placing their unsuspecting "Suitcases… side by side" and sharing "the same dream". This alone contains the making of a great lovers' triste. We are invited to peep in and note the feverish rendezvous, packed intimacies and night-time fantasies. It is as if all the paraphernalia that makes love, love, is already there. Love is just waiting for the lovers to identify it for what it is and seize it with both hands. The final stanza sums up the chase. It is a convincing reminder that the "sudden passion" is not so much a "beginning" but rather "a sequel". I love this idea that passion is a consequence of what has already occurred, unbeknownst to us. It seems the final message of this poem is that our reading of "the book of events" has so often been filled with folly. Most importantly, Szymborska is showing us that the signs of love are everywhere.

Tortures by Wislawa Szymborska (1986)
Translated by S. Baranczak & C. Cavanagh

Nothing has changed.
The body is susceptible to pain;
it has to eat and breathe the air, and sleep;
it has thin skin, and the blood is just beneath it;
an adequate supply of teeth and fingernails;
its bones can be broken; its joints can be stretched.
In tortures, all this is taken into account.

Nothing has changed.
The body shudders as it shuddered
before the founding of Rome and after,
in the twentieth century before and after Christ.
Tortures are just as they were, only the earth has frown smaller,
and what happens sounds as if it's happening in the next room.

Nothing has changed.
It's just that there are more people,
and beside the old offences new ones have sprung –

real, make-believe, short-lived, and non-existent.
But the howl with which the body answers to them,
was, is and ever will be a cry of innocence
according to the age-old scale and pitch.

Nothing has changed.
Except perhaps the manners, ceremonies, dances.
Yet the movement of hands to shield the head remains the same.
The body writhes, jerks and tries to pull away,
its legs fail, it falls, its knees jack-knife,
it bruises, swells, dribbles and bleeds.

Nothing has changed.
Except for the course of rivers,'
The lines of forests, coasts, deserts and glaciers.
Amid those landscapes roams the soul,
disappears, returns, draws nearer, moves away,
a stranger to itself, elusive,
now sure, now uncertain of its own existence,
while the body is and is and is
and has nowhere to go.

Here is a free verse poem, with the anaphora "Nothing has changed" headlining each of the five stanzas. It is a particularly accessible and direct poem in the message it conveys: that humanity has continued to imagine ways to inflict suffering on others since time immemorial. Whenever I read this poem, I am completely overwhelmed by all we are not. Szymborska is commenting on more than just the suffering we inflict, she is also considering the strictures we place around the body, be it boundaries established in the making of nation states or the rules and regulations imposed by certain expectations. At all times Szymborska is thinking about "bodies"; not humanity or people or society or individuals but bodies. This is interesting because in many ways she is stripping back the capital invested in making us more than just bodies. At the end of the day, indeed, at the end of a torturer's efforts, we are just bodies. I like the democratization of this idea. I like to think about the way we are part and parcel of the animal kingdom and should rethink our overdeveloped sense of superiority.

The first stanza is made up of three sentences. The first, as already noted, headlines the thesis which is that there is no alteration or transformation but rather existence is unchanged. The second sentence is the body of the stanza and so for five lines unpacks the way in which bodies have common characteristics such as being "susceptible to pain" and needing to eat, breath and sleep. The list continues and it is for the most part an innocent list recording the "adequate supply of teeth and fingernails" and that bones "can be broken" and "joints...stretched". The title and most of the first stanza could be a pleasant consideration of the after effects of exertion and nothing more. The final sentence in stanza one turns this completely on its head. With absolute surety we are told that the deliberate act of causing great suffering to others takes the body's vulnerability "into account". It is such a simple statement and arrests the irony with which liberal democracy uses this term "torture"

Let's look at the etymology of the word *torture*: it takes us back to Classical Latin to the word *torquere* meaning to twist; or the Late Latin *tortura* meaning twisting torment. This puts us in mind of the agony inflicted on those who are punished. A twisting torment, a harrowing ordeal. In the second stanza Szymborska takes us twisting through time, back and forwards we swing from "before the founding of Rome and after" and then back again from "the twentieth century before and after Christ". Dizzy with spiralling back and forth through time immemorial our minds "shudders", as did the bodies in these torturous scenarios. The last sentence of this stanza invokes the disarming characteristic of globalisation that the "sounds" are just more amplified, now that "the earth has grown smaller". The irony being of course that it still continues. During World War II Nazi occupied Poland endured a scale of torture never known before in its history; afterwards when the Soviets took over, the CHEKA, the secret police, used torture as a means to extract information or to force confessions.

By the third stanza the phrase, "Nothing has changed", is tolling like a bell. It is a wakeup call, an alarm that is sounding down throughout the ages. In this stanza the following two sentences offer a contrast between the punishable "offences" committed and the "howl" that "answers". On the one hand are the crimes: "old…new…real, make-believe, short-lived, and non-existent." A salient list and one that makes us think that the majority of crimes are not even real and so torture must serve another purpose besides the deterrent to crime. It must signal power. It must indicate control. It must measure the imagination of one and the vulnerability of the other. The tortured victim response is animalistic and primeval because it is one of howling: "a cry of innocence." In other words, there is no one sufficiently guilty of any crime who is worthy of torture. Contrast is mobilised deftly in the 4th stanza. Here Szymborska juxtaposes the gestures of "manners, ceremonies, dances", all of which evince specific cultural expression, to the movement of the body under torture. It is the dance of twisting torment of those being tortured: "The body writhes, jerks and tries to pull away,/ its legs fail, it falls, its knees jack-knife,/ it bruises, swells, dribbles and bleeds." It is a choreography of suffering.

The last stanza takes us to the body of nation space. This body is variously fought over and claimed; its borders arbitrarily established and re-established in the name of nationalism. The body of the nation space is the outcome of tribalism. The keeping in and keeping out of selected people. This random drawing up of territory is contingent on the powerful being able to take resources from the vulnerable. Indeed, the fear of the other underlies the formation of a nation, which in turn shapes the Nobel Laureates' oeuvre. Here in the 5th stanza Szymborska considers how the only variable to the axiom, that nothing changes, is the landscape: "Except for the course of rivers,/ the lines of forests, coasts, deserts and glaciers." These physical sites of belonging are constantly changing. Out there, beyond man-made power, "roams the soul". We have now moved into another stratosphere in this poem: from the physical to the metaphysical. Is this the thread of hope we have been waiting for? The soul is imagined as being forever in a state of metamorphoses: "disappears, returns, draws nearer, moves away,/ a stranger to itself, elusive,/ now sure, now uncertain." Unlike the body,

Szymborska is suggesting that the soul cannot be captured. Even the power of language fails to arrest it and smash it into submission. In contrast to the ephemeral state of the soul, with all its promise of salvation, "the body is and is and is/ and has nowhere to go." In the end, this is our inheritance to be locked into our bodily selves until we recognise the immutable power of our soul.

And the Winner is...

2016 Bob Dylan "for having created new poetic expressions within the great American song tradition"

Can Bob Dylan's lyrics ever be read without the soundscape of his nasal twang, guitar and harmonica, playing somewhere in the background of our mind? I am not too sure if this would ever be possible. When he sent Patti Smith to collect his Nobel Prize in 2016 it was said of him by a committee member that he was worthy of a place beside Greek bards, beside Ovid and beside Romantic visionaries. I have always said when teaching poetry that song is the first genre of literature and thus lyrics, the first poetry. The *Odyssey* and *Iliad* would have been sung. So, Dylan is in good company as we reflect on his considerable contribution of musical lyrics during the past six decades. His impact has been global as a result of the medium in which he reflected his times in the free world. His oeuvre is the very manifestation of Homer's declaration as the uber poet: "Sing in me, oh Muse and through me/ tell the story." He was born Robert Allen Zimmerman in 1941 and changed his name after reading the Welsh poet, Dylan Thomas. Bob Dylan articulated the political, social, philosophical and literary influences that shaped not only his generation but his nation. His lyrics and music move across sub genres including American folk, blues, country, gospel, rock and roll, rockabilly, English/Irish/Scottish folk, jazz, hip hop and contemporary. His lyrics express both his moral authority and non-conformity. He was and remains iconoclastic.

Dylan emerged as an American songwriter in the early 1960s, a time of great political and social change. This was the decade of the Vietnam War, hippies, drugs, rock and roll, protests, the Cuban Missile Crisis, the failed Bay of Pigs, the assassination of John F Kennedy and Martin Luther King, the freedom riders challenging ongoing segregation and the arrival of the birth control pill. During this decade Dylan expressed the emerging empowerment of the counter culture especially in the Civil Rights and Anti-War Movements. Indeed, his songs kept catching this tidal wave of change in the second half of the 20th century, reflecting and shaping the zeitgeist of his nation. His lyrics riff across the bars of despair, faith, sadness, triumph and the supernatural. The two quintessential protest songs of the early 60s civil rights and anti-war movements are *Blowin' in the Wind* (1962) and *The Times There Are A-Changing* (1963). *Blowin' in the Wind* in many ways makes the ground ready for *The Times There Are A-Changing*; *Blowin' in the Wind* is the call of alarm whereas *The Times There Are A-Changing* is the call to arms. *Blowin' in the Wind* offers a call and response lyric, a tradition deeply imbued in slave narratives and gospel music. This song is enriched by the intertextual references to the Slave spiritual *No More Auction Block* as well as the biblical reference, Ezekiel chapter 12: "you live in the midst of the rebellious house, who have eyes to see but do not see, ears to hear but do not hear." The question posed in this lyric is: when will certain ongoing attitudes cease and desist? The answer, which is sung in the refrain thrice, suggests that the end to such attitudes is a long way off. Less than 12 months later *The Times There Are A-Changing* takes the listening public into the battlefield.

The Times There Are A-Changing by Bob Dylan (1963)

Come gather 'round people
Wherever you roam
And admit that the waters
Around you have grown
And accept it that soon
You'll be drenched to the bone
If your time to you is worth savin'
Then you better start swimmin' or you'll sink like a stone
For the times they are a-changin'

Come writers and critics
Who prophesize with your pen
And keep your eyes wide
The chance won't come again
And don't speak too soon
For the wheel's still in spin
And there's no tellin' who that it's namin'
For the loser now will be later to win
For the times they are a-changin'

Come senators, congressmen
Please heed the call
Don't stand in the doorway
Don't block up the hall
For he that gets hurt
Will be he who has stalled
There's a battle outside and it is ragin'
It'll soon shake your windows and rattle your walls
For the times they are a-changin'

Come mothers and fathers
Throughout the land
And don't criticize
What you can't understand
Your sons and your daughters

Are beyond your command
Your old road is rapidly agin'
Please get out of the new one if you can't lend your hand
For the times they are a-changin'

The line it is drawn
The curse it is cast
The slow one now
Will later be fast
As the present now
Will later be past
The order is rapidly fadin'
And the first one now will later be last
For the times they are a-changin'

Times There Are A-Changing is written in September 1963; two months later President Kennedy would be dead and two years later US troops would be sent to fight in Vietnam. More specifically Martin Luther King had declared *I Have a Dream* at the *March on Washington for Jobs and Freedom*, just a month before Dylan penned this lyric. Thus, these early years of the 1960s were filled with unprecedented change. Kennedy had promised to radically invigorate USA's foreign policy and to be the super power of the Western nations. From his election in 1960 November a litany of trials and tribulations hit USA: the 1961 failed invasion of Cuba to oust President Castro and overthrow government by the CIA sponsored paramilitary; the 1961 building of the Berlin War; the 1962 Cuban Missile Crisis; and the deteriorating situation in South East Asia. Popular media and in particular television brought graphic images of these issues into people's homes. This impact cannot be underestimated. The American people responded by mobilising mass protests, building bomb shelters in their own backyard and sending telegrams to Washington DC demanding these crisis issues be solved.

Times There Are A-Changing opened Dylan's concert the night after Kennedy was assassinated. The first four stanzas commence with a powerful rhetorical device that commands the listening audience to move: "Come." From wherever they are the lyric's imperative is to move from that fixed point and to draw near to this voice. It is a call to the new world. The 5th stanza of the lyric indicates that the old world has collapsed. This final stanza tells us that the struggles, battles and suffering suggested in the transition from the old to the new world, is not only inevitable but fulfils the prophecies of old. In the New Testament, Mark Chapter 10, it is written: "But many that are first shall be last and the last first." Indeed, Dylan's lyrics reflect the belief that this was the dawning of a new age.

Stanza one commences with a folksy call to "gather 'round". The intimacy and immediacy suggested speaks to an ideal of grass root political activism. We are called to "admit" that the landscape upon which we find purchase is transforming rapidly. There is no longer footfall on this site of belonging. This is a nation drowning in the old world ways; and like the Genesis flood narrative we are called to hear the warning signs and get on board. Dylan asks whether we want to be "drenched to the bone ... or you'll sink like a stone". The rhyming couplet represents the critical point at which we have arrived: making the wrong choice here is a life and death situation. The refrain that ends this and every stanza, uses the archaic prefix "a" which intensifies the gerund verb change, as if reminding us that this is happening as we live and breathe, right now.

The second stanza moves us from the generic call of "people" in stanza one, to "writers and critics/ Who prophesize with your pen". The imperative here in bringing us out of a failed old world into the new is for composers to be the voice of truth. On some levels it is an instruction for writers and critics to predict honestly what this old world has install and what profits us in the possibility of the new world. These predications, paradoxically, need to have an element of hindsight in order to offer succor and sagacity: "And don't speak too soon/ For the wheel's still in spin." The frenetic temporality suggested is indicative of Dylan's own times and one that has, just a few years previous, seen the brutal outcome of the McCarthy trials, 1947 to 1956, where America witnessed the paranoia of "there's no tellin' who that it's namin'". This spinning wheel is a metaphor for the hysterical build-up within Dylan's own temporality. The penultimate line of stanza two is an intertextual play with the New Testament: "For the loser now will be later to win." This new world is one where the low will be brought high; the implied being that the powerholders will be overthrown. A revolutionary cry to gather arms.

The 3rd and 4th stanzas specifically identify these powerholders: "senators, congressmen... mothers and fathers." In both cases these powerholders are forming a blockade to the promised land of the new world, but they will not be tolerated, any longer: "Don't stand in the doorway/ Don't block up the hall" and in stanza four: "don't criticize/ What you can't understand". Here are the new set of commandments handed down by Dylan on behalf of his generation. In stanza three the commandments are associated with portals and reference the idea that there is an egress already in use moving people from the old to the new world and that this must remain clear. It also conjures images of the White House with its labyrinth of hallways and doorways, implying that the passage to a new political world must and will happen despite obstruction from the old vanguard. This is a battle as we enter the new world one where there will be casualties; one where such absolute axioms of, you are either with us or against us, reign supreme: "For he that gets hurt/Will be he who has stalled." A salient reminder that this is a song calling us to move and not remain fixed or stuck. In a clear threat to the icon of parliamentary democracy is this "battle outside ... ragin' [which will] soon shake your windows and rattle your walls". Again this revolutionary drive forward is made personal in stanza four; parents are reminded that their children are "beyond your command" and that they need to get out of the way if they cannot be constructive: "Your old road is rapidly agin'/ Please get out of the new one if you can't lend your hand." We are left with no doubt that the new world is not contingent on the old and could well be predicated solely by the energy and imagination of the young.

Kennedy believed it was a 33 to 55% chance that the Cuban Missile Crisis could become a nuclear war and over a 100,000,000 Americans would perish. It is no wonder that the youth of America demanded a new world. In stanza five Dylan uses symbols from the New Testament where truth is drawn in the sand and demons are cast out in order to create a new way forward, a new belief system and a new people: "The line it is drawn/ The curse it is cast." The new world is born anew, the power hierarchy will be inverted and thus the "slow ...Will ... be fast ... the present ... be past". Here is a promise for a new world order as the old one fades. The power of this lyric is immeasurable. Once this lyric was released its own democratic existence meant it became the call for all disenfranchised to strive for revolution. The lyric is remembered because of the melody and because of the contextual framework. It is transportable in popular media and so its reach is infinite. Dylan's *Times There Are A-Changing* is fearless and he writes it at age 22. Unbelievable.

All Along the Watchtower by Bob Dylan (1968)

"There must be some way out of here," said the joker to the thief
"There's too much confusion, I can't get no relief
Businessmen, they drink my wine, ploughmen dig my earth
None of them along the line know what any of it is worth"

"No reason to get excited," the thief, he kindly spoke
"There are many here among us who feel that life is but a joke
But you and I, we've been through that, and this is not our fate
So let us not talk falsely now, the hour is getting late"

All along the watchtower, princes kept the view
While all the women came and went, barefoot servants, too

Outside in the distance a wildcat did growl
Two riders were approaching, the wind began to howl

All Along the Watchtower is a mise en abyme: an image within an image within an image of self-reflection. I find this lyric haunting. I cannot tell whether we are looking backwards or forwards but either way there is catastrophic disaster pending. Written in 1968 the year of the assassination of Martin Luther King and during the appalling *Rolling Thunder* campaign in Vietnam, which was watched in every American living room on their television, this was a time when the poet songwriter seemed to be the only watchman. Yet I must also glance back to 740 BC when Isaiah wrote his prophecy of the fall of Babylon, the largest most important city in the world. Isaiah predicted it would be overthrown, like Sodom and Gomorrah, and never be settled again. Some 200 years later, Herodotus wrote about Persia and Medea diverting the Euphrates River that had previously filled the moat around Babylon city thus protecting it from enemies. The Babylonian Empire, built up by King Nebuchadnezzar, boasted the most beautiful palace, temples, city streets and double walls. This was later razed to the ground by the enemy. Rather than watching for their approach, the Babylonians had been celebrating and feasting their invincibility. Dylan's intertextual dialogue with Isaiah is worth a look:

"Like whirlwinds sweeping through the southland, an invader comes from the desert, from a land of terror.

A dire vision has been shown to me: The traitor betrays, the looter takes loot. Elam, attack! Media, lay siege! I will bring to an end all the groaning she caused. At this my body is racked with pain, pangs seize me, like those of a woman in labor; I am staggered by what I hear, I am bewildered by what I see. My heart falters, fear makes me tremble; the twilight I longed for has become a horror to me. They set the tables, they spread the rugs, they eat, they drink! Get up, you officers, oil the shields! This is what the Lord says to me: "Go, post a look out and have him report what he sees. When he sees chariots with teams of horses, riders on donkeys or riders on camels, let him be alert, fully alert." And the look out shouted, "Day after day, my lord, I stand on the watchtower; every night I stay at my post. Look, here comes a man in a chariot with a team of horses. And he gives back the answer: 'Babylon has fallen, has fallen! All the images of its gods lie shattered on the ground!'" My people who are crushed on the threshing floor, I tell you what I have heard from the Lord Almighty, from the God of Israel."

This Old Testament prophet conveys God's warning and it is dire! Disaster is roaring down upon the Babylonians and they are told that their enemies are preparing an offensive attack. Isaiah himself grows faint with all that God will let befall on Babylon. Rather than heed this warning and prepare for battle, the Babylonians continue feasting. They have a watchman on the tower looking for riders and indeed he calls out that he sees their approach. The rest, as they say, is history: Babylon is deaf to the warning, the city is captured, its idols smashed and its power razed to the ground.

Make no mistake, *All Along the Watchtower* is an augury for Dylan's own times. His lyric is made up of three quatrains and commences media res, as the joker talks to the thief about the rising pressure and unmitigated threat just beyond his peripheral vision. This is quintessential to Dylan's oeuvre because it sums up his creative project: the tension between the imperative to stand up for what is right and the impulse to escape. The joker is the archetypal jester, the truth teller but also the wild card. The thief is another sort of outrider because the thief works by stealth and cannot be trusted. The lyric is a dramatic dialogue between the joker and the thief. From the outset the joker wants an exit from his locus, his place of belonging, his nation space: "There must be some way out of here." He alone sees the truth of the situation and the high modal verb "must" speaks to the way he is unsettled and unnerved. In this place of excess with its pathological lack of honesty, "There's too much confusion...no relief".

The desperate need for exigency, called for by the joker in quatrain one, is replaced by the soothing voice of the thief. While the joker had spoken of what had been taken from him, the wine and food, the thief in quatrain two speaks of the shared perspective among many that "life is but a joke". There is an unsettling proximity between these two archetypes; they are untrustworthy to us and to each other. Moreover, they are not united in how they see the world unfolding. To the thief there is "No reason to get excited". In other words, the portents and auguries the joker sees are not taken seriously by the thief. Indeed, the thief's perspective is to deny any suggestion that their destiny is under threat, thus these incitements are false and misleading: "this is not our fate/ So let us not talk falsely now." For the thief, as it was for the Babylonians and is for some Americans in the late 60s, the only preoccupation is excessive consumption despite a growing sense of urgency: "the hour is getting late."

In the final quatrain we shift to a closer examination of the redoubt. We read that the sovereign powers are appraising the situation, while life goes on as usual: "All along the watchtower, princes kept the view/ While all the women came and went, barefoot servants, too." The watchtower is the panoptic eye that guards the city from the enemy. In the Old Testament we read that despite the prophecy to oil the shields in readiness for battle and place watchmen in the towers, the Babylonians continued to party. The chilling reference to not listening to the signs of their times, puts the tumultuous election year of 1968 in mind. The assassination of Martin Luther King led to riots throughout USA which was exacerbated by the widespread opposition to Vietnam War and the ongoing confrontations between police and anti-war protestors. The Democratic Lyndon B Johnson had decided not to run for office again and Richard Nixon became the Republican president. The final two lines of the lyric are a salient reminder of what can happen when a nation is not all along the watchtower: "Outside in the distance a wildcat did growl/ Two riders were approaching, the wind began to howl." The auguries contained in the alliterative rhyming couplet, "wildcat did growl... wind began to howl", speak to a soundscape that signals foreboding and change. The two riders are symbolic of Media and Persia, but also the carnage of the Vietnam War and bloody struggle for Civil Rights. This is an unquiet song in a time that desperately needed to hear.

Forever Young by Bob Dylan (1973)

May God bless and keep you always
May your wishes all come true
May you always do for others
And let others do for you

May you build a ladder to the stars
And climb on every rung
May you stay
Forever young

Forever young
Forever young
May you stay
Forever young

May you grow up to be righteous
May you grow up to be true
May you always know the truth
And see the lights surrounding you

May you always be courageous
Stand upright and be strong
And may you stay
Forever young

Forever young
Forever young
May you stay
Forever young

May your hands always be busy
May your feet always be swift
May you have a strong foundation
When the winds of changes shift

May your heart always be joyful
May your song always be sung
And may you stay
Forever young

Forever young
Forever young
May you stay
Forever young

This lyric was written in 1973 and is a lullaby to Dylan's son Jesse, born in 1966 when Dylan was only 22, but it also a lullaby to himself and to his nation. A cradle song is soothing and passes down cultural knowledge that is personal and value laden. Its lyrics sing to a tradition in simple and repetitive phrases. Lullabies indicate emotional intent, maintain the undivided attention of the listener and most curiously regulate behaviour. *Forever Young* is an emotional poem to read. It gathers up the longing we have for our children, for our lover and for loved ones departing too early. To desire eternal youth has been a hallmark of civilisation since Ancient Greece. Youth represents the best of us: vitality, energy, potential, beauty, curiosity and imagination. To exist in a world where these qualities are yours for ever, is to never have to come to terms with the great adventure offered us on the other side of dying. To remain eternally youthful means that one's mental and physical abilities will never decay. To discover the fountain of youth in Ancient Greece, is the equivalent of finding the Holy Grail. The Ancient gods were concerned with longevity and youthfulness; the pantheon of gods was immortal but not forever young. Indeed, we have the cautionary tale from Greek mythology where Eos, the goddess of dawn asked Zeus to grant her lover, Tithonus, immortality forgetting to add eternal youth. Unfortunately, Tithonus, a rhapsodist and performer of epic poetry, got to live on into eternity but as a more and more decrepit and aging creature who was eventually abandoned by Eos for a younger lover. Obviously when one climbs Mount Olympus one really needs to get the request right.

Why do we ask for eternal youth? Is it because life here on earth is so bountiful from which springs a myriad of possibilities? Is it because death and its unknown country is too frightening to contemplate? Youth reflects ourselves in our former glory. We ritualise this desire for eternal youth in the act of baptism. Our litany contains the promise for life everlasting. In the Book of Numbers

Chapter 6: 24-26, we read: "May the Lord bless you and guard you/ May the Lord make his face shed light upon you." It is this longing for eternity that makes its way into Dylan's lyric. *Forever Young* is made up of nine quatrains with the 3rd, 6th and 9th being a refrain. The modal verb "may", expressing hope, is used over 20 times in a poem that is made up of no more than 36 lines; in other words, the soothing and repetitious wish for the beloved not only dominates our reading but moves us into a quasi-incantatory state. The phrase "forever young" is repeated 12 times throughout the poem not counting its title. This is a spell being spun around the cradle; one that calls for protection, bounty, truth, courage and joy. It is a lyric that finds its way into the fairy-tale of a slumbering innocent. Moreover, its recitation demands a better world.

The first three quatrains are an invocation to "God". In fact, the poem opens as a blessing: "May God bless and keep you always." So, what is privileged here is an acknowledgement of cultural and traditional knowledge that God has promised eternal life to his people. Do you think this is oxymoronic for a singer song writer of Dylan's genius, temperament, atheism and recreational drug using to write? Or do you think that longing for eternal youth for one's beloved child can reduce your isms to their knees? We are given a litany of heart felt desires for a better world: "your wishes all come true...you always do for others...let other do for you." His lyric is full of sentiment but never sentimental. Dylan uses the metaphor of building and climbing "every rung" of a "ladder to the stars", suggesting the full and complete experience of life is the most valuable and it is only by surrendering to this that we can achieve our hopes, symbolised in the constellations. At the end of the second quatrain comes the ultimate wish for the beloved, that of eternal youth, which is taken up in the refrain of quatrain three: "May you stay/ Forever young." Perhaps this is a signature of complete love to want for the beloved what you cannot possess for yourself.

In quatrain four, five and six we are clearly shown the attributes desired for the eternal youth: truth and strength. Dylan implicitly speaks to the stewardship entrusted to those bringing up the child. It is their responsibility to ensure that the beloved understands what it is "to be righteous...to be true". What would the world be like if the beloved babe was brought up to be a person who was virtuous, worthy and decent? And to be faithful, sincere and honest? A better world. Once again, the lyric acknowledges the metaphysical or numinous element of self: "May you...see the lights surrounding you." It is articulated as a given, in that truth will lead to enlightenment beyond the physical self and world. For truth to take flight, fortitude and strength are needed and this is reflected in the metaphor: "May you...Stand upright." The lyrics Dylan had written throughout the 60s called for exactly that, to stand up for what one believed to be true and right. Again, the end of the 5th quatrain releases the call to be "forever young", which is intensified in the refrain of quatrain six.

The final three quatrains offer not only the beloved child but oneself and one's nation a litany of hope. Terms such as "hands", "feet", "heart" and "song" work as a synecdoche for the full and complete person or nation. Dylan asks that we are creative and that our energies are put to making a better place. Without this drive to be creative we will succumb to the "winds of change" which could well destroy our "strong foundation". It is a responsibility of each and every citizen of the nation to build and move forward: "May your hands always be busy/ May your feet always be swift." We have heard the messages blowing in the wind and we know that times are a-changing; therefore, it is up to us to make ourselves and our nation worthy of this new world. This better world must be created if America is to avoid being once again on the brink of nuclear destruction and civil war. It is in this new world that the new born and the reborn can "be joyful". Indeed, it is the voice of youth which should sing out their hopes and dreams, first and foremost. The most significant line, before we reverberate with the final refrain, is "May your song always be sung". Here Dylan reminds us that without the song of the young we are a nation without hope. Hence, we very much need the young to "stay/ Forever young".

A Hard Rain's A-Gonna Fall by Bob Dylan (1962)

Oh, where have you been, my blue-eyed son?
Oh, where have you been, my darling young one?
I've stumbled on the side of twelve misty mountains
I've walked and I've crawled on six crooked highways
I've stepped in the middle of seven sad forests
I've been out in front of a dozen dead oceans
I've been ten thousand miles in the mouth of a graveyard

And it's a hard, and it's a hard, it's a hard, and it's a hard
And it's a hard rain's a-gonna fall

Oh, what did you see, my blue-eyed son?
Oh, what did you see, my darling young one?
I saw a newborn baby with wild wolves all around it
I saw a highway of diamonds with nobody on it
I saw a black branch with blood that kept drippin'
I saw a room full of men with their hammers a-bleedin'
I saw a white ladder all covered with water
I saw ten thousand talkers whose tongues were all broken
I saw guns and sharp swords in the hands of young children

And it's a hard, and it's a hard, it's a hard, it's a hard
And it's a hard rain's a-gonna fall

And what did you hear, my blue-eyed son?
And what did you hear, my darling young one?
I heard the sound of a thunder, it roared out a warnin'
Heard the roar of a wave that could drown the whole world
Heard one person starve, I heard many people laughin'
Heard the song of a poet who died in the gutter
Heard the sound of a clown who cried in the alley

And it's a hard, and it's a hard, it's a hard, it's a hard
And it's a hard rain's a-gonna fall

Oh, who did you meet, my blue-eyed son?
Who did you meet, my darling young one?
I met a young child beside a dead pony
I met a white man who walked a black dog
I met a young woman whose body was burning
I met a young girl, she gave me a rainbow
I met one man who was wounded in love
I met another man who was wounded with hatred

And it's a hard, it's a hard, it's a hard, it's a hard
It's a hard rain's a-gonna fall

Oh, what'll you do now, my blue-eyed son?
Oh, what'll you do now, my darling young one?
I'm a-goin' back out 'fore the rain starts a-fallin'
I'll walk to the depths of the deepest black forest
Where the people are many and their hands are all empty
Where the pellets of poison are flooding their waters
Where the home in the valley meets the damp dirty prison
Where the executioner's face is always well-hidden
Where hunger is ugly, where souls are forgotten
Where black is the color, where none is the number
And I'll tell it and think it and speak it and breathe it
And reflect it from the mountain so all souls can see it
Then I'll stand on the ocean until I start sinkin'
But I'll know my song well before I start singin'

And it's a hard, it's a hard, it's a hard, it's a hard
It's a hard rain's a-gonna fall

    Although written in 1962 this song is seared into my brain by Patti Smith's rendition of it in 2016 at the Nobel Prize ceremony. A ceremony Dylan did not attend. I watched Smith's calm mesmeric version that was applauded by some politely and by others, not at all. Was it her long grey hair that appalled or her lack of make up or the obvious fact that she didn't care for the audience as much as she did for Dylan? Regardless, Dylan's songs made him the lyricist of his nation. This particular lyric sets up a haunting conversation with the Anglo-Scottish border ballad, *Lord Randall* that has its origins as far back as 1629. This 17th century ballad was a popular genre; one that told a story and was sold on the streets and at fairs and in taverns. This particular ballad recounts the fate of a lover whose femme fatale has induced him to satiate his appetite and in doing so, he has been poisoned. His tale is told to his mother. The call and response technique reflect the intimate anxiety between the mother asking the questions and the son responding. It is through the question and answer pattern that both arrive at the truth. This is an archetypical story. A preoccupation with the loved son by the doting parent; a cautionary tale about desire and the price one pays for satiating an appetite beyond the confines of one's site of belonging.

A Hard Rain's A-Gonna Fall is a ballad, and like *Lord Randall*, made up of five stanzas. Each stanza begins with a question posed by the parent. Each stanza ends with the two line refrain: "And it's a hard, it's a hard, it's a hard, it's a hard/ It's a hard rain's a-gonna fall." The lyrics were written a month or so before the Cuban Missile Crisis was announced by President Kennedy but this refrain was been interpreted as a premonition of the dark zeitgeist beneath which America crouched. The opening question from Dylan's lyric is the same as that of *Lord Randall*: "Where have you been..?" To this question concerning his absence the "blue-eyed son" replies he has "stumbled...walked...stepped" across iconic landscapes of "mountains ... highways ... forests". These places map the wandering son's country but one laden with indecipherable riddles. We work through the numbers and adjectives: "Twelve misty mountains...six crooked highways...seven sad forests." The site of belonging is beyond understanding. These travels have taken the "darling young one" to starting points of "dead oceans" and "graveyards". A journey through life and death.

Dylan's second stanza poses the question, "what did you see...?"; whereas the *Lord Randall*'s ballad asks "Where gat ye your dinner?" Both lyrics mobilise the colloquial dialect of its context. In dialogue with this earlier ballad, Dylan's son shares a vision that borders on the apocryphal: "a newborn baby... highway of diamonds... a black branch... a room full of men... a white ladder... ten thousand talkers... guns and sharp swords." His eyes have witnessed the beauty and terror of the home of his beloved. The lover hungers to know his beloved utterly and completely but in so doing risks his own life. The signatures of destruction are suggested in the nightmare periphery: "wild wolves... nobody on it... blood that kept drippin'... hammers a-bleedin'... covered with water... tongues were all broken... in the hands of young children." The 1629 addressee is "Lord Randall my son...my handsome young man" whereas the 1962 is "my blue-eyed son... my darling young one". These are questions posed to the all American hero, who is made hyperreal by Hollywood. What has the son, the American hero, seen on his travels across his place of belonging? Both an American Dream and Nightmare.

The third stanza moves away from location and vision to the sounds that make up this experience. The question posed to Lord Randall in 1629 is "what gat ye your dinner..?" the answer being the beloved. Lord Randall is so enamoured with his "true love" that he doesn't suspect foul play nor the noxious victuals of "eels boiled in broo'". Surely, a dead giveaway? Needless to say the soundscape heard by Dylan's "darling young one" is ominous and sinister: "thunder... roar of a wave... one person starve... a poet who died... a clown who cried." This is the song of urban America. A place imagined in the gutters and alleyways; one of decay and decadence and death. This is not the land of milk and honey, a promised land to the wandering son of America. *Lord Randall*'s, "mother, make my bed soon,/ For I'm weary wi' hunting, and fain wald lie down" is replaced by "And it's a hard, and it's a hard, it's a hard, it's a hard/ And it's a hard rain's a-gonna fall". Both refrains contain within them the truth and certainty of pending destruction. In the 17th century version, it is a lover's body poisoned; in the 20th century ballad, it is a nation gone rancid. In both cases, the beloved has turned on the lover. In Dylan's ballad, America has turned on the American hero. Meanwhile, the all-knowing parent keeps asking the questions until the son comes to self-awareness.

When asked in stanza four "who did you meet..?" the lover's response is indecipherable: "a dead pony...a black dog... body was burning....wounded in love...wounded with hatred." Enigmatically the only life affirming representation is "a rainbow" given by a young girl suggesting dreams and wishes, which is in stark contrast to the other portentous gifts. Similarly, in stanza four, the portent associated with Lord Randall's bloodhounds dying, "they swelled and they died", goes sadly unnoticed by the unsuspecting young son. In *Lord Randall* the mother replaces her questions with fears that he is poisoned, to which he affirms he is "sick at the heart". The ambiguity of the response suggests that he still longs for the femme fatale. The overwrought parent of Dylan's ballad seems to know the same fate has befallen her son. Thus, she asks: "what'll you do now...?" to which he replies "I'm a-goin' back out". Everything seems to turn on its head. Even in the face of pending death he chooses to return to the beloved. Into her arms he returns. Why? Because the lyricist can do nothing else: "And I'll tell it and think it and speak it and breathe it/ And reflect it from the mountain so all souls can see it." This is a ballad about the song of a nation and about the poet who must sing it. A love song to the beloved despite the fact that she is self-destructive: "Where the people are many and their hands are all empty...Where hunger is ugly, where souls are forgotten." This is what we have done to ourselves in our frenetic attempt to have; a place eschewed by pristine nature and transparent justice. To all of this the lover, the poet, cries out that he will sing until his dying breath the song to his beloved country.

11

List of Poems

Chapter 1. Poetry Confronting Art: Ekphrastic Poetry
W. H. Auden ... Musee des Beaux Arts
William Carlos Williams ... Landscape with the Fall of Icarus
Alfred Corn ... Seeing all the Vermeers
Edward Markham ... The Man with the Hoe
Matthew Olzmann ... Replica of The Thinker
Martha Ronk ... Why Knowing is (& Matisse's Woman with a Hat)
Mary Leader ... Girl at the Sewing Machine
William Carlos Williams ... The Great Figure
Rainer Maria Rilke ... Archaic Torso of Apollo
Homer ... The Iliad Book XVIII
John Keats ... Ode on a Grecian Urn
Percy Shelley ... On the Medusa of Leonardo Da Vinci

Chapter 2. Making Life Easier to Bear: The Sonnet
W. B. Yeats ... Leda and the Swan
W. H. Auden ... Who's Who
Sir Thomas Wyatt ... Whoso List to Hunt
Seamus Heaney ... Clearances V
Wilfred Owen ... Maundy Thursday
John Donne ... Batter my Heart, three-person'd God
William Wordsworth ... The world is too much with us
Tom Paulin ... In the Last Province
Lady Mary Wroth ... Sonnet 68
William Shakespeare .... Sonnet 73
Emily Dickinson ... Hope is the thing with feathers
Hartley Coleridge ... Long time a child

515

R. S. Thomas ... The bright field
Norman MacCaig ... Rag and Bone
Elizabeth Bishop ... Sonnet

Chapter 3. Go Seek the Kingdom: Pilgrimage and Poetry
Homer ... The Odyssey
Sons of Korah ... Psalm 84
Dante Alighieri ... Inferno Canto 1
Geoffrey Chaucer ... The Canterbury Tales: The General Prologue
William Shakespeare ... Romeo & Juliet Act 1 Scene 5
Sir Walter Raleigh ... The Passionate Man's Pilgrimage
John Donne ... Hymn to God, My God, in My Sickness
John Bunyan ... The Pilgrim
Lord Byron ... Childe Harold's Pilgrimage
Felicia Dorothea Hemans ... Landing of the Pilgrims
Walt Whitman ... Song of Myself: Section 46
Sophie Jewett ... The Pilgrim
Dylan Thomas ... Poem in October
Seamus Heaney ... Funeral Rites
Francie Lynch ... Pub Pilgrimage
Natasha Trethewey ... Pilgrimage

Chapter 4. Poetry with a Divine Will: Numinous Poetry
Vincent Buckley ... Day with its Dry Persistence
Les Murray ... Poetry and Religion
Noel Rowe ... Magnificat 5. Resurrection
Langston Hughes ... Christ in Alabama
W. H. Auden ... For the Time Being: Christmas Oratorio III
Charles Wright ... Last Supper
Howard Nemerov ... The Historical Judas
William Shakespeare ... To Be or Not To Be
John Donne ... Death Be Not Proud
Gerard Manley Hopkins ... God's Grandeur
G. K. Chesterton ... The Donkey
T. S. Eliot ... Journey of the Magi
Elizabeth Guy ... I Walk Through the Valley

Chapter 5. Troubled Pleasure: The Romantics
William Wordsworth ... Prelude
William Wordsworth ... Elegiac Stanzas Suggested by a Picture of Peele Castle in a Storm
William Wordsworth ... French Revolution

William Wordsworth ... Lines Composed a Few Miles above Tintern Abbey
William Wordsworth ... Inside of King's College Chapel, Cambridge
Samuel Taylor Coleridge ... This Lime-tree Bower my Prison
Samuel Taylor Coleridge ... France: An Ode
Samuel Taylor Coleridge ... Dejection: An Ode
Samuel Taylor Coleridge ... Youth and Age
Percy Bysshe Shelley ... England in 1819
Percy Bysshe Shelley ... Men of England
Percy Bysshe Shelley ... Ode to the West Wind
Percy Bysshe Shelley ... Lines Written in the Bay of Lerici
John Keats ... To Autumn
John Keats ... Ode to a Nightingale
John Keats ... The Eve of St Agnes
John Keats ... When I have fears that I may cease to be

Chapter 6. A Singularness of Heart: Pre-Raphaelite Poetry
John Keats ... La Belle Dame sans Merci
Alfred Tennyson ... The Lady of Shalott
Elizabeth Eleanor Siddal ... O Silent Wood
Elizabeth Eleanor Siddal ... Worn Out
William Morris ... The Defence of Guinevere
Christina Rossetti ... Goblin Market
George Meredith ... Modern Love
Algernon Charles Swinburne ... At a Month's End
Gabriel Dante Rossetti ... Willowwood 1
Gabriel Dante Rossetti ... Willowwood 2
Gabriel Dante Rossetti ... Willowwood 3
Gabriel Dante Rossetti ... Willowwood 4

Chapter 7. As We See Ourselves: Australian Poetry
Louisa Lawson ... Reverie
Banjo Patterson ... In Defence of the Bush
Kenneth Slessor ... Five Bells
Gwen Harwood ... Show me the order of the world
Les Murray ... A Poet Thinking Beyond Facts
Judith Wright ... South of my Days
David Malouf ... Ladybird
Dorothy Hewitt ... The Whistler
James McAuley ... Terra Australis
Rosemary Dobson ... Detail from an Annunciation by Crivelli
Fay Zwicky ... Soup and Jelly

Noel Rowe ... Next to Nothing

Chapter 8. A Terrible Beauty is Born: Irish Poetry
Anonymous ... The Hermitage
Seamus Heaney ... Lightenings viii
Eiléan Ní Chuilleanáin ... Swineherd
W. B. Yeats ... Second Coming
Paul Muldoon ... Anseo
Joseph Mary Plunkett ... I see his blood upon the rose
Patrick Pearse ... The Mother
Anonymous ... Kathleen Ni-Houlahan
Ciaran Carson ... Bomb Disposal
Seamus Heaney ... The Strand at Lough Beg
Catherine Twomey ... Cliona
W. B. Yeats ... A Prayer for Old Age
John Hewitt ... Ireland
Donagh MacDonald ... A Warning to the Conquerors
Seamus Heaney ... Requiem for the Croppies
Patrick Kavanagh ... Advent
Eavan Boland ... A Woman with a Country
Seamus Heaney ... The Skylight

Chapter 9. A Life Worth Living: The Russian Silver Age
Anna Akhmatova ... I wrung my hand under my dark veil
Anna Akhmatova ... Lot's Wife
Anna Akhmatova ... Requiem
Osip Mandelstam ... On the pale-blue enamel
Osip Mandelstam ... A flame is in my blood
Osip Mandelstam ... The night is irredeemable
Osip Mandelstam ... Tristia
Osip Mandelstam ... Night Piece
Osip Mandelstam ... Stalin Epigram
Osip Mandelstam ... Alone I stare into the frost's white face
Osip Mandelstam ... Yet to die. Unalone still
Marina Tsvetaeva ... Poems for Blok
Marina Tsvetaeva ... Bound for Hell
Marina Tsvetaeva ... I am happy simply living
Marina Tsvetaeva ... Wires
Marina Tsvetaeva ... An Attempt at Jealousy
Marina Tsvetaeva ... Poems for Czechoslovakia
Marina Tsvetaeva ... And there's no Grave

Boris Pasternak ... February
Boris Pasternak ... Storm, Instantaneous, Forever
Boris Pasternak ... In Memory of Marina Tsvetaeva
Boris Pasternak ... Hamlet

Chapter 10. Poetry that Saves a Nation: Nobel Laureates
Giorgos Seferis ... The Return of the Exile
Giorgos Seferis ... Denial
Giorgos Seferis ... Helen
Giorgos Seferis ... Argonauts
Pablo Neruda ... Central America
Pablo Neruda ... Pequena America
Pablo Neruda ... The Fugitive III
Pablo Neruda ... The Fable of the Siren and the Drunks
Pablo Neruda ... Ode to Salt
Derek Walcott ... Omeros: Book Two Chapter Eighteen
Derek Walcott ... The Spoiler's Return
Derek Walcott ... The Light of the World
Seamus Heaney ... Station Island IX
Seamus Heaney ... Punishment
Seamus Heaney ... Cassandra
Wislawa Szymborska ... The Joy of Writing
Wislawa Szymborska ... Nothing Twice
Wislawa Szymborska ... Love at First Sight
Wislawa Szymborska ... Tortures
Bob Dylan ... The Times There Are A-Changing
Bob Dylan ... All Along the Watchtower
Bob Dylan ... Forever Young
Bob Dylan ... A Hard Rain's A-Gonna Fall

Acknowledgements

This book owes its existence to the encouragement, faith and love of my husband, Roger and my daughter, Madelaine.

I am profoundly grateful for all the support and editorial assistance from First Rider Publishing.

Throughout my life I have learnt so much from students, at secondary and tertiary level, and I thank them for allowing me to share their epiphanies, joys and triumphs in unlocking some of the most challenging and life changing poems ever written. They have made me the writer and teacher I am today.

Finally, it is a gift to be able to dedicate this book to my parents who loved and believed in me, singularly and without end.

Contact:
Sign up to Elizabeth's newsletter on her website:
www.elizabeth-guy.com

Keep up to date with what Elizabeth is doing:
Instagram @elizabeth__guy | Facebook @elizabethguy01

www.ingramcontent.com/pod-product-compliance
Lightning Source LLC
Chambersburg PA
CBHW081143290426
44108CB00018B/2428